EVOLUTION OF THE WORD

Marcus J. Borg

EVOLUTION OF THE WORD

The New Testament in the Order the Books Were Written

HarperOne
An Imprint of HarperCollins*Publishers*

HarperOne

EVOLUTION OF THE WORD: *The New Testament in the Order the Books Were Written.* Copyright © 2012 by Marcus J. Borg. All rights reserved. Printed in the United States of America. No part of this book may be used or reproduced in any manner whatsoever without written permission except in the case of brief quotations embodied in critical articles and reviews. For information address HarperCollins Publishers, 10 East 53rd Street, New York, NY 10022.

HarperCollins books may be purchased for educational, business, or sales promotional use. For information please e-mail the Special Markets Department at SPsales@harpercollins.com.

HarperCollins website: http://www.harpercollins.com

HarperCollins®, 📖®, and HarperOne™ are trademarks of HarperCollins Publishers.

FIRST HARPERCOLLINS PAPERBACK EDITION PUBLISHED IN 2013

Library of Congress Cataloging-in-Publication Data
Borg, Marcus J.
    Evolution of the Word : the New Testament in the order the books were written
/ Marcus J. Borg. — 1st ed.
        p. cm.
    ISBN 978–0–06–208211–4
    1. Bible. N.T.—Chronology. 2. Bible. N.T.—Criticism, interpretation, etc.
I. Bible. N.T. English. New Revised Standard. 2012. II. Title.
    BS2409.B67   2012
    225.6'7—dc23   2012001947

13 14 15 16 17 RRD(H) 10 9 8 7 6 5 4 3 2 1

Contents

Foreword

I have long yearned for a New Testament that would put "first books first"—that would sequence the books of the New Testament in the chronological order in which they were written rather than in the order in which they appear in the New Testament familiar to Christians.

Scholars have known for a long time that the canonical sequence of the New Testament is not the same as its chronological sequence. The earliest documents are not the gospels, but at least seven of the letters of Paul, written in the 50s. The gospels come later, beginning around the year 70. And though Revelation ends the canonical New Testament, it was not the last to be written. That distinction almost certainly belongs to the second letter of Peter—and others are also later than Revelation.

I can still remember my surprise long ago when I learned that the first things written about Jesus and early Christianity were in the letters of Paul and not in the gospels. Since then I have heard and read a lot about all this and have tried to explain it to others, but fear that it probably sounds abstract and is soon forgotten.

I wish a seminary professor had shown me a "first books first" New Testament and that I'd had copies to "show and tell and sell" throughout my ministry. Presenting the book and having people young and old hold it in their hands and look at it would teach more than hundreds of words about dates and authorship.

If I were still a parish pastor, I'd hand out copies to all my Confirmation students and say, "Here's a different New Testament. You have never seen one like it. Take a good look at it and then tell me how it's different."

In a few minutes they would learn something that they had never thought of before and that many would never forget. We would spend the class thinking about how this can help us understand the New Testament. At the end of the class, I'd ask them to take this strange new New Testament home to show their families, asking them, "How is it different?" If they couldn't figure it out, the confirmands were to tell their families what they had learned in class that day.

I'd do something similar with adult Bible studies and forums. I would encourage members to buy a copy, read the New Testament in this chronological order, ponder the introductions, and join a group to share and discuss their experience of reading this New Testament with others.

I think every pastor, seminary professor, and seminary student should have a copy of this chronological New Testament. And every congregation should have a stack for purposes of "show and tell and sell." It will change the way we see the emergence and development of earliest Christianity. It will be an adventure of exploration and discovery.

—Bishop Lowell Erdahl
Evangelical Lutheran Church of America

EVOLUTION OF THE WORD

1

A Chronological New Testament
The Evolution of the Word

This chronological New Testament is the same as and yet different from the canonical New Testament. It contains the same twenty-seven documents, but it puts them in the order in which they were written.

The gospels do not come first. Rather, seven letters written by Paul do. Revelation is not at the end. Second Peter is, and eight other documents are later than Revelation.

Seeing the documents of the New Testament in chronological sequence illustrates and demonstrates a central theme of this book, namely, that the "Word"— shorthand for the "Word of God"—evolved. By "evolved," I mean simply that it developed and grew over time.

For Christians, the "Word of God" refers to both a book and a person. As a book, it includes both the Old and New Testaments. Though Christians have often (and wrongly) thought of the Old Testament as having inferior status, it does not cease to be the "Word of God" because of the New Testament. Rather, the New Testament is an evolution, a development, that does not leave the old behind.

The "Word of God" as the Bible evolved over a period of a thousand years. Most biblical scholars date the earliest written parts of the Old Testament to the 900s BCE and the latest parts of the New Testament to the 100s CE.

The "Word of God" as a person refers of course to Jesus. He is the "Word" made flesh, incarnate, embodied in a human life. Of course, he himself evolved—from childhood into early adulthood and into and through his public activity. But also— and this is what a chronological New Testament illustrates—understandings of his significance and meaning evolved, developed, in the decades and century after his historical life. The Word as book and as person is not static, but the product of a process.

The process, however, is not intrinsically about improvement. Later does not always mean better. Rather, as we will see, some of the later documents in the New Testament reflect a domestication of the radicalism of Jesus and early communities of his followers.

Canonical New Testament and Chronological New Testament

The canonical New Testament (in other words, the official ordering of the books in church Bibles) begins with the gospels and concludes with Revelation. Because Jesus is the central figure of Christianity, it makes sense that the New Testament begins with narratives of his life, teachings, and passion. Thus the gospels are "chronologically" first in a biographical sense. And because Revelation is about the "last things" and the second coming of Jesus, it makes sense that it comes at the end. Revelation and the gospels function as bookends for the New Testament; everything else comes in between.

By putting these documents in a quite different sequence, namely, the order in which they were written, this book presents a literary chronology—a panoramic view of how the ideas and stories of the New Testament changed over time. It also emphasizes chronology in a second important sense, namely, that of seeing, reading, and hearing these documents in their historical context, the world of the first century and a bit beyond.

Both of these emphases are the product of modern biblical scholarship. Its roots go back to the birth of modern thought in the Enlightenment of the sixteenth and seventeenth centuries. Though the Enlightenment began with science (Copernicus, Galileo, Newton, and so forth), it soon extended to other areas of inquiry, including the study of the past. It generated a historical approach to the Bible and early Christianity that emphasizes the importance of seeing its documents in their ancient settings. When were they written? What were the historical circumstances in which they were written? What did they mean in their ancient context?

This historical approach to the Bible and the New Testament is not universally embraced by Christians. Those in churches committed to biblical inerrancy and a literal interpretation of the Bible reject much historical scholarship, because it calls into question their understanding of the Bible as having a divine guarantee to be factually and absolutely true. Some Christians are unaware of the historical approach and thus neither reject nor affirm it. But it is taught in most universities and colleges and in mainline Protestant and Catholic seminaries.

Though modern biblical scholarship has not led to unanimity about how to sequence all of the New Testament, there is a consensus about a basic chronological framework:

- The earliest documents are seven of the thirteen letters attributed to Paul. There is universal agreement that these seven were written by Paul in the 50s. They are earlier than the gospels.

- The first gospel is Mark, written around the year 70. Matthew and Luke both used Mark when they later wrote their own gospels.

- Revelation (probably from the 90s) is not the last book of the New Testament to be written.

- Second Peter is almost certainly the latest, from near the middle of the second century.

And so this chronological New Testament does not begin with the gospels, but with seven of Paul's letters. Moreover, the gospels appear in a different order: Mark is first, not Matthew. It does not end with Revelation, but with several documents written later than Revelation.

Within this consensus framework, there is also uncertainty about the dates and sequence of some documents. Though seven letters of Paul are certainly by him and from the 50s, what about the other six attributed to him, but probably written a generation or two after his death? Are they from the 80s and 90s or from the early second century? So also how are we to date other letters—James, Hebrews, Jude, two attributed to Peter, and three attributed to John? Most are dated—estimated, guesstimated to be—from the 90s to the early 100s. How to sequence them is at best an educated guess. Should 1 Peter be before or after Hebrews or the letters of John? Hard to know.

But uncertainty about the sequence of some documents does not negate the twofold foundation of this chronological New Testament: the scholarly consensus that the chronological order and canonical order are different and that the general framework for ordering them is clear.

The Value of a Chronological New Testament

Seeing and reading the New Testament in chronological sequence is illuminating, making many things apparent:

- Starting with seven of Paul's letters illustrates that there were vibrant Christian communities spread throughout the Roman Empire before there were written gospels. These seven letters provide a "window" into the life of very early Christian communities.

- Placing the gospels after Paul's letters makes it clear that, as written documents, they are not the source of early Christianity, but its product. The gospel—the good news—of and about Jesus existed before the gospels. They were produced by early Christian communities several decades after Jesus's historical life.

- Reading the gospels in chronological order beginning with Mark demonstrates that early Christian understandings of Jesus and his significance developed over time. When Matthew and Luke used Mark as a source, they not only added to the Markan material, but often modified it.

- Seeing John separated from the other gospels and relatively late in the New Testament makes it clear how different from them John's gospel is.

- Realizing that many of the documents are from the 90s and later allows us to glimpse developments in early Christianity in the late first and early second centuries.

"Documents" Rather Than "Books"

Though it is conventional to call the writings in the New Testament "books," this is somewhat misleading. In ordinary English today, "book" refers to a relatively long document. We do not commonly use the word for a writing that is a few pages or ten, twenty, or even fifty pages long, though we might call the last a booklet.

In this modern sense, none of the writings in the New Testament is a "book." The longest is the gospel of Luke, with just under twenty thousand words. Depending upon type size, modern books typically have about four to five hundred words per page. Thus Luke is fewer than fifty pages—and even less in the small print of most Bibles. Mark, the earliest gospel, has about eleven thousand words—fewer than thirty pages. The longest of Paul's letters, Romans, has about seven thousand words—around fifteen pages. The shortest documents—Philemon, Jude, 2 John, and 3 John—are a page or less.

There is another reason that the modern meaning of "book" is misleading. In our world, books are typically written for people the author does not know and then published—they are for "the public." But the authors of the New Testament did not "publish" their works in this sense. They wrote for people they did know or knew about. They wrote from within Christian communities and for Christian communities. They weren't publishing books for a general reading audience. Indeed, in their largely preliterate and completely preprint world, doing so would have been a waste of time.

Chronology and Historical Contextualization

This New Testament has a second feature. It not only places the documents in chronological sequence, but also contextualizes them in their time and place. It emphasizes the importance and illuminating power of setting them in their historical context and seeking to discern their meanings in their ancient setting.

Context is not the same as "background." I recall from graduate school forty years ago books with titles like *"The Background of the New Testament"* and *"The New Testament in Its Background."* But context is more than background. Context is the world in which we live. Where we grew up is not only the background of our lives, but the context that shaped us. For example, I was born in the United States not long before the middle of the last century and thus grew up in the 1940s, 1950s, and 1960s. These decades not only contain the facts of my background; they also provide the context for the era that shaped me, as have the decades since.

Unlike background, context is interactive. We live in a particular time and place, and that affects what we think and how we respond and act. To illustrate from the recent past, American racism in the 1950s and 1960s was not simply the background for Martin Luther King's life, but the interactive context in which he lived and to which he responded. To imagine seeking to understand King's words and life by treating his time and place as a mere set of background facts rather than as the interactive context would be to miss understanding what shaped him, what guided him, why he made the decisions he did, and even why he matters so much to us today.

By viewing the documents of the New Testament in their historical context, we recognize that they were not written to us and for us, but to and for the ancient communities that produced them. They tell us how formative figures in early Christianity saw things within their historical context, their time and place. To try to read the New Testament without taking into account its historical context produces misunderstanding. What we read is about "their then," not directly about "our now."

Contextualizing the documents means asking:

- What did Paul's letters mean to him and to the communities that received them? What was going on in those communities that led Paul to address the issues he did?

- What did the gospels mean in and for the communities that produced them and to whom they were addressed?

- What did Revelation mean to the early Christian groups in western Asia Minor (modern Turkey) to whom it was addressed?

Not only do the New Testament texts come alive in their ancient settings, but we are saved from the fanciful misunderstandings that result from nonhistorical interpretations. For example, the book of Revelation tells us what some early Christians thought would happen soon in their time, not about what will happen in our time or some future time. Passages in the New Testament that affirm slavery and patriarchy and condemn same-sex relationships tell us how some of our spiritual ancestors saw things, not necessarily how we should see things. Of course, what they thought in their then matters—but it may or may not be normative for us in our now. Context matters.

The Threefold Historical Context

Taking the chronological context of the New Testament seriously involves paying attention to three contexts: Jesus and early Christianity, Judaism, and the Roman Empire. They are not successive chronological contexts, one after the other, but are more like three concentric circles, one within another. Jesus and his followers must be seen within the context of first-century Judaism, and all of that must be seen within the context of the Roman Empire.

The Context of Jesus and Early Christianity

Jesus's historical context was the Jewish homeland in the first third of the first century. He was born around 4 BCE and crucified around the year 30. The movement he had begun continued after his death among his followers. We commonly call the movement "early Christianity," though this is a bit anachronistic. The word "Christianity" does not appear in the New Testament, and "Christians" only appears twice. The people around Jesus understood themselves as followers of him and "the Way" that he proclaimed. For them, it was a movement within Judaism and not yet a new religion distinct from Judaism. That came later.

Soon after Jesus's death, the movement expanded geographically beyond the Jewish homeland—into Syria, Egypt, Asia Minor, Greece, and Rome. Initially, it spread within the Jewish Diaspora (Jewish communities outside of the homeland). Within no more than twenty years, it had begun to include Gentiles, that is, non-Jews.

These early Christian communities are the historical context for the oral traditions about Jesus and what it meant to follow him (more about this in Chapter 2).

They are also the context of the whole of the New Testament: its twenty-seven documents are the product of early Christians in the first hundred years or so after the end of Jesus's historical life.

The Context of Judaism

Early Christianity and the New Testament emerged within the larger context of Judaism. To say the obvious, Jesus, Paul, and most or perhaps all of the writers of the New Testament were Jewish. The exception may be the author of Luke and Acts, who may have been a Gentile—but if so, a Gentile who knew Judaism well.

First-century Judaism was diverse. In the Jewish homeland, there were a number of groups with different ways of being Jewish within the context of Roman rule, which began in 63 BCE, about sixty years before Jesus was born.

A group known as the Essenes advocated withdrawal from mainstream society and established monastic communities near the Dead Sea. Pharisees remained within society and advocated rigorous observance of laws that distinguished Jews from non-Jews as a way of maintaining Jewish identity. Violent resistance movements (sometimes called "Zealots," though this is historically inaccurate) opposed Roman rule through armed insurrection. There were three major Jewish revolts in the time around Jesus: in 4 BCE, 66–73 CE, and 132–135 CE. Sadducees (generally understood as a wealthy aristocratic group) took the opposite course and collaborated with Roman rule. A majority of Jews were not part of any of these groups, but lived their understanding of Judaism as they knew it. Many resigned themselves to Roman rule, even as they may also have resented it.

But within this diversity, Jews shared in common a core of convictions, sometimes called "covenantal theology" or "common Judaism." This common core included:

> *Radical monotheism.* God is one. God alone is Lord and is to be loved with heart, strength, soul, and mind.

> *Promise and hope.* In Genesis, God entered into a covenant with Abraham and Sarah and promised that they would have many descendants who would live in their own land—and land was the material basis of existence in the ancient and premodern world. God's promises continued as the prophets proclaimed God's dream of a world of justice and peace during the time of the monarchy and in the centuries of ancient Israel's subjugation by one empire after another. Except for a hundred-year period that ended in 63 BCE, the Jewish homeland had been ruled by foreign empires for roughly six centuries by the time of Jesus. Foreign rule created an urgent issue: When and how would God's promises be fulfilled?

Observance. Covenantal theology included living in accord with its way, its laws. What this meant varied among Jewish groups, but all affirmed that the covenant told them how they should live.

The Context of the Roman Empire

The third concentric circle of context is the Roman Empire. Jesus and his followers lived within it, and all of the documents in the New Testament were written within it. Though Christians are generally aware that Christianity began within the Roman Empire, the importance of this fact is not as widely recognized. In a sentence, its importance was that Rome was a particularly powerful form of an ancient domination system legitimated by an imperial theology.

An Ancient Domination System. "Domination system" is a semitechnical term for the most common form of structuring societies from the birth of agriculture and cities in the 3000s BCE until the industrial and democratic revolutions of the last few centuries. Premodern domination systems ranged in size from small kingdoms to large empires. Seeing their central features illuminates thousands of years of human history, from prebiblical through biblical times, to the Middle Ages, and the centuries that followed. Ancient domination systems were:

Politically oppressive. Societies were ruled by a few—by monarchies and aristocracies, the powerful and wealthy elites. Ordinary people, the vast majority of the population, had no voice in how these societies were structured.

Economically exploitative. The ruling elites structured society in their own economic self-interest. About half to two-thirds of the annual production of wealth went to the top few percent of the population. The great gap between the wealthy and the rest (90 percent or more) had calamitous effects on the latter, including a life expectancy about half that of the elite class.

Chronically violent. Elites maintained power by the threat and use of violence against their own populations. In addition, wars were frequent, initiated by one group of elites against another for the sake of expanding their wealth and power by controlling more people and land.

Legitimated by religious claims. Elite religion proclaimed that kings ruled by divine right and that the social order, the way the world was put together, reflected the will of God.

The world of the ancient domination system is the context not only of Jesus and early Christianity, but of the Bible as a whole. It is the context for the story of the exodus, which is about liberation from the domination system of ancient Egypt. It is the context for the prophetic protest against the re-creation of a domination system within Israel during the time of the monarchy. It is the context of Jewish voices, from the sixth century BCE on, crying out against oppression by a succession of foreign domination systems.

Rome was an especially large domination system, controlling much of Europe, the Middle East, and North Africa. Its military was both powerful and efficient. Its legions were highly trained professional soldiers and engineers who built a system of all-weather roads, so they could move quickly to quell resistance in any part of the empire.

It was even more economically exploitative than its predecessors. Not only were conquered provinces required to pay annual tribute to Rome (a form of taxation collected by local authorities), but Roman economic policy promoted the commercialization of agriculture. Small plots of land that had been farmed for centuries by families to produce food for their own use were combined into large estates owned by the wealthy to produce crops for sale and export. Having lost their land, many in the rural class became tenant farmers, sharecroppers, or day laborers, producing not their own food, but commercial crops like grains, olives, and grapes. Outside the Jewish homeland, the commercialization of agriculture also resulted in large-scale migration to cities, where former agricultural laborers became part of the urban working poor—a situation that becomes important for understanding the urban context of Paul's activity.

Roman Imperial Theology. Like most domination systems, Rome legitimated its rule with religion. Though Roman imperial theology began earlier, it was amplified during the reign of Caesar Augustus, emperor from 31 BCE to 14 CE. His birth name was Octavian, and he was about nineteen when Julius Caesar was assassinated, in 44 BCE. For the next thirteen years, Octavian and his rival, Mark Antony, carried on a devastating civil war—Roman legions fought each other on the battlefield—for the imperial throne. The war ended in 31 BCE when Octavian defeated Antony and Cleopatra in a naval battle at Actium, off the coast of Greece.

As a result, Octavian became "Augustus." The word means "he who is to be worshipped and revered." He was heralded not only as "Augustus," but also as "Son of God" and "Lord." He was called the "savior of the world" who had brought "peace on earth" by ending the civil war that was tearing the empire apart. His birth was the beginning of the "gospel," the "good news" (the Greek word used in the New Testament and translated into English as "good news" or "gospel"). Stories were even told about his divine conception: he was the son of the god Apollo.

The titles conferred upon Augustus continued to be used by his imperial successors, though some took their divine status more seriously than others. From

Augustus on, imperial theology imparted the message that Roman domination was divinely ordained. The gods had chosen Rome to rule the world.

Roman imperial theology is the oppositional context for much of early Christian language about Jesus. The gospels, Paul's letters, and the other New Testament writings use the language of imperial theology, but apply it to Jesus. Jesus is the "Son of God"—the emperor is not. Jesus is the "Lord"—the emperor is not. Jesus is the "Savior" who brings "peace on earth"—the emperor is not. The contrast is not just a matter of language. The contrast is also about two different visions of how the world should be. The world of the domination system is a world of political oppression, economic exploitation, and chronic violence. The alternative is a world in which everyone has enough and no one needs to be afraid. The gospel phrase for this is the "kingdom of God," the heart, as the gospels proclaim, of Jesus's message.

And so, throughout this chronological and contextual New Testament, the relationship of Jesus and early Christianity to the Jewish world that shaped them and the imperial context to which they responded will be emphasized. To take these ancient texts seriously requires taking their ancient contexts seriously. Contextualization matters.

2

Before Anything Was Written

Recall from Chapter 1 the scholarly consensus that Mark is the first gospel, written around the year 70, four decades after Jesus's historical life. During those decades his followers' memories of Jesus—what he said, what he did, and what he was like—circulated orally and were not yet in written form.

Though at least seven of Paul's letters were written in the 50s, they are not an exception. They say very little about the historical life of Jesus. Scholars have sometimes used this silence to argue that Jesus's earthly life didn't matter very much to Paul, but this is unpersuasive.

There is an obvious reason that Paul did not often refer to what Jesus said and did. He wrote to communities that he had taught in person, and so he would already have told them about Jesus. The one exception is his letter to Christians in Rome, but they also already knew about Jesus. The purpose of Paul's letters was not to tell people about Jesus, but to stay in touch with his communities and to address issues that had arisen in his absence. They are about applications of Paul's understanding of life "in Christ"—one of his most important phrases—to particular circumstances.

That the story of Jesus wasn't written down until several decades after his death is puzzling to many in our time. I have often been asked why his followers waited so long to do so. Indeed, why didn't Jesus himself put his message into writing? If it was so important, why didn't he write it down? These questions reflect our modern historical context and mind-set. In our time of widespread literacy and reliance on print (ink or electronic), writing something down is taken for granted as the way to preserve memory and accuracy.

But the historical context of the world of Jesus and his followers was very different. They lived in a preliterate and preprint culture. Most people—probably 95 percent or more—did not have the literacy necessary to read biblical documents—

whether from the Old Testament or the soon-to-be-born New Testament. Moreover, until the invention of the printing press in the 1400s, documents were expensive to produce. To say the obvious, copies had to be made by hand. So until relatively recently, most people knew their sacred stories and sacred teachings orally and aurally—by hearing them and holding them in memory.

Thus during the time of Jesus, written documents were not an effective way to spread a message. Writing, of course, did have a purpose. Letters—like the letters of Paul—were a way of communicating with a community that had somebody who could read the letter aloud to the rest. Gospels were a way of preserving an early Christian community's traditions about Jesus.

But putting traditions into written form was not the first thing that a new religious movement would put its energy into. Rather, doing so came later, as early Christian communities began the process of institutionalization, which included preserving their traditions for the future.

So we should not be surprised that the story of Jesus was not put into writing until the last third of the first century. How then did Paul and other early followers of Jesus know about him before anything was written about him? Some had known him during his historical life, but most knew about him through the oral tradition of the early Christian communities.

Early Christian Oral Tradition

In New Testament scholarship, "oral tradition" refers to both a time and a process. It refers to the time from Jesus's death until the gospels were written. The process—how Jesus was remembered—involved memory, development, and testimony.

It was a communal process. The traditions about Jesus—what he said, what he did, and what he was like—were remembered within communities of his followers. We should not imagine individuals remembering Jesus privately, alone, and then decades later putting their memories into writing. Nor should we imagine the authors of the gospels as independent researchers, seeking to contact as many people as possible who had known Jesus during his historical lifetime. Rather, they were themselves part of a Christian community and wrote from and to that community, even as they may also have thought that what they wrote might be of importance beyond their community.

Early Christian communities were small and intimate. According to a recent scholarly estimate, there were about two thousand followers of Jesus by the year 60. Perhaps half of these were in the Jewish homeland and the other half in other parts of the Roman Empire. Thus, with perhaps an exception or two, the size of a community would have been fifty or fewer. They were also committed and intentional: it took courage and passion to be part of an early Christian community.

In these communities the traditions about Jesus were remembered and used in a number of ways. They were used in recruitment, to enlist "outsiders" into the movement Jesus had begun. They formed the core of instruction, or catechesis, to teach those who desired to become part of the movement about Jesus. And they were used in devotion. Early followers loved Jesus and commemorated him in their worship. No doubt they also enjoyed talking about him. These communities are the context in which Jesus was remembered during the decades of oral tradition.

Oral Tradition and Memory

The oral tradition contains memory. It and the written gospels are about Jesus remembered. But memory is not the same as memorization. We should not imagine Jesus's followers memorizing what he said and did and then decades later putting their historically exact memories into writing.

One reason is that Jesus was an itinerant teacher whose most characteristic forms of speech were striking short sayings, called "aphorisms," and short stories, called "parables." The use of memorable aphorisms and parables is a brilliant and necessary strategy for a teacher in a preliterate and preprint culture.

As a teacher on the move, he would have spoken his aphorisms and told his parables many times. No itinerant teacher uses great one-liners like "Let the dead bury their own dead," or "Do you have eyes, but fail to see?" or "Blessed are the poor" only once. They would have been spoken many times in different contexts and with different "lead-ins." Their literary context in the gospels is one particular setting in which Jesus may have said them, but obviously they were not said only in that setting.

So also no itinerant teacher tells a story like the good Samaritan or the prodigal son only once. Moreover, there is no reason to think that Jesus would have told his parables exactly the same way each time. That's not how stories work. He most likely told them in shorter and longer versions. For example, the parable of the prodigal son in Luke 15.11–32 takes about four minutes to read out loud, but it is easy to imagine it being expanded into a thirty- or forty-minute story.

Thus his followers' memory of what Jesus taught is not about "memorization," but about "gist." We have the "gist" of sayings and the plot summaries of stories he would have spoken many times. "Gist" is what was remembered, not exact wording.

A second reason for saying that we do not have exact memory flows from a careful comparative reading of "gospel parallels," sayings and stories that appear in all three of the synoptic gospels, Mark, Matthew, and Luke. Most often the accounts of something Jesus said or did are not exactly the same. Sometimes they are quite different.

Some of the differences fall into the category of "copyediting." Matthew and Luke used Mark as they wrote their gospels. As they did so, they made changes. Some were grammatical, and some involved condensing a story. But sometimes the differences are about more than "copyediting." They are about the development of the tradition.

Oral Tradition and Development

The oral tradition involved development as well as memory. Traditions about Jesus sometimes developed in different ways in different Christian communities. For example, consider the prayer known by Catholics as the "Our Father" and by Protestants as "the Lord's Prayer." It appears in two quite different forms in Matthew and Luke. A third form is in an early Christian document known as the *Didache,* which many scholars think was written around 100 and thus earlier than some of the New Testament documents.

Matthew's version is best known, because it is used in Christian worship and devotion. It begins with the solemn "Our Father who art in heaven, hallowed be your name," and continues with "Your kingdom come, your will be done, on earth as in heaven," followed by petitions for daily bread, forgiveness of debts, and deliverance from temptation and evil. It lacks the concluding doxology familiar to Protestants: "For yours is the kingdom and the power and the glory forever."

Luke's begins with the simple "Father," continues with the brief "Your kingdom come," and lacks the final petition for deliverance from evil and, like Matthew's, the concluding doxology. A form of the latter is found in the *Didache:* "For yours is the power and the glory forever."

How do we account for these three forms of the Lord's Prayer in early Christian documents? A possible answer is that Jesus taught the three different forms on three different occasions, and those who were at any one session memorized the form they heard. A more plausible answer is that they are the way the prayer developed in three different communities.

Oral Tradition and Testimony

Testimony is testifying, witnessing, to what matters, to the truth that matters. In this sense, everything about Jesus in the oral tradition is testimony. Early Christian communities wouldn't have remembered a saying or story by Jesus or a story about something he did unless it mattered to them.

This realization impacts how we should hear, read, and understand the story of Jesus—of what he said and did, what he was like, and what happened to him. The stories are not simply "factual" reports—they are about what mattered to his followers. As such, they have a surplus of meaning. They are to be read for their meaning and not primarily for their factuality. If they also have a factual basis, fine—but it is their more-than-factual meaning that matters most.

Testimony involves both memory and development. It is grounded in early Christian memory of Jesus and the remarkable person that he was. And it developed beyond what Jesus himself said and did.

For example, in the earliest layers of the developing tradition, Jesus does not proclaim an extraordinary status for himself. Mark, the earliest gospel, affirms that Jesus is the "Son of God" and "Messiah," but, as Mark tells the story of Jesus, this extraordinary status was not part of Jesus's own teaching. The two times Jesus seems to affirm an exalted status in Mark do not take place in public, but in private—once alone with his disciples and then in the story of his trial at the end of his life. The fact that it was not part of Jesus's own public teaching in Mark has been called the "messianic secret." Jesus's identity as Son of God and Messiah was a secret, unknown by almost everybody while he was alive and only openly proclaimed after his death. Matthew and Luke change this a little, but not much.

John's gospel is very different. Jesus frequently speaks of himself in the most extraordinary language. He is the Light of the World; the Bread of Life; the Good Shepherd; the Way, the Truth, and the Life; and the True Vine; before Abraham was, he was. He identifies himself with God: "The Father and I are one"; "Whoever has seen me has seen the Father" (10.30; 14.9). John opens his gospel with a magnificent prologue that speaks of Jesus as the "Word of God," who was with God at creation and who has now become flesh. Jesus is the incarnation of God, the embodiment of what can be seen of God in a human life.

These affirmations go way beyond anything Jesus said about himself as reported by Mark, Matthew, and Luke. It is highly unlikely that Jesus ever said them. But that doesn't mean they are to be devalued and dismissed, because they are not factually accurate memory. Rather, they are testimony to the significance of Jesus as it had developed within the community (perhaps communities) that John wrote from and for. They testify to what Jesus had become in their experience, thought, and conviction. But it is a stage of development within the oral tradition that occurred much later than what is in Mark, Matthew, and Luke.

Testimony about Jesus within early Christian communities developed for more than one reason. In addition to people's memory of him as the extraordinary person he was, their understanding of his significance grew in the years after Easter. Some of them experienced him after his death as a living figure of the present, not simply as a remembered and dearly beloved figure from the past. Moreover, they did not experience him as a ghostly survivor, but in a radically new way as a divine reality now one with God. These experiences generated the conviction that God had vindicated Jesus and what he was doing. To echo language from Paul's letters, God had raised Jesus to God's right hand, exalted him, and given him the name above every name: Jesus is Lord.

Thus within modern biblical scholarship, there is a near consensus that the "titles" of Jesus—as the Son of God, Lord, Word of God, and so forth—are post-Easter developments; testimony, not memory. But they are testimony grounded in memory and experience.

The process of development within the oral tradition produced earlier and later layers. The earliest layer is closest in time to Jesus and represents a period when memory was still dominant and relatively little development had occurred. The latest layers—which are crystallized in written form in the gospels—do contain memory, but also include decades of development and testimony. They come from a time in which Jesus's followers affirmed him in the most exalted language.

What Is Most Likely Early?

What parts of the oral tradition are early? What did it say about Jesus in its early stages? How much was there by the time Paul wrote his letters? How much might Paul have known about Jesus from oral tradition?

The question is of more than historical interest. It is important for a chronological New Testament, in which seven of Paul's letters come first. They are a bewildering place to begin unless one already knows something about Jesus. His letters presuppose Jesus and knowing about Jesus, even though they do not presuppose the not-yet-written gospels.

But a growing number of people today do not know much about Jesus and the gospels. About half of American Christians cannot name the four gospels. Two-thirds do not know that the Sermon on the Mount is in Matthew. Moreover, more and more Americans are growing up outside the church and thus have little or no exposure to Jesus and the gospels.

I experienced this problem firsthand when I began my introductory New Testament course one year with Paul's letters rather than the gospels. About half of my students had grown up without any involvement in a church, and so they knew little or nothing about Jesus and the gospels. Paul knew about Jesus, but they didn't. They were lost as they tried to figure out what on earth Paul's letters were about. I taught the course that way only once.

So before we turn to Paul's letters, it is important and helpful to provide a concise summary of what is likely to be very early tradition about Jesus, already there by the time of Paul and from which Paul himself would have learned. The following are likely to be components of the early communities' historical memory of Jesus:

- Jesus was born shortly before the death of Herod the Great in 4 BCE and grew up in Nazareth, a peasant village in Galilee, in the northern part of the Jewish homeland.

- In his mid to late twenties, he went to a wilderness prophet known as John, who became his mentor. Presumably after some time (rather than immediately), he was baptized by John. After John was arrested by the ruler of Galilee, Jesus began his own public activity.

- At the center of Jesus's message was the kingdom of God. His first words in Mark, our earliest gospel, are about the coming of the kingdom of God. They are Mark's advance summary of what Jesus and his story are about.

- The kingdom of God was not about "heaven," but about the transformation of this world, the earth, which is clear from the Lord's Prayer: "Your kingdom come *on earth.*"

- He spoke primarily to the peasant class (90 percent of the population), which was made up of agricultural and manual laborers who lived in rural areas: small towns, villages, hamlets, the countryside. He didn't go to cities, except Jerusalem.

- As a teacher he consistently used arresting aphorisms and provocative parables to invite his hearers to image reality, life, and their lives differently.

- He was a healer and an exorcist. More stories of healings and exorcisms are told about him than about any other figure in the Jewish tradition.

- He broke social boundaries. He was known and criticized for eating with marginalized people, including virtual outcasts and untouchables, and for his associations with women.

- His followers spoke of him as "anointed by the Spirit." The Spirit of God was present in him and flowed through him.

- He went to Jerusalem at the season of Passover, most likely in the year 30. His last week was filled with confrontation and conflict, leading to arrest and execution by the imperial and religious authorities who ruled his world.

- Some of his followers experienced him after his death—not simply as a "ghost," but as a divine reality with the qualities of "Lord" and "God."

Details could be added to this list, but its purpose is not to provide an in-depth account of the historical pre-Easter Jesus. That would require a book-length treatment, and a multitude of books have been written that do just that. Rather, its purpose is twofold. It presents a scholarly consensus; most mainline scholars would agree that at least this much is early historical memory. And it is a crystallization of what Paul is likely to have known about Jesus. He may well have known more, but he knew at least this much. To Paul we now turn.

3

Paul and His Letters

Knowing what we can about Paul and his historical context greatly illuminates the seven letters that were definitely written by him. Indeed, it is not just illuminating, but essential. Without historical contextualization, Paul's letters remain opaque and subject to great misunderstanding, even as a number of verses virtually glow in the dark apart from context.

Next to Jesus, Paul is the most important person in the New Testament. Thirteen of its twenty-seven documents are attributed to him. More than half of Acts is about him. Paul's significance for Christianity extends beyond the New Testament. Augustine (356–430), the most important Christian theologian in the first thousand years of Christianity, was converted by a verse in Romans, and Paul's thought greatly influenced his theology for the rest of his life.

Paul's letters were the biblical foundation of the Reformation in the sixteenth century. He has been especially important for Protestants ever since. Many of their "big" words come from Paul: "justification," "grace," "faith," "sanctification," "Christ crucified," "dying and rising with Christ," "the body of Christ," and so forth. Some scholars call him the "founder of Christianity" or the "second founder of Christianity." Those who call him such often do so with a negative spin. They see Paul as the "spoiler" of Christianity, who turned the good religion *of* Jesus (what Jesus himself taught) into a not-so-good, or even bad, religion *about* Jesus (believing a collection of doctrines about Jesus). But admirers and detractors alike agree that Paul is very important for understanding Christianity.

He is also the only New Testament author about whom we know much. The others are essentially anonymous. Even when we think we know their names, our other information about them is negligible. Compared to Paul, we know very little about Peter, the other most important early follower of Jesus. But we know about Paul firsthand from what he says about himself in his letters and secondhand from Acts, where he is the central character. Acts is significantly later than Paul's letters and, like the gospels, combines memory, development, and testimony a generation or two after Paul. Thus it is a secondary source for knowing about Paul.

In contrast to Jesus, Paul has a mixed reputation. Jesus is almost universally admired, but Paul is not even admired by some Christians. Of course, he is highly regarded by Christians who see his letters (like the Bible as a whole) as the inerrant and infallible divine revelation of God. For them, his letters contain absolute truth.

Most Christians would not go that far. Many are troubled by some of what is in the thirteen letters attributed to Paul. There are passages they have difficulty believing are or ever were the will of God, texts, for example, that condone slavery, command the subordination of women, condemn same-sex relationships, and commend complete obedience to established authority.

So, to use language from an earlier book, is Paul appealing or appalling? The jury is out. The verdict depends on how we see the letters attributed to him. Were all thirteen written by him? If so, there is much in Paul that is appalling. But most of the problem passages referred to above appear in the six letters that modern scholarship puts in the disputed or definitely post-Pauline category. The seven letters universally accepted as coming from Paul in the 50s portray a Paul quite different from the Paul of the other six letters.

Paul's Life

Modern historical study of Paul's seven letters and Acts has produced a consensus about the following biographical sketch. The primary source is the letters; Acts is important, but secondary. When Acts and Paul's letters disagree, Paul's letters take precedence.

We do not know when Paul was born, but it was probably in the first decade of the first century. He was thus a near contemporary of Jesus, perhaps ten years or so younger. He lived vigorously into the 60s of that century, even though he was plagued by a recurrent malady. He was executed in Rome in the early to mid 60s.

He was born Jewish in the Diaspora, a term referring to Jews living outside of their ancestral homeland. Most did. Estimates of the number of Jews in the first century hover around six million, about one-tenth of the population of the Roman Empire. One to two million lived in the homeland. Two-thirds or more were in the Diaspora.

According to Acts, he was born in Tarsus, a cosmopolitan city in southern Asia Minor (today's Turkey). Capital of the Roman province of Cilicia and renowned for a university said to be as excellent as the one at Athens, Tarsus was, as Acts puts it, "an important city" (21.39).

We do not know how Paul's parents came to live there. The reasons Jews lived in areas other than the Jewish homeland were diverse, ranging from capture and enslavement to voluntary emigration. According to Acts, Paul's father was a Roman citizen, and thus Paul was a Roman citizen by birth. "Citizen" did not mean simply somebody who lived within the Roman Empire; it was an elevated status that belonged to a very small percentage of the population. If Paul's father was a Roman citizen, the most likely reason is that he had been a slave of a Roman citizen, who then liberated him. But Paul in his letters never refers to himself as a Roman citizen, and so scholars are uncertain whether this detail from Acts is correct.

Paul obviously had an excellent education. His letters reflect an intimate knowledge of the Jewish Bible, and his use of the Greek language and its rhetorical style is remarkable. He knew both Judaism and the Gentile world firsthand and may even have had a Greek education as well as a Jewish one. In Tarsus, he grew up in both worlds, a superb context for one who was to become the "apostle to the Gentiles" (that is, non-Jews, whom Paul frequently calls "Greeks").

He was a passionate Jew. He became a Pharisee, a member of a Jewish movement that sought through sharp social boundaries to preserve Jewish identity and community in a historical context in which accommodation to Hellenistic and Roman culture was a very real threat. According to Acts, he studied in Jerusalem under Gamaliel, one of the most renowned rabbis of the time. Paul himself does not mention this, and some scholars think this may be part of the "upgrading" of Paul's stature by the author of Acts. But whether or not he studied in Jerusalem, he was a brilliant, passionate, committed Pharisaic Jew.

Paul never met the historical Jesus. But almost immediately after Jesus's crucifixion, within at most a few years, he became a persecutor of Jesus's followers. That he did so is an indicator not only of his religious passion, but also that he knew enough about Jesus at this point in his life to think his movement should be stopped. That's the purpose of persecution.

Acts introduces Paul in the story of the first fatal persecution of a follower of Jesus, the martyrdom of Stephen in Jerusalem (Acts 7). Paul, still named "Saul" according to Acts, stands in the crowd consenting to Stephen's execution. Then Acts 9 narrates that Paul was given authority by the high priest in Jerusalem to arrest followers of Jesus in Damascus and bring them to Jerusalem in chains. For more than one reason, that is historically unlikely, perhaps even impossible.

But that Paul was a persecutor of followers of Jesus almost from the beginning is certain. He says so himself as he briefly refers to his life: he was "circumcised on the eighth day, a member of the people of Israel, of the tribe of Benjamin, a Hebrew born of Hebrews; as to the law, a Pharisee; as to zeal, a persecutor of the church; as to righteousness under the law, blameless" (Phil. 3.5–6). Paul was a young man when he was a persecutor. If he was born in the first decade of the first century, he would have been in his twenties or early thirties.

Then he had an experience that caused a dramatic reversal of his life. It happened in or near Damascus, the capital of Syria, then and now, three to five years after the death of Jesus. Paul's time as a persecutor was quite brief.

So famous is it that the phrase "Damascus road experience" has become a common metaphor for a life-changing experience. It changed Paul from persecutor of Jesus's followers to advocate of Jesus, from adversary of Jesus to Jesus's apostle to the Gentiles, the non-Jewish world.

Acts narrates the Damascus road story three times in slightly different ways (Acts 9; 22; 26). What they have in common is that Paul, while traveling to Damascus to arrest followers of Jesus, had an experience in which Jesus appeared to him as a living reality in the present, as Lord, and called Paul not only to be his follower, but his apostle to the Gentiles.

Paul refers to this experience in his letters, though he doesn't narrate the story. In Galatians, he acknowledges his past as a persecutor of the Jesus movement and then speaks of his transformation. Damascus is mentioned in the last verse:

> You have heard, no doubt, of my earlier life in Judaism. I was violently
> persecuting the church of God and was trying to destroy it. I advanced in
> Judaism beyond many among my people of the same age, for I was far more
> zealous for the traditions of my ancestors. But when God, who had set me
> apart before I was born and called me through his grace, was pleased to
> reveal his Son to me, so that I might proclaim him among the Gentiles, I did
> not confer with any human being, nor did I go up to Jerusalem to those who
> were already apostles before me, but I went away at once into Arabia, and
> afterwards I returned to Damascus. (1.13–17)

Both Acts and Paul's letters agree that Paul was radically transformed by this experience.

Though often called Paul's "conversion," the term can be misleading. In modern English, a common meaning of "conversion" is to convert from one religion to another or to convert from being nonreligious to being religious. Neither meaning applies in Paul's case. He was passionately religious before the experience, and he didn't think of himself as having converted from one religion (Judaism) to another (Christianity). He regarded himself as Jewish all of his life, not as a member of a new and different religion. His conversion was not from Judaism to Christianity, but from

Pharisaic Judaism to Christian Judaism. They were different ways of being Jewish. The division into two religions came later.

Paul's experience is commonly called a "vision." According to Acts, Paul saw a great light, and the light identified itself as Jesus. According to Paul's letters, Paul saw Jesus: "Have I not seen Jesus our Lord?" (1 Cor. 9.1); "he appeared also to me" (15.8). What he saw and experienced convinced him that he was wrong, that the Jesus whom he had been persecuting was not only alive, but Lord. The obvious inference was that if Jesus still lives and is Lord, it can only be because God had vindicated him. God had said "yes" to Jesus and "no" to the powers that had killed him. They were wrong. Paul had been wrong. Now Paul had been called to be Jesus's apostle to the Gentiles.

So, not later than five years after the death of Jesus, in the mid-30s of the first century, Paul began his vocation as a follower and apostle of Jesus. We know little about the next few years. He tells us he went to "Arabia" (not Saudi Arabia, but ancient Nabatea in present-day Jordan), presumably on a "mission" and not a desert retreat. He seems to have had no success there. Around the year 40, he went on his first mission to Asia Minor (Turkey) as an associate of Barnabas, an early Christian missionary to whom Paul was subordinate. Then Paul and Barnabas separated, and Paul traveled on his own to major cities in Asia Minor during most of the 40s. In the late 40s, he went to Greece, beginning in Macedonia in the north and continuing on to Athens and Corinth in the south. During most of the 50s, he traveled back and forth between Asia Minor and Greece, spending much of his time in Corinth and Ephesus.

Paul's life as an apostle often got him in trouble. Sometimes he had to flee cities because his message and activity caused conflict. He was arrested several times, often beaten, and thrown in prison more than once, in danger of being executed. Plus we need to imagine the privations and danger involved in his extensive travel. He walked thousands of miles, including through mountain passes and across high arid plateaus. Despite paintings that depict his being knocked off his horse during his Damascus experience, he didn't travel by horse. Only the military and the wealthy did. Sometimes he traveled by sea, and he was shipwrecked at least three times.

He refers to his trials as he defends himself against critics and opponents in his community in Corinth:

> Are they ministers of Christ? I am talking like a madman—I am a better one: with far greater labors, far more imprisonments, with countless floggings, and often near death. Five times I have received from the Jews the forty lashes minus one. Three times I was beaten with rods. Once I received a stoning. Three times I was shipwrecked; for a night and a day I was adrift

at sea; on frequent journeys, in danger from rivers, danger from bandits, danger from my own people, danger from Gentiles, danger in the city, danger in the wilderness, danger at sea, danger from false brothers and sisters; in toil and hardship, through many a sleepless night, hungry and thirsty, often without food, cold and naked. And, besides other things, I am under daily pressure because of my anxiety for all the churches. (2 Cor. 11.23–28)

In the late 50s, he traveled to Jerusalem. It resulted in his arrest and confinement for the rest of his life. His purpose was to bring a collection of money that he had raised in his largely Gentile communities to benefit followers of Jesus in Jerusalem. He planned to then take his apostolic vocation westward to Rome and Spain.

But in Jerusalem he was arrested by temple authorities and handed over to Roman authorities. Although the latter found him innocent, they did not release him. So Paul appealed to his right as a Roman citizen to have a hearing before the emperor himself, and he was transported to Rome as a prisoner. At the end of Acts, he has been living in Rome under house arrest for two years, "proclaiming the kingdom of God and teaching about the Lord Jesus Christ." Neither Acts nor any other New Testament document tells us what happened to Paul. But early Christian traditions, which report that he was executed in Rome around the year 64, during the reign of Nero, are generally accepted as historically factual. Like Jesus, Paul was killed by the powers that ruled his world.

The Urban Context of Paul's Apostleship and Letters

Paul was a city person. Unlike Jesus, who grew up in a small village and whose activity was among the peasant class in small towns and rural areas of the Jewish homeland, Paul was urban. He grew up in a city and carried out his vocation in major cities of Asia Minor and Greece, most of them capitals of Roman provinces. There is no report of his bringing his message to a small town or village.

Thus, to understand the historical context of Paul and his letters we need to know something of the cities in the Roman Empire of his time. The largest was Rome itself, with perhaps a million people. A number of others had six-figure populations: Alexandria in Egypt, Antioch in Syria, Ephesus in Asia Minor, perhaps Corinth in Greece. Most were smaller. Estimates for Jerusalem are around forty thousand, and for Tarsus, Paul's city of birth, around fifty thousand.

Cities in the Roman Empire shared a number of features. They were very densely populated. Because most were walled cities, population expansion occurred within the walls. For example, the walls of Antioch enclosed two square miles, within which lived two hundred thousand people. Its population density exceeded that of the most densely populated cities today, and without high-rise buildings. Most of the urban working class lived in four- or five-story tenements. Most families had only a room or two, used primarily for storage and sleeping.

There was no sanitation. Today's visitors to the remains of ancient cities of the Roman Empire often marvel at their water systems, including even toilets, but these were luxuries for the wealthy. In the tenement areas, where most of the population lived, water had to be carried, most often up several flights of stairs. Human waste was dumped into gutters. These conditions and crowding meant that contagious disease was rampant. Life expectancy was low, about thirty years for those who survived the high mortality rates of infancy and childhood.

The urban working population could be sustained only by continuing migration from rural areas. Roman agricultural policy virtually compelled migration to cities. Small peasant farms that had provided basic sustenance to the families that had lived on them for centuries were being combined into large estates that now produced grains and other agricultural products for export. Many of the rural class, now without their own land, moved to cities to find work. Most did so out of desperation, not because they desired city life.

Migration to cities destroyed the extended family and village relationships that marked traditional rural communities. Newcomers to cities, even if they arrived with their family, were severed from the familiarity and common concern of village life. They were, in an important sense, alone and on their own. Moreover, cities were populated by many ethnic and linguistic groups, in contrast to the homogeneity of village life. Ethnic estrangement and conflict were frequent.

Thus life was difficult for most of those who lived in cities. Earning enough money to pay for food and shelter was always an issue. Disease and death were constant threats. Community was no longer something that one was born into, but was either absent or newly formed.

Paul's Audience

Paul's purpose as apostle was to create and nurture urban communities of Christ-followers—from among Gentiles in particular. That was his commission: to go to Gentiles, not Jews. Preaching to the Jews was Peter's commission.

And yet when Paul arrived in a new city, he consistently went to a synagogue to tell people about Jesus. Why? Was he trying to convert Jews, in spite of his commission to go to the Gentiles, a vocation and restriction that he and other early Christian leaders had apparently agreed upon?

Almost certainly, the explanation is that synagogues in major cities were likely to have a number of Gentiles who were strongly attracted to Judaism, but not willing or ready to fully convert. Known variously in Acts and other ancient sources as "God-fearers," "God-worshippers," and "God-lovers," they were Gentiles involved in but still on the fringe of Judaism. They often attended synagogue services and thus knew quite a bit about Judaism, its scriptures, rituals, festivals, yearnings, and vision. Some became benefactors. No doubt they had Jewish friends. But the men did not get circumcised, and households may or may not have observed Jewish food and purity laws.

That Gentile "God-lovers" were Paul's primary audience not only is affirmed by Acts and implied in his letters, but makes great sense. The Gentiles to whom he had the most immediate access were the "God-lovers" whom he would find in synagogues. So when Paul arrived in a new city, he went first to the synagogue—not because his mission was to convert Jews, but because Gentile "God-lovers" would be there.

He sought to enlist them in communities of Christ-followers either by creating a new community in that city or by integrating them into an existing community. Christian groups existed in some cities before Paul got there, including Ephesus and Rome. In others, they were Paul's creation.

Other than synagogues, the other context in which Paul encountered Gentiles was in his work. Paul supported himself by "tent-making," an umbrella term that included making awnings, in great demand in the Mediterranean world, and perhaps also making leather goods more generally. Paul's skill gave him great mobility and self-sufficiency. The basic tools could be carried in a waist bag. He could travel light and find a job in any significant city. No doubt Paul met some of his Gentile converts while working next to them in a shop.

Paul's Approach

The above realizations about Paul's audience should affect our image of how Paul "preached" Jesus. Because of modern images of preaching, we tend to think of Paul standing in front of a crowd, large or small, and proclaiming the gospel. Acts sometimes portrays Paul this way; he preaches in synagogues and even in a theater filled with twenty thousand people. But it is unlikely that Paul preached in synagogues or to crowds of strangers who were completely unfamiliar with Judaism. What would his message, which makes so much use of Jewish language and tradition, have meant to Gentiles who knew nothing about Judaism?

We need to imagine Paul's approach as much more conversational. Consider the story in Acts 16 of Paul's conversion of a Gentile "God-lover" named Lydia, whom he met in a Jewish gathering just outside the gates of Philippi in northern Greece. Lydia was a successful and cosmopolitan businesswoman. A dealer in purple dye, which was highly valued and expensive in the ancient world, she was from Thyatira in Asia Minor and was now in Greece. Obviously very competent and intelligent, she had become attracted to Judaism.

According to Acts, Paul engaged her in conversation. Soon she and her whole household converted to become Christ-followers. What might Paul have said to Lydia? I cannot imagine that he simply proclaimed, as some Christian preaching today does, that we are all sinners and that Jesus died for our sins, so we can be forgiven and go to heaven if we believe in him. What reason would she have had for responding to that?

Instead, we need to imagine Paul telling her about Jesus, about the kind of man he was, what he taught, and what he did; about his execution by the authorities; about Paul's own experience of Jesus appearing to him, convincing him that the way of Jesus was the way of the God of the Bible; and that Jesus was Lord and Messiah, the promised one of Israel. In short, he would have talked about Jesus and testified to his meaning and significance. And he would have emphasized that in Jesus a new form of Judaism had been created in which Gentiles could be full participants. "In Christ," as he wrote in one of his most famous verses, "there is no longer Jew or Greek" (Gal. 3.28). He would have invited her into a new community in which she could be both Gentile and Jew. Indeed, Paul's purpose was to create communities of Christ-followers or to integrate converts into Christian communities that already existed.

Paul's Communities

Paul's communities of Christ-followers are called "churches" in most English translations of the New Testament. Doing so is potentially misleading, because of the modern associations with the word "church." It most commonly means a building and/or a community of Christians, large or small, organized for "religious" purposes with designated leadership roles and a set of beliefs or doctrines.

The communities of Paul were not churches in this modern sense. The first church building dates from the mid-200s, and churches were not common until after Constantine legalized and became a patron of Christianity in the 300s. So also the communities of Paul were not primarily intended for the practice of "religion" as one dimension of life; rather, they were groups learning about and practicing a comprehensive way of seeing and living.

The Greek word translated "church" is *ekklesia* (from which, for example, we get the word "ecclesiastical"). It means "assembly" and "those called out"—a community. Lacking the modern associations with "church," the Greek word is a good term for Paul's communities.

Another reason "church" is misleading is that Paul's communities were small, much smaller than most modern "churches." Recall from the previous chapter that the total number of followers of Jesus by the year 60 was about two thousand, half in the homeland and half in the Diaspora. Thus any particular community would have been small. We perhaps should imagine Paul's communities as small as fifteen or twenty people and perhaps as large as a hundred or two (as in Corinth?). And even when there were that many Christ-followers in a given city, they most often probably met in smaller groups.

One reason is the architecture of the ancient world. The spaces in which communities of Christ-followers could meet were small. It is common to speak of the earliest Christian communities as "house-churches." That term correctly makes the point that they did not have "church buildings." But it is misleading because it uses the words "church" and "house." "House" implies a private family home large enough for a gathering. Most early Christians, with some exceptions, however, lived in more modest accommodations in the four- and five-story tenement buildings mentioned earlier. They would not have had space for a gathering of fifteen or twenty or more.

But some of these tenement buildings and some homes of the wealthy on main streets had "shops" on the ground floor. These included retail shops and manufacturing and repair shops in which artisans like leatherworkers and others worked. These spaces were not large; they averaged about two hundred square feet. But, unlike residential space, they were unused some of the time. In them, small early Christian communities met. Thus some contemporary scholars speak of Paul's communities of Christ-followers not as "house-churches," but as "shop-churches." "Shop-communities" would be even more accurate, given the modern meaning of "church."

Paul's communities were not only small, but deeply committed and intentional. To become part of one was a serious undertaking. Jesus had been condemned and executed by Rome. Joining this movement meant risk—to call Jesus "Lord" and "Son of God" meant that the emperor was neither of these things. It meant becoming countercultural, rejecting the values of dominant culture and living in accord with another vision of how things should be. Paul referred to them as communities whose identity was "in Christ" and as "the body of Christ." They were "a new creation" in the midst of "this world" that subverted "this world."

The small size of these communities meant that they were intimate. Their members knew and were committed to taking care of each other. Paul's frequent use of the language of "brothers and sisters" is not just affectionate; it is "new family" imagery. People who became part of one of his communities took on the same responsibilities for each other that blood brothers and sisters had. In the first-century urban context in which many had lost their blood families because of migration and high mortality rates, this was a powerful image of community. It also meant that these were "share" communities: if you were part of this community, you would eat.

For the above reasons, I will not use the word "church" to refer to early Christian communities. Instead, I will use "Christ-communities" to refer to these small, committed, intentional, and intimate groups. Over time, what we call "churches" would emerge; but that time was not yet.

Paul's Letters in the Context of His Communities

Paul's relationship to urban Christian communities is the historical context of his letters. With one exception, the seven genuine letters of Paul were written to communities. The only one addressed to an individual is Philemon. But even it was to be read to the group of Christ-followers who gathered in his house. Again with one exception, the seven letters were written to communities Paul had founded and thus knew firsthand. The exception is Romans. When he wrote to the Christian community in Rome, he had not yet been there. But he planned to be, and Romans is to some extent an introduction to Paul's way of seeing things for Christians whom he planned to visit.

Paul's communities were sometimes conflicted, especially in Galatia and Corinth. Though they were all committed to Jesus, they sometimes differed about what that meant. Some who were deeply conflicted wrote to Paul with questions.

His letters are correspondence in context—as all correspondence is. Letters are not meant "for the world." They are meant for the person(s) to whom they are sent. They presuppose a relationship, a connection. And the context for understanding them is what we can know about that relationship.

Thus what we have in Paul's letters is not what he would have said to "outsiders," but what he wrote to Christian communities that already existed, whether he or somebody else had begun them. We do not have his "preaching"—used now as an umbrella term to refer to the content of what he said about Jesus. Instead, what we have is his very personal response to what he had learned was going on in these communities. With the mix depending on circumstances, his letters combine thanksgiving, tenderness, encouragement, teaching, affection, correction, conflict, and anger.

The Canonical and Chronological Sequences of Paul's Letters

In the canon, the thirteen letters attributed to Paul are organized according to two principles. The nine letters addressed to communities are placed first, followed by the four letters addressed to individuals. Then, within each category, the letters are arranged in descending order of length, from longest to shortest. The exception is Galatians; it comes before Ephesians, even though the latter is about two hundred words longer.

Thus the canonical order of the letters begins with Romans, the longest, continues with 1 and 2 Corinthians, Galatians, Ephesians, Philippians, Colossians, and 1 Thessalonians, and ends with 2 Thessalonians, the shortest. The letters addressed to individuals begin with 1 Timothy, the longest, continue with 2 Timothy and Titus, and end with Philemon, the shortest. To say the obvious, the organizing principle of the canonical order is not about chronological order.

In this chronological New Testament, the thirteen letters attributed to Paul appear in a very different sequence. The seven letters from Paul in the 50s begin not with Romans, but 1 Thessalonians. Indeed, Romans is the last of the seven. In between are Galatians, 1 and 2 Corinthians, Philemon, and Philippians.

The other six letters appear much later. Three—1 and 2 Timothy and Titus—appear almost at the end. The other three—Colossians, Ephesians, and 2 Thessalonians—are interspersed among the gospels and other early Christian documents. And so we turn to the first document in a chronological New Testament.

Time Line

30s

Execution of Jesus (30)

His followers continue his mission in the Jewish homeland, especially in Galilee

Conversion of Paul (ca. 33–35)

Christ-communities already in Syria, in the Jewish Diaspora beyond the homeland

40s

The emperor Caligula orders the erection of a statue of himself in the Jerusalem Temple, sparking massive nonviolent Jewish resistance

Paul in Asia Minor (Turkey)

Christ-communities reach Rome (how, we do not know)

Controversy about whether Gentile converts need to become Jewish (circumcision for males)

Jews expelled from Rome (49)

Paul enters Europe (Greece)

50s

Paul in Greece and Asia Minor

Near the end of the decade, he goes to Jerusalem where he is arrested, imprisoned, and finally sent to Rome in chains

Perhaps as early as the mid 50s, a collection of Jesus's teachings is put into writing for the first time (Q)

Seven genuine letters of Paul:
1 Thessalonians
Galatians
1 Corinthians
Philemon
Philippians
2 Corinthians
Romans

60s

Paul a prisoner in Rome

The emperor Nero blames Christians for a massive fire in Rome and kills many, including Paul and Peter (64)

Armed revolt against Roman rule in the Jewish homeland begins (66)

70s

In 70, Roman legions re-conquer Jerusalem and destroy the temple, the only place of Jewish sacrifice

The end of sacrifice begins to transform Judaism

Probably a majority of the followers of Jesus live in the Diaspora even though many are Jewish

The first gospel:
Mark

80s and onward

The center of Judaism in the homeland moves to Galilee	**James**
	Colossians
Judaism and followers of Jesus begin to separate into two different religions	**Matthew**
	Hebrews
Hostility between non-Christian Jews and Christian Jews grows	
Second- and third-generation Christians struggle with issues of adaptation to Roman culture	

90s

Earliest reference to Jesus in a non-Christian source (Josephus)	**John**
	Ephesians
The final part of the Jewish Bible is canonized, creating the three sections of Law, Prophets, and Writings	**Revelation**

100s

	Jude
	1 John
	2 John
	3 John

110s

Earliest references to Jesus and Christianity in Roman sources: Tacitus, Suetonius, and Pliny	**Luke**
	Acts
	2 Thessalonians
Unsuccessful Jewish revolt in Egypt because of tension between Jews and Gentiles	**1 Peter**
	1 Timothy
	2 Timothy
	Titus

120s

	2 Peter

130s

Jewish revolt against Roman rule in the Jewish homeland, brutally suppressed by the Romans; surviving Jews exiled from Jerusalem (132–135)

Christianity now largely in the Gentile world of the Roman Empire beyond the Jewish homeland, but perhaps the majority of Christians are Jewish in origin

New Testament

1 Thessalonians

The first document in this chronological New Testament is Paul's letter to a Christ-community in Thessalonica, the capital city of Macedonia, a province in northern Greece. It was written around the year 50, possibly a year or two earlier. Somewhat surprisingly, given the movement's origin among Jews in the Jewish homeland, the earliest Christian document is written to a community in Europe, which was largely Gentile.

Historical Context

According to Acts, Paul's mission to Europe began with a vision of "a man of Macedonia" urging him, "Come over to Macedonia and help us" (16.9). Paul's first stop was the city of Philippi, about which more will be said in the introduction to Philippians. Thessalonica was next. There, according to Acts, Paul went to the synagogue and converted some Jews and "a great many of the devout Greeks" (Gentile "God-lovers," 17.4). Then, presumably not immediately, but after some weeks or maybe a few months, riots broke out because of Paul. He left the city and went south to Athens and Corinth.

From the letter itself, we learn that while in Athens Paul sent his companion Timothy back to Thessalonica (about three hundred miles away) to find out how the community was doing (2.17–3.6). By foot, the journey took fifteen to twenty days each way; by boat, around a week each way. Timothy returned to Paul, who was possibly still in Athens but more likely in Corinth, with news of the community.

First Thessalonians is Paul's response to what he heard from Timothy. It follows the standard form of a Greek letter, as all of Paul's letters do: sender's name first, then the addressee, a brief greeting (often a blessing), a thanksgiving, the body of the letter, and the closing. To illustrate:

Sender: "Paul, Silvanus, and Timothy."

Addressee: "To the church of the Thessalonians in God the Father and the Lord Jesus Christ."

Greeting and blessing: "Grace to you and peace."

Thanksgiving: "We always give thanks to God for all of you and mention you in our prayers . . ." (1.2–10).

Body: Paul, responding to Timothy's report, wants to maintain his relationship with the community. It is full of gratitude and affection. Paul reminisces about his time with the Thessalonians and how he has longed to see them. He is also probably grateful—relieved—that they still want to be in touch with him despite his absence. Perhaps they and he had expected him to return to Thessalonica much sooner. Even now, he hadn't, but had sent Timothy instead. Perhaps he wondered if the community still thought well of him. He was obviously encouraged by Timothy's report.

Closing: "May the God of peace himself sanctify you entirely . . ." (5.23–28).

"New Family" Imagery

Paul fills this affectionate letter with family imagery. Fourteen times Paul calls the community "brothers and sisters." Though the Greek text has only "brothers," the inclusive language translation accurately communicates that these communities included women as well as men. "Brothers" did not mean "the men among you," but "all of you as siblings in a new family." Family imagery continues as Paul speaks of his relationship to them: he is like their mother (2.7) or father (2.11); he feels like an orphan when separated from them (2.17).

In this metaphor of the Christian community as a "new family," the relationship of the members to one another is not based solely on intimacy or sentiment, but also on mutual support, including material responsibility for each other. This was a "share" community, just as a family is a sharing community. Sharing in Paul's communities did not mean absolute equality of financial resources. But it did mean that the community would make sure that everybody was taken care of with regard to the material basis of life. Put simply, "You will eat, and you will be taken care of."

With one exception, texts in this letter have had little theological significance in Christian history. Paul's reminiscences and gratitude, over half of the letter, have not often been grist for theological mills. The letter does, however, contain "nuggets" that are central to Christianity. Twice Paul refers to the famous triad of faith, hope, and love" (1.3; 5.8). But when Christians think of these words, they are more likely to think of them as the climax of 1 Corinthians 13, often called the "great love chapter."

A "Second Coming"

For the last century or so, one text has been important to two very different groups. For millions of Christians, mostly in independent Protestant churches, the text is one of the foundations of "rapture theology." This is the belief that true believers will be raptured from the earth seven years before the second coming of Jesus. They will be spared the suffering—the trials and tribulations, plagues and wars and famines—that will engulf those left behind. The "rapture" is the premise of the recent bestselling Left Behind novels.

Rapture theology is almost always accompanied by the claim that the second coming of Jesus will be soon. Polls suggest that around 40 percent of American Christians believe that it will happen in the next fifty years. Most do so because they belong to churches that teach this.

The text is also important for mainstream biblical scholars. It is one of the reasons for the conclusion that Paul (and many early followers of Jesus) expected the second coming of Jesus soon relative to their point in time. The expectation was obviously wrong—it didn't happen.

The text is 4.13–18. Paul writes:

> But we do not want you to be uninformed, brothers and sisters, about those who have died, so that you may not grieve as others do who have no hope. For since we believe that Jesus died and rose again, even so, through Jesus, God will bring with him those who have died. For this we declare to you by the word of the Lord, that we who are alive, who are left until the coming of the Lord, will by no means precede those who have died. For the Lord himself, with a cry of command, with the archangel's call and with the sound of God's trumpet, will descend from heaven, and the dead in Christ will rise first. Then we who are alive, who are left, will be caught up in the clouds together with them to meet the Lord in the air; and so we will be with the Lord forever. Therefore encourage one another with these words.

The text is about the second coming of Jesus—rapture theology and modern scholarship agree about this. The imagery is vivid and obvious: the cry of the archangel, the sound of God's trumpet, the Lord himself descending from heaven, the raising of the dead, gathering them together with those still alive, meeting the Lord in the air, and being with the Lord forever.

Rapture theology and other future second-coming-of-Jesus scenarios begin with the premise that all of this will someday happen, for the obvious reason that it hasn't happened yet. Modern historical scholarship begins with a different premise, namely, that this text tells us what Paul wrote to the Christ-community in Thessalonica around the year 50. In that context, as best as we can discern, what did this text mean for Paul and those who heard it read in the community?

In the letter itself, the context is a question that had arisen in the community in Paul's absence. There had been deaths. Because he hadn't been gone very long (months? a year or two?), we should probably imagine only a few; possibly those who died were martyrs rather than people dying of natural causes. In either case, the Thessalonians' question (referred to in 4.13) was: What happens to those who have died before the second coming?

Note how 4.13–18 addresses their concern. When the second coming happens, the dead in Christ and the living will all be reunited and be with the Lord forever. In short, "Don't worry." As 4.18 says, "Encourage one another with these words." The purpose of the passage is primarily pastoral.

Within its historical and pastoral context, should its details be pressed, not only emphasized, but also more or less literalized? That there will be a last trumpet and the shout of an archangel, that the dead will be raised first, and at the same time the living will be taken up into clouds "to meet the Lord in the air"?

This is what rapture theology and most scenarios of an imminent second coming do. They maintain that all of this will happen someday. Some who believe this are willing to disagree about details. Note, for example, that 4.13–18 does not refer to a seven-year period between meeting "the Lord in the air" and the final judgment. The notion of seven years has to be imported from elsewhere. And so some Christians see this as a second coming text that does not necessarily affirm the rapture.

It is important to know that rapture theology—the notion that true Christians will be taken up into heaven seven years before the second coming and final judgment—is neither ancient nor traditional Christianity. It is thoroughly modern. It was conceived in the 1800s by John Nelson Darby (1800–1882), an Anglo-Irish clergyman active in Britain and North America. He not only originated the rapture, but is also the theological ancestor of the widely known "Scofield Bible," with its divisions of history into dispensations. Before him, no Christian had spoken of the "rapture."

Seeing this text in its ancient historical context dissolves a foundation of rapture theology. Paul was not providing detailed information about a second coming that is still future from our point in time, whose details are to be correlated with other biblical texts about the "last things"—the second coming, last judgment, and final state of affairs. Rather, using imagery from his time, he assured his community in Thessalonica of one thing—we shall all be together. Whether he meant any of the details in the text to be understood literally is impossible to know and seems unlikely.

But it is clear that the text in its historical context meant that Paul did think the second coming would be soon. He distinguished between "those who have died" and "we who are alive, who are left" when the Lord comes again. These words most naturally mean that Paul expected the second coming to occur while some of those he was writing to were still alive, including possibly himself. Paul makes a similar distinction in 1 Corinthians 15.51–52: "Listen, I will tell you a mystery! We will not all die, but we will all be changed," followed by language about the last trumpet and the raising of the dead. Other passages in Paul and the rest of the New Testament indicate that many early Christians expected the second coming soon. The author of Revelation says seven times that the time is near. That many early Christians expected this is one of the consensus conclusions of modern scholarship.

Seeing the text in this way, one has to conclude that it is in an important sense wrong. Paul expected the second coming soon, and it didn't happen. How central this expectation was for Paul is a different question. His passion, as we will see, was transformation, not preparation for the final judgment. The fact that Paul was wrong about the nearness of the second coming does not invalidate his thought as a whole. Nevertheless, the conclusion of most modern mainstream scholars is that Paul and many early Christians thought Jesus would return soon to complete what he had begun.

The conviction is a tribute to Jesus. Through him his followers had experienced a new world being born: the old had passed away and a new creation was beginning. Surely its culmination was near. Within this framework, the conviction is the product of enthusiasm and confidence.

Thus the first document in a chronological New Testament raises the central question of biblical interpretation that divides Christianity today. How are its documents to be understood? As coming from God in a sufficiently direct way as to have a divine guarantee to be true? If so, whatever they say is true or will someday be true.

Or do they tell us what formative figures in early Christianity said in their time and place? The question is about the divine or human origin of the Bible. If it is inerrant because of its direct origin in God, then it cannot be wrong; what Paul wrote about the second coming of Jesus in 4.13–18 will happen someday. But if it is the product of our spiritual ancestors, it tells us what they thought. It is not inerrant divine information to be integrated into a theological system, but expresses their understanding, conviction, and testimony.

SALUTATION

1 Paul, Silvanus, and Timothy,
To the church of the Thessalonians in God the Father and the Lord Jesus
Christ:
Grace to you and peace.

THE THESSALONIANS' FAITH AND EXAMPLE

2 We always give thanks to God for all of you and mention you in our prayers,
constantly ³remembering before our God and Father your work of faith and
labor of love and steadfastness of hope in our Lord Jesus Christ. ⁴For we know,
brothers and sisters*a* beloved by God, that he has chosen you, ⁵because our message of the gospel came to you not in word only, but also in power and in the
Holy Spirit and with full conviction; just as you know what kind of persons we
proved to be among you for your sake. ⁶And you became imitators of us and of
the Lord, for in spite of persecution you received the word with joy inspired by
the Holy Spirit, ⁷so that you became an example to all the believers in Macedonia and in Achaia. ⁸For the word of the Lord has sounded forth from you not
only in Macedonia and Achaia, but in every place your faith in God has become
known, so that we have no need to speak about it. ⁹For the people of those regions*b* report about us what kind of welcome we had among you, and how you
turned to God from idols, to serve a living and true God, ¹⁰and to wait for his
Son from heaven, whom he raised from the dead—Jesus, who rescues us from
the wrath that is coming.

---

a Gk *brothers*   *b* Gk *For they*

PAUL'S MINISTRY IN THESSALONICA

2 You yourselves know, brothers and sisters,[a] that our coming to you was not in vain, [2]but though we had already suffered and been shamefully mistreated at Philippi, as you know, we had courage in our God to declare to you the gospel of God in spite of great opposition. [3]For our appeal does not spring from deceit or impure motives or trickery, [4]but just as we have been approved by God to be entrusted with the message of the gospel, even so we speak, not to please mortals, but to please God who tests our hearts. [5]As you know and as God is our witness, we never came with words of flattery or with a pretext for greed; [6]nor did we seek praise from mortals, whether from you or from others, [7]though we might have made demands as apostles of Christ. But we were gentle[b] among you, like a nurse tenderly caring for her own children. [8]So deeply do we care for you that we are determined to share with you not only the gospel of God but also our own selves, because you have become very dear to us.

9 You remember our labor and toil, brothers and sisters;[a] we worked night and day, so that we might not burden any of you while we proclaimed to you the gospel of God. [10]You are witnesses, and God also, how pure, upright, and blameless our conduct was toward you believers. [11]As you know, we dealt with each one of you like a father with his children, [12]urging and encouraging you and pleading that you lead a life worthy of God, who calls you into his own kingdom and glory.

13 We also constantly give thanks to God for this, that when you received the word of God that you heard from us, you accepted it not as a human word but as what it really is, God's word, which is also at work in you believers. [14]For you, brothers and sisters,[a] became imitators of the churches of God in Christ Jesus that are in Judea, for you suffered the same things from your own compatriots as they did from the Jews, [15]who killed both the Lord Jesus and the prophets,[c] and drove us out; they displease God and oppose everyone [16]by hindering us from speaking to the Gentiles so that they may be saved. Thus they have constantly been filling up the measure of their sins; but God's wrath has overtaken them at last.[d]

PAUL'S DESIRE TO VISIT THE THESSALONIANS AGAIN

17 As for us, brothers and sisters,[a] when, for a short time, we were made orphans by being separated from you—in person, not in heart—we longed with great

---

a Gk brothers b Other ancient authorities read infants c Other ancient authorities read their own prophets d Or completely or forever eagerness to see you face to face. [18]For we wanted to come to you—certainly I, Paul, wanted to again and again—but Satan blocked our way. [19]For what is our hope or joy or crown of boasting before our Lord Jesus at his coming? Is it not you? [20]Yes, you are our glory and joy!

3 Therefore when we could bear it no longer, we decided to be left alone in Athens; [2]and we sent Timothy, our brother and co-worker for God in proclaiming[a] the gospel of Christ, to strengthen and encourage you for the sake of your faith, [3]so that no one would be shaken by these persecutions. Indeed, you yourselves know that this is what we are destined for. [4]In fact, when we were with you, we told you beforehand that we were to suffer persecution; so it turned out, as you know. [5]For this reason, when I could bear it no longer, I sent to find out about your faith; I was afraid that somehow the tempter had tempted you and that our labor had been in vain.

TIMOTHY'S ENCOURAGING REPORT

6 But Timothy has just now come to us from you, and has brought us the good news of your faith and love. He has told us also that you always remember us kindly and long to see us—just as we long to see you. [7]For this reason, brothers and sisters,[b] during all our distress and persecution we have been encouraged about you through your faith. [8]For we now live, if you continue to stand firm in the Lord. [9]How can we thank God enough for you in return for all the joy that we feel before our God because of you? [10]Night and day we pray most earnestly that we may see you face to face and restore whatever is lacking in your faith.

11 Now may our God and Father himself and our Lord Jesus direct our way to you. [12]And may the Lord make you increase and abound in love for one another and for all, just as we abound in love for you. [13]And may he so strengthen your hearts in holiness that you may be blameless before our God and Father at the coming of our Lord Jesus with all his saints.

A LIFE PLEASING TO GOD

4 Finally, brothers and sisters,[b] we ask and urge you in the Lord Jesus that, as you learned from us how you ought to live and to please God (as, in fact, you are doing), you should do so more and more. [2]For you know what instructions we gave you through the Lord Jesus. [3]For this is the will of God, your sanctification: that you abstain from fornication; [4]that each one of you know how to control your own body[c] in holiness and honor, [5]not with lustful passion, like the Gentiles who do not know God; [6]that no one wrong or exploit

---

a Gk lacks *proclaiming* b Gk *brothers* c Or *how to take a wife for himself* a brother or sister[a] in this matter, because the Lord is an avenger in all these things, just as we have already told you beforehand and solemnly warned you. [7]For God did not call us to impurity but in holiness. [8]Therefore whoever rejects this rejects not human authority but God, who also gives his Holy Spirit to you.

9 Now concerning love of the brothers and sisters,[b] you do not need to have anyone write to you, for you yourselves have been taught by God to love one another; [10]and indeed you do love all the brothers and sisters[b] throughout Macedonia. But we urge you, beloved,[b] to do so more and more, [11]to aspire to live quietly, to mind your own affairs, and to work with your hands, as we directed you, [12]so that you may behave properly toward outsiders and be dependent on no one.

THE COMING OF THE LORD

13 But we do not want you to be uninformed, brothers and sisters,[b] about those who have died,[c] so that you may not grieve as others do who have no hope. [14]For since we believe that Jesus died and rose again, even so, through Jesus, God will bring with him those who have died.[c] [15]For this we declare to you by the word of the Lord, that we who are alive, who are left until the coming of the Lord, will by no means precede those who have died.[c] [16]For the Lord himself, with a cry of command, with the archangel's call and with the sound of God's trumpet, will descend from heaven, and the dead in Christ will rise first. [17]Then we who are alive, who are left, will be caught up in the clouds together with them to meet the Lord in the air; and so we will be with the Lord forever. [18]Therefore encourage one another with these words.

5 Now concerning the times and the seasons, brothers and sisters,[b] you do not need to have anything written to you. [2]For you yourselves know very well that the day of the Lord will come like a thief in the night. [3]When they say, "There is peace and security," then sudden destruction will come upon them, as labor pains come upon a pregnant woman, and there will be no escape! [4]But you, beloved,[b] are not in darkness, for that day to surprise you like a thief; [5]for you are all children of light and children of the day; we are not of the night or of darkness. [6]So then let us not fall asleep as others do, but let us keep awake and be sober; [7]for those who sleep sleep at night, and those who are drunk get drunk at night. [8]But since we belong to the day, let us be sober, and put on the breastplate of faith and love, and for a helmet the hope of salvation. [9]For God has destined us not for wrath but for obtaining salvation through our Lord Jesus Christ, [10]who died for us, so that whether we are awake or asleep we may

---

a Gk *brother* *b* Gk *brothers* *c* Gk *fallen asleep*

live with him. [11]Therefore encourage one another and build up each other, as indeed you are doing.

FINAL EXHORTATIONS, GREETINGS, AND BENEDICTION

12 But we appeal to you, brothers and sisters,[a] to respect those who labor among you, and have charge of you in the Lord and admonish you; [13]esteem them very highly in love because of their work. Be at peace among yourselves. [14]And we urge you, beloved,[a] to admonish the idlers, encourage the fainthearted, help the weak, be patient with all of them. [15]See that none of you repays evil for evil, but always seek to do good to one another and to all. [16]Rejoice always, [17]pray without ceasing, [18]give thanks in all circumstances; for this is the will of God in Christ Jesus for you. [19]Do not quench the Spirit. [20]Do not despise the words of prophets,[b] [21]but test everything; hold fast to what is good; [22]abstain from every form of evil.

23 May the God of peace himself sanctify you entirely; and may your spirit and soul and body be kept sound[c] and blameless at the coming of our Lord Jesus Christ. [24]The one who calls you is faithful, and he will do this.

25 Beloved,[d] pray for us.

26 Greet all the brothers and sisters[a] with a holy kiss. [27]I solemnly command you by the Lord that this letter be read to all of them.[e]

28 The grace of our Lord Jesus Christ be with you.[f]

---

a Gk brothers b Gk despise prophecies c Or complete d Gk Brothers e Gk to all the brothers f Other ancient authorities add Amen

Galatians

No other relatively short New Testament document has had as much influence on Christian theology as Galatians. Its language of "justification" and the contrasts between "grace" and "law" and "faith" and "works" were central to Martin Luther's thought and have been for Protestants ever since. Though Paul also used this language in his letter to Christ-communities in Rome a half decade or so later, it first appears in Galatians.

Whether this letter should be second in a chronological New Testament is a toss-up. The other serious candidate is Paul's first letter to Corinth, customarily dated around 54. Because some scholars date Galatians as early as 50 and many others in the first half of the 50s, I have decided to put it before 1 Corinthians.

Some scholars date Galatians later because of similarities between it and Romans (especially the language of "justification," "faith," "law," and "works"). They argue that these suggest that the letters were written close to each other in time. Because Romans is by near unanimous consensus the last of Paul's seven letters, this would date Galatians, like Romans, in the late 50s.

However, nothing but the presence of these terms suggests that Romans and Galatians were written near each other in time. Nothing in Galatians refers to the plans Paul speaks about in Romans. Unless we think that Paul didn't develop the language of justification, grace, faith, law, and works until late in his activity, there is no reason to think that Galatians was written as late as Romans.

Audience and Historical Context

Galatians is the only one of Paul's seven letters to be addressed to a group of communities rather than to a particular community or individual; it is sent to the "churches of Galatia." Galatia was a region in central Asia Minor that contained several cities, including ancient Ankara, known as "Ancyra."

These communities had become deeply conflicted since Paul was there. Paul himself was under attack; some were accusing him of having falsified the gospel. The evidence is in the letter itself, the most polemical of all Paul's letters. Only in part of 2 Corinthians is Paul's tone as angry and combative. He accuses the Galatian communities of "deserting" and "turning to a different gospel," because of those who "pervert the gospel of Christ" (1.6–7). He pronounces a double curse on anyone who advocates a gospel other than the one they received from him (1.8–9). He calls them "foolish" and "bewitched" (3.1). He wishes that those who were troubling them "would castrate themselves" (5.12).

This explains another feature of Galatians: it is the only one of Paul's letters that does not include a thanksgiving after the greeting and blessing at the beginning. Clearly Paul was not feeling thankful for what was going on in his communities in Galatia. He was alarmed, furious, adamant. What was at stake was vitally and crucially important.

Those in the Christ-communities in Galatia were primarily Gentiles, most and perhaps nearly all of them "God-lovers" who had been attracted to Judaism. This is apparent from the central issue addressed by the letter. Did Gentile converts to life in Christ need to be circumcised? And did they need to follow at least some other Jewish laws, including food laws? While with them, Paul had taught "no." He had offered full participation in the Christ movement without circumcision and observance of Jewish laws.

After Paul left Galatia, probably some years earlier, other teachers—Paul's opponents in Galatia—had told them "yes." Gentile males had to be circumcised and follow Jewish food laws. For them, it seemed obvious that what Jesus began was a movement within Judaism, and that for Gentiles to become children of Abraham, they had to enter into God's covenant with Abraham, which included circumcision.

These teachers were also followers of Jesus. To use anachronistic language, they were Christians. Paul's converts in Galatia were not being tempted by non-Christian Jewish teachers. Rather, this was a conflict within early Christianity.

Whether Gentile converts had to observe Jewish laws was a major issue in early Christianity. The conflict and its resolution are a theme of Acts, which narrates the spread of the Jesus movement from Jerusalem and the Jewish homeland to the larger Gentile world, climaxing with Paul in Rome, the center of that world.

In the middle of Acts is the story of a meeting of early Christian leaders ("apostles and elders") in Jerusalem to decide whether Gentile converts needed to be circumcised and follow other Jewish laws (Acts 15). Paul and Barnabas were there, representing the Gentile mission, as were James and Peter, representing the mission to Jews. They resolved that Gentile converts did not need to be circumcised or follow all of Jewish law. Paul's mission to the Gentiles was blessed. Galatians refers to this meeting and the larger conflict. In 2.1–10, Paul reports that the leaders in Jerusalem had ratified his mission to Gentiles, including that males did not need to be circumcised.

The issue of food was more complex because of the common meal eaten by members of the Christ-communities. When they gathered together, was the food to be kosher or not? If the community was either all Jewish or all Gentile, the issue would not arise. But what if it was a mixed community of Christian Jews and Christian Gentiles? Was it to be kosher for all or kosher for none?

Paul refers to this issue as he recalls an episode in Antioch in northern Syria (2.11–14). Peter (Paul calls him "Cephas") and Barnabas withdrew from sharing the common meal of the Christ-community, because they would no longer eat with Gentile Christians. Paul tells the Galatians that he charged Peter with hypocrisy, because he changed his position. Paul's point was that even Peter accepted Gentile converts and ate with them, though he did backslide in Antioch.

Conflict about the status of Gentiles within the community is the context for what Paul says in Galatians about justification, faith, law, works, and life in the Spirit. He begins to develop these themes in 2.15, and they dominate the rest of the letter. To summarize his argument:

> Paul says, "We . . . Jews [referring to Christian Jews] . . . "know that a person is justified not by the works of the law but through faith in Jesus Christ" (2.15–16; the last phrase is better translated "through the faith of Jesus Christ"—that is, through the faith we see in Jesus).

> He reminds his largely Gentile communities that they had received the Spirit of God not "by doing the works of the law," but by faith (3.1–5).

> He argues that Abraham, the father of the Jewish people, was justified by faith, not by works of the law. Moreover, God promised Abraham that the Gentiles would be blessed through him, and this was now happening: "In Christ Jesus, the blessing of Abraham" had "come to the Gentiles . . . through faith" (3.6–18).

Requiring circumcision and observance of Jewish law would perpetuate the division between Jew and Gentile and thus destroy the unity of life "in Christ." As perhaps the best-known text in Galatians puts it:

> In Christ Jesus, you are all children of God through faith. As many of you as were baptized into Christ have clothed yourselves with Christ. There is no

longer Jew or Greek [Gentile], there is no longer slave or free, there is no longer male and female; for all of you are one in Christ Jesus. (3.26–28)

Note that Paul is not speaking about the ideal disappearance of these distinctions in "the world," but of their actual elimination within Christian community. The passage concludes with a link back to Abraham: "And if you belong to Christ, then you are Abraham's offspring" and "heirs" (3.29). Gentiles become children of Abraham not through circumcision, but by becoming "in Christ."

The theme of "freedom," one of Paul's favorite words, dominates much of the rest of the letter, beginning in chapter 4. He contrasts "slaves" and "heirs," creates an allegory of a slave woman and a free woman, and uses it to proclaim, "We are children not of the slave but of the free woman" (4.31). Then: "For freedom Christ has set us free. Stand firm, therefore, and do not submit again to a yoke of slavery" (5.1). And finally: "For you were called to freedom, brothers and sisters; only do not use your freedom as an opportunity for self-indulgence, but through love become slaves to one another. For the whole law is summed up in a single commandment: 'You shall love your neighbor as yourself'" (5.13–14). The law of freedom is love.

All of this was provoked by the issue of circumcision. Paul returns to the theme as his letter concludes:

Listen! I, Paul, am telling you that if you let yourselves be circumcised, Christ will be of no benefit to you. . . . For in Christ Jesus neither circumcision nor uncircumcision counts for anything; the only thing that counts is faith working through love. . . . For neither circumcision nor uncircumcision is anything; but a new creation is everything! (5.2, 6; 6.15)

Thus the letter is instructive for yet one more reason. Paul's theology comes to us from the concrete circumstances he encountered in his activity as an apostle of Christ. It soars to great heights, even as it is rooted in the ground of what was happening in early Christian communities.

Galatians

SALUTATION

1 Paul an apostle—sent neither by human commission nor from human authorities, but through Jesus Christ and God the Father, who raised him from the dead— ²and all the members of God's family *a* who are with me,

To the churches of Galatia:

3 Grace to you and peace from God our Father and the Lord Jesus Christ, ⁴who gave himself for our sins to set us free from the present evil age, according to the will of our God and Father, ⁵to whom be the glory forever and ever. Amen.

THERE IS NO OTHER GOSPEL

6 I am astonished that you are so quickly deserting the one who called you in the grace of Christ and are turning to a different gospel— ⁷not that there is another gospel, but there are some who are confusing you and want to pervert the gospel of Christ. ⁸But even if we or an angel *b* from heaven should proclaim to you a gospel contrary to what we proclaimed to you, let that one be accursed! ⁹As we have said before, so now I repeat, if anyone proclaims to you a gospel contrary to what you received, let that one be accursed!

10 Am I now seeking human approval, or God's approval? Or am I trying to please people? If I were still pleasing people, I would not be a servant *c* of Christ.

PAUL'S VINDICATION OF HIS APOSTLESHIP

11 For I want you to know, brothers and sisters, *d* that the gospel that was proclaimed by me is not of human origin; ¹²for I did not receive it from a

a Gk *all the brothers* *b* Or *a messenger* *c* Gk *slave* *d* Gk *brothers* human source, nor was I taught it, but I received it through a revelation of Jesus Christ.

13 You have heard, no doubt, of my earlier life in Judaism. I was violently persecuting the church of God and was trying to destroy it. [14]I advanced in Judaism beyond many among my people of the same age, for I was far more zealous for the traditions of my ancestors. [15]But when God, who had set me apart before I was born and called me through his grace, was pleased [16]to reveal his Son to me,[a] so that I might proclaim him among the Gentiles, I did not confer with any human being, [17]nor did I go up to Jerusalem to those who were already apostles before me, but I went away at once into Arabia, and afterwards I returned to Damascus.

18 Then after three years I did go up to Jerusalem to visit Cephas and stayed with him fifteen days; [19]but I did not see any other apostle except James the Lord's brother. [20]In what I am writing to you, before God, I do not lie! [21]Then I went into the regions of Syria and Cilicia, [22]and I was still unknown by sight to the churches of Judea that are in Christ; [23]they only heard it said, "The one who formerly was persecuting us is now proclaiming the faith he once tried to destroy." [24]And they glorified God because of me.

PAUL AND THE OTHER APOSTLES

2 Then after fourteen years I went up again to Jerusalem with Barnabas, taking Titus along with me. [2]I went up in response to a revelation. Then I laid before them (though only in a private meeting with the acknowledged leaders) the gospel that I proclaim among the Gentiles, in order to make sure that I was not running, or had not run, in vain. [3]But even Titus, who was with me, was not compelled to be circumcised, though he was a Greek. [4]But because of false believers[b] secretly brought in, who slipped in to spy on the freedom we have in Christ Jesus, so that they might enslave us— [5]we did not submit to them even for a moment, so that the truth of the gospel might always remain with you. [6]And from those who were supposed to be acknowledged leaders (what they actually were makes no difference to me; God shows no partiality)—those leaders contributed nothing to me. [7]On the contrary, when they saw that I had been entrusted with the gospel for the uncircumcised, just as Peter had been entrusted with the gospel for the circumcised [8](for he who worked through Peter making him an apostle to the circumcised also worked through me in sending me to the Gentiles), [9]and when James and Cephas and John, who were acknowledged pillars, recognized the grace that had been given to me, they

---

a Gk in me   b Gk false brothers

gave to Barnabas and me the right hand of fellowship, agreeing that we should go to the Gentiles and they to the circumcised. [10]They asked only one thing, that we remember the poor, which was actually what I was[a] eager to do.

PAUL REBUKES PETER AT ANTIOCH

11 But when Cephas came to Antioch, I opposed him to his face, because he stood self-condemned; [12]for until certain people came from James, he used to eat with the Gentiles. But after they came, he drew back and kept himself separate for fear of the circumcision faction. [13]And the other Jews joined him in this hypocrisy, so that even Barnabas was led astray by their hypocrisy. [14]But when I saw that they were not acting consistently with the truth of the gospel, I said to Cephas before them all, "If you, though a Jew, live like a Gentile and not like a Jew, how can you compel the Gentiles to live like Jews?"[b]

JEWS AND GENTILES ARE SAVED BY FAITH

15 We ourselves are Jews by birth and not Gentile sinners; [16]yet we know that a person is justified[c] not by the works of the law but through faith in Jesus Christ.[d] And we have come to believe in Christ Jesus, so that we might be justified by faith in Christ,[e] and not by doing the works of the law, because no one will be justified by the works of the law. [17]But if, in our effort to be justified in Christ, we ourselves have been found to be sinners, is Christ then a servant of sin? Certainly not! [18]But if I build up again the very things that I once tore down, then I demonstrate that I am a transgressor. [19]For through the law I died to the law, so that I might live to God. I have been crucified with Christ; [20]and it is no longer I who live, but it is Christ who lives in me. And the life I now live in the flesh I live by faith in the Son of God,[f] who loved me and gave himself for me. [21]I do not nullify the grace of God; for if justification[g] comes through the law, then Christ died for nothing.

LAW OR FAITH

3 You foolish Galatians! Who has bewitched you? It was before your eyes that Jesus Christ was publicly exhibited as crucified! [2]The only thing I want to learn from you is this: Did you receive the Spirit by doing the works of the law or by believing what you heard? [3]Are you so foolish? Having started with the Spirit, are you now ending with the flesh? [4]Did you experience so much for nothing?—if it really was for nothing. [5]Well then, does God[h] supply you with

---

a Or *had been* b Some interpreters hold that the quotation extends into the following paragraph c Or *reckoned as righteous;* and so elsewhere d Or *the faith of Jesus Christ* e Or *the faith of Christ* f Or *by the faith of the Son of God* g Or *righteousness* h Gk *he* the Spirit and work miracles among you by your doing the works of the law, or by your believing what you heard?

6 Just as Abraham "believed God, and it was reckoned to him as righteousness," ⁷so, you see, those who believe are the descendants of Abraham. ⁸And the scripture, foreseeing that God would justify the Gentiles by faith, declared the gospel beforehand to Abraham, saying, "All the Gentiles shall be blessed in you." ⁹For this reason, those who believe are blessed with Abraham who believed.

10 For all who rely on the works of the law are under a curse; for it is written, "Cursed is everyone who does not observe and obey all the things written in the book of the law." ¹¹Now it is evident that no one is justified before God by the law; for "The one who is righteous will live by faith."ᵃ ¹²But the law does not rest on faith; on the contrary, "Whoever does the works of the lawᵇ will live by them." ¹³Christ redeemed us from the curse of the law by becoming a curse for us—for it is written, "Cursed is everyone who hangs on a tree"— ¹⁴in order that in Christ Jesus the blessing of Abraham might come to the Gentiles, so that we might receive the promise of the Spirit through faith.

THE PROMISE TO ABRAHAM

15 Brothers and sisters,ᶜ I give an example from daily life: once a person's willᵈ has been ratified, no one adds to it or annuls it. ¹⁶Now the promises were made to Abraham and to his offspring;ᵉ it does not say, "And to offsprings,"ᶠ as of many; but it says, "And to your offspring,"ᵉ that is, to one person, who is Christ. ¹⁷My point is this: the law, which came four hundred thirty years later, does not annul a covenant previously ratified by God, so as to nullify the promise. ¹⁸For if the inheritance comes from the law, it no longer comes from the promise; but God granted it to Abraham through the promise.

THE PURPOSE OF THE LAW

19 Why then the law? It was added because of transgressions, until the offspringᵉ would come to whom the promise had been made; and it was ordained through angels by a mediator. ²⁰Now a mediator involves more than one party; but God is one.

21 Is the law then opposed to the promises of God? Certainly not! For if a law had been given that could make alive, then righteousness would indeed come through the law. ²²But the scripture has imprisoned all things under the power

---

a Or *The one who is righteous through faith will live*   b Gk *does them*   c Gk *Brothers*   d Or *covenant* (as in verse 17)   e Gk *seed*
f Gk *seeds*

of sin, so that what was promised through faith in Jesus Christ[a] might be given to those who believe.

23 Now before faith came, we were imprisoned and guarded under the law until faith would be revealed. [24]Therefore the law was our disciplinarian until Christ came, so that we might be justified by faith. [25]But now that faith has come, we are no longer subject to a disciplinarian, [26]for in Christ Jesus you are all children of God through faith. [27]As many of you as were baptized into Christ have clothed yourselves with Christ. [28]There is no longer Jew or Greek, there is no longer slave or free, there is no longer male and female; for all of you are one in Christ Jesus. [29]And if you belong to Christ, then you are Abraham's offspring,[b] heirs according to the promise.

4 My point is this: heirs, as long as they are minors, are no better than slaves, though they are the owners of all the property; [2]but they remain under guardians and trustees until the date set by the father. [3]So with us; while we were minors, we were enslaved to the elemental spirits[c] of the world. [4]But when the fullness of time had come, God sent his Son, born of a woman, born under the law, [5]in order to redeem those who were under the law, so that we might receive adoption as children. [6]And because you are children, God has sent the Spirit of his Son into our[d] hearts, crying, "Abba![e] Father!" [7]So you are no longer a slave but a child, and if a child then also an heir, through God.[f]

PAUL REPROVES THE GALATIANS

8 Formerly, when you did not know God, you were enslaved to beings that by nature are not gods. [9]Now, however, that you have come to know God, or rather to be known by God, how can you turn back again to the weak and beggarly elemental spirits?[g] How can you want to be enslaved to them again? [10]You are observing special days, and months, and seasons, and years. [11]I am afraid that my work for you may have been wasted.

12 Friends,[h] I beg you, become as I am, for I also have become as you are. You have done me no wrong. [13]You know that it was because of a physical infirmity that I first announced the gospel to you; [14]though my condition put you to the test, you did not scorn or despise me, but welcomed me as an angel of God, as Christ Jesus. [15]What has become of the goodwill you felt? For I testify that, had it been possible, you would have torn out your eyes and given them to me. [16]Have I now become your enemy by telling you the truth? [17]They make much of you, but for no good purpose; they want to exclude you, so that you may make much

---

a Or through the faith of Jesus Christ b Gk seed c Or the rudiments d Other ancient authorities read your e Aramaic for Father f Other ancient authorities read an heir of God through Christ g Or beggarly rudiments h Gk Brothers of them. [18]It is good to be made much of for a good purpose at all times, and not only when I am present with you. [19]My little children, for whom I am again in the pain of childbirth until Christ is formed in you, [20]I wish I were present with you now and could change my tone, for I am perplexed about you.

THE ALLEGORY OF HAGAR AND SARAH

21 Tell me, you who desire to be subject to the law, will you not listen to the law? [22]For it is written that Abraham had two sons, one by a slave woman and the other by a free woman. [23]One, the child of the slave, was born according to the flesh; the other, the child of the free woman, was born through the promise. [24]Now this is an allegory: these women are two covenants. One woman, in fact, is Hagar, from Mount Sinai, bearing children for slavery. [25]Now Hagar is Mount Sinai in Arabia[a] and corresponds to the present Jerusalem, for she is in slavery with her children. [26]But the other woman corresponds to the Jerusalem above; she is free, and she is our mother. [27]For it is written,

> "Rejoice, you childless one, you who bear no children,
>> burst into song and shout, you who endure no birth pangs;
> for the children of the desolate woman are more numerous
>> than the children of the one who is married."

28 Now you,[b] my friends,[c] are children of the promise, like Isaac. [29]But just as at that time the child who was born according to the flesh persecuted the child who was born according to the Spirit, so it is now also. [30]But what does the scripture say? "Drive out the slave and her child; for the child of the slave will not share the inheritance with the child of the free woman." [31]So then, friends,[c] we are children, not of the slave but of the free woman.

5 For freedom Christ has set us free. Stand firm, therefore, and do not submit again to a yoke of slavery.

THE NATURE OF CHRISTIAN FREEDOM

2 Listen! I, Paul, am telling you that if you let yourselves be circumcised, Christ will be of no benefit to you. [3]Once again I testify to every man who lets himself be circumcised that he is obliged to obey the entire law. [4]You who want to be justified by the law have cut yourselves off from Christ; you have fallen away from grace. [5]For through the Spirit, by faith, we eagerly wait for the hope of righteousness. [6]For in Christ Jesus neither circumcision nor uncircumcision counts for anything; the only thing that counts is faith working[d] through love.

---

a Other ancient authorities read For Sinai is a mountain in Arabia   b Other ancient authorities read we   c Gk brothers
d Or made effective

7 You were running well; who prevented you from obeying the truth? [8]Such persuasion does not come from the one who calls you. [9]A little yeast leavens the whole batch of dough. [10]I am confident about you in the Lord that you will not think otherwise. But whoever it is that is confusing you will pay the penalty. [11]But my friends,[a] why am I still being persecuted if I am still preaching circumcision? In that case the offense of the cross has been removed. [12]I wish those who unsettle you would castrate themselves!

13 For you were called to freedom, brothers and sisters;[a] only do not use your freedom as an opportunity for self-indulgence,[b] but through love become slaves to one another. [14]For the whole law is summed up in a single commandment, "You shall love your neighbor as yourself." [15]If, however, you bite and devour one another, take care that you are not consumed by one another.

THE WORKS OF THE FLESH

16 Live by the Spirit, I say, and do not gratify the desires of the flesh. [17]For what the flesh desires is opposed to the Spirit, and what the Spirit desires is opposed to the flesh; for these are opposed to each other, to prevent you from doing what you want. [18]But if you are led by the Spirit, you are not subject to the law. [19]Now the works of the flesh are obvious: fornication, impurity, licentiousness, [20]idolatry, sorcery, enmities, strife, jealousy, anger, quarrels, dissensions, factions, [21]envy,[c] drunkenness, carousing, and things like these. I am warning you, as I warned you before: those who do such things will not inherit the kingdom of God.

THE FRUIT OF THE SPIRIT

22 By contrast, the fruit of the Spirit is love, joy, peace, patience, kindness, generosity, faithfulness, [23]gentleness, and self-control. There is no law against such things. [24]And those who belong to Christ Jesus have crucified the flesh with its passions and desires. [25]If we live by the Spirit, let us also be guided by the Spirit. [26]Let us not become conceited, competing against one another, envying one another.

BEAR ONE ANOTHER'S BURDENS

6 My friends,[d] if anyone is detected in a transgression, you who have received the Spirit should restore such a one in a spirit of gentleness. Take care that you yourselves are not tempted. [2]Bear one another's burdens, and in this way you will fulfill[e] the law of Christ. [3]For if those who are nothing think they are

---

a Gk brothers b Gk the flesh c Other ancient authorities add murder d Gk Brothers e Other ancient authorities read in this way fulfill something, they deceive themselves. [4]All must test their own work; then that work, rather than their neighbor's work, will become a cause for pride. [5]For all must carry their own loads.

6 Those who are taught the word must share in all good things with their teacher.

7 Do not be deceived; God is not mocked, for you reap whatever you sow. [8]If you sow to your own flesh, you will reap corruption from the flesh; but if you sow to the Spirit, you will reap eternal life from the Spirit. [9]So let us not grow weary in doing what is right, for we will reap at harvest time, if we do not give up. [10]So then, whenever we have an opportunity, let us work for the good of all, and especially for those of the family of faith.

FINAL ADMONITIONS AND BENEDICTION

11 See what large letters I make when I am writing in my own hand! [12]It is those who want to make a good showing in the flesh that try to compel you to be circumcised—only that they may not be persecuted for the cross of Christ. [13]Even the circumcised do not themselves obey the law, but they want you to be circumcised so that they may boast about your flesh. [14]May I never boast of anything except the cross of our Lord Jesus Christ, by which[a] the world has been crucified to me, and I to the world. [15]For[b] neither circumcision nor uncircumcision is anything; but a new creation is everything! [16]As for those who will follow this rule—peace be upon them, and mercy, and upon the Israel of God.

17 From now on, let no one make trouble for me; for I carry the marks of Jesus branded on my body.

18 May the grace of our Lord Jesus Christ be with your spirit, brothers and sisters.[c] Amen.

---

a Or *through whom* *b* Other ancient authorities add *in Christ Jesus* *c* Gk *brothers*

1 Corinthians

First Corinthians is the second longest of Paul's letters. Only Romans is longer, and thus this letter comes right after Romans in the canonical New Testament. But in this chronological New Testament, it comes after 1 Thessalonians and Galatians.

According to Acts, Paul created a Christ-community in Corinth in southern Greece around the year 50. Corinth was a major city, seaport, and capital of the Roman province of Achaia, which included Athens. In Paul's world, Corinth (not Athens) was the most important city in Greece.

Though there was a Jewish synagogue there, the city was almost completely Gentile, cosmopolitan, and multi-ethnic. According to Acts, Paul spent eighteen months in Corinth on his first visit, probably from about 50 through 51. When he wrote this letter a few years later, he was in Ephesus in Asia Minor, just over two hundred miles across the Aegean from Corinth. It was not his first letter to the community in Corinth. He refers to a previous letter (5.9) and to a letter he has received from them (7.1).

Historical Context

The historical context of the letter is Paul's relationship to the Christ-community he had founded in Corinth. Paul has been away from it for a few years—probably at least two. Now he has learned that divisions and conflicts have developed within the community.

Much of the letter addresses these conflicts. But the "mood" of conflict is not nearly as intense as in Galatians or, as we will see, in 2 Corinthians. Other parts respond to questions the Corinthians have sent to him.

From the letter itself, we know that the community was divided into factions, apparently based on who their mentors were. Paul refers to this in the first chapter. Some were saying, "I belong to Paul"; others were saying, "I belong to Apollos," or "I belong to Cephas [Peter]," or "I belong to Christ" (1.12). Paul responds by contrasting the "wisdom of *this* world" with the "wisdom of God" (which he also calls "God's foolishness"—foolish in the eyes of *this* world). He proclaims that the heart of the gospel is "Christ crucified" (1.23). Paul is referring not merely to the fact that Jesus died, but that he was *crucified*—executed by the powers and authorities that ruled his world, by the wisdom of "*this* world." The gospel is "Christ crucified"—not loyalty to a particular teacher or humanly constructed system of thought.

Second, we learn from the letter that the community was divided over spiritual gifts. Are those who have particular spiritual gifts (especially ecstatic experiences like visions or speaking in tongues) more advanced spiritually and thus superior to those who do not? This conflict is the subject of chapters 12–14. In the middle of this section is the most familiar chapter in the New Testament because of its widespread use at weddings and funerals. Though verses from elsewhere in the New Testament may be as well known, no chapter is. It begins with the familiar, "If I speak in the tongues of mortals and of angels but do not have love, I am a noisy gong and a clanging cymbal," and ends with, "Faith, hope, and love abide, these three; and the greatest of these is love" (13.1–13).

In the context of Paul's addressing the conflict about spiritual gifts, this text affirms that the greatest spiritual gifts are faith, hope, and love, and love is the most important one. Paul is telling the community in Corinth that there is no hierarchy, no superiority, to be built on the more ecstatic spiritual gifts. The most central gifts of the Spirit are faith, hope, and love. They are the signs of Christian maturity.

Third, we learn that there were divisions within the community between "the rich" and "the rest." The letter tells us that few were wealthy: "Not many of you were wise by human standards, not many were powerful, not many were of noble birth" (1.26). But obviously some were. In this respect, the Christ-community in Corinth may have been an exception among Paul's communities. It was mostly made up of urban workers, many of them God-fearers from the merchant and artisan classes. Some were prosperous enough to have become Paul's patrons and benefactors. Although not from the super-wealthy class, they may have been what we might call "well-to-do."

This conflict surfaces in chapter 11 and is the context for what Paul writes about the meaning of the common meal that he calls the "Lord's supper." This is the earliest Christian text about the sacramental meal at the center of Christian worship, also known as the "Eucharist," "Mass," and "Communion."

In first-century Christianity, the Lord's supper was a real meal. It was not just a pinch of bread and a sip of wine, but a full meal shared in common by the community, during which bread and wine would be celebrated as the body and blood of Christ. What we call the Eucharist was part of the common meal. We do not know how often Paul's communities shared this meal, but they probably did so at least weekly, following the rhythm of the Sabbath, even if celebrated on a different day.

In Corinth, the meal had ceased to be a common meal. According to chapter 11, the wealthy (who didn't have to work) would gather early for the meal. By the time the people who worked (most of the community) got to the meal, the wealthy had already eaten, and some were tipsy. They may also have served the best wine and best food to themselves before the others arrived. Such was common among the wealthy in that world. For Paul, this violated the "one body" understanding of life "in Christ." It meant bringing the hierarchical distinctions of "this world" into the body of Christ. But these differences were not to be replicated in the community that Paul called "a new creation."

Paul describes the situation:

> For when the time comes to eat, each of you goes ahead with your own supper, and one goes hungry and another becomes drunk. What! Do you not have homes to eat and drink in? Or do you show contempt for the church of God and humiliate those who have nothing? What should I say to you? Should I commend you? In this matter I do not commend you! (11.21–22)

This conflict is the context in which Paul then recalls for the Corinthians what are commonly called the "words of institution" of the sacrament of bread and wine:

> For I received from the Lord what I also handed on to you, that the Lord Jesus on the night when he was betrayed took a loaf of bread, and when he had given thanks, he broke it and said, "This is my body that is for you. Do this in remembrance of me." In the same way he took the cup also, after supper, saying, "This cup is the new covenant in my blood. Do this, as often as you drink it, in remembrance of me." For as often as you eat this bread and drink the cup, you proclaim the Lord's death until he comes. (11.23–26)

The text concludes: "Whoever, therefore, eats the bread or drinks the cup of the Lord in an unworthy manner will be answerable for the body and blood of the Lord" (11.27). In this context, eating and drinking the bread and wine "in an unworthy manner" refers to the behavior of the wealthy in perpetuating the divisions of "this world." In Christian communities, those divisions were abolished.

Portions of the rest of the letter respond to questions that the community has directed to Paul. The beginning of chapter 7 refers explicitly to this: "Now concerning the matters about which you wrote." The verse continues: "It is well for a man not to touch a woman" (7.1). Is this what Paul thought? No. That sentence is from a letter to Paul from the community in Corinth. Some were advocating total abstinence, and others in the community wanted to know Paul's teaching on the matter. The sentence functions as a section heading for Paul's comments on marriage, conjugal relations, and divorce, which occupy the rest of the chapter.

In the next chapter, Paul addresses the question of whether food sacrificed to idols, especially meat, can be eaten by Christians. In the urban Gentile world, most meat was from animals that had been sacrificed to various deities—idols from a Jewish and Christian point of view. So could Christ-followers eat it? Paul's answer: yes.

The Resurrection

The earliest extended treatment of the resurrection of Jesus in the New Testament is in 1 Corinthians 15. Although Paul's earlier letters to the Thessalonians and Galatians presuppose and affirm it, they say nothing more about it. Here almost an entire chapter is devoted to it.

Paul reports a list of people to whom the risen Christ "appeared" (15.5–8; he uses the word four times in the list): Cephas (Peter), the twelve, more than five hundred brothers and sisters at one time, James, and all the apostles. He includes himself in the list: "Last of all, as to one untimely born, he appeared also to me." The risen Christ had appeared to Paul in a vision, and his inclusion of himself in the list and his repeated use of "appeared" suggest that he saw his experience as similar to the experiences of the others.

Then he emphasizes the utter centrality of the resurrection: "If Christ has not been raised, then our proclamation has been in vain and your faith has been in vain. . . . If Christ has not been raised, your faith is futile" (15.14, 17). The language could not be stronger: the resurrection of Jesus is the bedrock of Christianity. Without it, Christian faith is "in vain" and "futile."

These verses are often quoted by Christians who insist upon the physical, bodily resurrection of Jesus as the factual foundation of Christianity. For them, if his physical body wasn't raised, if the tomb wasn't really empty, Christianity is not true. But in the context of 1 Corinthians 15 as a whole, this is not what the words mean.

This is clear in part from Paul's list early in the chapter of those to whom the risen Christ appeared. Did Paul's vision (and their experiences) involve an encounter with a physical, bodily Jesus? Paul's certainly didn't; those traveling with him in the three accounts in Acts did not experience what he did.

It is also clear from the last part of the chapter. There Paul addresses the question of "what kind of body" the resurrected body is (15.35–50). His images affirm continuity even as they emphasize radical discontinuity between the earthly body and the resurrection body. It is like the difference between a seed and a full-grown plant:

> What is sown is perishable, what is raised is imperishable. It is sown in dishonor, it is raised in glory. It is sown in weakness, it is raised in power. It is sown a physical body, it is raised a spiritual body. (15.42–44)

What exactly Paul means by a "spiritual body" is not completely clear, but it is not a physical body. He even explicitly denies that the resurrected body is a flesh and blood body (15.50).

Modern scholarship has often noted that Paul never mentions that Jesus's tomb was empty—neither in this chapter nor anywhere else in his letters. Is this because Paul took it for granted that affirming the resurrection of Jesus meant that of course Jesus's tomb was empty? Or is it because for Paul the resurrection of Jesus was not about something spectacular happening to the corpse of Jesus?

In either case, the resurrection of Jesus mattered utterly to Paul. For him, it meant "Jesus lives" and "Jesus is Lord"—and he lives and is Lord because God vindicated him against the powers that had crucified him. To vindicate means to say "yes" to what Jesus was doing and "no" to "this world," the world that crucified him. This is the heart of Paul's experience and thought.

The Conclusion

Chapter 16 begins with a reference to the "collection for the saints." Paul is raising money from his largely Gentile Christian communities for Christian Jews in Jerusalem. This collection was a major reason for Paul's final journey to Jerusalem in the late 50s, where he was arrested and then spent the rest of his life in confinement, initially in Jerusalem, then in Caesarea, and then in Rome.

The chapter continues with Paul sharing his travel plans, including a perhaps extended visit to Corinth in the near future. It concludes with comments about Timothy, Apollos, and a few other Christian leaders, plus an admonition and a blessing:

> Keep alert, stand firm in your faith, be courageous, be strong. Let all that you do be done in love. . . . The grace of the Lord Jesus be with you. My love be with all of you in Christ Jesus. (16.13–14, 23–24)

As we will see, the conflicts in Corinth continued and perhaps became more intense. That is the tale of 2 Corinthians. But on the whole, 1 Corinthians is not primarily a conflict letter. Its tone includes affection and tenderness as well as passages remarkable for their profundity, insight, and beauty.

Corinthians

SALUTATION

1 Paul, called to be an apostle of Christ Jesus by the will of God, and our brother Sosthenes,

2 To the church of God that is in Corinth, to those who are sanctified in Christ Jesus, called to be saints, together with all those who in every place call on the name of our Lord Jesus Christ, both their Lord[a] and ours:

3 Grace to you and peace from God our Father and the Lord Jesus Christ.

4 I give thanks to my[b] God always for you because of the grace of God that has been given you in Christ Jesus, [5]for in every way you have been enriched in him, in speech and knowledge of every kind— [6]just as the testimony of[c] Christ has been strengthened among you— [7]so that you are not lacking in any spiritual gift as you wait for the revealing of our Lord Jesus Christ. [8]He will also strengthen you to the end, so that you may be blameless on the day of our Lord Jesus Christ. [9]God is faithful; by him you were called into the fellowship of his Son, Jesus Christ our Lord.

DIVISIONS IN THE CHURCH

10 Now I appeal to you, brothers and sisters,[d] by the name of our Lord Jesus Christ, that all of you be in agreement and that there be no divisions among you, but that you be united in the same mind and the same purpose. [11]For it has been reported to me by Chloe's people that there are quarrels among you, my brothers and sisters.[e] [12]What I mean is that each of you says, "I belong to

---

a Gk *theirs*   b Other ancient authorities lack *my*   c Or *to*   d Gk *brothers*   e Gk *my brothers*

Paul," or "I belong to Apollos," or "I belong to Cephas," or "I belong to Christ." [13]Has Christ been divided? Was Paul crucified for you? Or were you baptized in the name of Paul? [14]I thank God[a] that I baptized none of you except Crispus and Gaius, [15]so that no one can say that you were baptized in my name. [16](I did baptize also the household of Stephanas; beyond that, I do not know whether I baptized anyone else.) [17]For Christ did not send me to baptize but to proclaim the gospel, and not with eloquent wisdom, so that the cross of Christ might not be emptied of its power.

CHRIST THE POWER AND WISDOM OF GOD

18 For the message about the cross is foolishness to those who are perishing, but to us who are being saved it is the power of God. [19]For it is written,

> "I will destroy the wisdom of the wise,
>
>   and the discernment of the discerning I will thwart."

20 Where is the one who is wise? Where is the scribe? Where is the debater of this age? Has not God made foolish the wisdom of the world? [21]For since, in the wisdom of God, the world did not know God through wisdom, God decided, through the foolishness of our proclamation, to save those who believe. [22]For Jews demand signs and Greeks desire wisdom, [23]but we proclaim Christ crucified, a stumbling block to Jews and foolishness to Gentiles, [24]but to those who are the called, both Jews and Greeks, Christ the power of God and the wisdom of God. [25]For God's foolishness is wiser than human wisdom, and God's weakness is stronger than human strength.

26 Consider your own call, brothers and sisters:[b] not many of you were wise by human standards,[c] not many were powerful, not many were of noble birth. [27]But God chose what is foolish in the world to shame the wise; God chose what is weak in the world to shame the strong; [28]God chose what is low and despised in the world, things that are not, to reduce to nothing things that are, [29]so that no one[d] might boast in the presence of God. [30]He is the source of your life in Christ Jesus, who became for us wisdom from God, and righteousness and sanctification and redemption, [31]in order that, as it is written, "Let the one who boasts, boast in[e] the Lord."

PROCLAIMING CHRIST CRUCIFIED

2 When I came to you, brothers and sisters,[b] I did not come proclaiming the mystery[f] of God to you in lofty words or wisdom. [2]For I decided to know nothing among you except Jesus Christ, and him crucified. [3]And I came to you

---

a Other ancient authorities read *I am thankful*   b Gk *brothers*   c Gk *according to the flesh*   d Gk *no flesh*   e Or *of*   f Other ancient authorities read *testimony* in weakness and in fear and in much trembling. [4]My speech and my proclamation were not with plausible words of wisdom,[a] but with a demonstration of the Spirit and of power, [5]so that your faith might rest not on human wisdom but on the power of God.

THE TRUE WISDOM OF GOD

6 Yet among the mature we do speak wisdom, though it is not a wisdom of this age or of the rulers of this age, who are doomed to perish. [7]But we speak God's wisdom, secret and hidden, which God decreed before the ages for our glory. [8]None of the rulers of this age understood this; for if they had, they would not have crucified the Lord of glory. [9]But, as it is written,

"What no eye has seen, nor ear heard,
    nor the human heart conceived,
what God has prepared for those who love him"—

10 these things God has revealed to us through the Spirit; for the Spirit searches everything, even the depths of God. [11]For what human being knows what is truly human except the human spirit that is within? So also no one comprehends what is truly God's except the Spirit of God. [12]Now we have received not the spirit of the world, but the Spirit that is from God, so that we may understand the gifts bestowed on us by God. [13]And we speak of these things in words not taught by human wisdom but taught by the Spirit, interpreting spiritual things to those who are spiritual.[b]

14 Those who are unspiritual[c] do not receive the gifts of God's Spirit, for they are foolishness to them, and they are unable to understand them because they are spiritually discerned. [15]Those who are spiritual discern all things, and they are themselves subject to no one else's scrutiny.

16 "For who has known the mind of the Lord
    so as to instruct him?"
But we have the mind of Christ.

ON DIVISIONS IN THE CORINTHIAN CHURCH

3 And so, brothers and sisters,[d] I could not speak to you as spiritual people, but rather as people of the flesh, as infants in Christ. [2]I fed you with milk, not solid food, for you were not ready for solid food. Even now you are still not ready, [3]for you are still of the flesh. For as long as there is jealousy and quarreling among you, are you not of the flesh, and behaving according to human

---

a Other ancient authorities read *the persuasiveness of wisdom*   b Or *interpreting spiritual things in spiritual language,* or *comparing spiritual things with spiritual*   c Or *natural*   d Gk *brothers* inclinations? ⁴For when one says, "I belong to Paul," and another, "I belong to Apollos," are you not merely human?

5 What then is Apollos? What is Paul? Servants through whom you came to believe, as the Lord assigned to each. ⁶I planted, Apollos watered, but God gave the growth. ⁷So neither the one who plants nor the one who waters is anything, but only God who gives the growth. ⁸The one who plants and the one who waters have a common purpose, and each will receive wages according to the labor of each. ⁹For we are God's servants, working together; you are God's field, God's building.

10 According to the grace of God given to me, like a skilled master builder I laid a foundation, and someone else is building on it. Each builder must choose with care how to build on it. ¹¹For no one can lay any foundation other than the one that has been laid; that foundation is Jesus Christ. ¹²Now if anyone builds on the foundation with gold, silver, precious stones, wood, hay, straw— ¹³the work of each builder will become visible, for the Day will disclose it, because it will be revealed with fire, and the fire will test what sort of work each has done. ¹⁴If what has been built on the foundation survives, the builder will receive a reward. ¹⁵If the work is burned up, the builder will suffer loss; the builder will be saved, but only as through fire.

16 Do you not know that you are God's temple and that God's Spirit dwells in you?*ᵃ* ¹⁷If anyone destroys God's temple, God will destroy that person. For God's temple is holy, and you are that temple.

18 Do not deceive yourselves. If you think that you are wise in this age, you should become fools so that you may become wise. ¹⁹For the wisdom of this world is foolishness with God. For it is written,

"He catches the wise in their craftiness,"
20 and again,

"The Lord knows the thoughts of the wise,
        that they are futile."

21 So let no one boast about human leaders. For all things are yours, ²²whether Paul or Apollos or Cephas or the world or life or death or the present or the future— all belong to you, ²³and you belong to Christ, and Christ belongs to God.

THE MINISTRY OF THE APOSTLES

4 Think of us in this way, as servants of Christ and stewards of God's mysteries. ²Moreover, it is required of stewards that they be found trustworthy. ³But with me it is a very small thing that I should be judged by you or by any

---

a In verses 16 and 17 the Greek word for *you* is plural

human court. I do not even judge myself. [4]I am not aware of anything against myself, but I am not thereby acquitted. It is the Lord who judges me. [5]Therefore do not pronounce judgment before the time, before the Lord comes, who will bring to light the things now hidden in darkness and will disclose the purposes of the heart. Then each one will receive commendation from God.

6 I have applied all this to Apollos and myself for your benefit, brothers and sisters,[a] so that you may learn through us the meaning of the saying, "Nothing beyond what is written," so that none of you will be puffed up in favor of one against another. [7]For who sees anything different in you?[b] What do you have that you did not receive? And if you received it, why do you boast as if it were not a gift?

8 Already you have all you want! Already you have become rich! Quite apart from us you have become kings! Indeed, I wish that you had become kings, so that we might be kings with you! [9]For I think that God has exhibited us apostles as last of all, as though sentenced to death, because we have become a spectacle to the world, to angels and to mortals. [10]We are fools for the sake of Christ, but you are wise in Christ. We are weak, but you are strong. You are held in honor, but we in disrepute. [11]To the present hour we are hungry and thirsty, we are poorly clothed and beaten and homeless, [12]and we grow weary from the work of our own hands. When reviled, we bless; when persecuted, we endure; [13]when slandered, we speak kindly. We have become like the rubbish of the world, the dregs of all things, to this very day.

FATHERLY ADMONITION

14 I am not writing this to make you ashamed, but to admonish you as my beloved children. [15]For though you might have ten thousand guardians in Christ, you do not have many fathers. Indeed, in Christ Jesus I became your father through the gospel. [16]I appeal to you, then, be imitators of me. [17]For this reason I sent[c] you Timothy, who is my beloved and faithful child in the Lord, to remind you of my ways in Christ Jesus, as I teach them everywhere in every church. [18]But some of you, thinking that I am not coming to you, have become arrogant. [19]But I will come to you soon, if the Lord wills, and I will find out not the talk of these arrogant people but their power. [20]For the kingdom of God depends not on talk but on power. [21]What would you prefer? Am I to come to you with a stick, or with love in a spirit of gentleness?

---

a Gk brothers   b Or Who makes you different from another?   c Or am sending

SEXUAL IMMORALITY DEFILES THE CHURCH

5 It is actually reported that there is sexual immorality among you, and of a kind that is not found even among pagans; for a man is living with his father's wife. ²And you are arrogant! Should you not rather have mourned, so that he who has done this would have been removed from among you?

3 For though absent in body, I am present in spirit; and as if present I have already pronounced judgment ⁴in the name of the Lord Jesus on the man who has done such a thing.ª When you are assembled, and my spirit is present with the power of our Lord Jesus, ⁵you are to hand this man over to Satan for the destruction of the flesh, so that his spirit may be saved in the day of the Lord.ᵇ

6 Your boasting is not a good thing. Do you not know that a little yeast leavens the whole batch of dough? ⁷Clean out the old yeast so that you may be a new batch, as you really are unleavened. For our paschal lamb, Christ, has been sacrificed. ⁸Therefore, let us celebrate the festival, not with the old yeast, the yeast of malice and evil, but with the unleavened bread of sincerity and truth.

SEXUAL IMMORALITY MUST BE JUDGED

9 I wrote to you in my letter not to associate with sexually immoral persons— ¹⁰not at all meaning the immoral of this world, or the greedy and robbers, or idolaters, since you would then need to go out of the world. ¹¹But now I am writing to you not to associate with anyone who bears the name of brother or sisterᶜ who is sexually immoral or greedy, or is an idolater, reviler, drunkard, or robber. Do not even eat with such a one. ¹²For what have I to do with judging those outside? Is it not those who are inside that you are to judge? ¹³God will judge those outside. "Drive out the wicked person from among you."

LAWSUITS AMONG BELIEVERS

6 When any of you has a grievance against another, do you dare to take it to court before the unrighteous, instead of taking it before the saints? ²Do you not know that the saints will judge the world? And if the world is to be judged by you, are you incompetent to try trivial cases? ³Do you not know that we are to judge angels—to say nothing of ordinary matters? ⁴If you have ordinary cases, then, do you appoint as judges those who have no standing in the church? ⁵I say this to your shame. Can it be that there is no one among you

---

a Or on the man who has done such a thing in the name of the Lord Jesus b Other ancient authorities add Jesus c Gk brother wise enough to decide between one believer[a] and another, [6]but a believer[a] goes to court against a believer[a]—and before unbelievers at that?

7 In fact, to have lawsuits at all with one another is already a defeat for you. Why not rather be wronged? Why not rather be defrauded? [8]But you yourselves wrong and defraud—and believers[b] at that.

9 Do you not know that wrongdoers will not inherit the kingdom of God? Do not be deceived! Fornicators, idolaters, adulterers, male prostitutes, sodomites, [10]thieves, the greedy, drunkards, revilers, robbers—none of these will inherit the kingdom of God. [11]And this is what some of you used to be. But you were washed, you were sanctified, you were justified in the name of the Lord Jesus Christ and in the Spirit of our God.

GLORIFY GOD IN BODY AND SPIRIT

12 "All things are lawful for me," but not all things are beneficial. "All things are lawful for me," but I will not be dominated by anything. [13]"Food is meant for the stomach and the stomach for food,"[c] and God will destroy both one and the other. The body is meant not for fornication but for the Lord, and the Lord for the body. [14]And God raised the Lord and will also raise us by his power. [15]Do you not know that your bodies are members of Christ? Should I therefore take the members of Christ and make them members of a prostitute? Never! [16]Do you not know that whoever is united to a prostitute becomes one body with her? For it is said, "The two shall be one flesh." [17]But anyone united to the Lord becomes one spirit with him. [18]Shun fornication! Every sin that a person commits is outside the body; but the fornicator sins against the body itself. [19]Or do you not know that your body is a temple[d] of the Holy Spirit within you, which you have from God, and that you are not your own? [20]For you were bought with a price; therefore glorify God in your body.

DIRECTIONS CONCERNING MARRIAGE

7 Now concerning the matters about which you wrote: "It is well for a man not to touch a woman." [2]But because of cases of sexual immorality, each man should have his own wife and each woman her own husband. [3]The husband should give to his wife her conjugal rights, and likewise the wife to her husband. [4]For the wife does not have authority over her own body, but the husband does; likewise the husband does not have authority over his own body, but the wife does. [5]Do not deprive one another except perhaps by agreement for a set time, to devote yourselves to prayer, and then come together again, so

---

a Gk *brother*   *b* Gk *brothers*   *c* The quotation may extend to the word *other*   *d* Or *sanctuary* that Satan may not tempt you because of your lack of self-control. ⁶This I say by way of concession, not of command. ⁷I wish that all were as I myself am. But each has a particular gift from God, one having one kind and another a different kind.

8 To the unmarried and the widows I say that it is well for them to remain unmarried as I am. ⁹But if they are not practicing self-control, they should marry. For it is better to marry than to be aflame with passion.

10 To the married I give this command—not I but the Lord—that the wife should not separate from her husband ¹¹(but if she does separate, let her remain unmarried or else be reconciled to her husband), and that the husband should not divorce his wife.

12 To the rest I say—I and not the Lord—that if any believer*a* has a wife who is an unbeliever, and she consents to live with him, he should not divorce her. ¹³And if any woman has a husband who is an unbeliever, and he consents to live with her, she should not divorce him. ¹⁴For the unbelieving husband is made holy through his wife, and the unbelieving wife is made holy through her husband. Otherwise, your children would be unclean, but as it is, they are holy. ¹⁵But if the unbelieving partner separates, let it be so; in such a case the brother or sister is not bound. It is to peace that God has called you.*b* ¹⁶Wife, for all you know, you might save your husband. Husband, for all you know, you might save your wife.

THE LIFE THAT THE LORD HAS ASSIGNED

17 However that may be, let each of you lead the life that the Lord has assigned, to which God called you. This is my rule in all the churches. ¹⁸Was anyone at the time of his call already circumcised? Let him not seek to remove the marks of circumcision. Was anyone at the time of his call uncircumcised? Let him not seek circumcision. ¹⁹Circumcision is nothing, and uncircumcision is nothing; but obeying the commandments of God is everything. ²⁰Let each of you remain in the condition in which you were called.

21 Were you a slave when called? Do not be concerned about it. Even if you can gain your freedom, make use of your present condition now more than ever.*c* ²²For whoever was called in the Lord as a slave is a freed person belonging to the Lord, just as whoever was free when called is a slave of Christ. ²³You were bought with a price; do not become slaves of human masters. ²⁴In whatever condition you were called, brothers and sisters,*d* there remain with God.

---

a Gk *brother*   *b* Other ancient authorities read *us*   *c* Or *avail yourself of the opportunity*   *d* Gk *brothers*

THE UNMARRIED AND THE WIDOWS

25 Now concerning virgins, I have no command of the Lord, but I give my opinion as one who by the Lord's mercy is trustworthy. [26]I think that, in view of the impending[a] crisis, it is well for you to remain as you are. [27]Are you bound to a wife? Do not seek to be free. Are you free from a wife? Do not seek a wife. [28]But if you marry, you do not sin, and if a virgin marries, she does not sin. Yet those who marry will experience distress in this life,[b] and I would spare you that. [29]I mean, brothers and sisters,[c] the appointed time has grown short; from now on, let even those who have wives be as though they had none, [30]and those who mourn as though they were not mourning, and those who rejoice as though they were not rejoicing, and those who buy as though they had no possessions, [31]and those who deal with the world as though they had no dealings with it. For the present form of this world is passing away.

32 I want you to be free from anxieties. The unmarried man is anxious about the affairs of the Lord, how to please the Lord; [33]but the married man is anxious about the affairs of the world, how to please his wife, [34]and his interests are divided. And the unmarried woman and the virgin are anxious about the affairs of the Lord, so that they may be holy in body and spirit; but the married woman is anxious about the affairs of the world, how to please her husband. [35]I say this for your own benefit, not to put any restraint upon you, but to promote good order and unhindered devotion to the Lord.

36 If anyone thinks that he is not behaving properly toward his fiancée,[d] if his passions are strong, and so it has to be, let him marry as he wishes; it is no sin. Let them marry. [37]But if someone stands firm in his resolve, being under no necessity but having his own desire under control, and has determined in his own mind to keep her as his fiancée,[d] he will do well. [38]So then, he who marries his fiancée[d] does well; and he who refrains from marriage will do better.

39 A wife is bound as long as her husband lives. But if the husband dies,[e] she is free to marry anyone she wishes, only in the Lord. [40]But in my judgment she is more blessed if she remains as she is. And I think that I too have the Spirit of God.

FOOD OFFERED TO IDOLS

8 Now concerning food sacrificed to idols: we know that "all of us possess knowledge." Knowledge puffs up, but love builds up. [2]Anyone who claims

---

a Or present   b Gk in the flesh   c Gk brothers   d Gk virgin   e Gk falls asleep to know something does not yet have the necessary knowledge; ³but anyone who loves God is known by him.

4 Hence, as to the eating of food offered to idols, we know that "no idol in the world really exists," and that "there is no God but one." ⁵Indeed, even though there may be so-called gods in heaven or on earth—as in fact there are many gods and many lords— ⁶yet for us there is one God, the Father, from whom are all things and for whom we exist, and one Lord, Jesus Christ, through whom are all things and through whom we exist.

7 It is not everyone, however, who has this knowledge. Since some have become so accustomed to idols until now, they still think of the food they eat as food offered to an idol; and their conscience, being weak, is defiled. ⁸"Food will not bring us close to God."ᵃ We are no worse off if we do not eat, and no better off if we do. ⁹But take care that this liberty of yours does not somehow become a stumbling block to the weak. ¹⁰For if others see you, who possess knowledge, eating in the temple of an idol, might they not, since their conscience is weak, be encouraged to the point of eating food sacrificed to idols? ¹¹So by your knowledge those weak believers for whom Christ died are destroyed.ᵇ ¹²But when you thus sin against members of your family,ᶜ and wound their conscience when it is weak, you sin against Christ. ¹³Therefore, if food is a cause of their falling,ᵈ I will never eat meat, so that I may not cause one of themᵉ to fall.

THE RIGHTS OF AN APOSTLE

9 Am I not free? Am I not an apostle? Have I not seen Jesus our Lord? Are you not my work in the Lord? ²If I am not an apostle to others, at least I am to you; for you are the seal of my apostleship in the Lord.

3 This is my defense to those who would examine me. ⁴Do we not have the right to our food and drink? ⁵Do we not have the right to be accompanied by a believing wife,ᶠ as do the other apostles and the brothers of the Lord and Cephas? ⁶Or is it only Barnabas and I who have no right to refrain from working for a living? ⁷Who at any time pays the expenses for doing military service? Who plants a vineyard and does not eat any of its fruit? Or who tends a flock and does not get any of its milk?

8 Do I say this on human authority? Does not the law also say the same? ⁹For it is written in the law of Moses, "You shall not muzzle an ox while it is treading out the grain." Is it for oxen that God is concerned? ¹⁰Or does he not speak entirely

---

a The quotation may extend to the end of the verse   b Gk *the weak brother . . . is destroyed*   c Gk *against the brothers*   d Gk *my brother's falling*   e Gk *cause my brother*   f Gk *a sister as wife* for our sake? It was indeed written for our sake, for whoever plows should plow in hope and whoever threshes should thresh in hope of a share in the crop. [11]If we have sown spiritual good among you, is it too much if we reap your material benefits? [12]If others share this rightful claim on you, do not we still more?

Nevertheless, we have not made use of this right, but we endure anything rather than put an obstacle in the way of the gospel of Christ. [13]Do you not know that those who are employed in the temple service get their food from the temple, and those who serve at the altar share in what is sacrificed on the altar? [14]In the same way, the Lord commanded that those who proclaim the gospel should get their living by the gospel.

15 But I have made no use of any of these rights, nor am I writing this so that they may be applied in my case. Indeed, I would rather die than that—no one will deprive me of my ground for boasting! [16]If I proclaim the gospel, this gives me no ground for boasting, for an obligation is laid on me, and woe to me if I do not proclaim the gospel! [17]For if I do this of my own will, I have a reward; but if not of my own will, I am entrusted with a commission. [18]What then is my reward? Just this: that in my proclamation I may make the gospel free of charge, so as not to make full use of my rights in the gospel.

19 For though I am free with respect to all, I have made myself a slave to all, so that I might win more of them. [20]To the Jews I became as a Jew, in order to win Jews. To those under the law I became as one under the law (though I myself am not under the law) so that I might win those under the law. [21]To those outside the law I became as one outside the law (though I am not free from God's law but am under Christ's law) so that I might win those outside the law. [22]To the weak I became weak, so that I might win the weak. I have become all things to all people, that I might by all means save some. [23]I do it all for the sake of the gospel, so that I may share in its blessings.

24 Do you not know that in a race the runners all compete, but only one receives the prize? Run in such a way that you may win it. [25]Athletes exercise self-control in all things; they do it to receive a perishable wreath, but we an imperishable one. [26]So I do not run aimlessly, nor do I box as though beating the air; [27]but I punish my body and enslave it, so that after proclaiming to others I myself should not be disqualified.

WARNINGS FROM ISRAEL'S HISTORY

10 I do not want you to be unaware, brothers and sisters,[a] that our ancestors were all under the cloud, and all passed through the sea, [2]and all

---

a Gk brothers

were baptized into Moses in the cloud and in the sea, [3]and all ate the same spiritual food, [4]and all drank the same spiritual drink. For they drank from the spiritual rock that followed them, and the rock was Christ. [5]Nevertheless, God was not pleased with most of them, and they were struck down in the wilderness.

6 Now these things occurred as examples for us, so that we might not desire evil as they did. [7]Do not become idolaters as some of them did; as it is written, "The people sat down to eat and drink, and they rose up to play." [8]We must not indulge in sexual immorality as some of them did, and twenty-three thousand fell in a single day. [9]We must not put Christ[a] to the test, as some of them did, and were destroyed by serpents. [10]And do not complain as some of them did, and were destroyed by the destroyer. [11]These things happened to them to serve as an example, and they were written down to instruct us, on whom the ends of the ages have come. [12]So if you think you are standing, watch out that you do not fall. [13]No testing has overtaken you that is not common to everyone. God is faithful, and he will not let you be tested beyond your strength, but with the testing he will also provide the way out so that you may be able to endure it.

14 Therefore, my dear friends,[b] flee from the worship of idols. [15]I speak as to sensible people; judge for yourselves what I say. [16]The cup of blessing that we bless, is it not a sharing in the blood of Christ? The bread that we break, is it not a sharing in the body of Christ? [17]Because there is one bread, we who are many are one body, for we all partake of the one bread. [18]Consider the people of Israel;[c] are not those who eat the sacrifices partners in the altar? [19]What do I imply then? That food sacrificed to idols is anything, or that an idol is anything? [20]No, I imply that what pagans sacrifice, they sacrifice to demons and not to God. I do not want you to be partners with demons. [21]You cannot drink the cup of the Lord and the cup of demons. You cannot partake of the table of the Lord and the table of demons. [22]Or are we provoking the Lord to jealousy? Are we stronger than he?

DO ALL TO THE GLORY OF GOD

23 "All things are lawful," but not all things are beneficial. "All things are lawful," but not all things build up. [24]Do not seek your own advantage, but that of the other. [25]Eat whatever is sold in the meat market without raising any question on the ground of conscience, [26]for "the earth and its fullness are the Lord's." [27]If an unbeliever invites you to a meal and you are disposed to go, eat

---

a Other ancient authorities read *the Lord*   *b* Gk *my beloved*   *c* Gk *Israel according to the flesh* whatever is set before you without raising any question on the ground of conscience. ²⁸But if someone says to you, "This has been offered in sacrifice," then do not eat it, out of consideration for the one who informed you, and for the sake of conscience— ²⁹I mean the other's conscience, not your own. For why should my liberty be subject to the judgment of someone else's conscience? ³⁰If I partake with thankfulness, why should I be denounced because of that for which I give thanks?

31 So, whether you eat or drink, or whatever you do, do everything for the glory of God. ³²Give no offense to Jews or to Greeks or to the church of God, ³³just as I try to please everyone in everything I do, not seeking my own advantage, but that of many, so that they may be saved.

11

Be imitators of me, as I am of Christ.

HEAD COVERINGS

2 I commend you because you remember me in everything and maintain the traditions just as I handed them on to you. ³But I want you to understand that Christ is the head of every man, and the husband*a* is the head of his wife,*b* and God is the head of Christ. ⁴Any man who prays or prophesies with something on his head disgraces his head, ⁵but any woman who prays or prophesies with her head unveiled disgraces her head—it is one and the same thing as having her head shaved. ⁶For if a woman will not veil herself, then she should cut off her hair; but if it is disgraceful for a woman to have her hair cut off or to be shaved, she should wear a veil. ⁷For a man ought not to have his head veiled, since he is the image and reflection*c* of God; but woman is the reflection*c* of man. ⁸Indeed, man was not made from woman, but woman from man. ⁹Neither was man created for the sake of woman, but woman for the sake of man. ¹⁰For this reason a woman ought to have a symbol of*d* authority on her head,*e* because of the angels. ¹¹Nevertheless, in the Lord woman is not independent of man or man independent of woman. ¹²For just as woman came from man, so man comes through woman; but all things come from God. ¹³Judge for yourselves: is it proper for a woman to pray to God with her head unveiled? ¹⁴Does not nature itself teach you that if a man wears long hair, it is degrading to him, ¹⁵but if a woman has long hair, it is her glory? For her hair is given to her for a covering. ¹⁶But if anyone is disposed to be contentious—we have no such custom, nor do the churches of God.

---

a The same Greek word means *man* or *husband*   *b* Or *head of the woman*   *c* Or *glory*   *d* Gk lacks *a symbol of*   *e* Or *have freedom of choice regarding her head*

ABUSES AT THE LORD'S SUPPER

17 Now in the following instructions I do not commend you, because when you come together it is not for the better but for the worse. [18]For, to begin with, when you come together as a church, I hear that there are divisions among you; and to some extent I believe it. [19]Indeed, there have to be factions among you, for only so will it become clear who among you are genuine. [20]When you come together, it is not really to eat the Lord's supper. [21]For when the time comes to eat, each of you goes ahead with your own supper, and one goes hungry and another becomes drunk. [22]What! Do you not have homes to eat and drink in? Or do you show contempt for the church of God and humiliate those who have nothing? What should I say to you? Should I commend you? In this matter I do not commend you!

THE INSTITUTION OF THE LORD'S SUPPER

23 For I received from the Lord what I also handed on to you, that the Lord Jesus on the night when he was betrayed took a loaf of bread, [24]and when he had given thanks, he broke it and said, "This is my body that is for[a] you. Do this in remembrance of me." [25]In the same way he took the cup also, after supper, saying, "This cup is the new covenant in my blood. Do this, as often as you drink it, in remembrance of me." [26]For as often as you eat this bread and drink the cup, you proclaim the Lord's death until he comes.

PARTAKING OF THE SUPPER UNWORTHILY

27 Whoever, therefore, eats the bread or drinks the cup of the Lord in an unworthy manner will be answerable for the body and blood of the Lord. [28]Examine yourselves, and only then eat of the bread and drink of the cup. [29]For all who eat and drink[b] without discerning the body,[c] eat and drink judgment against themselves. [30]For this reason many of you are weak and ill, and some have died.[d] [31]But if we judged ourselves, we would not be judged. [32]But when we are judged by the Lord, we are disciplined[e] so that we may not be condemned along with the world.

33 So then, my brothers and sisters,[f] when you come together to eat, wait for one another. [34]If you are hungry, eat at home, so that when you come together, it will not be for your condemnation. About the other things I will give instructions when I come.

---

a Other ancient authorities read *is broken for*   b Other ancient authorities add *in an unworthy manner*   c Other ancient authorities read *the Lord's body*   d Gk *fallen asleep*   e Or *When we are judged, we are being disciplined by the Lord*   f Gk *brothers*

SPIRITUAL GIFTS

12 Now concerning spiritual gifts,[a] brothers and sisters,[b] I do not want you to be uninformed. [2]You know that when you were pagans, you were enticed and led astray to idols that could not speak. [3]Therefore I want you to understand that no one speaking by the Spirit of God ever says "Let Jesus be cursed!" and no one can say "Jesus is Lord" except by the Holy Spirit.

4 Now there are varieties of gifts, but the same Spirit; [5]and there are varieties of services, but the same Lord; [6]and there are varieties of activities, but it is the same God who activates all of them in everyone. [7]To each is given the manifestation of the Spirit for the common good. [8]To one is given through the Spirit the utterance of wisdom, and to another the utterance of knowledge according to the same Spirit, [9]to another faith by the same Spirit, to another gifts of healing by the one Spirit, [10]to another the working of miracles, to another prophecy, to another the discernment of spirits, to another various kinds of tongues, to another the interpretation of tongues. [11]All these are activated by one and the same Spirit, who allots to each one individually just as the Spirit chooses.

ONE BODY WITH MANY MEMBERS

12 For just as the body is one and has many members, and all the members of the body, though many, are one body, so it is with Christ. [13]For in the one Spirit we were all baptized into one body—Jews or Greeks, slaves or free—and we were all made to drink of one Spirit.

14 Indeed, the body does not consist of one member but of many. [15]If the foot would say, "Because I am not a hand, I do not belong to the body," that would not make it any less a part of the body. [16]And if the ear would say, "Because I am not an eye, I do not belong to the body," that would not make it any less a part of the body. [17]If the whole body were an eye, where would the hearing be? If the whole body were hearing, where would the sense of smell be? [18]But as it is, God arranged the members in the body, each one of them, as he chose. [19]If all were a single member, where would the body be? [20]As it is, there are many members, yet one body. [21]The eye cannot say to the hand, "I have no need of you," nor again the head to the feet, "I have no need of you." [22]On the contrary, the members of the body that seem to be weaker are indispensable, [23]and those members of the body that we think less honorable we clothe with greater honor, and our less respectable members are treated with greater respect; [24]whereas our more respectable members do not need this. But God has so arranged the

---

a Or spiritual persons b Gk brothers

body, giving the greater honor to the inferior member, [25]that there may be no dissension within the body, but the members may have the same care for one another. [26]If one member suffers, all suffer together with it; if one member is honored, all rejoice together with it.

27 Now you are the body of Christ and individually members of it. [28]And God has appointed in the church first apostles, second prophets, third teachers; then deeds of power, then gifts of healing, forms of assistance, forms of leadership, various kinds of tongues. [29]Are all apostles? Are all prophets? Are all teachers? Do all work miracles? [30]Do all possess gifts of healing? Do all speak in tongues? Do all interpret? [31]But strive for the greater gifts. And I will show you a still more excellent way.

THE GIFT OF LOVE

13 If I speak in the tongues of mortals and of angels, but do not have love, I am a noisy gong or a clanging cymbal. [2]And if I have prophetic powers, and understand all mysteries and all knowledge, and if I have all faith, so as to remove mountains, but do not have love, I am nothing. [3]If I give away all my possessions, and if I hand over my body so that I may boast,[a] but do not have love, I gain nothing.

4 Love is patient; love is kind; love is not envious or boastful or arrogant [5]or rude. It does not insist on its own way; it is not irritable or resentful; [6]it does not rejoice in wrongdoing, but rejoices in the truth. [7]It bears all things, believes all things, hopes all things, endures all things.

8 Love never ends. But as for prophecies, they will come to an end; as for tongues, they will cease; as for knowledge, it will come to an end. [9]For we know only in part, and we prophesy only in part; [10]but when the complete comes, the partial will come to an end. [11]When I was a child, I spoke like a child, I thought like a child, I reasoned like a child; when I became an adult, I put an end to childish ways. [12]For now we see in a mirror, dimly,[b] but then we will see face to face. Now I know only in part; then I will know fully, even as I have been fully known. [13]And now faith, hope, and love abide, these three; and the greatest of these is love.

GIFTS OF PROPHECY AND TONGUES

14 Pursue love and strive for the spiritual gifts, and especially that you may prophesy. [2]For those who speak in a tongue do not speak to other people but to God; for nobody understands them, since they are speaking mysteries

---

a Other ancient authorities read *body to be burned*   b Gk *in a riddle* in the Spirit. [3]On the other hand, those who prophesy speak to other people for their upbuilding and encouragement and consolation. [4]Those who speak in a tongue build up themselves, but those who prophesy build up the church. [5]Now I would like all of you to speak in tongues, but even more to prophesy. One who prophesies is greater than one who speaks in tongues, unless someone interprets, so that the church may be built up.

6 Now, brothers and sisters,[a] if I come to you speaking in tongues, how will I benefit you unless I speak to you in some revelation or knowledge or prophecy or teaching? [7]It is the same way with lifeless instruments that produce sound, such as the flute or the harp. If they do not give distinct notes, how will anyone know what is being played? [8]And if the bugle gives an indistinct sound, who will get ready for battle? [9]So with yourselves; if in a tongue you utter speech that is not intelligible, how will anyone know what is being said? For you will be speaking into the air. [10]There are doubtless many different kinds of sounds in the world, and nothing is without sound. [11]If then I do not know the meaning of a sound, I will be a foreigner to the speaker and the speaker a foreigner to me. [12]So with yourselves; since you are eager for spiritual gifts, strive to excel in them for building up the church.

13 Therefore, one who speaks in a tongue should pray for the power to interpret. [14]For if I pray in a tongue, my spirit prays but my mind is unproductive. [15]What should I do then? I will pray with the spirit, but I will pray with the mind also; I will sing praise with the spirit, but I will sing praise with the mind also. [16]Otherwise, if you say a blessing with the spirit, how can anyone in the position of an outsider say the "Amen" to your thanksgiving, since the outsider does not know what you are saying? [17]For you may give thanks well enough, but the other person is not built up. [18]I thank God that I speak in tongues more than all of you; [19]nevertheless, in church I would rather speak five words with my mind, in order to instruct others also, than ten thousand words in a tongue.

20 Brothers and sisters,[b] do not be children in your thinking; rather, be infants in evil, but in thinking be adults. [21]In the law it is written,

> "By people of strange tongues
>   and by the lips of foreigners
> I will speak to this people;
>   yet even then they will not listen
>   to me,"

says the Lord. [22]Tongues, then, are a sign not for believers but for unbelievers, while prophecy is not for unbelievers but for believers. [23]If, therefore, the whole

---

a Gk brothers b Gk Brothers

church comes together and all speak in tongues, and outsiders or unbelievers enter, will they not say that you are out of your mind? [24]But if all prophesy, an unbeliever or outsider who enters is reproved by all and called to account by all. [25]After the secrets of the unbeliever's heart are disclosed, that person will bow down before God and worship him, declaring, "God is really among you."

ORDERLY WORSHIP

26 What should be done then, my friends?[a] When you come together, each one has a hymn, a lesson, a revelation, a tongue, or an interpretation. Let all things be done for building up. [27]If anyone speaks in a tongue, let there be only two or at most three, and each in turn; and let one interpret. [28]But if there is no one to interpret, let them be silent in church and speak to themselves and to God. [29]Let two or three prophets speak, and let the others weigh what is said. [30]If a revelation is made to someone else sitting nearby, let the first person be silent. [31]For you can all prophesy one by one, so that all may learn and all be encouraged. [32]And the spirits of prophets are subject to the prophets, [33]for God is a God not of disorder but of peace.

(As in all the churches of the saints, [34]women should be silent in the churches. For they are not permitted to speak, but should be subordinate, as the law also says. [35]If there is anything they desire to know, let them ask their husbands at home. For it is shameful for a woman to speak in church.[b] [36]Or did the word of God originate with you? Or are you the only ones it has reached?)

37 Anyone who claims to be a prophet, or to have spiritual powers, must acknowledge that what I am writing to you is a command of the Lord. [38]Anyone who does not recognize this is not to be recognized. [39]So, my friends,[c] be eager to prophesy, and do not forbid speaking in tongues; [40]but all things should be done decently and in order.

THE RESURRECTION OF CHRIST

15 Now I would remind you, brothers and sisters,[a] of the good news[d] that I proclaimed to you, which you in turn received, in which also you stand, [2]through which also you are being saved, if you hold firmly to the message that I proclaimed to you—unless you have come to believe in vain.

3 For I handed on to you as of first importance what I in turn had received: that Christ died for our sins in accordance with the scriptures, [4]and that he was buried, and that he was raised on the third day in accordance with the scriptures, [5]and that he appeared to Cephas, then to the twelve. [6]Then he appeared

---

a Gk brothers b Other ancient authorities put verses 34–35 after verse 40 c Gk my brothers d Or gospel to more than five hundred brothers and sisters*a* at one time, most of whom are still alive, though some have died.*b* *7*Then he appeared to James, then to all the apostles. *8*Last of all, as to one untimely born, he appeared also to me. *9*For I am the least of the apostles, unfit to be called an apostle, because I persecuted the church of God. *10*But by the grace of God I am what I am, and his grace toward me has not been in vain. On the contrary, I worked harder than any of them— though it was not I, but the grace of God that is with me. *11*Whether then it was I or they, so we proclaim and so you have come to believe.

THE RESURRECTION OF THE DEAD

12 Now if Christ is proclaimed as raised from the dead, how can some of you say there is no resurrection of the dead? *13*If there is no resurrection of the dead, then Christ has not been raised; *14*and if Christ has not been raised, then our proclamation has been in vain and your faith has been in vain. *15*We are even found to be misrepresenting God, because we testified of God that he raised Christ—whom he did not raise if it is true that the dead are not raised. *16*For if the dead are not raised, then Christ has not been raised. *17*If Christ has not been raised, your faith is futile and you are still in your sins. *18*Then those also who have died*b* in Christ have perished. *19*If for this life only we have hoped in Christ, we are of all people most to be pitied.

20 But in fact Christ has been raised from the dead, the first fruits of those who have died.*b* *21*For since death came through a human being, the resurrection of the dead has also come through a human being; *22*for as all die in Adam, so all will be made alive in Christ. *23*But each in his own order: Christ the first fruits, then at his coming those who belong to Christ. *24*Then comes the end,*c* when he hands over the kingdom to God the Father, after he has destroyed every ruler and every authority and power. *25*For he must reign until he has put all his enemies under his feet. *26*The last enemy to be destroyed is death. *27*For "God*d* has put all things in subjection under his feet." But when it says, "All things are put in subjection," it is plain that this does not include the one who put all things in subjection under him. *28*When all things are subjected to him, then the Son himself will also be subjected to the one who put all things in subjection under him, so that God may be all in all.

29 Otherwise, what will those people do who receive baptism on behalf of the dead? If the dead are not raised at all, why are people baptized on their behalf?

30 And why are we putting ourselves in danger every hour? *31*I die every

---

a Gk *brothers*   *b* Gk *fallen asleep*   *c* Or *Then come the rest*   *d* Gk *he* day! That is as certain, brothers and sisters,*a* as my boasting of you—a boast that I make in Christ Jesus our Lord. ³²If with merely human hopes I fought with wild animals at Ephesus, what would I have gained by it? If the dead are not raised,

> "Let us eat and drink,
>> for tomorrow we die."

33 Do not be deceived:

> "Bad company ruins good morals."

34 Come to a sober and right mind, and sin no more; for some people have no knowledge of God. I say this to your shame.

THE RESURRECTION BODY

35 But someone will ask, "How are the dead raised? With what kind of body do they come?" ³⁶Fool! What you sow does not come to life unless it dies. ³⁷And as for what you sow, you do not sow the body that is to be, but a bare seed, perhaps of wheat or of some other grain. ³⁸But God gives it a body as he has chosen, and to each kind of seed its own body. ³⁹Not all flesh is alike, but there is one flesh for human beings, another for animals, another for birds, and another for fish. ⁴⁰There are both heavenly bodies and earthly bodies, but the glory of the heavenly is one thing, and that of the earthly is another. ⁴¹There is one glory of the sun, and another glory of the moon, and another glory of the stars; indeed, star differs from star in glory.

42 So it is with the resurrection of the dead. What is sown is perishable, what is raised is imperishable. ⁴³It is sown in dishonor, it is raised in glory. It is sown in weakness, it is raised in power. ⁴⁴It is sown a physical body, it is raised a spiritual body. If there is a physical body, there is also a spiritual body. ⁴⁵Thus it is written, "The first man, Adam, became a living being"; the last Adam became a life-giving spirit. ⁴⁶But it is not the spiritual that is first, but the physical, and then the spiritual. ⁴⁷The first man was from the earth, a man of dust; the second man is*b* from heaven. ⁴⁸As was the man of dust, so are those who are of the dust; and as is the man of heaven, so are those who are of heaven. ⁴⁹Just as we have borne the image of the man of dust, we will*c* also bear the image of the man of heaven.

50 What I am saying, brothers and sisters,*a* is this: flesh and blood cannot inherit the kingdom of God, nor does the perishable inherit the imperishable. ⁵¹Listen, I will tell you a mystery! We will not all die,*d* but we will all be changed, ⁵²in a moment, in the twinkling of an eye, at the last trumpet. For

---

a Gk *brothers*   *b* Other ancient authorities add *the Lord*   *c* Other ancient authorities read *let us*   *d* Gk *fall asleep* the trumpet will sound, and the dead will be raised imperishable, and we will be changed. [53]For this perishable body must put on imperishability, and this mortal body must put on immortality. [54]When this perishable body puts on imperishability, and this mortal body puts on immortality, then the saying that is written will be fulfilled:

"Death has been swallowed up in victory."
55 "Where, O death, is your victory?
Where, O death, is your sting?"

56 The sting of death is sin, and the power of sin is the law. [57]But thanks be to God, who gives us the victory through our Lord Jesus Christ.

58 Therefore, my beloved,[a] be steadfast, immovable, always excelling in the work of the Lord, because you know that in the Lord your labor is not in vain.

THE COLLECTION FOR THE SAINTS

16 Now concerning the collection for the saints: you should follow the directions I gave to the churches of Galatia. [2]On the first day of every week, each of you is to put aside and save whatever extra you earn, so that collections need not be taken when I come. [3]And when I arrive, I will send any whom you approve with letters to take your gift to Jerusalem. [4]If it seems advisable that I should go also, they will accompany me.

PLANS FOR TRAVEL

5 I will visit you after passing through Macedonia—for I intend to pass through Macedonia— [6]and perhaps I will stay with you or even spend the winter, so that you may send me on my way, wherever I go. [7]I do not want to see you now just in passing, for I hope to spend some time with you, if the Lord permits. [8]But I will stay in Ephesus until Pentecost, [9]for a wide door for effective work has opened to me, and there are many adversaries.

10 If Timothy comes, see that he has nothing to fear among you, for he is doing the work of the Lord just as I am; [11]therefore let no one despise him. Send him on his way in peace, so that he may come to me; for I am expecting him with the brothers.

12 Now concerning our brother Apollos, I strongly urged him to visit you with the other brothers, but he was not at all willing[b] to come now. He will come when he has the opportunity.

---

a Gk beloved brothers   b Or it was not at all God's will for him

FINAL MESSAGES AND GREETINGS

13 Keep alert, stand firm in your faith, be courageous, be strong. [14]Let all that you do be done in love.

15 Now, brothers and sisters,[a] you know that members of the household of Stephanas were the first converts in Achaia, and they have devoted themselves to the service of the saints; [16]I urge you to put yourselves at the service of such people, and of everyone who works and toils with them. [17]I rejoice at the coming of Stephanas and Fortunatus and Achaicus, because they have made up for your absence; [18]for they refreshed my spirit as well as yours. So give recognition to such persons.

19 The churches of Asia send greetings. Aquila and Prisca, together with the church in their house, greet you warmly in the Lord. [20]All the brothers and sisters[a] send greetings. Greet one another with a holy kiss.

21 I, Paul, write this greeting with my own hand. [22]Let anyone be accursed who has no love for the Lord. Our Lord, come![b] [23]The grace of the Lord Jesus be with you. [24]My love be with all of you in Christ Jesus.[c]

---

a Gk brothers   b Gk Marana tha. These Aramaic words can also be read Maran atha, meaning Our Lord has come   c Other ancient authorities add Amen

Philemon

In the canonical New Testament, Philemon is the last of the thirteen letters attributed to Paul because it is the shortest, only twenty-five verses long, so brief it is not even divided into chapters. But in this chronological New Testament, it comes early, in the middle of the seven letters universally accepted as by Paul himself.

Philemon is one of Paul's "prison letters" (the other in the seven genuine letters is Philippians). From details in the letter, we know that it was a Roman prison. Some scholars think it was in the city of Rome and thus date Philemon (and Philippians) to Paul's imprisonment there in the early 60s. But there were Roman prisons throughout the empire, especially in provincial capitals such as Ephesus in Asia Minor. A majority think these two letters were written during an imprisonment in Ephesus in the mid-50s. Because they were written near each other in time, it is arbitrary to place one ahead of the other. For didactic rather than historical reasons, I have put Philemon before Philippians.

Historical Context

Philemon is unique among Paul's seven letters not only because it is the shortest, but also because it is the only one written to a person rather than to a community. The two main characters are Philemon and Onesimus. Philemon was a member of a Christ-community, maybe even its leader, for the community met in his house (vv. 1–2). Onesimus was Philemon's slave who had fled from him for reasons we do not know. To be a runaway slave was a very serious matter in that world. Onesimus went to Paul in prison, presumably because he knew Philemon admired Paul, and he wanted Paul to intercede on his behalf. There he became a convert, a Christ-follower. Now Paul has sent Onesimus back to Philemon with this letter.

Paul's intercession could have recommended mitigating punishment, counseling Philemon not to punish Onesimus too harshly, or perhaps not at all. But that was not Paul's purpose. Rather, it was to persuade Philemon to free Onesimus.

Paul's Rhetorical Strategy of Persuasion

This letter illustrates Paul's exceptional gifts of persuasion as well as the theological foundation of his conviction. Though the letter is addressed to Philemon, Paul also addressed it to the Christ-community that met in his house. The letter would have been read to the community. It was personal, but not private.

Note Paul's rhetorical strategy:

> Paul praises Philemon, calling him "our dear friend and co-worker" (v. 1). He tells him, "I hear of your love for all the saints and your faith toward the Lord Jesus. . . . The hearts of the saints have been refreshed through you, my brother" (vv. 5, 7).

> Paul emphasizes his own situation as "an old man" (v. 9) and a prisoner of Christ Jesus (vv. 1, 9, 13).

> Paul tells Philemon that he could command him to do his duty, but would rather appeal to him on the basis of love (vv. 8–9), so that his "good deed might be voluntary and not something forced" (v. 14).

> Paul calls Onesimus "my child" (v. 10) and "my own heart" (v. 12) and mentions how "useful" (v. 11; the meaning of the name Onesimus) he has been during Paul's imprisonment and that he would like to keep Onesimus "to be of service" to him while in prison (v. 13). He adds "in your place." Is there a barb in this? Is Paul implying that Philemon should be doing something for him in prison, but isn't? Or that Philemon could feel virtuous by freeing Onesimus, so he can serve Paul in his place—that he would be doing a good deed by doing so?

> Paul then makes his appeal. His instructions to Philemon are: "Have him back forever, no longer as a slave, but more than a slave, a beloved brother—especially to me but how much more to you, both in the flesh and in the Lord. . . . Welcome him as you would welcome me" (vv. 15–17).

> Then he tells Philemon that if Onesimus has wronged him in any way or owes him anything, Philemon is to charge that to Paul's account and he will repay it. He adds, "I say nothing about your owing me even your own self" (vv. 18–19).

Paul concludes his appeal by praising Philemon once again: "Confident of your obedience, I am writing to you, knowing that you will do even more than I say" (v. 21).

He adds, "One more thing—prepare a guest room for me, for I am hoping through your prayers to be restored to you" (v. 22). The words may suggest that Paul thought he would be set free, but their rhetorical function in the letter is clear: if and when Paul gets out of prison, he will come and see Philemon. The words suggest affection (he matters that much to Paul) and also inspection (Paul might be there soon to see how this has worked out).

The letter ends with greetings from five Christ-followers who were known to Philemon, at least by name: Epaphras, Mark, Aristarchus, Demas, and Luke. The implicit message is that they know what Paul is asking Philemon to do. Just as this personal letter was also very public because Philemon's community would hear it, so also Paul's co-workers knew what it said. They would be watching.

The letter is a masterpiece of persuasion. Some see it as "manipulative" and decry it as such. Paul does back Philemon into a corner that he couldn't get out of without looking really bad. It can also be seen as "loving persuasion." How do you lead somebody to do the right thing without ordering it? Whatever the mixture, it is a masterpiece.

The Underlying Issue

In addition to illustrating Paul's rhetoric of persuasion, the letter provides a case study of what life "in Christ" (one of Paul's most frequently used phrases), in the "new creation," in Christ-communities was to be like. The issue was larger than resolving a conflict between Philemon and Onesimus. It was whether slavery was acceptable within life "in Christ." Philemon is a Christ-follower who has slaves. Onesimus has become a Christ-follower—he has become "in Christ." Thus the issue is: May a Christian have a slave who has become a Christian?

Paul's answer is no. A Christian master may not have a Christian slave. That this larger claim underlies his appeal to Philemon is apparent from the language he uses. Receive Onesimus back as "a beloved brother." That is "new family" language again. And the two are to be brothers "both in the flesh and in the Lord"—indicating not just spiritual equality, but equality "in the flesh."

This letter is a concrete application of what Paul wrote about life in Christ in Galatians. If you have been "baptized into Christ" and "clothed yourselves with Christ," there is no longer Jew or Gentile, slave or free, male or female, "for all of you are one in Christ Jesus" (3.27–28). Life "in Christ" abolishes the hierarchical relations of conventional culture. Its equality is not only spiritual, but also "in the flesh."

We do not know how Philemon acted in response to Paul's appeal. Did he free Onesimus immediately? Did he grumble and maybe even resist for a while? Though we do not know, early Christian tradition reports that Onesimus eventually became a bishop in Ephesus. He was at some point freed—and this letter may be in the New Testament because of him.

Philemon

SALUTATION

1 Paul, a prisoner of Christ Jesus, and Timothy our brother,*a*

To Philemon our dear friend and co-worker, ²to Apphia our sister,*b* to Archippus our fellow soldier, and to the church in your house:

3 Grace to you and peace from God our Father and the Lord Jesus Christ.

PHILEMON'S LOVE AND FAITH

4 When I remember you*c* in my prayers, I always thank my God ⁵because I hear of your love for all the saints and your faith toward the Lord Jesus. ⁶I pray that the sharing of your faith may become effective when you perceive all the good that we*d* may do for Christ. ⁷I have indeed received much joy and encouragement from your love, because the hearts of the saints have been refreshed through you, my brother.

PAUL'S PLEA FOR ONESIMUS

8 For this reason, though I am bold enough in Christ to command you to do your duty, ⁹yet I would rather appeal to you on the basis of love—and I, Paul, do this as an old man, and now also as a prisoner of Christ Jesus.*e* ¹⁰I am appealing to you for my child, Onesimus, whose father I have become during my imprisonment. ¹¹Formerly he was useless to you, but now he is indeed useful*f* both to you and to me. ¹²I am sending him, that is, my own heart, back to you.

---

a Gk *the brother*   *b* Gk *the sister*   *c* From verse 4 through verse 21, *you* is singular   *d* Other ancient authorities read *you* (plural)   *e* Or *as an ambassador of Christ Jesus, and now also his prisoner*   *f* The name Onesimus means *useful* or (compare verse 20) *beneficial*

¹³I wanted to keep him with me, so that he might be of service to me in your place during my imprisonment for the gospel; ¹⁴but I preferred to do nothing without your consent, in order that your good deed might be voluntary and not something forced. ¹⁵Perhaps this is the reason he was separated from you for a while, so that you might have him back forever, ¹⁶no longer as a slave but more than a slave, a beloved brother—especially to me but how much more to you, both in the flesh and in the Lord.

17 So if you consider me your partner, welcome him as you would welcome me. ¹⁸If he has wronged you in any way, or owes you anything, charge that to my account. ¹⁹I, Paul, am writing this with my own hand: I will repay it. I say nothing about your owing me even your own self. ²⁰Yes, brother, let me have this benefit from you in the Lord! Refresh my heart in Christ. ²¹Confident of your obedience, I am writing to you, knowing that you will do even more than I say.

22 One thing more—prepare a guest room for me, for I am hoping through your prayers to be restored to you.

FINAL GREETINGS AND BENEDICTION

23 Epaphras, my fellow prisoner in Christ Jesus, sends greetings to you,ᵃ ²⁴and so do Mark, Aristarchus, Demas, and Luke, my fellow workers.

25 The grace of the Lord Jesus Christ be with your spirit.ᵇ

---

a Here *you* is singular   b Other ancient authorities add *Amen*

Philippians

Philippians is the most consistently affectionate of Paul's letters. Philippi was the capital of ancient Macedonia, in northern Greece. According to Acts 16, it was the first city in Europe in which Paul founded a Christ-community after leaving Asia Minor in the late 40s. We do not know if he had visited it in the years since, though it seems likely, given his visits to Macedonia. In any case, his relationship to the community seems to have been uncomplicated. The tone of the letter is not only affectionate, but filled with gratitude. It also contains important and extraordinary passages.

Like Philemon, Philippians was written from a Roman prison, probably from the same imprisonment in Ephesus in the mid-50s. Unlike in the closing of Philemon, in which Paul writes that he hopes to be freed, in this letter he is uncertain about whether his imprisonment might end in execution.

The letter begins with the typical Pauline opening: "Paul and Timothy, servants of Christ Jesus, to all the saints in Christ Jesus who are in Philippi. . . . Grace to you and peace from God our Father and the Lord Jesus Christ" (1.1–2). The opening continues with an extended thanksgiving (1.3–11). The letter ends with a reiteration of Paul's thankfulness for the Philippians and their gifts to him (4.10–23).

Joy

Given that Paul was in prison and uncertain about whether he would be executed, it is remarkable that the letter is so filled with the language of "joy" and "rejoicing." They are among Paul's favorite words when he speaks of life "in Christ" and are especially prominent in this letter.

> I thank my God, . . . constantly praying with joy. (1.3–4)
>
> I rejoice . . . and I will continue to rejoice. (1.18)
>
> Make my joy complete. (2.2)
>
> I am glad and rejoice with all of you. . . . You also must . . . rejoice with me. (2.17–18)
>
> That you may rejoice . . . (2.28)
>
> Rejoice in the Lord. (3.1)
>
> Rejoice in the Lord always; again I will say, Rejoice. (4.4)
>
> I rejoice in the Lord greatly. (4.10)

Paul's joy is grounded "in Christ." Life "in Christ" has led him to a state he describes as follows:

> I have learned to be content with whatever I have. I know what it is to have little, and I know what it is to have plenty. In any and all circumstances I have learned the secret of being well-fed and of going hungry, of having plenty and of being in need. I can do all things through him [Christ] who strengthens me. (4.11–13)

Imitating Christ

One of the most important and best-known passages in this letter speaks of imitating the life that we see in Jesus (2.1–11). It begins:

> If then there is any encouragement in Christ, any consolation from love, any sharing in the Spirit, any compassion and sympathy, make my joy complete: *be of the same mind, having the same love, being in full accord and of one mind.* (italics added)

It continues with "the mind," "the love," Christ-followers are to have:

> Let the same mind be in you that was in Christ Jesus, who, though he was in the form of God, did not regard equality with God as something to be exploited, but emptied himself, taking the form of a slave, being born in human likeness. And being found in human form, he humbled himself and became obedient to the point of death—even death on a cross. Therefore God also highly exalted him and gave him the name that is above every name, so that at the name of Jesus every knee should bend, in heaven and on earth and under the earth, and every tongue should confess that Jesus Christ is Lord, to the glory of God the Father.

It is an extraordinary passage, concisely crystallizing Paul's gospel: what we see in Jesus is self-emptying and obedience to God "to the point of death—even death on a cross." Paul's gospel, as in 1 Corinthians, is "Christ crucified," executed by the powers of domination that rule "this world." Furthermore, God has vindicated Jesus, so that Jesus is Lord over all other lords, whether in heaven, on earth, or under the earth, the three-story universe of the ancient imagination. Paul is telling the Philippians to have the mind we see in Jesus, who followed God even when other lords seemed to have the last word.

Most scholars see this passage as containing an early Christian hymn that Paul either wrote or is quoting. If it is a hymn that Paul knew his hearers would recognize, it provides a glimpse into how early Christian communities celebrated and remembered Jesus and the significance of his life and death. And if it is not a hymn, it still tells us what Paul thought was most central about Jesus. Follow him; live the life you see in him, for he is Lord, and the lords of this world are not.

Whatever Is True and Honorable

Near the end of the letter is another remarkable passage. Paul urges the members of the Christ-community in Philippi to follow what they have learned and seen in him. In the previous passage, he spoke of imitating Christ. In 3.17 he urges the community to imitate him and in 4.8–9 describes what that means:

> Finally, beloved, whatever is true, whatever is honorable, whatever is just, whatever is pure, whatever is pleasing, whatever is commendable, if there is any excellence and if there is anything worthy of praise, think about these things. Keep on doing the things that you have learned and received and heard and seen in me, and the God of peace will be with you.

When Paul wrote this letter, he thought it might be his farewell letter. But if locating this letter during an imprisonment in Ephesus is correct, he was released and lived for several more years. Thus this letter was not his last. But it stands as testimony to what Paul wanted most to communicate as he faced the possibility of his own imminent death. In this sense, it was his last will and testament.

THE LETTER OF PAUL TO THE
Philippians

SALUTATION

1 Paul and Timothy, servants*a* of Christ Jesus,

To all the saints in Christ Jesus who are in Philippi, with the bishops*b* and deacons:*c*

2 Grace to you and peace from God our Father and the Lord Jesus Christ.

PAUL'S PRAYER FOR THE PHILIPPIANS

3 I thank my God every time I remember you, [4]constantly praying with joy in every one of my prayers for all of you, [5]because of your sharing in the gospel from the first day until now. [6]I am confident of this, that the one who began a good work among you will bring it to completion by the day of Jesus Christ. [7]It is right for me to think this way about all of you, because you hold me in your heart,*d* for all of you share in God's grace*e* with me, both in my imprisonment and in the defense and confirmation of the gospel. [8]For God is my witness, how I long for all of you with the compassion of Christ Jesus. [9]And this is my prayer, that your love may overflow more and more with knowledge and full insight [10]to help you to determine what is best, so that in the day of Christ you may be pure and blameless, [11]having produced the harvest of righteousness that comes through Jesus Christ for the glory and praise of God.

PAUL'S PRESENT CIRCUMSTANCES

12 I want you to know, beloved,*f* that what has happened to me has actually helped to spread the gospel, [13]so that it has become known throughout

---

a Gk *slaves* *b* Or *overseers* *c* Or *overseers and helpers* *d* Or *because I hold you in my heart* *e* Gk *in grace* *f* Gk *brothers* the whole imperial guard*a* and to everyone else that my imprisonment is for Christ; [14]and most of the brothers and sisters,*b* having been made confident in the Lord by my imprisonment, dare to speak the word*c* with greater boldness and without fear.

15 Some proclaim Christ from envy and rivalry, but others from goodwill. [16]These proclaim Christ out of love, knowing that I have been put here for the defense of the gospel; [17]the others proclaim Christ out of selfish ambition, not sincerely but intending to increase my suffering in my imprisonment. [18]What does it matter? Just this, that Christ is proclaimed in every way, whether out of false motives or true; and in that I rejoice.

Yes, and I will continue to rejoice, [19]for I know that through your prayers and the help of the Spirit of Jesus Christ this will turn out for my deliverance. [20]It is my eager expectation and hope that I will not be put to shame in any way, but that by my speaking with all boldness, Christ will be exalted now as always in my body, whether by life or by death. [21]For to me, living is Christ and dying is gain. [22]If I am to live in the flesh, that means fruitful labor for me; and I do not know which I prefer. [23]I am hard pressed between the two: my desire is to depart and be with Christ, for that is far better; [24]but to remain in the flesh is more necessary for you. [25]Since I am convinced of this, I know that I will remain and continue with all of you for your progress and joy in faith, [26]so that I may share abundantly in your boasting in Christ Jesus when I come to you again.

27 Only, live your life in a manner worthy of the gospel of Christ, so that, whether I come and see you or am absent and hear about you, I will know that you are standing firm in one spirit, striving side by side with one mind for the faith of the gospel, [28]and are in no way intimidated by your opponents. For them this is evidence of their destruction, but of your salvation. And this is God's doing. [29]For he has graciously granted you the privilege not only of believing in Christ, but of suffering for him as well— [30]since you are having the same struggle that you saw I had and now hear that I still have.

IMITATING CHRIST'S HUMILITY

2 If then there is any encouragement in Christ, any consolation from love, any sharing in the Spirit, any compassion and sympathy, [2]make my joy complete: be of the same mind, having the same love, being in full accord and of one mind. [3]Do nothing from selfish ambition or conceit, but in humility regard others as better than yourselves. [4]Let each of you look not to your own

---

a Gk *whole praetorium*   *b* Gk *brothers*   *c* Other ancient authorities read *word of God*

interests, but to the interests of others. ⁵Let the same mind be in you that was*ᵃ
in Christ Jesus,

> 6 who, though he was in the form of God,
>   did not regard equality with God
>   as something to be exploited,
> 7 but emptied himself,
>   taking the form of a slave,
>   being born in human likeness.
>   And being found in human form,
>   8 he humbled himself
>   and became obedient to the point of death—
>   even death on a cross.
>
> 9 Therefore God also highly exalted him
>   and gave him the name
>   that is above every name,
> 10 so that at the name of Jesus
>   every knee should bend,
>   in heaven and on earth and under the earth,
> 11 and every tongue should confess
>   that Jesus Christ is Lord,
>   to the glory of God the Father.

SHINING AS LIGHTS IN THE WORLD

12 Therefore, my beloved, just as you have always obeyed me, not only in my
presence, but much more now in my absence, work out your own salvation
with fear and trembling; ¹³for it is God who is at work in you, enabling you both
to will and to work for his good pleasure.

14 Do all things without murmuring and arguing, ¹⁵so that you may be
blameless and innocent, children of God without blemish in the midst of a
crooked and perverse generation, in which you shine like stars in the world. ¹⁶It
is by your holding fast to the word of life that I can boast on the day of Christ
that I did not run in vain or labor in vain. ¹⁷But even if I am being poured out
as a libation over the sacrifice and the offering of your faith, I am glad and rejoice with all of you— ¹⁸and in the same way you also must be glad and rejoice
with me.

---

a Or that you have

TIMOTHY AND EPAPHRODITUS

19 I hope in the Lord Jesus to send Timothy to you soon, so that I may be cheered by news of you. [20]I have no one like him who will be genuinely concerned for your welfare. [21]All of them are seeking their own interests, not those of Jesus Christ. [22]But Timothy's[a] worth you know, how like a son with a father he has served with me in the work of the gospel. [23]I hope therefore to send him as soon as I see how things go with me; [24]and I trust in the Lord that I will also come soon.

25 Still, I think it necessary to send to you Epaphroditus—my brother and co-worker and fellow soldier, your messenger[b] and minister to my need; [26]for he has been longing for[c] all of you, and has been distressed because you heard that he was ill. [27]He was indeed so ill that he nearly died. But God had mercy on him, and not only on him but on me also, so that I would not have one sorrow after another. [28]I am the more eager to send him, therefore, in order that you may rejoice at seeing him again, and that I may be less anxious. [29]Welcome him then in the Lord with all joy, and honor such people, [30]because he came close to death for the work of Christ,[d] risking his life to make up for those services that you could not give me.

3 Finally, my brothers and sisters,[e] rejoice[f] in the Lord.

BREAKING WITH THE PAST

To write the same things to you is not troublesome to me, and for you it is a safeguard.

2 Beware of the dogs, beware of the evil workers, beware of those who mutilate the flesh![g] [3]For it is we who are the circumcision, who worship in the Spirit of God[h] and boast in Christ Jesus and have no confidence in the flesh— [4]even though I, too, have reason for confidence in the flesh.

If anyone else has reason to be confident in the flesh, I have more: [5]circumcised on the eighth day, a member of the people of Israel, of the tribe of Benjamin, a Hebrew born of Hebrews; as to the law, a Pharisee; [6]as to zeal, a persecutor of the church; as to righteousness under the law, blameless.

7 Yet whatever gains I had, these I have come to regard as loss because of Christ. [8]More than that, I regard everything as loss because of the surpassing value of knowing Christ Jesus my Lord. For his sake I have suffered the loss of

---

a Gk *his*   b Gk *apostle*   c Other ancient authorities read *longing to see*   d Other ancient authorities read *of the Lord*   e Gk *my brothers*   f Or *farewell*   g Gk *the mutilation*   h Other ancient authorities read *worship God in spirit* all things, and I regard them as rubbish, in order that I may gain Christ [9]and be found in him, not having a righteousness of my own that comes from the law, but one that comes through faith in Christ,[a] the righteousness from God based on faith. [10]I want to know Christ[b] and the power of his resurrection and the sharing of his sufferings by becoming like him in his death, [11]if somehow I may attain the resurrection from the dead.

PRESSING TOWARD THE GOAL

12 Not that I have already obtained this or have already reached the goal;[c] but I press on to make it my own, because Christ Jesus has made me his own. [13]Beloved,[d] I do not consider that I have made it my own;[e] but this one thing I do: forgetting what lies behind and straining forward to what lies ahead, [14]I press on toward the goal for the prize of the heavenly[f] call of God in Christ Jesus. [15]Let those of us then who are mature be of the same mind; and if you think differently about anything, this too God will reveal to you. [16]Only let us hold fast to what we have attained.

17 Brothers and sisters,[d] join in imitating me, and observe those who live according to the example you have in us. [18]For many live as enemies of the cross of Christ; I have often told you of them, and now I tell you even with tears. [19]Their end is destruction; their god is the belly; and their glory is in their shame; their minds are set on earthly things. [20]But our citizenship[g] is in heaven, and it is from there that we are expecting a Savior, the Lord Jesus Christ. [21]He will transform the body of our humiliation[h] that it may be conformed to the body of his glory,[i] by the power that also enables him to make all things subject to himself.

4 Therefore, my brothers and sisters,[j] whom I love and long for, my joy and crown, stand firm in the Lord in this way, my beloved.

EXHORTATIONS

2 I urge Euodia and I urge Syntyche to be of the same mind in the Lord. [3]Yes, and I ask you also, my loyal companion,[k] help these women, for they have struggled beside me in the work of the gospel, together with Clement and the rest of my co-workers, whose names are in the book of life.

4 Rejoice[l] in the Lord always; again I will say, Rejoice.[l] [5]Let your gentleness be known to everyone. The Lord is near. [6]Do not worry about anything, but in everything by prayer and supplication with thanksgiving let your requests be

---

a Or through the faith of Christ   b Gk him   c Or have already been made perfect   d Gk Brothers   e Other ancient authorities read my own yet   f Gk upward   g Or commonwealth   h Or our humble bodies   i Or his glorious body   j Gk my brothers   k Or loyal Syzygus   l Or Farewell made known to God. [7]And the peace of God, which surpasses all understanding, will guard your hearts and your minds in Christ Jesus.

8 Finally, beloved,[a] whatever is true, whatever is honorable, whatever is just, whatever is pure, whatever is pleasing, whatever is commendable, if there is any excellence and if there is anything worthy of praise, think about[b] these things. [9]Keep on doing the things that you have learned and received and heard and seen in me, and the God of peace will be with you.

ACKNOWLEDGMENT OF THE PHILIPPIANS' GIFT

10 I rejoice[c] in the Lord greatly that now at last you have revived your concern for me; indeed, you were concerned for me, but had no opportunity to show it.[d] [11]Not that I am referring to being in need; for I have learned to be content with whatever I have. [12]I know what it is to have little, and I know what it is to have plenty. In any and all circumstances I have learned the secret of being well-fed and of going hungry, of having plenty and of being in need. [13]I can do all things through him who strengthens me. [14]In any case, it was kind of you to share my distress.

15 You Philippians indeed know that in the early days of the gospel, when I left Macedonia, no church shared with me in the matter of giving and receiving, except you alone. [16]For even when I was in Thessalonica, you sent me help for my needs more than once. [17]Not that I seek the gift, but I seek the profit that accumulates to your account. [18]I have been paid in full and have more than enough; I am fully satisfied, now that I have received from Epaphroditus the gifts you sent, a fragrant offering, a sacrifice acceptable and pleasing to God. [19]And my God will fully satisfy every need of yours according to his riches in glory in Christ Jesus. [20]To our God and Father be glory forever and ever. Amen.

FINAL GREETINGS AND BENEDICTION

21 Greet every saint in Christ Jesus. The friends[a] who are with me greet you. [22]All the saints greet you, especially those of the emperor's household.

23 The grace of the Lord Jesus Christ be with your spirit.[e]

---

a Gk brothers   b Gk take account of   c Gk I rejoiced   d Gk lacks to show it   e Other ancient authorities add Amen

2 Corinthians

Second Corinthians is not a single letter, but a combination of at least three letters from Paul to the Christ-community in Corinth. Though there is consensus within modern scholarship about its composite character, there is no unanimity about the extent of each letter. The most common divisions are chapters 1–7, 8–9, and 10–13, though probably not in that sequence. The community in Corinth preserved these letters and later combined them into one letter as 2 Corinthians.

That this letter combines several letters is important not only for reading and interpreting it, but also because it provides a vivid glimpse of Paul's continuing relationship to one of his communities. Recall that Paul founded the community in Corinth around the year 50 and spent a year or two there. Recall also that 1 Corinthians refers to a previous letter that he had written to the Corinthians and also to a letter he had received from them.

Second Corinthians adds to this correspondence. First Corinthians reports that Paul had sent Timothy to Corinth and promised to come soon himself in a context that speaks of conflict (4.17–19). In 2 Corinthians, Paul refers to a "painful visit" (2.1), perhaps the visit he promised in his earlier letter. He mentions a letter to Corinth for which he partially apologizes (2.4; 7.8). Written in "distress and anguish" and with "many tears" (2.4), it may have been lost or it may be preserved in 2 Corinthians 10–13, angry chapters in which Paul vigorously defends himself and aggressively attacks those who have been maligning him.

Whether chapters 1–7 are a single letter or a composite, their tone and content are very different from those in 10–13. There is no combativeness, no anger; instead, we find some of the most radiant and luminous language in all of Paul's letters. Chapters 8–9 seem to be yet another letter or even two letters. They are about the collection that Paul is taking up for the Christ-community in Jerusalem. As in chapters 1–7, the tone is completely different from that in 10–13.

Paul's multiple letters to Corinth provide a window into the life of one of his Christ-communities and his continuing affectionate, passionate, and sometimes troubled relationship with its members. Like Galatians, they disclose that the early decades of Christianity were not an ideal time of original perfection and harmony, but a time of conflict as well among followers of Jesus as they struggled to discern what it meant to follow him and his way.

Chapters 10–13

Though there is no scholarly consensus about the sequence of the letters combined in 2 Corinthians, probably a majority think that chapters 10–13 are earlier than the rest. In these chapters, Paul defends himself against teachers who have come to Corinth and sought to undermine him and his message. They were also followers of Jesus. Some in the Corinthian Christ-community had been persuaded by them and become critics of Paul.

Paul attacks the teachers as "super-apostles" (11.5) and "false apostles, deceitful workers" (11.13). Then he superlatively compares himself to them, even as he apologizes for sounding like a boastful fool (11.21):

> "Are they Hebrews? So am I. Are they Israelites? So am I. Are they descendants of Abraham? So am I. Are they ministers of Christ? I am talking like a madman—I am a better one." (11.22–23)

Then Paul lists his sufferings as an apostle: imprisonments, floggings, stonings, shipwrecks, and the dangers and hardships of long journeys on land: bandits, rivers, hunger, thirst, cold, and the toil of walking hundreds of miles across the terrain of Asia Minor and Greece. To which he adds the daily pressure that he feels because of his anxiety for all of his communities (11.23–28).

Then, acknowledging once again his embarrassment about continuing to "boast," he writes, "I will go on to visions and revelations of the Lord" (12.1). He describes an ecstatic religious experience that seems to have involved an out-of-body state of consciousness and traveling to another layer or level of reality—what Paul calls the "third heaven" and "Paradise" (12.2–4). There he "heard things that are not to be told" (12.4). To the extent that these words suggest that Paul heard something that could in principle be told, be put into words, but he had been ordered not to, the translation is unfortunate. What he heard, what he experienced, was ineffable—beyond all words.

In the context of this letter, this text is part of Paul's defense of his credentials as an apostle and interpreter of Jesus. That is its function. Without that context of conflict, Paul would almost certainly never have written these words. Thus the conflict setting drew something out of Paul that we otherwise would not have known about.

In the rest of this letter within a letter, Paul acknowledges a "thorn in the flesh," which he three times asked God to deliver him from. Instead, the message came, "My grace is sufficient for you, for power is made perfect in weakness" (12.9). Even Paul's "thorn"—whatever it was—was confirmation of God's grace present in Paul's weakness. Then Paul tells the Corinthians that he would be visiting them a third time and that he feared finding a community full of "quarreling, jealousy, anger, selfishness, slander, gossip, conceit, and disorder" (12.20). The letter concludes with urgent appeals to those in the community to "examine" and "test" themselves and the hope that when Paul comes to them again he will not need to be so severe.

Chapters 8–9

Chapters 8–9 could have been written anytime in the sequence of letters combined in 2 Corinthians. Their subject matter is the "collection for the saints" that Paul referred to at the end of 1 Corinthians. Paul was raising money from his largely Gentile communities for the impoverished Christian Jewish community in Jerusalem, both as a sign of solidarity and to meet their need for help. Because of the way chapters 8 and 9 are written, scholars suspect that they were originally separate; note that chapter 9 begins as if Paul were introducing a new subject.

These chapters disclose how important the collection for the Jerusalem community was to Paul. They abound with appeals to generosity, grace, bounty, sharing, and fairness. They also suggest something about Paul's strategy. In chapter 8, he tells the Corinthians how generous the Christ-communities in Macedonia (northern Greece) have been in order to motivate the Corinthians. In chapter 9, he tells them that he has been boasting about their generosity to the Macedonians in order to motivate them. And he asks them not to embarrass him by not having the gift ready.

Chapters 1–7

The first seven chapters of 2 Corinthians may have been written last. Though they do reflect a situation of conflict, it seems to be in the past and more or less resolved. Paul refers to the conflict and urges forgiveness of the person (singular) who caused it (2.5–11). But conflict is not the dominant theme. Instead, these chapters combine relief and gratitude with an exposition of a number of Paul's central affirmations:

The ministry of the Spirit (which is life in Christ, the new covenant) is superior to the ministry of death in tablets of stone (3.2–8): "The letter kills, but the Spirit gives life" (3.6).

In the metaphor of "unveiled faces" (3.12–18), Paul refers to "a veil" that lies over our minds and continues with the good news that in Christ it is set aside: "When one turns to the Lord, the veil is removed. Now the Lord is the Spirit, and where the Spirit of the Lord is, there is freedom." He continues: "And all of us, with unveiled faces, seeing the glory of the Lord as though reflected in a mirror, are being transformed into the same image from one degree of glory to another." The gospel, the Christian message, is about being transformed into the likeness of Christ.

Then comes a comparison between the blindness of "this world" and the light of Jesus Christ (4.1–6): "The god of *this world* has blinded the minds of the unbelievers, to keep them from seeing the light of the gospel of the glory of Christ, who is the image of God" (4.4; italics added). "This world" is the world of cultural normalcy with its categories, hierarchies, and domination. But God as revealed in Jesus is the light: "It is the God who said, 'Let light shine out of darkness' [an echo of Gen. 1], who has shone in our hearts to give the light of the knowledge of the glory of God in the face of Jesus Christ" (4.6). Jesus is the light and "the face" who shows us what God is like.

Paul also affirms that "we have this treasure in clay jars" ("earthen vessels" in an earlier English translation, 4.7–12). It is a recognition that the treasure of the gospel always comes to us in clay jars, earthen vessels—that is, through us. The jars, the vessels, are not the treasure; the gospel is. Anything "earthen" can at best be a sacrament, a mediator of the sacred.

He refers to what has happened in Jesus as the "new creation": "From now on, therefore, we regard no one from a human point of view; even though we once knew Christ from a human point of view, we know him no longer in that way. So if anyone is in Christ, there is a new creation: everything old has passed away; see, everything has become new! All this is from God, who reconciled us to himself through Christ" (5.16–18). The new creation, the new age, the turning of the epochs, the transformation of "this world" has begun.

These are among the most remarkable and important passages in Paul's letters. Thus, though parts of this letter are among the most angry in the New Testament, it also includes passages of great radiance.

THE SECOND LETTER OF PAUL TO THE

we have set our hope that he will rescue us again, [11]as you also join in helping us by your prayers, so that many will give thanks on our[a] behalf for the blessing granted us through the prayers of many.

THE POSTPONEMENT OF PAUL'S VISIT

12　Indeed, this is our boast, the testimony of our conscience: we have behaved in the world with frankness[b] and godly sincerity, not by earthly wisdom but by the grace of God—and all the more toward you. [13]For we write you nothing other than what you can read and also understand; I hope you will understand until the end— [14]as you have already understood us in part—that on the day of the Lord Jesus we are your boast even as you are our boast.

15　Since I was sure of this, I wanted to come to you first, so that you might have a double favor;[c] [16]I wanted to visit you on my way to Macedonia, and to come back to you from Macedonia and have you send me on to Judea. [17]Was I vacillating when I wanted to do this? Do I make my plans according to ordinary human standards,[d] ready to say "Yes, yes" and "No, no" at the same time? [18]As surely as God is faithful, our word to you has not been "Yes and No." [19]For the Son of God, Jesus Christ, whom we proclaimed among you, Silvanus and Timothy and I, was not "Yes and No"; but in him it is always "Yes." [20]For in him every one of God's promises is a "Yes." For this reason it is through him that we say the "Amen," to the glory of God. [21]But it is God who establishes us with you in Christ and has anointed us, [22]by putting his seal on us and giving us his Spirit in our hearts as a first installment.

23　But I call on God as witness against me: it was to spare you that I did not come again to Corinth. [24]I do not mean to imply that we lord it over your faith; rather, we are workers with you for your joy, because you stand firm in the faith. 2 So I made up my mind not to make you another painful visit. [2]For if I cause you pain, who is there to make me glad but the one whom I have pained? [3]And I wrote as I did, so that when I came, I might not suffer pain from those who should have made me rejoice; for I am confident about all of you, that my joy would be the joy of all of you. [4]For I wrote you out of much distress and anguish of heart and with many tears, not to cause you pain, but to let you know the abundant love that I have for you.

FORGIVENESS FOR THE OFFENDER

5　But if anyone has caused pain, he has caused it not to me, but to some extent—not to exaggerate it—to all of you. [6]This punishment by the majority

---

a Other ancient authorities read *your*　b Other ancient authorities read *holiness*　c Other ancient authorities read *pleasure*
d Gk *according to the flesh*

is enough for such a person; [7]so now instead you should forgive and console him, so that he may not be overwhelmed by excessive sorrow. [8]So I urge you to reaffirm your love for him. [9]I wrote for this reason: to test you and to know whether you are obedient in everything. [10]Anyone whom you forgive, I also forgive. What I have forgiven, if I have forgiven anything, has been for your sake in the presence of Christ. [11]And we do this so that we may not be outwitted by Satan; for we are not ignorant of his designs.

PAUL'S ANXIETY IN TROAS

12 When I came to Troas to proclaim the good news of Christ, a door was opened for me in the Lord; [13]but my mind could not rest because I did not find my brother Titus there. So I said farewell to them and went on to Macedonia.

14 But thanks be to God, who in Christ always leads us in triumphal procession, and through us spreads in every place the fragrance that comes from knowing him. [15]For we are the aroma of Christ to God among those who are being saved and among those who are perishing; [16]to the one a fragrance from death to death, to the other a fragrance from life to life. Who is sufficient for these things? [17]For we are not peddlers of God's word like so many;[a] but in Christ we speak as persons of sincerity, as persons sent from God and standing in his presence.

MINISTERS OF THE NEW COVENANT

3 Are we beginning to commend ourselves again? Surely we do not need, as some do, letters of recommendation to you or from you, do we? [2]You yourselves are our letter, written on our[b] hearts, to be known and read by all; [3]and you show that you are a letter of Christ, prepared by us, written not with ink but with the Spirit of the living God, not on tablets of stone but on tablets of human hearts.

4 Such is the confidence that we have through Christ toward God. [5]Not that we are competent of ourselves to claim anything as coming from us; our competence is from God, [6]who has made us competent to be ministers of a new covenant, not of letter but of spirit; for the letter kills, but the Spirit gives life.

7 Now if the ministry of death, chiseled in letters on stone tablets,[c] came in glory so that the people of Israel could not gaze at Moses' face because of the glory of his face, a glory now set aside, [8]how much more will the ministry of the Spirit come in glory? [9]For if there was glory in the ministry of condemnation, much more does the ministry of justification abound in glory! [10]Indeed, what

---

a Other ancient authorities read *like the others*   b Other ancient authorities read *your*   c Gk *on stones* once had glory has lost its glory because of the greater glory; [11]for if what was set aside came through glory, much more has the permanent come in glory!

12 Since, then, we have such a hope, we act with great boldness, [13]not like Moses, who put a veil over his face to keep the people of Israel from gazing at the end of the glory that*a* was being set aside. [14]But their minds were hardened. Indeed, to this very day, when they hear the reading of the old covenant, that same veil is still there, since only in Christ is it set aside. [15]Indeed, to this very day whenever Moses is read, a veil lies over their minds; [16]but when one turns to the Lord, the veil is removed. [17]Now the Lord is the Spirit, and where the Spirit of the Lord is, there is freedom. [18]And all of us, with unveiled faces, seeing the glory of the Lord as though reflected in a mirror, are being transformed into the same image from one degree of glory to another; for this comes from the Lord, the Spirit.

TREASURE IN CLAY JARS

4 Therefore, since it is by God's mercy that we are engaged in this ministry, we do not lose heart. [2]We have renounced the shameful things that one hides; we refuse to practice cunning or to falsify God's word; but by the open statement of the truth we commend ourselves to the conscience of everyone in the sight of God. [3]And even if our gospel is veiled, it is veiled to those who are perishing. [4]In their case the god of this world has blinded the minds of the unbelievers, to keep them from seeing the light of the gospel of the glory of Christ, who is the image of God. [5]For we do not proclaim ourselves; we proclaim Jesus Christ as Lord and ourselves as your slaves for Jesus' sake. [6]For it is the God who said, "Let light shine out of darkness," who has shone in our hearts to give the light of the knowledge of the glory of God in the face of Jesus Christ.

7 But we have this treasure in clay jars, so that it may be made clear that this extraordinary power belongs to God and does not come from us. [8]We are afflicted in every way, but not crushed; perplexed, but not driven to despair; [9]persecuted, but not forsaken; struck down, but not destroyed; [10]always carrying in the body the death of Jesus, so that the life of Jesus may also be made visible in our bodies. [11]For while we live, we are always being given up to death for Jesus' sake, so that the life of Jesus may be made visible in our mortal flesh. [12]So death is at work in us, but life in you.

13 But just as we have the same spirit of faith that is in accordance with scripture—"I believed, and so I spoke"—we also believe, and so we speak, [14]because we know that the one who raised the Lord Jesus will raise us also with Jesus, and will bring us with you into his presence. [15]Yes, everything is for

---

a Gk *of what*

your sake, so that grace, as it extends to more and more people, may increase thanksgiving, to the glory of God.

LIVING BY FAITH

16 So we do not lose heart. Even though our outer nature is wasting away, our inner nature is being renewed day by day. [17]For this slight momentary affliction is preparing us for an eternal weight of glory beyond all measure, [18]because we look not at what can be seen but at what cannot be seen; for what can be seen is temporary, but what cannot be seen is eternal.

5 For we know that if the earthly tent we live in is destroyed, we have a building from God, a house not made with hands, eternal in the heavens. [2]For in this tent we groan, longing to be clothed with our heavenly dwelling— [3]if indeed, when we have taken it off[a] we will not be found naked. [4]For while we are still in this tent, we groan under our burden, because we wish not to be unclothed but to be further clothed, so that what is mortal may be swallowed up by life. [5]He who has prepared us for this very thing is God, who has given us the Spirit as a guarantee.

6 So we are always confident; even though we know that while we are at home in the body we are away from the Lord— [7]for we walk by faith, not by sight. [8]Yes, we do have confidence, and we would rather be away from the body and at home with the Lord. [9]So whether we are at home or away, we make it our aim to please him. [10]For all of us must appear before the judgment seat of Christ, so that each may receive recompense for what has been done in the body, whether good or evil.

THE MINISTRY OF RECONCILIATION

11 Therefore, knowing the fear of the Lord, we try to persuade others; but we ourselves are well known to God, and I hope that we are also well known to your consciences. [12]We are not commending ourselves to you again, but giving you an opportunity to boast about us, so that you may be able to answer those who boast in outward appearance and not in the heart. [13]For if we are beside ourselves, it is for God; if we are in our right mind, it is for you. [14]For the love of Christ urges us on, because we are convinced that one has died for all; therefore all have died. [15]And he died for all, so that those who live might live no longer for themselves, but for him who died and was raised for them.

16 From now on, therefore, we regard no one from a human point of view;[b] even though we once knew Christ from a human point of view,[b] we know him

---

a Other ancient authorities read *put it on*   *b* Gk *according to the flesh* no longer in that way. [17]So if anyone is in Christ, there is a new creation: everything old has passed away; see, everything has become new! [18]All this is from God, who reconciled us to himself through Christ, and has given us the ministry of reconciliation; [19]that is, in Christ God was reconciling the world to himself,[a] not counting their trespasses against them, and entrusting the message of reconciliation to us. [20]So we are ambassadors for Christ, since God is making his appeal through us; we entreat you on behalf of Christ, be reconciled to God. [21]For our sake he made him to be sin who knew no sin, so that in him we might become the righteousness of God.

6 As we work together with him,[b] we urge you also not to accept the grace of God in vain. [2]For he says,

"At an acceptable time I have listened to you,
    and on a day of salvation I have helped you."

See, now is the acceptable time; see, now is the day of salvation! [3]We are putting no obstacle in anyone's way, so that no fault may be found with our ministry, [4]but as servants of God we have commended ourselves in every way: through great endurance, in afflictions, hardships, calamities, [5]beatings, imprisonments, riots, labors, sleepless nights, hunger; [6]by purity, knowledge, patience, kindness, holiness of spirit, genuine love, [7]truthful speech, and the power of God; with the weapons of righteousness for the right hand and for the left; [8]in honor and dishonor, in ill repute and good repute. We are treated as impostors, and yet are true; [9]as unknown, and yet are well known; as dying, and see—we are alive; as punished, and yet not killed; [10]as sorrowful, yet always rejoicing; as poor, yet making many rich; as having nothing, and yet possessing everything.

11 We have spoken frankly to you Corinthians; our heart is wide open to you. [12]There is no restriction in our affections, but only in yours. [13]In return—I speak as to children—open wide your hearts also.

THE TEMPLE OF THE LIVING GOD

14 Do not be mismatched with unbelievers. For what partnership is there between righteousness and lawlessness? Or what fellowship is there between light and darkness? [15]What agreement does Christ have with Beliar? Or what does a believer share with an unbeliever? [16]What agreement has the temple of God with idols? For we[c] are the temple of the living God; as God said,

"I will live in them and walk among them,
    and I will be their God,
    and they shall be my people.

---

a Or *God was in Christ reconciling the world to himself*   *b* Gk *As we work together*   *c* Other ancient authorities read *you*

17 Therefore come out from them,
>   and be separate from them, says the Lord,
> and touch nothing unclean;
>   then I will welcome you,
18 and I will be your father,
>   and you shall be my sons and daughters,
> says the Lord Almighty.'"

7 Since we have these promises, beloved, let us cleanse ourselves from every defilement of body and of spirit, making holiness perfect in the fear of God.

PAUL'S JOY AT THE CHURCH'S REPENTANCE

2 Make room in your hearts*a* for us; we have wronged no one, we have corrupted no one, we have taken advantage of no one. ³I do not say this to condemn you, for I said before that you are in our hearts, to die together and to live together. ⁴I often boast about you; I have great pride in you; I am filled with consolation; I am overjoyed in all our affliction.

5 For even when we came into Macedonia, our bodies had no rest, but we were afflicted in every way—disputes without and fears within. ⁶But God, who consoles the downcast, consoled us by the arrival of Titus, ⁷and not only by his coming, but also by the consolation with which he was consoled about you, as he told us of your longing, your mourning, your zeal for me, so that I rejoiced still more. ⁸For even if I made you sorry with my letter, I do not regret it (though I did regret it, for I see that I grieved you with that letter, though only briefly). ⁹Now I rejoice, not because you were grieved, but because your grief led to repentance; for you felt a godly grief, so that you were not harmed in any way by us. ¹⁰For godly grief produces a repentance that leads to salvation and brings no regret, but worldly grief produces death. ¹¹For see what earnestness this godly grief has produced in you, what eagerness to clear yourselves, what indignation, what alarm, what longing, what zeal, what punishment! At every point you have proved yourselves guiltless in the matter. ¹²So although I wrote to you, it was not on account of the one who did the wrong, nor on account of the one who was wronged, but in order that your zeal for us might be made known to you before God. ¹³In this we find comfort.

In addition to our own consolation, we rejoiced still more at the joy of Titus, because his mind has been set at rest by all of you. ¹⁴For if I have been somewhat boastful about you to him, I was not disgraced; but just as everything we said to you was true, so our boasting to Titus has proved true as well. ¹⁵And his

---

a Gk lacks *in your hearts*

heart goes out all the more to you, as he remembers the obedience of all of you, and how you welcomed him with fear and trembling. [16]I rejoice, because I have complete confidence in you.

ENCOURAGEMENT TO BE GENEROUS

8 We want you to know, brothers and sisters,[a] about the grace of God that has been granted to the churches of Macedonia; [2]for during a severe ordeal of affliction, their abundant joy and their extreme poverty have overflowed in a wealth of generosity on their part. [3]For, as I can testify, they voluntarily gave according to their means, and even beyond their means, [4]begging us earnestly for the privilege[b] of sharing in this ministry to the saints— [5]and this, not merely as we expected; they gave themselves first to the Lord and, by the will of God, to us, [6]so that we might urge Titus that, as he had already made a beginning, so he should also complete this generous undertaking[c] among you. [7]Now as you excel in everything—in faith, in speech, in knowledge, in utmost eagerness, and in our love for you[d]—so we want you to excel also in this generous undertaking.[c]

8 I do not say this as a command, but I am testing the genuineness of your love against the earnestness of others. [9]For you know the generous act[e] of our Lord Jesus Christ, that though he was rich, yet for your sakes he became poor, so that by his poverty you might become rich. [10]And in this matter I am giving my advice: it is appropriate for you who began last year not only to do something but even to desire to do something— [11]now finish doing it, so that your eagerness may be matched by completing it according to your means. [12]For if the eagerness is there, the gift is acceptable according to what one has—not according to what one does not have. [13]I do not mean that there should be relief for others and pressure on you, but it is a question of a fair balance between [14]your present abundance and their need, so that their abundance may be for your need, in order that there may be a fair balance. [15]As it is written,

"The one who had much did not have too much,
and the one who had little did not have too little."

COMMENDATION OF TITUS

16 But thanks be to God who put in the heart of Titus the same eagerness for you that I myself have. [17]For he not only accepted our appeal, but since he is more eager than ever, he is going to you of his own accord. [18]With him we are

---

a Gk brothers   b Gk grace   c Gk this grace   d Other ancient authorities read your love for us   e Gk the grace

sending the brother who is famous among all the churches for his proclaiming the good news;*[a] [19]and not only that, but he has also been appointed by the
churches to travel with us while we are administering this generous undertaking*[b] for the glory of the Lord himself*[c] and to show our goodwill. [20]We intend
that no one should blame us about this generous gift that we are administering,
[21]for we intend to do what is right not only in the Lord's sight but also in the
sight of others. [22]And with them we are sending our brother whom we have
often tested and found eager in many matters, but who is now more eager than
ever because of his great confidence in you. [23]As for Titus, he is my partner
and co-worker in your service; as for our brothers, they are messengers*[d] of
the churches, the glory of Christ. [24]Therefore openly before the churches, show
them the proof of your love and of our reason for boasting about you.

THE COLLECTION FOR CHRISTIANS AT JERUSALEM

9 Now it is not necessary for me to write you about the ministry to the saints,
[2]for I know your eagerness, which is the subject of my boasting about you
to the people of Macedonia, saying that Achaia has been ready since last year;
and your zeal has stirred up most of them. [3]But I am sending the brothers in
order that our boasting about you may not prove to have been empty in this
case, so that you may be ready, as I said you would be; [4]otherwise, if some
Macedonians come with me and find that you are not ready, we would be hu-
miliated—to say nothing of you—in this undertaking.*[e] [5]So I thought it necessary to urge the brothers to go on ahead to you, and arrange in advance for this
bountiful gift that you have promised, so that it may be ready as a voluntary
gift and not as an extortion.

6 The point is this: the one who sows sparingly will also reap sparingly, and
the one who sows bountifully will also reap bountifully. [7]Each of you must
give as you have made up your mind, not reluctantly or under compulsion, for
God loves a cheerful giver. [8]And God is able to provide you with every blessing
in abundance, so that by always having enough of everything, you may share
abundantly in every good work. [9]As it is written,

> "He scatters abroad, he gives to the poor;
>   his righteousness*[f] endures forever."

10 He who supplies seed to the sower and bread for food will supply and multiply your seed for sowing and increase the harvest of your righteousness.*[f] [11]You
will be enriched in every way for your great generosity, which will produce

---

a Or *the gospel* *b* Gk *this grace* *c* Other ancient authorities lack *himself* *d* Gk *apostles* *e* Other ancient authorities add *of
boasting* *f* Or *benevolence*

thanksgiving to God through us; [12]for the rendering of this ministry not only supplies the needs of the saints but also overflows with many thanksgivings to God. [13]Through the testing of this ministry you glorify God by your obedience to the confession of the gospel of Christ and by the generosity of your sharing with them and with all others, [14]while they long for you and pray for you because of the surpassing grace of God that he has given you. [15]Thanks be to God for his indescribable gift!

PAUL DEFENDS HIS MINISTRY

10 I myself, Paul, appeal to you by the meekness and gentleness of Christ—I who am humble when face to face with you, but bold toward you when I am away!— [2]I ask that when I am present I need not show boldness by daring to oppose those who think we are acting according to human standards.[a] [3]Indeed, we live as human beings,[b] but we do not wage war according to human standards;[a] [4]for the weapons of our warfare are not merely human,[c] but they have divine power to destroy strongholds. We destroy arguments [5]and every proud obstacle raised up against the knowledge of God, and we take every thought captive to obey Christ. [6]We are ready to punish every disobedience when your obedience is complete.

7 Look at what is before your eyes. If you are confident that you belong to Christ, remind yourself of this, that just as you belong to Christ, so also do we. [8]Now, even if I boast a little too much of our authority, which the Lord gave for building you up and not for tearing you down, I will not be ashamed of it. [9]I do not want to seem as though I am trying to frighten you with my letters. [10]For they say, "His letters are weighty and strong, but his bodily presence is weak, and his speech contemptible." [11]Let such people understand that what we say by letter when absent, we will also do when present.

12 We do not dare to classify or compare ourselves with some of those who commend themselves. But when they measure themselves by one another, and compare themselves with one another, they do not show good sense. [13]We, however, will not boast beyond limits, but will keep within the field that God has assigned to us, to reach out even as far as you. [14]For we were not overstepping our limits when we reached you; we were the first to come all the way to you with the good news[d] of Christ. [15]We do not boast beyond limits, that is, in the labors of others; but our hope is that, as your faith increases, our sphere of action among you may be greatly enlarged, [16]so that we may proclaim the good news[d] in lands beyond you, without boasting of work already done in someone

---

a Gk *according to the flesh*   *b* Gk *in the flesh*   *c* Gk *fleshly*   *d* Or *the gospel* else's sphere of action. [17]"Let the one who boasts, boast in the Lord." [18]For it is not those who commend themselves that are approved, but those whom the Lord commends.

PAUL AND THE FALSE APOSTLES

11 I wish you would bear with me in a little foolishness. Do bear with me! [2]I feel a divine jealousy for you, for I promised you in marriage to one husband, to present you as a chaste virgin to Christ. [3]But I am afraid that as the serpent deceived Eve by its cunning, your thoughts will be led astray from a sincere and pure[a] devotion to Christ. [4]For if someone comes and proclaims another Jesus than the one we proclaimed, or if you receive a different spirit from the one you received, or a different gospel from the one you accepted, you submit to it readily enough. [5]I think that I am not in the least inferior to these super-apostles. [6]I may be untrained in speech, but not in knowledge; certainly in every way and in all things we have made this evident to you.

7 Did I commit a sin by humbling myself so that you might be exalted, because I proclaimed God's good news[b] to you free of charge? [8]I robbed other churches by accepting support from them in order to serve you. [9]And when I was with you and was in need, I did not burden anyone, for my needs were supplied by the friends[c] who came from Macedonia. So I refrained and will continue to refrain from burdening you in any way. [10]As the truth of Christ is in me, this boast of mine will not be silenced in the regions of Achaia. [11]And why? Because I do not love you? God knows I do!

12 And what I do I will also continue to do, in order to deny an opportunity to those who want an opportunity to be recognized as our equals in what they boast about. [13]For such boasters are false apostles, deceitful workers, disguising themselves as apostles of Christ. [14]And no wonder! Even Satan disguises himself as an angel of light. [15]So it is not strange if his ministers also disguise themselves as ministers of righteousness. Their end will match their deeds.

PAUL'S SUFFERINGS AS AN APOSTLE

16 I repeat, let no one think that I am a fool; but if you do, then accept me as a fool, so that I too may boast a little. [17]What I am saying in regard to this boastful confidence, I am saying not with the Lord's authority, but as a fool; [18]since many boast according to human standards,[d] I will also boast. [19]For you gladly put up with fools, being wise yourselves! [20]For you put up with it when someone makes slaves of you, or preys upon you, or takes advantage of you, or

---

a Other ancient authorities lack *and pure* *b* Gk *the gospel of God* *c* Gk *brothers* *d* Gk *according to the flesh* puts on airs, or gives you a slap in the face. [21]To my shame, I must say, we were too weak for that!

But whatever anyone dares to boast of—I am speaking as a fool—I also dare to boast of that. [22]Are they Hebrews? So am I. Are they Israelites? So am I. Are they descendants of Abraham? So am I. [23]Are they ministers of Christ? I am talking like a madman—I am a better one: with far greater labors, far more imprisonments, with countless floggings, and often near death. [24]Five times I have received from the Jews the forty lashes minus one. [25]Three times I was beaten with rods. Once I received a stoning. Three times I was shipwrecked; for a night and a day I was adrift at sea; [26]on frequent journeys, in danger from rivers, danger from bandits, danger from my own people, danger from Gentiles, danger in the city, danger in the wilderness, danger at sea, danger from false brothers and sisters;[a] [27]in toil and hardship, through many a sleepless night, hungry and thirsty, often without food, cold and naked. [28]And, besides other things, I am under daily pressure because of my anxiety for all the churches. [29]Who is weak, and I am not weak? Who is made to stumble, and I am not indignant?

30 If I must boast, I will boast of the things that show my weakness. [31]The God and Father of the Lord Jesus (blessed be he forever!) knows that I do not lie. [32]In Damascus, the governor[b] under King Aretas guarded the city of Damascus in order to[c] seize me, [33]but I was let down in a basket through a window in the wall,[d] and escaped from his hands.

PAUL'S VISIONS AND REVELATIONS

12 It is necessary to boast; nothing is to be gained by it, but I will go on to visions and revelations of the Lord. [2]I know a person in Christ who fourteen years ago was caught up to the third heaven—whether in the body or out of the body I do not know; God knows. [3]And I know that such a person—whether in the body or out of the body I do not know; God knows— [4]was caught up into Paradise and heard things that are not to be told, that no mortal is permitted to repeat. [5]On behalf of such a one I will boast, but on my own behalf I will not boast, except of my weaknesses. [6]But if I wish to boast, I will not be a fool, for I will be speaking the truth. But I refrain from it, so that no one may think better of me than what is seen in me or heard from me, [7]even considering the exceptional character of the revelations. Therefore, to keep[e] me from being too elated, a thorn was given me in the flesh, a messenger of Satan

---

a Gk brothers   b Gk ethnarch   c Other ancient authorities read and wanted to   d Gk through the wall   e Other ancient authorities read To keep to torment me, to keep me from being too elated.[a] [8]Three times I appealed to the Lord about this, that it would leave me, [9]but he said to me, "My grace is sufficient for you, for power[b] is made perfect in weakness." So, I will boast all the more gladly of my weaknesses, so that the power of Christ may dwell in me. [10]Therefore I am content with weaknesses, insults, hardships, persecutions, and calamities for the sake of Christ; for whenever I am weak, then I am strong.

PAUL'S CONCERN FOR THE CORINTHIAN CHURCH

11 I have been a fool! You forced me to it. Indeed you should have been the ones commending me, for I am not at all inferior to these super-apostles, even though I am nothing. [12]The signs of a true apostle were performed among you with utmost patience, signs and wonders and mighty works. [13]How have you been worse off than the other churches, except that I myself did not burden you? Forgive me this wrong!

14 Here I am, ready to come to you this third time. And I will not be a burden, because I do not want what is yours but you; for children ought not to lay up for their parents, but parents for their children. [15]I will most gladly spend and be spent for you. If I love you more, am I to be loved less? [16]Let it be assumed that I did not burden you. Nevertheless (you say) since I was crafty, I took you in by deceit. [17]Did I take advantage of you through any of those whom I sent to you? [18]I urged Titus to go, and sent the brother with him. Titus did not take advantage of you, did he? Did we not conduct ourselves with the same spirit? Did we not take the same steps?

19 Have you been thinking all along that we have been defending ourselves before you? We are speaking in Christ before God. Everything we do, beloved, is for the sake of building you up. [20]For I fear that when I come, I may find you not as I wish, and that you may find me not as you wish; I fear that there may perhaps be quarreling, jealousy, anger, selfishness, slander, gossip, conceit, and disorder. [21]I fear that when I come again, my God may humble me before you, and that I may have to mourn over many who previously sinned and have not repented of the impurity, sexual immorality, and licentiousness that they have practiced.

FURTHER WARNING

13 This is the third time I am coming to you. "Any charge must be sustained by the evidence of two or three witnesses." [2]I warned those who

---

a Other ancient authorities lack *to keep me from being too elated*   b Other ancient authorities read *my power*   g Other ancient authorities read *with him* sinned previously and all the others, and I warn them now while absent, as I did when present on my second visit, that if I come again, I will not be lenient—³since you desire proof that Christ is speaking in me. He is not weak in dealing with you, but is powerful in you. ⁴For he was crucified in weakness, but lives by the power of God. For we are weak in him,ᵃ but in dealing with you we will live with him by the power of God.

5 Examine yourselves to see whether you are living in the faith. Test yourselves. Do you not realize that Jesus Christ is in you?—unless, indeed, you fail to meet the test! ⁶I hope you will find out that we have not failed. ⁷But we pray to God that you may not do anything wrong—not that we may appear to have met the test, but that you may do what is right, though we may seem to have failed. ⁸For we cannot do anything against the truth, but only for the truth. ⁹For we rejoice when we are weak and you are strong. This is what we pray for, that you may become perfect. ¹⁰So I write these things while I am away from you, so that when I come, I may not have to be severe in using the authority that the Lord has given me for building up and not for tearing down.

FINAL GREETINGS AND BENEDICTION

11 Finally, brothers and sisters,ᵇ farewell.ᶜ Put things in order, listen to my appeal,ᵈ agree with one another, live in peace; and the God of love and peace will be with you. ¹²Greet one another with a holy kiss. All the saints greet you.

13 The grace of the Lord Jesus Christ, the love of God, and the communion ofᵉ the Holy Spirit be with all of you.

---

a Other ancient authorities read *with him*   b Gk *brothers*   c Or *rejoice*   d Or *encourage one another*   e Or *and the sharing in*

Romans

Paul's letter to the Christ-communities in Rome is distinctive in many ways. It is his longest letter. Only 1 Corinthians is a serious rival. It is the only letter he wrote to people he didn't know; Paul had never been to Rome. Unlike his other letters, it does not deal with highly specific issues like whether it's acceptable to eat meat sacrificed to idols (1 Cor. 8), for women to prophesy with their heads uncovered (1 Cor. 11), for male Gentile converts to remain uncircumcised (Galatians), or for a Christian master to have a Christian slave (Philemon). Except for a brief section near the end on "weak" and "strong" within the community, Romans has none of this specificity.

It is probably his last letter. Though a small minority of scholars think that the "prison letters"—Philippians, Philemon, and Colossians—are later, most think Romans is the last of the universally agreed upon seven genuine letters of Paul. He wrote it from Corinth around the year 58, just before he began what became his final journey to Jerusalem, arrest, imprisonment, and eventual execution in Rome itself.

So this letter is not about interacting with a community he had founded or with which he had a continuing relationship. Rather, its main purpose was to introduce himself to a group of Christ-followers whom he planned to visit and from whom he hoped to receive support for a mission to Spain. He did so by telling them about his "theology" in the broad sense of that word; that is, how he saw the significance of Jesus and its meaning for thinking about God, transformation, and the new life in Christ.

Romans thus has an additional distinction. It is the most theological of Paul's letters, and the most important of his letters in the history of Christian theology. St. Augustine in the late fourth century was converted by a passage in Romans. In the sixteenth century, it was the theological centerpiece of the Protestant Reformation. Its language of justification, grace, and faith, usually shortened to justification by faith, has been central to Protestant theology ever since.

Historical Context

In addition to introducing Paul to Christians in Rome, the letter has another primary purpose, namely, explicating its central theme of the relationship between Jew and Gentile in the context of God's covenant with Israel. The first verse of the body of the letter announces it. The gospel is the power of God for salvation "to everyone who has faith, to the Jew first and also to the Greek" (1.16; recall that "Greek" means "Gentile"). In chapters 9–11, the theme of God's covenant with Israel, including Jews who had not become followers of Jesus, is explicit. Some scholars think these chapters are the climax and heart of the letter.

Why this emphasis is so strong in Romans is explained by the historical context of the Christ-communities in Rome. There is much that we do not know about them. We do not know who founded them. Were they established by followers of Jesus who came to Rome from the Jewish homeland? Or were they founded by Jewish pilgrims from Rome to Jerusalem who had encountered followers there? We do not know exactly when they were founded, though we do know that there were Christ-communities in Rome by the mid-40s at the latest. Some in them would have been Christian Jews, and some would have been Christian Gentiles, most of them "God-lovers."

In the year 49, the emperor Claudius ordered the expulsion of Jews from Rome. Christian Jews, of course, were also expelled. The report of the Roman historian Suetonius is confirmed in Acts 18.2, which tells the story of Paul meeting Aquila and Priscilla, Christian Jews expelled from Rome under Claudius.

Thus, from roughly 49 or 50 on, the Christ-communities in Rome would have become primarily and perhaps completely Gentile. The Christian Jews were gone. Then, in 54, Claudius's edict was rescinded. How many Jews returned and how quickly they did so are unknown. But the process was under way in the years immediately before and as Paul wrote this letter.

Though we can only imagine some of the issues, it is not difficult to do so. Would the Christian Gentile communities have welcomed Christian Jews back? During the years that Christian Jews had been gone, positions of leadership (however informal) would have been filled by Christian Gentiles. Might these Gentiles even have seen the returned Christian Jews as relative outsiders? And would Christian Jews have felt like outsiders? Might they have formed their own communities, so that there would have been separate kinds of Christ-communities in Rome? This setting, this historical context, accounts for Paul's emphasis in this letter on the relationship between Jews and Gentiles.

Jews and Gentiles, and the Mess the World Is In

After Paul announces his theme in 1.16–17—that the gospel is for both Jew and Gentile—much of the rest of chapters 1–3 is about the mutual responsibility of both Gentiles and Jews for the mess the world is in. Both are guilty; all are guilty and responsible.

The section begins with Paul's indictment of the Gentile world (1.18–2.16). He recites standard Jewish stereotypes of what Gentiles are like; they are idolaters who should know better, exchanging the truth for a lie and worshipping the creation rather than the creator. A long list of Gentile vices follows, beginning with unnatural sexual relationships and continuing with "wickedness, evil, covetousness, malice, . . . envy, murder, strife, deceit, craftiness." Gentiles are "gossips, slanderers, God-haters, insolent, haughty, boastful, inventors of evil, . . . foolish, faithless, heartless, ruthless" (1.29–31).

This is pretty harsh rhetoric. Does this mean that Paul thought that all Gentiles were like this? No, as 2.12–16 make clear—there can be good Gentiles. His indictment is of the Gentile "world"—"*this* world," as he commonly refers to it.

In 2.17, he turns to the guilt and responsibility of Jews for the way the world is. His main claim is that having the "law" (the Torah, the Bible) does not exempt you from judgment unless you live it. So also circumcision is of no value unless it is internal, not merely external. Yet Jews have priority; to them were revealed the promises of God. But the section ends with a common indictment of Jews and Gentiles as responsible for the mess the world is in (3.9–20). They share a solidarity of failure.

Both Jews and Gentiles Justified by Grace Through Faith

Then Paul turns from indictment to proclamation, an announcement and pronouncement that something decisive has happened:

> But now [the construction is emphatic], apart from law [that is, not only to Jews], the righteousness of God has been disclosed, and is attested by the law and the prophets [that is, grounded in Judaism], the righteousness of God through faith in Jesus Christ for all who believe. (3.21–22)

These verses and the ones that follow include some of the most important words in the history of Christian theology, especially in Protestant forms: "justification" (and its siblings "justify" and "justified"), "grace," and "faith." To highlight these three words in the rest of this section:

> Since all have sinned and fall short of the glory of God; they are now *justi-fied* by his *grace* as a gift, through the redemption that is in Christ Jesus, whom God put forward as a sacrifice of atonement by his blood, effective through *faith*. . . . He himself [God] is righteous and . . . *justifies* the one who has *faith* in Jesus. (3.23–26)

The three words are commonly combined in the phrase "justification by grace through faith," often shortened to "justification by faith." Both phrases have become theological shorthand for a widespread Protestant emphasis: *we are saved by believing in Jesus.* As commonly understood, "to be saved" and "salvation" mean a blessed afterlife—going to heaven when we die. The means by which we are saved are not good works, even though they matter. What ultimately matters is faith, understood as believing in Jesus. From this good works will flow. But faith (as believing in Jesus) is primary. It is the gateway to heaven.

The preceding interpretation is a serious misunderstanding of Paul's use of these words. The greatest distortion is caused by imagining that Paul was writing about "how to get to heaven," that is, that his concern was primarily the afterlife and how a concern for that life should affect how we lead this life. Within this framework, "If you want to go to heaven, believe in Jesus."

But heaven, the afterlife, was not central to Paul and early Christianity. Did they believe in an afterlife? Most, perhaps all, did. But was that the main focus for how they saw Jesus? That he provides the way to get to heaven? No. For Paul, "salvation" was not primarily about an afterlife, but about transformation this side of death—the transformation of ourselves and of "this world." Justification by grace through faith is not about how we get to heaven, but how we are transformed here and now.

So Paul was not addressing the question of eternal salvation in heaven and how to get there. Rather, as he wrote about justification and grace and faith, he was addressing the issue of Christian Jews and Christian Gentiles; both, he affirms, are justified by grace through faith in Jesus. They are equals in the solidarity of failure and in the solidarity of grace, and equally dependent on the same grace.

Paul continues this theme in chapter 4 as he invokes the example of Abraham, the primordial ancestor of the Jewish people. Was he, Paul asks, justified (made right with God) by works of the law or by faith? "Faith" is Paul's unambiguous answer. Abraham (as in Galatians) becomes a hero of Paul's understanding of faith and of Paul's proclamation about Jesus.

Finally, as we leave this section of Romans, which has been so important for

Protestant theology, we note that just as "salvation" meant something different for Paul than it does for many Christians today, we note also that "faith" and what it means to "believe in Jesus" have often been misunderstood. The misunderstanding is that "faith" means "believing" a set of teachings/doctrines/beliefs/statements about Jesus.

This misunderstanding has grown in Western culture over the last three centuries or so. Beliefs about Jesus—that he was born of a virgin, that he walked on water and changed water into wine, that he died for our sins and rose again on the third day, that he is the Son of God and the only way, and so forth—have changed from what everybody took for granted to claims that are questionable in the minds of many. So "faith," "believing," has come to mean believing a particular set of claims about Jesus to be true in spite of perhaps somewhat persuasive reasons to question them.

But this is not what Paul (and early Christians generally and their spiritual ancestors in the Jewish Bible) meant by "faith." The word had two primary meanings: loyalty and trust. Loyalty was about commitment and allegiance—not to a set of statements, but to a person. Its opposite was not doubt, but betrayal. Trust was about who or what you trusted. Its opposite was not intellectual doubt, but anxiety. Faith for Paul was about loyalty to and trust in Christ, not about believing a set of statements to be true.

To crystallize Paul's affirmation in this section: Christian Jews and Christian Gentiles alike are justified together by God's grace and by faith—loyalty and trust—in what God has revealed in Jesus.

Romans 5–8

Chapters 5–8 include some of the most magnificent passages in Paul's letters. They expand Paul's theme to the new life "in Christ." They occasionally echo the contrast to the failure of both Gentile and Jew in the construction of "this world," but their dominant tone is vibrant and hope-filled.

The section begins with "Therefore," a characteristic Pauline way of flagging a conclusion. It continues: "Since we are *justified* by *faith,* we have peace with God through our Lord Jesus Christ, through whom we have obtained access to this *grace* in which we stand" (5.1–2; italics added).

Then in a relatively brief contrast between Adam and Christ, "Adam" becomes a symbol of the universality of sin—the disordering of creation caused and sustained by Jew and Gentile alike. But in Christ there is a new possibility. Just as we are all involved universally in sin, so now in Jesus there is the possibility of a new kind of life (5.12–21). Then Paul treats the following in chapters 6–8:

The Christian life as dying and rising with Christ

The inner conflict (between life in Adam and life in Christ?)

Life in the Spirit

The transformation of creation

No separation from the love of God in Christ

Romans 9–11

Then Paul returns to the explicit theme of Jew and Gentile. In chapters 9–11, he agonizes about the nonresponse of many Jews to Jesus, emphasizes his own Jewish roots, and ponders what God's promises to the Jews mean. The issue is no longer simply the relationship between Christian Jews and Christian Gentiles, but God's relationship to Jews as a whole. His conclusion is that God's promises to Israel are still valid: all of Israel will be saved. In the twenty-first century, both Christians and Jews need to be careful not to misunderstand. Paul was not saying that all Jews would become believers in Jesus; their relationship with God was prior to Jesus. And Paul was not saying that the promises to Israel included the land as a geographical possession.

Romans 12–14

As the letter nears its end, Paul turns to what is mostly ethical instruction. It begins with another emphatic "therefore," after which Paul tells his readers what follows from what he had written thus far, the "so what." This section begins with one of the most concise summations of Paul's message:

> I appeal to you therefore, brothers and sisters, by the mercies of God, to present your bodies as a living sacrifice, holy and acceptable to God, which is your spiritual worship. Do not be conformed to this world, but be transformed by the renewing of your minds. (12.1–2)

Paul emphasizes that Christ-followers should present their "bodies as a living sacrifice." We would say "selves." That is their spiritual worship, which is about dying and rising with Christ. Note also the emphasis on transformation. They are not to be conformed to "this world," but to be transformed by the renewing of their minds—"minds" as a comprehensive image for a way of seeing reality. Following Jesus is about transformation.

The rest of these chapters emphasize love, nonviolence, acceptance of imperial authority (even as you resist it), nonjudgment of one another, and so forth. Though the letter has a significance beyond its historical context, it clearly was shaped by the fact that Paul wrote it to Roman Christians.

Romans 15–16

The letter seems to end twice, once at the end of chapter 15 and again at the end of chapter 16. Scholars have wondered if Romans once ended with chapter 15 and if chapter 16 was added later (or perhaps even sent to a different community). But most scholars think both of these chapters were written by Paul to Christ-communities in Rome, however they came to be combined.

What is most striking about these chapters is the list of people in Romans 16. It begins by commending to them a woman named Phoebe, named as a deacon or minister and benefactor. Presumably she carried the letter to Rome and read it to the Christ-communities there. Reading it would also have involved explaining it whenever there were questions. The list continues with greetings to a number of individuals in the Roman communities. Of those who are named, some are clearly Christian Jews and others Christian Gentiles. Even more striking is the number of women's names. Of the twenty-eight individuals mentioned, ten are women. Of the eleven singled out for special praise, five are women. Paul uses the Greek verb for dedicated apostolic activity to refer to four of these women. One, Junia, is spoken of as "prominent among the apostles." Leadership by women was a fact in early Christ-communities. Not only did Paul not challenge it; he obviously approved of it.

Romans concludes the seven letters certainly written by Paul. Christian tradition later than the New Testament reports that Paul was released from his imprisonment in Rome and traveled to Spain, as he planned to according to Romans. Then he was again arrested and executed in Rome in the late 60s. Scholars who take this seriously are inclined to date some of his letters in the 60s, including even some of the disputed letters. But most scholars are skeptical that he was released or went to Spain. Rather, soon after Paul wrote this letter, he was arrested in Jerusalem and spent the rest of his life as a prisoner. His desire to visit the Christ-communities in Rome was fulfilled—but as a prisoner of Jesus Christ.

SALUTATION

1 Paul, a servant*ᵃ* of Jesus Christ, called to be an apostle, set apart for the gospel of God, ²which he promised beforehand through his prophets in the holy scriptures, ³the gospel concerning his Son, who was descended from David according to the flesh ⁴and was declared to be Son of God with power according to the spirit*ᵇ* of holiness by resurrection from the dead, Jesus Christ our Lord, ⁵through whom we have received grace and apostleship to bring about the obedience of faith among all the Gentiles for the sake of his name, ⁶including yourselves who are called to belong to Jesus Christ,

7 To all God's beloved in Rome, who are called to be saints:

Grace to you and peace from God our Father and the Lord Jesus Christ.

PRAYER OF THANKSGIVING

8 First, I thank my God through Jesus Christ for all of you, because your faith is proclaimed throughout the world. ⁹For God, whom I serve with my spirit by announcing the gospel*ᶜ* of his Son, is my witness that without ceasing I remember you always in my prayers, ¹⁰asking that by God's will I may somehow at last succeed in coming to you. ¹¹For I am longing to see you so that I may share with you some spiritual gift to strengthen you— ¹²or rather so that we may be mutually encouraged by each other's faith, both yours and mine. ¹³I want you to know, brothers and sisters,*ᵈ* that I have often intended to come to you (but thus far have been prevented), in order that I may reap some harvest among

---

a Gk *slave*   *b* Or *Spirit*   *c* Gk *my spirit in the gospel*   *d* Gk *brothers* you as I have among the rest of the Gentiles. [14]I am a debtor both to Greeks and to barbarians, both to the wise and to the foolish [15]—hence my eagerness to proclaim the gospel to you also who are in Rome.

THE POWER OF THE GOSPEL

16 For I am not ashamed of the gospel; it is the power of God for salvation to everyone who has faith, to the Jew first and also to the Greek. [17]For in it the righteousness of God is revealed through faith for faith; as it is written, "The one who is righteous will live by faith."[a]

THE GUILT OF HUMANKIND

18 For the wrath of God is revealed from heaven against all ungodliness and wickedness of those who by their wickedness suppress the truth. [19]For what can be known about God is plain to them, because God has shown it to them. [20]Ever since the creation of the world his eternal power and divine nature, invisible though they are, have been understood and seen through the things he has made. So they are without excuse; [21]for though they knew God, they did not honor him as God or give thanks to him, but they became futile in their thinking, and their senseless minds were darkened. [22]Claiming to be wise, they became fools; [23]and they exchanged the glory of the immortal God for images resembling a mortal human being or birds or four-footed animals or reptiles.

24 Therefore God gave them up in the lusts of their hearts to impurity, to the degrading of their bodies among themselves, [25]because they exchanged the truth about God for a lie and worshiped and served the creature rather than the Creator, who is blessed forever! Amen.

26 For this reason God gave them up to degrading passions. Their women exchanged natural intercourse for unnatural, [27]and in the same way also the men, giving up natural intercourse with women, were consumed with passion for one another. Men committed shameless acts with men and received in their own persons the due penalty for their error.

28 And since they did not see fit to acknowledge God, God gave them up to a debased mind and to things that should not be done. [29]They were filled with every kind of wickedness, evil, covetousness, malice. Full of envy, murder, strife, deceit, craftiness, they are gossips, [30]slanderers, God-haters,[b] insolent, haughty, boastful, inventors of evil, rebellious toward parents, [31]foolish, faithless, heartless, ruthless. [32]They know God's decree, that those who practice such things deserve to die—yet they not only do them but even applaud others who practice them.

---

a Or *The one who is righteous through faith will live*   b Or *God-hated*

THE RIGHTEOUS JUDGMENT OF GOD

2 Therefore you have no excuse, whoever you are, when you judge others; for in passing judgment on another you condemn yourself, because you, the judge, are doing the very same things. ²You say,ᵃ "We know that God's judgment on those who do such things is in accordance with truth." ³Do you imagine, whoever you are, that when you judge those who do such things and yet do them yourself, you will escape the judgment of God? ⁴Or do you despise the riches of his kindness and forbearance and patience? Do you not realize that God's kindness is meant to lead you to repentance? ⁵But by your hard and impenitent heart you are storing up wrath for yourself on the day of wrath, when God's righteous judgment will be revealed. ⁶For he will repay according to each one's deeds: ⁷to those who by patiently doing good seek for glory and honor and immortality, he will give eternal life; ⁸while for those who are self-seeking and who obey not the truth but wickedness, there will be wrath and fury. ⁹There will be anguish and distress for everyone who does evil, the Jew first and also the Greek, ¹⁰but glory and honor and peace for everyone who does good, the Jew first and also the Greek. ¹¹For God shows no partiality.

12 All who have sinned apart from the law will also perish apart from the law, and all who have sinned under the law will be judged by the law. ¹³For it is not the hearers of the law who are righteous in God's sight, but the doers of the law who will be justified. ¹⁴When Gentiles, who do not possess the law, do instinctively what the law requires, these, though not having the law, are a law to themselves. ¹⁵They show that what the law requires is written on their hearts, to which their own conscience also bears witness; and their conflicting thoughts will accuse or perhaps excuse them ¹⁶on the day when, according to my gospel, God, through Jesus Christ, will judge the secret thoughts of all.

THE JEWS AND THE LAW

17 But if you call yourself a Jew and rely on the law and boast of your relation to God ¹⁸and know his will and determine what is best because you are instructed in the law, ¹⁹and if you are sure that you are a guide to the blind, a light to those who are in darkness, ²⁰a corrector of the foolish, a teacher of children, having in the law the embodiment of knowledge and truth, ²¹you, then, that teach others, will you not teach yourself? While you preach against stealing, do you steal? ²²You that forbid adultery, do you commit adultery? You that abhor idols, do you rob temples? ²³You that boast in the law, do you dishonor God

---

a Gk lacks *You say*

by breaking the law? ²⁴For, as it is written, "The name of God is blasphemed among the Gentiles because of you."

25 Circumcision indeed is of value if you obey the law; but if you break the law, your circumcision has become uncircumcision. ²⁶So, if those who are uncircumcised keep the requirements of the law, will not their uncircumcision be regarded as circumcision? ²⁷Then those who are physically uncircumcised but keep the law will condemn you that have the written code and circumcision but break the law. ²⁸For a person is not a Jew who is one outwardly, nor is true circumcision something external and physical. ²⁹Rather, a person is a Jew who is one inwardly, and real circumcision is a matter of the heart—it is spiritual and not literal. Such a person receives praise not from others but from God.

3 Then what advantage has the Jew? Or what is the value of circumcision? ²Much, in every way. For in the first place the Jews*ᵃ* were entrusted with the oracles of God. ³What if some were unfaithful? Will their faithlessness nullify the faithfulness of God? ⁴By no means! Although everyone is a liar, let God be proved true, as it is written,

> "So that you may be justified in your words,
>   and prevail in your judging."*ᵇ*

⁵But if our injustice serves to confirm the justice of God, what should we say? That God is unjust to inflict wrath on us? (I speak in a human way.) ⁶By no means! For then how could God judge the world? ⁷But if through my falsehood God's truthfulness abounds to his glory, why am I still being condemned as a sinner? ⁸And why not say (as some people slander us by saying that we say), "Let us do evil so that good may come"? Their condemnation is deserved!

NONE IS RIGHTEOUS

9 What then? Are we any better off?*ᶜ* No, not at all; for we have already charged that all, both Jews and Greeks, are under the power of sin, ¹⁰as it is written:

> "There is no one who is righteous, not even one;
> 11 there is no one who has understanding,
>   there is no one who seeks God.
> 12 All have turned aside, together they have become worthless;
>   there is no one who shows kindness,
>   there is not even one."
> 13 "Their throats are opened graves;
>   they use their tongues to deceive."
>   "The venom of vipers is under their lips."

---

a Gk *they*   *b* Gk *when you are being judged*   *c* Or *at any disadvantage?*

14 "Their mouths are full of cursing and bitterness."

15 "Their feet are swift to shed blood;

16 ruin and misery are in their paths,

17 and the way of peace they have not known."

18 "There is no fear of God before their eyes."

19 Now we know that whatever the law says, it speaks to those who are under the law, so that every mouth may be silenced, and the whole world may be held accountable to God. 20For "no human being will be justified in his sight" by deeds prescribed by the law, for through the law comes the knowledge of sin.

RIGHTEOUSNESS THROUGH FAITH

21 But now, apart from law, the righteousness of God has been disclosed, and is attested by the law and the prophets, 22the righteousness of God through faith in Jesus Christ*a* for all who believe. For there is no distinction, 23since all have sinned and fall short of the glory of God; 24they are now justified by his grace as a gift, through the redemption that is in Christ Jesus, 25whom God put forward as a sacrifice of atonement*b* by his blood, effective through faith. He did this to show his righteousness, because in his divine forbearance he had passed over the sins previously committed; 26it was to prove at the present time that he himself is righteous and that he justifies the one who has faith in Jesus.*c*

27 Then what becomes of boasting? It is excluded. By what law? By that of works? No, but by the law of faith. 28For we hold that a person is justified by faith apart from works prescribed by the law. 29Or is God the God of Jews only? Is he not the God of Gentiles also? Yes, of Gentiles also, 30since God is one; and he will justify the circumcised on the ground of faith and the uncircumcised through that same faith. 31Do we then overthrow the law by this faith? By no means! On the contrary, we uphold the law.

THE EXAMPLE OF ABRAHAM

4 What then are we to say was gained by*d* Abraham, our ancestor according to the flesh? 2For if Abraham was justified by works, he has something to boast about, but not before God. 3For what does the scripture say? "Abraham believed God, and it was reckoned to him as righteousness." 4Now to one who works, wages are not reckoned as a gift but as something due. 5But to one who without works trusts him who justifies the ungodly, such faith is reckoned as

---

a Or *through the faith of Jesus Christ*   *b* Or *a place of atonement*   *c* Or *who has the faith of Jesus*   *d* Other ancient authorities read *say about* righteousness. ⁶So also David speaks of the blessedness of those to whom God reckons righteousness apart from works:

7 "Blessed are those whose iniquities are forgiven,

and whose sins are covered;

8 blessed is the one against whom the Lord will not reckon sin."

9 Is this blessedness, then, pronounced only on the circumcised, or also on the uncircumcised? We say, "Faith was reckoned to Abraham as righteousness." ¹⁰How then was it reckoned to him? Was it before or after he had been circumcised? It was not after, but before he was circumcised. ¹¹He received the sign of circumcision as a seal of the righteousness that he had by faith while he was still uncircumcised. The purpose was to make him the ancestor of all who believe without being circumcised and who thus have righteousness reckoned to them, ¹²and likewise the ancestor of the circumcised who are not only circumcised but who also follow the example of the faith that our ancestor Abraham had before he was circumcised.

GOD'S PROMISE REALIZED THROUGH FAITH

13 For the promise that he would inherit the world did not come to Abraham or to his descendants through the law but through the righteousness of faith. ¹⁴If it is the adherents of the law who are to be the heirs, faith is null and the promise is void. ¹⁵For the law brings wrath; but where there is no law, neither is there violation.

16 For this reason it depends on faith, in order that the promise may rest on grace and be guaranteed to all his descendants, not only to the adherents of the law but also to those who share the faith of Abraham (for he is the father of all of us, ¹⁷as it is written, "I have made you the father of many nations")—in the presence of the God in whom he believed, who gives life to the dead and calls into existence the things that do not exist. ¹⁸Hoping against hope, he believed that he would become "the father of many nations," according to what was said, "So numerous shall your descendants be." ¹⁹He did not weaken in faith when he considered his own body, which was already *a* as good as dead (for he was about a hundred years old), or when he considered the barrenness of Sarah's womb. ²⁰No distrust made him waver concerning the promise of God, but he grew strong in his faith as he gave glory to God, ²¹being fully convinced that God was able to do what he had promised. ²²Therefore his faith*b* "was reckoned to him as righteousness." ²³Now the words, "it was reckoned to him," were written not for his sake alone, ²⁴but for ours also. It will be reckoned to us who

---

a Other ancient authorities lack *already*   *b* Gk *Therefore it* believe in him who raised Jesus our Lord from the dead, [25]who was handed over to death for our trespasses and was raised for our justification.

RESULTS OF JUSTIFICATION

5 Therefore, since we are justified by faith, we[a] have peace with God through our Lord Jesus Christ, [2]through whom we have obtained access[b] to this grace in which we stand; and we[c] boast in our hope of sharing the glory of God. [3]And not only that, but we[c] also boast in our sufferings, knowing that suffering produces endurance, [4]and endurance produces character, and character produces hope, [5]and hope does not disappoint us, because God's love has been poured into our hearts through the Holy Spirit that has been given to us.

6 For while we were still weak, at the right time Christ died for the ungodly. [7]Indeed, rarely will anyone die for a righteous person—though perhaps for a good person someone might actually dare to die. [8]But God proves his love for us in that while we still were sinners Christ died for us. [9]Much more surely then, now that we have been justified by his blood, will we be saved through him from the wrath of God.[d] [10]For if while we were enemies, we were reconciled to God through the death of his Son, much more surely, having been reconciled, will we be saved by his life. [11]But more than that, we even boast in God through our Lord Jesus Christ, through whom we have now received reconciliation.

ADAM AND CHRIST

12 Therefore, just as sin came into the world through one man, and death came through sin, and so death spread to all because all have sinned— [13]sin was indeed in the world before the law, but sin is not reckoned when there is no law. [14]Yet death exercised dominion from Adam to Moses, even over those whose sins were not like the transgression of Adam, who is a type of the one who was to come.

15 But the free gift is not like the trespass. For if the many died through the one man's trespass, much more surely have the grace of God and the free gift in the grace of the one man, Jesus Christ, abounded for the many. [16]And the free gift is not like the effect of the one man's sin. For the judgment following one trespass brought condemnation, but the free gift following many trespasses brings justification. [17]If, because of the one man's trespass, death exercised dominion through that one, much more surely will those who receive

---

a Other ancient authorities read *let us*   b Other ancient authorities add *by faith*   c Or *let us*   d Gk *the wrath* the abundance of grace and the free gift of righteousness exercise dominion in life through the one man, Jesus Christ.

18 Therefore just as one man's trespass led to condemnation for all, so one man's act of righteousness leads to justification and life for all. [19]For just as by the one man's disobedience the many were made sinners, so by the one man's obedience the many will be made righteous. [20]But law came in, with the result that the trespass multiplied; but where sin increased, grace abounded all the more, [21]so that, just as sin exercised dominion in death, so grace might also exercise dominion through justification[a] leading to eternal life through Jesus Christ our Lord.

DYING AND RISING WITH CHRIST

6 What then are we to say? Should we continue in sin in order that grace may abound? [2]By no means! How can we who died to sin go on living in it? [3]Do you not know that all of us who have been baptized into Christ Jesus were baptized into his death? [4]Therefore we have been buried with him by baptism into death, so that, just as Christ was raised from the dead by the glory of the Father, so we too might walk in newness of life.

5 For if we have been united with him in a death like his, we will certainly be united with him in a resurrection like his. [6]We know that our old self was crucified with him so that the body of sin might be destroyed, and we might no longer be enslaved to sin. [7]For whoever has died is freed from sin. [8]But if we have died with Christ, we believe that we will also live with him. [9]We know that Christ, being raised from the dead, will never die again; death no longer has dominion over him. [10]The death he died, he died to sin, once for all; but the life he lives, he lives to God. [11]So you also must consider yourselves dead to sin and alive to God in Christ Jesus.

12 Therefore, do not let sin exercise dominion in your mortal bodies, to make you obey their passions. [13]No longer present your members to sin as instruments[b] of wickedness, but present yourselves to God as those who have been brought from death to life, and present your members to God as instruments[b] of righteousness. [14]For sin will have no dominion over you, since you are not under law but under grace.

SLAVES OF RIGHTEOUSNESS

15 What then? Should we sin because we are not under law but under grace? By no means! [16]Do you not know that if you present yourselves to anyone as

---

a Or *righteousness*   *b* Or *weapons*

obedient slaves, you are slaves of the one whom you obey, either of sin, which leads to death, or of obedience, which leads to righteousness? [17]But thanks be to God that you, having once been slaves of sin, have become obedient from the heart to the form of teaching to which you were entrusted, [18]and that you, having been set free from sin, have become slaves of righteousness. [19]I am speaking in human terms because of your natural limitations.[a] For just as you once presented your members as slaves to impurity and to greater and greater iniquity, so now present your members as slaves to righteousness for sanctification.

20 When you were slaves of sin, you were free in regard to righteousness. [21]So what advantage did you then get from the things of which you now are ashamed? The end of those things is death. [22]But now that you have been freed from sin and enslaved to God, the advantage you get is sanctification. The end is eternal life. [23]For the wages of sin is death, but the free gift of God is eternal life in Christ Jesus our Lord.

AN ANALOGY FROM MARRIAGE

7 Do you not know, brothers and sisters[b]—for I am speaking to those who know the law—that the law is binding on a person only during that person's lifetime? [2]Thus a married woman is bound by the law to her husband as long as he lives; but if her husband dies, she is discharged from the law concerning the husband. [3]Accordingly, she will be called an adulteress if she lives with another man while her husband is alive. But if her husband dies, she is free from that law, and if she marries another man, she is not an adulteress.

4 In the same way, my friends,[b] you have died to the law through the body of Christ, so that you may belong to another, to him who has been raised from the dead in order that we may bear fruit for God. [5]While we were living in the flesh, our sinful passions, aroused by the law, were at work in our members to bear fruit for death. [6]But now we are discharged from the law, dead to that which held us captive, so that we are slaves not under the old written code but in the new life of the Spirit.

THE LAW AND SIN

7 What then should we say? That the law is sin? By no means! Yet, if it had not been for the law, I would not have known sin. I would not have known what it is to covet if the law had not said, "You shall not covet." [8]But sin, seizing an opportunity in the commandment, produced in me all kinds of covetousness. Apart from the law sin lies dead. [9]I was once alive apart from the law, but when

---

a Gk *the weakness of your flesh*   *b* Gk *brothers*

the commandment came, sin revived [10]and I died, and the very commandment that promised life proved to be death to me. [11]For sin, seizing an opportunity in the commandment, deceived me and through it killed me. [12]So the law is holy, and the commandment is holy and just and good.

13 Did what is good, then, bring death to me? By no means! It was sin, working death in me through what is good, in order that sin might be shown to be sin, and through the commandment might become sinful beyond measure.

THE INNER CONFLICT

14 For we know that the law is spiritual; but I am of the flesh, sold into slavery under sin.[a] [15]I do not understand my own actions. For I do not do what I want, but I do the very thing I hate. [16]Now if I do what I do not want, I agree that the law is good. [17]But in fact it is no longer I that do it, but sin that dwells within me. [18]For I know that nothing good dwells within me, that is, in my flesh. I can will what is right, but I cannot do it. [19]For I do not do the good I want, but the evil I do not want is what I do. [20]Now if I do what I do not want, it is no longer I that do it, but sin that dwells within me.

21 So I find it to be a law that when I want to do what is good, evil lies close at hand. [22]For I delight in the law of God in my inmost self, [23]but I see in my members another law at war with the law of my mind, making me captive to the law of sin that dwells in my members. [24]Wretched man that I am! Who will rescue me from this body of death? [25]Thanks be to God through Jesus Christ our Lord!

So then, with my mind I am a slave to the law of God, but with my flesh I am a slave to the law of sin.

LIFE IN THE SPIRIT

8 There is therefore now no condemnation for those who are in Christ Jesus. [2]For the law of the Spirit[b] of life in Christ Jesus has set you[c] free from the law of sin and of death. [3]For God has done what the law, weakened by the flesh, could not do: by sending his own Son in the likeness of sinful flesh, and to deal with sin,[d] he condemned sin in the flesh, [4]so that the just requirement of the law might be fulfilled in us, who walk not according to the flesh but according to the Spirit.[b] [5]For those who live according to the flesh set their minds on the things of the flesh, but those who live according to the Spirit[b] set their minds on the things of the Spirit.[b] [6]To set the mind on the flesh is death, but to set the

---

a Gk *sold under sin*   b Or *spirit*   c Here the Greek word *you* is singular number; other ancient authorities read *me* or *us*
d Or *and as a sin offering*

mind on the Spirit^a is life and peace. ⁷For this reason the mind that is set on the flesh is hostile to God; it does not submit to God's law—indeed it cannot, ⁸and those who are in the flesh cannot please God.

9 But you are not in the flesh; you are in the Spirit,^a since the Spirit of God dwells in you. Anyone who does not have the Spirit of Christ does not belong to him. ¹⁰But if Christ is in you, though the body is dead because of sin, the Spirit^a is life because of righteousness. ¹¹If the Spirit of him who raised Jesus from the dead dwells in you, he who raised Christ^b from the dead will give life to your mortal bodies also through^c his Spirit that dwells in you.

12 So then, brothers and sisters,^d we are debtors, not to the flesh, to live according to the flesh— ¹³for if you live according to the flesh, you will die; but if by the Spirit you put to death the deeds of the body, you will live. ¹⁴For all who are led by the Spirit of God are children of God. ¹⁵For you did not receive a spirit of slavery to fall back into fear, but you have received a spirit of adoption. When we cry, "Abba!^e Father!" ¹⁶it is that very Spirit bearing witness^f with our spirit that we are children of God, ¹⁷and if children, then heirs, heirs of God and joint heirs with Christ—if, in fact, we suffer with him so that we may also be glorified with him.

FUTURE GLORY

18 I consider that the sufferings of this present time are not worth comparing with the glory about to be revealed to us. ¹⁹For the creation waits with eager longing for the revealing of the children of God; ²⁰for the creation was subjected to futility, not of its own will but by the will of the one who subjected it, in hope ²¹that the creation itself will be set free from its bondage to decay and will obtain the freedom of the glory of the children of God. ²²We know that the whole creation has been groaning in labor pains until now; ²³and not only the creation, but we ourselves, who have the first fruits of the Spirit, groan inwardly while we wait for adoption, the redemption of our bodies. ²⁴For in^g hope we were saved. Now hope that is seen is not hope. For who hopes^h for what is seen? ²⁵But if we hope for what we do not see, we wait for it with patience.

26 Likewise the Spirit helps us in our weakness; for we do not know how to pray as we ought, but that very Spirit intercedesⁱ with sighs too deep for words. ²⁷And God,^j who searches the heart, knows what is the mind of the Spirit, because the Spirit^k intercedes for the saints according to the will of God.^l

---

a Or *spirit* b Other ancient authorities read *the Christ* or *Christ Jesus* or *Jesus Christ* c Other ancient authorities read *on account of* d Gk *brothers* e Aramaic for *Father* f Or *¹⁵a spirit of adoption, by which we cry, "Abba! Father!"* *¹⁶The Spirit itself bears witness* g Or *by* h Other ancient authorities read *awaits* i Other ancient authorities add *for us* j Gk *the one* k Gk *he* or *it* l Gk *according to God*

28 We know that all things work together for good[a] for those who love God, who are called according to his purpose. [29]For those whom he foreknew he also predestined to be conformed to the image of his Son, in order that he might be the firstborn within a large family.[b] [30]And those whom he predestined he also called; and those whom he called he also justified; and those whom he justified he also glorified.

GOD'S LOVE IN CHRIST JESUS

31 What then are we to say about these things? If God is for us, who is against us? [32]He who did not withhold his own Son, but gave him up for all of us, will he not with him also give us everything else? [33]Who will bring any charge against God's elect? It is God who justifies. [34]Who is to condemn? It is Christ Jesus, who died, yes, who was raised, who is at the right hand of God, who indeed intercedes for us.[c] [35]Who will separate us from the love of Christ? Will hardship, or distress, or persecution, or famine, or nakedness, or peril, or sword? [36]As it is written,

> "For your sake we are being killed all day long;
> we are accounted as sheep to be slaughtered."

37 No, in all these things we are more than conquerors through him who loved us. [38]For I am convinced that neither death, nor life, nor angels, nor rulers, nor things present, nor things to come, nor powers, [39]nor height, nor depth, nor anything else in all creation, will be able to separate us from the love of God in Christ Jesus our Lord.

GOD'S ELECTION OF ISRAEL

9 I am speaking the truth in Christ—I am not lying; my conscience confirms it by the Holy Spirit— [2]I have great sorrow and unceasing anguish in my heart. [3]For I could wish that I myself were accursed and cut off from Christ for the sake of my own people,[d] my kindred according to the flesh. [4]They are Israelites, and to them belong the adoption, the glory, the covenants, the giving of the law, the worship, and the promises; [5]to them belong the patriarchs, and from them, according to the flesh, comes the Messiah,[e] who is over all, God blessed forever.[f] Amen.

6 It is not as though the word of God had failed. For not all Israelites truly belong to Israel, [7]and not all of Abraham's children are his true descendants; but "It is through Isaac that descendants shall be named for you." [8]This means

---

a Other ancient authorities read *God makes all things work together for good*, or *in all things God works for good* b Gk *among many brothers* c Or *Is it Christ Jesus . . . for us?* d Gk *my brothers* e Or *the Christ* f Or *Messiah, who is God over all, blessed forever;* or *Messiah. May he who is God over all be blessed forever* that it is not the children of the flesh who are the children of God, but the children of the promise are counted as descendants. ⁹For this is what the promise said, "About this time I will return and Sarah shall have a son." ¹⁰Nor is that all; something similar happened to Rebecca when she had conceived children by one husband, our ancestor Isaac. ¹¹Even before they had been born or had done anything good or bad (so that God's purpose of election might continue, ¹²not by works but by his call) she was told, "The elder shall serve the younger." ¹³As it is written,

> "I have loved Jacob,
> > but I have hated Esau."

14 What then are we to say? Is there injustice on God's part? By no means! ¹⁵For he says to Moses,

> "I will have mercy on whom I have mercy,
> > and I will have compassion on whom I have compassion."

16 So it depends not on human will or exertion, but on God who shows mercy. ¹⁷For the scripture says to Pharaoh, "I have raised you up for the very purpose of showing my power in you, so that my name may be proclaimed in all the earth." ¹⁸So then he has mercy on whomever he chooses, and he hardens the heart of whomever he chooses.

GOD'S WRATH AND MERCY

19 You will say to me then, "Why then does he still find fault? For who can resist his will?" ²⁰But who indeed are you, a human being, to argue with God? Will what is molded say to the one who molds it, "Why have you made me like this?" ²¹Has the potter no right over the clay, to make out of the same lump one object for special use and another for ordinary use? ²²What if God, desiring to show his wrath and to make known his power, has endured with much patience the objects of wrath that are made for destruction; ²³and what if he has done so in order to make known the riches of his glory for the objects of mercy, which he has prepared beforehand for glory— ²⁴including us whom he has called, not from the Jews only but also from the Gentiles? ²⁵As indeed he says in Hosea,

> "Those who were not my people I will call 'my people,'
> > and her who was not beloved I will call 'beloved.'"

> 26 "And in the very place where it was said to them, 'You are not my
> > people,'
> > there they shall be called children of the living God."

27 And Isaiah cries out concerning Israel, "Though the number of the children of Israel were like the sand of the sea, only a remnant of them will be saved;

²⁸for the Lord will execute his sentence on the earth quickly and decisively."ᵃ
²⁹And as Isaiah predicted,

> "If the Lord of hosts had not left survivorsᵇ to us,
>> we would have fared like Sodom
>> and been made like Gomorrah."

ISRAEL'S UNBELIEF

30 What then are we to say? Gentiles, who did not strive for righteousness, have attained it, that is, righteousness through faith; ³¹but Israel, who did strive for the righteousness that is based on the law, did not succeed in fulfilling that law. ³²Why not? Because they did not strive for it on the basis of faith, but as if it were based on works. They have stumbled over the stumbling stone, ³³as it is written,

> "See, I am laying in Zion a stone that will make people stumble,
>> a rock that will make them fall,
>> and whoever believes in himᶜ will not be put to shame."

10 Brothers and sisters,ᵈ my heart's desire and prayer to God for them is that they may be saved. ²I can testify that they have a zeal for God, but it is not enlightened. ³For, being ignorant of the righteousness that comes from God, and seeking to establish their own, they have not submitted to God's righteousness. ⁴For Christ is the end of the law so that there may be righteousness for everyone who believes.

SALVATION IS FOR ALL

5 Moses writes concerning the righteousness that comes from the law, that "the person who does these things will live by them." ⁶But the righteousness that comes from faith says, "Do not say in your heart, 'Who will ascend into heaven?'" (that is, to bring Christ down) ⁷"or 'Who will descend into the abyss?'" (that is, to bring Christ up from the dead). ⁸But what does it say?

> "The word is near you,
>> on your lips and in your heart"

(that is, the word of faith that we proclaim); ⁹becauseᵉ if you confess with your lips that Jesus is Lord and believe in your heart that God raised him from the dead, you will be saved. ¹⁰For one believes with the heart and so is justified, and one confesses with the mouth and so is saved. ¹¹The scripture says, "No one who believes in him will be put to shame." ¹²For there is no distinction between

---

a Other ancient authorities read *for he will finish his work and cut it short in righteousness, because the Lord will make the sentence shortened on the earth*   *b* Or *descendants;* Gk *seed*   *c* Or *trusts in it*   *d* Gk *Brothers*   *e* Or *namely, that*

Jew and Greek; the same Lord is Lord of all and is generous to all who call on him. [13]For, "Everyone who calls on the name of the Lord shall be saved."

14 But how are they to call on one in whom they have not believed? And how are they to believe in one of whom they have never heard? And how are they to hear without someone to proclaim him? [15]And how are they to proclaim him unless they are sent? As it is written, "How beautiful are the feet of those who bring good news!" [16]But not all have obeyed the good news;[a] for Isaiah says, "Lord, who has believed our message?" [17]So faith comes from what is heard, and what is heard comes through the word of Christ.[b]

18 But I ask, have they not heard? Indeed they have; for

> "Their voice has gone out to all the earth,
>> and their words to the ends of the world."

19 Again I ask, did Israel not understand? First Moses says,

> "I will make you jealous of those who are not a nation;
>> with a foolish nation I will make you angry."

20 Then Isaiah is so bold as to say,

> "I have been found by those who did not seek me;
>> I have shown myself to those who did not ask for me."

21 But of Israel he says, "All day long I have held out my hands to a disobedient and contrary people."

ISRAEL'S REJECTION IS NOT FINAL

11 I ask, then, has God rejected his people? By no means! I myself am an Israelite, a descendant of Abraham, a member of the tribe of Benjamin. [2]God has not rejected his people whom he foreknew. Do you not know what the scripture says of Elijah, how he pleads with God against Israel? [3]"Lord, they have killed your prophets, they have demolished your altars; I alone am left, and they are seeking my life." [4]But what is the divine reply to him? "I have kept for myself seven thousand who have not bowed the knee to Baal." [5]So too at the present time there is a remnant, chosen by grace. [6]But if it is by grace, it is no longer on the basis of works, otherwise grace would no longer be grace.[c]

7 What then? Israel failed to obtain what it was seeking. The elect obtained it, but the rest were hardened, [8]as it is written,

> "God gave them a sluggish spirit,
>> eyes that would not see
>> and ears that would not hear,
> down to this very day."

---

a Or gospel b Or about Christ; other ancient authorities read of God c Other ancient authorities add But if it is by works, it is no longer on the basis of grace, otherwise work would no longer be work

9 And David says,

> "Let their table become a snare and a trap,
> > a stumbling block and a retribution for them;
> 10 let their eyes be darkened so that they cannot see,
> > and keep their backs forever bent."

THE SALVATION OF THE GENTILES

11 So I ask, have they stumbled so as to fall? By no means! But through their stumbling[a] salvation has come to the Gentiles, so as to make Israel[b] jealous. [12]Now if their stumbling[a] means riches for the world, and if their defeat means riches for Gentiles, how much more will their full inclusion mean!

13 Now I am speaking to you Gentiles. Inasmuch then as I am an apostle to the Gentiles, I glorify my ministry [14]in order to make my own people[c] jealous, and thus save some of them. [15]For if their rejection is the reconciliation of the world, what will their acceptance be but life from the dead! [16]If the part of the dough offered as first fruits is holy, then the whole batch is holy; and if the root is holy, then the branches also are holy.

17 But if some of the branches were broken off, and you, a wild olive shoot, were grafted in their place to share the rich root[d] of the olive tree, [18]do not boast over the branches. If you do boast, remember that it is not you that support the root, but the root that supports you. [19]You will say, "Branches were broken off so that I might be grafted in." [20]That is true. They were broken off because of their unbelief, but you stand only through faith. So do not become proud, but stand in awe. [21]For if God did not spare the natural branches, perhaps he will not spare you.[e] [22]Note then the kindness and the severity of God: severity toward those who have fallen, but God's kindness toward you, provided you continue in his kindness; otherwise you also will be cut off. [23]And even those of Israel,[f] if they do not persist in unbelief, will be grafted in, for God has the power to graft them in again. [24]For if you have been cut from what is by nature a wild olive tree and grafted, contrary to nature, into a cultivated olive tree, how much more will these natural branches be grafted back into their own olive tree.

ALL ISRAEL WILL BE SAVED

25 So that you may not claim to be wiser than you are, brothers and sisters,[g] I want you to understand this mystery: a hardening has come upon part of Israel,

---

a Gk transgression b Gk them c Gk my flesh d Other ancient authorities read the richness e Other ancient authorities read neither will he spare you f Gk lacks of Israel g Gk brothers until the full number of the Gentiles has come in. [26]And so all Israel will be saved; as it is written,

> "Out of Zion will come the Deliverer;
>> he will banish ungodliness from Jacob."
> 27 "And this is my covenant with them,
>> when I take away their sins."

28 As regards the gospel they are enemies of God[a] for your sake; but as regards election they are beloved, for the sake of their ancestors; [29]for the gifts and the calling of God are irrevocable. [30]Just as you were once disobedient to God but have now received mercy because of their disobedience, [31]so they have now been disobedient in order that, by the mercy shown to you, they too may now[b] receive mercy. [32]For God has imprisoned all in disobedience so that he may be merciful to all.

33 O the depth of the riches and wisdom and knowledge of God! How unsearchable are his judgments and how inscrutable his ways!

> 34 "For who has known the mind of the Lord?
>> Or who has been his counselor?"
> 35 "Or who has given a gift to him,
>> to receive a gift in return?"

36 For from him and through him and to him are all things. To him be the glory forever. Amen.

THE NEW LIFE IN CHRIST

12 I appeal to you therefore, brothers and sisters,[c] by the mercies of God, to present your bodies as a living sacrifice, holy and acceptable to God, which is your spiritual[d] worship. [2]Do not be conformed to this world,[e] but be transformed by the renewing of your minds, so that you may discern what is the will of God—what is good and acceptable and perfect.[f]

3 For by the grace given to me I say to everyone among you not to think of yourself more highly than you ought to think, but to think with sober judgment, each according to the measure of faith that God has assigned. [4]For as in one body we have many members, and not all the members have the same function, [5]so we, who are many, are one body in Christ, and individually we are members one of another. [6]We have gifts that differ according to the grace given to us: prophecy, in proportion to faith; [7]ministry, in ministering; the teacher, in teaching; [8]the exhorter, in exhortation; the giver, in generosity; the leader, in diligence; the compassionate, in cheerfulness.

---

a Gk lacks of God   b Other ancient authorities lack now   c Gk brothers   d Or reasonable   e Gk age   f Or what is the good and acceptable and perfect will of God

MARKS OF THE TRUE CHRISTIAN

9 Let love be genuine; hate what is evil, hold fast to what is good; [10]love one another with mutual affection; outdo one another in showing honor. [11]Do not lag in zeal, be ardent in spirit, serve the Lord.[a] [12]Rejoice in hope, be patient in suffering, persevere in prayer. [13]Contribute to the needs of the saints; extend hospitality to strangers.

14 Bless those who persecute you; bless and do not curse them. [15]Rejoice with those who rejoice, weep with those who weep. [16]Live in harmony with one another; do not be haughty, but associate with the lowly;[b] do not claim to be wiser than you are. [17]Do not repay anyone evil for evil, but take thought for what is noble in the sight of all. [18]If it is possible, so far as it depends on you, live peaceably with all. [19]Beloved, never avenge yourselves, but leave room for the wrath of God;[c] for it is written, "Vengeance is mine, I will repay, says the Lord." [20]No, "if your enemies are hungry, feed them; if they are thirsty, give them something to drink; for by doing this you will heap burning coals on their heads." [21]Do not be overcome by evil, but overcome evil with good.

BEING SUBJECT TO AUTHORITIES

13 Let every person be subject to the governing authorities; for there is no authority except from God, and those authorities that exist have been instituted by God. [2]Therefore whoever resists authority resists what God has appointed, and those who resist will incur judgment. [3]For rulers are not a terror to good conduct, but to bad. Do you wish to have no fear of the authority? Then do what is good, and you will receive its approval; [4]for it is God's servant for your good. But if you do what is wrong, you should be afraid, for the authority[d] does not bear the sword in vain! It is the servant of God to execute wrath on the wrongdoer. [5]Therefore one must be subject, not only because of wrath but also because of conscience. [6]For the same reason you also pay taxes, for the authorities are God's servants, busy with this very thing. [7]Pay to all what is due them—taxes to whom taxes are due, revenue to whom revenue is due, respect to whom respect is due, honor to whom honor is due.

LOVE FOR ONE ANOTHER

8 Owe no one anything, except to love one another; for the one who loves another has fulfilled the law. [9]The commandments, "You shall not commit adultery; You shall not murder; You shall not steal; You shall not covet"; and

---

a Other ancient authorities read *serve the opportune time*   *b* Or *give yourselves to humble tasks*   *c* Gk *the wrath*   *d* Gk *it* any other commandment, are summed up in this word, "Love your neighbor as yourself." [10]Love does no wrong to a neighbor; therefore, love is the fulfilling of the law.

AN URGENT APPEAL

11 Besides this, you know what time it is, how it is now the moment for you to wake from sleep. For salvation is nearer to us now than when we became believers; [12]the night is far gone, the day is near. Let us then lay aside the works of darkness and put on the armor of light; [13]let us live honorably as in the day, not in reveling and drunkenness, not in debauchery and licentiousness, not in quarreling and jealousy. [14]Instead, put on the Lord Jesus Christ, and make no provision for the flesh, to gratify its desires.

DO NOT JUDGE ANOTHER

14 Welcome those who are weak in faith,[a] but not for the purpose of quarreling over opinions. [2]Some believe in eating anything, while the weak eat only vegetables. [3]Those who eat must not despise those who abstain, and those who abstain must not pass judgment on those who eat; for God has welcomed them. [4]Who are you to pass judgment on servants of another? It is before their own lord that they stand or fall. And they will be upheld, for the Lord[b] is able to make them stand.

5 Some judge one day to be better than another, while others judge all days to be alike. Let all be fully convinced in their own minds. [6]Those who observe the day, observe it in honor of the Lord. Also those who eat, eat in honor of the Lord, since they give thanks to God; while those who abstain, abstain in honor of the Lord and give thanks to God.

7 We do not live to ourselves, and we do not die to ourselves. [8]If we live, we live to the Lord, and if we die, we die to the Lord; so then, whether we live or whether we die, we are the Lord's. [9]For to this end Christ died and lived again, so that he might be Lord of both the dead and the living.

10 Why do you pass judgment on your brother or sister?[c] Or you, why do you despise your brother or sister?[c] For we will all stand before the judgment seat of God.[d] [11]For it is written,

> "As I live, says the Lord, every knee shall bow to me,
>   and every tongue shall give praise to[e] God."

12 So then, each of us will be accountable to God.[f]

---

a Or *conviction*   b Other ancient authorities read *for God*   c Gk *brother*   d Other ancient authorities read *of Christ*
e Or *confess*   f Other ancient authorities lack *to God*

DO NOT MAKE ANOTHER STUMBLE

13 Let us therefore no longer pass judgment on one another, but resolve instead never to put a stumbling block or hindrance in the way of another.[a] [14]I know and am persuaded in the Lord Jesus that nothing is unclean in itself; but it is unclean for anyone who thinks it unclean. [15]If your brother or sister[b] is being injured by what you eat, you are no longer walking in love. Do not let what you eat cause the ruin of one for whom Christ died. [16]So do not let your good be spoken of as evil. [17]For the kingdom of God is not food and drink but righteousness and peace and joy in the Holy Spirit. [18]The one who thus serves Christ is acceptable to God and has human approval. [19]Let us then pursue what makes for peace and for mutual upbuilding. [20]Do not, for the sake of food, destroy the work of God. Everything is indeed clean, but it is wrong for you to make others fall by what you eat; [21]it is good not to eat meat or drink wine or do anything that makes your brother or sister[b] stumble.[c] [22]The faith that you have, have as your own conviction before God. Blessed are those who have no reason to condemn themselves because of what they approve. [23]But those who have doubts are condemned if they eat, because they do not act from faith;[d] for whatever does not proceed from faith[d] is sin.[e]

PLEASE OTHERS, NOT YOURSELVES

15 We who are strong ought to put up with the failings of the weak, and not to please ourselves. [2]Each of us must please our neighbor for the good purpose of building up the neighbor. [3]For Christ did not please himself; but, as it is written, "The insults of those who insult you have fallen on me." [4]For whatever was written in former days was written for our instruction, so that by steadfastness and by the encouragement of the scriptures we might have hope. [5]May the God of steadfastness and encouragement grant you to live in harmony with one another, in accordance with Christ Jesus, [6]so that together you may with one voice glorify the God and Father of our Lord Jesus Christ.

THE GOSPEL FOR JEWS AND GENTILES ALIKE

7 Welcome one another, therefore, just as Christ has welcomed you, for the glory of God. [8]For I tell you that Christ has become a servant of the circumcised on behalf of the truth of God in order that he might confirm the promises given to the patriarchs, [9]and in order that the Gentiles might glorify God for his mercy. As it is written,

---

a Gk *of a brother* b Gk *brother* c Other ancient authorities add *or be upset or be weakened* d Or *conviction* e Other authorities, some ancient, add here 16.25–27

"Therefore I will confess[a] you among the Gentiles,
    and sing praises to your name";

10 and again he says,
    "Rejoice, O Gentiles, with his people";

11 and again,
    "Praise the Lord, all you Gentiles,
    and let all the peoples praise him";

12 and again Isaiah says,
    "The root of Jesse shall come,
      the one who rises to rule the Gentiles;
    in him the Gentiles shall hope."

13 May the God of hope fill you with all joy and peace in believing, so that you may abound in hope by the power of the Holy Spirit.

PAUL'S REASON FOR WRITING SO BOLDLY

14 I myself feel confident about you, my brothers and sisters,[b] that you yourselves are full of goodness, filled with all knowledge, and able to instruct one another. [15]Nevertheless on some points I have written to you rather boldly by way of reminder, because of the grace given me by God [16]to be a minister of Christ Jesus to the Gentiles in the priestly service of the gospel of God, so that the offering of the Gentiles may be acceptable, sanctified by the Holy Spirit. [17]In Christ Jesus, then, I have reason to boast of my work for God. [18]For I will not venture to speak of anything except what Christ has accomplished[c] through me to win obedience from the Gentiles, by word and deed, [19]by the power of signs and wonders, by the power of the Spirit of God,[d] so that from Jerusalem and as far around as Illyricum I have fully proclaimed the good news[e] of Christ. [20]Thus I make it my ambition to proclaim the good news,[e] not where Christ has already been named, so that I do not build on someone else's foundation, [21]but as it is written,

    "Those who have never been told of him shall see,
    and those who have never heard of him shall understand."

PAUL'S PLAN TO VISIT ROME

22 This is the reason that I have so often been hindered from coming to you. [23]But now, with no further place for me in these regions, I desire, as I have for many years, to come to you [24]when I go to Spain. For I do hope to see you on

---

a Or thank b Gk brothers c Gk speak of those things that Christ has not accomplished d Other ancient authorities read of the Spirit or of the Holy Spirit e Or gospel my journey and to be sent on by you, once I have enjoyed your company for a little while. ²⁵At present, however, I am going to Jerusalem in a ministry to the saints; ²⁶for Macedonia and Achaia have been pleased to share their resources with the poor among the saints at Jerusalem. ²⁷They were pleased to do this, and indeed they owe it to them; for if the Gentiles have come to share in their spiritual blessings, they ought also to be of service to them in material things. ²⁸So, when I have completed this, and have delivered to them what has been collected,ᵃ I will set out by way of you to Spain; ²⁹and I know that when I come to you, I will come in the fullness of the blessingᵇ of Christ.

30 I appeal to you, brothers and sisters,ᶜ by our Lord Jesus Christ and by the love of the Spirit, to join me in earnest prayer to God on my behalf, ³¹that I may be rescued from the unbelievers in Judea, and that my ministryᵈ to Jerusalem may be acceptable to the saints, ³²so that by God's will I may come to you with joy and be refreshed in your company. ³³The God of peace be with all of you.ᵉ Amen.

PERSONAL GREETINGS

16 I commend to you our sister Phoebe, a deaconᶠ of the church at Cenchreae, ²so that you may welcome her in the Lord as is fitting for the saints, and help her in whatever she may require from you, for she has been a benefactor of many and of myself as well.

3 Greet Prisca and Aquila, who work with me in Christ Jesus, ⁴and who risked their necks for my life, to whom not only I give thanks, but also all the churches of the Gentiles. ⁵Greet also the church in their house. Greet my beloved Epaenetus, who was the first convertᵍ in Asia for Christ. ⁶Greet Mary, who has worked very hard among you. ⁷Greet Andronicus and Junia,ʰ my relativesⁱ who were in prison with me; they are prominent among the apostles, and they were in Christ before I was. ⁸Greet Ampliatus, my beloved in the Lord. ⁹Greet Urbanus, our co-worker in Christ, and my beloved Stachys. ¹⁰Greet Apelles, who is approved in Christ. Greet those who belong to the family of Aristobulus. ¹¹Greet my relativeʲ Herodion. Greet those in the Lord who belong to the family of Narcissus. ¹²Greet those workers in the Lord, Tryphaena and Tryphosa. Greet the beloved Persis, who has worked hard in the Lord. ¹³Greet Rufus, chosen in the Lord; and greet his mother—a mother to me also. ¹⁴Greet Asyncritus, Phlegon, Hermes, Patrobas, Hermas, and the brothers and sistersᶜ who are with them. ¹⁵Greet Philologus, Julia, Nereus and his sister, and Olympas, and

---

a Gk *have sealed to them this fruit*   *b* Other ancient authorities add *of the gospel*   *c* Gk *brothers*   *d* Other ancient authorities read *my bringing of a gift*   *e* One ancient authority adds 16.25–27 here   *f* Or *minister*   *g* Gk *first fruits*   *h* Or *Junias*; other ancient authorities read *Julia*   *i* Or *compatriots*   *j* Or *compatriot* all the saints who are with them. [16]Greet one another with a holy kiss. All the churches of Christ greet you.

FINAL INSTRUCTIONS

17 I urge you, brothers and sisters,[a] to keep an eye on those who cause dissensions and offenses, in opposition to the teaching that you have learned; avoid them. [18]For such people do not serve our Lord Christ, but their own appetites,[b] and by smooth talk and flattery they deceive the hearts of the simple-minded. [19]For while your obedience is known to all, so that I rejoice over you, I want you to be wise in what is good and guileless in what is evil. [20]The God of peace will shortly crush Satan under your feet. The grace of our Lord Jesus Christ be with you.[c]

21 Timothy, my co-worker, greets you; so do Lucius and Jason and Sosipater, my relatives.[d]

22 I Tertius, the writer of this letter, greet you in the Lord.[e]

23 Gaius, who is host to me and to the whole church, greets you. Erastus, the city treasurer, and our brother Quartus, greet you.[f]

FINAL DOXOLOGY

25 Now to God[g] who is able to strengthen you according to my gospel and the proclamation of Jesus Christ, according to the revelation of the mystery that was kept secret for long ages [26]but is now disclosed, and through the prophetic writings is made known to all the Gentiles, according to the command of the eternal God, to bring about the obedience of faith— [27]to the only wise God, through Jesus Christ, to whom[h] be the glory forever! Amen.[i]

---

a Gk brothers   b Gk their own belly   c Other ancient authorities lack this sentence   d Or compatriots   e Or I Tertius, writing this letter in the Lord, greet you   f Other ancient authorities add verse 24, The grace of our Lord Jesus Christ be with all of you. Amen.   g Gk the one   h Other ancient authorities lack to whom. The verse then reads, to the only wise God be the glory through Jesus Christ forever. Amen.   i Other ancient authorities lack 16.25–27 or include it after 14.23 or 15.33; others put verse 24 after verse 27

Mark

Around the year 70, an early Christian put the story of Jesus into written form for the first time. Though the location is uncertain, the best guess is a Christ-community near the northern border of Galilee in the Jewish homeland. We call the document "Mark," though it is not certain that somebody named "Mark" wrote it. The gospel does not name the author; he did not write "The Gospel According to Mark" at the top of the first page. So also the authors of Matthew, Luke, and John do not name themselves. Names were assigned only in the second century when the existence of several gospels required a way of distinguishing among them. Perhaps somebody named "Mark" wrote the earliest gospel, and perhaps not. It really doesn't matter; its value doesn't depend upon who wrote it. But we will call him and his gospel "Mark."

Mark is the first narrative gospel. Even if, as seems likely, a major part of Jesus's teaching was committed to writing in the 50s or early 60s in the hypothetical document Q, that is a collection of teachings, not a narrative.

Mark is also the shortest gospel. It has sixteen chapters, compared to Matthew's twenty-eight, Luke's twenty-four, and John's twenty-one. In percentages based on the number of words in each, Mark is about 60 percent as long as Matthew, 57 percent as long as Luke, and 72 percent as long as John.

Mark's importance is greater than its relative brevity might suggest. It is the fountainhead of the other two synoptic gospels, Matthew and Luke. Both authors not only had a copy of Mark when they wrote, but also used Mark's threefold narrative pattern:

- Part one: Galilee, where most of Jesus's public activity happens

- Part two: Journey from Galilee to Jerusalem for Passover

- Part three: Jerusalem and Jesus's final week, including confrontation with authorities, execution, and the discovery of the empty tomb

In Mark (and in Matthew and Luke), all of this fits into one year, though the authors do not say so explicitly. But only one Passover and one journey to Jerusalem are mentioned. Only in John's gospel does Jesus go to Jerusalem several times, including more than one Passover. His narrative time frame for Jesus's public activity is thus three or four years.

Mark's Story of Jesus

It is challenging to read Mark as the first gospel—as if the other gospels didn't exist and this is our first encounter with the story of Jesus. It requires imagining that we haven't already heard about Jesus from the other gospels, from Christian preaching and teaching, and from what is taken for granted about Jesus in Christian and popular culture.

Mark's story is striking because of what it does include and what it does not include. We begin with the latter. Much of what is most familiar about the story of Jesus is not in Mark:

Mark has no stories of Jesus's birth or early years. Instead, it begins with Jesus as an adult going to a wilderness prophet named John and being baptized by him.

Though Mark includes some of Jesus's teaching, there is much that is not present. In particular, the collection of teachings (about two hundred verses) shared by Matthew and Luke and commonly assigned to Q do not appear in Mark—perhaps because Mark knew they had already been put into writing and thus felt no need to include them in his narrative.

The Lord's Prayer is not in Mark. It is found in somewhat different versions in Matthew, Luke, and the *Didache,* a late first-century writing not included in the New Testament.

Many of Jesus's best-known parables are not in Mark. The missing include the good Samaritan and the prodigal son (only in Luke); the unmerciful servant, workers in the vineyard, and the sheep and the goats (only in Matthew); and the talents and the lost sheep (in both Matthew and Luke). Mark's best-known parables are the sower and the seeds (4.1–9) and the wicked vineyard tenants (12.1–12).

Mark does not portray Jesus as publicly proclaiming his identity as "Son of God" or "Messiah." Of course, Mark affirms that Jesus is both, but he does not present the titles as part of the message of Jesus himself. The two affirmations of an exceptional status for Jesus are in private and not part of Jesus's public teaching (8.27–30; 14.61–62). According to Mark, Jesus is Messiah and Son of God—but this was a secret during Jesus's lifetime (a feature commonly called the "messianic secret").

Mark has no stories of the risen Jesus appearing to his followers ("appearance stories," as they are commonly called). Instead, his gospel ends with the story of women finding Jesus's tomb empty and the promise that his followers will see him in Galilee. Appearance stories are found in Matthew, Luke, and John—but not in Mark.

How Mark Tells the Story

Mark's story begins with a prologue to the public activity of Jesus and then narrates it in the threefold pattern of Galilee, journey to Jerusalem, and final week, including crucifixion and resurrection.

The Prologue: Mark 1.1–15. The first verse is the title of the gospel: "The beginning of the good news of Jesus Christ, the Son of God." It affirms that Jesus is "Christ," the Messiah, the one promised to Israel, that he is the "Son of God," and that his story is "good news" (the Greek word *evangellion* is translated into English as both "gospel" and "good news").

One of Mark's central themes is announced in 1.2–3: "the Way." Italicized words emphasize "way" imagery: "See, I am sending my messenger ahead of you, who will prepare your *way;* the voice of one crying out in the wilderness: 'Prepare *the way of the Lord,* make his *paths* straight.'" The words echo language from ancient Israel's experience of exile in Babylon six centuries earlier. Mark's story of Jesus is about "the way," "the way of the Lord," "the way" of Jesus, and what it means to follow that way.

The next verses introduce John the Baptizer. Jesus leaves home in Nazareth to go to John. He is baptized by John, has a vision of God's Spirit descending on him, and hears God's voice, "You are my Son, the Beloved; with you I am well pleased." Immediately thereafter, "the Spirit drove him out into the wilderness" for forty days, where he was tempted by Satan.

In 1.14–15, the second theme of the gospel is announced: the coming of the kingdom of God. John has been arrested by Herod Antipas, son of Herod the Great and ruler of Galilee. The arrest of Jesus's mentor is the trigger for him to begin his public activity in Galilee. Jesus's first words—Mark's advance summary of Jesus's message—proclaim the "good news" as the coming of the kingdom of God.

Part One: Galilee. The rest of chapter 1 through most of chapter 8—roughly half of the gospel—narrates Jesus's activity in Galilee. He calls disciples who leave everything—livelihood and family—to follow him. He teaches "with authority," and he often uses parables. He exorcises demons and heals people. He stills a storm on the sea (twice) and feeds a multitude with a few loaves and fish (twice).

Almost from the beginning, the Galilee section foreshadows the conflict that will lead to Jesus's death in Jerusalem in Part Three. Chapters 2–3 contain a series of conflict stories in which Jesus is challenged by representatives of the authorities. Already the shadow of the cross darkens the story.

Part Two: Journey to Jerusalem. Toward the end of chapter 8, Jesus's final journey to Jerusalem begins to dominate Mark's narrative. For the first time, a follower of Jesus (Peter) calls Jesus "the Messiah" (8.27–30). Jesus immediately tells his disciples that he will be rejected and killed by the authorities in Jerusalem. Following him means to "take up their cross"—to join him on "the way" that leads to Jerusalem, confrontation, death, and resurrection. Twice more in this section Jesus announces his impending execution (9.30–32; 10.32–34). As the journey section draws to its end, Mark's theme of "the way" is again emphasized; after Jesus restores the sight of a blind man at the end of chapter 10, he "followed Jesus on *the way*"—the way or path or road to Jerusalem, the next stop.

Part Three: Jerusalem. Chapters 11–16—about 40 percent of Mark—narrate Jesus's final week in Jerusalem. Sunday, he rides into Jerusalem on a donkey, provocatively acting out an Old Testament text that speaks of a king of peace coming to Jerusalem on a donkey; he will banish the weapons of war from the land and speak peace to the nations. Monday, he performs another public prophetic protest by indicting the temple—the center of native collaboration with imperial power—as a den of violent robbers.

Tuesday, representatives of the authorities challenge him with a series of questions in the presence of crowds of pilgrims. They plan to arrest him, but want first to discredit him with "the crowd," who like what he is saying. They fail. Wednesday, he is betrayed by a follower named Judas. Thursday, after he and his followers share a final meal, they go to the Garden of Gethsemane, where the authorities arrest him. Friday, he is condemned to death and crucified.

On Saturday it was the Sabbath, and nothing happened according to Mark. The descent into hell on Holy Saturday came later.

Mark's gospel concludes with what is now known as Easter Sunday. His story is very brief, only eight verses long (16.1–8), and it all fits into an hour or so of early

Easter morning shortly after dawn. The other gospels have significantly longer Easter stories and continue them into the next days and perhaps weeks. Compared to Mark's eight verses, Matthew has twenty-eight, Luke fifty-three, and John fifty-six.

Mark's Story of Easter

As Mark tells the story: "And very early on the first day of the week, . . . when the sun had risen," three women, named as "Mary Magdalene, and Mary the mother of James, and Salome," go to the tomb of Jesus to anoint him with spices (16.1–2). Expecting to find his body, they walk into his tomb. They are met by "a young man, dressed in a white robe," presumably an angel, who tells the women, "Do not be alarmed" (a frequent biblical expression also translated "Fear not" and "Be not afraid"). The white-robed figure continues: "You are looking for Jesus of Nazareth, who was crucified. He has been raised; he is not here. Look, there is the place they laid him." "Look" is the old "behold": "Behold, there is the place they laid him." And he was no longer there.

Then the white-robed figure promises that the women and Jesus's other follow-ers (the disciples and Peter are mentioned) will see Jesus in Galilee: "There you will see him, just as he told you" (16.7). This promise, along with the empty tomb and the white-robed figure's interpretation of it, are the heart and climax of Mark's Easter story. It would have been a grand ending to the first gospel. But Mark has one more verse. It is the end not only of his Easter story, but of his gospel as a whole. The women "fled from the tomb, for terror and amazement had seized them; and they said nothing to anyone, for they were afraid."

Mark's ending has been puzzling for a long time, beginning in Christian antiquity. New endings were added in the early centuries of Christianity, a shorter one from no earlier than the fourth century and a longer one from the late second century. The longer endings are often printed in English translations and often (though not always) identified as such. But our best ancient manuscripts end with "they said nothing to anyone, for they were afraid."

In the modern period, Mark's ending has attracted scholarly attention. Some scholars have argued that Mark either didn't have a chance to finish his gospel or that it did originally have a longer ending that got lost very early. Their primary reason is that they find it hard to believe that a gospel could end the way Mark does. But the majority of scholars think the gospel did originally end with 16.8.

Though Mark's ending may be strange and puzzling to us, it may not have been to his community. Local circumstances may have made the ending exquisitely ap-propriate. Perhaps it was enough to trigger connections to what they all knew.

Moreover, the oddness of Mark's last verse should not distract from the central affirmation of the story, spoken by the angel to the women. The angel begins with the obvious: "You are looking for Jesus of Nazareth, who was crucified." Then the proclamation: "He has been raised; he is not here."

Thus Mark's story, in spite of its puzzling ending, unambiguously proclaims the central conviction of Jesus's followers in the post-Easter period. Jesus was not just a figure of the past, but is a figure of the present. You won't find him in a tomb, won't find him in the land of the dead; imperial execution and a rich man's tomb couldn't hold him, couldn't stop him. God has raised and vindicated him—he lives and is Lord. This conviction, the foundation of early Christianity and the New Testament, is expressed with great economy in Mark's Easter story. It's all there. The tomb is empty. Jesus is still loose in the world.

Historical Context: The Year 70

Dating Mark's gospel around 70 puts it during a momentous time for Jews and early Christians, the majority of whom were Jewish. It was especially calamitous in the Jewish homeland. In the year 66, a revolt against Roman rule broke out. The Jewish revolutionaries were initially successful. They took control of Jerusalem, deposed the high priest appointed by Rome, and installed one of their own. War immediately followed. Rome sent several legions to crush the revolt. After four years, in the year 70, the legions reconquered Jerusalem and destroyed both the city and the temple. It was perhaps the most devastating event in ancient Jewish history, rivaled only by the Babylonian destruction of Jerusalem and the temple some six centuries earlier.

The destruction of the temple was almost unimaginable for first-century Jews. Herod the Great (ruler of the Jewish homeland from 37 to 4 BCE) and his successors had turned the temple into a magnificent combination of courtyards and buildings that had features of a fortress. It walls were high (over 300 feet at one point) and massive (some stones were 40 feet long, 15 feet wide, and 7 feet high and weighed 200 tons). It seemed like an impregnable fortress. Moreover, according to temple theology it was the dwelling place on earth of the God of Israel. God had promised to dwell in it forever, and only there were sacrifices offered to God. Surely nothing could destroy it. But in 70 the unimaginable happened.

The war with its climax in the destruction of Jerusalem and the temple was central to the historical context of Mark. This is especially apparent in Mark 13, sometimes called the "little apocalypse" to distinguish it from the "big apocalypse" of Revelation. An apocalypse is a revelation of "the end" and the creation of "the new," sometimes with a list of "signs" indicating what will happen near "the end."

Mark 13 begins with followers of Jesus marveling at the magnificence of the temple and its huge stones. Then Jesus warns them that it will all be cast down.

The rest of the chapter speaks of what will soon happen: wars and rumors of wars, suffering and persecution, "the desolating sacrilege" in the temple (almost certainly referring to the legions offering sacrifices to Caesar in the temple after its conquest in 70), and then after a few more events, the coming of the "Son of Man" in clouds "with great power and glory," language commonly and naturally understood to refer to the second coming of Jesus. It will happen soon, Mark says: "This generation will not pass away until all these things have taken place" (13.30).

Thus the gospel of Mark is marked by "imminent eschatology," to use a scholarly phrase. Eschatology is about "the end"—not the end of the created world, but the end of "this age." Imminent eschatology means the end is near. It appears in Mark not only in chapter 13, but also earlier, in 9.1: "Truly, I tell you, there are some standing here who will not taste death until they see that the kingdom of God has come with power." The coming of the kingdom of God "with power" and the coming of the Son of Man "with power" seem to refer to the same thing.

Mark and his community expected the second coming of Jesus soon. So did Paul and many others in first-century Christianity. The language they use suggests that they expected it to involve a dramatic divine intervention. God would do this, soon. Obviously, they were wrong—it didn't happen.

There is vigorous scholarly disagreement about whether this expectation goes back to Jesus himself and his message about the kingdom of God or whether this conviction emerged after Easter within early Christian communities. To relate this to Mark's story of Jesus, as the earliest gospel, does Mark's imminent eschatology accurately report that Jesus expected God to intervene in a dramatic way in the near future? Or is it (and other New Testament expressions of it) the product of a process that began after Jesus's historical life? That is, is imminent eschatology a post-Easter development?

The issues are complex. It is clear from Paul's letters that he and his communities thought the second coming could be near. But was that because Jesus said so or at least taught that God would dramatically intervene in an unmistakable way in the very near future? Or was it because of their conviction that in Jesus something dramatically new and decisive had happened and that its culmination must therefore be close at hand? Is imminent eschatology an extension of what Jesus taught? Or is it the product of early Christian testimony, enthusiasm, and conviction?

To return to the historical context of Mark's gospel, it is both easy and plausible to imagine that events around 70 generated an intensified expectation among Jews and Christian Jews that the end might indeed be near. God would soon intervene dramatically. Mark was a wartime gospel—a war between the empire that ruled his world and the people from whom Jesus came and who had been given the promises of God. Maybe this was the end that would make all things new.

As you read Mark, keep in mind that it is the first gospel—the first extended telling of the story of Jesus put into writing. Seek to read it without what you have heard about Jesus shaping what you hear. Imagine that this is the way the story of Jesus was told in a Christ-community around the year 70. What Matthew and Luke add to Mark some decades later is not wrong. Nor is John's very different telling of the story of Jesus wrong. Rather, in each case, we hear different authors and communities telling the story. Mark is the first.

Mark

THE PROCLAMATION OF JOHN THE BAPTIST

1 The beginning of the good news*a* of Jesus Christ, the Son of God.*b* 2 As it is written in the prophet Isaiah,*c*

"See, I am sending my messenger ahead of you,*d*
    who will prepare your way;
3 the voice of one crying out in the wilderness:
    'Prepare the way of the Lord,
    make his paths straight,'"

4 John the baptizer appeared*e* in the wilderness, proclaiming a baptism of repentance for the forgiveness of sins. 5And people from the whole Judean countryside and all the people of Jerusalem were going out to him, and were baptized by him in the river Jordan, confessing their sins. 6Now John was clothed with camel's hair, with a leather belt around his waist, and he ate locusts and wild honey. 7He proclaimed, "The one who is more powerful than I is coming after me; I am not worthy to stoop down and untie the thong of his sandals. 8I have baptized you with*f* water; but he will baptize you with*f* the Holy Spirit."

THE BAPTISM OF JESUS

9 In those days Jesus came from Nazareth of Galilee and was baptized by John in the Jordan. 10And just as he was coming up out of the water, he saw the heavens torn apart and the Spirit descending like a dove on him. 11And a voice came from heaven, "You are my Son, the Beloved;*g* with you I am well pleased."

---

a Or *gospel* *b* Other ancient authorities lack *the Son of God* *c* Other ancient authorities read *in the prophets* *d* Gk *before your face* *e* Other ancient authorities read *John was baptizing* *f* Or *in* *g* Or *my beloved Son*

THE TEMPTATION OF JESUS

12 And the Spirit immediately drove him out into the wilderness. [13]He was in the wilderness forty days, tempted by Satan; and he was with the wild beasts; and the angels waited on him.

THE BEGINNING OF THE GALILEAN MINISTRY

14 Now after John was arrested, Jesus came to Galilee, proclaiming the good news[a] of God,[b] [15]and saying, "The time is fulfilled, and the kingdom of God has come near;[c] repent, and believe in the good news."[a]

JESUS CALLS THE FIRST DISCIPLES

16 As Jesus passed along the Sea of Galilee, he saw Simon and his brother Andrew casting a net into the sea—for they were fishermen. [17]And Jesus said to them, "Follow me and I will make you fish for people." [18]And immediately they left their nets and followed him. [19]As he went a little farther, he saw James son of Zebedee and his brother John, who were in their boat mending the nets. [20]Immediately he called them; and they left their father Zebedee in the boat with the hired men, and followed him.

THE MAN WITH AN UNCLEAN SPIRIT

21 They went to Capernaum; and when the sabbath came, he entered the synagogue and taught. [22]They were astounded at his teaching, for he taught them as one having authority, and not as the scribes. [23]Just then there was in their synagogue a man with an unclean spirit, [24]and he cried out, "What have you to do with us, Jesus of Nazareth? Have you come to destroy us? I know who you are, the Holy One of God." [25]But Jesus rebuked him, saying, "Be silent, and come out of him!" [26]And the unclean spirit, convulsing him and crying with a loud voice, came out of him. [27]They were all amazed, and they kept on asking one another, "What is this? A new teaching—with authority! He[d] commands even the unclean spirits, and they obey him." [28]At once his fame began to spread throughout the surrounding region of Galilee.

JESUS HEALS MANY AT SIMON'S HOUSE

29 As soon as they[e] left the synagogue, they entered the house of Simon and Andrew, with James and John. [30]Now Simon's mother-in-law was in bed with a

---

a Or *gospel*   *b* Other ancient authorities read *of the kingdom*   *c* Or *is at hand*   *d* Or *A new teaching! With authority he*   *e* Other ancient authorities read *he* fever, and they told him about her at once. ³¹He came and took her by the hand and lifted her up. Then the fever left her, and she began to serve them.

32 That evening, at sunset, they brought to him all who were sick or possessed with demons. ³³And the whole city was gathered around the door. ³⁴And he cured many who were sick with various diseases, and cast out many demons; and he would not permit the demons to speak, because they knew him.

A PREACHING TOUR IN GALILEE

35 In the morning, while it was still very dark, he got up and went out to a deserted place, and there he prayed. ³⁶And Simon and his companions hunted for him. ³⁷When they found him, they said to him, "Everyone is searching for you." ³⁸He answered, "Let us go on to the neighboring towns, so that I may proclaim the message there also; for that is what I came out to do." ³⁹And he went throughout Galilee, proclaiming the message in their synagogues and casting out demons.

JESUS CLEANSES A LEPER

40 A leper[a] came to him begging him, and kneeling[b] he said to him, "If you choose, you can make me clean." ⁴¹Moved with pity,[c] Jesus[d] stretched out his hand and touched him, and said to him, "I do choose. Be made clean!" ⁴²Immediately the leprosy[a] left him, and he was made clean. ⁴³After sternly warning him he sent him away at once, ⁴⁴saying to him, "See that you say nothing to anyone; but go, show yourself to the priest, and offer for your cleansing what Moses commanded, as a testimony to them." ⁴⁵But he went out and began to proclaim it freely, and to spread the word, so that Jesus[d] could no longer go into a town openly, but stayed out in the country; and people came to him from every quarter.

JESUS HEALS A PARALYTIC

2 When he returned to Capernaum after some days, it was reported that he was at home. ²So many gathered around that there was no longer room for them, not even in front of the door; and he was speaking the word to them. ³Then some people[e] came, bringing to him a paralyzed man, carried by four of them. ⁴And when they could not bring him to Jesus because of the crowd, they removed the roof above him; and after having dug through it, they let down the mat on which the paralytic lay. ⁵When Jesus saw their faith, he said to the paralytic, "Son, your sins are forgiven." ⁶Now some of the scribes were sitting

---

a The terms *leper* and *leprosy* can refer to several diseases   *b* Other ancient authorities lack *kneeling*   *c* Other ancient authorities read *anger*   *d* Gk *he*   *e* Gk *they* there, questioning in their hearts, [7]"Why does this fellow speak in this way? It is blasphemy! Who can forgive sins but God alone?" [8]At once Jesus perceived in his spirit that they were discussing these questions among themselves; and he said to them, "Why do you raise such questions in your hearts? [9]Which is easier, to say to the paralytic, 'Your sins are forgiven,' or to say, 'Stand up and take your mat and walk'? [10]But so that you may know that the Son of Man has authority on earth to forgive sins"—he said to the paralytic— [11]"I say to you, stand up, take your mat and go to your home." [12]And he stood up, and immediately took the mat and went out before all of them; so that they were all amazed and glorified God, saying, "We have never seen anything like this!"

JESUS CALLS LEVI

13 Jesus[a] went out again beside the sea; the whole crowd gathered around him, and he taught them. [14]As he was walking along, he saw Levi son of Alphaeus sitting at the tax booth, and he said to him, "Follow me." And he got up and followed him.

15 And as he sat at dinner[b] in Levi's[c] house, many tax collectors and sinners were also sitting[d] with Jesus and his disciples—for there were many who followed him. [16]When the scribes of[e] the Pharisees saw that he was eating with sinners and tax collectors, they said to his disciples, "Why does he eat[f] with tax collectors and sinners?" [17]When Jesus heard this, he said to them, "Those who are well have no need of a physician, but those who are sick; I have come to call not the righteous but sinners."

THE QUESTION ABOUT FASTING

18 Now John's disciples and the Pharisees were fasting; and people[g] came and said to him, "Why do John's disciples and the disciples of the Pharisees fast, but your disciples do not fast?" [19]Jesus said to them, "The wedding guests cannot fast while the bridegroom is with them, can they? As long as they have the bridegroom with them, they cannot fast. [20]The days will come when the bridegroom is taken away from them, and then they will fast on that day.

21 "No one sews a piece of unshrunk cloth on an old cloak; otherwise, the patch pulls away from it, the new from the old, and a worse tear is made. [22]And no one puts new wine into old wineskins; otherwise, the wine will burst the skins, and the wine is lost, and so are the skins; but one puts new wine into fresh wineskins."[h]

---

a Gk He   b Gk reclined   c Gk his   d Gk reclining   e Other ancient authorities read and   f Other ancient authorities add and drink   g Gk they   h Other ancient authorities lack but one puts new wine into fresh wineskins

PRONOUNCEMENT ABOUT THE SABBATH

23 One sabbath he was going through the grainfields; and as they made their way his disciples began to pluck heads of grain. ²⁴The Pharisees said to him, "Look, why are they doing what is not lawful on the sabbath?" ²⁵And he said to them, "Have you never read what David did when he and his companions were hungry and in need of food? ²⁶He entered the house of God, when Abiathar was high priest, and ate the bread of the Presence, which it is not lawful for any but the priests to eat, and he gave some to his companions." ²⁷Then he said to them, "The sabbath was made for humankind, and not humankind for the sabbath; ²⁸so the Son of Man is lord even of the sabbath."

THE MAN WITH A WITHERED HAND

3 Again he entered the synagogue, and a man was there who had a withered hand. ²They watched him to see whether he would cure him on the sabbath, so that they might accuse him. ³And he said to the man who had the withered hand, "Come forward." ⁴Then he said to them, "Is it lawful to do good or to do harm on the sabbath, to save life or to kill?" But they were silent. ⁵He looked around at them with anger; he was grieved at their hardness of heart and said to the man, "Stretch out your hand." He stretched it out, and his hand was restored. ⁶The Pharisees went out and immediately conspired with the Herodians against him, how to destroy him.

A MULTITUDE AT THE SEASIDE

7 Jesus departed with his disciples to the sea, and a great multitude from Galilee followed him; ⁸hearing all that he was doing, they came to him in great numbers from Judea, Jerusalem, Idumea, beyond the Jordan, and the region around Tyre and Sidon. ⁹He told his disciples to have a boat ready for him because of the crowd, so that they would not crush him; ¹⁰for he had cured many, so that all who had diseases pressed upon him to touch him. ¹¹Whenever the unclean spirits saw him, they fell down before him and shouted, "You are the Son of God!" ¹²But he sternly ordered them not to make him known.

JESUS APPOINTS THE TWELVE

13 He went up the mountain and called to him those whom he wanted, and they came to him. ¹⁴And he appointed twelve, whom he also named apostles,ᵃ to be with him, and to be sent out to proclaim the message, ¹⁵and to have

---

a Other ancient authorities lack *whom he also named apostles* authority to cast out demons. [16]So he appointed the twelve:[a] Simon (to whom he gave the name Peter); [17]James son of Zebedee and John the brother of James (to whom he gave the name Boanerges, that is, Sons of Thunder); [18]and Andrew, and Philip, and Bartholomew, and Matthew, and Thomas, and James son of Alphaeus, and Thaddaeus, and Simon the Cananaean, [19]and Judas Iscariot, who betrayed him.

JESUS AND BEELZEBUL

Then he went home; [20]and the crowd came together again, so that they could not even eat. [21]When his family heard it, they went out to restrain him, for people were saying, "He has gone out of his mind." [22]And the scribes who came down from Jerusalem said, "He has Beelzebul, and by the ruler of the demons he casts out demons." [23]And he called them to him, and spoke to them in parables, "How can Satan cast out Satan? [24]If a kingdom is divided against itself, that kingdom cannot stand. [25]And if a house is divided against itself, that house will not be able to stand. [26]And if Satan has risen up against himself and is divided, he cannot stand, but his end has come. [27]But no one can enter a strong man's house and plunder his property without first tying up the strong man; then indeed the house can be plundered.

28 "Truly I tell you, people will be forgiven for their sins and whatever blasphemies they utter; [29]but whoever blasphemes against the Holy Spirit can never have forgiveness, but is guilty of an eternal sin"— [30]for they had said, "He has an unclean spirit."

THE TRUE KINDRED OF JESUS

31 Then his mother and his brothers came; and standing outside, they sent to him and called him. [32]A crowd was sitting around him; and they said to him, "Your mother and your brothers and sisters[b] are outside, asking for you." [33]And he replied, "Who are my mother and my brothers?" [34]And looking at those who sat around him, he said, "Here are my mother and my brothers! [35]Whoever does the will of God is my brother and sister and mother."

THE PARABLE OF THE SOWER

4 Again he began to teach beside the sea. Such a very large crowd gathered around him that he got into a boat on the sea and sat there, while the whole crowd was beside the sea on the land. [2]He began to teach them many things in parables, and in his teaching he said to them: [3]"Listen! A sower went out to sow.

---

a Other ancient authorities lack *So he appointed the twelve*   *b* Other ancient authorities lack *and sisters*

[4]And as he sowed, some seed fell on the path, and the birds came and ate it up. [5]Other seed fell on rocky ground, where it did not have much soil, and it sprang up quickly, since it had no depth of soil. [6]And when the sun rose, it was scorched; and since it had no root, it withered away. [7]Other seed fell among thorns, and the thorns grew up and choked it, and it yielded no grain. [8]Other seed fell into good soil and brought forth grain, growing up and increasing and yielding thirty and sixty and a hundredfold." [9]And he said, "Let anyone with ears to hear listen!"

THE PURPOSE OF THE PARABLES

10 When he was alone, those who were around him along with the twelve asked him about the parables. [11]And he said to them, "To you has been given the secret[a] of the kingdom of God, but for those outside, everything comes in parables; [12]in order that

'they may indeed look, but not perceive,
   and may indeed listen, but not understand;
so that they may not turn again and be forgiven.'"

13 And he said to them, "Do you not understand this parable? Then how will you understand all the parables? [14]The sower sows the word. [15]These are the ones on the path where the word is sown: when they hear, Satan immediately comes and takes away the word that is sown in them. [16]And these are the ones sown on rocky ground: when they hear the word, they immediately receive it with joy. [17]But they have no root, and endure only for a while; then, when trouble or persecution arises on account of the word, immediately they fall away.[b] [18]And others are those sown among the thorns: these are the ones who hear the word, [19]but the cares of the world, and the lure of wealth, and the desire for other things come in and choke the word, and it yields nothing. [20]And these are the ones sown on the good soil: they hear the word and accept it and bear fruit, thirty and sixty and a hundredfold."

A LAMP UNDER A BUSHEL BASKET

21 He said to them, "Is a lamp brought in to be put under the bushel basket, or under the bed, and not on the lampstand? [22]For there is nothing hidden, except to be disclosed; nor is anything secret, except to come to light. [23]Let anyone with ears to hear listen!" [24]And he said to them, "Pay attention to what you hear; the measure you give will be the measure you get, and still more will be given you. [25]For to those who have, more will be given; and from those who have nothing, even what they have will be taken away."

---

a Or *mystery*   *b* Or *stumble*

THE PARABLE OF THE GROWING SEED

26 He also said, "The kingdom of God is as if someone would scatter seed on the ground, ²⁷and would sleep and rise night and day, and the seed would sprout and grow, he does not know how. ²⁸The earth produces of itself, first the stalk, then the head, then the full grain in the head. ²⁹But when the grain is ripe, at once he goes in with his sickle, because the harvest has come."

THE PARABLE OF THE MUSTARD SEED

30 He also said, "With what can we compare the kingdom of God, or what parable will we use for it? ³¹It is like a mustard seed, which, when sown upon the ground, is the smallest of all the seeds on earth; ³²yet when it is sown it grows up and becomes the greatest of all shrubs, and puts forth large branches, so that the birds of the air can make nests in its shade."

THE USE OF PARABLES

33 With many such parables he spoke the word to them, as they were able to hear it; ³⁴he did not speak to them except in parables, but he explained everything in private to his disciples.

JESUS STILLS A STORM

35 On that day, when evening had come, he said to them, "Let us go across to the other side." ³⁶And leaving the crowd behind, they took him with them in the boat, just as he was. Other boats were with him. ³⁷A great windstorm arose, and the waves beat into the boat, so that the boat was already being swamped. ³⁸But he was in the stern, asleep on the cushion; and they woke him up and said to him, "Teacher, do you not care that we are perishing?" ³⁹He woke up and rebuked the wind, and said to the sea, "Peace! Be still!" Then the wind ceased, and there was a dead calm. ⁴⁰He said to them, "Why are you afraid? Have you still no faith?" ⁴¹And they were filled with great awe and said to one another, "Who then is this, that even the wind and the sea obey him?"

JESUS HEALS THE GERASENE DEMONIAC

5 They came to the other side of the sea, to the country of the Gerasenes.ᵃ ²And when he had stepped out of the boat, immediately a man out of the tombs with an unclean spirit met him. ³He lived among the tombs; and no one could restrain him any more, even with a chain; ⁴for he had often been

---

a Other ancient authorities read *Gergesenes;* others, *Gadarenes* restrained with shackles and chains, but the chains he wrenched apart, and the shackles he broke in pieces; and no one had the strength to subdue him. [5]Night and day among the tombs and on the mountains he was always howling and bruising himself with stones. [6]When he saw Jesus from a distance, he ran and bowed down before him; [7]and he shouted at the top of his voice, "What have you to do with me, Jesus, Son of the Most High God? I adjure you by God, do not torment me." [8]For he had said to him, "Come out of the man, you unclean spirit!" [9]Then Jesus[a] asked him, "What is your name?" He replied, "My name is Legion; for we are many." [10]He begged him earnestly not to send them out of the country. [11]Now there on the hillside a great herd of swine was feeding; [12]and the unclean spirits[b] begged him, "Send us into the swine; let us enter them." [13]So he gave them permission. And the unclean spirits came out and entered the swine; and the herd, numbering about two thousand, rushed down the steep bank into the sea, and were drowned in the sea.

14 The swineherds ran off and told it in the city and in the country. Then people came to see what it was that had happened. [15]They came to Jesus and saw the demoniac sitting there, clothed and in his right mind, the very man who had had the legion; and they were afraid. [16]Those who had seen what had happened to the demoniac and to the swine reported it. [17]Then they began to beg Jesus[c] to leave their neighborhood. [18]As he was getting into the boat, the man who had been possessed by demons begged him that he might be with him. [19]But Jesus[a] refused, and said to him, "Go home to your friends, and tell them how much the Lord has done for you, and what mercy he has shown you." [20]And he went away and began to proclaim in the Decapolis how much Jesus had done for him; and everyone was amazed.

A GIRL RESTORED TO LIFE AND A WOMAN HEALED

21 When Jesus had crossed again in the boat[d] to the other side, a great crowd gathered around him; and he was by the sea. [22]Then one of the leaders of the synagogue named Jairus came and, when he saw him, fell at his feet [23]and begged him repeatedly, "My little daughter is at the point of death. Come and lay your hands on her, so that she may be made well, and live." [24]So he went with him.

And a large crowd followed him and pressed in on him. [25]Now there was a woman who had been suffering from hemorrhages for twelve years. [26]She had endured much under many physicians, and had spent all that she had; and she was no better, but rather grew worse. [27]She had heard about Jesus, and came up

---

a Gk *he* b Gk *they* c Gk *him* d Other ancient authorities lack *in the boat*

behind him in the crowd and touched his cloak, ²⁸for she said, "If I but touch
his clothes, I will be made well." ²⁹Immediately her hemorrhage stopped; and
she felt in her body that she was healed of her disease. ³⁰Immediately aware
that power had gone forth from him, Jesus turned about in the crowd and
said, "Who touched my clothes?" ³¹And his disciples said to him, "You see the
crowd pressing in on you; how can you say, 'Who touched me?'" ³²He looked
all around to see who had done it. ³³But the woman, knowing what had happened to her, came in fear and trembling, fell down before him, and told him
the whole truth. ³⁴He said to her, "Daughter, your faith has made you well; go
in peace, and be healed of your disease."

35 While he was still speaking, some people came from the leader's house
to say, "Your daughter is dead. Why trouble the teacher any further?" ³⁶But
overhearing*a* what they said, Jesus said to the leader of the synagogue, "Do not
fear, only believe." ³⁷He allowed no one to follow him except Peter, James, and
John, the brother of James. ³⁸When they came to the house of the leader of the
synagogue, he saw a commotion, people weeping and wailing loudly. ³⁹When
he had entered, he said to them, "Why do you make a commotion and weep?
The child is not dead but sleeping." ⁴⁰And they laughed at him. Then he put
them all outside, and took the child's father and mother and those who were
with him, and went in where the child was. ⁴¹He took her by the hand and said
to her, "Talitha cum," which means, "Little girl, get up!" ⁴²And immediately the
girl got up and began to walk about (she was twelve years of age). At this they
were overcome with amazement. ⁴³He strictly ordered them that no one should
know this, and told them to give her something to eat.

THE REJECTION OF JESUS AT NAZARETH

6 He left that place and came to his hometown, and his disciples followed
him. ²On the sabbath he began to teach in the synagogue, and many who
heard him were astounded. They said, "Where did this man get all this? What
is this wisdom that has been given to him? What deeds of power are being done
by his hands! ³Is not this the carpenter, the son of Mary*b* and brother of James
and Joses and Judas and Simon, and are not his sisters here with us?" And
they took offense*c* at him. ⁴Then Jesus said to them, "Prophets are not without
honor, except in their hometown, and among their own kin, and in their own
house." ⁵And he could do no deed of power there, except that he laid his hands
on a few sick people and cured them. ⁶And he was amazed at their unbelief.

---

a Or *ignoring;* other ancient authorities read *hearing*   *b* Other ancient authorities read *son of the carpenter and of Mary*
c Or *stumbled*

THE MISSION OF THE TWELVE

Then he went about among the villages teaching. [7]He called the twelve and began to send them out two by two, and gave them authority over the unclean spirits. [8]He ordered them to take nothing for their journey except a staff; no bread, no bag, no money in their belts; [9]but to wear sandals and not to put on two tunics. [10]He said to them, "Wherever you enter a house, stay there until you leave the place. [11]If any place will not welcome you and they refuse to hear you, as you leave, shake off the dust that is on your feet as a testimony against them." [12]So they went out and proclaimed that all should repent. [13]They cast out many demons, and anointed with oil many who were sick and cured them.

THE DEATH OF JOHN THE BAPTIST

14 King Herod heard of it, for Jesus'[a] name had become known. Some were[b] saying, "John the baptizer has been raised from the dead; and for this reason these powers are at work in him." [15]But others said, "It is Elijah." And others said, "It is a prophet, like one of the prophets of old." [16]But when Herod heard of it, he said, "John, whom I beheaded, has been raised."

17 For Herod himself had sent men who arrested John, bound him, and put him in prison on account of Herodias, his brother Philip's wife, because Herod[c] had married her. [18]For John had been telling Herod, "It is not lawful for you to have your brother's wife." [19]And Herodias had a grudge against him, and wanted to kill him. But she could not, [20]for Herod feared John, knowing that he was a righteous and holy man, and he protected him. When he heard him, he was greatly perplexed;[d] and yet he liked to listen to him. [21]But an opportunity came when Herod on his birthday gave a banquet for his courtiers and officers and for the leaders of Galilee. [22]When his daughter Herodias[e] came in and danced, she pleased Herod and his guests; and the king said to the girl, "Ask me for whatever you wish, and I will give it." [23]And he solemnly swore to her, "Whatever you ask me, I will give you, even half of my kingdom." [24]She went out and said to her mother, "What should I ask for?" She replied, "The head of John the baptizer." [25]Immediately she rushed back to the king and requested, "I want you to give me at once the head of John the Baptist on a platter." [26]The king was deeply grieved; yet out of regard for his oaths and for the guests, he did not want to refuse her. [27]Immediately the king sent a soldier of the guard with orders to bring John's[a] head. He went and beheaded him in the prison, [28]brought his head on a platter, and gave it to the girl. Then the girl gave it to

---

a Gk *his*   *b* Other ancient authorities read *He was*   *c* Gk *he*   *d* Other ancient authorities read *he did many things*   *e* Other ancient authorities read *the daughter of Herodias herself* her mother. ²⁹When his disciples heard about it, they came and took his body, and laid it in a tomb.

FEEDING THE FIVE THOUSAND

30 The apostles gathered around Jesus, and told him all that they had done and taught. ³¹He said to them, "Come away to a deserted place all by yourselves and rest a while." For many were coming and going, and they had no leisure even to eat. ³²And they went away in the boat to a deserted place by themselves. ³³Now many saw them going and recognized them, and they hurried there on foot from all the towns and arrived ahead of them. ³⁴As he went ashore, he saw a great crowd; and he had compassion for them, because they were like sheep without a shepherd; and he began to teach them many things. ³⁵When it grew late, his disciples came to him and said, "This is a deserted place, and the hour is now very late; ³⁶send them away so that they may go into the surrounding country and villages and buy something for themselves to eat." ³⁷But he answered them, "You give them something to eat." They said to him, "Are we to go and buy two hundred denarii*a* worth of bread, and give it to them to eat?" ³⁸And he said to them, "How many loaves have you? Go and see." When they had found out, they said, "Five, and two fish." ³⁹Then he ordered them to get all the people to sit down in groups on the green grass. ⁴⁰So they sat down in groups of hundreds and of fifties. ⁴¹Taking the five loaves and the two fish, he looked up to heaven, and blessed and broke the loaves, and gave them to his disciples to set before the people; and he divided the two fish among them all. ⁴²And all ate and were filled; ⁴³and they took up twelve baskets full of broken pieces and of the fish. ⁴⁴Those who had eaten the loaves numbered five thousand men.

JESUS WALKS ON THE WATER

45 Immediately he made his disciples get into the boat and go on ahead to the other side, to Bethsaida, while he dismissed the crowd. ⁴⁶After saying farewell to them, he went up on the mountain to pray.

47 When evening came, the boat was out on the sea, and he was alone on the land. ⁴⁸When he saw that they were straining at the oars against an adverse wind, he came towards them early in the morning, walking on the sea. He intended to pass them by. ⁴⁹But when they saw him walking on the sea, they thought it was a ghost and cried out; ⁵⁰for they all saw him and were terrified. But immediately he spoke to them and said, "Take heart, it is I; do not

---

a The denarius was the usual day's wage for a laborer

be afraid." [51]Then he got into the boat with them and the wind ceased. And they were utterly astounded, [52]for they did not understand about the loaves, but their hearts were hardened.

HEALING THE SICK IN GENNESARET

53 When they had crossed over, they came to land at Gennesaret and moored the boat. [54]When they got out of the boat, people at once recognized him, [55]and rushed about that whole region and began to bring the sick on mats to wherever they heard he was. [56]And wherever he went, into villages or cities or farms, they laid the sick in the marketplaces, and begged him that they might touch even the fringe of his cloak; and all who touched it were healed.

THE TRADITION OF THE ELDERS

7 Now when the Pharisees and some of the scribes who had come from Jerusalem gathered around him, [2]they noticed that some of his disciples were eating with defiled hands, that is, without washing them. [3](For the Pharisees, and all the Jews, do not eat unless they thoroughly wash their hands,[a] thus observing the tradition of the elders; [4]and they do not eat anything from the market unless they wash it;[b] and there are also many other traditions that they observe, the washing of cups, pots, and bronze kettles.[c]) [5]So the Pharisees and the scribes asked him, "Why do your disciples not live[d] according to the tradition of the elders, but eat with defiled hands?" [6]He said to them, "Isaiah prophesied rightly about you hypocrites, as it is written,

> 'This people honors me with their lips,
>> but their hearts are far from me;
> 7 in vain do they worship me,
>> teaching human precepts as doctrines.'

8 You abandon the commandment of God and hold to human tradition."

9 Then he said to them, "You have a fine way of rejecting the commandment of God in order to keep your tradition! [10]For Moses said, 'Honor your father and your mother'; and, 'Whoever speaks evil of father or mother must surely die.' [11]But you say that if anyone tells father or mother, 'Whatever support you might have had from me is Corban' (that is, an offering to God[e])— [12]then you no longer permit doing anything for a father or mother, [13]thus making void the word of God through your tradition that you have handed on. And you do many things like this."

---

a Meaning of Gk uncertain   b Other ancient authorities read *and when they come from the marketplace, they do not eat unless they purify themselves*   c Other ancient authorities add *and beds*   d Gk *walk*   e Gk lacks *to God*

14 Then he called the crowd again and said to them, "Listen to me, all of you, and understand: ¹⁵there is nothing outside a person that by going in can defile, but the things that come out are what defile."ᵃ

17 When he had left the crowd and entered the house, his disciples asked him about the parable. ¹⁸He said to them, "Then do you also fail to understand? Do you not see that whatever goes into a person from outside cannot defile, ¹⁹since it enters, not the heart but the stomach, and goes out into the sewer?" (Thus he declared all foods clean.) ²⁰And he said, "It is what comes out of a person that defiles. ²¹For it is from within, from the human heart, that evil intentions come: fornication, theft, murder, ²²adultery, avarice, wickedness, deceit, licentiousness, envy, slander, pride, folly. ²³All these evil things come from within, and they defile a person."

THE SYROPHOENICIAN WOMAN'S FAITH

24 From there he set out and went away to the region of Tyre.ᵇ He entered a house and did not want anyone to know he was there. Yet he could not escape notice, ²⁵but a woman whose little daughter had an unclean spirit immediately heard about him, and she came and bowed down at his feet. ²⁶Now the woman was a Gentile, of Syrophoenician origin. She begged him to cast the demon out of her daughter. ²⁷He said to her, "Let the children be fed first, for it is not fair to take the children's food and throw it to the dogs." ²⁸But she answered him, "Sir,ᶜ even the dogs under the table eat the children's crumbs." ²⁹Then he said to her, "For saying that, you may go—the demon has left your daughter." ³⁰So she went home, found the child lying on the bed, and the demon gone.

JESUS CURES A DEAF MAN

31 Then he returned from the region of Tyre, and went by way of Sidon towards the Sea of Galilee, in the region of the Decapolis. ³²They brought to him a deaf man who had an impediment in his speech; and they begged him to lay his hand on him. ³³He took him aside in private, away from the crowd, and put his fingers into his ears, and he spat and touched his tongue. ³⁴Then looking up to heaven, he sighed and said to him, "Ephphatha," that is, "Be opened." ³⁵And immediately his ears were opened, his tongue was released, and he spoke plainly. ³⁶Then Jesusᵈ ordered them to tell no one; but the more he ordered them, the more zealously they proclaimed it. ³⁷They were astounded beyond measure, saying, "He has done everything well; he even makes the deaf to hear and the mute to speak."

---

a Other ancient authorities add verse 16, "Let anyone with ears to hear listen"   b Other ancient authorities add and Sidon
c Or Lord; other ancient authorities prefix Yes   d Gk he

FEEDING THE FOUR THOUSAND

8 In those days when there was again a great crowd without anything to eat, he called his disciples and said to them, [2]"I have compassion for the crowd, because they have been with me now for three days and have nothing to eat. [3]If I send them away hungry to their homes, they will faint on the way—and some of them have come from a great distance." [4]His disciples replied, "How can one feed these people with bread here in the desert?" [5]He asked them, "How many loaves do you have?" They said, "Seven." [6]Then he ordered the crowd to sit down on the ground; and he took the seven loaves, and after giving thanks he broke them and gave them to his disciples to distribute; and they distributed them to the crowd. [7]They had also a few small fish; and after blessing them, he ordered that these too should be distributed. [8]They ate and were filled; and they took up the broken pieces left over, seven baskets full. [9]Now there were about four thousand people. And he sent them away. [10]And immediately he got into the boat with his disciples and went to the district of Dalmanutha.[a]

THE DEMAND FOR A SIGN

11 The Pharisees came and began to argue with him, asking him for a sign from heaven, to test him. [12]And he sighed deeply in his spirit and said, "Why does this generation ask for a sign? Truly I tell you, no sign will be given to this generation." [13]And he left them, and getting into the boat again, he went across to the other side.

THE YEAST OF THE PHARISEES AND OF HEROD

14 Now the disciples[b] had forgotten to bring any bread; and they had only one loaf with them in the boat. [15]And he cautioned them, saying, "Watch out— beware of the yeast of the Pharisees and the yeast of Herod."[c] [16]They said to one another, "It is because we have no bread." [17]And becoming aware of it, Jesus said to them, "Why are you talking about having no bread? Do you still not perceive or understand? Are your hearts hardened? [18]Do you have eyes, and fail to see? Do you have ears, and fail to hear? And do you not remember? [19]When I broke the five loaves for the five thousand, how many baskets full of broken pieces did you collect?" They said to him, "Twelve." [20]"And the seven for the four thousand, how many baskets full of broken pieces did you collect?" And they said to him, "Seven." [21]Then he said to them, "Do you not yet understand?"

---

a Other ancient authorities read *Mageda* or *Magdala*   b Gk *they*   c Other ancient authorities read *the Herodians*

JESUS CURES A BLIND MAN AT BETHSAIDA

22 They came to Bethsaida. Some people*a* brought a blind man to him and begged him to touch him. ²³He took the blind man by the hand and led him out of the village; and when he had put saliva on his eyes and laid his hands on him, he asked him, "Can you see anything?" ²⁴And the man*b* looked up and said, "I can see people, but they look like trees, walking." ²⁵Then Jesus*b* laid his hands on his eyes again; and he looked intently and his sight was restored, and he saw everything clearly. ²⁶Then he sent him away to his home, saying, "Do not even go into the village."*c*

PETER'S DECLARATION ABOUT JESUS

27 Jesus went on with his disciples to the villages of Caesarea Philippi; and on the way he asked his disciples, "Who do people say that I am?" ²⁸And they answered him, "John the Baptist; and others, Elijah; and still others, one of the prophets." ²⁹He asked them, "But who do you say that I am?" Peter answered him, "You are the Messiah."*d* ³⁰And he sternly ordered them not to tell anyone about him.

JESUS FORETELLS HIS DEATH AND RESURRECTION

31 Then he began to teach them that the Son of Man must undergo great suffering, and be rejected by the elders, the chief priests, and the scribes, and be killed, and after three days rise again. ³²He said all this quite openly. And Peter took him aside and began to rebuke him. ³³But turning and looking at his disciples, he rebuked Peter and said, "Get behind me, Satan! For you are setting your mind not on divine things but on human things."

34 He called the crowd with his disciples, and said to them, "If any want to become my followers, let them deny themselves and take up their cross and follow me. ³⁵For those who want to save their life will lose it, and those who lose their life for my sake, and for the sake of the gospel,*e* will save it. ³⁶For what will it profit them to gain the whole world and forfeit their life? ³⁷Indeed, what can they give in return for their life? ³⁸Those who are ashamed of me and of my words*f* in this adulterous and sinful generation, of them the Son of Man will also be ashamed when he comes in the glory of his Father with the holy angels."

9 And he said to them, "Truly I tell you, there are some standing here who will not taste death until they see that the kingdom of God has come with*g* power."

---

a Gk *They*   b Gk *he*   c Other ancient authorities add *or tell anyone in the village*   d Or *the Christ*   e Other ancient authorities read *lose their life for the sake of the gospel*   f Other ancient authorities read *and of mine*   g Or *in*

THE TRANSFIGURATION

2 Six days later, Jesus took with him Peter and James and John, and led them up a high mountain apart, by themselves. And he was transfigured before them, ³and his clothes became dazzling white, such as no one*a* on earth could bleach them. ⁴And there appeared to them Elijah with Moses, who were talking with Jesus. ⁵Then Peter said to Jesus, "Rabbi, it is good for us to be here; let us make three dwellings,*b* one for you, one for Moses, and one for Elijah." ⁶He did not know what to say, for they were terrified. ⁷Then a cloud overshadowed them, and from the cloud there came a voice, "This is my Son, the Beloved;*c* listen to him!" ⁸Suddenly when they looked around, they saw no one with them any more, but only Jesus.

THE COMING OF ELIJAH

9 As they were coming down the mountain, he ordered them to tell no one about what they had seen, until after the Son of Man had risen from the dead. ¹⁰So they kept the matter to themselves, questioning what this rising from the dead could mean. ¹¹Then they asked him, "Why do the scribes say that Elijah must come first?" ¹²He said to them, "Elijah is indeed coming first to restore all things. How then is it written about the Son of Man, that he is to go through many sufferings and be treated with contempt? ¹³But I tell you that Elijah has come, and they did to him whatever they pleased, as it is written about him."

THE HEALING OF A BOY WITH A SPIRIT

14 When they came to the disciples, they saw a great crowd around them, and some scribes arguing with them. ¹⁵When the whole crowd saw him, they were immediately overcome with awe, and they ran forward to greet him. ¹⁶He asked them, "What are you arguing about with them?" ¹⁷Someone from the crowd answered him, "Teacher, I brought you my son; he has a spirit that makes him unable to speak; ¹⁸and whenever it seizes him, it dashes him down; and he foams and grinds his teeth and becomes rigid; and I asked your disciples to cast it out, but they could not do so." ¹⁹He answered them, "You faithless generation, how much longer must I be among you? How much longer must I put up with you? Bring him to me." ²⁰And they brought the boy*d* to him. When the spirit saw him, immediately it convulsed the boy,*d* and he fell on the ground and rolled about, foaming at the mouth. ²¹Jesus*e* asked the father, "How long has this been happening to him?" And he said, "From childhood. ²²It has often

---

a Gk *no fuller*   *b* Or *tents*   *c* Or *my beloved Son*   *d* Gk *him*   *e* Gk *He* cast him into the fire and into the water, to destroy him; but if you are able to do anything, have pity on us and help us." ²³Jesus said to him, "If you are able!—All things can be done for the one who believes." ²⁴Immediately the father of the child cried out,ᵃ "I believe; help my unbelief!" ²⁵When Jesus saw that a crowd came running together, he rebuked the unclean spirit, saying to it, "You spirit that keeps this boy from speaking and hearing, I command you, come out of him, and never enter him again!" ²⁶After crying out and convulsing him terribly, it came out, and the boy was like a corpse, so that most of them said, "He is dead." ²⁷But Jesus took him by the hand and lifted him up, and he was able to stand. ²⁸When he had entered the house, his disciples asked him privately, "Why could we not cast it out?" ²⁹He said to them, "This kind can come out only through prayer."ᵇ

JESUS AGAIN FORETELLS HIS DEATH AND RESURRECTION

30 They went on from there and passed through Galilee. He did not want anyone to know it; ³¹for he was teaching his disciples, saying to them, "The Son of Man is to be betrayed into human hands, and they will kill him, and three days after being killed, he will rise again." ³²But they did not understand what he was saying and were afraid to ask him.

WHO IS THE GREATEST?

33 Then they came to Capernaum; and when he was in the house he asked them, "What were you arguing about on the way?" ³⁴But they were silent, for on the way they had argued with one another who was the greatest. ³⁵He sat down, called the twelve, and said to them, "Whoever wants to be first must be last of all and servant of all." ³⁶Then he took a little child and put it among them; and taking it in his arms, he said to them, ³⁷"Whoever welcomes one such child in my name welcomes me, and whoever welcomes me welcomes not me but the one who sent me."

ANOTHER EXORCIST

38 John said to him, "Teacher, we saw someoneᶜ casting out demons in your name, and we tried to stop him, because he was not following us." ³⁹But Jesus said, "Do not stop him; for no one who does a deed of power in my name will be able soon afterward to speak evil of me. ⁴⁰Whoever is not against us is for us. ⁴¹For truly I tell you, whoever gives you a cup of water to drink because you bear the name of Christ will by no means lose the reward.

---

a Other ancient authorities add *with tears*   b Other ancient authorities add *and fasting*   c Other ancient authorities add *who does not follow us*

TEMPTATIONS TO SIN

42 "If any of you put a stumbling block before one of these little ones who believe in me,*ᵃ* it would be better for you if a great millstone were hung around your neck and you were thrown into the sea. ⁴³If your hand causes you to stumble, cut it off; it is better for you to enter life maimed than to have two hands and to go to hell,*ᵇ* to the unquenchable fire.*ᶜ* ⁴⁵And if your foot causes you to stumble, cut it off; it is better for you to enter life lame than to have two feet and to be thrown into hell.*ᵇ, ᶜ* ⁴⁷And if your eye causes you to stumble, tear it out; it is better for you to enter the kingdom of God with one eye than to have two eyes and to be thrown into hell,*ᵇ* ⁴⁸where their worm never dies, and the fire is never quenched.

49 "For everyone will be salted with fire.*ᵈ* ⁵⁰Salt is good; but if salt has lost its saltiness, how can you season it?*ᵉ* Have salt in yourselves, and be at peace with one another."

TEACHING ABOUT DIVORCE

10 He left that place and went to the region of Judea and*ᶠ* beyond the Jordan. And crowds again gathered around him; and, as was his custom, he again taught them.

2 Some Pharisees came, and to test him they asked, "Is it lawful for a man to divorce his wife?" ³He answered them, "What did Moses command you?" ⁴They said, "Moses allowed a man to write a certificate of dismissal and to divorce her." ⁵But Jesus said to them, "Because of your hardness of heart he wrote this commandment for you. ⁶But from the beginning of creation, 'God made them male and female.' ⁷'For this reason a man shall leave his father and mother and be joined to his wife,*ᵍ* ⁸and the two shall become one flesh.' So they are no longer two, but one flesh. ⁹Therefore what God has joined together, let no one separate."

10 Then in the house the disciples asked him again about this matter. ¹¹He said to them, "Whoever divorces his wife and marries another commits adultery against her; ¹²and if she divorces her husband and marries another, she commits adultery."

JESUS BLESSES LITTLE CHILDREN

13 People were bringing little children to him in order that he might touch them; and the disciples spoke sternly to them. ¹⁴But when Jesus saw this, he

---

a Other ancient authorities lack *in me*   *b* Gk *Gehenna*   *c* Verses 44 and 46 (which are identical with verse 48) are lacking in the best ancient authorities   *d* Other ancient authorities either add or substitute *and every sacrifice will be salted with salt*   *e* Or *how can you restore its saltiness?*   *f* Other ancient authorities lack *and*   *g* Other ancient authorities lack *and be joined to his wife* was indignant and said to them, "Let the little children come to me; do not stop them; for it is to such as these that the kingdom of God belongs. [15]Truly I tell you, whoever does not receive the kingdom of God as a little child will never enter it." [16]And he took them up in his arms, laid his hands on them, and blessed them.

THE RICH MAN

17 As he was setting out on a journey, a man ran up and knelt before him, and asked him, "Good Teacher, what must I do to inherit eternal life?" [18]Jesus said to him, "Why do you call me good? No one is good but God alone. [19]You know the commandments: 'You shall not murder; You shall not commit adultery; You shall not steal; You shall not bear false witness; You shall not defraud; Honor your father and mother.'" [20]He said to him, "Teacher, I have kept all these since my youth." [21]Jesus, looking at him, loved him and said, "You lack one thing; go, sell what you own, and give the money[a] to the poor, and you will have treasure in heaven; then come, follow me." [22]When he heard this, he was shocked and went away grieving, for he had many possessions.

23 Then Jesus looked around and said to his disciples, "How hard it will be for those who have wealth to enter the kingdom of God!" [24]And the disciples were perplexed at these words. But Jesus said to them again, "Children, how hard it is[b] to enter the kingdom of God! [25]It is easier for a camel to go through the eye of a needle than for someone who is rich to enter the kingdom of God." [26]They were greatly astounded and said to one another,[c] "Then who can be saved?" [27]Jesus looked at them and said, "For mortals it is impossible, but not for God; for God all things are possible."

28 Peter began to say to him, "Look, we have left everything and followed you." [29]Jesus said, "Truly I tell you, there is no one who has left house or brothers or sisters or mother or father or children or fields, for my sake and for the sake of the good news,[d] [30]who will not receive a hundredfold now in this age—houses, brothers and sisters, mothers and children, and fields, with persecutions—and in the age to come eternal life. [31]But many who are first will be last, and the last will be first."

A THIRD TIME JESUS FORETELLS HIS DEATH AND RESURRECTION

32 They were on the road, going up to Jerusalem, and Jesus was walking ahead of them; they were amazed, and those who followed were afraid. He took the

---

a Gk lacks *the money*   b Other ancient authorities add *for those who trust in riches*   c Other ancient authorities read *to him*
d Or *gospel*

twelve aside again and began to tell them what was to happen to him, ³³saying, "See, we are going up to Jerusalem, and the Son of Man will be handed over to the chief priests and the scribes, and they will condemn him to death; then they will hand him over to the Gentiles; ³⁴they will mock him, and spit upon him, and flog him, and kill him; and after three days he will rise again."

THE REQUEST OF JAMES AND JOHN

35 James and John, the sons of Zebedee, came forward to him and said to him, "Teacher, we want you to do for us whatever we ask of you." ³⁶And he said to them, "What is it you want me to do for you?" ³⁷And they said to him, "Grant us to sit, one at your right hand and one at your left, in your glory." ³⁸But Jesus said to them, "You do not know what you are asking. Are you able to drink the cup that I drink, or be baptized with the baptism that I am baptized with?" ³⁹They replied, "We are able." Then Jesus said to them, "The cup that I drink you will drink; and with the baptism with which I am baptized, you will be baptized; ⁴⁰but to sit at my right hand or at my left is not mine to grant, but it is for those for whom it has been prepared."

41 When the ten heard this, they began to be angry with James and John. ⁴²So Jesus called them and said to them, "You know that among the Gentiles those whom they recognize as their rulers lord it over them, and their great ones are tyrants over them. ⁴³But it is not so among you; but whoever wishes to become great among you must be your servant, ⁴⁴and whoever wishes to be first among you must be slave of all. ⁴⁵For the Son of Man came not to be served but to serve, and to give his life a ransom for many."

THE HEALING OF BLIND BARTIMAEUS

46 They came to Jericho. As he and his disciples and a large crowd were leaving Jericho, Bartimaeus son of Timaeus, a blind beggar, was sitting by the roadside. ⁴⁷When he heard that it was Jesus of Nazareth, he began to shout out and say, "Jesus, Son of David, have mercy on me!" ⁴⁸Many sternly ordered him to be quiet, but he cried out even more loudly, "Son of David, have mercy on me!" ⁴⁹Jesus stood still and said, "Call him here." And they called the blind man, saying to him, "Take heart; get up, he is calling you." ⁵⁰So throwing off his cloak, he sprang up and came to Jesus. ⁵¹Then Jesus said to him, "What do you want me to do for you?" The blind man said to him, "My teacher,[a] let me see again." ⁵²Jesus said to him, "Go; your faith has made you well." Immediately he regained his sight and followed him on the way.

---

a Aramaic *Rabbouni*

JESUS' TRIUMPHAL ENTRY INTO JERUSALEM

11 When they were approaching Jerusalem, at Bethphage and Bethany, near the Mount of Olives, he sent two of his disciples ²and said to them, "Go into the village ahead of you, and immediately as you enter it, you will find tied there a colt that has never been ridden; untie it and bring it. ³If anyone says to you, 'Why are you doing this?' just say this, 'The Lord needs it and will send it back here immediately.'" ⁴They went away and found a colt tied near a door, outside in the street. As they were untying it, ⁵some of the bystanders said to them, "What are you doing, untying the colt?" ⁶They told them what Jesus had said; and they allowed them to take it. ⁷Then they brought the colt to Jesus and threw their cloaks on it; and he sat on it. ⁸Many people spread their cloaks on the road, and others spread leafy branches that they had cut in the fields. ⁹Then those who went ahead and those who followed were shouting,

"Hosanna!
　　Blessed is the one who comes in the name of the Lord!
　10　Blessed is the coming kingdom of our ancestor David!
　　Hosanna in the highest heaven!"

11　Then he entered Jerusalem and went into the temple; and when he had looked around at everything, as it was already late, he went out to Bethany with the twelve.

JESUS CURSES THE FIG TREE

12　On the following day, when they came from Bethany, he was hungry. ¹³Seeing in the distance a fig tree in leaf, he went to see whether perhaps he would find anything on it. When he came to it, he found nothing but leaves, for it was not the season for figs. ¹⁴He said to it, "May no one ever eat fruit from you again." And his disciples heard it.

JESUS CLEANSES THE TEMPLE

15　Then they came to Jerusalem. And he entered the temple and began to drive out those who were selling and those who were buying in the temple, and he overturned the tables of the money changers and the seats of those who sold doves; ¹⁶and he would not allow anyone to carry anything through the temple. ¹⁷He was teaching and saying, "Is it not written,

　　'My house shall be called a house of prayer for all the nations'?
　　But you have made it a den of robbers."

¹⁸And when the chief priests and the scribes heard it, they kept looking for a way to kill him; for they were afraid of him, because the whole crowd was

spellbound by his teaching. [19]And when evening came, Jesus and his disciples[a] went out of the city.

THE LESSON FROM THE WITHERED FIG TREE

20 In the morning as they passed by, they saw the fig tree withered away to its roots. [21]Then Peter remembered and said to him, "Rabbi, look! The fig tree that you cursed has withered." [22]Jesus answered them, "Have[b] faith in God. [23]Truly I tell you, if you say to this mountain, 'Be taken up and thrown into the sea,' and if you do not doubt in your heart, but believe that what you say will come to pass, it will be done for you. [24]So I tell you, whatever you ask for in prayer, believe that you have received[c] it, and it will be yours.

25 "Whenever you stand praying, forgive, if you have anything against anyone; so that your Father in heaven may also forgive you your trespasses."[d]

JESUS' AUTHORITY IS QUESTIONED

27 Again they came to Jerusalem. As he was walking in the temple, the chief priests, the scribes, and the elders came to him [28]and said, "By what authority are you doing these things? Who gave you this authority to do them?" [29]Jesus said to them, "I will ask you one question; answer me, and I will tell you by what authority I do these things. [30]Did the baptism of John come from heaven, or was it of human origin? Answer me." [31]They argued with one another, "If we say, 'From heaven,' he will say, 'Why then did you not believe him?' [32]But shall we say, 'Of human origin'?"—they were afraid of the crowd, for all regarded John as truly a prophet. [33]So they answered Jesus, "We do not know." And Jesus said to them, "Neither will I tell you by what authority I am doing these things."

THE PARABLE OF THE WICKED TENANTS

12 Then he began to speak to them in parables. "A man planted a vineyard, put a fence around it, dug a pit for the wine press, and built a watchtower; then he leased it to tenants and went to another country. [2]When the season came, he sent a slave to the tenants to collect from them his share of the produce of the vineyard. [3]But they seized him, and beat him, and sent him away empty-handed. [4]And again he sent another slave to them; this one they beat over the head and insulted. [5]Then he sent another, and that one they killed. And so it was with many others; some they beat, and others they killed. [6]He had still one other, a beloved son. Finally he sent him to them, saying,

---

a Gk *they:* other ancient authorities read *he*   b Other ancient authorities read *"If you have*   c Other ancient authorities read *are receiving*   d Other ancient authorities add verse 26, *"But if you do not forgive, neither will your Father in heaven forgive your trespasses."*

'They will respect my son.' [7]But those tenants said to one another, 'This is the heir; come, let us kill him, and the inheritance will be ours.' [8]So they seized him, killed him, and threw him out of the vineyard. [9]What then will the owner of the vineyard do? He will come and destroy the tenants and give the vineyard to others. [10]Have you not read this scripture:

> 'The stone that the builders rejected
>> has become the cornerstone;[a]

> 11 this was the Lord's doing,
>> and it is amazing in our eyes'?"

12 When they realized that he had told this parable against them, they wanted to arrest him, but they feared the crowd. So they left him and went away.

THE QUESTION ABOUT PAYING TAXES

13 Then they sent to him some Pharisees and some Herodians to trap him in what he said. [14]And they came and said to him, "Teacher, we know that you are sincere, and show deference to no one; for you do not regard people with partiality, but teach the way of God in accordance with truth. Is it lawful to pay taxes to the emperor, or not? [15]Should we pay them, or should we not?" But knowing their hypocrisy, he said to them, "Why are you putting me to the test? Bring me a denarius and let me see it." [16]And they brought one. Then he said to them, "Whose head is this, and whose title?" They answered, "The emperor's." [17]Jesus said to them, "Give to the emperor the things that are the emperor's, and to God the things that are God's." And they were utterly amazed at him.

THE QUESTION ABOUT THE RESURRECTION

18 Some Sadducees, who say there is no resurrection, came to him and asked him a question, saying, [19]"Teacher, Moses wrote for us that if a man's brother dies, leaving a wife but no child, the man[b] shall marry the widow and raise up children for his brother. [20]There were seven brothers; the first married and, when he died, left no children; [21]and the second married the widow[c] and died, leaving no children; and the third likewise; [22]none of the seven left children. Last of all the woman herself died. [23]In the resurrection[d] whose wife will she be? For the seven had married her."

24 Jesus said to them, "Is not this the reason you are wrong, that you know neither the scriptures nor the power of God? [25]For when they rise from the dead,

---

a Or *keystone*   b Gk *his brother*   c Gk *her*   d Other ancient authorities add *when they rise* they neither marry nor are given in marriage, but are like angels in heaven. [26] And as for the dead being raised, have you not read in the book of Moses, in the story about the bush, how God said to him, 'I am the God of Abraham, the God of Isaac, and the God of Jacob'? [27] He is God not of the dead, but of the living; you are quite wrong."

THE FIRST COMMANDMENT

28 One of the scribes came near and heard them disputing with one another, and seeing that he answered them well, he asked him, "Which commandment is the first of all?" [29] Jesus answered, "The first is, 'Hear, O Israel: the Lord our God, the Lord is one; [30] you shall love the Lord your God with all your heart, and with all your soul, and with all your mind, and with all your strength.' [31] The second is this, 'You shall love your neighbor as yourself.' There is no other commandment greater than these." [32] Then the scribe said to him, "You are right, Teacher; you have truly said that 'he is one, and besides him there is no other'; [33] and 'to love him with all the heart, and with all the understanding, and with all the strength,' and 'to love one's neighbor as oneself,'—this is much more important than all whole burnt offerings and sacrifices." [34] When Jesus saw that he answered wisely, he said to him, "You are not far from the kingdom of God." After that no one dared to ask him any question.

THE QUESTION ABOUT DAVID'S SON

35 While Jesus was teaching in the temple, he said, "How can the scribes say that the Messiah[a] is the son of David? [36] David himself, by the Holy Spirit, declared,

> 'The Lord said to my Lord,
> "Sit at my right hand,
>   until I put your enemies under your feet."'

[37] David himself calls him Lord; so how can he be his son?" And the large crowd was listening to him with delight.

JESUS DENOUNCES THE SCRIBES

38 As he taught, he said, "Beware of the scribes, who like to walk around in long robes, and to be greeted with respect in the marketplaces, [39] and to have the best seats in the synagogues and places of honor at banquets! [40] They devour widows' houses and for the sake of appearance say long prayers. They will receive the greater condemnation."

---

a Or the Christ

THE WIDOW'S OFFERING

41 He sat down opposite the treasury, and watched the crowd putting money into the treasury. Many rich people put in large sums. ⁴²A poor widow came and put in two small copper coins, which are worth a penny. ⁴³Then he called his disciples and said to them, "Truly I tell you, this poor widow has put in more than all those who are contributing to the treasury. ⁴⁴For all of them have contributed out of their abundance; but she out of her poverty has put in everything she had, all she had to live on."

THE DESTRUCTION OF THE TEMPLE FORETOLD

13 As he came out of the temple, one of his disciples said to him, "Look, Teacher, what large stones and what large buildings!" ²Then Jesus asked him, "Do you see these great buildings? Not one stone will be left here upon another; all will be thrown down."

3 When he was sitting on the Mount of Olives opposite the temple, Peter, James, John, and Andrew asked him privately, ⁴"Tell us, when will this be, and what will be the sign that all these things are about to be accomplished?" ⁵Then Jesus began to say to them, "Beware that no one leads you astray. ⁶Many will come in my name and say, 'I am he!'ᵃ and they will lead many astray. ⁷When you hear of wars and rumors of wars, do not be alarmed; this must take place, but the end is still to come. ⁸For nation will rise against nation, and kingdom against kingdom; there will be earthquakes in various places; there will be famines. This is but the beginning of the birth pangs.

PERSECUTION FORETOLD

9 "As for yourselves, beware; for they will hand you over to councils; and you will be beaten in synagogues; and you will stand before governors and kings because of me, as a testimony to them. ¹⁰And the good newsᵇ must first be proclaimed to all nations. ¹¹When they bring you to trial and hand you over, do not worry beforehand about what you are to say; but say whatever is given you at that time, for it is not you who speak, but the Holy Spirit. ¹²Brother will betray brother to death, and a father his child, and children will rise against parents and have them put to death; ¹³and you will be hated by all because of my name. But the one who endures to the end will be saved.

---

a Gk *I am*   *b* Gk *gospel*

THE DESOLATING SACRILEGE

14 "But when you see the desolating sacrilege set up where it ought not to be (let the reader understand), then those in Judea must flee to the mountains; ¹⁵the one on the housetop must not go down or enter the house to take anything away; ¹⁶the one in the field must not turn back to get a coat. ¹⁷Woe to those who are pregnant and to those who are nursing infants in those days! ¹⁸Pray that it may not be in winter. ¹⁹For in those days there will be suffering, such as has not been from the beginning of the creation that God created until now, no, and never will be. ²⁰And if the Lord had not cut short those days, no one would be saved; but for the sake of the elect, whom he chose, he has cut short those days. ²¹And if anyone says to you at that time, 'Look! Here is the Messiah!'[a] or 'Look! There he is!'—do not believe it. ²²False messiahs[b] and false prophets will appear and produce signs and omens, to lead astray, if possible, the elect. ²³But be alert; I have already told you everything.

THE COMING OF THE SON OF MAN

24 "But in those days, after that suffering,
> the sun will be darkened,
>> and the moon will not give its light,
> 25 and the stars will be falling from heaven,
>> and the powers in the heavens will be shaken.

26 Then they will see 'the Son of Man coming in clouds' with great power and glory. ²⁷Then he will send out the angels, and gather his elect from the four winds, from the ends of the earth to the ends of heaven.

THE LESSON OF THE FIG TREE

28 "From the fig tree learn its lesson: as soon as its branch becomes tender and puts forth its leaves, you know that summer is near. ²⁹So also, when you see these things taking place, you know that he[c] is near, at the very gates. ³⁰Truly I tell you, this generation will not pass away until all these things have taken place. ³¹Heaven and earth will pass away, but my words will not pass away.

THE NECESSITY FOR WATCHFULNESS

32 "But about that day or hour no one knows, neither the angels in heaven, nor the Son, but only the Father. ³³Beware, keep alert;[d] for you do not know

---

a Or *the Christ* *b* Or *christs* *c* Or *it* *d* Other ancient authorities add *and pray* when the time will come. [34]It is like a man going on a journey, when he leaves home and puts his slaves in charge, each with his work, and commands the doorkeeper to be on the watch. [35]Therefore, keep awake—for you do not know when the master of the house will come, in the evening, or at midnight, or at cockcrow, or at dawn, [36]or else he may find you asleep when he comes suddenly. [37]And what I say to you I say to all: Keep awake."

THE PLOT TO KILL JESUS

14 It was two days before the Passover and the festival of Unleavened Bread. The chief priests and the scribes were looking for a way to arrest Jesus[a] by stealth and kill him; [2]for they said, "Not during the festival, or there may be a riot among the people."

THE ANOINTING AT BETHANY

3 While he was at Bethany in the house of Simon the leper,[b] as he sat at the table, a woman came with an alabaster jar of very costly ointment of nard, and she broke open the jar and poured the ointment on his head. [4]But some were there who said to one another in anger, "Why was the ointment wasted in this way? [5]For this ointment could have been sold for more than three hundred denarii,[c] and the money given to the poor." And they scolded her. [6]But Jesus said, "Let her alone; why do you trouble her? She has performed a good service for me. [7]For you always have the poor with you, and you can show kindness to them whenever you wish; but you will not always have me. [8]She has done what she could; she has anointed my body beforehand for its burial. [9]Truly I tell you, wherever the good news[d] is proclaimed in the whole world, what she has done will be told in remembrance of her."

JUDAS AGREES TO BETRAY JESUS

10 Then Judas Iscariot, who was one of the twelve, went to the chief priests in order to betray him to them. [11]When they heard it, they were greatly pleased, and promised to give him money. So he began to look for an opportunity to betray him.

THE PASSOVER WITH THE DISCIPLES

12 On the first day of Unleavened Bread, when the Passover lamb is sacrificed, his disciples said to him, "Where do you want us to go and make the preparations for you to eat the Passover?" [13]So he sent two of his disciples, saying to

---

a Gk him　b The terms *leper* and *leprosy* can refer to several diseases　c The denarius was the usual day's wage for a laborer
d Or *gospel*

them, "Go into the city, and a man carrying a jar of water will meet you; follow him, [14]and wherever he enters, say to the owner of the house, 'The Teacher asks, Where is my guest room where I may eat the Passover with my disciples?' [15]He will show you a large room upstairs, furnished and ready. Make preparations for us there." [16]So the disciples set out and went to the city, and found everything as he had told them; and they prepared the Passover meal.

17 When it was evening, he came with the twelve. [18]And when they had taken their places and were eating, Jesus said, "Truly I tell you, one of you will betray me, one who is eating with me." [19]They began to be distressed and to say to him one after another, "Surely, not I?" [20]He said to them, "It is one of the twelve, one who is dipping bread[a] into the bowl[b] with me. [21]For the Son of Man goes as it is written of him, but woe to that one by whom the Son of Man is betrayed! It would have been better for that one not to have been born."

THE INSTITUTION OF THE LORD'S SUPPER

22 While they were eating, he took a loaf of bread, and after blessing it he broke it, gave it to them, and said, "Take; this is my body." [23]Then he took a cup, and after giving thanks he gave it to them, and all of them drank from it. [24]He said to them, "This is my blood of the[c] covenant, which is poured out for many. [25]Truly I tell you, I will never again drink of the fruit of the vine until that day when I drink it new in the kingdom of God."

PETER'S DENIAL FORETOLD

26 When they had sung the hymn, they went out to the Mount of Olives. [27]And Jesus said to them, "You will all become deserters; for it is written,

> 'I will strike the shepherd,
> and the sheep will be scattered.'

28 But after I am raised up, I will go before you to Galilee." [29]Peter said to him, "Even though all become deserters, I will not." [30]Jesus said to him, "Truly I tell you, this day, this very night, before the cock crows twice, you will deny me three times." [31]But he said vehemently, "Even though I must die with you, I will not deny you." And all of them said the same.

JESUS PRAYS IN GETHSEMANE

32 They went to a place called Gethsemane; and he said to his disciples, "Sit here while I pray." [33]He took with him Peter and James and John, and began to be distressed and agitated. [34]And he said to them, "I am deeply grieved, even

---

a Gk lacks *bread*   b Other ancient authorities read *same bowl*   c Other ancient authorities add *new* to death; remain here, and keep awake." [35]And going a little farther, he threw himself on the ground and prayed that, if it were possible, the hour might pass from him. [36]He said, "Abba,[a] Father, for you all things are possible; remove this cup from me; yet, not what I want, but what you want." [37]He came and found them sleeping; and he said to Peter, "Simon, are you asleep? Could you not keep awake one hour? [38]Keep awake and pray that you may not come into the time of trial;[b] the spirit indeed is willing, but the flesh is weak." [39]And again he went away and prayed, saying the same words. [40]And once more he came and found them sleeping, for their eyes were very heavy; and they did not know what to say to him. [41]He came a third time and said to them, "Are you still sleeping and taking your rest? Enough! The hour has come; the Son of Man is betrayed into the hands of sinners. [42]Get up, let us be going. See, my betrayer is at hand."

THE BETRAYAL AND ARREST OF JESUS

43 Immediately, while he was still speaking, Judas, one of the twelve, arrived; and with him there was a crowd with swords and clubs, from the chief priests, the scribes, and the elders. [44]Now the betrayer had given them a sign, saying, "The one I will kiss is the man; arrest him and lead him away under guard." [45]So when he came, he went up to him at once and said, "Rabbi!" and kissed him. [46]Then they laid hands on him and arrested him. [47]But one of those who stood near drew his sword and struck the slave of the high priest, cutting off his ear. [48]Then Jesus said to them, "Have you come out with swords and clubs to arrest me as though I were a bandit? [49]Day after day I was with you in the temple teaching, and you did not arrest me. But let the scriptures be fulfilled." [50]All of them deserted him and fled.

51 A certain young man was following him, wearing nothing but a linen cloth. They caught hold of him, [52]but he left the linen cloth and ran off naked.

JESUS BEFORE THE COUNCIL

53 They took Jesus to the high priest; and all the chief priests, the elders, and the scribes were assembled. [54]Peter had followed him at a distance, right into the courtyard of the high priest; and he was sitting with the guards, warming himself at the fire. [55]Now the chief priests and the whole council were looking for testimony against Jesus to put him to death; but they found none. [56]For many gave false testimony against him, and their testimony did not agree. [57]Some stood up and gave false testimony against him, saying, [58]"We heard

---

a Aramaic for *Father* *b* Or *into temptation*

him say, 'I will destroy this temple that is made with hands, and in three days I will build another, not made with hands.'" [59]But even on this point their testimony did not agree. [60]Then the high priest stood up before them and asked Jesus, "Have you no answer? What is it that they testify against you?" [61]But he was silent and did not answer. Again the high priest asked him, "Are you the Messiah,[a] the Son of the Blessed One?" [62]Jesus said, "I am; and

> 'you will see the Son of Man
> seated at the right hand of the Power,'
> and 'coming with the clouds of heaven.'"

63 Then the high priest tore his clothes and said, "Why do we still need witnesses? [64]You have heard his blasphemy! What is your decision?" All of them condemned him as deserving death. [65]Some began to spit on him, to blindfold him, and to strike him, saying to him, "Prophesy!" The guards also took him over and beat him.

PETER DENIES JESUS

66 While Peter was below in the courtyard, one of the servant-girls of the high priest came by. [67]When she saw Peter warming himself, she stared at him and said, "You also were with Jesus, the man from Nazareth." [68]But he denied it, saying, "I do not know or understand what you are talking about." And he went out into the forecourt.[b] Then the cock crowed.[c] [69]And the servant-girl, on seeing him, began again to say to the bystanders, "This man is one of them." [70]But again he denied it. Then after a little while the bystanders again said to Peter, "Certainly you are one of them; for you are a Galilean." [71]But he began to curse, and he swore an oath, "I do not know this man you are talking about." [72]At that moment the cock crowed for the second time. Then Peter remembered that Jesus had said to him, "Before the cock crows twice, you will deny me three times." And he broke down and wept.

JESUS BEFORE PILATE

15 As soon as it was morning, the chief priests held a consultation with the elders and scribes and the whole council. They bound Jesus, led him away, and handed him over to Pilate. [2]Pilate asked him, "Are you the King of the Jews?" He answered him, "You say so." [3]Then the chief priests accused him of many things. [4]Pilate asked him again, "Have you no answer? See how many charges they bring against you." [5]But Jesus made no further reply, so that Pilate was amazed.

---

a Or *the Christ* b Or *gateway* c Other ancient authorities lack *Then the cock crowed*

PILATE HANDS JESUS OVER TO BE CRUCIFIED

6 Now at the festival he used to release a prisoner for them, anyone for whom they asked. [7]Now a man called Barabbas was in prison with the rebels who had committed murder during the insurrection. [8]So the crowd came and began to ask Pilate to do for them according to his custom. [9]Then he answered them, "Do you want me to release for you the King of the Jews?" [10]For he realized that it was out of jealousy that the chief priests had handed him over. [11]But the chief priests stirred up the crowd to have him release Barabbas for them instead. [12]Pilate spoke to them again, "Then what do you wish me to do[a] with the man you call[b] the King of the Jews?" [13]They shouted back, "Crucify him!" [14]Pilate asked them, "Why, what evil has he done?" But they shouted all the more, "Crucify him!" [15]So Pilate, wishing to satisfy the crowd, released Barabbas for them; and after flogging Jesus, he handed him over to be crucified.

THE SOLDIERS MOCK JESUS

16 Then the soldiers led him into the courtyard of the palace (that is, the governor's headquarters[c]); and they called together the whole cohort. [17]And they clothed him in a purple cloak; and after twisting some thorns into a crown, they put it on him. [18]And they began saluting him, "Hail, King of the Jews!" [19]They struck his head with a reed, spat upon him, and knelt down in homage to him. [20]After mocking him, they stripped him of the purple cloak and put his own clothes on him. Then they led him out to crucify him.

THE CRUCIFIXION OF JESUS

21 They compelled a passer-by, who was coming in from the country, to carry his cross; it was Simon of Cyrene, the father of Alexander and Rufus. [22]Then they brought Jesus[d] to the place called Golgotha (which means the place of a skull). [23]And they offered him wine mixed with myrrh; but he did not take it. [24]And they crucified him, and divided his clothes among them, casting lots to decide what each should take.

25 It was nine o'clock in the morning when they crucified him. [26]The inscription of the charge against him read, "The King of the Jews." [27]And with him they crucified two bandits, one on his right and one on his left.[e] [29]Those who passed by derided[f] him, shaking their heads and saying, "Aha! You who would

---

a Other ancient authorities read *what should I do*   *b* Other ancient authorities lack *the man you call*   *c* Gk *the praetorium*   *d* Gk *him*   *e* Other ancient authorities add verse 28, *And the scripture was fulfilled that says, "And he was counted among the lawless."*   *f* Or *blasphemed* destroy the temple and build it in three days, [30]save yourself, and come down from the cross!" [31]In the same way the chief priests, along with the scribes, were also mocking him among themselves and saying, "He saved others; he cannot save himself. [32]Let the Messiah,[a] the King of Israel, come down from the cross now, so that we may see and believe." Those who were crucified with him also taunted him.

THE DEATH OF JESUS

33 When it was noon, darkness came over the whole land[b] until three in the afternoon. [34]At three o'clock Jesus cried out with a loud voice, "Eloi, Eloi, lema sabachthani?" which means, "My God, my God, why have you forsaken me?"[c] [35]When some of the bystanders heard it, they said, "Listen, he is calling for Elijah." [36]And someone ran, filled a sponge with sour wine, put it on a stick, and gave it to him to drink, saying, "Wait, let us see whether Elijah will come to take him down." [37]Then Jesus gave a loud cry and breathed his last. [38]And the curtain of the temple was torn in two, from top to bottom. [39]Now when the centurion, who stood facing him, saw that in this way he[d] breathed his last, he said, "Truly this man was God's Son!"[e]

40 There were also women looking on from a distance; among them were Mary Magdalene, and Mary the mother of James the younger and of Joses, and Salome. [41]These used to follow him and provided for him when he was in Galilee; and there were many other women who had come up with him to Jerusalem.

THE BURIAL OF JESUS

42 When evening had come, and since it was the day of Preparation, that is, the day before the sabbath, [43]Joseph of Arimathea, a respected member of the council, who was also himself waiting expectantly for the kingdom of God, went boldly to Pilate and asked for the body of Jesus. [44]Then Pilate wondered if he were already dead; and summoning the centurion, he asked him whether he had been dead for some time. [45]When he learned from the centurion that he was dead, he granted the body to Joseph. [46]Then Joseph[f] bought a linen cloth, and taking down the body,[g] wrapped it in the linen cloth, and laid it in a tomb that had been hewn out of the rock. He then rolled a stone against the door of the tomb. [47]Mary Magdalene and Mary the mother of Joses saw where the body[g] was laid.

---

a Or *the Christ*   b Or *earth*   c Other ancient authorities read *made me a reproach*   d Other ancient authorities add *cried out and*   e Or *a son of God*   f Gk *he*   g Gk *it*

THE RESURRECTION OF JESUS

16 When the sabbath was over, Mary Magdalene, and Mary the mother of James, and Salome bought spices, so that they might go and anoint him. ²And very early on the first day of the week, when the sun had risen, they went to the tomb. ³They had been saying to one another, "Who will roll away the stone for us from the entrance to the tomb?" ⁴When they looked up, they saw that the stone, which was very large, had already been rolled back. ⁵As they entered the tomb, they saw a young man, dressed in a white robe, sitting on the right side; and they were alarmed. ⁶But he said to them, "Do not be alarmed; you are looking for Jesus of Nazareth, who was crucified. He has been raised; he is not here. Look, there is the place they laid him. ⁷But go, tell his disciples and Peter that he is going ahead of you to Galilee; there you will see him, just as he told you." ⁸So they went out and fled from the tomb, for terror and amazement had seized them; and they said nothing to anyone, for they were afraid.*ᵃ*

THE SHORTER ENDING OF MARK

[[And all that had been commanded them they told briefly to those around Peter. And afterward Jesus himself sent out through them, from east to west, the sacred and imperishable proclamation of eternal salvation.*ᵇ*]]

THE LONGER ENDING OF MARK

JESUS APPEARS TO MARY MAGDALENE

9 [[Now after he rose early on the first day of the week, he appeared first to Mary Magdalene, from whom he had cast out seven demons. ¹⁰She went out and told those who had been with him, while they were mourning and weeping. ¹¹But when they heard that he was alive and had been seen by her, they would not believe it.

JESUS APPEARS TO TWO DISCIPLES

12 After this he appeared in another form to two of them, as they were walking into the country. ¹³And they went back and told the rest, but they did not believe them.

---

a Some of the most ancient authorities bring the book to a close at the end of verse 8. One authority concludes the book with the shorter ending; others include the shorter ending and then continue with verses 9–20. In most authorities verses 9–20 follow immediately after verse 8, though in some of these authorities the passage is marked as being doubtful.   *b* Other ancient authorities add *Amen*

JESUS COMMISSIONS THE DISCIPLES

14 Later he appeared to the eleven themselves as they were sitting at the table; and he upbraided them for their lack of faith and stubbornness, because they had not believed those who saw him after he had risen.[a] [15]And he said to them, "Go into all the world and proclaim the good news[b] to the whole creation. [16]The one who believes and is baptized will be saved; but the one who does not believe will be condemned. [17]And these signs will accompany those who believe: by using my name they will cast out demons; they will speak in new tongues; [18]they will pick up snakes in their hands,[c] and if they drink any deadly thing, it will not hurt them; they will lay their hands on the sick, and they will recover."

THE ASCENSION OF JESUS

19 So then the Lord Jesus, after he had spoken to them, was taken up into heaven and sat down at the right hand of God. [20]And they went out and proclaimed the good news everywhere, while the Lord worked with them and confirmed the message by the signs that accompanied it.[d]]]

---

a Other ancient authorities add, in whole or in part, *And they excused themselves, saying, "This age of lawlessness and unbelief is under Satan, who does not allow the truth and power of God to prevail over the unclean things of the spirits. Therefore reveal your righteousness now"—thus they spoke to Christ. And Christ replied to them, "The term of years of Satan's power has been fulfilled, but other terrible things draw near. And for those who have sinned I was handed over to death, that they may return to the truth and sin no more, that they may inherit the spiritual and imperishable glory of righteousness that is in heaven."* b Or *gospel* c Other ancient authorities lack *in their hands* d Other ancient authorities add *Amen*

James

The dating and authorship of James are inextricably intertwined. The author identifies himself as "James" (1.1). For centuries, Christian tradition took it for granted that the author was James, the brother of Jesus. According to Acts and Paul, James was the "leader" or "head" of the Christian community in Jerusalem. He was executed in the early 60s.

If by this James, the letter must have been written before the early 60s, thus making it earlier than any of the gospels. Indeed, some scholars argue that it could have been written in the 40s or 50s, which would make it as early or even earlier than the letters of Paul—perhaps the earliest document in the New Testament.

But the majority of mainstream scholars do not think the author was the brother of Jesus. The author does not say so, but describes himself simply as "James, a servant of God and of the Lord Jesus Christ." Moreover, his use of Greek language and grammar is quite sophisticated—not impossible for a brother of Jesus from the peasant class whose native language was Aramaic, but at least somewhat unlikely.

If the author was not the brother of Jesus, then its date becomes wide open. There is no scholarly consensus. Estimates range from the 70s or 80s to as late as the early 100s. I have decided to place it in the 70s or 80s, later than Mark, but before Matthew, because much of James seems like early tradition. It echoes sayings of Jesus included in Matthew (and Luke), but never exactly. It is likely that the author knew the teachings of Jesus from the oral tradition or from Q and not from Matthew or Luke.

Though called a "letter," James does not have the typical characteristics of a letter. It was not sent to a particular Christ-community as the letters of Paul were. Rather, it was written to the "twelve tribes" (a traditional designation for the Jewish people) "in the Diaspora" (Jews living outside the homeland). Moreover, it lacks the traditional closing of a letter.

Despite being written to the "twelve tribes in the Diaspora," its audience was not Jews in general, but Christian Jews who had become followers of Jesus. That James is a Christian Jewish document is suggested not only by its content, but also by a detail in 2.2. A gathering of this Christian group is referred to as an "assembly"—the Greek word for "assembly" is the one from which we derive "synagogue."

There is little in this document that is overtly theological, nothing about the death and resurrection of Jesus, nothing about "doctrines" that are to be believed. Its focus is primarily practical, combining wisdom about how to live and prophetic indictment of how people commonly do live. Half of James's 108 verses are imperatives.

The author emphasizes the importance of doing and acting. Two of the best-known passages are: "Be doers of the word, and not merely hearers . . . doers who act" (1.22–25) and "Faith without works is dead" (2.14–26). His examples of "works" are concretely compassionate: clothing the naked, feeding the hungry, supplying their bodily needs.

"Wisdom"—how to live, the way—is a frequent theme in James. One passage contrasts two kinds, the "wisdom from above" and "earthly" wisdom (3.13–18). The former, of course, is from God. It is "peaceable, gentle, willing to yield, full of mercy and good fruits, without a trace of partiality or hypocrisy," with "a harvest of righteousness . . . for those who make peace." The latter is marked by "envy and selfish ambition," leading to "disorder and wickedness of every kind." The contrast is similar to Paul's contrast between the wisdom of God and the wisdom of "this world."

James recognizes that this conflict goes on within individuals, including presumably within the Christians for whom he writes. He speaks of people who are "double-minded" (1.8; 4.8). The Greek word means to have two minds, two *psyches*. To play with language, this condition can be called "di-psychosis."

In this state people have a divided commitment and thus lack grounding and stability. They are "like a wave of the sea, driven and tossed by the wind" (1.6). James contrasts loyalty to God with "friendship with the world" (4.1–10): "Friendship with the world is enmity with God." As James uses the phrase, it does not refer to God's created world. Rather, it indicts the humanly created world of covetousness and violence—earthly wisdom, the way "this world" most often is. In this context, he commands: "Purify your hearts, you double-minded." The choice is friendship with the world or friendship with God.

James also includes harsh indictments of "the rich" and their position in the world. The first passage speaks of them withering away like beautiful flowers, the second criticizes the favoritism they often receive, and the third indicts them for not paying their workers adequately and living lives of luxury and pleasure, fattening their hearts:

> The rich will disappear like a flower in the field. For the sun rises with its scorching heat and withers the field; its flower falls, and its beauty perishes. It is the same way with the rich; in the midst of a busy life, they will wither away. (1.10–11)

> My brothers and sisters, do you with your acts of favoritism really believe in our glorious Lord Jesus Christ? For if a person with gold rings and in fine clothes comes into your assembly, and if a poor person in dirty clothes also comes in, and if you take notice of the one wearing the fine clothes and say, "Have a seat here, please," while to the one who is poor you say, "Stand there," or, "Sit at my feet," have you not made distinctions among your-selves, and become judges with evil thoughts? Listen, my beloved brothers and sisters. Has not God chosen the poor in the world to be rich in faith and to be heirs of the kingdom that he has promised to those who love him? But you have dishonored the poor. Is it not the rich who oppress you? Is it not they who drag you into court? (2.1–6)

> Come now, you rich people, weep and wail for the miseries that are coming to you. Your riches have rotted, and your clothes are moth-eaten. Your gold and silver have rusted, and their rust will be evidence against you, and it will eat your flesh like fire. You have laid up treasure for the last days. Listen! The wages of the laborers who mowed your fields, which you kept back by fraud, cry out, and the cries of the harvesters have reached the ears of the Lord of hosts. You have lived on the earth in luxury and in pleasure; you have fattened your hearts in a day of slaughter. (5.1–5)

Not surprisingly, the message of James has been called "scandalous"—a scandal to much of today's Christianity.

Most American Christians will never hear these passages read or preached in church. They do not appear in *The Revised Common Lectionary,* the set of biblical texts designated for mainline Protestant and Catholic worship services. Thus Chris-tians will be unaware of them unless they study James on their own.

In Christian history, James has sometimes been controversial. Martin Luther called it "an epistle of straw" and wanted to excise it from the New Testament. Paul's message of "justification by grace through faith" was for him the heart of Christianity, and he thought James emphasized "works" too much. Luther's passion for Paul led him to misunderstand James. The kind of faith that James castigated was believing something to be true, but not acting on it. As James puts it, even the demons believe in God (2.19).

Few Christians today would be bold enough to advocate throwing a book out of the Bible. But many have perhaps unknowingly sided with Luther's verdict on James, that what matters most is what we believe and not what we do. James called his audience beyond belief to action: "Be doers of the word, and not merely hearers." Rather than being an epistle of straw, it is a fiery and passionate letter.

Finally, we note that James echoes more sayings of Jesus than any document in the New Testament other than the gospels themselves. Its fiery passion reflects the passion of Jesus himself.

THE LETTER OF
James

SALUTATION

1 James, a servant*a* of God and of the Lord Jesus Christ,
To the twelve tribes in the Dispersion:
Greetings.

FAITH AND WISDOM

2 My brothers and sisters,*b* whenever you face trials of any kind, consider it nothing but joy, ³because you know that the testing of your faith produces endurance; ⁴and let endurance have its full effect, so that you may be mature and complete, lacking in nothing.

5 If any of you is lacking in wisdom, ask God, who gives to all generously and ungrudgingly, and it will be given you. ⁶But ask in faith, never doubting, for the one who doubts is like a wave of the sea, driven and tossed by the wind; ⁷, ⁸for the doubter, being double-minded and unstable in every way, must not expect to receive anything from the Lord.

POVERTY AND RICHES

9 Let the believer*c* who is lowly boast in being raised up, ¹⁰and the rich in being brought low, because the rich will disappear like a flower in the field. ¹¹For the sun rises with its scorching heat and withers the field; its flower falls, and its beauty perishes. It is the same way with the rich; in the midst of a busy life, they will wither away.

---

a Gk *slave*   *b* Gk *brothers*   *c* Gk *brother*

TRIAL AND TEMPTATION

12 Blessed is anyone who endures temptation. Such a one has stood the test and will receive the crown of life that the Lord[a] has promised to those who love him. [13]No one, when tempted, should say, "I am being tempted by God"; for God cannot be tempted by evil and he himself tempts no one. [14]But one is tempted by one's own desire, being lured and enticed by it; [15]then, when that desire has conceived, it gives birth to sin, and that sin, when it is fully grown, gives birth to death. [16]Do not be deceived, my beloved.[b]

17 Every generous act of giving, with every perfect gift, is from above, coming down from the Father of lights, with whom there is no variation or shadow due to change.[c] [18]In fulfillment of his own purpose he gave us birth by the word of truth, so that we would become a kind of first fruits of his creatures.

HEARING AND DOING THE WORD

19 You must understand this, my beloved:[b] let everyone be quick to listen, slow to speak, slow to anger; [20]for your anger does not produce God's righteousness. [21]Therefore rid yourselves of all sordidness and rank growth of wickedness, and welcome with meekness the implanted word that has the power to save your souls.

22 But be doers of the word, and not merely hearers who deceive themselves. [23]For if any are hearers of the word and not doers, they are like those who look at themselves[d] in a mirror; [24]for they look at themselves and, on going away, immediately forget what they were like. [25]But those who look into the perfect law, the law of liberty, and persevere, being not hearers who forget but doers who act—they will be blessed in their doing.

26 If any think they are religious, and do not bridle their tongues but deceive their hearts, their religion is worthless. [27]Religion that is pure and undefiled before God, the Father, is this: to care for orphans and widows in their distress, and to keep oneself unstained by the world.

WARNING AGAINST PARTIALITY

2 My brothers and sisters,[e] do you with your acts of favoritism really believe in our glorious Lord Jesus Christ?[f] [2]For if a person with gold rings and in fine clothes comes into your assembly, and if a poor person in dirty clothes also comes in, [3]and if you take notice of the one wearing the fine clothes and say,

---

a Gk *he;* other ancient authorities read *God*   b Gk *my beloved brothers*   c Other ancient authorities read *variation due to a shadow of turning*   d Gk *at the face of his birth*   e Gk *My brothers*   f Or *hold the faith of our glorious Lord Jesus Christ without acts of favoritism*

"Have a seat here, please," while to the one who is poor you say, "Stand there," or, "Sit at my feet,"[a] [4]have you not made distinctions among yourselves, and become judges with evil thoughts? [5]Listen, my beloved brothers and sisters.[b] Has not God chosen the poor in the world to be rich in faith and to be heirs of the kingdom that he has promised to those who love him? [6]But you have dishonored the poor. Is it not the rich who oppress you? Is it not they who drag you into court? [7]Is it not they who blaspheme the excellent name that was invoked over you?

8 You do well if you really fulfill the royal law according to the scripture, "You shall love your neighbor as yourself." [9]But if you show partiality, you commit sin and are convicted by the law as transgressors. [10]For whoever keeps the whole law but fails in one point has become accountable for all of it. [11]For the one who said, "You shall not commit adultery," also said, "You shall not murder." Now if you do not commit adultery but if you murder, you have become a transgressor of the law. [12]So speak and so act as those who are to be judged by the law of liberty. [13]For judgment will be without mercy to anyone who has shown no mercy; mercy triumphs over judgment.

FAITH WITHOUT WORKS IS DEAD

14 What good is it, my brothers and sisters,[b] if you say you have faith but do not have works? Can faith save you? [15]If a brother or sister is naked and lacks daily food, [16]and one of you says to them, "Go in peace; keep warm and eat your fill," and yet you do not supply their bodily needs, what is the good of that? [17]So faith by itself, if it has no works, is dead.

18 But someone will say, "You have faith and I have works." Show me your faith apart from your works, and I by my works will show you my faith. [19]You believe that God is one; you do well. Even the demons believe—and shudder. [20]Do you want to be shown, you senseless person, that faith apart from works is barren? [21]Was not our ancestor Abraham justified by works when he offered his son Isaac on the altar? [22]You see that faith was active along with his works, and faith was brought to completion by the works. [23]Thus the scripture was fulfilled that says, "Abraham believed God, and it was reckoned to him as righteousness," and he was called the friend of God. [24]You see that a person is justified by works and not by faith alone. [25]Likewise, was not Rahab the prostitute also justified by works when she welcomed the messengers and sent them out by another road? [26]For just as the body without the spirit is dead, so faith without works is also dead.

---

a Gk *Sit under my footstool*   *b* Gk *brothers*

TAMING THE TONGUE

3 Not many of you should become teachers, my brothers and sisters,[a] for you know that we who teach will be judged with greater strictness. [2]For all of us make many mistakes. Anyone who makes no mistakes in speaking is perfect, able to keep the whole body in check with a bridle. [3]If we put bits into the mouths of horses to make them obey us, we guide their whole bodies. [4]Or look at ships: though they are so large that it takes strong winds to drive them, yet they are guided by a very small rudder wherever the will of the pilot directs. [5]So also the tongue is a small member, yet it boasts of great exploits.

How great a forest is set ablaze by a small fire! [6]And the tongue is a fire. The tongue is placed among our members as a world of iniquity; it stains the whole body, sets on fire the cycle of nature,[b] and is itself set on fire by hell.[c] [7]For every species of beast and bird, of reptile and sea creature, can be tamed and has been tamed by the human species, [8]but no one can tame the tongue—a restless evil, full of deadly poison. [9]With it we bless the Lord and Father, and with it we curse those who are made in the likeness of God. [10]From the same mouth come blessing and cursing. My brothers and sisters,[d] this ought not to be so. [11]Does a spring pour forth from the same opening both fresh and brackish water? [12]Can a fig tree, my brothers and sisters,[e] yield olives, or a grapevine figs? No more can salt water yield fresh.

TWO KINDS OF WISDOM

13 Who is wise and understanding among you? Show by your good life that your works are done with gentleness born of wisdom. [14]But if you have bitter envy and selfish ambition in your hearts, do not be boastful and false to the truth. [15]Such wisdom does not come down from above, but is earthly, unspiritual, devilish. [16]For where there is envy and selfish ambition, there will also be disorder and wickedness of every kind. [17]But the wisdom from above is first pure, then peaceable, gentle, willing to yield, full of mercy and good fruits, without a trace of partiality or hypocrisy. [18]And a harvest of righteousness is sown in peace for[f] those who make peace.

FRIENDSHIP WITH THE WORLD

4 Those conflicts and disputes among you, where do they come from? Do they not come from your cravings that are at war within you? [2]You want something and do not have it; so you commit murder. And you covet[g] some-

---

a Gk brothers   b Or wheel of birth   c Gk Gehenna   d Gk My brothers   e Gk my brothers   f Or by   g Or you murder and you covet thing and cannot obtain it; so you engage in disputes and conflicts. You do not have, because you do not ask. ³You ask and do not receive, because you ask wrongly, in order to spend what you get on your pleasures. ⁴Adulterers! Do you not know that friendship with the world is enmity with God? Therefore whoever wishes to be a friend of the world becomes an enemy of God. ⁵Or do you suppose that it is for nothing that the scripture says, "God*a* yearns jealously for the spirit that he has made to dwell in us"? ⁶But he gives all the more grace; therefore it says,

> "God opposes the proud,
>> but gives grace to the humble."

7 Submit yourselves therefore to God. Resist the devil, and he will flee from you. ⁸Draw near to God, and he will draw near to you. Cleanse your hands, you sinners, and purify your hearts, you double-minded. ⁹Lament and mourn and weep. Let your laughter be turned into mourning and your joy into dejection. ¹⁰Humble yourselves before the Lord, and he will exalt you.

WARNING AGAINST JUDGING ANOTHER

11 Do not speak evil against one another, brothers and sisters.*b* Whoever speaks evil against another or judges another, speaks evil against the law and judges the law; but if you judge the law, you are not a doer of the law but a judge. ¹²There is one lawgiver and judge who is able to save and to destroy. So who, then, are you to judge your neighbor?

BOASTING ABOUT TOMORROW

13 Come now, you who say, "Today or tomorrow we will go to such and such a town and spend a year there, doing business and making money." ¹⁴Yet you do not even know what tomorrow will bring. What is your life? For you are a mist that appears for a little while and then vanishes. ¹⁵Instead you ought to say, "If the Lord wishes, we will live and do this or that." ¹⁶As it is, you boast in your arrogance; all such boasting is evil. ¹⁷Anyone, then, who knows the right thing to do and fails to do it, commits sin.

WARNING TO RICH OPPRESSORS

5 Come now, you rich people, weep and wail for the miseries that are coming to you. ²Your riches have rotted, and your clothes are moth-eaten. ³Your gold and silver have rusted, and their rust will be evidence against you, and it will eat your flesh like fire. You have laid up treasure*c* for the last days. ⁴Listen!

---

a Gk *He* *b* Gk *brothers* *c* Or *will eat your flesh, since you have stored up fire*

The wages of the laborers who mowed your fields, which you kept back by fraud, cry out, and the cries of the harvesters have reached the ears of the Lord of hosts. [5]You have lived on the earth in luxury and in pleasure; you have fattened your hearts in a day of slaughter. [6]You have condemned and murdered the righteous one, who does not resist you.

PATIENCE IN SUFFERING

7 Be patient, therefore, beloved,[a] until the coming of the Lord. The farmer waits for the precious crop from the earth, being patient with it until it receives the early and the late rains. [8]You also must be patient. Strengthen your hearts, for the coming of the Lord is near.[b] [9]Beloved,[c] do not grumble against one another, so that you may not be judged. See, the Judge is standing at the doors! [10]As an example of suffering and patience, beloved,[a] take the prophets who spoke in the name of the Lord. [11]Indeed we call blessed those who showed endurance. You have heard of the endurance of Job, and you have seen the purpose of the Lord, how the Lord is compassionate and merciful.

12 Above all, my beloved,[a] do not swear, either by heaven or by earth or by any other oath, but let your "Yes" be yes and your "No" be no, so that you may not fall under condemnation.

THE PRAYER OF FAITH

13 Are any among you suffering? They should pray. Are any cheerful? They should sing songs of praise. [14]Are any among you sick? They should call for the elders of the church and have them pray over them, anointing them with oil in the name of the Lord. [15]The prayer of faith will save the sick, and the Lord will raise them up; and anyone who has committed sins will be forgiven. [16]Therefore confess your sins to one another, and pray for one another, so that you may be healed. The prayer of the righteous is powerful and effective. [17]Elijah was a human being like us, and he prayed fervently that it might not rain, and for three years and six months it did not rain on the earth. [18]Then he prayed again, and the heaven gave rain and the earth yielded its harvest.

19 My brothers and sisters,[d] if anyone among you wanders from the truth and is brought back by another, [20]you should know that whoever brings back a sinner from wandering will save the sinner's[e] soul from death and will cover a multitude of sins.

---

a Gk *brothers*   *b* Or *is at hand*   *c* Gk *Brothers*   *d* Gk *My brothers*   *e* Gk *his*

Colossians

Colossians is almost certainly the earliest of the letters attributed to Paul but not actually written by him. Its strongest literary connections are to Ephesians, whose author most likely knew Colossians. Ephesians was most likely written no later than around the year 90, and thus Colossians must have been written earlier, probably in the 80s.

A minority of mainline scholars argue that Colossians is even earlier, because it was written by Paul himself. The letter not only says so, but it has the classic form of a Pauline letter. It begins with the author identifying himself, the naming of the addressees, and an introductory blessing: "Grace to you and peace from God our Father." It continues with a prayer of thanksgiving and, after the body of the letter, concludes with a closing greeting and blessing: "Grace be with you."

But in style and content, it differs significantly from the seven genuine letters of Paul. Its sentences are much longer and more complex (obscured in the NRSV, because it breaks them up into shorter units for sake of clarity). Its content not only goes beyond what is in the seven genuine letters, but sometimes conflicts with them.

For example, recall that Paul's letter to the Galatians affirms that Jew and Gentile, male and female, and slave and free are all one in Christ (3.28) and that his letter to Philemon asserts that a Christian master may not have a Christian slave. When Colossians 3.11 echoes Galatians 3.28, it does not mention the equality of male and female. A few verses later, the earliest New Testament example of what are called "household codes" begins. It includes the subordination of wives to husbands and slaves to masters. "Wives, be subject to your husbands, as is fitting in the Lord" (3.18). Slaves are to be obedient to their "earthly masters in everything, not only while being watched and in order to please them, but wholeheartedly, fearing the Lord" (3.22). The radicalism of Paul's early communities is being accommodated to the hierarchical normalcy of the Roman world.

The letter is addressed to Christians in Colossae (1.2) and Laodicea (4.16), two cities near each other in western Asia Minor. According to the letter itself, Paul did not know these communities in person; he was not their founder and had not visited them. The letter is called one of the "prison letters" because of its closing: "Remember my chains." The author, assuming it was not Paul, knew that Paul had been imprisoned.

Content

One of this letter's most striking passages speaks of the "cosmic Christ"; that is, its language about the status and significance of Jesus transcends his historical life and goes back to the beginning of creation, the *cosmos*. What is seen in Jesus is

> the image of the invisible God, the firstborn of all creation; for in him all things in heaven and on earth were created, things visible and invisible, whether thrones or dominions or rulers or powers—all things have been created through him and for him. He himself is before all things, and in him all things hold together. He is the head of the body, the church; he is the beginning, the firstborn from the dead, so that he might come to have first place in everything. For in him all the fullness of God was pleased to dwell, and through him God was pleased to reconcile to himself all things, whether on earth or in heaven. (1.15–20)

These extraordinary statements affirm in slightly different language what we will see in the first chapter of John's gospel. There Jesus is the "Word of God" become flesh, the Word who was "in the beginning" with God and through whom God created everything. Here, Jesus "is the image of the invisible God" and "in him all the fullness of God was pleased to dwell." As "the firstborn of all creation," all things were "created through him and for him." Through him and his death all things on earth and heaven have been reconciled. As in John's gospel, this is incarnational theology: in Jesus, we see what God is like.

Many scholars think this text is an early Christian hymn used and perhaps adapted by the author. If so, these affirmations are earlier than Colossians and shared by other developing streams of Christian traditions such as what we will see in John's gospel.

The author also cautions the community about the teachings and practices advocated by unnamed teachers. There is no scholarly agreement about who they were. But the author's message is clear: live the life you see in Jesus.

As you therefore have received Christ Jesus the Lord, continue to live your lives in him, rooted and built up in him and established in the faith, just as you were taught, abounding in thanksgiving. (2.6–7)

So also in a longer passage:

As God's chosen ones, holy and beloved, clothe yourselves with compassion, kindness, humility, meekness, and patience. Bear with one another and, if anyone has a complaint against another, forgive each other; just as the Lord has forgiven you, so you also must forgive. Above all, clothe yourselves with love, which binds everything together in perfect harmony. And let the peace of Christ rule in your hearts, to which indeed you were called in the one body. And be thankful. Let the word of Christ dwell in you richly; teach and admonish one another in all wisdom; and with gratitude in your hearts sing psalms, hymns, and spiritual songs to God. And whatever you do, in word or deed, do everything in the name of the Lord Jesus, giving thanks to God the Father through him. (3.12–17)

Note the virtues: compassion, kindness, humility, meekness, patience, forgiveness, love, harmony, peace, thankfulness, wisdom, gratitude, singing, and doing everything in Jesus.

The letter closes in chapter 4 with final words of advice and greetings. Specific persons are named. This specificity is one of the major reasons some think Paul himself wrote the letter. But if Paul didn't write this letter, what are we to make of the specificity of the greetings? Was it part of a deliberate forgery—was somebody deceitfully and maliciously pretending to be Paul? Or was it a follower of Paul seeking to adapt his message to a later generation? Is Colossians an extension of Paul's thought? Or the beginning of a subversion of Paul's radicalism? The jury is still out.

Colossians

SALUTATION

1 Paul, an apostle of Christ Jesus by the will of God, and Timothy our brother, 2 To the saints and faithful brothers and sisters*a* in Christ in Colossae: Grace to you and peace from God our Father.

PAUL THANKS GOD FOR THE COLOSSIANS

3 In our prayers for you we always thank God, the Father of our Lord Jesus Christ, ⁴for we have heard of your faith in Christ Jesus and of the love that you have for all the saints, ⁵because of the hope laid up for you in heaven. You have heard of this hope before in the word of the truth, the gospel ⁶that has come to you. Just as it is bearing fruit and growing in the whole world, so it has been bearing fruit among yourselves from the day you heard it and truly comprehended the grace of God. ⁷This you learned from Epaphras, our beloved fellow servant.*b* He is a faithful minister of Christ on your*c* behalf, ⁸and he has made known to us your love in the Spirit.

9 For this reason, since the day we heard it, we have not ceased praying for you and asking that you may be filled with the knowledge of God's*d* will in all spiritual wisdom and understanding, ¹⁰so that you may lead lives worthy of the Lord, fully pleasing to him, as you bear fruit in every good work and as you grow in the knowledge of God. ¹¹May you be made strong with all the strength that comes from his glorious power, and may you be prepared to endure everything with patience, while joyfully ¹²giving thanks to the Father,

---

a Gk *brothers* *b* Gk *slave* *c* Other ancient authorities read *our* *d* Gk *his* who has enabled[a] you[b] to share in the inheritance of the saints in the light. [13]He has rescued us from the power of darkness and transferred us into the kingdom of his beloved Son, [14]in whom we have redemption, the forgiveness of sins.[c]

THE SUPREMACY OF CHRIST

15 He is the image of the invisible God, the firstborn of all creation; [16]for in[d] him all things in heaven and on earth were created, things visible and invisible, whether thrones or dominions or rulers or powers—all things have been created through him and for him. [17]He himself is before all things, and in[d] him all things hold together. [18]He is the head of the body, the church; he is the beginning, the firstborn from the dead, so that he might come to have first place in everything. [19]For in him all the fullness of God was pleased to dwell, [20]and through him God was pleased to reconcile to himself all things, whether on earth or in heaven, by making peace through the blood of his cross.

21 And you who were once estranged and hostile in mind, doing evil deeds, [22]he has now reconciled[e] in his fleshly body[f] through death, so as to present you holy and blameless and irreproachable before him— [23]provided that you continue securely established and steadfast in the faith, without shifting from the hope promised by the gospel that you heard, which has been proclaimed to every creature under heaven. I, Paul, became a servant of this gospel.

PAUL'S INTEREST IN THE COLOSSIANS

24 I am now rejoicing in my sufferings for your sake, and in my flesh I am completing what is lacking in Christ's afflictions for the sake of his body, that is, the church. [25]I became its servant according to God's commission that was given to me for you, to make the word of God fully known, [26]the mystery that has been hidden throughout the ages and generations but has now been revealed to his saints. [27]To them God chose to make known how great among the Gentiles are the riches of the glory of this mystery, which is Christ in you, the hope of glory. [28]It is he whom we proclaim, warning everyone and teaching everyone in all wisdom, so that we may present everyone mature in Christ. [29]For this I toil and struggle with all the energy that he powerfully inspires within me.

2 For I want you to know how much I am struggling for you, and for those in Laodicea, and for all who have not seen me face to face. [2]I want their hearts to be encouraged and united in love, so that they may have all the riches of assured understanding and have the knowledge of God's mystery, that is, Christ

---

a Other ancient authorities read *called*   b Other ancient authorities read *us*   c Other ancient authorities add *through his blood*
d Or *by*   e Other ancient authorities read *you have now been reconciled*   f Gk *in the body of his flesh*

himself,[a] [3]in whom are hidden all the treasures of wisdom and knowledge. [4]I am saying this so that no one may deceive you with plausible arguments. [5]For though I am absent in body, yet I am with you in spirit, and I rejoice to see your morale and the firmness of your faith in Christ.

FULLNESS OF LIFE IN CHRIST

6 As you therefore have received Christ Jesus the Lord, continue to live your lives[b] in him, [7]rooted and built up in him and established in the faith, just as you were taught, abounding in thanksgiving.

8 See to it that no one takes you captive through philosophy and empty deceit, according to human tradition, according to the elemental spirits of the universe,[c] and not according to Christ. [9]For in him the whole fullness of deity dwells bodily, [10]and you have come to fullness in him, who is the head of every ruler and authority. [11]In him also you were circumcised with a spiritual circumcision,[d] by putting off the body of the flesh in the circumcision of Christ; [12]when you were buried with him in baptism, you were also raised with him through faith in the power of God, who raised him from the dead. [13]And when you were dead in trespasses and the uncircumcision of your flesh, God[e] made you[f] alive together with him, when he forgave us all our trespasses, [14]erasing the record that stood against us with its legal demands. He set this aside, nailing it to the cross. [15]He disarmed[g] the rulers and authorities and made a public example of them, triumphing over them in it.

16 Therefore do not let anyone condemn you in matters of food and drink or of observing festivals, new moons, or sabbaths. [17]These are only a shadow of what is to come, but the substance belongs to Christ. [18]Do not let anyone disqualify you, insisting on self-abasement and worship of angels, dwelling[h] on visions,[i] puffed up without cause by a human way of thinking,[j] [19]and not holding fast to the head, from whom the whole body, nourished and held together by its ligaments and sinews, grows with a growth that is from God.

WARNINGS AGAINST FALSE TEACHERS

20 If with Christ you died to the elemental spirits of the universe,[c] why do you live as if you still belonged to the world? Why do you submit to regulations, [21]"Do not handle, Do not taste, Do not touch"? [22]All these regulations refer to things that perish with use; they are simply human commands and teachings.

---

a Other ancient authorities read *of the mystery of God, both of the Father and of Christ*   b Gk *to walk*   c Or *the rudiments of the world*   d Gk *a circumcision made without hands*   e Gk *he*   f Other ancient authorities read *made us;* others, *made* g Or *divested himself of*   h Other ancient authorities read *not dwelling*   i Meaning of Gk uncertain   j Gk *by the mind of his flesh*

[23]These have indeed an appearance of wisdom in promoting self-imposed piety, humility, and severe treatment of the body, but they are of no value in checking self-indulgence.[a]

THE NEW LIFE IN CHRIST

3 So if you have been raised with Christ, seek the things that are above, where Christ is, seated at the right hand of God. [2]Set your minds on things that are above, not on things that are on earth, [3]for you have died, and your life is hidden with Christ in God. [4]When Christ who is your[b] life is revealed, then you also will be revealed with him in glory.

5 Put to death, therefore, whatever in you is earthly: fornication, impurity, passion, evil desire, and greed (which is idolatry). [6]On account of these the wrath of God is coming on those who are disobedient.[c] [7]These are the ways you also once followed, when you were living that life.[d] [8]But now you must get rid of all such things—anger, wrath, malice, slander, and abusive[e] language from your mouth. [9]Do not lie to one another, seeing that you have stripped off the old self with its practices [10]and have clothed yourselves with the new self, which is being renewed in knowledge according to the image of its creator. [11]In that renewal[f] there is no longer Greek and Jew, circumcised and uncircumcised, barbarian, Scythian, slave and free; but Christ is all and in all!

12 As God's chosen ones, holy and beloved, clothe yourselves with compassion, kindness, humility, meekness, and patience. [13]Bear with one another and, if anyone has a complaint against another, forgive each other; just as the Lord[g] has forgiven you, so you also must forgive. [14]Above all, clothe yourselves with love, which binds everything together in perfect harmony. [15]And let the peace of Christ rule in your hearts, to which indeed you were called in the one body. And be thankful. [16]Let the word of Christ[h] dwell in you richly; teach and admonish one another in all wisdom; and with gratitude in your hearts sing psalms, hymns, and spiritual songs to God.[i] [17]And whatever you do, in word or deed, do everything in the name of the Lord Jesus, giving thanks to God the Father through him.

RULES FOR CHRISTIAN HOUSEHOLDS

18 Wives, be subject to your husbands, as is fitting in the Lord. [19]Husbands, love your wives and never treat them harshly.

---

a Or are of no value, serving only to indulge the flesh   b Other authorities read our   c Other ancient authorities lack on those who are disobedient (Gk the children of disobedience)   d Or living among such people   e Or filthy   f Gk its creator, [11]where   g Other ancient authorities read just as Christ   h Other ancient authorities read of God, or of the Lord   i Other ancient authorities read to the Lord

20 Children, obey your parents in everything, for this is your acceptable duty in the Lord. ²¹Fathers, do not provoke your children, or they may lose heart. ²²Slaves, obey your earthly masters*a* in everything, not only while being watched and in order to please them, but wholeheartedly, fearing the Lord.*a* ²³Whatever your task, put yourselves into it, as done for the Lord and not for your masters,*b* ²⁴since you know that from the Lord you will receive the inheritance as your reward; you serve*c* the Lord Christ. ²⁵For the wrongdoer will be paid back for whatever wrong has been done, and there is no partiality.

4 Masters, treat your slaves justly and fairly, for you know that you also have a Master in heaven.

FURTHER INSTRUCTIONS

2 Devote yourselves to prayer, keeping alert in it with thanksgiving. ³At the same time pray for us as well that God will open to us a door for the word, that we may declare the mystery of Christ, for which I am in prison, ⁴so that I may reveal it clearly, as I should.

5 Conduct yourselves wisely toward outsiders, making the most of the time.*d* ⁶Let your speech always be gracious, seasoned with salt, so that you may know how you ought to answer everyone.

FINAL GREETINGS AND BENEDICTION

7 Tychicus will tell you all the news about me; he is a beloved brother, a faithful minister, and a fellow servant*e* in the Lord. ⁸I have sent him to you for this very purpose, so that you may know how we are*f* and that he may encourage your hearts; ⁹he is coming with Onesimus, the faithful and beloved brother, who is one of you. They will tell you about everything here.

10 Aristarchus my fellow prisoner greets you, as does Mark the cousin of Barnabas, concerning whom you have received instructions—if he comes to you, welcome him. ¹¹And Jesus who is called Justus greets you. These are the only ones of the circumcision among my co-workers for the kingdom of God, and they have been a comfort to me. ¹²Epaphras, who is one of you, a servant*e* of Christ Jesus, greets you. He is always wrestling in his prayers on your behalf, so that you may stand mature and fully assured in everything that God wills. ¹³For I testify for him that he has worked hard for you and for those in Laodicea and in Hierapolis. ¹⁴Luke, the beloved physician, and Demas greet you. ¹⁵Give

---

a In Greek the same word is used for *master* and *Lord*   *b* Gk *not for men*   *c* Or *you are slaves of,* or *be slaves of*   *d* Or *opportunity*   *e* Gk *slave*   *f* Other authorities read *that I may know how you are* my greetings to the brothers and sisters*a* in Laodicea, and to Nympha and the church in her house. ¹⁶And when this letter has been read among you, have it read also in the church of the Laodiceans; and see that you read also the letter from Laodicea. ¹⁷And say to Archippus, "See that you complete the task that you have received in the Lord."

18 I, Paul, write this greeting with my own hand. Remember my chains. Grace be with you.*b*

---

a Gk *brothers*   *b* Other ancient authorities add *Amen*

Matthew

Matthew was written a decade or two after Mark, in the 80s or perhaps early 90s. Along with John, it is one of two gospels named after a disciple of Jesus. According to 9.9, Matthew was a tax collector before Jesus called him to be a disciple. Mark and Luke tell the same story, but name the tax collector "Levi." They could be different names for the same person. The name Matthew also appears in all the lists of the twelve disciples in the gospels and Acts.

For centuries, it has been taken for granted that this gospel was written by this Matthew, and thus by an eyewitness to the historical life of Jesus. And not just any eyewitness, but one of the inner circle of twelve.

Mainstream modern scholarship does not think this to be likely. Recall that names were assigned to the gospels only in the second century. The gospel of Matthew does not claim to be written by Matthew, one of the twelve disciples. Moreover, its date in the last decades of the first century makes it unlikely that it was written by somebody who knew the historical Jesus. Finally, the author used Mark as his major source. Would an eyewitness have done this? Used a source written by somebody who was not an eyewitness?

But ultimately, who the author was does not matter, for all we can know can only be inferred from the way the author puts the story of Jesus together. As we did with Mark, we will call both the gospel and its author Matthew.

In an important sense, Matthew is an expanded version of Mark. Matthew used 90 percent of Mark (about 600 of Mark's 678 verses) in his 1,071 verses. To Mark he added birth stories (48 verses) and about 400 verses mostly of Jesus's teaching. About 200 of those come from Q, the collection of Jesus's teaching shared with Luke. The rest are mostly sayings and parables not found in the other gospels (sometimes called "special Matthew" or "M" by New Testament scholars). These include parts of the Sermon on the Mount and parables like the weeds, the hidden treasure, the pearl of great value, the unmerciful servant, and the workers in the vineyard.

Fivefold Structure

Though Matthew takes over Mark's threefold narrative pattern of Galilee, journey to Jerusalem, and Jerusalem, he also imposes his own fivefold structure. In between the stories of Jesus's birth in chapters 1–2 and his final days in 26–28, the body of Matthew's gospel has five "blocks" or "sections" of material, as scholars have long noted. Each combines narrative and teaching and ends with a distinctive formula (7.28; 11.1; 13.53; 19.1; 26.1).

This fivefold structure reflects the five books of the Pentateuch, the Torah, and perhaps also the traditional division of Psalms into five sections. But the resonance with the Pentateuch, the foundational document of Judaism, is more important. At its heart is the story of Moses and the exodus from Egypt, the creation of a new community under God, and the giving of the laws at Mt. Sinai by which it was to live.

Matthew's fivefold structure suggests that the story of Jesus is analogous to the story of Moses and the exodus in both importance and content. Jesus's story is about a new exodus from a new pharaoh and the creation of a new community under God—and it is deeply grounded in the story of ancient Israel.

The theme expressed in this structure also shows up in particular details. For example, the first of the five blocks of teaching in Matthew begins with Jesus going "up the mountain"—which is why what follows in chapters 5–7 is known as "the Sermon on the Mount." Matthew is the only gospel that says that Jesus taught this from a mountain. Jesus is like Moses, a new Moses, revealing God's will from a mountain, a new Sinai.

Connections with Moses and the exodus also appear in Matthew's story of Jesus's birth. After a genealogy that underlines Jesus's origin in Israel's heritage going back to Abraham, it is dominated by King Herod's plot to kill the newborn "king of the Jews." Even the story of the wise men is integrated into this theme. Herod's behavior echoes Pharaoh's in the story of the exodus, including especially ordering the killing of Jewish infants. Other details in first-century Jewish versions of the story of Moses's birth also shape Matthew's birth story. (See my book *The First Christmas*, coauthored with John Dominic Crossan.) It functions as an overture to the gospel, announcing its central theme: Jesus is a new Moses leading a new exodus from a new pharaoh into a new way of life.

Affirmation of Judaism

Matthew's fivefold structure and the theme it expresses indicate the gospel's deep roots within Judaism. Of course, the other gospels and the New Testament are also rooted in Judaism, but Matthew emphasizes this more.

Not counting allusions or echoes, he quotes the Jewish Bible forty times with an explicit phrase such as "It is written" and another twenty-one times without such a phrase. Matthew affirms the eternal validity of the "law" and the "prophets," designations for sections of the Jewish Bible in his time. Jesus says in this gospel (and only in this gospel): "Do not think that I have come to abolish the law or the prophets; I have come not to abolish but to fulfill. For truly I tell you, until heaven and earth pass away, not one letter, not one stroke of a letter, will pass from the law until all is accomplished" (5.17–18).

Finally, in Matthew, Jesus restricts his mission during his lifetime to Jews. When he gives his disciples mission instructions, he tells them: "Go nowhere among the Gentiles, and enter no town of the Samaritans, but go rather to the lost sheep of the house of Israel" (10.5–6). Later he says about himself: "I was sent only to the lost sheep of the house of Israel" (15.24). It is only the risen Jesus, the post-Easter Jesus, in the last verse of the gospel, who commissions his followers to go to "the nations" (the Gentiles).

Hostility Toward Judaism

Yet Matthew is deeply hostile toward "Jews"—meaning those who opposed Jesus or at least did not respond to him. Of course, the other gospels also report conflict between Jesus and some of his Jewish contemporaries, including groups like scribes, lawyers, Pharisees, Sadducees and temple authorities. But Matthew intensifies it. His language is harsher and more intemperate, condemnatory, vindictive, and filled with invective. Along with John, as we will see, Matthew has been for many centuries the major scriptural justification for Christian anti-Semitism and often deadly persecution of Jews.

The sharpness of Matthew's hostility is seen in small details and in larger ways. In a detail involving pronouns, Matthew three times refers to "their" synagogues (4.23; 12.9; 13.54), as if Jews in synagogues were already "other."

The hostility dominates a whole chapter in Matthew's story of Jesus's final week in Jerusalem. Matthew 23, added to the story of Jesus's last week as told by Mark, is a sustained indictment of the "scribes and Pharisees." "Scribes" were a highly skilled, literate class who could read and write complex religious and legal documents. Most worked for the powerful and wealthy elite. "Pharisees," by the time Matthew wrote in the late first century, were in the process of becoming the dominant interpreters of Judaism, now that the temple and its authorities no longer existed.

Though some of the content of Matthew's indictment of scribes and Pharisees is also found in Luke (and is thus from Q), Matthew's language is stridently condemnatory and includes name-calling. They are not just hypocrites, but children of hell, "blind guides," "blind fools." They are "whitewashed tombs" that look great outside, but are filled with rot and death inside. They are "snakes," a "brood of vipers," and "descendants of those who murdered the prophets." The chapter then ends with a passage proclaiming the coming destruction of Jerusalem and the temple. Matthew interprets what happened in 70—the Roman destruction of Jerusalem and the temple—as God's judgment on those who rejected Jesus.

So also in a detail in Matthew's version of the parable of the wedding banquet (22.1–14). The destruction of the city of those who rejected the invitation to the wedding banquet—which occurs in the midst of gathering people for a wedding feast that remains ready, presumably still hot—is a detail added by Matthew to an earlier form of the parable. For Matthew, it refers to the destruction of Jerusalem, a decade or so before he wrote his gospel.

Most seriously of all with regard to its effects on subsequent history, a text in Matthew assigns primary responsibility for Jesus's death to the Jewish people. To Mark's story of Jesus before Pilate, the Roman governor, he adds an episode. After Pilate concludes that Jesus is innocent, he washes his hands and declares, "I am innocent of this man's blood; see to it yourselves." Then "the people as a whole" take responsibility for Jesus's death: "His blood be *on us and on our children*" (27.24–25; italics added).

This verse is only in Matthew, not in any other gospel. Sometimes called the "blood curse," it is the scriptural basis for the deadly Christian notion that "the Jews" were responsible for the death of Jesus. And not just Jews back then, but also their children—presumably forever. They are "Christ-killers," a phrase used during the frequent and often fatal Christian persecution of Jews for many centuries. In fairness to Matthew, that term does not appear in his gospel. But some of his language did become the scriptural basis for Christian violence against Jews.

Why the Hostility?

Why does the most Jewish of the gospels include such heightened hostility toward Jews? Historical contextualization provides the answer. Matthew wrote during a time of growing conflict between Christian Jews and non-Christian Jews in the last decades of the first century. His community, composed mostly of Jews who had become followers of Jesus as well as perhaps a few Gentiles, was very much affected by it.

The conflict was particularly intense in and near the Jewish homeland, where there were large Jewish communities. Two factors were primarily responsible. The first was the Roman destruction of Jerusalem in the year 70. Not only did the Roman reconquest mean the loss of the temple and the traditional center of Judaism; it also resulted in a sharp decrease in the Jewish population. Many were killed. These circumstances naturally led to a greater emphasis on Jewish identity and the social boundaries that maintained that identity and distinguished Jews from non-Jews.

The second reason was the growing number of Gentile Christians, especially outside of the homeland. Though Gentiles were still a minority of Christians and would remain so for perhaps another century or so, early Christian communities increasingly included Gentiles who had not become Jews. The men remained uncircumcised, and adherence to Jewish food and purity laws was not required.

The more Gentiles there were, the less the movement struck other Jews as a form of Judaism. Rather, it seemed to transgress and transcend the boundaries of Judaism. Its success in the Gentile world began the process of separation from Judaism, the parting of the ways.

The conflict led to what has been called "Jewish persecution of Christians." It began in the decades around the time Matthew wrote. Compared to later Christian persecution of Jews, it was mild and seldom lethal. We have only two stories of Jewish followers of Jesus being killed by other Jews, in both cases by temple authorities: the martyrdom of Stephen (Acts 7) and of James (executed in the early 60s). That is all.

Rather, Jewish persecution of Christian Jews in the decades after 70 took the form of social ostracism. Commonly called "expulsion from the synagogue," it was far more serious than being expelled from a church today. We can always find another one. To be expelled from the synagogue, "the gathering" or "assembly," which is what the word meant, resulted in exclusion from the Jewish community. Though we do not know the details of what this included, presumably it meant no marriage between Christian Jews and non-Christian Jews and perhaps the severing of family and economic relationships. In locations where Jews were the majority of the population, the consequences could have been severe.

This is the historical context in which Matthew wrote. His intensified invective against Jews flows from conflicts between his community of Christian Jews and other Jews in his setting. This realization does not legitimate his language. Rather, it contextualizes it. We can understand why he wrote what he wrote in his contextual circumstances.

To return to Matthew's affirmation of Judaism, Matthew and his community are also claiming that what happened in Jesus is the fulfillment of Judaism, not its negation. The affirmation is made in a setting in which two Jewish groups are making the claim to be the true descendants of Abraham. Matthew's affirmation, without its polemical edge, continues to be true: what happened in Jesus and early Christianity is deeply rooted in Judaism. To separate Christianity from its Jewish roots invariably leads not only to a diminishment of Judaism, but to a serious distortion of Christianity.

The Ending of the Gospel

Recall that Mark's gospel ends with the story of an angel promising the women at the empty tomb that Jesus would appear to his followers in Galilee, though no appearance is narrated. In his last chapter, Matthew adds a story of Jesus appearing to his disciples in Galilee, thereby fulfilling the promise in Mark.

In a significant detail in the last chapter of Matthew, Jesus appears on "the mountain" (28.16). Just as the first block of Jesus's teaching in this gospel happened on "the mountain" (5.1), so the gospel ends on "the mountain." Big things happen on mountains in Matthew and often in the Bible, including the story of Moses on Mt. Sinai in particular.

There Jesus speaks his final words to his followers. The last three sentences of Matthew combine affirmation, imperative, and promise:

> *Affirmation:* "All authority in heaven and on earth has been given to me." This is the familiar New Testament affirmation that Jesus is Lord and all authority has been given to him by God. Note that in Matthew it is the risen Jesus who proclaims this, not the pre-Easter Jesus.

> *Imperative:* "Go therefore and make disciples of all nations, baptizing them in the name of the Father and of the Son and of the Holy Spirit, and teaching them to obey everything that I have commanded you." Commonly known as "the Great Commission," this has been the classic foundation for Christian missionary work, especially since about 1800 and the birth of the modern missionary movement. Its purpose has been to convert "all nations"—the whole world—to Jesus and Christianity.

> In Matthew, "nations" has a more limited meaning. In first-century Judaism and Christianity, it meant "Gentiles." It did not mean then what it means today when we speak of the nations of the world. Rather, Matthew

was affirming the validity of the mission to Gentiles, even though Jesus during his earthly life restricted his mission to Jews and told his followers to do likewise. Now, as the gospel ends, the risen Christ authorizes the mission to non-Jews.

Promise: In the final words of the gospel, the Jesus of Matthew promises his followers: "Remember, I am with you always, to the end of the age." The ending returns to a theme announced at the beginning of Matthew's gospel. In his story of Jesus's birth, he names Jesus as "Emmanuel" (citing Isa. 7.14) and explains that it means "God is with us" (1.23). Now the risen Christ says the same thing about himself in first-person language: "I am with you always."

Jesus is Emmanuel, "God with us." Thus Matthew ends.

THE GOSPEL ACCORDING TO

Matthew

THE GENEALOGY OF JESUS THE MESSIAH

1 An account of the genealogy*a* of Jesus the Messiah,*b* the son of David, the son of Abraham.

2 Abraham was the father of Isaac, and Isaac the father of Jacob, and Jacob the father of Judah and his brothers, ³and Judah the father of Perez and Zerah by Tamar, and Perez the father of Hezron, and Hezron the father of Aram, ⁴and Aram the father of Aminadab, and Aminadab the father of Nahshon, and Nahshon the father of Salmon, ⁵and Salmon the father of Boaz by Rahab, and Boaz the father of Obed by Ruth, and Obed the father of Jesse, ⁶and Jesse the father of King David.

And David was the father of Solomon by the wife of Uriah, ⁷and Solomon the father of Rehoboam, and Rehoboam the father of Abijah, and Abijah the father of Asaph,*c* ⁸and Asaph*c* the father of Jehoshaphat, and Jehoshaphat the father of Joram, and Joram the father of Uzziah, ⁹and Uzziah the father of Jotham, and Jotham the father of Ahaz, and Ahaz the father of Hezekiah, ¹⁰and Hezekiah the father of Manasseh, and Manasseh the father of Amos,*d* and Amos*d* the father of Josiah, ¹¹and Josiah the father of Jechoniah and his brothers, at the time of the deportation to Babylon.

12 And after the deportation to Babylon: Jechoniah was the father of Salathiel, and Salathiel the father of Zerubbabel, ¹³and Zerubbabel the father of Abiud, and Abiud the father of Eliakim, and Eliakim the father of Azor, ¹⁴and Azor the father of Zadok, and Zadok the father of Achim, and Achim the father

---

a Or *birth*   *b* Or *Jesus Christ*   *c* Other ancient authorities read *Asa*   *d* Other ancient authorities read *Amon* of Eliud, [15]and Eliud the father of Eleazar, and Eleazar the father of Matthan, and Matthan the father of Jacob, [16]and Jacob the father of Joseph the husband of Mary, of whom Jesus was born, who is called the Messiah.[a]

17 So all the generations from Abraham to David are fourteen generations; and from David to the deportation to Babylon, fourteen generations; and from the deportation to Babylon to the Messiah,[a] fourteen generations.

THE BIRTH OF JESUS THE MESSIAH

18 Now the birth of Jesus the Messiah[b] took place in this way. When his mother Mary had been engaged to Joseph, but before they lived together, she was found to be with child from the Holy Spirit. [19]Her husband Joseph, being a righteous man and unwilling to expose her to public disgrace, planned to dismiss her quietly. [20]But just when he had resolved to do this, an angel of the Lord appeared to him in a dream and said, "Joseph, son of David, do not be afraid to take Mary as your wife, for the child conceived in her is from the Holy Spirit. [21]She will bear a son, and you are to name him Jesus, for he will save his people from their sins." [22]All this took place to fulfill what had been spoken by the Lord through the prophet:

23 "Look, the virgin shall conceive and bear a son,
 and they shall name him Emmanuel,"
which means, "God is with us." [24]When Joseph awoke from sleep, he did as the angel of the Lord commanded him; he took her as his wife, [25]but had no marital relations with her until she had borne a son;[c] and he named him Jesus.

THE VISIT OF THE WISE MEN

2 In the time of King Herod, after Jesus was born in Bethlehem of Judea, wise men[d] from the East came to Jerusalem, [2]asking, "Where is the child who has been born king of the Jews? For we observed his star at its rising,[e] and have come to pay him homage." [3]When King Herod heard this, he was frightened, and all Jerusalem with him; [4]and calling together all the chief priests and scribes of the people, he inquired of them where the Messiah[a] was to be born. [5]They told him, "In Bethlehem of Judea; for so it has been written by the prophet:

6 'And you, Bethlehem, in the land of Judah,
 are by no means least among the rulers of Judah;
 for from you shall come a ruler
  who is to shepherd[f] my people Israel.'"

---

a Or *the Christ* *b* Or *Jesus Christ* *c* Other ancient authorities read *her firstborn son* *d* Or *astrologers;* Gk *magi* *e* Or *in the East* *f* Or *rule*

7 Then Herod secretly called for the wise men*a* and learned from them the exact time when the star had appeared. [8]Then he sent them to Bethlehem, saying, "Go and search diligently for the child; and when you have found him, bring me word so that I may also go and pay him homage." [9]When they had heard the king, they set out; and there, ahead of them, went the star that they had seen at its rising,*b* until it stopped over the place where the child was. [10]When they saw that the star had stopped,*c* they were overwhelmed with joy. [11]On entering the house, they saw the child with Mary his mother; and they knelt down and paid him homage. Then, opening their treasure chests, they offered him gifts of gold, frankincense, and myrrh. [12]And having been warned in a dream not to return to Herod, they left for their own country by another road.

THE ESCAPE TO EGYPT

13 Now after they had left, an angel of the Lord appeared to Joseph in a dream and said, "Get up, take the child and his mother, and flee to Egypt, and remain there until I tell you; for Herod is about to search for the child, to destroy him." [14]Then Joseph*d* got up, took the child and his mother by night, and went to Egypt, [15]and remained there until the death of Herod. This was to fulfill what had been spoken by the Lord through the prophet, "Out of Egypt I have called my son."

THE MASSACRE OF THE INFANTS

16 When Herod saw that he had been tricked by the wise men,*a* he was infuriated, and he sent and killed all the children in and around Bethlehem who were two years old or under, according to the time that he had learned from the wise men.*a* [17]Then was fulfilled what had been spoken through the prophet Jeremiah:

18 "A voice was heard in Ramah,
        wailing and loud lamentation,
    Rachel weeping for her children;
        she refused to be consoled, because they are no more."

THE RETURN FROM EGYPT

19 When Herod died, an angel of the Lord suddenly appeared in a dream to Joseph in Egypt and said, [20]"Get up, take the child and his mother, and go to the land of Israel, for those who were seeking the child's life are dead." [21]Then Joseph*d* got up, took the child and his mother, and went to the land of Israel.

---

a Or *astrologers;* Gk *magi*   *b* Or *in the East*   *c* Gk *saw the star*   *d* Gk *he*

²²But when he heard that Archelaus was ruling over Judea in place of his father Herod, he was afraid to go there. And after being warned in a dream, he went away to the district of Galilee. ²³There he made his home in a town called Nazareth, so that what had been spoken through the prophets might be fulfilled, "He will be called a Nazorean."

THE PROCLAMATION OF JOHN THE BAPTIST

3 In those days John the Baptist appeared in the wilderness of Judea, proclaiming, ²"Repent, for the kingdom of heaven has come near."ᵃ ³This is the one of whom the prophet Isaiah spoke when he said,

>"The voice of one crying out in the wilderness:
>'Prepare the way of the Lord,
>>make his paths straight.'"

4 Now John wore clothing of camel's hair with a leather belt around his waist, and his food was locusts and wild honey. ⁵Then the people of Jerusalem and all Judea were going out to him, and all the region along the Jordan, ⁶and they were baptized by him in the river Jordan, confessing their sins.

7 But when he saw many Pharisees and Sadducees coming for baptism, he said to them, "You brood of vipers! Who warned you to flee from the wrath to come? ⁸Bear fruit worthy of repentance. ⁹Do not presume to say to yourselves, 'We have Abraham as our ancestor'; for I tell you, God is able from these stones to raise up children to Abraham. ¹⁰Even now the ax is lying at the root of the trees; every tree therefore that does not bear good fruit is cut down and thrown into the fire.

11 "I baptize you withᵇ water for repentance, but one who is more powerful than I is coming after me; I am not worthy to carry his sandals. He will baptize you withᵇ the Holy Spirit and fire. ¹²His winnowing fork is in his hand, and he will clear his threshing floor and will gather his wheat into the granary; but the chaff he will burn with unquenchable fire."

THE BAPTISM OF JESUS

13 Then Jesus came from Galilee to John at the Jordan, to be baptized by him. ¹⁴John would have prevented him, saying, "I need to be baptized by you, and do you come to me?" ¹⁵But Jesus answered him, "Let it be so now; for it is proper for us in this way to fulfill all righteousness." Then he consented. ¹⁶And when Jesus had been baptized, just as he came up from the water, suddenly the heavens were opened to him and he saw the Spirit of God descending like

---

a Or *is at hand*   *b* Or *in*

a dove and alighting on him. [17]And a voice from heaven said, "This is my Son, the Beloved,[a] with whom I am well pleased."

THE TEMPTATION OF JESUS

4 Then Jesus was led up by the Spirit into the wilderness to be tempted by the devil. [2]He fasted forty days and forty nights, and afterwards he was famished. [3]The tempter came and said to him, "If you are the Son of God, command these stones to become loaves of bread." [4]But he answered, "It is written,

'One does not live by bread alone,
>   but by every word that comes from the mouth of God.'"

5 Then the devil took him to the holy city and placed him on the pinnacle of the temple, [6]saying to him, "If you are the Son of God, throw yourself down; for it is written,

'He will command his angels concerning you,'
>   and 'On their hands they will bear you up,
>   so that you will not dash your foot against a stone.'"

7 Jesus said to him, "Again it is written, 'Do not put the Lord your God to the test.'"

8 Again, the devil took him to a very high mountain and showed him all the kingdoms of the world and their splendor; [9]and he said to him, "All these I will give you, if you will fall down and worship me." [10]Jesus said to him, "Away with you, Satan! for it is written,

'Worship the Lord your God,
>   and serve only him.'"

11 Then the devil left him, and suddenly angels came and waited on him.

JESUS BEGINS HIS MINISTRY IN GALILEE

12 Now when Jesus[b] heard that John had been arrested, he withdrew to Galilee. [13]He left Nazareth and made his home in Capernaum by the sea, in the territory of Zebulun and Naphtali, [14]so that what had been spoken through the prophet Isaiah might be fulfilled:

15 "Land of Zebulun, land of Naphtali,
>   on the road by the sea, across the Jordan, Galilee of the Gentiles—
16 the people who sat in darkness
>   have seen a great light,
> and for those who sat in the region and shadow of death
>   light has dawned."

---

a Or my beloved Son   b Gk he

17 From that time Jesus began to proclaim, "Repent, for the kingdom of heaven has come near."[a]

JESUS CALLS THE FIRST DISCIPLES

18 As he walked by the Sea of Galilee, he saw two brothers, Simon, who is called Peter, and Andrew his brother, casting a net into the sea—for they were fishermen. [19]And he said to them, "Follow me, and I will make you fish for people." [20]Immediately they left their nets and followed him. [21]As he went from there, he saw two other brothers, James son of Zebedee and his brother John, in the boat with their father Zebedee, mending their nets, and he called them. [22]Immediately they left the boat and their father, and followed him.

JESUS MINISTERS TO CROWDS OF PEOPLE

23 Jesus[b] went throughout Galilee, teaching in their synagogues and proclaiming the good news[c] of the kingdom and curing every disease and every sickness among the people. [24]So his fame spread throughout all Syria, and they brought to him all the sick, those who were afflicted with various diseases and pains, demoniacs, epileptics, and paralytics, and he cured them. [25]And great crowds followed him from Galilee, the Decapolis, Jerusalem, Judea, and from beyond the Jordan.

THE BEATITUDES

5 When Jesus[d] saw the crowds, he went up the mountain; and after he sat down, his disciples came to him. [2]Then he began to speak, and taught them, saying:

3 "Blessed are the poor in spirit, for theirs is the kingdom of heaven.

4 "Blessed are those who mourn, for they will be comforted.

5 "Blessed are the meek, for they will inherit the earth.

6 "Blessed are those who hunger and thirst for righteousness, for they will be filled.

7 "Blessed are the merciful, for they will receive mercy.

8 "Blessed are the pure in heart, for they will see God.

9 "Blessed are the peacemakers, for they will be called children of God.

10 "Blessed are those who are persecuted for righteousness' sake, for theirs is the kingdom of heaven.

11 "Blessed are you when people revile you and persecute you and utter all kinds of evil against you falsely[e] on my account. [12]Rejoice and be glad, for your

---

a Or *is at hand*   *b* Gk *He*   *c* Gk *gospel*   *d* Gk *he*   *e* Other ancient authorities lack *falsely* reward is great in heaven, for in the same way they persecuted the prophets who were before you.

SALT AND LIGHT

13 "You are the salt of the earth; but if salt has lost its taste, how can its salt-iness be restored? It is no longer good for anything, but is thrown out and trampled under foot.

14 "You are the light of the world. A city built on a hill cannot be hid. [15]No one after lighting a lamp puts it under the bushel basket, but on the lampstand, and it gives light to all in the house. [16]In the same way, let your light shine before others, so that they may see your good works and give glory to your Father in heaven.

THE LAW AND THE PROPHETS

17 "Do not think that I have come to abolish the law or the prophets; I have come not to abolish but to fulfill. [18]For truly I tell you, until heaven and earth pass away, not one letter,[a] not one stroke of a letter, will pass from the law until all is accomplished. [19]Therefore, whoever breaks[b] one of the least of these com-mandments, and teaches others to do the same, will be called least in the king-dom of heaven; but whoever does them and teaches them will be called great in the kingdom of heaven. [20]For I tell you, unless your righteousness exceeds that of the scribes and Pharisees, you will never enter the kingdom of heaven.

CONCERNING ANGER

21 "You have heard that it was said to those of ancient times, 'You shall not murder'; and 'whoever murders shall be liable to judgment.' [22]But I say to you that if you are angry with a brother or sister,[c] you will be liable to judgment; and if you insult[d] a brother or sister,[e] you will be liable to the council; and if you say, 'You fool,' you will be liable to the hell[f] of fire. [23]So when you are of-fering your gift at the altar, if you remember that your brother or sister[g] has something against you, [24]leave your gift there before the altar and go; first be reconciled to your brother or sister,[g] and then come and offer your gift. [25]Come to terms quickly with your accuser while you are on the way to court[h] with him, or your accuser may hand you over to the judge, and the judge to the guard, and you will be thrown into prison. [26]Truly I tell you, you will never get out until you have paid the last penny.

---

a Gk *one iota*   b Or *annuls*   c Gk *a brother;* other ancient authorities add *without cause*   d Gk *say Raca to* (an obscure term of abuse)   e Gk *a brother*   f Gk *Gehenna*   g Gk *your brother*   h Gk lacks *to court*

CONCERNING ADULTERY

27 "You have heard that it was said, 'You shall not commit adultery.' [28]But I say to you that everyone who looks at a woman with lust has already committed adultery with her in his heart. [29]If your right eye causes you to sin, tear it out and throw it away; it is better for you to lose one of your members than for your whole body to be thrown into hell.[a] [30]And if your right hand causes you to sin, cut it off and throw it away; it is better for you to lose one of your members than for your whole body to go into hell.[a]

CONCERNING DIVORCE

31 "It was also said, 'Whoever divorces his wife, let him give her a certificate of divorce.' [32]But I say to you that anyone who divorces his wife, except on the ground of unchastity, causes her to commit adultery; and whoever marries a divorced woman commits adultery.

CONCERNING OATHS

33 "Again, you have heard that it was said to those of ancient times, 'You shall not swear falsely, but carry out the vows you have made to the Lord.' [34]But I say to you, Do not swear at all, either by heaven, for it is the throne of God, [35]or by the earth, for it is his footstool, or by Jerusalem, for it is the city of the great King. [36]And do not swear by your head, for you cannot make one hair white or black. [37]Let your word be 'Yes, Yes' or 'No, No'; anything more than this comes from the evil one.[b]

CONCERNING RETALIATION

38 "You have heard that it was said, 'An eye for an eye and a tooth for a tooth.' [39]But I say to you, Do not resist an evildoer. But if anyone strikes you on the right cheek, turn the other also; [40]and if anyone wants to sue you and take your coat, give your cloak as well; [41]and if anyone forces you to go one mile, go also the second mile. [42]Give to everyone who begs from you, and do not refuse anyone who wants to borrow from you.

LOVE FOR ENEMIES

43 "You have heard that it was said, 'You shall love your neighbor and hate your enemy.' [44]But I say to you, Love your enemies and pray for those who persecute you, [45]so that you may be children of your Father in heaven; for he makes

---

a Gk *Gehenna*   *b* Or *evil*

his sun rise on the evil and on the good, and sends rain on the righteous and on the unrighteous. ⁴⁶For if you love those who love you, what reward do you have? Do not even the tax collectors do the same? ⁴⁷And if you greet only your brothers and sisters,ᵃ what more are you doing than others? Do not even the Gentiles do the same? ⁴⁸Be perfect, therefore, as your heavenly Father is perfect.

CONCERNING ALMSGIVING

6 "Beware of practicing your piety before others in order to be seen by them; for then you have no reward from your Father in heaven.

2 "So whenever you give alms, do not sound a trumpet before you, as the hypocrites do in the synagogues and in the streets, so that they may be praised by others. Truly I tell you, they have received their reward. ³But when you give alms, do not let your left hand know what your right hand is doing, ⁴so that your alms may be done in secret; and your Father who sees in secret will reward you.ᵇ

CONCERNING PRAYER

5 "And whenever you pray, do not be like the hypocrites; for they love to stand and pray in the synagogues and at the street corners, so that they may be seen by others. Truly I tell you, they have received their reward. ⁶But whenever you pray, go into your room and shut the door and pray to your Father who is in secret; and your Father who sees in secret will reward you.ᵇ

7 "When you are praying, do not heap up empty phrases as the Gentiles do; for they think that they will be heard because of their many words. ⁸Do not be like them, for your Father knows what you need before you ask him.

9 "Pray then in this way:

Our Father in heaven,
    hallowed be your name.
10 Your kingdom come.
    Your will be done,
        on earth as it is in heaven.
11 Give us this day our daily bread.ᶜ
12 And forgive us our debts,
        as we also have forgiven our debtors.
13 And do not bring us to the time of trial,ᵈ
        but rescue us from the evil one.ᵉ

---

a Gk *your brothers* b Other ancient authorities add *openly* c Or *our bread for tomorrow* d Or *us into temptation* e Or *from evil*. Other ancient authorities add, in some form, *For the kingdom and the power and the glory are yours forever. Amen.*

14 For if you forgive others their trespasses, your heavenly Father will also forgive you; [15]but if you do not forgive others, neither will your Father forgive your trespasses.

CONCERNING FASTING

16 "And whenever you fast, do not look dismal, like the hypocrites, for they disfigure their faces so as to show others that they are fasting. Truly I tell you, they have received their reward. [17]But when you fast, put oil on your head and wash your face, [18]so that your fasting may be seen not by others but by your Father who is in secret; and your Father who sees in secret will reward you.[a]

CONCERNING TREASURES

19 "Do not store up for yourselves treasures on earth, where moth and rust[b] consume and where thieves break in and steal; [20]but store up for yourselves treasures in heaven, where neither moth nor rust[b] consumes and where thieves do not break in and steal. [21]For where your treasure is, there your heart will be also.

THE SOUND EYE

22 "The eye is the lamp of the body. So, if your eye is healthy, your whole body will be full of light; [23]but if your eye is unhealthy, your whole body will be full of darkness. If then the light in you is darkness, how great is the darkness!

SERVING TWO MASTERS

24 "No one can serve two masters; for a slave will either hate the one and love the other, or be devoted to the one and despise the other. You cannot serve God and wealth.[c]

DO NOT WORRY

25 "Therefore I tell you, do not worry about your life, what you will eat or what you will drink,[d] or about your body, what you will wear. Is not life more than food, and the body more than clothing? [26]Look at the birds of the air; they neither sow nor reap nor gather into barns, and yet your heavenly Father feeds them. Are you not of more value than they? [27]And can any of you by worrying add a single hour to your span of life?[e] [28]And why do you worry about clothing? Consider the lilies of the field, how they grow; they neither toil nor spin,

---

a Other ancient authorities add *openly*   b Gk *eating*   c Gk *mammon*   d Other ancient authorities lack *or what you will drink*
e Or *add one cubit to your height*

²⁹yet I tell you, even Solomon in all his glory was not clothed like one of these. ³⁰But if God so clothes the grass of the field, which is alive today and tomorrow is thrown into the oven, will he not much more clothe you—you of little faith? ³¹Therefore do not worry, saying, 'What will we eat?' or 'What will we drink?' or 'What will we wear?' ³²For it is the Gentiles who strive for all these things; and indeed your heavenly Father knows that you need all these things. ³³But strive first for the kingdom of God*a* and his*b* righteousness, and all these things will be given to you as well.

34 "So do not worry about tomorrow, for tomorrow will bring worries of its own. Today's trouble is enough for today.

JUDGING OTHERS

7 "Do not judge, so that you may not be judged. ²For with the judgment you make you will be judged, and the measure you give will be the measure you get. ³Why do you see the speck in your neighbor's*c* eye, but do not notice the log in your own eye? ⁴Or how can you say to your neighbor,*d* 'Let me take the speck out of your eye,' while the log is in your own eye? ⁵You hypocrite, first take the log out of your own eye, and then you will see clearly to take the speck out of your neighbor's*c* eye.

PROFANING THE HOLY

6 "Do not give what is holy to dogs; and do not throw your pearls before swine, or they will trample them under foot and turn and maul you.

ASK, SEARCH, KNOCK

7 "Ask, and it will be given you; search, and you will find; knock, and the door will be opened for you. ⁸For everyone who asks receives, and everyone who searches finds, and for everyone who knocks, the door will be opened. ⁹Is there anyone among you who, if your child asks for bread, will give a stone? ¹⁰Or if the child asks for a fish, will give a snake? ¹¹If you then, who are evil, know how to give good gifts to your children, how much more will your Father in heaven give good things to those who ask him!

THE GOLDEN RULE

12 "In everything do to others as you would have them do to you; for this is the law and the prophets.

---

a Other ancient authorities lack *of God*　*b* Or *its*　*c* Gk *brother's*　*d* Gk *brother*

THE NARROW GATE

13 "Enter through the narrow gate; for the gate is wide and the road is easy*a* that leads to destruction, and there are many who take it. ¹⁴For the gate is narrow and the road is hard that leads to life, and there are few who find it.

A TREE AND ITS FRUIT

15 "Beware of false prophets, who come to you in sheep's clothing but inwardly are ravenous wolves. ¹⁶You will know them by their fruits. Are grapes gathered from thorns, or figs from thistles? ¹⁷In the same way, every good tree bears good fruit, but the bad tree bears bad fruit. ¹⁸A good tree cannot bear bad fruit, nor can a bad tree bear good fruit. ¹⁹Every tree that does not bear good fruit is cut down and thrown into the fire. ²⁰Thus you will know them by their fruits.

CONCERNING SELF-DECEPTION

21 "Not everyone who says to me, 'Lord, Lord,' will enter the kingdom of heaven, but only the one who does the will of my Father in heaven. ²²On that day many will say to me, 'Lord, Lord, did we not prophesy in your name, and cast out demons in your name, and do many deeds of power in your name?' ²³Then I will declare to them, 'I never knew you; go away from me, you evildoers.'

HEARERS AND DOERS

24 "Everyone then who hears these words of mine and acts on them will be like a wise man who built his house on rock. ²⁵The rain fell, the floods came, and the winds blew and beat on that house, but it did not fall, because it had been founded on rock. ²⁶And everyone who hears these words of mine and does not act on them will be like a foolish man who built his house on sand. ²⁷The rain fell, and the floods came, and the winds blew and beat against that house, and it fell—and great was its fall!"

28 Now when Jesus had finished saying these things, the crowds were astounded at his teaching, ²⁹for he taught them as one having authority, and not as their scribes.

JESUS CLEANSES A LEPER

8 When Jesus*b* had come down from the mountain, great crowds followed him; ²and there was a leper*c* who came to him and knelt before him, saying,

---

a Other ancient authorities read *for the road is wide and easy*   *b* Gk *he*   *c* The terms *leper* and *leprosy* can refer to several diseases

"Lord, if you choose, you can make me clean." [3]He stretched out his hand and touched him, saying, "I do choose. Be made clean!" Immediately his leprosy[a] was cleansed. [4]Then Jesus said to him, "See that you say nothing to anyone; but go, show yourself to the priest, and offer the gift that Moses commanded, as a testimony to them."

JESUS HEALS A CENTURION'S SERVANT

5 When he entered Capernaum, a centurion came to him, appealing to him [6]and saying, "Lord, my servant is lying at home paralyzed, in terrible distress." [7]And he said to him, "I will come and cure him." [8]The centurion answered, "Lord, I am not worthy to have you come under my roof; but only speak the word, and my servant will be healed. [9]For I also am a man under authority, with soldiers under me; and I say to one, 'Go,' and he goes, and to another, 'Come,' and he comes, and to my slave, 'Do this,' and the slave does it." [10]When Jesus heard him, he was amazed and said to those who followed him, "Truly I tell you, in no one[b] in Israel have I found such faith. [11]I tell you, many will come from east and west and will eat with Abraham and Isaac and Jacob in the kingdom of heaven, [12]while the heirs of the kingdom will be thrown into the outer darkness, where there will be weeping and gnashing of teeth." [13]And to the centurion Jesus said, "Go; let it be done for you according to your faith." And the servant was healed in that hour.

JESUS HEALS MANY AT PETER'S HOUSE

14 When Jesus entered Peter's house, he saw his mother-in-law lying in bed with a fever; [15]he touched her hand, and the fever left her, and she got up and began to serve him. [16]That evening they brought to him many who were possessed with demons; and he cast out the spirits with a word, and cured all who were sick. [17]This was to fulfill what had been spoken through the prophet Isaiah, "He took our infirmities and bore our diseases."

WOULD-BE FOLLOWERS OF JESUS

18 Now when Jesus saw great crowds around him, he gave orders to go over to the other side. [19]A scribe then approached and said, "Teacher, I will follow you wherever you go." [20]And Jesus said to him, "Foxes have holes, and birds of the air have nests; but the Son of Man has nowhere to lay his head." [21]Another of his disciples said to him, "Lord, first let me go and bury my father." [22]But Jesus said to him, "Follow me, and let the dead bury their own dead."

---

a The terms *leper* and *leprosy* can refer to several diseases   b Other ancient authorities read *Truly I tell you, not even*

JESUS STILLS THE STORM

23 And when he got into the boat, his disciples followed him. [24]A windstorm arose on the sea, so great that the boat was being swamped by the waves; but he was asleep. [25]And they went and woke him up, saying, "Lord, save us! We are perishing!" [26]And he said to them, "Why are you afraid, you of little faith?" Then he got up and rebuked the winds and the sea; and there was a dead calm. [27]They were amazed, saying, "What sort of man is this, that even the winds and the sea obey him?"

JESUS HEALS THE GADARENE DEMONIACS

28 When he came to the other side, to the country of the Gadarenes,[a] two demoniacs coming out of the tombs met him. They were so fierce that no one could pass that way. [29]Suddenly they shouted, "What have you to do with us, Son of God? Have you come here to torment us before the time?" [30]Now a large herd of swine was feeding at some distance from them. [31]The demons begged him, "If you cast us out, send us into the herd of swine." [32]And he said to them, "Go!" So they came out and entered the swine; and suddenly, the whole herd rushed down the steep bank into the sea and perished in the water. [33]The swineherds ran off, and on going into the town, they told the whole story about what had happened to the demoniacs. [34]Then the whole town came out to meet Jesus; and when they saw him, they begged him to leave their neighborhood.

9 And after getting into a boat he crossed the sea and came to his own town.

JESUS HEALS A PARALYTIC

2 And just then some people were carrying a paralyzed man lying on a bed. When Jesus saw their faith, he said to the paralytic, "Take heart, son; your sins are forgiven." [3]Then some of the scribes said to themselves, "This man is blaspheming." [4]But Jesus, perceiving their thoughts, said, "Why do you think evil in your hearts? [5]For which is easier, to say, 'Your sins are forgiven,' or to say, 'Stand up and walk'? [6]But so that you may know that the Son of Man has authority on earth to forgive sins"—he then said to the paralytic—"Stand up, take your bed and go to your home." [7]And he stood up and went to his home. [8]When the crowds saw it, they were filled with awe, and they glorified God, who had given such authority to human beings.

---

a Other ancient authorities read *Gergesenes;* others, *Gerasenes*

THE CALL OF MATTHEW

9 As Jesus was walking along, he saw a man called Matthew sitting at the tax booth; and he said to him, "Follow me." And he got up and followed him.

10 And as he sat at dinner*a* in the house, many tax collectors and sinners came and were sitting*b* with him and his disciples. [11]When the Pharisees saw this, they said to his disciples, "Why does your teacher eat with tax collectors and sinners?" [12]But when he heard this, he said, "Those who are well have no need of a physician, but those who are sick. [13]Go and learn what this means, 'I desire mercy, not sacrifice.' For I have come to call not the righteous but sinners."

THE QUESTION ABOUT FASTING

14 Then the disciples of John came to him, saying, "Why do we and the Pharisees fast often,*c* but your disciples do not fast?" [15]And Jesus said to them, "The wedding guests cannot mourn as long as the bridegroom is with them, can they? The days will come when the bridegroom is taken away from them, and then they will fast. [16]No one sews a piece of unshrunk cloth on an old cloak, for the patch pulls away from the cloak, and a worse tear is made. [17]Neither is new wine put into old wineskins; otherwise, the skins burst, and the wine is spilled, and the skins are destroyed; but new wine is put into fresh wineskins, and so both are preserved."

A GIRL RESTORED TO LIFE AND A WOMAN HEALED

18 While he was saying these things to them, suddenly a leader of the synagogue*d* came in and knelt before him, saying, "My daughter has just died; but come and lay your hand on her, and she will live." [19]And Jesus got up and followed him, with his disciples. [20]Then suddenly a woman who had been suffering from hemorrhages for twelve years came up behind him and touched the fringe of his cloak, [21]for she said to herself, "If I only touch his cloak, I will be made well." [22]Jesus turned, and seeing her he said, "Take heart, daughter; your faith has made you well." And instantly the woman was made well. [23]When Jesus came to the leader's house and saw the flute players and the crowd making a commotion, [24]he said, "Go away; for the girl is not dead but sleeping." And they laughed at him. [25]But when the crowd had been put outside, he went in and took her by the hand, and the girl got up. [26]And the report of this spread throughout that district.

---

a Gk *reclined*   *b* Gk *were reclining*   *c* Other ancient authorities lack *often*   *d* Gk lacks *of the synagogue*

JESUS HEALS TWO BLIND MEN

27 As Jesus went on from there, two blind men followed him, crying loudly, "Have mercy on us, Son of David!" [28]When he entered the house, the blind men came to him; and Jesus said to them, "Do you believe that I am able to do this?" They said to him, "Yes, Lord." [29]Then he touched their eyes and said, "According to your faith let it be done to you." [30]And their eyes were opened. Then Jesus sternly ordered them, "See that no one knows of this." [31]But they went away and spread the news about him throughout that district.

JESUS HEALS ONE WHO WAS MUTE

32 After they had gone away, a demoniac who was mute was brought to him. [33]And when the demon had been cast out, the one who had been mute spoke; and the crowds were amazed and said, "Never has anything like this been seen in Israel." [34]But the Pharisees said, "By the ruler of the demons he casts out the demons."[a]

THE HARVEST IS GREAT, THE LABORERS FEW

35 Then Jesus went about all the cities and villages, teaching in their synagogues, and proclaiming the good news of the kingdom, and curing every disease and every sickness. [36]When he saw the crowds, he had compassion for them, because they were harassed and helpless, like sheep without a shepherd. [37]Then he said to his disciples, "The harvest is plentiful, but the laborers are few; [38]therefore ask the Lord of the harvest to send out laborers into his harvest."

THE TWELVE APOSTLES

10 Then Jesus[b] summoned his twelve disciples and gave them authority over unclean spirits, to cast them out, and to cure every disease and every sickness. [2]These are the names of the twelve apostles: first, Simon, also known as Peter, and his brother Andrew; James son of Zebedee, and his brother John; [3]Philip and Bartholomew; Thomas and Matthew the tax collector; James son of Alphaeus, and Thaddaeus;[c] [4]Simon the Cananaean, and Judas Iscariot, the one who betrayed him.

THE MISSION OF THE TWELVE

5 These twelve Jesus sent out with the following instructions: "Go nowhere among the Gentiles, and enter no town of the Samaritans, [6]but go rather to

---

a Other ancient authorities lack this verse   *b* Gk *he*   *c* Other ancient authorities read *Lebbaeus,* or *Lebbaeus called Thaddaeus* the lost sheep of the house of Israel. [7]As you go, proclaim the good news, 'The kingdom of heaven has come near.'[a] [8]Cure the sick, raise the dead, cleanse the lepers,[b] cast out demons. You received without payment; give without payment. [9]Take no gold, or silver, or copper in your belts, [10]no bag for your journey, or two tunics, or sandals, or a staff; for laborers deserve their food. [11]Whatever town or village you enter, find out who in it is worthy, and stay there until you leave. [12]As you enter the house, greet it. [13]If the house is worthy, let your peace come upon it; but if it is not worthy, let your peace return to you. [14]If anyone will not welcome you or listen to your words, shake off the dust from your feet as you leave that house or town. [15]Truly I tell you, it will be more tolerable for the land of Sodom and Gomorrah on the day of judgment than for that town.

COMING PERSECUTIONS

16 "See, I am sending you out like sheep into the midst of wolves; so be wise as serpents and innocent as doves. [17]Beware of them, for they will hand you over to councils and flog you in their synagogues; [18]and you will be dragged before governors and kings because of me, as a testimony to them and the Gentiles. [19]When they hand you over, do not worry about how you are to speak or what you are to say; for what you are to say will be given to you at that time; [20]for it is not you who speak, but the Spirit of your Father speaking through you. [21]Brother will betray brother to death, and a father his child, and children will rise against parents and have them put to death; [22]and you will be hated by all because of my name. But the one who endures to the end will be saved. [23]When they persecute you in one town, flee to the next; for truly I tell you, you will not have gone through all the towns of Israel before the Son of Man comes.

24 "A disciple is not above the teacher, nor a slave above the master; [25]it is enough for the disciple to be like the teacher, and the slave like the master. If they have called the master of the house Beelzebul, how much more will they malign those of his household!

WHOM TO FEAR

26 "So have no fear of them; for nothing is covered up that will not be uncovered, and nothing secret that will not become known. [27]What I say to you in the dark, tell in the light; and what you hear whispered, proclaim from the housetops. [28]Do not fear those who kill the body but cannot kill the soul; rather fear him who can destroy both soul and body in hell.[c] [29]Are not two sparrows

---

a Or *is at hand*   *b* The terms *leper* and *leprosy* can refer to several diseases   *c* Gk *Gehenna* sold for a penny? Yet not one of them will fall to the ground apart from your Father. ³⁰And even the hairs of your head are all counted. ³¹So do not be afraid; you are of more value than many sparrows.

32 "Everyone therefore who acknowledges me before others, I also will acknowledge before my Father in heaven; ³³but whoever denies me before others, I also will deny before my Father in heaven.

NOT PEACE, BUT A SWORD

34 "Do not think that I have come to bring peace to the earth; I have not come to bring peace, but a sword.

> 35 For I have come to set a man against his father,
> and a daughter against her mother,
> and a daughter-in-law against her mother-in-law;
> 36 and one's foes will be members of one's own household.

37 Whoever loves father or mother more than me is not worthy of me; and whoever loves son or daughter more than me is not worthy of me; ³⁸and whoever does not take up the cross and follow me is not worthy of me. ³⁹Those who find their life will lose it, and those who lose their life for my sake will find it.

REWARDS

40 "Whoever welcomes you welcomes me, and whoever welcomes me welcomes the one who sent me. ⁴¹Whoever welcomes a prophet in the name of a prophet will receive a prophet's reward; and whoever welcomes a righteous person in the name of a righteous person will receive the reward of the righteous; ⁴²and whoever gives even a cup of cold water to one of these little ones in the name of a disciple—truly I tell you, none of these will lose their reward."

11 Now when Jesus had finished instructing his twelve disciples, he went on from there to teach and proclaim his message in their cities.

MESSENGERS FROM JOHN THE BAPTIST

2 When John heard in prison what the Messiah*a* was doing, he sent word by his*b* disciples ³and said to him, "Are you the one who is to come, or are we to wait for another?" ⁴Jesus answered them, "Go and tell John what you hear and see: ⁵the blind receive their sight, the lame walk, the lepers*c* are cleansed, the deaf hear, the dead are raised, and the poor have good news brought to them. ⁶And blessed is anyone who takes no offense at me."

---

a Or *the Christ* *b* Other ancient authorities read *two of his* *c* The terms *leper* and *leprosy* can refer to several diseases

JESUS PRAISES JOHN THE BAPTIST

7 As they went away, Jesus began to speak to the crowds about John: "What did you go out into the wilderness to look at? A reed shaken by the wind? ⁸What then did you go out to see? Someone*ᵃ* dressed in soft robes? Look, those who wear soft robes are in royal palaces. ⁹What then did you go out to see? A prophet?*ᵇ* Yes, I tell you, and more than a prophet. ¹⁰This is the one about whom it is written,

> 'See, I am sending my messenger ahead of you,
> who will prepare your way before you.'

11 Truly I tell you, among those born of women no one has arisen greater than John the Baptist; yet the least in the kingdom of heaven is greater than he. ¹²From the days of John the Baptist until now the kingdom of heaven has suffered violence,*ᶜ* and the violent take it by force. ¹³For all the prophets and the law prophesied until John came; ¹⁴and if you are willing to accept it, he is Elijah who is to come. ¹⁵Let anyone with ears*ᵈ* listen!

16 "But to what will I compare this generation? It is like children sitting in the marketplaces and calling to one another,

> 17 'We played the flute for you, and you did not dance;
> we wailed, and you did not mourn.'

18 For John came neither eating nor drinking, and they say, 'He has a demon'; ¹⁹the Son of Man came eating and drinking, and they say, 'Look, a glutton and a drunkard, a friend of tax collectors and sinners!' Yet wisdom is vindicated by her deeds."*ᵉ*

WOES TO UNREPENTANT CITIES

20 Then he began to reproach the cities in which most of his deeds of power had been done, because they did not repent. ²¹"Woe to you, Chorazin! Woe to you, Bethsaida! For if the deeds of power done in you had been done in Tyre and Sidon, they would have repented long ago in sackcloth and ashes. ²²But I tell you, on the day of judgment it will be more tolerable for Tyre and Sidon than for you. ²³And you, Capernaum,

> will you be exalted to heaven?
> No, you will be brought down to Hades.

For if the deeds of power done in you had been done in Sodom, it would have remained until this day. ²⁴But I tell you that on the day of judgment it will be more tolerable for the land of Sodom than for you."

---

a Or Why then did you go out? To see someone   b Other ancient authorities read Why then did you go out? To see a prophet?
c Or has been coming violently   d Other ancient authorities add to hear   e Other ancient authorities read children

JESUS THANKS HIS FATHER

25 At that time Jesus said, "I thank*a* you, Father, Lord of heaven and earth, because you have hidden these things from the wise and the intelligent and have revealed them to infants; ²⁶yes, Father, for such was your gracious will.*b* ²⁷All things have been handed over to me by my Father; and no one knows the Son except the Father, and no one knows the Father except the Son and anyone to whom the Son chooses to reveal him.

28 "Come to me, all you that are weary and are carrying heavy burdens, and I will give you rest. ²⁹Take my yoke upon you, and learn from me; for I am gentle and humble in heart, and you will find rest for your souls. ³⁰For my yoke is easy, and my burden is light."

PLUCKING GRAIN ON THE SABBATH

12 At that time Jesus went through the grainfields on the sabbath; his disciples were hungry, and they began to pluck heads of grain and to eat. ²When the Pharisees saw it, they said to him, "Look, your disciples are doing what is not lawful to do on the sabbath." ³He said to them, "Have you not read what David did when he and his companions were hungry? ⁴He entered the house of God and ate the bread of the Presence, which it was not lawful for him or his companions to eat, but only for the priests. ⁵Or have you not read in the law that on the sabbath the priests in the temple break the sabbath and yet are guiltless? ⁶I tell you, something greater than the temple is here. ⁷But if you had known what this means, 'I desire mercy and not sacrifice,' you would not have condemned the guiltless. ⁸For the Son of Man is lord of the sabbath."

THE MAN WITH A WITHERED HAND

9 He left that place and entered their synagogue; ¹⁰a man was there with a withered hand, and they asked him, "Is it lawful to cure on the sabbath?" so that they might accuse him. ¹¹He said to them, "Suppose one of you has only one sheep and it falls into a pit on the sabbath; will you not lay hold of it and lift it out? ¹²How much more valuable is a human being than a sheep! So it is lawful to do good on the sabbath." ¹³Then he said to the man, "Stretch out your hand." He stretched it out, and it was restored, as sound as the other. ¹⁴But the Pharisees went out and conspired against him, how to destroy him.

---

a Or *praise*   *b* Or *for so it was well-pleasing in your sight*

GOD'S CHOSEN SERVANT

15 When Jesus became aware of this, he departed. Many crowds*a* followed him, and he cured all of them, ¹⁶and he ordered them not to make him known. ¹⁷This was to fulfill what had been spoken through the prophet Isaiah:

18 "Here is my servant, whom I have chosen,
    my beloved, with whom my soul is well pleased.
  I will put my Spirit upon him,
    and he will proclaim justice to the Gentiles.
19 He will not wrangle or cry aloud,
    nor will anyone hear his voice in the streets.
20 He will not break a bruised reed
    or quench a smoldering wick
  until he brings justice to victory.
    21 And in his name the Gentiles will hope."

JESUS AND BEELZEBUL

22 Then they brought to him a demoniac who was blind and mute; and he cured him, so that the one who had been mute could speak and see. ²³All the crowds were amazed and said, "Can this be the Son of David?" ²⁴But when the Pharisees heard it, they said, "It is only by Beelzebul, the ruler of the demons, that this fellow casts out the demons." ²⁵He knew what they were thinking and said to them, "Every kingdom divided against itself is laid waste, and no city or house divided against itself will stand. ²⁶If Satan casts out Satan, he is divided against himself; how then will his kingdom stand? ²⁷If I cast out demons by Beelzebul, by whom do your own exorcists*b* cast them out? Therefore they will be your judges. ²⁸But if it is by the Spirit of God that I cast out demons, then the kingdom of God has come to you. ²⁹Or how can one enter a strong man's house and plunder his property, without first tying up the strong man? Then indeed the house can be plundered. ³⁰Whoever is not with me is against me, and whoever does not gather with me scatters. ³¹Therefore I tell you, people will be forgiven for every sin and blasphemy, but blasphemy against the Spirit will not be forgiven. ³²Whoever speaks a word against the Son of Man will be forgiven, but whoever speaks against the Holy Spirit will not be forgiven, either in this age or in the age to come.

---

a Other ancient authorities lack *crowds* *b* Gk *sons*

A TREE AND ITS FRUIT

33 "Either make the tree good, and its fruit good; or make the tree bad, and its fruit bad; for the tree is known by its fruit. [34]You brood of vipers! How can you speak good things, when you are evil? For out of the abundance of the heart the mouth speaks. [35]The good person brings good things out of a good treasure, and the evil person brings evil things out of an evil treasure. [36]I tell you, on the day of judgment you will have to give an account for every careless word you utter; [37]for by your words you will be justified, and by your words you will be condemned."

THE SIGN OF JONAH

38 Then some of the scribes and Pharisees said to him, "Teacher, we wish to see a sign from you." [39]But he answered them, "An evil and adulterous generation asks for a sign, but no sign will be given to it except the sign of the prophet Jonah. [40]For just as Jonah was three days and three nights in the belly of the sea monster, so for three days and three nights the Son of Man will be in the heart of the earth. [41]The people of Nineveh will rise up at the judgment with this generation and condemn it, because they repented at the proclamation of Jonah, and see, something greater than Jonah is here! [42]The queen of the South will rise up at the judgment with this generation and condemn it, because she came from the ends of the earth to listen to the wisdom of Solomon, and see, something greater than Solomon is here!

THE RETURN OF THE UNCLEAN SPIRIT

43 "When the unclean spirit has gone out of a person, it wanders through waterless regions looking for a resting place, but it finds none. [44]Then it says, 'I will return to my house from which I came.' When it comes, it finds it empty, swept, and put in order. [45]Then it goes and brings along seven other spirits more evil than itself, and they enter and live there; and the last state of that person is worse than the first. So will it be also with this evil generation."

THE TRUE KINDRED OF JESUS

46 While he was still speaking to the crowds, his mother and his brothers were standing outside, wanting to speak to him. [47]Someone told him, "Look, your mother and your brothers are standing outside, wanting to speak to you."[a]

---

a Other ancient authorities lack verse 47

⁴⁸But to the one who had told him this, Jesus*ᵃ* replied, "Who is my mother, and who are my brothers?" ⁴⁹And pointing to his disciples, he said, "Here are my mother and my brothers! ⁵⁰For whoever does the will of my Father in heaven is my brother and sister and mother."

THE PARABLE OF THE SOWER

13 That same day Jesus went out of the house and sat beside the sea. ²Such great crowds gathered around him that he got into a boat and sat there, while the whole crowd stood on the beach. ³And he told them many things in parables, saying: "Listen! A sower went out to sow. ⁴And as he sowed, some seeds fell on the path, and the birds came and ate them up. ⁵Other seeds fell on rocky ground, where they did not have much soil, and they sprang up quickly, since they had no depth of soil. ⁶But when the sun rose, they were scorched; and since they had no root, they withered away. ⁷Other seeds fell among thorns, and the thorns grew up and choked them. ⁸Other seeds fell on good soil and brought forth grain, some a hundredfold, some sixty, some thirty. ⁹Let anyone with ears*ᵇ* listen!"

THE PURPOSE OF THE PARABLES

10 Then the disciples came and asked him, "Why do you speak to them in parables?" ¹¹He answered, "To you it has been given to know the secrets*ᶜ* of the kingdom of heaven, but to them it has not been given. ¹²For to those who have, more will be given, and they will have an abundance; but from those who have nothing, even what they have will be taken away. ¹³The reason I speak to them in parables is that 'seeing they do not perceive, and hearing they do not listen, nor do they understand.' ¹⁴With them indeed is fulfilled the prophecy of Isaiah that says:

> 'You will indeed listen, but never understand,
>> and you will indeed look, but never perceive.
> 15 For this people's heart has grown dull,
>> and their ears are hard of hearing,
>>> and they have shut their eyes;
>>> so that they might not look with their eyes,
>> and listen with their ears,
> and understand with their heart and turn—
>> and I would heal them.'

---

a Gk *he*   *b* Other ancient authorities add *to hear*   *c* Or *mysteries*

16 But blessed are your eyes, for they see, and your ears, for they hear. ¹⁷Truly I tell you, many prophets and righteous people longed to see what you see, but did not see it, and to hear what you hear, but did not hear it.

THE PARABLE OF THE SOWER EXPLAINED

18 "Hear then the parable of the sower. ¹⁹When anyone hears the word of the kingdom and does not understand it, the evil one comes and snatches away what is sown in the heart; this is what was sown on the path. ²⁰As for what was sown on rocky ground, this is the one who hears the word and immediately receives it with joy; ²¹yet such a person has no root, but endures only for a while, and when trouble or persecution arises on account of the word, that person immediately falls away.ᵃ ²²As for what was sown among thorns, this is the one who hears the word, but the cares of the world and the lure of wealth choke the word, and it yields nothing. ²³But as for what was sown on good soil, this is the one who hears the word and understands it, who indeed bears fruit and yields, in one case a hundredfold, in another sixty, and in another thirty."

THE PARABLE OF WEEDS AMONG THE WHEAT

24 He put before them another parable: "The kingdom of heaven may be compared to someone who sowed good seed in his field; ²⁵but while everybody was asleep, an enemy came and sowed weeds among the wheat, and then went away. ²⁶So when the plants came up and bore grain, then the weeds appeared as well. ²⁷And the slaves of the householder came and said to him, 'Master, did you not sow good seed in your field? Where, then, did these weeds come from?' ²⁸He answered, 'An enemy has done this.' The slaves said to him, 'Then do you want us to go and gather them?' ²⁹But he replied, 'No; for in gathering the weeds you would uproot the wheat along with them. ³⁰Let both of them grow together until the harvest; and at harvest time I will tell the reapers, Collect the weeds first and bind them in bundles to be burned, but gather the wheat into my barn.'"

THE PARABLE OF THE MUSTARD SEED

31 He put before them another parable: "The kingdom of heaven is like a mustard seed that someone took and sowed in his field; ³²it is the smallest of all the seeds, but when it has grown it is the greatest of shrubs and becomes a tree, so that the birds of the air come and make nests in its branches."

---

a Gk *stumbles*

THE PARABLE OF THE YEAST

33 He told them another parable: "The kingdom of heaven is like yeast that a woman took and mixed in with*a* three measures of flour until all of it was leavened."

THE USE OF PARABLES

34 Jesus told the crowds all these things in parables; without a parable he told them nothing. [35]This was to fulfill what had been spoken through the prophet:*b*
> "I will open my mouth to speak in parables;
> I will proclaim what has been hidden from the foundation of the world."*c*

JESUS EXPLAINS THE PARABLE OF THE WEEDS

36 Then he left the crowds and went into the house. And his disciples approached him, saying, "Explain to us the parable of the weeds of the field." [37]He answered, "The one who sows the good seed is the Son of Man; [38]the field is the world, and the good seed are the children of the kingdom; the weeds are the children of the evil one, [39]and the enemy who sowed them is the devil; the harvest is the end of the age, and the reapers are angels. [40]Just as the weeds are collected and burned up with fire, so will it be at the end of the age. [41]The Son of Man will send his angels, and they will collect out of his kingdom all causes of sin and all evildoers, [42]and they will throw them into the furnace of fire, where there will be weeping and gnashing of teeth. [43]Then the righteous will shine like the sun in the kingdom of their Father. Let anyone with ears*d* listen!

THREE PARABLES

44 "The kingdom of heaven is like treasure hidden in a field, which someone found and hid; then in his joy he goes and sells all that he has and buys that field.

45 "Again, the kingdom of heaven is like a merchant in search of fine pearls; [46]on finding one pearl of great value, he went and sold all that he had and bought it.

47 "Again, the kingdom of heaven is like a net that was thrown into the sea and caught fish of every kind; [48]when it was full, they drew it ashore, sat down, and put the good into baskets but threw out the bad. [49]So it will be at the end of

---

a Gk *hid in*   *b* Other ancient authorities read *the prophet Isaiah*   *c* Other ancient authorities lack *of the world*   *d* Other ancient authorities add *to hear* the age. The angels will come out and separate the evil from the righteous [50]and throw them into the furnace of fire, where there will be weeping and gnashing of teeth.

TREASURES NEW AND OLD

51 "Have you understood all this?" They answered, "Yes." [52]And he said to them, "Therefore every scribe who has been trained for the kingdom of heaven is like the master of a household who brings out of his treasure what is new and what is old." [53]When Jesus had finished these parables, he left that place.

THE REJECTION OF JESUS AT NAZARETH

54 He came to his hometown and began to teach the people[a] in their synagogue, so that they were astounded and said, "Where did this man get this wisdom and these deeds of power? [55]Is not this the carpenter's son? Is not his mother called Mary? And are not his brothers James and Joseph and Simon and Judas? [56]And are not all his sisters with us? Where then did this man get all this?" [57]And they took offense at him. But Jesus said to them, "Prophets are not without honor except in their own country and in their own house." [58]And he did not do many deeds of power there, because of their unbelief.

THE DEATH OF JOHN THE BAPTIST

14 At that time Herod the ruler[b] heard reports about Jesus; [2]and he said to his servants, "This is John the Baptist; he has been raised from the dead, and for this reason these powers are at work in him." [3]For Herod had arrested John, bound him, and put him in prison on account of Herodias, his brother Philip's wife,[c] [4]because John had been telling him, "It is not lawful for you to have her." [5]Though Herod[d] wanted to put him to death, he feared the crowd, because they regarded him as a prophet. [6]But when Herod's birthday came, the daughter of Herodias danced before the company, and she pleased Herod [7]so much that he promised on oath to grant her whatever she might ask. [8]Prompted by her mother, she said, "Give me the head of John the Baptist here on a platter." [9]The king was grieved, yet out of regard for his oaths and for the guests, he commanded it to be given; [10]he sent and had John beheaded in the prison. [11]The head was brought on a platter and given to the girl, who brought it to her mother. [12]His disciples came and took the body and buried it; then they went and told Jesus.

_a_ Gk _them_ _b_ Gk _tetrarch_ _c_ Other ancient authorities read _his brother's wife_ _d_ Gk _he_

FEEDING THE FIVE THOUSAND

13 Now when Jesus heard this, he withdrew from there in a boat to a deserted place by himself. But when the crowds heard it, they followed him on foot from the towns. ¹⁴When he went ashore, he saw a great crowd; and he had compassion for them and cured their sick. ¹⁵When it was evening, the disciples came to him and said, "This is a deserted place, and the hour is now late; send the crowds away so that they may go into the villages and buy food for themselves." ¹⁶Jesus said to them, "They need not go away; you give them something to eat." ¹⁷They replied, "We have nothing here but five loaves and two fish." ¹⁸And he said, "Bring them here to me." ¹⁹Then he ordered the crowds to sit down on the grass. Taking the five loaves and the two fish, he looked up to heaven, and blessed and broke the loaves, and gave them to the disciples, and the disciples gave them to the crowds. ²⁰And all ate and were filled; and they took up what was left over of the broken pieces, twelve baskets full. ²¹And those who ate were about five thousand men, besides women and children.

JESUS WALKS ON THE WATER

22 Immediately he made the disciples get into the boat and go on ahead to the other side, while he dismissed the crowds. ²³And after he had dismissed the crowds, he went up the mountain by himself to pray. When evening came, he was there alone, ²⁴but by this time the boat, battered by the waves, was far from the land,ᵃ for the wind was against them. ²⁵And early in the morning he came walking toward them on the sea. ²⁶But when the disciples saw him walking on the sea, they were terrified, saying, "It is a ghost!" And they cried out in fear. ²⁷But immediately Jesus spoke to them and said, "Take heart, it is I; do not be afraid."

28 Peter answered him, "Lord, if it is you, command me to come to you on the water." ²⁹He said, "Come." So Peter got out of the boat, started walking on the water, and came toward Jesus. ³⁰But when he noticed the strong wind,ᵇ he became frightened, and beginning to sink, he cried out, "Lord, save me!" ³¹Jesus immediately reached out his hand and caught him, saying to him, "You of little faith, why did you doubt?" ³²When they got into the boat, the wind ceased. ³³And those in the boat worshiped him, saying, "Truly you are the Son of God."

ᵃ Other ancient authorities read *was out on the sea*   ᵇ Other ancient authorities read *the wind*

JESUS HEALS THE SICK IN GENNESARET

34 When they had crossed over, they came to land at Gennesaret. [35]After the people of that place recognized him, they sent word throughout the region and brought all who were sick to him, [36]and begged him that they might touch even the fringe of his cloak; and all who touched it were healed.

THE TRADITION OF THE ELDERS

15 Then Pharisees and scribes came to Jesus from Jerusalem and said, [2]"Why do your disciples break the tradition of the elders? For they do not wash their hands before they eat." [3]He answered them, "And why do you break the commandment of God for the sake of your tradition? [4]For God said,[a] 'Honor your father and your mother,' and, 'Whoever speaks evil of father or mother must surely die.' [5]But you say that whoever tells father or mother, 'Whatever support you might have had from me is given to God,'[b] then that person need not honor the father.[c] [6]So, for the sake of your tradition, you make void the word[d] of God. [7]You hypocrites! Isaiah prophesied rightly about you when he said:

8 'This people honors me with their lips,
       but their hearts are far from me;
9 in vain do they worship me,
       teaching human precepts as doctrines.'"

THINGS THAT DEFILE

10 Then he called the crowd to him and said to them, "Listen and understand: [11]it is not what goes into the mouth that defiles a person, but it is what comes out of the mouth that defiles." [12]Then the disciples approached and said to him, "Do you know that the Pharisees took offense when they heard what you said?" [13]He answered, "Every plant that my heavenly Father has not planted will be uprooted. [14]Let them alone; they are blind guides of the blind.[e] And if one blind person guides another, both will fall into a pit." [15]But Peter said to him, "Explain this parable to us." [16]Then he said, "Are you also still without understanding? [17]Do you not see that whatever goes into the mouth enters the stomach, and goes out into the sewer? [18]But what comes out of the mouth proceeds from the heart, and this is what defiles. [19]For out of the heart come evil

---

a Other ancient authorities read *commanded, saying*   b Or *is an offering*   c Other ancient authorities add *or the mother*
d Other ancient authorities read *law;* others, *commandment*   e Other ancient authorities lack *of the blind*

intentions, murder, adultery, fornication, theft, false witness, slander. ²⁰These are what defile a person, but to eat with unwashed hands does not defile."

THE CANAANITE WOMAN'S FAITH

21 Jesus left that place and went away to the district of Tyre and Sidon. ²²Just then a Canaanite woman from that region came out and started shouting, "Have mercy on me, Lord, Son of David; my daughter is tormented by a demon." ²³But he did not answer her at all. And his disciples came and urged him, saying, "Send her away, for she keeps shouting after us." ²⁴He answered, "I was sent only to the lost sheep of the house of Israel." ²⁵But she came and knelt before him, saying, "Lord, help me." ²⁶He answered, "It is not fair to take the children's food and throw it to the dogs." ²⁷She said, "Yes, Lord, yet even the dogs eat the crumbs that fall from their masters' table." ²⁸Then Jesus answered her, "Woman, great is your faith! Let it be done for you as you wish." And her daughter was healed instantly.

JESUS CURES MANY PEOPLE

29 After Jesus had left that place, he passed along the Sea of Galilee, and he went up the mountain, where he sat down. ³⁰Great crowds came to him, bringing with them the lame, the maimed, the blind, the mute, and many others. They put them at his feet, and he cured them, ³¹so that the crowd was amazed when they saw the mute speaking, the maimed whole, the lame walking, and the blind seeing. And they praised the God of Israel.

FEEDING THE FOUR THOUSAND

32 Then Jesus called his disciples to him and said, "I have compassion for the crowd, because they have been with me now for three days and have nothing to eat; and I do not want to send them away hungry, for they might faint on the way." ³³The disciples said to him, "Where are we to get enough bread in the desert to feed so great a crowd?" ³⁴Jesus asked them, "How many loaves have you?" They said, "Seven, and a few small fish." ³⁵Then ordering the crowd to sit down on the ground, ³⁶he took the seven loaves and the fish; and after giving thanks he broke them and gave them to the disciples, and the disciples gave them to the crowds. ³⁷And all of them ate and were filled; and they took up the broken pieces left over, seven baskets full. ³⁸Those who had eaten were four thousand men, besides women and children. ³⁹After sending away the crowds, he got into the boat and went to the region of Magadan.^a

---

a Other ancient authorities read *Magdala* or *Magdalan*

THE DEMAND FOR A SIGN

16 The Pharisees and Sadducees came, and to test Jesus[a] they asked him to show them a sign from heaven. [2]He answered them, "When it is evening, you say, 'It will be fair weather, for the sky is red.' [3]And in the morning, 'It will be stormy today, for the sky is red and threatening.' You know how to interpret the appearance of the sky, but you cannot interpret the signs of the times.[b] [4]An evil and adulterous generation asks for a sign, but no sign will be given to it except the sign of Jonah." Then he left them and went away.

THE YEAST OF THE PHARISEES AND SADDUCEES

5 When the disciples reached the other side, they had forgotten to bring any bread. [6]Jesus said to them, "Watch out, and beware of the yeast of the Pharisees and Sadducees." [7]They said to one another, "It is because we have brought no bread." [8]And becoming aware of it, Jesus said, "You of little faith, why are you talking about having no bread? [9]Do you still not perceive? Do you not remember the five loaves for the five thousand, and how many baskets you gathered? [10]Or the seven loaves for the four thousand, and how many baskets you gathered? [11]How could you fail to perceive that I was not speaking about bread? Beware of the yeast of the Pharisees and Sadducees!" [12]Then they understood that he had not told them to beware of the yeast of bread, but of the teaching of the Pharisees and Sadducees.

PETER'S DECLARATION ABOUT JESUS

13 Now when Jesus came into the district of Caesarea Philippi, he asked his disciples, "Who do people say that the Son of Man is?" [14]And they said, "Some say John the Baptist, but others Elijah, and still others Jeremiah or one of the prophets." [15]He said to them, "But who do you say that I am?" [16]Simon Peter answered, "You are the Messiah,[c] the Son of the living God." [17]And Jesus answered him, "Blessed are you, Simon son of Jonah! For flesh and blood has not revealed this to you, but my Father in heaven. [18]And I tell you, you are Peter,[d] and on this rock[e] I will build my church, and the gates of Hades will not prevail against it. [19]I will give you the keys of the kingdom of heaven, and whatever you bind on earth will be bound in heaven, and whatever you loose on earth will be loosed in heaven." [20]Then he sternly ordered the disciples not to tell anyone that he was[f] the Messiah.[c]

---

a Gk *him*   b Other ancient authorities lack [2]*When it is . . . of the times*   c Or *the Christ*   d Gk *Petros*   e Gk *petra*   f Other ancient authorities add *Jesus*

JESUS FORETELLS HIS DEATH AND RESURRECTION

21 From that time on, Jesus began to show his disciples that he must go to Jerusalem and undergo great suffering at the hands of the elders and chief priests and scribes, and be killed, and on the third day be raised. ²²And Peter took him aside and began to rebuke him, saying, "God forbid it, Lord! This must never happen to you." ²³But he turned and said to Peter, "Get behind me, Satan! You are a stumbling block to me; for you are setting your mind not on divine things but on human things."

THE CROSS AND SELF-DENIAL

24 Then Jesus told his disciples, "If any want to become my followers, let them deny themselves and take up their cross and follow me. ²⁵For those who want to save their life will lose it, and those who lose their life for my sake will find it. ²⁶For what will it profit them if they gain the whole world but forfeit their life? Or what will they give in return for their life?

27 "For the Son of Man is to come with his angels in the glory of his Father, and then he will repay everyone for what has been done. ²⁸Truly I tell you, there are some standing here who will not taste death before they see the Son of Man coming in his kingdom."

THE TRANSFIGURATION

17 Six days later, Jesus took with him Peter and James and his brother John and led them up a high mountain, by themselves. ²And he was transfigured before them, and his face shone like the sun, and his clothes became dazzling white. ³Suddenly there appeared to them Moses and Elijah, talking with him. ⁴Then Peter said to Jesus, "Lord, it is good for us to be here; if you wish, I*a* will make three dwellings*b* here, one for you, one for Moses, and one for Elijah." ⁵While he was still speaking, suddenly a bright cloud overshadowed them, and from the cloud a voice said, "This is my Son, the Beloved;*c* with him I am well pleased; listen to him!" ⁶When the disciples heard this, they fell to the ground and were overcome by fear. ⁷But Jesus came and touched them, saying, "Get up and do not be afraid." ⁸And when they looked up, they saw no one except Jesus himself alone.

9 As they were coming down the mountain, Jesus ordered them, "Tell no one about the vision until after the Son of Man has been raised from the dead."

---

a Other ancient authorities read *we*   *b* Or *tents*   *c* Or *my beloved Son*

¹⁰And the disciples asked him, "Why, then, do the scribes say that Elijah must come first?" ¹¹He replied, "Elijah is indeed coming and will restore all things; ¹²but I tell you that Elijah has already come, and they did not recognize him, but they did to him whatever they pleased. So also the Son of Man is about to suffer at their hands." ¹³Then the disciples understood that he was speaking to them about John the Baptist.

JESUS CURES A BOY WITH A DEMON

14 When they came to the crowd, a man came to him, knelt before him, ¹⁵and said, "Lord, have mercy on my son, for he is an epileptic and he suffers terribly; he often falls into the fire and often into the water. ¹⁶And I brought him to your disciples, but they could not cure him." ¹⁷Jesus answered, "You faithless and perverse generation, how much longer must I be with you? How much longer must I put up with you? Bring him here to me." ¹⁸And Jesus rebuked the demon,ᵃ and itᵇ came out of him, and the boy was cured instantly. ¹⁹Then the disciples came to Jesus privately and said, "Why could we not cast it out?" ²⁰He said to them, "Because of your little faith. For truly I tell you, if you have faith the size of aᶜ mustard seed, you will say to this mountain, 'Move from here to there,' and it will move; and nothing will be impossible for you."ᵈ

JESUS AGAIN FORETELLS HIS DEATH AND RESURRECTION

22 As they were gatheringᵉ in Galilee, Jesus said to them, "The Son of Man is going to be betrayed into human hands, ²³and they will kill him, and on the third day he will be raised." And they were greatly distressed.

JESUS AND THE TEMPLE TAX

24 When they reached Capernaum, the collectors of the temple taxᶠ came to Peter and said, "Does your teacher not pay the temple tax?"ᶠ ²⁵He said, "Yes, he does." And when he came home, Jesus spoke of it first, asking, "What do you think, Simon? From whom do kings of the earth take toll or tribute? From their children or from others?" ²⁶When Peterᵍ said, "From others," Jesus said to him, "Then the children are free. ²⁷However, so that we do not give offense to them, go to the sea and cast a hook; take the first fish that comes up; and when you open its mouth, you will find a coin;ʰ take that and give it to them for you and me."

---

a Gk *it* or *him* b Gk *the demon* c Gk *faith as a grain of* d Other ancient authorities add verse 21, *But this kind does not come out except by prayer and fasting* e Other ancient authorities read *living* f Gk *didrachma* g Gk *he* h Gk *stater;* the stater was worth two didrachmas

TRUE GREATNESS

18 At that time the disciples came to Jesus and asked, "Who is the greatest in the kingdom of heaven?" [2]He called a child, whom he put among them, [3]and said, "Truly I tell you, unless you change and become like children, you will never enter the kingdom of heaven. [4]Whoever becomes humble like this child is the greatest in the kingdom of heaven. [5]Whoever welcomes one such child in my name welcomes me.

TEMPTATIONS TO SIN

6 "If any of you put a stumbling block before one of these little ones who believe in me, it would be better for you if a great millstone were fastened around your neck and you were drowned in the depth of the sea. [7]Woe to the world because of stumbling blocks! Occasions for stumbling are bound to come, but woe to the one by whom the stumbling block comes!

8 "If your hand or your foot causes you to stumble, cut it off and throw it away; it is better for you to enter life maimed or lame than to have two hands or two feet and to be thrown into the eternal fire. [9]And if your eye causes you to stumble, tear it out and throw it away; it is better for you to enter life with one eye than to have two eyes and to be thrown into the hell[a] of fire.

THE PARABLE OF THE LOST SHEEP

10 "Take care that you do not despise one of these little ones; for, I tell you, in heaven their angels continually see the face of my Father in heaven.[b] [12]What do you think? If a shepherd has a hundred sheep, and one of them has gone astray, does he not leave the ninety-nine on the mountains and go in search of the one that went astray? [13]And if he finds it, truly I tell you, he rejoices over it more than over the ninety-nine that never went astray. [14]So it is not the will of your[c] Father in heaven that one of these little ones should be lost.

REPROVING ANOTHER WHO SINS

15 "If another member of the church[d] sins against you,[e] go and point out the fault when the two of you are alone. If the member listens to you, you have regained that one.[f] [16]But if you are not listened to, take one or two others along with you, so that every word may be confirmed by the evidence of two or three witnesses. [17]If the member refuses to listen to them, tell it to the church; and

---

a Gk *Gehenna*   b Other ancient authorities add verse 11, *For the Son of Man came to save the lost*   c Other ancient authorities read *my*   d Gk *If your brother*   e Other ancient authorities lack *against you*   f Gk *the brother* if the offender refuses to listen even to the church, let such a one be to you as a Gentile and a tax collector. [18]Truly I tell you, whatever you bind on earth will be bound in heaven, and whatever you loose on earth will be loosed in heaven. [19]Again, truly I tell you, if two of you agree on earth about anything you ask, it will be done for you by my Father in heaven. [20]For where two or three are gathered in my name, I am there among them."

FORGIVENESS

21 Then Peter came and said to him, "Lord, if another member of the church[a] sins against me, how often should I forgive? As many as seven times?" [22]Jesus said to him, "Not seven times, but, I tell you, seventy-seven[b] times.

THE PARABLE OF THE UNFORGIVING SERVANT

23 "For this reason the kingdom of heaven may be compared to a king who wished to settle accounts with his slaves. [24]When he began the reckoning, one who owed him ten thousand talents[c] was brought to him; [25]and, as he could not pay, his lord ordered him to be sold, together with his wife and children and all his possessions, and payment to be made. [26]So the slave fell on his knees before him, saying, 'Have patience with me, and I will pay you everything.' [27]And out of pity for him, the lord of that slave released him and forgave him the debt. [28]But that same slave, as he went out, came upon one of his fellow slaves who owed him a hundred denarii;[d] and seizing him by the throat, he said, 'Pay what you owe.' [29]Then his fellow slave fell down and pleaded with him, 'Have patience with me, and I will pay you.' [30]But he refused; then he went and threw him into prison until he would pay the debt. [31]When his fellow slaves saw what had happened, they were greatly distressed, and they went and reported to their lord all that had taken place. [32]Then his lord summoned him and said to him, 'You wicked slave! I forgave you all that debt because you pleaded with me. [33]Should you not have had mercy on your fellow slave, as I had mercy on you?' [34]And in anger his lord handed him over to be tortured until he would pay his entire debt. [35]So my heavenly Father will also do to every one of you, if you do not forgive your brother or sister[e] from your heart."

TEACHING ABOUT DIVORCE

19 When Jesus had finished saying these things, he left Galilee and went to the region of Judea beyond the Jordan. [2]Large crowds followed him, and he cured them there.

---

a Gk *if my brother*   b Or *seventy times seven*   c A talent was worth more than fifteen years' wages of a laborer   d The denarius was the usual day's wage for a laborer   e Gk *brother*

3 Some Pharisees came to him, and to test him they asked, "Is it lawful for a man to divorce his wife for any cause?" [4]He answered, "Have you not read that the one who made them at the beginning 'made them male and female,' [5]and said, 'For this reason a man shall leave his father and mother and be joined to his wife, and the two shall become one flesh'? [6]So they are no longer two, but one flesh. Therefore what God has joined together, let no one separate." [7]They said to him, "Why then did Moses command us to give a certificate of dismissal and to divorce her?" [8]He said to them, "It was because you were so hard-hearted that Moses allowed you to divorce your wives, but from the beginning it was not so. [9]And I say to you, whoever divorces his wife, except for unchastity, and marries another commits adultery."[a]

10 His disciples said to him, "If such is the case of a man with his wife, it is better not to marry." [11]But he said to them, "Not everyone can accept this teaching, but only those to whom it is given. [12]For there are eunuchs who have been so from birth, and there are eunuchs who have been made eunuchs by others, and there are eunuchs who have made themselves eunuchs for the sake of the kingdom of heaven. Let anyone accept this who can."

JESUS BLESSES LITTLE CHILDREN

13 Then little children were being brought to him in order that he might lay his hands on them and pray. The disciples spoke sternly to those who brought them; [14]but Jesus said, "Let the little children come to me, and do not stop them; for it is to such as these that the kingdom of heaven belongs." [15]And he laid his hands on them and went on his way.

THE RICH YOUNG MAN

16 Then someone came to him and said, "Teacher, what good deed must I do to have eternal life?" [17]And he said to him, "Why do you ask me about what is good? There is only one who is good. If you wish to enter into life, keep the commandments." [18]He said to him, "Which ones?" And Jesus said, "You shall not murder; You shall not commit adultery; You shall not steal; You shall not bear false witness; [19]Honor your father and mother; also, You shall love your neighbor as yourself." [20]The young man said to him, "I have kept all these;[b] what do I still lack?" [21]Jesus said to him, "If you wish to be perfect, go, sell your possessions, and give the money[c] to the poor, and you will have treasure

---

a Other ancient authorities read *except on the ground of unchastity, causes her to commit adultery*; others add at the end of the verse *and he who marries a divorced woman commits adultery* b Other ancient authorities add *from my youth* c Gk lacks *the money* in heaven; then come, follow me." ²²When the young man heard this word, he went away grieving, for he had many possessions.

23 Then Jesus said to his disciples, "Truly I tell you, it will be hard for a rich person to enter the kingdom of heaven. ²⁴Again I tell you, it is easier for a camel to go through the eye of a needle than for someone who is rich to enter the kingdom of God." ²⁵When the disciples heard this, they were greatly astounded and said, "Then who can be saved?" ²⁶But Jesus looked at them and said, "For mortals it is impossible, but for God all things are possible."

27 Then Peter said in reply, "Look, we have left everything and followed you. What then will we have?" ²⁸Jesus said to them, "Truly I tell you, at the renewal of all things, when the Son of Man is seated on the throne of his glory, you who have followed me will also sit on twelve thrones, judging the twelve tribes of Israel. ²⁹And everyone who has left houses or brothers or sisters or father or mother or children or fields, for my name's sake, will receive a hundred-fold,ᵃ and will inherit eternal life. ³⁰But many who are first will be last, and the last will be first.

THE LABORERS IN THE VINEYARD

20 "For the kingdom of heaven is like a landowner who went out early in the morning to hire laborers for his vineyard. ²After agreeing with the laborers for the usual daily wage,ᵇ he sent them into his vineyard. ³When he went out about nine o'clock, he saw others standing idle in the marketplace; ⁴and he said to them, 'You also go into the vineyard, and I will pay you whatever is right.' So they went. ⁵When he went out again about noon and about three o'clock, he did the same. ⁶And about five o'clock he went out and found others standing around; and he said to them, 'Why are you standing here idle all day?' ⁷They said to him, 'Because no one has hired us.' He said to them, 'You also go into the vineyard.' ⁸When evening came, the owner of the vineyard said to his manager, 'Call the laborers and give them their pay, beginning with the last and then going to the first.' ⁹When those hired about five o'clock came, each of them received the usual daily wage.ᵇ ¹⁰Now when the first came, they thought they would receive more; but each of them also received the usual daily wage.ᵇ ¹¹And when they received it, they grumbled against the landowner, ¹²saying, 'These last worked only one hour, and you have made them equal to us who have borne the burden of the day and the scorching heat.' ¹³But he replied to one of them, 'Friend, I am doing you no wrong; did you not agree with me for the usual daily wage?ᵇ ¹⁴Take what belongs

---

a Other ancient authorities read *manifold*   *b* Gk *a denarius* to you and go; I choose to give to this last the same as I give to you. ¹⁵Am I not allowed to do what I choose with what belongs to me? Or are you envious because I am generous?'ᵃ ¹⁶So the last will be first, and the first will be last."ᵇ

A THIRD TIME JESUS FORETELLS HIS DEATH AND RESURRECTION

17 While Jesus was going up to Jerusalem, he took the twelve disciples aside by themselves, and said to them on the way, ¹⁸"See, we are going up to Jerusalem, and the Son of Man will be handed over to the chief priests and scribes, and they will condemn him to death; ¹⁹then they will hand him over to the Gentiles to be mocked and flogged and crucified; and on the third day he will be raised."

THE REQUEST OF THE MOTHER OF JAMES AND JOHN

20 Then the mother of the sons of Zebedee came to him with her sons, and kneeling before him, she asked a favor of him. ²¹And he said to her, "What do you want?" She said to him, "Declare that these two sons of mine will sit, one at your right hand and one at your left, in your kingdom." ²²But Jesus answered, "You do not know what you are asking. Are you able to drink the cup that I am about to drink?"ᶜ They said to him, "We are able." ²³He said to them, "You will indeed drink my cup, but to sit at my right hand and at my left, this is not mine to grant, but it is for those for whom it has been prepared by my Father."

24 When the ten heard it, they were angry with the two brothers. ²⁵But Jesus called them to him and said, "You know that the rulers of the Gentiles lord it over them, and their great ones are tyrants over them. ²⁶It will not be so among you; but whoever wishes to be great among you must be your servant, ²⁷and whoever wishes to be first among you must be your slave; ²⁸just as the Son of Man came not to be served but to serve, and to give his life a ransom for many."

JESUS HEALS TWO BLIND MEN

29 As they were leaving Jericho, a large crowd followed him. ³⁰There were two blind men sitting by the roadside. When they heard that Jesus was passing by, they shouted, "Lord,ᵈ have mercy on us, Son of David!" ³¹The crowd sternly ordered them to be quiet; but they shouted even more loudly, "Have mercy on us, Lord, Son of David!" ³²Jesus stood still and called them, saying, "What do you want me to do for you?" ³³They said to him, "Lord, let our eyes be opened." ³⁴Moved with compassion, Jesus touched their eyes. Immediately they regained their sight and followed him.

---

a Gk *is your eye evil because I am good?*   *b* Other ancient authorities add *for many are called but few are chosen*   *c* Other ancient authorities add *or to be baptized with the baptism that I am baptized with?*   *d* Other ancient authorities lack *Lord*

JESUS' TRIUMPHAL ENTRY INTO JERUSALEM

21 When they had come near Jerusalem and had reached Bethphage, at the Mount of Olives, Jesus sent two disciples, ²saying to them, "Go into the village ahead of you, and immediately you will find a donkey tied, and a colt with her; untie them and bring them to me. ³If anyone says anything to you, just say this, 'The Lord needs them.' And he will send them immediately."*ᵃ* ⁴This took place to fulfill what had been spoken through the prophet, saying,

5 "Tell the daughter of Zion,
    Look, your king is coming to you,
        humble, and mounted on a donkey,
           and on a colt, the foal of a donkey."

6 The disciples went and did as Jesus had directed them; ⁷they brought the donkey and the colt, and put their cloaks on them, and he sat on them. ⁸A very large crowd*ᵇ* spread their cloaks on the road, and others cut branches from the trees and spread them on the road. ⁹The crowds that went ahead of him and that followed were shouting,

    "Hosanna to the Son of David!
      Blessed is the one who comes in the name of the Lord!
    Hosanna in the highest heaven!"

10 When he entered Jerusalem, the whole city was in turmoil, asking, "Who is this?" ¹¹The crowds were saying, "This is the prophet Jesus from Nazareth in Galilee."

JESUS CLEANSES THE TEMPLE

12 Then Jesus entered the temple*ᶜ* and drove out all who were selling and buying in the temple, and he overturned the tables of the money changers and the seats of those who sold doves. ¹³He said to them, "It is written,

    'My house shall be called a house of prayer';
        but you are making it a den of robbers."

14 The blind and the lame came to him in the temple, and he cured them. ¹⁵But when the chief priests and the scribes saw the amazing things that he did, and heard*ᵈ* the children crying out in the temple, "Hosanna to the Son of David," they became angry ¹⁶and said to him, "Do you hear what these are saying?" Jesus said to them, "Yes; have you never read,

    'Out of the mouths of infants and nursing babies

---

a Or 'The Lord needs them and will send them back immediately.' *b* Or Most of the crowd *c* Other ancient authorities add of God
d Gk lacks heard

you have prepared praise for yourself'?"

17 He left them, went out of the city to Bethany, and spent the night there.

JESUS CURSES THE FIG TREE

18 In the morning, when he returned to the city, he was hungry. [19]And seeing a fig tree by the side of the road, he went to it and found nothing at all on it but leaves. Then he said to it, "May no fruit ever come from you again!" And the fig tree withered at once. [20]When the disciples saw it, they were amazed, saying, "How did the fig tree wither at once?" [21]Jesus answered them, "Truly I tell you, if you have faith and do not doubt, not only will you do what has been done to the fig tree, but even if you say to this mountain, 'Be lifted up and thrown into the sea,' it will be done. [22]Whatever you ask for in prayer with faith, you will receive."

THE AUTHORITY OF JESUS QUESTIONED

23 When he entered the temple, the chief priests and the elders of the people came to him as he was teaching, and said, "By what authority are you doing these things, and who gave you this authority?" [24]Jesus said to them, "I will also ask you one question; if you tell me the answer, then I will also tell you by what authority I do these things. [25]Did the baptism of John come from heaven, or was it of human origin?" And they argued with one another, "If we say, 'From heaven,' he will say to us, 'Why then did you not believe him?' [26]But if we say, 'Of human origin,' we are afraid of the crowd; for all regard John as a prophet." [27]So they answered Jesus, "We do not know." And he said to them, "Neither will I tell you by what authority I am doing these things.

THE PARABLE OF THE TWO SONS

28 "What do you think? A man had two sons; he went to the first and said, 'Son, go and work in the vineyard today.' [29]He answered, 'I will not'; but later he changed his mind and went. [30]The father[a] went to the second and said the same; and he answered, 'I go, sir'; but did not go. [31]Which of the two did the will of his father?" They said, "The first." Jesus said to them, "Truly I tell you, the tax collectors and the prostitutes are going into the kingdom of God ahead of you. [32]For John came to you in the way of righteousness and you did not believe him, but the tax collectors and the prostitutes believed him; and even after you saw it, you did not change your minds and believe him.

---

a Gk *He*

THE PARABLE OF THE WICKED TENANTS

33 "Listen to another parable. There was a landowner who planted a vineyard, put a fence around it, dug a wine press in it, and built a watchtower. Then he leased it to tenants and went to another country. ³⁴When the harvest time had come, he sent his slaves to the tenants to collect his produce. ³⁵But the tenants seized his slaves and beat one, killed another, and stoned another. ³⁶Again he sent other slaves, more than the first; and they treated them in the same way. ³⁷Finally he sent his son to them, saying, 'They will respect my son.' ³⁸But when the tenants saw the son, they said to themselves, 'This is the heir; come, let us kill him and get his inheritance.' ³⁹So they seized him, threw him out of the vineyard, and killed him. ⁴⁰Now when the owner of the vineyard comes, what will he do to those tenants?" ⁴¹They said to him, "He will put those wretches to a miserable death, and lease the vineyard to other tenants who will give him the produce at the harvest time."

42 Jesus said to them, "Have you never read in the scriptures:

'The stone that the builders rejected
    has become the cornerstone;ᵃ
this was the Lord's doing,
    and it is amazing in our eyes'?

43 Therefore I tell you, the kingdom of God will be taken away from you and given to a people that produces the fruits of the kingdom.ᵇ ⁴⁴The one who falls on this stone will be broken to pieces; and it will crush anyone on whom it falls."ᶜ

45 When the chief priests and the Pharisees heard his parables, they realized that he was speaking about them. ⁴⁶They wanted to arrest him, but they feared the crowds, because they regarded him as a prophet.

THE PARABLE OF THE WEDDING BANQUET

22 Once more Jesus spoke to them in parables, saying: ²"The kingdom of heaven may be compared to a king who gave a wedding banquet for his son. ³He sent his slaves to call those who had been invited to the wedding banquet, but they would not come. ⁴Again he sent other slaves, saying, 'Tell those who have been invited: Look, I have prepared my dinner, my oxen and my fat calves have been slaughtered, and everything is ready; come to the wedding banquet.' ⁵But they made light of it and went away, one to his farm, another to his business, ⁶while the rest seized his slaves, mistreated them, and killed

---

a Or keystone b Gk the fruits of it c Other ancient authorities lack verse 44 them. [7]The king was enraged. He sent his troops, destroyed those murderers, and burned their city. [8]Then he said to his slaves, 'The wedding is ready, but those invited were not worthy. [9]Go therefore into the main streets, and invite everyone you find to the wedding banquet.' [10]Those slaves went out into the streets and gathered all whom they found, both good and bad; so the wedding hall was filled with guests.

11 "But when the king came in to see the guests, he noticed a man there who was not wearing a wedding robe, [12]and he said to him, 'Friend, how did you get in here without a wedding robe?' And he was speechless. [13]Then the king said to the attendants, 'Bind him hand and foot, and throw him into the outer darkness, where there will be weeping and gnashing of teeth.' [14]For many are called, but few are chosen."

THE QUESTION ABOUT PAYING TAXES

15 Then the Pharisees went and plotted to entrap him in what he said. [16]So they sent their disciples to him, along with the Herodians, saying, "Teacher, we know that you are sincere, and teach the way of God in accordance with truth, and show deference to no one; for you do not regard people with partiality. [17]Tell us, then, what you think. Is it lawful to pay taxes to the emperor, or not?" [18]But Jesus, aware of their malice, said, "Why are you putting me to the test, you hypocrites? [19]Show me the coin used for the tax." And they brought him a denarius. [20]Then he said to them, "Whose head is this, and whose title?" [21]They answered, "The emperor's." Then he said to them, "Give therefore to the emperor the things that are the emperor's, and to God the things that are God's." [22]When they heard this, they were amazed; and they left him and went away.

THE QUESTION ABOUT THE RESURRECTION

23 The same day some Sadducees came to him, saying there is no resurrection;[a] and they asked him a question, saying, [24]"Teacher, Moses said, 'If a man dies childless, his brother shall marry the widow, and raise up children for his brother.' [25]Now there were seven brothers among us; the first married, and died childless, leaving the widow to his brother. [26]The second did the same, so also the third, down to the seventh. [27]Last of all, the woman herself died. [28]In the resurrection, then, whose wife of the seven will she be? For all of them had married her."

29 Jesus answered them, "You are wrong, because you know neither the scriptures nor the power of God. [30]For in the resurrection they neither marry

---

a Other ancient authorities read *who say that there is no resurrection* nor are given in marriage, but are like angels*a* in heaven. ³¹And as for the resurrection of the dead, have you not read what was said to you by God, ³²'I am the God of Abraham, the God of Isaac, and the God of Jacob'? He is God not of the dead, but of the living." ³³And when the crowd heard it, they were astounded at his teaching.

THE GREATEST COMMANDMENT

34 When the Pharisees heard that he had silenced the Sadducees, they gathered together, ³⁵and one of them, a lawyer, asked him a question to test him. ³⁶"Teacher, which commandment in the law is the greatest?" ³⁷He said to him, "'You shall love the Lord your God with all your heart, and with all your soul, and with all your mind.' ³⁸This is the greatest and first commandment. ³⁹And a second is like it: 'You shall love your neighbor as yourself.' ⁴⁰On these two commandments hang all the law and the prophets."

THE QUESTION ABOUT DAVID'S SON

41 Now while the Pharisees were gathered together, Jesus asked them this question: ⁴²"What do you think of the Messiah?*b* Whose son is he?" They said to him, "The son of David." ⁴³He said to them, "How is it then that David by the Spirit*c* calls him Lord, saying,

> 44 'The Lord said to my Lord,
>> "Sit at my right hand,
>>> until I put your enemies under your feet"'?

45 If David thus calls him Lord, how can he be his son?" ⁴⁶No one was able to give him an answer, nor from that day did anyone dare to ask him any more questions.

JESUS DENOUNCES SCRIBES AND PHARISEES

23 Then Jesus said to the crowds and to his disciples, ²"The scribes and the Pharisees sit on Moses' seat; ³therefore, do whatever they teach you and follow it; but do not do as they do, for they do not practice what they teach. ⁴They tie up heavy burdens, hard to bear,*d* and lay them on the shoulders of others; but they themselves are unwilling to lift a finger to move them. ⁵They do all their deeds to be seen by others; for they make their phylacteries broad and their fringes long. ⁶They love to have the place of honor at banquets and the best seats in the synagogues, ⁷and to be greeted with respect in the marketplaces, and to have people call them rabbi. ⁸But you are not to be called rabbi,

---

a Other ancient authorities add *of God*   *b* Or *Christ*   *c* Gk *in spirit*   *d* Other ancient authorities lack *hard to bear* for you have one teacher, and you are all students.*⁹And call no one your father on earth, for you have one Father—the one in heaven. ¹⁰Nor are you to be called instructors, for you have one instructor, the Messiah.* ¹¹The greatest among you will be your servant. ¹²All who exalt themselves will be humbled, and all who humble themselves will be exalted.

13 "But woe to you, scribes and Pharisees, hypocrites! For you lock people out of the kingdom of heaven. For you do not go in yourselves, and when others are going in, you stop them.* ¹⁵Woe to you, scribes and Pharisees, hypocrites! For you cross sea and land to make a single convert, and you make the new convert twice as much a child of hell* as yourselves.

16 "Woe to you, blind guides, who say, 'Whoever swears by the sanctuary is bound by nothing, but whoever swears by the gold of the sanctuary is bound by the oath.' ¹⁷You blind fools! For which is greater, the gold or the sanctuary that has made the gold sacred? ¹⁸And you say, 'Whoever swears by the altar is bound by nothing, but whoever swears by the gift that is on the altar is bound by the oath.' ¹⁹How blind you are! For which is greater, the gift or the altar that makes the gift sacred? ²⁰So whoever swears by the altar, swears by it and by everything on it; ²¹and whoever swears by the sanctuary, swears by it and by the one who dwells in it; ²²and whoever swears by heaven, swears by the throne of God and by the one who is seated upon it.

23 "Woe to you, scribes and Pharisees, hypocrites! For you tithe mint, dill, and cummin, and have neglected the weightier matters of the law: justice and mercy and faith. It is these you ought to have practiced without neglecting the others. ²⁴You blind guides! You strain out a gnat but swallow a camel!

25 "Woe to you, scribes and Pharisees, hypocrites! For you clean the outside of the cup and of the plate, but inside they are full of greed and self-indulgence. ²⁶You blind Pharisee! First clean the inside of the cup,* so that the outside also may become clean.

27 "Woe to you, scribes and Pharisees, hypocrites! For you are like white-washed tombs, which on the outside look beautiful, but inside they are full of the bones of the dead and of all kinds of filth. ²⁸So you also on the outside look righteous to others, but inside you are full of hypocrisy and lawlessness.

29 "Woe to you, scribes and Pharisees, hypocrites! For you build the tombs of the prophets and decorate the graves of the righteous, ³⁰and you say, 'If we had lived in the days of our ancestors, we would not have taken part with them in shedding the blood of the prophets.' ³¹Thus you testify against yourselves

---

a Gk brothers   b Or the Christ   c Other authorities add here (or after verse 12) verse 14, Woe to you, scribes and Pharisees, hypocrites! For you devour widows' houses and for the sake of appearance you make long prayers; therefore you will receive the greater condemnation   d Gk Gehenna   e Other ancient authorities add and of the plate that you are descendants of those who murdered the prophets. [32]Fill up, then, the measure of your ancestors. [33]You snakes, you brood of vipers! How can you escape being sentenced to hell?[a] [34]Therefore I send you prophets, sages, and scribes, some of whom you will kill and crucify, and some you will flog in your synagogues and pursue from town to town, [35]so that upon you may come all the righteous blood shed on earth, from the blood of righteous Abel to the blood of Zechariah son of Barachiah, whom you murdered between the sanctuary and the altar. [36]Truly I tell you, all this will come upon this generation.

THE LAMENT OVER JERUSALEM

37 "Jerusalem, Jerusalem, the city that kills the prophets and stones those who are sent to it! How often have I desired to gather your children together as a hen gathers her brood under her wings, and you were not willing! [38]See, your house is left to you, desolate.[b] [39]For I tell you, you will not see me again until you say, 'Blessed is the one who comes in the name of the Lord.'"

THE DESTRUCTION OF THE TEMPLE FORETOLD

24 As Jesus came out of the temple and was going away, his disciples came to point out to him the buildings of the temple. [2]Then he asked them, "You see all these, do you not? Truly I tell you, not one stone will be left here upon another; all will be thrown down."

SIGNS OF THE END OF THE AGE

3 When he was sitting on the Mount of Olives, the disciples came to him privately, saying, "Tell us, when will this be, and what will be the sign of your coming and of the end of the age?" [4]Jesus answered them, "Beware that no one leads you astray. [5]For many will come in my name, saying, 'I am the Messiah!'[c] and they will lead many astray. [6]And you will hear of wars and rumors of wars; see that you are not alarmed; for this must take place, but the end is not yet. [7]For nation will rise against nation, and kingdom against kingdom, and there will be famines[d] and earthquakes in various places: [8]all this is but the beginning of the birth pangs.

PERSECUTIONS FORETOLD

9 "Then they will hand you over to be tortured and will put you to death, and you will be hated by all nations because of my name. [10]Then many will fall away,[e] and they will betray one another and hate one another. [11]And many

---

a Gk *Gehenna*   b Other ancient authorities lack *desolate*   c Or *the Christ*   d Other ancient authorities add *and pestilences*
e Or *stumble*

false prophets will arise and lead many astray. [12]And because of the increase of lawlessness, the love of many will grow cold. [13]But the one who endures to the end will be saved. [14]And this good news[a] of the kingdom will be proclaimed throughout the world, as a testimony to all the nations; and then the end will come.

THE DESOLATING SACRILEGE

15 "So when you see the desolating sacrilege standing in the holy place, as was spoken of by the prophet Daniel (let the reader understand), [16]then those in Judea must flee to the mountains; [17]the one on the housetop must not go down to take what is in the house; [18]the one in the field must not turn back to get a coat. [19]Woe to those who are pregnant and to those who are nursing infants in those days! [20]Pray that your flight may not be in winter or on a sabbath. [21]For at that time there will be great suffering, such as has not been from the beginning of the world until now, no, and never will be. [22]And if those days had not been cut short, no one would be saved; but for the sake of the elect those days will be cut short. [23]Then if anyone says to you, 'Look! Here is the Messiah!'[b] or 'There he is!'—do not believe it. [24]For false messiahs[c] and false prophets will appear and produce great signs and omens, to lead astray, if possible, even the elect. [25]Take note, I have told you beforehand. [26]So, if they say to you, 'Look! He is in the wilderness,' do not go out. If they say, 'Look! He is in the inner rooms,' do not believe it. [27]For as the lightning comes from the east and flashes as far as the west, so will be the coming of the Son of Man. [28]Wherever the corpse is, there the vultures will gather.

THE COMING OF THE SON OF MAN

29 "Immediately after the suffering of those days
> the sun will be darkened,
>> and the moon will not give its light;
> the stars will fall from heaven,
>> and the powers of heaven will be shaken.

30 Then the sign of the Son of Man will appear in heaven, and then all the tribes of the earth will mourn, and they will see 'the Son of Man coming on the clouds of heaven' with power and great glory. [31]And he will send out his angels with a loud trumpet call, and they will gather his elect from the four winds, from one end of heaven to the other.

---

a Or gospel b Or the Christ c Or christs

THE LESSON OF THE FIG TREE

32 "From the fig tree learn its lesson: as soon as its branch becomes tender and puts forth its leaves, you know that summer is near. ³³So also, when you see all these things, you know that he*a* is near, at the very gates. ³⁴Truly I tell you, this generation will not pass away until all these things have taken place. ³⁵Heaven and earth will pass away, but my words will not pass away.

THE NECESSITY FOR WATCHFULNESS

36 "But about that day and hour no one knows, neither the angels of heaven, nor the Son,*b* but only the Father. ³⁷For as the days of Noah were, so will be the coming of the Son of Man. ³⁸For as in those days before the flood they were eating and drinking, marrying and giving in marriage, until the day Noah entered the ark, ³⁹and they knew nothing until the flood came and swept them all away, so too will be the coming of the Son of Man. ⁴⁰Then two will be in the field; one will be taken and one will be left. ⁴¹Two women will be grinding meal together; one will be taken and one will be left. ⁴²Keep awake therefore, for you do not know on what day*c* your Lord is coming. ⁴³But understand this: if the owner of the house had known in what part of the night the thief was coming, he would have stayed awake and would not have let his house be broken into. ⁴⁴Therefore you also must be ready, for the Son of Man is coming at an unexpected hour.

THE FAITHFUL OR THE UNFAITHFUL SLAVE

45 "Who then is the faithful and wise slave, whom his master has put in charge of his household, to give the other slaves*d* their allowance of food at the proper time? ⁴⁶Blessed is that slave whom his master will find at work when he arrives. ⁴⁷Truly I tell you, he will put that one in charge of all his possessions. ⁴⁸But if that wicked slave says to himself, 'My master is delayed,' ⁴⁹and he begins to beat his fellow slaves, and eats and drinks with drunkards, ⁵⁰the master of that slave will come on a day when he does not expect him and at an hour that he does not know. ⁵¹He will cut him in pieces*e* and put him with the hypocrites, where there will be weeping and gnashing of teeth.

THE PARABLE OF THE TEN BRIDESMAIDS

25 "Then the kingdom of heaven will be like this. Ten bridesmaids*f* took their lamps and went to meet the bridegroom.*g* ²Five of them were

---

a Or *it*   *b* Other ancient authorities lack *nor the Son*   *c* Other ancient authorities read *at what hour*   *d* Gk *to give them*
e Or *cut him off*   *f* Gk *virgins*   *g* Other ancient authorities add *and the bride*

foolish, and five were wise. [3]When the foolish took their lamps, they took no oil with them; [4]but the wise took flasks of oil with their lamps. [5]As the bridegroom was delayed, all of them became drowsy and slept. [6]But at midnight there was a shout, 'Look! Here is the bridegroom! Come out to meet him.' [7]Then all those bridesmaids[a] got up and trimmed their lamps. [8]The foolish said to the wise, 'Give us some of your oil, for our lamps are going out.' [9]But the wise replied, 'No! there will not be enough for you and for us; you had better go to the dealers and buy some for yourselves.' [10]And while they went to buy it, the bridegroom came, and those who were ready went with him into the wedding banquet; and the door was shut. [11]Later the other bridesmaids[a] came also, saying, 'Lord, lord, open to us.' [12]But he replied, 'Truly I tell you, I do not know you.' [13]Keep awake therefore, for you know neither the day nor the hour.[b]

THE PARABLE OF THE TALENTS

14 "For it is as if a man, going on a journey, summoned his slaves and entrusted his property to them; [15]to one he gave five talents,[c] to another two, to another one, to each according to his ability. Then he went away. [16]The one who had received the five talents went off at once and traded with them, and made five more talents. [17]In the same way, the one who had the two talents made two more talents. [18]But the one who had received the one talent went off and dug a hole in the ground and hid his master's money. [19]After a long time the master of those slaves came and settled accounts with them. [20]Then the one who had received the five talents came forward, bringing five more talents, saying, 'Master, you handed over to me five talents; see, I have made five more talents.' [21]His master said to him, 'Well done, good and trustworthy slave; you have been trustworthy in a few things, I will put you in charge of many things; enter into the joy of your master.' [22]And the one with the two talents also came forward, saying, 'Master, you handed over to me two talents; see, I have made two more talents.' [23]His master said to him, 'Well done, good and trustworthy slave; you have been trustworthy in a few things, I will put you in charge of many things; enter into the joy of your master.' [24]Then the one who had received the one talent also came forward, saying, 'Master, I knew that you were a harsh man, reaping where you did not sow, and gathering where you did not scatter seed; [25]so I was afraid, and I went and hid your talent in the ground. Here you have what is yours.' [26]But his master replied, 'You wicked and lazy slave! You knew, did you, that I reap where I did not sow, and gather where I did not scatter? [27]Then you ought to have invested my money with the bankers, and on my return I would

---

a Other ancient authorities add *and the bride*   b Other ancient authorities add *in which the Son of Man is coming*   c A talent was worth more than fifteen years' wages of a laborer have received what was my own with interest. [28]So take the talent from him, and give it to the one with the ten talents. [29]For to all those who have, more will be given, and they will have an abundance; but from those who have nothing, even what they have will be taken away. [30]As for this worthless slave, throw him into the outer darkness, where there will be weeping and gnashing of teeth.'

THE JUDGMENT OF THE NATIONS

31 "When the Son of Man comes in his glory, and all the angels with him, then he will sit on the throne of his glory. [32]All the nations will be gathered before him, and he will separate people one from another as a shepherd separates the sheep from the goats, [33]and he will put the sheep at his right hand and the goats at the left. [34]Then the king will say to those at his right hand, 'Come, you that are blessed by my Father, inherit the kingdom prepared for you from the foundation of the world; [35]for I was hungry and you gave me food, I was thirsty and you gave me something to drink, I was a stranger and you welcomed me, [36]I was naked and you gave me clothing, I was sick and you took care of me, I was in prison and you visited me.' [37]Then the righteous will answer him, 'Lord, when was it that we saw you hungry and gave you food, or thirsty and gave you something to drink? [38]And when was it that we saw you a stranger and welcomed you, or naked and gave you clothing? [39]And when was it that we saw you sick or in prison and visited you?' [40]And the king will answer them, 'Truly I tell you, just as you did it to one of the least of these who are members of my family,[a] you did it to me.' [41]Then he will say to those at his left hand, 'You that are accursed, depart from me into the eternal fire prepared for the devil and his angels; [42]for I was hungry and you gave me no food, I was thirsty and you gave me nothing to drink, [43]I was a stranger and you did not welcome me, naked and you did not give me clothing, sick and in prison and you did not visit me.' [44]Then they also will answer, 'Lord, when was it that we saw you hungry or thirsty or a stranger or naked or sick or in prison, and did not take care of you?' [45]Then he will answer them, 'Truly I tell you, just as you did not do it to one of the least of these, you did not do it to me.' [46]And these will go away into eternal punishment, but the righteous into eternal life."

THE PLOT TO KILL JESUS

26 When Jesus had finished saying all these things, he said to his disciples, [2]"You know that after two days the Passover is coming, and the Son of Man will be handed over to be crucified."

---

a Gk *these my brothers*

3 Then the chief priests and the elders of the people gathered in the palace of the high priest, who was called Caiaphas, ⁴and they conspired to arrest Jesus by stealth and kill him. ⁵But they said, "Not during the festival, or there may be a riot among the people."

THE ANOINTING AT BETHANY

6 Now while Jesus was at Bethany in the house of Simon the leper,ᵃ ⁷a woman came to him with an alabaster jar of very costly ointment, and she poured it on his head as he sat at the table. ⁸But when the disciples saw it, they were angry and said, "Why this waste? ⁹For this ointment could have been sold for a large sum, and the money given to the poor." ¹⁰But Jesus, aware of this, said to them, "Why do you trouble the woman? She has performed a good service for me. ¹¹For you always have the poor with you, but you will not always have me. ¹²By pouring this ointment on my body she has prepared me for burial. ¹³Truly I tell you, wherever this good newsᵇ is proclaimed in the whole world, what she has done will be told in remembrance of her."

JUDAS AGREES TO BETRAY JESUS

14 Then one of the twelve, who was called Judas Iscariot, went to the chief priests ¹⁵and said, "What will you give me if I betray him to you?" They paid him thirty pieces of silver. ¹⁶And from that moment he began to look for an opportunity to betray him.

THE PASSOVER WITH THE DISCIPLES

17 On the first day of Unleavened Bread the disciples came to Jesus, saying, "Where do you want us to make the preparations for you to eat the Passover?" ¹⁸He said, "Go into the city to a certain man, and say to him, 'The Teacher says, My time is near; I will keep the Passover at your house with my disciples.'" ¹⁹So the disciples did as Jesus had directed them, and they prepared the Passover meal.

20 When it was evening, he took his place with the twelve;ᶜ ²¹and while they were eating, he said, "Truly I tell you, one of you will betray me." ²²And they became greatly distressed and began to say to him one after another, "Surely not I, Lord?" ²³He answered, "The one who has dipped his hand into the bowl with me will betray me. ²⁴The Son of Man goes as it is written of him, but woe to that one by whom the Son of Man is betrayed! It would have been better for that one

---

a The terms *leper* and *leprosy* can refer to several diseases   b Or *gospel*   c Other ancient authorities add *disciples* not to have been born." ²⁵Judas, who betrayed him, said, "Surely not I, Rabbi?" He replied, "You have said so."

THE INSTITUTION OF THE LORD'S SUPPER

26 While they were eating, Jesus took a loaf of bread, and after blessing it he broke it, gave it to the disciples, and said, "Take, eat; this is my body." ²⁷Then he took a cup, and after giving thanks he gave it to them, saying, "Drink from it, all of you; ²⁸for this is my blood of the* covenant, which is poured out for many for the forgiveness of sins. ²⁹I tell you, I will never again drink of this fruit of the vine until that day when I drink it new with you in my Father's kingdom."

30 When they had sung the hymn, they went out to the Mount of Olives.

PETER'S DENIAL FORETOLD

31 Then Jesus said to them, "You will all become deserters because of me this night; for it is written,

> 'I will strike the shepherd,
>> and the sheep of the flock will be scattered.'

32 But after I am raised up, I will go ahead of you to Galilee." ³³Peter said to him, "Though all become deserters because of you, I will never desert you." ³⁴Jesus said to him, "Truly I tell you, this very night, before the cock crows, you will deny me three times." ³⁵Peter said to him, "Even though I must die with you, I will not deny you." And so said all the disciples.

JESUS PRAYS IN GETHSEMANE

36 Then Jesus went with them to a place called Gethsemane; and he said to his disciples, "Sit here while I go over there and pray." ³⁷He took with him Peter and the two sons of Zebedee, and began to be grieved and agitated. ³⁸Then he said to them, "I am deeply grieved, even to death; remain here, and stay awake with me." ³⁹And going a little farther, he threw himself on the ground and prayed, "My Father, if it is possible, let this cup pass from me; yet not what I want but what you want." ⁴⁰Then he came to the disciples and found them sleeping; and he said to Peter, "So, could you not stay awake with me one hour? ⁴¹Stay awake and pray that you may not come into the time of trial;ᵇ the spirit indeed is willing, but the flesh is weak." ⁴²Again he went away for the second time and prayed, "My Father, if this cannot pass unless I drink it, your will be done."

---

a Other ancient authorities add *new* *b* Or *into temptation*

[43]Again he came and found them sleeping, for their eyes were heavy. [44]So leaving them again, he went away and prayed for the third time, saying the same words. [45]Then he came to the disciples and said to them, "Are you still sleeping and taking your rest? See, the hour is at hand, and the Son of Man is betrayed into the hands of sinners. [46]Get up, let us be going. See, my betrayer is at hand."

THE BETRAYAL AND ARREST OF JESUS

47 While he was still speaking, Judas, one of the twelve, arrived; with him was a large crowd with swords and clubs, from the chief priests and the elders of the people. [48]Now the betrayer had given them a sign, saying, "The one I will kiss is the man; arrest him." [49]At once he came up to Jesus and said, "Greetings, Rabbi!" and kissed him. [50]Jesus said to him, "Friend, do what you are here to do." Then they came and laid hands on Jesus and arrested him. [51]Suddenly, one of those with Jesus put his hand on his sword, drew it, and struck the slave of the high priest, cutting off his ear. [52]Then Jesus said to him, "Put your sword back into its place; for all who take the sword will perish by the sword. [53]Do you think that I cannot appeal to my Father, and he will at once send me more than twelve legions of angels? [54]But how then would the scriptures be fulfilled, which say it must happen in this way?" [55]At that hour Jesus said to the crowds, "Have you come out with swords and clubs to arrest me as though I were a bandit? Day after day I sat in the temple teaching, and you did not arrest me. [56]But all this has taken place, so that the scriptures of the prophets may be fulfilled." Then all the disciples deserted him and fled.

JESUS BEFORE THE HIGH PRIEST

57 Those who had arrested Jesus took him to Caiaphas the high priest, in whose house the scribes and the elders had gathered. [58]But Peter was following him at a distance, as far as the courtyard of the high priest; and going inside, he sat with the guards in order to see how this would end. [59]Now the chief priests and the whole council were looking for false testimony against Jesus so that they might put him to death, [60]but they found none, though many false witnesses came forward. At last two came forward [61]and said, "This fellow said, 'I am able to destroy the temple of God and to build it in three days.'" [62]The high priest stood up and said, "Have you no answer? What is it that they testify against you?" [63]But Jesus was silent. Then the high priest said to him, "I put you under oath before the living God, tell us if you are the Messiah,[a] the Son of God." [64]Jesus said to him, "You have said so. But I tell you,

---

a Or Christ

> From now on you will see the Son of Man
> > seated at the right hand of Power
> > and coming on the clouds of heaven."

65 Then the high priest tore his clothes and said, "He has blasphemed! Why do we still need witnesses? You have now heard his blasphemy. ⁶⁶What is your verdict?" They answered, "He deserves death." ⁶⁷Then they spat in his face and struck him; and some slapped him, ⁶⁸saying, "Prophesy to us, you Messiah!ᵃ Who is it that struck you?"

PETER'S DENIAL OF JESUS

69 Now Peter was sitting outside in the courtyard. A servant-girl came to him and said, "You also were with Jesus the Galilean." ⁷⁰But he denied it before all of them, saying, "I do not know what you are talking about." ⁷¹When he went out to the porch, another servant-girl saw him, and she said to the bystanders, "This man was with Jesus of Nazareth."ᵇ ⁷²Again he denied it with an oath, "I do not know the man." ⁷³After a little while the bystanders came up and said to Peter, "Certainly you are also one of them, for your accent betrays you." ⁷⁴Then he began to curse, and he swore an oath, "I do not know the man!" At that moment the cock crowed. ⁷⁵Then Peter remembered what Jesus had said: "Before the cock crows, you will deny me three times." And he went out and wept bitterly.

JESUS BROUGHT BEFORE PILATE

27 When morning came, all the chief priests and the elders of the people conferred together against Jesus in order to bring about his death. ²They bound him, led him away, and handed him over to Pilate the governor.

THE SUICIDE OF JUDAS

3 When Judas, his betrayer, saw that Jesusᶜ was condemned, he repented and brought back the thirty pieces of silver to the chief priests and the elders. ⁴He said, "I have sinned by betraying innocentᵈ blood." But they said, "What is that to us? See to it yourself." ⁵Throwing down the pieces of silver in the temple, he departed; and he went and hanged himself. ⁶But the chief priests, taking the pieces of silver, said, "It is not lawful to put them into the treasury, since they are blood money." ⁷After conferring together, they used them to buy the potter's field as a place to bury foreigners. ⁸For this reason that field has been called the Field of Blood to this day. ⁹Then was fulfilled what had been spoken

---

a Or *Christ*   *b* Gk *the Nazorean*   *c* Gk *he*   *d* Other ancient authorities read *righteous* through the prophet Jeremiah,[a] "And they took[b] the thirty pieces of silver, the price of the one on whom a price had been set,[c] on whom some of the people of Israel had set a price, [10]and they gave[d] them for the potter's field, as the Lord commanded me."

PILATE QUESTIONS JESUS

11 Now Jesus stood before the governor; and the governor asked him, "Are you the King of the Jews?" Jesus said, "You say so." [12]But when he was accused by the chief priests and elders, he did not answer. [13]Then Pilate said to him, "Do you not hear how many accusations they make against you?" [14]But he gave him no answer, not even to a single charge, so that the governor was greatly amazed.

BARABBAS OR JESUS?

15 Now at the festival the governor was accustomed to release a prisoner for the crowd, anyone whom they wanted. [16]At that time they had a notorious prisoner, called Jesus[e] Barabbas. [17]So after they had gathered, Pilate said to them, "Whom do you want me to release for you, Jesus[e] Barabbas or Jesus who is called the Messiah?"[f] [18]For he realized that it was out of jealousy that they had handed him over. [19]While he was sitting on the judgment seat, his wife sent word to him, "Have nothing to do with that innocent man, for today I have suffered a great deal because of a dream about him." [20]Now the chief priests and the elders persuaded the crowds to ask for Barabbas and to have Jesus killed. [21]The governor again said to them, "Which of the two do you want me to release for you?" And they said, "Barabbas." [22]Pilate said to them, "Then what should I do with Jesus who is called the Messiah?"[f] All of them said, "Let him be crucified!" [23]Then he asked, "Why, what evil has he done?" But they shouted all the more, "Let him be crucified!"

PILATE HANDS JESUS OVER TO BE CRUCIFIED

24 So when Pilate saw that he could do nothing, but rather that a riot was beginning, he took some water and washed his hands before the crowd, saying, "I am innocent of this man's blood;[g] see to it yourselves." [25]Then the people as a whole answered, "His blood be on us and on our children!" [26]So he released Barabbas for them; and after flogging Jesus, he handed him over to be crucified.

---

a Other ancient authorities read *Zechariah* or *Isaiah*　*b* Or *I took*　*c* Or *the price of the precious One*　*d* Other ancient authorities read *I gave*　*e* Other ancient authorities lack *Jesus*　*f* Or *the Christ*　*g* Other ancient authorities read *this righteous blood,* or *this righteous man's blood*

THE SOLDIERS MOCK JESUS

27 Then the soldiers of the governor took Jesus into the governor's head-quarters,*a* and they gathered the whole cohort around him. ²⁸They stripped him and put a scarlet robe on him, ²⁹and after twisting some thorns into a crown, they put it on his head. They put a reed in his right hand and knelt before him and mocked him, saying, "Hail, King of the Jews!" ³⁰They spat on him, and took the reed and struck him on the head. ³¹After mocking him, they stripped him of the robe and put his own clothes on him. Then they led him away to crucify him.

THE CRUCIFIXION OF JESUS

32 As they went out, they came upon a man from Cyrene named Simon; they compelled this man to carry his cross. ³³And when they came to a place called Golgotha (which means Place of a Skull), ³⁴they offered him wine to drink, mixed with gall; but when he tasted it, he would not drink it. ³⁵And when they had crucified him, they divided his clothes among themselves by casting lots;*b* ³⁶then they sat down there and kept watch over him. ³⁷Over his head they put the charge against him, which read, "This is Jesus, the King of the Jews."

38 Then two bandits were crucified with him, one on his right and one on his left. ³⁹Those who passed by derided*c* him, shaking their heads ⁴⁰and saying, "You who would destroy the temple and build it in three days, save yourself! If you are the Son of God, come down from the cross." ⁴¹In the same way the chief priests also, along with the scribes and elders, were mocking him, saying, ⁴²"He saved others; he cannot save himself.*d* He is the King of Israel; let him come down from the cross now, and we will believe in him. ⁴³He trusts in God; let God deliver him now, if he wants to; for he said, 'I am God's Son.'" ⁴⁴The bandits who were crucified with him also taunted him in the same way.

THE DEATH OF JESUS

45 From noon on, darkness came over the whole land*e* until three in the afternoon. ⁴⁶And about three o'clock Jesus cried with a loud voice, "Eli, Eli, lema sabachthani?" that is, "My God, my God, why have you forsaken me?" ⁴⁷When some of the bystanders heard it, they said, "This man is calling for Elijah." ⁴⁸At once one of them ran and got a sponge, filled it with sour wine, put it on a stick, and gave it to him to drink. ⁴⁹But the others said, "Wait, let us see whether

---

a Gk *the praetorium*   *b* Other ancient authorities add *in order that what had been spoken through the prophet might be fulfilled,* *"They divided my clothes among themselves, and for my clothing they cast lots."*   *c* Or *blasphemed*   *d* Or *is he unable to save himself?*   *e* Or *earth*

Elijah will come to save him."[a] [50]Then Jesus cried again with a loud voice and breathed his last.[b] [51]At that moment the curtain of the temple was torn in two, from top to bottom. The earth shook, and the rocks were split. [52]The tombs also were opened, and many bodies of the saints who had fallen asleep were raised. [53]After his resurrection they came out of the tombs and entered the holy city and appeared to many. [54]Now when the centurion and those with him, who were keeping watch over Jesus, saw the earthquake and what took place, they were terrified and said, "Truly this man was God's Son!"[c]

55 Many women were also there, looking on from a distance; they had followed Jesus from Galilee and had provided for him. [56]Among them were Mary Magdalene, and Mary the mother of James and Joseph, and the mother of the sons of Zebedee.

THE BURIAL OF JESUS

57 When it was evening, there came a rich man from Arimathea, named Joseph, who was also a disciple of Jesus. [58]He went to Pilate and asked for the body of Jesus; then Pilate ordered it to be given to him. [59]So Joseph took the body and wrapped it in a clean linen cloth [60]and laid it in his own new tomb, which he had hewn in the rock. He then rolled a great stone to the door of the tomb and went away. [61]Mary Magdalene and the other Mary were there, sitting opposite the tomb.

THE GUARD AT THE TOMB

62 The next day, that is, after the day of Preparation, the chief priests and the Pharisees gathered before Pilate [63]and said, "Sir, we remember what that impostor said while he was still alive, 'After three days I will rise again.' [64]Therefore command the tomb to be made secure until the third day; otherwise his disciples may go and steal him away, and tell the people, 'He has been raised from the dead,' and the last deception would be worse than the first." [65]Pilate said to them, "You have a guard[d] of soldiers; go, make it as secure as you can."[e] [66]So they went with the guard and made the tomb secure by sealing the stone.

THE RESURRECTION OF JESUS

28 After the sabbath, as the first day of the week was dawning, Mary Magdalene and the other Mary went to see the tomb. [2]And suddenly there was a great earthquake; for an angel of the Lord, descending from heaven,

---

a Other ancient authorities add And another took a spear and pierced his side, and out came water and blood   b Or gave up his spirit   c Or a son of God   d Or Take a guard   e Gk you know how came and rolled back the stone and sat on it. ³His appearance was like lightning, and his clothing white as snow. ⁴For fear of him the guards shook and became like dead men. ⁵But the angel said to the women, "Do not be afraid; I know that you are looking for Jesus who was crucified. ⁶He is not here; for he has been raised, as he said. Come, see the place where he*ᵃ* lay. ⁷Then go quickly and tell his disciples, 'He has been raised from the dead,*ᵇ* and indeed he is going ahead of you to Galilee; there you will see him.' This is my message for you." ⁸So they left the tomb quickly with fear and great joy, and ran to tell his disciples. ⁹Suddenly Jesus met them and said, "Greetings!" And they came to him, took hold of his feet, and worshiped him. ¹⁰Then Jesus said to them, "Do not be afraid; go and tell my brothers to go to Galilee; there they will see me."

THE REPORT OF THE GUARD

11 While they were going, some of the guard went into the city and told the chief priests everything that had happened. ¹²After the priests*ᶜ* had assembled with the elders, they devised a plan to give a large sum of money to the soldiers, ¹³telling them, "You must say, 'His disciples came by night and stole him away while we were asleep.' ¹⁴If this comes to the governor's ears, we will satisfy him and keep you out of trouble." ¹⁵So they took the money and did as they were directed. And this story is still told among the Jews to this day.

THE COMMISSIONING OF THE DISCIPLES

16 Now the eleven disciples went to Galilee, to the mountain to which Jesus had directed them. ¹⁷When they saw him, they worshiped him; but some doubted. ¹⁸And Jesus came and said to them, "All authority in heaven and on earth has been given to me. ¹⁹Go therefore and make disciples of all nations, baptizing them in the name of the Father and of the Son and of the Holy Spirit, ²⁰and teaching them to obey everything that I have commanded you. And remember, I am with you always, to the end of the age."*ᵈ*

---

a Other ancient authorities read *the Lord*   *b* Other ancient authorities lack *from the dead*   *c* Gk *they*   *d* Other ancient authorities add *Amen*

Hebrews

The document we know as "the letter to the Hebrews" is exceptionally rich. Its central and best-known metaphor presents Jesus as the "great high priest" who offers himself as the "once for all" sacrifice. Its chapter on faith is one of the most famous in the New Testament. Its creative use of texts from the Jewish Bible, especially from Psalms and the prophets, is powerful.

We do not know who wrote it. In the 200s, an early Christian theologian named Origen said that its author "was known only to God." In the centuries since, there have been guesses. Around the year 400, Augustine and Jerome suggested it was written by Paul, and thus it has sometimes been called the fourteenth letter of Paul. But there is no reason to think Paul wrote it, and many reasons to think he did not. Other guesses have included Barnabas, Apollos, and Priscilla. None is persuasive, and modern scholarship agrees with Origen: God only knows who wrote it.

We also do not know to whom it was written. Unlike most New Testament letters, it does not name its audience. The title "to the Hebrews" was added in the second century and is potentially misleading. "Hebrews" is most commonly a synonym for "Jews," but the document is clearly written to Christians. Moreover, though the document does not have the typical characteristics of a letter, its contents make it clear that it was meant for a particular community, not for a category of people like "the Hebrews" or "the Jews" or Christians in general.

From the document itself, we learn a few things about the author. His use of Greek and his literary style were very sophisticated, perhaps the best in the New Testament. He knew the Old Testament very well, quoting it thirty times, sometimes at considerable length, and alluding to it another seventy times. He was brilliant, creatively weaving together evocative readings of texts from the Jewish Bible with a presentation of Jesus as the Son of God, who is also the great high priest and sacrifice.

We also learn some things about the community. It was made up of second-generation or later Christians. They had experienced suffering and persecution (though apparently not fatal). Some were considering abandoning Christianity, and perhaps some had. The community may have been in Italy. "Those from Italy send you greetings" (13.24) probably refers to the destination of the letter, not the location of the author. If in Italy, then perhaps it was sent to Rome.

The author's repeated use of the Jewish Bible also tells us something about the community. Not only does it suggest that the Old Testament was of great importance to its members, but also that he could count on their recognizing the verses he quoted and the allusions he made. This suggests it was made up of Christian Jews or "God-lovers" and most likely both. Most "God-lovers" knew the Jewish Bible well from their attachment to Jewish synagogues.

Dating

There is no consensus about the date of Hebrews. Estimates range from 60 to the early 90s. Though the document emphasizes the temple, the high priesthood, and sacrifice, it does not mention the destruction of the temple and the end of sacrifice in the year 70. Thus some scholars argue that it must have been written before 70. Other scholars, at least a slight majority, are not persuaded by the lack of reference to the events of 70. The circumstances of the letter—second-generation or later Christians who had experienced persecution, some of whom were tempted to abandon Christianity—suggest a later date. That the author did not refer to the destruction of the temple may be because it was part of what he and his audience took for granted as common knowledge.

On the whole, a date later than 70 seems likely. The situation of the community is similar to the time period implied in Matthew's gospel, the 80s or perhaps very early 90s. So I have sequenced it after Matthew and before other documents from the 90s.

Jesus as God's Son

"Long ago," Hebrews begins, "God spoke to our ancestors in many and various ways by the prophets, but in these last days . . . has spoken to us by a Son." God has appointed him "heir of all things," and through him God "also created the worlds." He is no less than "the reflection of God's glory and the exact imprint of God's very being, . . . he sustains all things by his powerful words," and he is now "at the right hand of the Majesty on high" (1.1–3). These affirmations about Jesus are similar to those in Colossians and the gospel of John, both of which speak of the cosmic Christ present with God at creation.

Hebrews also emphasizes the importance of Jesus's humanity. As the pioneer of our salvation (2.10), he had to experience what we do in every respect; only so could he be a faithful and compassionate high priest able to sympathize with our weakness (2.17; 4.15). Hebrews even says that Jesus had to learn obedience and did so through suffering (5.8). Incarnation matters for Hebrews, as it does for John's gospel.

Jesus as the Great High Priest

The author's central metaphor for Jesus dominates most of the document. Announced in 2.17 and 3.1, it becomes central from 4.14 though chapter 10. The linguistic home of the metaphor, the framework within which it has its meaning, is the temple in Jerusalem, the high priest, and temple sacrifice.

Though the meaning of this language would have been well known to the community to whom Hebrews was written, it is not so among us. Within Judaism, the temple in Jerusalem was the dwelling place of God on earth. Because it was God's dwelling place, it was there and only there that sacrifices were offered to God.

Sacrifices had various purposes. Because many people today automatically think of sacrifice and sin as intrinsically connected, it is important to know that not all sacrifices had to do with sin. Some were about hosting God—about "feeding" the God who dwelled in the temple. Some were sacrifices of thanksgiving, petition, and purification, none of which intrinsically involved forgiveness of sin as the motivation. Sacrifices that did involve sin were sacrifices of reconciliation in which the community, represented by temple priests, offered a sacrifice as a way of making peace with God.

Within this system, the high priest, appointed from the tribe of Levi, was the chief official of the temple. There was only one at a time and, according to Jewish law, he served for life (although during the Roman period Rome appointed and deposed Jewish high priests at will). He represented God to the people and the people to God. Only he could enter "the Holy of Holies," the innermost chamber of the temple, and only on one day of the year, the Day of Atonement.

This is the context in which Hebrews proclaims that Jesus is the "great high priest." He—not the temple high priest—is the mediator between God and God's people. He has entered the inner shrine behind the curtain (6.19–20). The author knew that Jesus was not descended from the tribe of Levi and thus did not have a genetic qualification to be high priest, so in chapter 7 he presents Jesus as a priest from the "order of Melchizedek," a figure from Genesis who blessed Abraham. Melchizedek, Hebrews tells us, was a "king of justice" and "king of peace." Jesus is descended from him.

For Hebrews, Jesus is not only the great high priest, but also the sacrifice. What he sacrificed was his life. Moreover, his sacrifice rendered temple sacrifice unnecessary. His death was the "once for all" sacrifice for sin (9.12, 26). Therefore, Jesus is the "mediator of a new covenant" (9.15), and we have a great high priest over the house of God (10.21).

The image of Jesus as the "once for all" sacrifice for sin has often been misunderstood in Christian history. It has been placed within a theological framework that emphasizes that we are all sinners, that our sins must be paid for in order for God to forgive us, and that Jesus is the sacrifice who paid the price. This theological framework is a later development, not present in the first thousand years of Christianity. It was first theologically articulated by St. Anselm in 1098.

Within this framework, God cannot or will not forgive sins unless adequate payment is made; for God to forgive without payment would imply that sin doesn't matter all that much to God. Somebody had to pay the price. But ordinary humans couldn't pay the price; they would be dying only for their own sins. Only a perfect human, a sinless human who didn't deserve to die, could be the sacrifice. For Anselm, this explained the necessity of the incarnation: God became human in Jesus so that he could be the perfect sacrifice that paid for our sins.

The theological terms for this understanding of Jesus's death include "substitutionary atonement" and the "satisfaction theory of the atonement." The first emphasizes that Jesus died in our place, the second that he satisfied the debt we owe to God. Though less than a thousand years old, many people today (perhaps most) think that this is orthodox Christianity—the official, traditional, ancient understanding of Jesus's death. It is the "default" position for many when they hear the words "sacrifice" and "atonement" and when they think about the death of Jesus.

Note what this view implicitly (and sometimes explicitly) affirms about Jesus. His death was necessary—God required a perfect sacrifice, and Jesus was it. His death was the most important thing about his life. This is the heart of the most widespread contemporary understanding of Christianity's gospel: Jesus died for our sins, so that we can be forgiven. It is usually accompanied by the promise of a blessed afterlife: if we believe that he died for us, we can go to heaven.

This theological framework is the result of literalizing the metaphorical language of Hebrews and some other passages in the New Testament. It also involves a rationalizing of this language, reducing it to statements in doctrinal formulations.

All of this goes far beyond what the language of Hebrews communicated near the end of the first century. The author is obviously using metaphorical language. He did not think Jesus was literally a high priest; he knew that Jesus was from the tribe of Judah and not Levi. He knew that Jesus never served as the high priest of Jerusalem. He knew that Jesus never entered the Holy of Holies in the Jerusalem temple. All of this is metaphor. And it is meaningful metaphor. For Christians, Jesus is the great high priest, even though he was never the high priest of the Jerusalem temple.

So also the language of Jesus as sacrifice is metaphorical. He was not literally a divine-human sacrifice planned and required by God, so that our sins can be paid for and we can be forgiven. In Hebrews (and in the New Testament generally when the language of sacrifice is used), what Jesus sacrificed was his life because of his passion for God. To sacrifice is to make a gift of one's life to God. That is what Jesus did—not because God required it, but because of his passion for God and God's will.

Within its late first-century historical context, the language of Hebrews is thoroughly subversive. It subverts the foundation of temple theology—the claim that only through the temple is reconciliation with God possible. The author argues that what we see in Jesus means that the need for temple sacrifice is over with. "Where there is forgiveness of these [sins], there is no longer any offering for sin" (10.18). Hebrews is about the end of the system of sacrifice, not about its reestablishment in Christian doctrinal form.

The metaphorical meaning of its presentation of Jesus as high priest and sacrifice is radical: God through Jesus has taken away whatever you think separates you from God. The "once for all" sacrifice has been made. The system of requirements is over with. This meaning is confirmed by the author's use of "new covenant" language from Jeremiah 31.31–34. He refers to the passage more than once (8.8–13; 9.15–20; 10.9–18). The "new covenant" is written in minds and hearts, not in a list of requirements. It is about "knowing God," who remembers sins no more.

Faith

After the multichapter exposition of Jesus as great high priest and sacrifice, Hebrews 11 speaks about faith. It begins with a definition: "Faith is the assurance of things hoped for, the conviction of things not seen." It continues with a litany of heroes of faith in the Jewish Bible: Abel, Enoch, Noah, Abraham, Isaac, Jacob, Joseph, Moses, the people of the exodus generation, Rahab, and others whom the author says he doesn't have time to describe. His examples of faith combine trust, obedience, and hope—the desire for a better country, a homeland, a city whose architect and builder is God (11.10, 13–16).

Concluding Counsel

The rest of the document (chaps. 12–13) contains practical counsel for the community in its specific circumstances. Some of it is encouragement to a community under pressure. The recipients are told to persevere, to endure trials, to lift their drooping hands and strengthen their weak knees, to avoid bitterness, and not to sell their birthright.

   Some of it is a reminder of ethical teachings that are to shape their lives. They are to let mutual love continue, show hospitality to strangers, and remember those in prison; be faithful in marriage, free from the love of money, and content with what they have; and do good and share. In the midst of these is one of the best-known verses from Hebrews: "Jesus Christ is the same yesterday and today and forever" (13.8). The context is ethical; they are to remember what they had been taught. Thus after its unique presentation of Jesus as high priest and sacrifice, Hebrews ends with ethical teachings common to early Christian communities.

Hebrews

GOD HAS SPOKEN BY HIS SON

1 Long ago God spoke to our ancestors in many and various ways by the prophets, ²but in these last days he has spoken to us by a Son,ᵃ whom he appointed heir of all things, through whom he also created the worlds. ³He is the reflection of God's glory and the exact imprint of God's very being, and he sustainsᵇ all things by his powerful word. When he had made purification for sins, he sat down at the right hand of the Majesty on high, ⁴having become as much superior to angels as the name he has inherited is more excellent than theirs.

THE SON IS SUPERIOR TO ANGELS

5 For to which of the angels did God ever say,

> "You are my Son;
>> today I have begotten you"?

Or again,

> "I will be his Father,
>> and he will be my Son"?

6 And again, when he brings the firstborn into the world, he says,

> "Let all God's angels worship him."

7 Of the angels he says,

> "He makes his angels winds,
>> and his servants flames of fire."

---

a Or the Son *b* Or bears along

8 But of the Son he says,

> "Your throne, O God, is^a forever and ever,
>   and the righteous scepter is the scepter of your^b kingdom.
> 9 You have loved righteousness and hated wickedness;
>   therefore God, your God, has anointed you
>   with the oil of gladness beyond your companions."

10 And,

> "In the beginning, Lord, you founded the earth,
>   and the heavens are the work of your hands;
> 11 they will perish, but you remain;
>   they will all wear out like
>   clothing;
> 12 like a cloak you will roll them up,
>   and like clothing^c they will be changed.
>   But you are the same,
>   and your years will never end."

13 But to which of the angels has he ever said,

> "Sit at my right hand
>   until I make your enemies a footstool for your feet"?

14 Are not all angels^d spirits in the divine service, sent to serve for the sake of those who are to inherit salvation?

WARNING TO PAY ATTENTION

2 Therefore we must pay greater attention to what we have heard, so that we do not drift away from it. ²For if the message declared through angels was valid, and every transgression or disobedience received a just penalty, ³how can we escape if we neglect so great a salvation? It was declared at first through the Lord, and it was attested to us by those who heard him, ⁴while God added his testimony by signs and wonders and various miracles, and by gifts of the Holy Spirit, distributed according to his will.

EXALTATION THROUGH ABASEMENT

5 Now God^e did not subject the coming world, about which we are speaking, to angels. ⁶But someone has testified somewhere,

> "What are human beings that you are mindful of them,^f
>   or mortals, that you care for them?^g

---

a Or *God is your throne*   b Other ancient authorities read *his*   c Other ancient authorities lack *like clothing*   d Gk *all of them*
e Gk *he*   f Gk *What is man that you are mindful of him?*   g Gk *or the son of man that you care for him?* In the Hebrew of Psalm
8.4–6 both *man* and *son of man* refer to all humankind

7 You have made them for a little while lower[a] than the angels;

    you have crowned them with glory and honor,[b]

8 subjecting all things under their feet."

Now in subjecting all things to them, God[c] left nothing outside their control. As it is, we do not yet see everything in subjection to them, [9]but we do see Jesus, who for a little while was made lower[d] than the angels, now crowned with glory and honor because of the suffering of death, so that by the grace of God[e] he might taste death for everyone.

10 It was fitting that God,[c] for whom and through whom all things exist, in bringing many children to glory, should make the pioneer of their salvation perfect through sufferings. [11]For the one who sanctifies and those who are sanctified all have one Father.[f] For this reason Jesus[c] is not ashamed to call them brothers and sisters,[g] [12]saying,

    "I will proclaim your name to my brothers and sisters,[g]

    in the midst of the congregation I will praise you."

13 And again,

    "I will put my trust in him."

And again,

    "Here am I and the children whom God has given me."

14 Since, therefore, the children share flesh and blood, he himself likewise shared the same things, so that through death he might destroy the one who has the power of death, that is, the devil, [15]and free those who all their lives were held in slavery by the fear of death. [16]For it is clear that he did not come to help angels, but the descendants of Abraham. [17]Therefore he had to become like his brothers and sisters[g] in every respect, so that he might be a merciful and faithful high priest in the service of God, to make a sacrifice of atonement for the sins of the people. [18]Because he himself was tested by what he suffered, he is able to help those who are being tested.

MOSES A SERVANT, CHRIST A SON

3 Therefore, brothers and sisters,[g] holy partners in a heavenly calling, consider that Jesus, the apostle and high priest of our confession, [2]was faithful to the one who appointed him, just as Moses also "was faithful in all[h] God's[i] house." [3]Yet Jesus[j] is worthy of more glory than Moses, just as the builder of a house has more honor than the house itself. [4](For every house is built by someone, but the builder of all things is God.) [5]Now Moses was faithful in all God's[i]

---

a Or *them only a little lower* b Other ancient authorities add *and set them over the works of your hands* c Gk *he* d Or *who was made a little lower* e Other ancient authorities read *apart from God* f Gk *are all of one* g Gk *brothers* h Other ancient authorities lack *all* i Gk *his* j Gk *this one* house as a servant, to testify to the things that would be spoken later. [6]Christ, however, was faithful over God's[a] house as a son, and we are his house if we hold firm[b] the confidence and the pride that belong to hope.

WARNING AGAINST UNBELIEF

7 Therefore, as the Holy Spirit says,

> "Today, if you hear his voice,
>   8 do not harden your hearts as in the rebellion,
>   as on the day of testing in the wilderness,
>   9 where your ancestors put me to the test,
>   though they had seen my works [10]for forty years.
>   Therefore I was angry with that generation,
>   and I said, 'They always go astray in their hearts,
>   and they have not known my ways.'
>   11 As in my anger I swore,
>   'They will not enter my rest.'"

12 Take care, brothers and sisters,[c] that none of you may have an evil, unbelieving heart that turns away from the living God. [13]But exhort one another every day, as long as it is called "today," so that none of you may be hardened by the deceitfulness of sin. [14]For we have become partners of Christ, if only we hold our first confidence firm to the end. [15]As it is said,

> "Today, if you hear his voice,
>   do not harden your hearts as in the rebellion."

[16]Now who were they who heard and yet were rebellious? Was it not all those who left Egypt under the leadership of Moses? [17]But with whom was he angry forty years? Was it not those who sinned, whose bodies fell in the wilderness? [18]And to whom did he swear that they would not enter his rest, if not to those who were disobedient? [19]So we see that they were unable to enter because of unbelief.

THE REST THAT GOD PROMISED

4 Therefore, while the promise of entering his rest is still open, let us take care that none of you should seem to have failed to reach it. [2]For indeed the good news came to us just as to them; but the message they heard did not benefit them, because they were not united by faith with those who listened.[d] [3]For we who have believed enter that rest, just as God[e] has said,

---

a Gk *his*   b Other ancient authorities add *to the end*   c Gk *brothers*   d Other ancient authorities read *it did not meet with faith in those who listened*   e Gk *he*

"As in my anger I swore,
    'They shall not enter my rest,'"

though his works were finished at the foundation of the world. ⁴For in one place it speaks about the seventh day as follows, "And God rested on the seventh day from all his works." ⁵And again in this place it says, "They shall not enter my rest." ⁶Since therefore it remains open for some to enter it, and those who formerly received the good news failed to enter because of disobedience, ⁷again he sets a certain day—"today"—saying through David much later, in the words already quoted,

"Today, if you hear his voice,
    do not harden your hearts."

8 For if Joshua had given them rest, God*a* would not speak later about another day. ⁹So then, a sabbath rest still remains for the people of God; ¹⁰for those who enter God's rest also cease from their labors as God did from his. ¹¹Let us therefore make every effort to enter that rest, so that no one may fall through such disobedience as theirs.

12 Indeed, the word of God is living and active, sharper than any two-edged sword, piercing until it divides soul from spirit, joints from marrow; it is able to judge the thoughts and intentions of the heart. ¹³And before him no creature is hidden, but all are naked and laid bare to the eyes of the one to whom we must render an account.

JESUS THE GREAT HIGH PRIEST

14 Since, then, we have a great high priest who has passed through the heavens, Jesus, the Son of God, let us hold fast to our confession. ¹⁵For we do not have a high priest who is unable to sympathize with our weaknesses, but we have one who in every respect has been tested*b* as we are, yet without sin. ¹⁶Let us therefore approach the throne of grace with boldness, so that we may receive mercy and find grace to help in time of need.

5 Every high priest chosen from among mortals is put in charge of things pertaining to God on their behalf, to offer gifts and sacrifices for sins. ²He is able to deal gently with the ignorant and wayward, since he himself is subject to weakness; ³and because of this he must offer sacrifice for his own sins as well as for those of the people. ⁴And one does not presume to take this honor, but takes it only when called by God, just as Aaron was.

5 So also Christ did not glorify himself in becoming a high priest, but was appointed by the one who said to him,

---

a Gk *he*   *b* Or *tempted*

"You are my Son,
today I have begotten you";

6 as he says also in another place,

"You are a priest forever,
according to the order of Melchizedek."

7 In the days of his flesh, Jesus[a] offered up prayers and supplications, with loud cries and tears, to the one who was able to save him from death, and he was heard because of his reverent submission. [8]Although he was a Son, he learned obedience through what he suffered; [9]and having been made perfect, he became the source of eternal salvation for all who obey him, [10]having been designated by God a high priest according to the order of Melchizedek.

WARNING AGAINST FALLING AWAY

11 About this[b] we have much to say that is hard to explain, since you have become dull in understanding. [12]For though by this time you ought to be teachers, you need someone to teach you again the basic elements of the oracles of God. You need milk, not solid food; [13]for everyone who lives on milk, being still an infant, is unskilled in the word of righteousness. [14]But solid food is for the mature, for those whose faculties have been trained by practice to distinguish good from evil.

THE PERIL OF FALLING AWAY

6 Therefore let us go on toward perfection,[c] leaving behind the basic teaching about Christ, and not laying again the foundation: repentance from dead works and faith toward God, [2]instruction about baptisms, laying on of hands, resurrection of the dead, and eternal judgment. [3]And we will do[d] this, if God permits. [4]For it is impossible to restore again to repentance those who have once been enlightened, and have tasted the heavenly gift, and have shared in the Holy Spirit, [5]and have tasted the goodness of the word of God and the powers of the age to come, [6]and then have fallen away, since on their own they are crucifying again the Son of God and are holding him up to contempt. [7]Ground that drinks up the rain falling on it repeatedly, and that produces a crop useful to those for whom it is cultivated, receives a blessing from God. [8]But if it produces thorns and thistles, it is worthless and on the verge of being cursed; its end is to be burned over.

9 Even though we speak in this way, beloved, we are confident of better things in your case, things that belong to salvation. [10]For God is not unjust; he

---

a Gk he   b Or him   c Or toward maturity   d Other ancient authorities read let us do will not overlook your work and the love that you showed for his sake[a] in serving the saints, as you still do. [11]And we want each one of you to show the same diligence so as to realize the full assurance of hope to the very end, [12]so that you may not become sluggish, but imitators of those who through faith and patience inherit the promises.

THE CERTAINTY OF GOD'S PROMISE

13 When God made a promise to Abraham, because he had no one greater by whom to swear, he swore by himself, [14]saying, "I will surely bless you and multiply you." [15]And thus Abraham,[b] having patiently endured, obtained the promise. [16]Human beings, of course, swear by someone greater than themselves, and an oath given as confirmation puts an end to all dispute. [17]In the same way, when God desired to show even more clearly to the heirs of the promise the unchangeable character of his purpose, he guaranteed it by an oath, [18]so that through two unchangeable things, in which it is impossible that God would prove false, we who have taken refuge might be strongly encouraged to seize the hope set before us. [19]We have this hope, a sure and steadfast anchor of the soul, a hope that enters the inner shrine behind the curtain, [20]where Jesus, a forerunner on our behalf, has entered, having become a high priest forever according to the order of Melchizedek.

THE PRIESTLY ORDER OF MELCHIZEDEK

7 This "King Melchizedek of Salem, priest of the Most High God, met Abraham as he was returning from defeating the kings and blessed him"; [2]and to him Abraham apportioned "one-tenth of everything." His name, in the first place, means "king of righteousness"; next he is also king of Salem, that is, "king of peace." [3]Without father, without mother, without genealogy, having neither beginning of days nor end of life, but resembling the Son of God, he remains a priest forever.

4 See how great he is! Even[c] Abraham the patriarch gave him a tenth of the spoils. [5]And those descendants of Levi who receive the priestly office have a commandment in the law to collect tithes[d] from the people, that is, from their kindred,[e] though these also are descended from Abraham. [6]But this man, who does not belong to their ancestry, collected tithes[d] from Abraham and blessed him who had received the promises. [7]It is beyond dispute that the inferior is blessed by the superior. [8]In the one case, tithes are received by those who are mortal; in the other, by one of whom it is testified that he lives. [9]One might

---

a Gk *for his name*   *b* Gk *he*   *c* Other ancient authorities lack *Even*   *d* Or *a tenth*   *e* Gk *brothers* even say that Levi himself, who receives tithes, paid tithes through Abraham, [10]for he was still in the loins of his ancestor when Melchizedek met him.

ANOTHER PRIEST, LIKE MELCHIZEDEK

11 Now if perfection had been attainable through the levitical priesthood—for the people received the law under this priesthood—what further need would there have been to speak of another priest arising according to the order of Melchizedek, rather than one according to the order of Aaron? [12]For when there is a change in the priesthood, there is necessarily a change in the law as well. [13]Now the one of whom these things are spoken belonged to another tribe, from which no one has ever served at the altar. [14]For it is evident that our Lord was descended from Judah, and in connection with that tribe Moses said nothing about priests.

15 It is even more obvious when another priest arises, resembling Melchizedek, [16]one who has become a priest, not through a legal requirement concerning physical descent, but through the power of an indestructible life. [17]For it is attested of him,

> "You are a priest forever,
>> according to the order of Melchizedek."

18 There is, on the one hand, the abrogation of an earlier commandment because it was weak and ineffectual [19](for the law made nothing perfect); there is, on the other hand, the introduction of a better hope, through which we approach God.

20 This was confirmed with an oath; for others who became priests took their office without an oath, [21]but this one became a priest with an oath, because of the one who said to him,

> "The Lord has sworn
>> and will not change his mind,
> 'You are a priest forever'"—

22 accordingly Jesus has also become the guarantee of a better covenant.

23 Furthermore, the former priests were many in number, because they were prevented by death from continuing in office; [24]but he holds his priesthood permanently, because he continues forever. [25]Consequently he is able for all time to save[a] those who approach God through him, since he always lives to make intercession for them.

26 For it was fitting that we should have such a high priest, holy, blameless, undefiled, separated from sinners, and exalted above the heavens. [27]Unlike the

---

a Or able to save completely

other[a] high priests, he has no need to offer sacrifices day after day, first for his own sins, and then for those of the people; this he did once for all when he offered himself. [28]For the law appoints as high priests those who are subject to weakness, but the word of the oath, which came later than the law, appoints a Son who has been made perfect forever.

MEDIATOR OF A BETTER COVENANT

8 Now the main point in what we are saying is this: we have such a high priest, one who is seated at the right hand of the throne of the Majesty in the heavens, [2]a minister in the sanctuary and the true tent[b] that the Lord, and not any mortal, has set up. [3]For every high priest is appointed to offer gifts and sacrifices; hence it is necessary for this priest also to have something to offer. [4]Now if he were on earth, he would not be a priest at all, since there are priests who offer gifts according to the law. [5]They offer worship in a sanctuary that is a sketch and shadow of the heavenly one; for Moses, when he was about to erect the tent,[b] was warned, "See that you make everything according to the pattern that was shown you on the mountain." [6]But Jesus[c] has now obtained a more excellent ministry, and to that degree he is the mediator of a better covenant, which has been enacted through better promises. [7]For if that first covenant had been faultless, there would have been no need to look for a second one.

   8 God[d] finds fault with them when he says:
   "The days are surely coming, says the Lord,
       when I will establish a new covenant with the house of Israel
       and with the house of Judah;
   9 not like the covenant that I made with their ancestors,
       on the day when I took them by the hand to lead them out of the
       land of Egypt;
   for they did not continue in my covenant,
       and so I had no concern for them, says the Lord.
   10 This is the covenant that I will make with the house of Israel
       after those days, says the Lord:
   I will put my laws in their minds,
       and write them on their hearts,
   and I will be their God,
       and they shall be my people.
   11 And they shall not teach one another
       or say to each other, 'Know the Lord,'

---

a Gk lacks *other*   *b* Or *tabernacle*   *c* Gk *he*   *d* Gk *He*

for they shall all know me,
    from the least of them to the greatest.
12 For I will be merciful toward their iniquities,
    and I will remember their sins no more."

13 In speaking of "a new covenant," he has made the first one obsolete. And what is obsolete and growing old will soon disappear.

THE EARTHLY AND THE HEAVENLY SANCTUARIES

9 Now even the first covenant had regulations for worship and an earthly sanctuary. [2]For a tent[a] was constructed, the first one, in which were the lampstand, the table, and the bread of the Presence;[b] this is called the Holy Place. [3]Behind the second curtain was a tent[a] called the Holy of Holies. [4]In it stood the golden altar of incense and the ark of the covenant overlaid on all sides with gold, in which there were a golden urn holding the manna, and Aaron's rod that budded, and the tablets of the covenant; [5]above it were the cherubim of glory overshadowing the mercy seat.[c] Of these things we cannot speak now in detail.

6 Such preparations having been made, the priests go continually into the first tent[a] to carry out their ritual duties; [7]but only the high priest goes into the second, and he but once a year, and not without taking the blood that he offers for himself and for the sins committed unintentionally by the people. [8]By this the Holy Spirit indicates that the way into the sanctuary has not yet been disclosed as long as the first tent[a] is still standing. [9]This is a symbol[d] of the present time, during which gifts and sacrifices are offered that cannot perfect the conscience of the worshiper, [10]but deal only with food and drink and various baptisms, regulations for the body imposed until the time comes to set things right.

11 But when Christ came as a high priest of the good things that have come,[e] then through the greater and perfect[f] tent[a] (not made with hands, that is, not of this creation), [12]he entered once for all into the Holy Place, not with the blood of goats and calves, but with his own blood, thus obtaining eternal redemption. [13]For if the blood of goats and bulls, with the sprinkling of the ashes of a heifer, sanctifies those who have been defiled so that their flesh is purified, [14]how much more will the blood of Christ, who through the eternal Spirit[g] offered himself without blemish to God, purify our[h] conscience from dead works to worship the living God!

---

a Or *tabernacle*   b Gk *the presentation of the loaves*   c Or *the place of atonement*   d Gk *parable*   e Other ancient authorities read *good things to come*   f Gk *more perfect*   g Other ancient authorities read *Holy Spirit*   h Other ancient authorities read *your*

15 For this reason he is the mediator of a new covenant, so that those who are called may receive the promised eternal inheritance, because a death has occurred that redeems them from the transgressions under the first covenant.*ᵃ* ¹⁶Where a will*ᵃ* is involved, the death of the one who made it must be established. ¹⁷For a will*ᵃ* takes effect only at death, since it is not in force as long as the one who made it is alive. ¹⁸Hence not even the first covenant was inaugurated without blood. ¹⁹For when every commandment had been told to all the people by Moses in accordance with the law, he took the blood of calves and goats,*ᵇ* with water and scarlet wool and hyssop, and sprinkled both the scroll itself and all the people, ²⁰saying, "This is the blood of the covenant that God has ordained for you." ²¹And in the same way he sprinkled with the blood both the tent*ᶜ* and all the vessels used in worship. ²²Indeed, under the law almost everything is purified with blood, and without the shedding of blood there is no forgiveness of sins.

CHRIST'S SACRIFICE TAKES AWAY SIN

23 Thus it was necessary for the sketches of the heavenly things to be purified with these rites, but the heavenly things themselves need better sacrifices than these. ²⁴For Christ did not enter a sanctuary made by human hands, a mere copy of the true one, but he entered into heaven itself, now to appear in the presence of God on our behalf. ²⁵Nor was it to offer himself again and again, as the high priest enters the Holy Place year after year with blood that is not his own; ²⁶for then he would have had to suffer again and again since the foundation of the world. But as it is, he has appeared once for all at the end of the age to remove sin by the sacrifice of himself. ²⁷And just as it is appointed for mortals to die once, and after that the judgment, ²⁸so Christ, having been offered once to bear the sins of many, will appear a second time, not to deal with sin, but to save those who are eagerly waiting for him.

CHRIST'S SACRIFICE ONCE FOR ALL

10 Since the law has only a shadow of the good things to come and not the true form of these realities, it*ᵈ* can never, by the same sacrifices that are continually offered year after year, make perfect those who approach. ²Otherwise, would they not have ceased being offered, since the worshipers, cleansed once for all, would no longer have any consciousness of sin? ³But in these sacrifices there is a reminder of sin year after year. ⁴For it is impossible for the blood

---

a The Greek word used here means both *covenant* and *will*   *b* Other ancient authorities lack *and goats*   *c* Or *tabernacle*
d Other ancient authorities read *they*

of bulls and goats to take away sins. [5]Consequently, when Christ[a] came into the world, he said,

> "Sacrifices and offerings you have not desired,
>> but a body you have prepared for me;
> 6 in burnt offerings and sin offerings
>> you have taken no pleasure.
> 7 Then I said, 'See, God, I have come to do your will, O God'
>> (in the scroll of the book[b] it is written of me)."

[8]When he said above, "You have neither desired nor taken pleasure in sacrifices and offerings and burnt offerings and sin offerings" (these are offered according to the law), [9]then he added, "See, I have come to do your will." He abolishes the first in order to establish the second. [10]And it is by God's will[c] that we have been sanctified through the offering of the body of Jesus Christ once for all.

11 And every priest stands day after day at his service, offering again and again the same sacrifices that can never take away sins. [12]But when Christ[d] had offered for all time a single sacrifice for sins, "he sat down at the right hand of God," [13]and since then has been waiting "until his enemies would be made a footstool for his feet." [14]For by a single offering he has perfected for all time those who are sanctified. [15]And the Holy Spirit also testifies to us, for after saying,

> 16 "This is the covenant that I will make with them
>> after those days, says the Lord:
> I will put my laws in their hearts,
>> and I will write them on their minds,"

17 he also adds,

> "I will remember[e] their sins and their lawless deeds no more."

[18]Where there is forgiveness of these, there is no longer any offering for sin.

A CALL TO PERSEVERE

19 Therefore, my friends,[f] since we have confidence to enter the sanctuary by the blood of Jesus, [20]by the new and living way that he opened for us through the curtain (that is, through his flesh), [21]and since we have a great priest over the house of God, [22]let us approach with a true heart in full assurance of faith, with our hearts sprinkled clean from an evil conscience and our bodies washed with pure water. [23]Let us hold fast to the confession of our hope without wavering, for he who has promised is faithful. [24]And let us consider how to provoke one another to love and good deeds, [25]not neglecting to meet together,

---

a Gk *he*   *b* Meaning of Gk uncertain   *c* Gk *by that will*   *d* Gk *this one*   *e* Gk *on their minds and I will remember*
f Gk *Therefore, brothers*

as is the habit of some, but encouraging one another, and all the more as you see the Day approaching.

26 For if we willfully persist in sin after having received the knowledge of the truth, there no longer remains a sacrifice for sins, [27]but a fearful prospect of judgment, and a fury of fire that will consume the adversaries. [28]Anyone who has violated the law of Moses dies without mercy "on the testimony of two or three witnesses." [29]How much worse punishment do you think will be deserved by those who have spurned the Son of God, profaned the blood of the covenant by which they were sanctified, and outraged the Spirit of grace? [30]For we know the one who said, "Vengeance is mine, I will repay." And again, "The Lord will judge his people." [31]It is a fearful thing to fall into the hands of the living God.

32 But recall those earlier days when, after you had been enlightened, you endured a hard struggle with sufferings, [33]sometimes being publicly exposed to abuse and persecution, and sometimes being partners with those so treated. [34]For you had compassion for those who were in prison, and you cheerfully accepted the plundering of your possessions, knowing that you yourselves possessed something better and more lasting. [35]Do not, therefore, abandon that confidence of yours; it brings a great reward. [36]For you need endurance, so that when you have done the will of God, you may receive what was promised. [37]For yet

>   "in a very little while,
>   the one who is coming will come and will not delay;
>   38 but my righteous one will live by faith.
>   My soul takes no pleasure in anyone who shrinks back."

39 But we are not among those who shrink back and so are lost, but among those who have faith and so are saved.

THE MEANING OF FAITH

11 Now faith is the assurance of things hoped for, the conviction of things not seen. [2]Indeed, by faith[a] our ancestors received approval. [3]By faith we understand that the worlds were prepared by the word of God, so that what is seen was made from things that are not visible.[b]

THE EXAMPLES OF ABEL, ENOCH, AND NOAH

4 By faith Abel offered to God a more acceptable[c] sacrifice than Cain's. Through this he received approval as righteous, God himself giving approval

---

a Gk *by this*   b Or *was not made out of visible things*   c Gk *greater* to his gifts; he died, but through his faith*a* he still speaks. ⁵By faith Enoch was taken so that he did not experience death; and "he was not found, because God had taken him." For it was attested before he was taken away that "he had pleased God." ⁶And without faith it is impossible to please God, for whoever would approach him must believe that he exists and that he rewards those who seek him. ⁷By faith Noah, warned by God about events as yet unseen, respected the warning and built an ark to save his household; by this he condemned the world and became an heir to the righteousness that is in accordance with faith.

THE FAITH OF ABRAHAM

8 By faith Abraham obeyed when he was called to set out for a place that he was to receive as an inheritance; and he set out, not knowing where he was going. ⁹By faith he stayed for a time in the land he had been promised, as in a foreign land, living in tents, as did Isaac and Jacob, who were heirs with him of the same promise. ¹⁰For he looked forward to the city that has foundations, whose architect and builder is God. ¹¹By faith he received power of procreation, even though he was too old—and Sarah herself was barren—because he considered him faithful who had promised.*b* ¹²Therefore from one person, and this one as good as dead, descendants were born, "as many as the stars of heaven and as the innumerable grains of sand by the seashore."

13 All of these died in faith without having received the promises, but from a distance they saw and greeted them. They confessed that they were strangers and foreigners on the earth, ¹⁴for people who speak in this way make it clear that they are seeking a homeland. ¹⁵If they had been thinking of the land that they had left behind, they would have had opportunity to return. ¹⁶But as it is, they desire a better country, that is, a heavenly one. Therefore God is not ashamed to be called their God; indeed, he has prepared a city for them.

17 By faith Abraham, when put to the test, offered up Isaac. He who had received the promises was ready to offer up his only son, ¹⁸of whom he had been told, "It is through Isaac that descendants shall be named for you." ¹⁹He considered the fact that God is able even to raise someone from the dead—and figuratively speaking, he did receive him back. ²⁰By faith Isaac invoked blessings for the future on Jacob and Esau. ²¹By faith Jacob, when dying, blessed each of the sons of Joseph, "bowing in worship over the top of his staff." ²²By faith Joseph, at the end of his life, made mention of the exodus of the Israelites and gave instructions about his burial.*c*

---

a Gk through it   b Or By faith Sarah herself, though barren, received power to conceive, even when she was too old, because she considered him faithful who had promised.   c Gk his bones

THE FAITH OF MOSES

23 By faith Moses was hidden by his parents for three months after his birth, because they saw that the child was beautiful; and they were not afraid of the king's edict.*ᵃ* ²⁴By faith Moses, when he was grown up, refused to be called a son of Pharaoh's daughter, ²⁵choosing rather to share ill-treatment with the people of God than to enjoy the fleeting pleasures of sin. ²⁶He considered abuse suffered for the Christ*ᵇ* to be greater wealth than the treasures of Egypt, for he was looking ahead to the reward. ²⁷By faith he left Egypt, unafraid of the king's anger; for he persevered as though*ᶜ* he saw him who is invisible. ²⁸By faith he kept the Passover and the sprinkling of blood, so that the destroyer of the firstborn would not touch the firstborn of Israel.*ᵈ*

THE FAITH OF OTHER ISRAELITE HEROES

29 By faith the people passed through the Red Sea as if it were dry land, but when the Egyptians attempted to do so they were drowned. ³⁰By faith the walls of Jericho fell after they had been encircled for seven days. ³¹By faith Rahab the prostitute did not perish with those who were disobedient,*ᵉ* because she had received the spies in peace.

32 And what more should I say? For time would fail me to tell of Gideon, Barak, Samson, Jephthah, of David and Samuel and the prophets— ³³who through faith conquered kingdoms, administered justice, obtained promises, shut the mouths of lions, ³⁴quenched raging fire, escaped the edge of the sword, won strength out of weakness, became mighty in war, put foreign armies to flight. ³⁵Women received their dead by resurrection. Others were tortured, refusing to accept release, in order to obtain a better resurrection. ³⁶Others suffered mocking and flogging, and even chains and imprisonment. ³⁷They were stoned to death, they were sawn in two,*ᶠ* they were killed by the sword; they went about in skins of sheep and goats, destitute, persecuted, tormented— ³⁸of whom the world was not worthy. They wandered in deserts and mountains, and in caves and holes in the ground.

39 Yet all these, though they were commended for their faith, did not receive what was promised, ⁴⁰since God had provided something better so that they would not, apart from us, be made perfect.

---

a Other ancient authorities add *By faith Moses, when he was grown up, killed the Egyptian, because he observed the humiliation of his people* (Gk *brothers*) *b* Or *the Messiah* *c* Or *because* *d* Gk *would not touch them* *e* Or *unbelieving* *f* Other ancient authorities add *they were tempted*

THE EXAMPLE OF JESUS

12 Therefore, since we are surrounded by so great a cloud of witnesses, let us also lay aside every weight and the sin that clings so closely,[a] and let us run with perseverance the race that is set before us, [2]looking to Jesus the pioneer and perfecter of our faith, who for the sake of[b] the joy that was set before him endured the cross, disregarding its shame, and has taken his seat at the right hand of the throne of God.

3 Consider him who endured such hostility against himself from sinners,[c] so that you may not grow weary or lose heart. [4]In your struggle against sin you have not yet resisted to the point of shedding your blood. [5]And you have forgotten the exhortation that addresses you as children—

> "My child, do not regard lightly the discipline of the Lord,
> or lose heart when you are punished by him;
> 6 for the Lord disciplines those whom he loves,
> and chastises every child whom he accepts."

7 Endure trials for the sake of discipline. God is treating you as children; for what child is there whom a parent does not discipline? [8]If you do not have that discipline in which all children share, then you are illegitimate and not his children. [9]Moreover, we had human parents to discipline us, and we respected them. Should we not be even more willing to be subject to the Father of spirits and live? [10]For they disciplined us for a short time as seemed best to them, but he disciplines us for our good, in order that we may share his holiness. [11]Now, discipline always seems painful rather than pleasant at the time, but later it yields the peaceful fruit of righteousness to those who have been trained by it.

12 Therefore lift your drooping hands and strengthen your weak knees, [13]and make straight paths for your feet, so that what is lame may not be put out of joint, but rather be healed.

WARNINGS AGAINST REJECTING GOD'S GRACE

14 Pursue peace with everyone, and the holiness without which no one will see the Lord. [15]See to it that no one fails to obtain the grace of God; that no root of bitterness springs up and causes trouble, and through it many become defiled. [16]See to it that no one becomes like Esau, an immoral and godless person, who sold his birthright for a single meal. [17]You know that later, when he wanted to inherit the blessing, he was rejected, for he found no chance to repent,[d] even though he sought the blessing[e] with tears.

---

a Other ancient authorities read *sin that easily distracts*   b Or *who instead of*   c Other ancient authorities read *such hostility from sinners against themselves*   d Or *no chance to change his father's mind*   e Gk *it*

18 You have not come to something*a* that can be touched, a blazing fire, and darkness, and gloom, and a tempest, [19]and the sound of a trumpet, and a voice whose words made the hearers beg that not another word be spoken to them. [20](For they could not endure the order that was given, "If even an animal touches the mountain, it shall be stoned to death." [21]Indeed, so terrifying was the sight that Moses said, "I tremble with fear.") [22]But you have come to Mount Zion and to the city of the living God, the heavenly Jerusalem, and to innumerable angels in festal gathering, [23]and to the assembly*b* of the firstborn who are enrolled in heaven, and to God the judge of all, and to the spirits of the righteous made perfect, [24]and to Jesus, the mediator of a new covenant, and to the sprinkled blood that speaks a better word than the blood of Abel.

25 See that you do not refuse the one who is speaking; for if they did not escape when they refused the one who warned them on earth, how much less will we escape if we reject the one who warns from heaven! [26]At that time his voice shook the earth; but now he has promised, "Yet once more I will shake not only the earth but also the heaven." [27]This phrase, "Yet once more," indicates the removal of what is shaken—that is, created things—so that what cannot be shaken may remain. [28]Therefore, since we are receiving a kingdom that cannot be shaken, let us give thanks, by which we offer to God an acceptable worship with reverence and awe; [29]for indeed our God is a consuming fire.

SERVICE WELL-PLEASING TO GOD

13 Let mutual love continue. [2]Do not neglect to show hospitality to strangers, for by doing that some have entertained angels without knowing it. [3]Remember those who are in prison, as though you were in prison with them; those who are being tortured, as though you yourselves were being tortured.*c* [4]Let marriage be held in honor by all, and let the marriage bed be kept undefiled; for God will judge fornicators and adulterers. [5]Keep your lives free from the love of money, and be content with what you have; for he has said, "I will never leave you or forsake you." [6]So we can say with confidence,

> "The Lord is my helper;
> I will not be afraid.
> What can anyone do to me?"

7 Remember your leaders, those who spoke the word of God to you; consider the outcome of their way of life, and imitate their faith. [8]Jesus Christ is the same yesterday and today and forever. [9]Do not be carried away by all kinds of strange teachings; for it is well for the heart to be strengthened by grace, not

---

a Other ancient authorities read *a mountain*   *b* Or *angels, and to the festal gathering* [23]*and assembly*   *c* Gk *were in the body* by regulations about food,*a* which have not benefited those who observe them. ¹⁰We have an altar from which those who officiate in the tent*b* have no right to eat. ¹¹For the bodies of those animals whose blood is brought into the sanctuary by the high priest as a sacrifice for sin are burned outside the camp. ¹²Therefore Jesus also suffered outside the city gate in order to sanctify the people by his own blood. ¹³Let us then go to him outside the camp and bear the abuse he endured. ¹⁴For here we have no lasting city, but we are looking for the city that is to come. ¹⁵Through him, then, let us continually offer a sacrifice of praise to God, that is, the fruit of lips that confess his name. ¹⁶Do not neglect to do good and to share what you have, for such sacrifices are pleasing to God.

17　Obey your leaders and submit to them, for they are keeping watch over your souls and will give an account. Let them do this with joy and not with sighing—for that would be harmful to you.

18　Pray for us; we are sure that we have a clear conscience, desiring to act honorably in all things. ¹⁹I urge you all the more to do this, so that I may be restored to you very soon.

BENEDICTION

20　Now may the God of peace, who brought back from the dead our Lord Jesus, the great shepherd of the sheep, by the blood of the eternal covenant, ²¹make you complete in everything good so that you may do his will, working among us*c* that which is pleasing in his sight, through Jesus Christ, to whom be the glory forever and ever. Amen.

FINAL EXHORTATION AND GREETINGS

22　I appeal to you, brothers and sisters,*d* bear with my word of exhortation, for I have written to you briefly. ²³I want you to know that our brother Timothy has been set free; and if he comes in time, he will be with me when I see you. ²⁴Greet all your leaders and all the saints. Those from Italy send you greetings. ²⁵Grace be with all of you.*e*

---

a Gk *not by foods*　*b* Or *tabernacle*　*c* Other ancient authorities read *you*　*d* Gk *brothers*　*e* Other ancient authorities add *Amen*

John

The gospel of John is very different from the synoptic gospels, as we will see. And yet its language has shaped Christian understandings of Jesus and his significance perhaps even more than the first three gospels. Its language is both familiar and beloved by many Christians:

- Jesus is the "Word of God" become flesh—the Word that was in the beginning with God and was God. The language is not only familiar, but also the basis of the Christian doctrine of the incarnation (literally, "being in the flesh," "embodiment").

- Probably the best-known verse in the New Testament is John 3.16: "For God so loved the world that he gave his only Son, so that everyone who believes in him may not perish but may have eternal life." It is often quoted as a summary of the Christian message and even shows up behind the goal posts at professional football games.

- John's well-known stories include the wedding feast at Cana, where Jesus changed water into wine, Nicodemus and the teaching on being "born again," the Samaritan woman at the well, Lazarus and "resurrection," Jesus's appearance to Mary Magdalene near the empty tomb, and his showing of his wounds to "doubting" Thomas.

- John's series of "I am" statements presents familiar metaphors for Jesus: the Bread of Life; the Light of the World; the Good Shepherd; the Gate or the Door; the Resurrection and the Life; the Way, and the Truth, and the Life; the True Vine; and also simply "I am." Because John presents these as statements of Jesus, Christians for centuries have taken it for granted that Jesus said these things about himself.

Dissimilarities with Mark, Matthew, and Luke

None of the above is found in the synoptic gospels. Moreover, there are other differences. In the synoptics, Jesus frequently teaches with parables. In John, he does not; instead, he often speaks in extended and complex discourses. One is five chapters long (13–17). In the synoptics, Jesus is an exorcist; in John, there are no exorcisms. In the synoptics, Jesus's public activity is mostly in Galilee; only his final journey to Jerusalem takes him south to Judea. In John, Jesus has several periods of public activity in Judea and Jerusalem. In the synoptics, there is one Passover; in John, three. And, perhaps most strikingly, in the synoptics, Jesus's divine identity and status are not part of his teaching; in John, they are.

Yet John and the synoptic gospels also share some things in common:

- The story of Jesus's adult life begins with John the Baptizer.

- Jesus's public activity begins in Galilee.

- He walks on water and comes to his disciples on a stormy sea.

- He feeds a multitude with a few loaves and fish.

- He gives sight to a blind man.

- He raises a dead person.

- He heals a paralytic.

Finally and importantly, John and the synoptics emphasize Jesus's final week in Jerusalem and his crucifixion and resurrection. Indeed, John devotes more of his gospel to this than the other gospels do.

But even when John and the synoptics share similar stories, John most often tells them differently. For example:

> John the Baptizer proclaims Jesus as "the Lamb of God who takes away the sin of the world" and as the "Son of God" (1.29–34). In the synoptics, John does not explicitly proclaim who Jesus is; only in Matthew is there a conversation in which John recognizes that Jesus is greater than he.

> Though Jesus begins his public activity in Galilee, the first scene in John is not about proclaiming the kingdom of God (Mark and Matthew)

or announcing that "the Spirit of the Lord is upon" Jesus (Luke), but a wedding banquet in the village of Cana.

Though both John and the synoptics narrate a dramatic act in which Jesus drove money changers out of the temple, the chronology is very different. In the synoptics, it happens during the last week of Jesus's life and is the reason the authorities decide to arrest him. In John, it happens very near the beginning of Jesus's public activity, immediately after the story of the wedding at Cana.

When Jesus feeds five thousand people with a few loaves and fish, in John it becomes the occasion for a lengthy discourse by Jesus in which he affirms, "I am the bread of life," "the living bread that came down from heaven."

When Jesus restores sight to a blind man, it becomes the occasion for him to say, "I am the light of the world."

When Jesus raises a person from the dead, it becomes the occasion for him to say, "I am the resurrection and the life."

So also the story of Jesus's final week is told very differently. In John, much of it consists of Jesus's "farewell discourses" (chaps. 13–17), spoken on the evening of his arrest. The story of Jesus before Pilate is significantly different. In the synoptics, Jesus is basically silent. In John, the two engage in conversation in which Jesus bests Pilate. Indeed, Jesus seems to be in control of the process.

They even differ on the day of Jesus's crucifixion. In the synoptics, it happens on the day of Passover (Passover was both a weeklong festival and a particular day). The day of Passover began at dusk, so the whole sequence in the synoptics from Jesus's last supper with his followers through his arrest, torture, and death all happened on Passover. In John, it all happens the day before Passover. Jesus dies at the same hour that the Passover lambs are being slaughtered for that evening's Passover meal. Jesus is dead before the Passover begins.

These differences and similarities have led mainline scholars to wonder whether John knew any of the synoptic gospels. Had he read or heard one or more of them? There is no consensus. Some think he knew Mark, and perhaps Luke. The majority are undecided, because the case is inconclusive. Verbal parallels—the kind that are precise enough to imply that an author knew another document—are few. They could be accounted for if both John and the synoptic authors knew some of the same oral tradition. But whether or not John knew any of the other gospels, he went his own way. His gospel is very different.

John's difference from the synoptics was recognized in Christian antiquity. Around the year 200, an early Christian named Clement of Alexandria described it as "a spiritual gospel." He was probably not the first to notice, but the first whose comments have survived. Exactly what Clement meant, beyond naming a difference, is not clear. The most obvious meaning is that John's story—his language—is more symbolic than literal and factual. Such is also the conclusion of mainstream modern scholarship.

Some who think of "history" as "the facts," as "what happened," dismiss John because his story is not straightforwardly factual. They are right to regard John as less "historical" in this sense than the earlier layers of the synoptic gospels. But to dismiss or set John aside would be a mistake. John is a remarkable testimony to what Jesus had become in the early Christian milieu in which the gospel was written. Its language is rich and powerful, and it has shaped Christianity ever since.

Dating

Mainline scholars commonly date John around the year 90. Most also think that John has earlier and later layers. The clearest example is that the gospel seems to end twice—once at the end of chapter 20 and again at the end of chapter 21. The most plausible explanation is that John 21 was added to a "first edition" that ended with John 20. Scholars have also argued that the author may have had what is commonly called a "signs source." Despite uncertainty about what might be earlier and what is likely later, there is a strong consensus that the form in which we have John came from the decade of the 90s. It tells us how Jesus was spoken of in a Christian community near the end of the first century. It does not tell us very much about how Jesus himself spoke.

The Prologue

Whereas Matthew and Luke begin their stories of Jesus with his birth and Mark with John the Baptizer, John begins his with creation—indeed, before creation. His gospel opens with a magnificent prologue that is perhaps an adaptation of an early Christian hymn. Its first words are the same as the first words of Genesis: "In the beginning." The allusion is deliberate, not accidental.

John's prologue continues. What was in the beginning "was the Word, and the Word was with God, and the Word was God." The Greek word translated into English as "word" is *logos,* sometimes capitalized. In Greek philosophy, the *logos* referred to the principle of reason ordering the universe. It was the opposite of chaos. Though John's meaning might include this, his context was thoroughly Jewish. Within

Judaism, God created by "word," speaking the world into being. Prophets spoke "the word of the Lord," God's countercultural word and also promise-filled word.

The "word of God" in Judaism is closely associated with the "wisdom of God," especially in documents written in the five hundred years or so before Jesus, some of them perhaps more or less contemporary with him. There the "wisdom of God" and the "word of God" become virtually interchangeable. God created the world through wisdom, wisdom spoke through the prophets, and wisdom (like the Spirit of God) permeates everything. In both Hebrew and Greek, the word for "wisdom" is grammatically feminine, and in Jewish writings about the wisdom of God, wisdom is often personified as a woman, commonly called "Sophia" in scholarship today.

Given the equivalence between the "word" and "wisdom" of God, John could just as well have written, "In the beginning was Wisdom, and Wisdom was with God, and Wisdom was God." But John chose the word *logos,* a masculine noun in Greek, even though what is meant is without gender and beyond gender. And so the text continues with the masculine pronoun: "He was in the beginning with God." Furthermore, he was not only with God, but active in the process of creation: "All things came into being through him [the Word], and without him not one thing came into being." If John had written about the wisdom of God rather than the word of God, the pronouns would have been feminine.

As John's prologue continues, it announces more major themes of his gospel: life, light, and enlightenment. The Word is the "life" of the world and the "light of all people," the true light that enlightens everyone. Then John declares: "The Word became flesh and lived among us" (1.14). He is, of course referring to Jesus. Jesus is the Word of God become flesh, the incarnation of the Word.

What John says about Jesus and the Word is sometimes misunderstood. For many Christians, "Jesus" and the "Word of God" have become identical and inter-changeable terms. Thus they understand John's opening words to mean, "In the beginning was Jesus, and Jesus was with God, and Jesus was God." But that is not what John says. What was in the beginning with God was the Word/Wisdom of God. But Jesus wasn't there "in the beginning"; that which became flesh in him was. Jesus is the embodiment and revelation of what can be seen of the Word/Wisdom of God in a human life.

The Power of John's Language

John's use of symbolic language is extraordinarily powerful. His images are often "archetypal" (literally, imprinted in human psyches from the beginning). They flow out of the depths of human experience and longing. We see this with great clarity in the "I am" statements that he attributes to Jesus:

"I am the light of the world" (8.12). The archetypal image is darkness and light and its close relative blindness and seeing. The image is not only in John's prologue, but also in the story of Nicodemus (John 3), who comes to Jesus "by night"—he is still in the dark. In John 9, the overcoming of blindness and Jesus as the "light of the world" are juxtaposed.

"I am the bread of life" (6.35). Here the archetypal image is hunger— we hunger for food, and for more than food. Jesus is the "bread of life." John 4 uses the closely related image of thirst: Jesus is the "living water."

"I am the gate" (10.7). Jesus is the gate or door of the sheepfold as well as the Good Shepherd who leads the sheep through the gate (10.11). The larger application of the image is "gate" and "door" as threshold, or point of entry, into a new way of life.

"I am the way" (14.6). The statement, "I am the way, and the truth, and the life," is for some Christians one of the troublesome passages in the New Testament, because it is commonly used to proclaim the superiority and exclusive truth of Christianity. John may have meant it this way in his historical context of conflict between Christian Jews and non-Christian Jews; to his community, he was saying, "What you see in Jesus is the way to true life; don't go back to the way you came from." But to draw the conclusion that Christianity is the only true religion is to go beyond what he meant in his historical context. For John, the image of Jesus as "the way" means the same as Jesus as "the gate," the threshold into new life.

"I am . . . the truth" (14.6). To continue with the second term in the triad, the opposite of truth is falsehood, the lie. What is seen and embodied in Jesus is "the truth," not what is seen and embodied in the world the way it is. In John's story of Jesus's trial, Pilate asks, "What is truth?" (18.38). Given John's use of symbolic language, the irony is apparent: "the truth"— Jesus—is standing right in front of him, and Pilate is about to condemn him—and thus condemn "the truth."

"I am . . . the life" (14.6). The opposite of the third term in the series is death. Jesus is "the life"—what we see embodied in him is "the life." He is the "abundant life" referred to in 10.10. So also in the story of the raising of Lazarus, Jesus says, "I am the resurrection and the life" (11.25). What we see in Jesus is life in contrast to confinement in a tomb.

John's symbolic use of language is magnificently signaled in his inaugural story of Jesus's public activity. At a wedding in Cana, Jesus changed a very large amount of water into wine (150 gallons—750 bottles in modern terms). The story in John 2 begins, "On the third day," but John provides no chronological context for the phrase. Rather, its meaning is symbolic. Big things happen in the Bible on "the third day," and in particular the phrase points forward to the resurrection of Jesus "on the third day."

The next phrase is "there was a wedding." Just as "the third day" has symbolic meaning in the Bible, so also does marriage imagery. God's relationship to Israel, the union between heaven and earth, the divine-human union. This, John is saying, is what the story of Jesus is about—the marriage between heaven and earth. And more, it is about a wedding at which the wine never runs out and the best is saved for last.

"Eternal Life"

John is especially fond of a phrase translated into English as "eternal life" (NRSV) or "everlasting life" (KJV). Though the phrase appears a few times in the other gospels, John uses it seventeen times. It is commonly misunderstood. It suggests to most people an "afterlife"—going to heaven and living forever. John's frequent use of the term has contributed to the widespread Christian notion that Jesus and Christianity are primarily about life after death.

This is unfortunate. Jesus and early Christianity were primarily focused on the transformation of lives and the world this side of death. Of course, Jesus and Paul and other early Christians believed in an afterlife—that death was not the end. But that was not the heart of their message. Rather, it was about the kingdom of God on earth and what the world would be like under the lordship of God rather than the lords of this world.

This understanding was shared by John. The Greek phrase translated into English as "eternal or everlasting life" is better translated "the life of the age to come," the Jewish hope for the transformation of life on earth in the here and now. "The life of the age to come" is roughly equivalent to the "kingdom of God." And for John, this life is not just a future hope, but a present reality. John speaks of "eternal life" in the present tense and names its content: "This is eternal life, that they may know you, the only true God, and Jesus Christ whom you have sent" (17.3). To know God as known in Jesus is to enter "the life of the age to come" now, in the present, this side of death. Is there also confidence that death is not the end? Yes. But the message is not primarily about the promise of life after death and how to enter it.

"The Jews"

John's language about "the Jews" is even more condemnatory than Matthew's. Consistently, Jesus's opponents are called "the Jews." They are "from below," from "this world" (8.23). They are children of the devil: "You are from your father the devil, and you choose to do your father's desires. He was a murderer from the beginning, ... a liar and the father of lies" (8.44).

Such language is dangerous, especially when separated from its first-century historical context. The author of John was Jewish, and most or perhaps all of the people for whom he wrote were originally Jewish. He knew that Jesus and his disciples were all Jewish. The reason for his harsh language was because his community of Christian Jews, like Matthew's, was experiencing rejection by non-Christian Jews. The rejection is reflected in the story of Jesus healing a blind man in John 9, especially verses 22, 34–35.

Scholars correctly point out that the term "the Jews" in John should be translated "the Jewish authorities" or simply "the authorities." Despite his language, John is not indicting *all* Jews, but those responsible for Jesus's rejection and for his own community's rejection. To fail to recognize the historical circumstances and the limited intention of these passages is to perpetuate the long history of Christian anti-Semitism. What do Christians who take the Bible literally and absolutely do with passages that say that Jews are children of the devil? But recognizing John's late first-century historical context enables us to understand why he said what he said even as it delegitimates continuing to say what he said.

Thus John, like Matthew, comes from a time when conflict between non-Christian Jews and Christian Jews was intensifying. What historians often call the "parting of the ways" between Judaism and what was becoming early Christianity was well under way.

John does not preserve as much of the memory of the pre-Easter Jesus as the synoptics do. But its use of archetypal imagery to testify to the significance of Jesus is magnificent and powerful. For millions of Christians ever since, Jesus has been "the Word" become flesh, the Light of the World, the Bread of Life, the Way, the Truth, and the Life. Much of John's language speaks to the deepest of human yearnings. In the gospel's final scene, the post-Easter Jesus speaks words that are also central to the synoptics: "Follow me" (21.19). Follow Jesus; he is the word and wisdom of God incarnate, the light, the food that satisfies our hunger, the way, the truth, and the life. Jesus is the embodiment of what can be seen of God in a human life; follow him.

THE GOSPEL ACCORDING TO
John

THE WORD BECAME FLESH

1 In the beginning was the Word, and the Word was with God, and the Word was God. [2]He was in the beginning with God. [3]All things came into being through him, and without him not one thing came into being. What has come into being [4]in him was life,*a* and the life was the light of all people. [5]The light shines in the darkness, and the darkness did not overcome it.

6 There was a man sent from God, whose name was John. [7]He came as a witness to testify to the light, so that all might believe through him. [8]He himself was not the light, but he came to testify to the light. [9]The true light, which enlightens everyone, was coming into the world.*b*

10 He was in the world, and the world came into being through him; yet the world did not know him. [11]He came to what was his own,*c* and his own people did not accept him. [12]But to all who received him, who believed in his name, he gave power to become children of God, [13]who were born, not of blood or of the will of the flesh or of the will of man, but of God.

14 And the Word became flesh and lived among us, and we have seen his glory, the glory as of a father's only son,*d* full of grace and truth. [15](John testified to him and cried out, "This was he of whom I said, 'He who comes after me ranks ahead of me because he was before me.' ") [16]From his fullness we have all received, grace upon grace. [17]The law indeed was given through Moses; grace and truth came through Jesus Christ. [18]No one has ever seen

---

a Or [3]*through him. And without him not one thing came into being that has come into being.* [4]*In him was life* *b* Or *He was the true light that enlightens everyone coming into the world* *c* Or *to his own home* *d* Or *the Father's only Son*

God. It is God the only Son,[a] who is close to the Father's heart,[b] who has made him known.

THE TESTIMONY OF JOHN THE BAPTIST

19 This is the testimony given by John when the Jews sent priests and Levites from Jerusalem to ask him, "Who are you?" [20]He confessed and did not deny it, but confessed, "I am not the Messiah."[c] [21]And they asked him, "What then? Are you Elijah?" He said, "I am not." "Are you the prophet?" He answered, "No." [22]Then they said to him, "Who are you? Let us have an answer for those who sent us. What do you say about yourself?" [23]He said,

> "I am the voice of one crying out in the wilderness,
> 'Make straight the way of the Lord,' "

as the prophet Isaiah said.

24 Now they had been sent from the Pharisees. [25]They asked him, "Why then are you baptizing if you are neither the Messiah,[c] nor Elijah, nor the prophet?" [26]John answered them, "I baptize with water. Among you stands one whom you do not know, [27]the one who is coming after me; I am not worthy to untie the thong of his sandal." [28]This took place in Bethany across the Jordan where John was baptizing.

THE LAMB OF GOD

29 The next day he saw Jesus coming toward him and declared, "Here is the Lamb of God who takes away the sin of the world! [30]This is he of whom I said, 'After me comes a man who ranks ahead of me because he was before me.' [31]I myself did not know him; but I came baptizing with water for this reason, that he might be revealed to Israel." [32]And John testified, "I saw the Spirit descending from heaven like a dove, and it remained on him. [33]I myself did not know him, but the one who sent me to baptize with water said to me, 'He on whom you see the Spirit descend and remain is the one who baptizes with the Holy Spirit.' [34]And I myself have seen and have testified that this is the Son of God."[d]

THE FIRST DISCIPLES OF JESUS

35 The next day John again was standing with two of his disciples, [36]and as he watched Jesus walk by, he exclaimed, "Look, here is the Lamb of God!" [37]The two disciples heard him say this, and they followed Jesus. [38]When Jesus turned and saw them following, he said to them, "What are you looking for?" They said to him, "Rabbi" (which translated means Teacher), "where are you

---

a Other ancient authorities read *It is an only Son, God,* or *It is the only Son*   b Gk *bosom*   c Or *the Christ*   d Other ancient authorities read *is God's chosen one* staying?" ³⁹He said to them, "Come and see." They came and saw where he was staying, and they remained with him that day. It was about four o'clock in the afternoon. ⁴⁰One of the two who heard John speak and followed him was Andrew, Simon Peter's brother. ⁴¹He first found his brother Simon and said to him, "We have found the Messiah" (which is translated Anointed*ᵃ*). ⁴²He brought Simon*ᵇ* to Jesus, who looked at him and said, "You are Simon son of John. You are to be called Cephas" (which is translated Peter*ᶜ*).

JESUS CALLS PHILIP AND NATHANAEL

43 The next day Jesus decided to go to Galilee. He found Philip and said to him, "Follow me." ⁴⁴Now Philip was from Bethsaida, the city of Andrew and Peter. ⁴⁵Philip found Nathanael and said to him, "We have found him about whom Moses in the law and also the prophets wrote, Jesus son of Joseph from Nazareth." ⁴⁶Nathanael said to him, "Can anything good come out of Nazareth?" Philip said to him, "Come and see." ⁴⁷When Jesus saw Nathanael coming toward him, he said of him, "Here is truly an Israelite in whom there is no deceit!" ⁴⁸Nathanael asked him, "Where did you get to know me?" Jesus answered, "I saw you under the fig tree before Philip called you." ⁴⁹Nathanael replied, "Rabbi, you are the Son of God! You are the King of Israel!" ⁵⁰Jesus answered, "Do you believe because I told you that I saw you under the fig tree? You will see greater things than these." ⁵¹And he said to him, "Very truly, I tell you,*ᵈ* you will see heaven opened and the angels of God ascending and descending upon the Son of Man."

THE WEDDING AT CANA

2 On the third day there was a wedding in Cana of Galilee, and the mother of Jesus was there. ²Jesus and his disciples had also been invited to the wedding. ³When the wine gave out, the mother of Jesus said to him, "They have no wine." ⁴And Jesus said to her, "Woman, what concern is that to you and to me? My hour has not yet come." ⁵His mother said to the servants, "Do whatever he tells you." ⁶Now standing there were six stone water jars for the Jewish rites of purification, each holding twenty or thirty gallons. ⁷Jesus said to them, "Fill the jars with water." And they filled them up to the brim. ⁸He said to them, "Now draw some out, and take it to the chief steward." So they took it. ⁹When the steward tasted the water that had become wine, and did not know where it came from (though the servants who had drawn the water knew), the steward called the bridegroom ¹⁰and said to him, "Everyone serves the good wine first,

---

a Or *Christ*   *b* Gk *him*   *c* From the word for *rock* in Aramaic (*kepha*) and Greek (*petra*), respectively   *d* Both instances of the Greek word for *you* in this verse are plural and then the inferior wine after the guests have become drunk. But you have kept the good wine until now." ¹¹Jesus did this, the first of his signs, in Cana of Galilee, and revealed his glory; and his disciples believed in him.

12 After this he went down to Capernaum with his mother, his brothers, and his disciples; and they remained there a few days.

JESUS CLEANSES THE TEMPLE

13 The Passover of the Jews was near, and Jesus went up to Jerusalem. ¹⁴In the temple he found people selling cattle, sheep, and doves, and the money changers seated at their tables. ¹⁵Making a whip of cords, he drove all of them out of the temple, both the sheep and the cattle. He also poured out the coins of the money changers and overturned their tables. ¹⁶He told those who were selling the doves, "Take these things out of here! Stop making my Father's house a marketplace!" ¹⁷His disciples remembered that it was written, "Zeal for your house will consume me." ¹⁸The Jews then said to him, "What sign can you show us for doing this?" ¹⁹Jesus answered them, "Destroy this temple, and in three days I will raise it up." ²⁰The Jews then said, "This temple has been under construction for forty-six years, and will you raise it up in three days?" ²¹But he was speaking of the temple of his body. ²²After he was raised from the dead, his disciples remembered that he had said this; and they believed the scripture and the word that Jesus had spoken.

23 When he was in Jerusalem during the Passover festival, many believed in his name because they saw the signs that he was doing. ²⁴But Jesus on his part would not entrust himself to them, because he knew all people ²⁵and needed no one to testify about anyone; for he himself knew what was in everyone.

NICODEMUS VISITS JESUS

3 Now there was a Pharisee named Nicodemus, a leader of the Jews. ²He came to Jesus*ᵃ* by night and said to him, "Rabbi, we know that you are a teacher who has come from God; for no one can do these signs that you do apart from the presence of God." ³Jesus answered him, "Very truly, I tell you, no one can see the kingdom of God without being born from above."ᵇ ⁴Nicodemus said to him, "How can anyone be born after having grown old? Can one enter a second time into the mother's womb and be born?" ⁵Jesus answered, "Very truly, I tell you, no one can enter the kingdom of God without being born of water and Spirit. ⁶What is born of the flesh is flesh, and what is born of the Spirit is spirit.ᶜ ⁷Do not be astonished that I said to you, 'Youᵈ

---

a Gk him   b Or born anew   c The same Greek word means both wind and spirit   d The Greek word for you here is plural must be born from above.'*a* *8*The wind*b* blows where it chooses, and you hear the sound of it, but you do not know where it comes from or where it goes. So it is with everyone who is born of the Spirit." *9*Nicodemus said to him, "How can these things be?" *10*Jesus answered him, "Are you a teacher of Israel, and yet you do not understand these things?

11 "Very truly, I tell you, we speak of what we know and testify to what we have seen; yet you*c* do not receive our testimony. *12*If I have told you about earthly things and you do not believe, how can you believe if I tell you about heavenly things? *13*No one has ascended into heaven except the one who descended from heaven, the Son of Man.*d* *14*And just as Moses lifted up the serpent in the wilderness, so must the Son of Man be lifted up, *15*that whoever believes in him may have eternal life.*e*

16 "For God so loved the world that he gave his only Son, so that everyone who believes in him may not perish but may have eternal life.

17 "Indeed, God did not send the Son into the world to condemn the world, but in order that the world might be saved through him. *18*Those who believe in him are not condemned; but those who do not believe are condemned already, because they have not believed in the name of the only Son of God. *19*And this is the judgment, that the light has come into the world, and people loved darkness rather than light because their deeds were evil. *20*For all who do evil hate the light and do not come to the light, so that their deeds may not be exposed. *21*But those who do what is true come to the light, so that it may be clearly seen that their deeds have been done in God."*e*

JESUS AND JOHN THE BAPTIST

22 After this Jesus and his disciples went into the Judean countryside, and he spent some time there with them and baptized. *23*John also was baptizing at Aenon near Salim because water was abundant there; and people kept coming and were being baptized *24*—John, of course, had not yet been thrown into prison.

25 Now a discussion about purification arose between John's disciples and a Jew.*f* *26*They came to John and said to him, "Rabbi, the one who was with you across the Jordan, to whom you testified, here he is baptizing, and all are going to him." *27*John answered, "No one can receive anything except what has been given from heaven. *28*You yourselves are my witnesses that I said, 'I am not the Messiah,*g* but I have been sent ahead of him.' *29*He who has the bride is the

---

a Or *anew*   *b* The same Greek word means both *wind* and *spirit*   *c* The Greek word for *you* here and in verse 12 is plural
d Other ancient authorities add *who is in heaven*   *e* Some interpreters hold that the quotation concludes with verse 15   *f* Other ancient authorities read *the Jews*   *g* Or *the Christ*

bridegroom. The friend of the bridegroom, who stands and hears him, rejoices greatly at the bridegroom's voice. For this reason my joy has been fulfilled. [30]He must increase, but I must decrease."[a]

THE ONE WHO COMES FROM HEAVEN

31 The one who comes from above is above all; the one who is of the earth belongs to the earth and speaks about earthly things. The one who comes from heaven is above all. [32]He testifies to what he has seen and heard, yet no one accepts his testimony. [33]Whoever has accepted his testimony has certified[b] this, that God is true. [34]He whom God has sent speaks the words of God, for he gives the Spirit without measure. [35]The Father loves the Son and has placed all things in his hands. [36]Whoever believes in the Son has eternal life; whoever disobeys the Son will not see life, but must endure God's wrath.

JESUS AND THE WOMAN OF SAMARIA

4 Now when Jesus[c] learned that the Pharisees had heard, "Jesus is making and baptizing more disciples than John" [2]—although it was not Jesus himself but his disciples who baptized— [3]he left Judea and started back to Galilee. [4]But he had to go through Samaria. [5]So he came to a Samaritan city called Sychar, near the plot of ground that Jacob had given to his son Joseph. [6]Jacob's well was there, and Jesus, tired out by his journey, was sitting by the well. It was about noon.

7 A Samaritan woman came to draw water, and Jesus said to her, "Give me a drink." [8](His disciples had gone to the city to buy food.) [9]The Samaritan woman said to him, "How is it that you, a Jew, ask a drink of me, a woman of Samaria?" (Jews do not share things in common with Samaritans.)[d] [10]Jesus answered her, "If you knew the gift of God, and who it is that is saying to you, 'Give me a drink,' you would have asked him, and he would have given you living water." [11]The woman said to him, "Sir, you have no bucket, and the well is deep. Where do you get that living water? [12]Are you greater than our ancestor Jacob, who gave us the well, and with his sons and his flocks drank from it?" [13]Jesus said to her, "Everyone who drinks of this water will be thirsty again, [14]but those who drink of the water that I will give them will never be thirsty. The water that I will give will become in them a spring of water gushing up to eternal life." [15]The woman said to him, "Sir, give me this water, so that I may never be thirsty or have to keep coming here to draw water."

---

a Some interpreters hold that the quotation continues through verse 36   b Gk *set a seal to*   c Other ancient authorities read *the Lord*   d Other ancient authorities lack this sentence

16 Jesus said to her, "Go, call your husband, and come back." ¹⁷The woman answered him, "I have no husband." Jesus said to her, "You are right in saying, 'I have no husband'; ¹⁸for you have had five husbands, and the one you have now is not your husband. What you have said is true!" ¹⁹The woman said to him, "Sir, I see that you are a prophet. ²⁰Our ancestors worshiped on this mountain, but you*ᵃ* say that the place where people must worship is in Jerusalem." ²¹Jesus said to her, "Woman, believe me, the hour is coming when you will worship the Father neither on this mountain nor in Jerusalem. ²²You worship what you do not know; we worship what we know, for salvation is from the Jews. ²³But the hour is coming, and is now here, when the true worshipers will worship the Father in spirit and truth, for the Father seeks such as these to worship him. ²⁴God is spirit, and those who worship him must worship in spirit and truth." ²⁵The woman said to him, "I know that Messiah is coming" (who is called Christ). "When he comes, he will proclaim all things to us." ²⁶Jesus said to her, "I am he,*ᵇ* the one who is speaking to you."

27 Just then his disciples came. They were astonished that he was speaking with a woman, but no one said, "What do you want?" or, "Why are you speaking with her?" ²⁸Then the woman left her water jar and went back to the city. She said to the people, ²⁹"Come and see a man who told me everything I have ever done! He cannot be the Messiah,*ᶜ* can he?" ³⁰They left the city and were on their way to him.

31 Meanwhile the disciples were urging him, "Rabbi, eat something." ³²But he said to them, "I have food to eat that you do not know about." ³³So the disciples said to one another, "Surely no one has brought him something to eat?" ³⁴Jesus said to them, "My food is to do the will of him who sent me and to complete his work. ³⁵Do you not say, 'Four months more, then comes the harvest'? But I tell you, look around you, and see how the fields are ripe for harvesting. ³⁶The reaper is already receiving*ᵈ* wages and is gathering fruit for eternal life, so that sower and reaper may rejoice together. ³⁷For here the saying holds true, 'One sows and another reaps.' ³⁸I sent you to reap that for which you did not labor. Others have labored, and you have entered into their labor."

39 Many Samaritans from that city believed in him because of the woman's testimony, "He told me everything I have ever done." ⁴⁰So when the Samaritans came to him, they asked him to stay with them; and he stayed there two days. ⁴¹And many more believed because of his word. ⁴²They said to the woman, "It is no longer because of what you said that we believe, for we have heard for ourselves, and we know that this is truly the Savior of the world."

---

a The Greek word for *you* here and in verses 21 and 22 is plural   *b* Gk *I am*   *c* Or *the Christ*   *d* Or ³⁵. . . *the fields are already ripe for harvesting.* ³⁶*The reaper is receiving*

JESUS RETURNS TO GALILEE

43 When the two days were over, he went from that place to Galilee ⁴⁴(for Jesus himself had testified that a prophet has no honor in the prophet's own country). ⁴⁵When he came to Galilee, the Galileans welcomed him, since they had seen all that he had done in Jerusalem at the festival; for they too had gone to the festival.

JESUS HEALS AN OFFICIAL'S SON

46 Then he came again to Cana in Galilee where he had changed the water into wine. Now there was a royal official whose son lay ill in Capernaum. ⁴⁷When he heard that Jesus had come from Judea to Galilee, he went and begged him to come down and heal his son, for he was at the point of death. ⁴⁸Then Jesus said to him, "Unless you[a] see signs and wonders you will not believe." ⁴⁹The official said to him, "Sir, come down before my little boy dies." ⁵⁰Jesus said to him, "Go; your son will live." The man believed the word that Jesus spoke to him and started on his way. ⁵¹As he was going down, his slaves met him and told him that his child was alive. ⁵²So he asked them the hour when he began to recover, and they said to him, "Yesterday at one in the afternoon the fever left him." ⁵³The father realized that this was the hour when Jesus had said to him, "Your son will live." So he himself believed, along with his whole household. ⁵⁴Now this was the second sign that Jesus did after coming from Judea to Galilee.

JESUS HEALS ON THE SABBATH

5 After this there was a festival of the Jews, and Jesus went up to Jerusalem. 2 Now in Jerusalem by the Sheep Gate there is a pool, called in Hebrew[b] Beth-zatha,[c] which has five porticoes. ³In these lay many invalids—blind, lame, and paralyzed.[d] ⁵One man was there who had been ill for thirty-eight years. ⁶When Jesus saw him lying there and knew that he had been there a long time, he said to him, "Do you want to be made well?" ⁷The sick man answered him, "Sir, I have no one to put me into the pool when the water is stirred up; and while I am making my way, someone else steps down ahead of me." ⁸Jesus said to him, "Stand up, take your mat and walk." ⁹At once the man was made well, and he took up his mat and began to walk.

---

a Both instances of the Greek word for *you* in this verse are plural   *b* That is, *Aramaic*   *c* Other ancient authorities read *Bethesda*, others *Bethsaida*   *d* Other ancient authorities add, wholly or in part, *waiting for the stirring of the water;* *'for an angel of the Lord went down at certain seasons into the pool, and stirred up the water; whoever stepped in first after the stirring of the water was made well from whatever disease that person had.*

Now that day was a sabbath. ¹⁰So the Jews said to the man who had been cured, "It is the sabbath; it is not lawful for you to carry your mat." ¹¹But he answered them, "The man who made me well said to me, 'Take up your mat and walk.'" ¹²They asked him, "Who is the man who said to you, 'Take it up and walk'?" ¹³Now the man who had been healed did not know who it was, for Jesus had disappeared in*a* the crowd that was there. ¹⁴Later Jesus found him in the temple and said to him, "See, you have been made well! Do not sin any more, so that nothing worse happens to you." ¹⁵The man went away and told the Jews that it was Jesus who had made him well. ¹⁶Therefore the Jews started persecuting Jesus, because he was doing such things on the sabbath. ¹⁷But Jesus answered them, "My Father is still working, and I also am working." ¹⁸For this reason the Jews were seeking all the more to kill him, because he was not only breaking the sabbath, but was also calling God his own Father, thereby making himself equal to God.

THE AUTHORITY OF THE SON

19 Jesus said to them, "Very truly, I tell you, the Son can do nothing on his own, but only what he sees the Father doing; for whatever the Father*b* does, the Son does likewise. ²⁰The Father loves the Son and shows him all that he himself is doing; and he will show him greater works than these, so that you will be astonished. ²¹Indeed, just as the Father raises the dead and gives them life, so also the Son gives life to whomever he wishes. ²²The Father judges no one but has given all judgment to the Son, ²³so that all may honor the Son just as they honor the Father. Anyone who does not honor the Son does not honor the Father who sent him. ²⁴Very truly, I tell you, anyone who hears my word and believes him who sent me has eternal life, and does not come under judgment, but has passed from death to life.

25 "Very truly, I tell you, the hour is coming, and is now here, when the dead will hear the voice of the Son of God, and those who hear will live. ²⁶For just as the Father has life in himself, so he has granted the Son also to have life in himself; ²⁷and he has given him authority to execute judgment, because he is the Son of Man. ²⁸Do not be astonished at this; for the hour is coming when all who are in their graves will hear his voice ²⁹and will come out—those who have done good, to the resurrection of life, and those who have done evil, to the resurrection of condemnation.

---

a Or *had left because of*   *b* Gk *that one*

WITNESSES TO JESUS

30 "I can do nothing on my own. As I hear, I judge; and my judgment is just, because I seek to do not my own will but the will of him who sent me.

31 "If I testify about myself, my testimony is not true. ³²There is another who testifies on my behalf, and I know that his testimony to me is true. ³³You sent messengers to John, and he testified to the truth. ³⁴Not that I accept such human testimony, but I say these things so that you may be saved. ³⁵He was a burning and shining lamp, and you were willing to rejoice for a while in his light. ³⁶But I have a testimony greater than John's. The works that the Father has given me to complete, the very works that I am doing, testify on my behalf that the Father has sent me. ³⁷And the Father who sent me has himself testified on my behalf. You have never heard his voice or seen his form, ³⁸and you do not have his word abiding in you, because you do not believe him whom he has sent.

39 "You search the scriptures because you think that in them you have eternal life; and it is they that testify on my behalf. ⁴⁰Yet you refuse to come to me to have life. ⁴¹I do not accept glory from human beings. ⁴²But I know that you do not have the love of God in^a you. ⁴³I have come in my Father's name, and you do not accept me; if another comes in his own name, you will accept him. ⁴⁴How can you believe when you accept glory from one another and do not seek the glory that comes from the one who alone is God? ⁴⁵Do not think that I will accuse you before the Father; your accuser is Moses, on whom you have set your hope. ⁴⁶If you believed Moses, you would believe me, for he wrote about me. ⁴⁷But if you do not believe what he wrote, how will you believe what I say?"

FEEDING THE FIVE THOUSAND

6 After this Jesus went to the other side of the Sea of Galilee, also called the Sea of Tiberias.^{b} ²A large crowd kept following him, because they saw the signs that he was doing for the sick. ³Jesus went up the mountain and sat down there with his disciples. ⁴Now the Passover, the festival of the Jews, was near. ⁵When he looked up and saw a large crowd coming toward him, Jesus said to Philip, "Where are we to buy bread for these people to eat?" ⁶He said this to test him, for he himself knew what he was going to do. ⁷Philip answered him, "Six months' wages^c would not buy enough bread for each of them to get a little." ⁸One of his disciples, Andrew, Simon Peter's brother, said to him, ⁹"There is a boy here who has five barley loaves and two fish. But what are they among so

---

a Or *among* b Gk *of Galilee of Tiberias* c Gk *Two hundred denarii;* the denarius was the usual day's wage for a laborer many people?" [10]Jesus said, "Make the people sit down." Now there was a great deal of grass in the place; so they[a] sat down, about five thousand in all. [11]Then Jesus took the loaves, and when he had given thanks, he distributed them to those who were seated; so also the fish, as much as they wanted. [12]When they were satisfied, he told his disciples, "Gather up the fragments left over, so that nothing may be lost." [13]So they gathered them up, and from the fragments of the five barley loaves, left by those who had eaten, they filled twelve baskets. [14]When the people saw the sign that he had done, they began to say, "This is indeed the prophet who is to come into the world."

15 When Jesus realized that they were about to come and take him by force to make him king, he withdrew again to the mountain by himself.

JESUS WALKS ON THE WATER

16 When evening came, his disciples went down to the sea, [17]got into a boat, and started across the sea to Capernaum. It was now dark, and Jesus had not yet come to them. [18]The sea became rough because a strong wind was blowing. [19]When they had rowed about three or four miles,[b] they saw Jesus walking on the sea and coming near the boat, and they were terrified. [20]But he said to them, "It is I;[c] do not be afraid." [21]Then they wanted to take him into the boat, and immediately the boat reached the land toward which they were going.

THE BREAD FROM HEAVEN

22 The next day the crowd that had stayed on the other side of the sea saw that there had been only one boat there. They also saw that Jesus had not got into the boat with his disciples, but that his disciples had gone away alone. [23]Then some boats from Tiberias came near the place where they had eaten the bread after the Lord had given thanks.[d] [24]So when the crowd saw that neither Jesus nor his disciples were there, they themselves got into the boats and went to Capernaum looking for Jesus.

25 When they found him on the other side of the sea, they said to him, "Rabbi, when did you come here?" [26]Jesus answered them, "Very truly, I tell you, you are looking for me, not because you saw signs, but because you ate your fill of the loaves. [27]Do not work for the food that perishes, but for the food that endures for eternal life, which the Son of Man will give you. For it is on him that God the Father has set his seal." [28]Then they said to him, "What must we do to perform the works of God?" [29]Jesus answered them, "This is the

---

a Gk *the men* *b* Gk *about twenty-five or thirty stadia* *c* Gk *I am* *d* Other ancient authorities lack *after the Lord had given thanks* work of God, that you believe in him whom he has sent." ³⁰So they said to him, "What sign are you going to give us then, so that we may see it and believe you? What work are you performing? ³¹Our ancestors ate the manna in the wilderness; as it is written, 'He gave them bread from heaven to eat.'" ³²Then Jesus said to them, "Very truly, I tell you, it was not Moses who gave you the bread from heaven, but it is my Father who gives you the true bread from heaven. ³³For the bread of God is that which*ᵃ* comes down from heaven and gives life to the world." ³⁴They said to him, "Sir, give us this bread always."

35 Jesus said to them, "I am the bread of life. Whoever comes to me will never be hungry, and whoever believes in me will never be thirsty. ³⁶But I said to you that you have seen me and yet do not believe. ³⁷Everything that the Father gives me will come to me, and anyone who comes to me I will never drive away; ³⁸for I have come down from heaven, not to do my own will, but the will of him who sent me. ³⁹And this is the will of him who sent me, that I should lose nothing of all that he has given me, but raise it up on the last day. ⁴⁰This is indeed the will of my Father, that all who see the Son and believe in him may have eternal life; and I will raise them up on the last day."

41 Then the Jews began to complain about him because he said, "I am the bread that came down from heaven." ⁴²They were saying, "Is not this Jesus, the son of Joseph, whose father and mother we know? How can he now say, 'I have come down from heaven'?" ⁴³Jesus answered them, "Do not complain among yourselves. ⁴⁴No one can come to me unless drawn by the Father who sent me; and I will raise that person up on the last day. ⁴⁵It is written in the prophets, 'And they shall all be taught by God.' Everyone who has heard and learned from the Father comes to me. ⁴⁶Not that anyone has seen the Father except the one who is from God; he has seen the Father. ⁴⁷Very truly, I tell you, whoever believes has eternal life. ⁴⁸I am the bread of life. ⁴⁹Your ancestors ate the manna in the wilderness, and they died. ⁵⁰This is the bread that comes down from heaven, so that one may eat of it and not die. ⁵¹I am the living bread that came down from heaven. Whoever eats of this bread will live forever; and the bread that I will give for the life of the world is my flesh."

52 The Jews then disputed among themselves, saying, "How can this man give us his flesh to eat?" ⁵³So Jesus said to them, "Very truly, I tell you, unless you eat the flesh of the Son of Man and drink his blood, you have no life in you. ⁵⁴Those who eat my flesh and drink my blood have eternal life, and I will raise them up on the last day; ⁵⁵for my flesh is true food and my blood is true drink.

---

a Or *he who*

⁵⁶Those who eat my flesh and drink my blood abide in me, and I in them. ⁵⁷Just as the living Father sent me, and I live because of the Father, so whoever eats me will live because of me. ⁵⁸This is the bread that came down from heaven, not like that which your ancestors ate, and they died. But the one who eats this bread will live forever." ⁵⁹He said these things while he was teaching in the synagogue at Capernaum.

THE WORDS OF ETERNAL LIFE

60 When many of his disciples heard it, they said, "This teaching is difficult; who can accept it?" ⁶¹But Jesus, being aware that his disciples were complaining about it, said to them, "Does this offend you? ⁶²Then what if you were to see the Son of Man ascending to where he was before? ⁶³It is the spirit that gives life; the flesh is useless. The words that I have spoken to you are spirit and life. ⁶⁴But among you there are some who do not believe." For Jesus knew from the first who were the ones that did not believe, and who was the one that would betray him. ⁶⁵And he said, "For this reason I have told you that no one can come to me unless it is granted by the Father."

66 Because of this many of his disciples turned back and no longer went about with him. ⁶⁷So Jesus asked the twelve, "Do you also wish to go away?" ⁶⁸Simon Peter answered him, "Lord, to whom can we go? You have the words of eternal life. ⁶⁹We have come to believe and know that you are the Holy One of God."*ᵃ* ⁷⁰Jesus answered them, "Did I not choose you, the twelve? Yet one of you is a devil." ⁷¹He was speaking of Judas son of Simon Iscariot,*ᵇ* for he, though one of the twelve, was going to betray him.

THE UNBELIEF OF JESUS' BROTHERS

7 After this Jesus went about in Galilee. He did not wish*ᶜ* to go about in Judea because the Jews were looking for an opportunity to kill him. ²Now the Jewish festival of Booths*ᵈ* was near. ³So his brothers said to him, "Leave here and go to Judea so that your disciples also may see the works you are doing; ⁴for no one who wants*ᵉ* to be widely known acts in secret. If you do these things, show yourself to the world." ⁵(For not even his brothers believed in him.) ⁶Jesus said to them, "My time has not yet come, but your time is always here. ⁷The world cannot hate you, but it hates me because I testify against it that its works are evil. ⁸Go to the festival yourselves. I am not*ᶠ* going to this festival, for my time has not yet fully come." ⁹After saying this, he remained in Galilee.

---

a Other ancient authorities read *the Christ, the Son of the living God*   b Other ancient authorities read *Judas Iscariot son of Simon;* others, *Judas son of Simon from Karyot* (Kerioth)   c Other ancient authorities read *was not at liberty*   d Or *Tabernacles*   e Other ancient authorities read *wants it*   f Other ancient authorities add *yet*

JESUS AT THE FESTIVAL OF BOOTHS

10 But after his brothers had gone to the festival, then he also went, not publicly but as it were*a* in secret. [11]The Jews were looking for him at the festival and saying, "Where is he?" [12]And there was considerable complaining about him among the crowds. While some were saying, "He is a good man," others were saying, "No, he is deceiving the crowd." [13]Yet no one would speak openly about him for fear of the Jews.

14 About the middle of the festival Jesus went up into the temple and began to teach. [15]The Jews were astonished at it, saying, "How does this man have such learning,*b* when he has never been taught?" [16]Then Jesus answered them, "My teaching is not mine but his who sent me. [17]Anyone who resolves to do the will of God will know whether the teaching is from God or whether I am speaking on my own. [18]Those who speak on their own seek their own glory; but the one who seeks the glory of him who sent him is true, and there is nothing false in him.

19 "Did not Moses give you the law? Yet none of you keeps the law. Why are you looking for an opportunity to kill me?" [20]The crowd answered, "You have a demon! Who is trying to kill you?" [21]Jesus answered them, "I performed one work, and all of you are astonished. [22]Moses gave you circumcision (it is, of course, not from Moses, but from the patriarchs), and you circumcise a man on the sabbath. [23]If a man receives circumcision on the sabbath in order that the law of Moses may not be broken, are you angry with me because I healed a man's whole body on the sabbath? [24]Do not judge by appearances, but judge with right judgment."

IS THIS THE CHRIST?

25 Now some of the people of Jerusalem were saying, "Is not this the man whom they are trying to kill? [26]And here he is, speaking openly, but they say nothing to him! Can it be that the authorities really know that this is the Messiah?*c* [27]Yet we know where this man is from; but when the Messiah*c* comes, no one will know where he is from." [28]Then Jesus cried out as he was teaching in the temple, "You know me, and you know where I am from. I have not come on my own. But the one who sent me is true, and you do not know him. [29]I know him, because I am from him, and he sent me." [30]Then they tried to arrest him, but no one laid hands on him, because his hour had not yet come. [31]Yet many in the crowd believed in him and were saying, "When the Messiah*c* comes, will he do more signs than this man has done?"*d*

---

a Other ancient authorities lack *as it were*   *b* Or *this man know his letters*   *c* Or *the Christ*   *d* Other ancient authorities read *is doing*

OFFICERS ARE SENT TO ARREST JESUS

32 The Pharisees heard the crowd muttering such things about him, and the chief priests and Pharisees sent temple police to arrest him. [33]Jesus then said, "I will be with you a little while longer, and then I am going to him who sent me. [34]You will search for me, but you will not find me; and where I am, you cannot come." [35]The Jews said to one another, "Where does this man intend to go that we will not find him? Does he intend to go to the Dispersion among the Greeks and teach the Greeks? [36]What does he mean by saying, 'You will search for me and you will not find me' and 'Where I am, you cannot come'?"

RIVERS OF LIVING WATER

37 On the last day of the festival, the great day, while Jesus was standing there, he cried out, "Let anyone who is thirsty come to me, [38]and let the one who believes in me drink. As[a] the scripture has said, 'Out of the believer's heart[b] shall flow rivers of living water.'" [39]Now he said this about the Spirit, which believers in him were to receive; for as yet there was no Spirit,[c] because Jesus was not yet glorified.

DIVISION AMONG THE PEOPLE

40 When they heard these words, some in the crowd said, "This is really the prophet." [41]Others said, "This is the Messiah."[d] But some asked, "Surely the Messiah[d] does not come from Galilee, does he? [42]Has not the scripture said that the Messiah[d] is descended from David and comes from Bethlehem, the village where David lived?" [43]So there was a division in the crowd because of him. [44]Some of them wanted to arrest him, but no one laid hands on him.

THE UNBELIEF OF THOSE IN AUTHORITY

45 Then the temple police went back to the chief priests and Pharisees, who asked them, "Why did you not arrest him?" [46]The police answered, "Never has anyone spoken like this!" [47]Then the Pharisees replied, "Surely you have not been deceived too, have you? [48]Has any one of the authorities or of the Pharisees believed in him? [49]But this crowd, which does not know the law—they are accursed." [50]Nicodemus, who had gone to Jesus[e] before, and who was one of them, asked, [51]"Our law does not judge people without first giving them a hearing to find out what they are doing, does it?" [52]They replied, "Surely you

---

a Or come to me and drink. [38]The one who believes in me, as   b Gk out of his belly   c Other ancient authorities read for as yet the Spirit (others, Holy Spirit) had not been given   d Or the Christ   e Gk him are not also from Galilee, are you? Search and you will see that no prophet is to arise from Galilee."

THE WOMAN CAUGHT IN ADULTERY

[[⁵³Then each of them went home,

8while Jesus went to the Mount of Olives. ²Early in the morning he came again to the temple. All the people came to him and he sat down and began to teach them. ³The scribes and the Pharisees brought a woman who had been caught in adultery; and making her stand before all of them, ⁴they said to him, "Teacher, this woman was caught in the very act of committing adultery. ⁵Now in the law Moses commanded us to stone such women. Now what do you say?" ⁶They said this to test him, so that they might have some charge to bring against him. Jesus bent down and wrote with his finger on the ground. ⁷When they kept on questioning him, he straightened up and said to them, "Let anyone among you who is without sin be the first to throw a stone at her." ⁸And once again he bent down and wrote on the ground.*ᵃ* ⁹When they heard it, they went away, one by one, beginning with the elders; and Jesus was left alone with the woman standing before him. ¹⁰Jesus straightened up and said to her, "Woman, where are they? Has no one condemned you?" ¹¹She said, "No one, sir."*ᵇ* And Jesus said, "Neither do I condemn you. Go your way, and from now on do not sin again."]]*ᶜ*

JESUS THE LIGHT OF THE WORLD

12 Again Jesus spoke to them, saying, "I am the light of the world. Whoever follows me will never walk in darkness but will have the light of life." ¹³Then the Pharisees said to him, "You are testifying on your own behalf; your testimony is not valid." ¹⁴Jesus answered, "Even if I testify on my own behalf, my testimony is valid because I know where I have come from and where I am going, but you do not know where I come from or where I am going. ¹⁵You judge by human standards;*ᵈ* I judge no one. ¹⁶Yet even if I do judge, my judgment is valid; for it is not I alone who judge, but I and the Father*ᵉ* who sent me. ¹⁷In your law it is written that the testimony of two witnesses is valid. ¹⁸I testify on my own behalf, and the Father who sent me testifies on my behalf." ¹⁹Then they said to him, "Where is your Father?" Jesus answered, "You know neither me nor my Father. If you knew me, you would know my Father also." ²⁰He spoke these words while he was teaching in the treasury of the temple, but no one arrested him, because his hour had not yet come.

---

a Other ancient authorities add *the sins of each of them*   *b* Or *Lord*   *c* The most ancient authorities lack 7.53–8.11; other authorities add the passage here or after 7.36 or after 21.25 or after Luke 21.38, with variations of text; some mark the passage as doubtful.   *d* Gk *according to the flesh*   *e* Other ancient authorities read *he*

JESUS FORETELLS HIS DEATH

21 Again he said to them, "I am going away, and you will search for me, but you will die in your sin. Where I am going, you cannot come." [22]Then the Jews said, "Is he going to kill himself? Is that what he means by saying, 'Where I am going, you cannot come'?" [23]He said to them, "You are from below, I am from above; you are of this world, I am not of this world. [24]I told you that you would die in your sins, for you will die in your sins unless you believe that I am he."[a] [25]They said to him, "Who are you?" Jesus said to them, "Why do I speak to you at all?[b] [26]I have much to say about you and much to condemn; but the one who sent me is true, and I declare to the world what I have heard from him." [27]They did not understand that he was speaking to them about the Father. [28]So Jesus said, "When you have lifted up the Son of Man, then you will realize that I am he,[a] and that I do nothing on my own, but I speak these things as the Father instructed me. [29]And the one who sent me is with me; he has not left me alone, for I always do what is pleasing to him." [30]As he was saying these things, many believed in him.

TRUE DISCIPLES

31 Then Jesus said to the Jews who had believed in him, "If you continue in my word, you are truly my disciples; [32]and you will know the truth, and the truth will make you free." [33]They answered him, "We are descendants of Abraham and have never been slaves to anyone. What do you mean by saying, 'You will be made free'?"

34 Jesus answered them, "Very truly, I tell you, everyone who commits sin is a slave to sin. [35]The slave does not have a permanent place in the household; the son has a place there forever. [36]So if the Son makes you free, you will be free indeed. [37]I know that you are descendants of Abraham; yet you look for an opportunity to kill me, because there is no place in you for my word. [38]I declare what I have seen in the Father's presence; as for you, you should do what you have heard from the Father."[c]

JESUS AND ABRAHAM

39 They answered him, "Abraham is our father." Jesus said to them, "If you were Abraham's children, you would be doing[d] what Abraham did, [40]but now you are trying to kill me, a man who has told you the truth that I heard from God. This is not what Abraham did. [41]You are indeed doing what your father

---

a Gk I am   b Or What I have told you from the beginning?   c Other ancient authorities read you do what you have heard from your father   d Other ancient authorities read If you are Abraham's children, then do does." They said to him, "We are not illegitimate children; we have one father, God himself." [42]Jesus said to them, "If God were your Father, you would love me, for I came from God and now I am here. I did not come on my own, but he sent me. [43]Why do you not understand what I say? It is because you cannot accept my word. [44]You are from your father the devil, and you choose to do your father's desires. He was a murderer from the beginning and does not stand in the truth, because there is no truth in him. When he lies, he speaks according to his own nature, for he is a liar and the father of lies. [45]But because I tell the truth, you do not believe me. [46]Which of you convicts me of sin? If I tell the truth, why do you not believe me? [47]Whoever is from God hears the words of God. The reason you do not hear them is that you are not from God."

48 The Jews answered him, "Are we not right in saying that you are a Samaritan and have a demon?" [49]Jesus answered, "I do not have a demon; but I honor my Father, and you dishonor me. [50]Yet I do not seek my own glory; there is one who seeks it and he is the judge. [51]Very truly, I tell you, whoever keeps my word will never see death." [52]The Jews said to him, "Now we know that you have a demon. Abraham died, and so did the prophets; yet you say, 'Whoever keeps my word will never taste death.' [53]Are you greater than our father Abraham, who died? The prophets also died. Who do you claim to be?" [54]Jesus answered, "If I glorify myself, my glory is nothing. It is my Father who glorifies me, he of whom you say, 'He is our God,' [55]though you do not know him. But I know him; if I would say that I do not know him, I would be a liar like you. But I do know him and I keep his word. [56]Your ancestor Abraham rejoiced that he would see my day; he saw it and was glad." [57]Then the Jews said to him, "You are not yet fifty years old, and have you seen Abraham?"[a] [58]Jesus said to them, "Very truly, I tell you, before Abraham was, I am." [59]So they picked up stones to throw at him, but Jesus hid himself and went out of the temple.

A MAN BORN BLIND RECEIVES SIGHT

9 As he walked along, he saw a man blind from birth. [2]His disciples asked him, "Rabbi, who sinned, this man or his parents, that he was born blind?" [3]Jesus answered, "Neither this man nor his parents sinned; he was born blind so that God's works might be revealed in him. [4]We[b] must work the works of him who sent me[c] while it is day; night is coming when no one can work. [5]As long as I am in the world, I am the light of the world." [6]When he had said this, he spat on the ground and made mud with the saliva and spread the mud on the man's eyes, [7]saying to him, "Go, wash in the pool of Siloam" (which means

---

a Other ancient authorities read *has Abraham seen you?* *b* Other ancient authorities read *I* *c* Other ancient authorities read *us*

Sent). Then he went and washed and came back able to see. [8]The neighbors and those who had seen him before as a beggar began to ask, "Is this not the man who used to sit and beg?" [9]Some were saying, "It is he." Others were saying, "No, but it is someone like him." He kept saying, "I am the man." [10]But they kept asking him, "Then how were your eyes opened?" [11]He answered, "The man called Jesus made mud, spread it on my eyes, and said to me, 'Go to Siloam and wash.' Then I went and washed and received my sight." [12]They said to him, "Where is he?" He said, "I do not know."

THE PHARISEES INVESTIGATE THE HEALING

13 They brought to the Pharisees the man who had formerly been blind. [14]Now it was a sabbath day when Jesus made the mud and opened his eyes. [15]Then the Pharisees also began to ask him how he had received his sight. He said to them, "He put mud on my eyes. Then I washed, and now I see." [16]Some of the Pharisees said, "This man is not from God, for he does not observe the sabbath." But others said, "How can a man who is a sinner perform such signs?" And they were divided. [17]So they said again to the blind man, "What do you say about him? It was your eyes he opened." He said, "He is a prophet."

18 The Jews did not believe that he had been blind and had received his sight until they called the parents of the man who had received his sight [19]and asked them, "Is this your son, who you say was born blind? How then does he now see?" [20]His parents answered, "We know that this is our son, and that he was born blind; [21]but we do not know how it is that now he sees, nor do we know who opened his eyes. Ask him; he is of age. He will speak for himself." [22]His parents said this because they were afraid of the Jews; for the Jews had already agreed that anyone who confessed Jesus[a] to be the Messiah[b] would be put out of the synagogue. [23]Therefore his parents said, "He is of age; ask him."

24 So for the second time they called the man who had been blind, and they said to him, "Give glory to God! We know that this man is a sinner." [25]He answered, "I do not know whether he is a sinner. One thing I do know, that though I was blind, now I see." [26]They said to him, "What did he do to you? How did he open your eyes?" [27]He answered them, "I have told you already, and you would not listen. Why do you want to hear it again? Do you also want to become his disciples?" [28]Then they reviled him, saying, "You are his disciple, but we are disciples of Moses. [29]We know that God has spoken to Moses, but as for this man, we do not know where he comes from." [30]The man answered, "Here is an astonishing thing! You do not know where he comes from, and yet

---

a Gk *him*   *b* Or *the Christ*

he opened my eyes. [31]We know that God does not listen to sinners, but he does listen to one who worships him and obeys his will. [32]Never since the world began has it been heard that anyone opened the eyes of a person born blind. [33]If this man were not from God, he could do nothing." [34]They answered him, "You were born entirely in sins, and are you trying to teach us?" And they drove him out.

SPIRITUAL BLINDNESS

35 Jesus heard that they had driven him out, and when he found him, he said, "Do you believe in the Son of Man?"[a] [36]He answered, "And who is he, sir?[b] Tell me, so that I may believe in him." [37]Jesus said to him, "You have seen him, and the one speaking with you is he." [38]He said, "Lord,[b] I believe." And he worshiped him. [39]Jesus said, "I came into this world for judgment so that those who do not see may see, and those who do see may become blind." [40]Some of the Pharisees near him heard this and said to him, "Surely we are not blind, are we?" [41]Jesus said to them, "If you were blind, you would not have sin. But now that you say, 'We see,' your sin remains.

JESUS THE GOOD SHEPHERD

10 "Very truly, I tell you, anyone who does not enter the sheepfold by the gate but climbs in by another way is a thief and a bandit. [2]The one who enters by the gate is the shepherd of the sheep. [3]The gatekeeper opens the gate for him, and the sheep hear his voice. He calls his own sheep by name and leads them out. [4]When he has brought out all his own, he goes ahead of them, and the sheep follow him because they know his voice. [5]They will not follow a stranger, but they will run from him because they do not know the voice of strangers." [6]Jesus used this figure of speech with them, but they did not understand what he was saying to them.

7 So again Jesus said to them, "Very truly, I tell you, I am the gate for the sheep. [8]All who came before me are thieves and bandits; but the sheep did not listen to them. [9]I am the gate. Whoever enters by me will be saved, and will come in and go out and find pasture. [10]The thief comes only to steal and kill and destroy. I came that they may have life, and have it abundantly.

11 "I am the good shepherd. The good shepherd lays down his life for the sheep. [12]The hired hand, who is not the shepherd and does not own the sheep, sees the wolf coming and leaves the sheep and runs away—and the wolf snatches them and scatters them. [13]The hired hand runs away because a hired

---

a Other ancient authorities read *the Son of God*   b *Sir* and *Lord* translate the same Greek word hand does not care for the sheep. ¹⁴I am the good shepherd. I know my own and my own know me, ¹⁵just as the Father knows me and I know the Father. And I lay down my life for the sheep. ¹⁶I have other sheep that do not belong to this fold. I must bring them also, and they will listen to my voice. So there will be one flock, one shepherd. ¹⁷For this reason the Father loves me, because I lay down my life in order to take it up again. ¹⁸No one takes*ᵃ* it from me, but I lay it down of my own accord. I have power to lay it down, and I have power to take it up again. I have received this command from my Father."

19 Again the Jews were divided because of these words. ²⁰Many of them were saying, "He has a demon and is out of his mind. Why listen to him?" ²¹Others were saying, "These are not the words of one who has a demon. Can a demon open the eyes of the blind?"

JESUS IS REJECTED BY THE JEWS

22 At that time the festival of the Dedication took place in Jerusalem. It was winter, ²³and Jesus was walking in the temple, in the portico of Solomon. ²⁴So the Jews gathered around him and said to him, "How long will you keep us in suspense? If you are the Messiah,*ᵇ* tell us plainly." ²⁵Jesus answered, "I have told you, and you do not believe. The works that I do in my Father's name testify to me; ²⁶but you do not believe, because you do not belong to my sheep. ²⁷My sheep hear my voice. I know them, and they follow me. ²⁸I give them eternal life, and they will never perish. No one will snatch them out of my hand. ²⁹What my Father has given me is greater than all else, and no one can snatch it out of the Father's hand.*ᶜ* ³⁰The Father and I are one."

31 The Jews took up stones again to stone him. ³²Jesus replied, "I have shown you many good works from the Father. For which of these are you going to stone me?" ³³The Jews answered, "It is not for a good work that we are going to stone you, but for blasphemy, because you, though only a human being, are making yourself God." ³⁴Jesus answered, "Is it not written in your law,*ᵈ* 'I said, you are gods'? ³⁵If those to whom the word of God came were called 'gods'— and the scripture cannot be annulled— ³⁶can you say that the one whom the Father has sanctified and sent into the world is blaspheming because I said, 'I am God's Son'? ³⁷If I am not doing the works of my Father, then do not believe me. ³⁸But if I do them, even though you do not believe me, believe the works, so that you may know and understand*ᵉ* that the Father is in me and I am in the Father." ³⁹Then they tried to arrest him again, but he escaped from their hands.

---

a Other ancient authorities read *has taken*   *b* Or *the Christ*   *c* Other ancient authorities read *My Father who has given them to me is greater than all, and no one can snatch them out of the Father's hand*   *d* Other ancient authorities read *in the law*   *e* Other ancient authorities lack *and understand;* others read *and believe*

40 He went away again across the Jordan to the place where John had been baptizing earlier, and he remained there. [41]Many came to him, and they were saying, "John performed no sign, but everything that John said about this man was true." [42]And many believed in him there.

THE DEATH OF LAZARUS

11 Now a certain man was ill, Lazarus of Bethany, the village of Mary and her sister Martha. [2]Mary was the one who anointed the Lord with perfume and wiped his feet with her hair; her brother Lazarus was ill. [3]So the sisters sent a message to Jesus,[a] "Lord, he whom you love is ill." [4]But when Jesus heard it, he said, "This illness does not lead to death; rather it is for God's glory, so that the Son of God may be glorified through it." [5]Accordingly, though Jesus loved Martha and her sister and Lazarus, [6]after having heard that Lazarus[b] was ill, he stayed two days longer in the place where he was.

7 Then after this he said to the disciples, "Let us go to Judea again." [8]The disciples said to him, "Rabbi, the Jews were just now trying to stone you, and are you going there again?" [9]Jesus answered, "Are there not twelve hours of daylight? Those who walk during the day do not stumble, because they see the light of this world. [10]But those who walk at night stumble, because the light is not in them." [11]After saying this, he told them, "Our friend Lazarus has fallen asleep, but I am going there to awaken him." [12]The disciples said to him, "Lord, if he has fallen asleep, he will be all right." [13]Jesus, however, had been speaking about his death, but they thought that he was referring merely to sleep. [14]Then Jesus told them plainly, "Lazarus is dead. [15]For your sake I am glad I was not there, so that you may believe. But let us go to him." [16]Thomas, who was called the Twin,[c] said to his fellow disciples, "Let us also go, that we may die with him."

JESUS THE RESURRECTION AND THE LIFE

17 When Jesus arrived, he found that Lazarus[b] had already been in the tomb four days. [18]Now Bethany was near Jerusalem, some two miles[d] away, [19]and many of the Jews had come to Martha and Mary to console them about their brother. [20]When Martha heard that Jesus was coming, she went and met him, while Mary stayed at home. [21]Martha said to Jesus, "Lord, if you had been here, my brother would not have died. [22]But even now I know that God will give you whatever you ask of him." [23]Jesus said to her, "Your brother will rise again." [24]Martha said to him, "I know that he will rise again in the resurrection on the

---

a Gk *him*   *b* Gk *he*   *c* Gk *Didymus*   *d* Gk *fifteen stadia* last day." ²⁵Jesus said to her, "I am the resurrection and the life.ᵃ Those who believe in me, even though they die, will live, ²⁶and everyone who lives and believes in me will never die. Do you believe this?" ²⁷She said to him, "Yes, Lord, I believe that you are the Messiah,ᵇ the Son of God, the one coming into the world."

JESUS WEEPS

28 When she had said this, she went back and called her sister Mary, and told her privately, "The Teacher is here and is calling for you." ²⁹And when she heard it, she got up quickly and went to him. ³⁰Now Jesus had not yet come to the village, but was still at the place where Martha had met him. ³¹The Jews who were with her in the house, consoling her, saw Mary get up quickly and go out. They followed her because they thought that she was going to the tomb to weep there. ³²When Mary came where Jesus was and saw him, she knelt at his feet and said to him, "Lord, if you had been here, my brother would not have died." ³³When Jesus saw her weeping, and the Jews who came with her also weeping, he was greatly disturbed in spirit and deeply moved. ³⁴He said, "Where have you laid him?" They said to him, "Lord, come and see." ³⁵Jesus began to weep. ³⁶So the Jews said, "See how he loved him!" ³⁷But some of them said, "Could not he who opened the eyes of the blind man have kept this man from dying?"

JESUS RAISES LAZARUS TO LIFE

38 Then Jesus, again greatly disturbed, came to the tomb. It was a cave, and a stone was lying against it. ³⁹Jesus said, "Take away the stone." Martha, the sister of the dead man, said to him, "Lord, already there is a stench because he has been dead four days." ⁴⁰Jesus said to her, "Did I not tell you that if you believed, you would see the glory of God?" ⁴¹So they took away the stone. And Jesus looked upward and said, "Father, I thank you for having heard me. ⁴²I knew that you always hear me, but I have said this for the sake of the crowd standing here, so that they may believe that you sent me." ⁴³When he had said this, he cried with a loud voice, "Lazarus, come out!" ⁴⁴The dead man came out, his hands and feet bound with strips of cloth, and his face wrapped in a cloth. Jesus said to them, "Unbind him, and let him go."

THE PLOT TO KILL JESUS

45 Many of the Jews therefore, who had come with Mary and had seen what Jesus did, believed in him. ⁴⁶But some of them went to the Pharisees and told

---

ᵃ Other ancient authorities lack *and the life*   ᵇ Or *the Christ* them what he had done. ⁴⁷So the chief priests and the Pharisees called a meeting of the council, and said, "What are we to do? This man is performing many signs. ⁴⁸If we let him go on like this, everyone will believe in him, and the Romans will come and destroy both our holy place*ᵃ* and our nation." ⁴⁹But one of them, Caiaphas, who was high priest that year, said to them, "You know nothing at all! ⁵⁰You do not understand that it is better for you to have one man die for the people than to have the whole nation destroyed." ⁵¹He did not say this on his own, but being high priest that year he prophesied that Jesus was about to die for the nation, ⁵²and not for the nation only, but to gather into one the dispersed children of God. ⁵³So from that day on they planned to put him to death.

54 Jesus therefore no longer walked about openly among the Jews, but went from there to a town called Ephraim in the region near the wilderness; and he remained there with the disciples.

55 Now the Passover of the Jews was near, and many went up from the country to Jerusalem before the Passover to purify themselves. ⁵⁶They were looking for Jesus and were asking one another as they stood in the temple, "What do you think? Surely he will not come to the festival, will he?" ⁵⁷Now the chief priests and the Pharisees had given orders that anyone who knew where Jesus*ᵇ* was should let them know, so that they might arrest him.

MARY ANOINTS JESUS

12 Six days before the Passover Jesus came to Bethany, the home of Lazarus, whom he had raised from the dead. ²There they gave a dinner for him. Martha served, and Lazarus was one of those at the table with him. ³Mary took a pound of costly perfume made of pure nard, anointed Jesus' feet, and wiped them*ᶜ* with her hair. The house was filled with the fragrance of the perfume. ⁴But Judas Iscariot, one of his disciples (the one who was about to betray him), said, ⁵"Why was this perfume not sold for three hundred denarii*ᵈ* and the money given to the poor?" ⁶(He said this not because he cared about the poor, but because he was a thief; he kept the common purse and used to steal what was put into it.) ⁷Jesus said, "Leave her alone. She bought it*ᵉ* so that she might keep it for the day of my burial. ⁸You always have the poor with you, but you do not always have me."

THE PLOT TO KILL LAZARUS

9 When the great crowd of the Jews learned that he was there, they came not only because of Jesus but also to see Lazarus, whom he had raised from the

---

a Or *our temple*; Greek *our place*   *b* Gk *he*   *c* Gk *his feet*   *d* Three hundred denarii would be nearly a year's wages for a laborer
e Gk lacks *She bought it*

dead. [10]So the chief priests planned to put Lazarus to death as well, [11]since it was on account of him that many of the Jews were deserting and were believing in Jesus.

JESUS' TRIUMPHAL ENTRY INTO JERUSALEM

12 The next day the great crowd that had come to the festival heard that Jesus was coming to Jerusalem. [13]So they took branches of palm trees and went out to meet him, shouting,

> "Hosanna!
> Blessed is the one who comes in the name of the Lord—
>   the King of Israel!"

14 Jesus found a young donkey and sat on it; as it is written:
15 "Do not be afraid, daughter of Zion.
>   Look, your king is coming,
>   sitting on a donkey's colt!"

16 His disciples did not understand these things at first; but when Jesus was glorified, then they remembered that these things had been written of him and had been done to him. [17]So the crowd that had been with him when he called Lazarus out of the tomb and raised him from the dead continued to testify.[a] [18]It was also because they heard that he had performed this sign that the crowd went to meet him. [19]The Pharisees then said to one another, "You see, you can do nothing. Look, the world has gone after him!"

SOME GREEKS WISH TO SEE JESUS

20 Now among those who went up to worship at the festival were some Greeks. [21]They came to Philip, who was from Bethsaida in Galilee, and said to him, "Sir, we wish to see Jesus." [22]Philip went and told Andrew; then Andrew and Philip went and told Jesus. [23]Jesus answered them, "The hour has come for the Son of Man to be glorified. [24]Very truly, I tell you, unless a grain of wheat falls into the earth and dies, it remains just a single grain; but if it dies, it bears much fruit. [25]Those who love their life lose it, and those who hate their life in this world will keep it for eternal life. [26]Whoever serves me must follow me, and where I am, there will my servant be also. Whoever serves me, the Father will honor.

JESUS SPEAKS ABOUT HIS DEATH

27 "Now my soul is troubled. And what should I say—'Father, save me from this hour'? No, it is for this reason that I have come to this hour. [28]Father,

---

a Other ancient authorities read *with him began to testify that he had called . . . from the dead* glorify your name." Then a voice came from heaven, "I have glorified it, and I will glorify it again." [29]The crowd standing there heard it and said that it was thunder. Others said, "An angel has spoken to him." [30]Jesus answered, "This voice has come for your sake, not for mine. [31]Now is the judgment of this world; now the ruler of this world will be driven out. [32]And I, when I am lifted up from the earth, will draw all people[a] to myself." [33]He said this to indicate the kind of death he was to die. [34]The crowd answered him, "We have heard from the law that the Messiah[b] remains forever. How can you say that the Son of Man must be lifted up? Who is this Son of Man?" [35]Jesus said to them, "The light is with you for a little longer. Walk while you have the light, so that the darkness may not overtake you. If you walk in the darkness, you do not know where you are going. [36]While you have the light, believe in the light, so that you may become children of light."

THE UNBELIEF OF THE PEOPLE

After Jesus had said this, he departed and hid from them. [37]Although he had performed so many signs in their presence, they did not believe in him. [38]This was to fulfill the word spoken by the prophet Isaiah:

> "Lord, who has believed our message,
>> and to whom has the arm of the Lord been revealed?"

39 And so they could not believe, because Isaiah also said,

40 "He has blinded their eyes
>> and hardened their heart,
> so that they might not look with their eyes,
>> and understand with their heart and turn—
>> and I would heal them."

41 Isaiah said this because[c] he saw his glory and spoke about him. [42]Nevertheless many, even of the authorities, believed in him. But because of the Pharisees they did not confess it, for fear that they would be put out of the synagogue; [43]for they loved human glory more than the glory that comes from God.

SUMMARY OF JESUS' TEACHING

44 Then Jesus cried aloud: "Whoever believes in me believes not in me but in him who sent me. [45]And whoever sees me sees him who sent me. [46]I have come as light into the world, so that everyone who believes in me should not remain in the darkness. [47]I do not judge anyone who hears my words and does not keep them, for I came not to judge the world, but to save the world. [48]The one who

---

a Other ancient authorities read *all things*   *b* Or *the Christ*   *c* Other ancient witnesses read *when* rejects me and does not receive my word has a judge; on the last day the word that I have spoken will serve as judge, [49]for I have not spoken on my own, but the Father who sent me has himself given me a commandment about what to say and what to speak. [50]And I know that his commandment is eternal life. What I speak, therefore, I speak just as the Father has told me."

JESUS WASHES THE DISCIPLES' FEET

13 Now before the festival of the Passover, Jesus knew that his hour had come to depart from this world and go to the Father. Having loved his own who were in the world, he loved them to the end. [2]The devil had already put it into the heart of Judas son of Simon Iscariot to betray him. And during supper [3]Jesus, knowing that the Father had given all things into his hands, and that he had come from God and was going to God, [4]got up from the table,[a] took off his outer robe, and tied a towel around himself. [5]Then he poured water into a basin and began to wash the disciples' feet and to wipe them with the towel that was tied around him. [6]He came to Simon Peter, who said to him, "Lord, are you going to wash my feet?" [7]Jesus answered, "You do not know now what I am doing, but later you will understand." [8]Peter said to him, "You will never wash my feet." Jesus answered, "Unless I wash you, you have no share with me." [9]Simon Peter said to him, "Lord, not my feet only but also my hands and my head!" [10]Jesus said to him, "One who has bathed does not need to wash, except for the feet,[b] but is entirely clean. And you[c] are clean, though not all of you." [11]For he knew who was to betray him; for this reason he said, "Not all of you are clean."

12 After he had washed their feet, had put on his robe, and had returned to the table, he said to them, "Do you know what I have done to you? [13]You call me Teacher and Lord—and you are right, for that is what I am. [14]So if I, your Lord and Teacher, have washed your feet, you also ought to wash one another's feet. [15]For I have set you an example, that you also should do as I have done to you. [16]Very truly, I tell you, servants[d] are not greater than their master, nor are messengers greater than the one who sent them. [17]If you know these things, you are blessed if you do them. [18]I am not speaking of all of you; I know whom I have chosen. But it is to fulfill the scripture, 'The one who ate my bread[e] has lifted his heel against me.' [19]I tell you this now, before it occurs, so that when it does occur, you may believe that I am he.[f] [20]Very truly, I tell you, whoever receives one whom I send receives me; and whoever receives me receives him who sent me."

---

a Gk *from supper*   b Other ancient authorities lack *except for the feet*   c The Greek word for *you* here is plural   d Gk *slaves*
e Other ancient authorities read *ate bread with me*   f Gk *I am*

JESUS FORETELLS HIS BETRAYAL

21 After saying this Jesus was troubled in spirit, and declared, "Very truly, I tell you, one of you will betray me." ²²The disciples looked at one another, uncertain of whom he was speaking. ²³One of his disciples—the one whom Jesus loved—was reclining next to him; ²⁴Simon Peter therefore motioned to him to ask Jesus of whom he was speaking. ²⁵So while reclining next to Jesus, he asked him, "Lord, who is it?" ²⁶Jesus answered, "It is the one to whom I give this piece of bread when I have dipped it in the dish."*a* So when he had dipped the piece of bread, he gave it to Judas son of Simon Iscariot.*b* ²⁷After he received the piece of bread,*c* Satan entered into him. Jesus said to him, "Do quickly what you are going to do." ²⁸Now no one at the table knew why he said this to him. ²⁹Some thought that, because Judas had the common purse, Jesus was telling him, "Buy what we need for the festival"; or, that he should give something to the poor. ³⁰So, after receiving the piece of bread, he immediately went out. And it was night.

THE NEW COMMANDMENT

31 When he had gone out, Jesus said, "Now the Son of Man has been glorified, and God has been glorified in him. ³²If God has been glorified in him,*d* God will also glorify him in himself and will glorify him at once. ³³Little children, I am with you only a little longer. You will look for me; and as I said to the Jews so now I say to you, 'Where I am going, you cannot come.' ³⁴I give you a new commandment, that you love one another. Just as I have loved you, you also should love one another. ³⁵By this everyone will know that you are my disciples, if you have love for one another."

JESUS FORETELLS PETER'S DENIAL

36 Simon Peter said to him, "Lord, where are you going?" Jesus answered, "Where I am going, you cannot follow me now; but you will follow afterward." ³⁷Peter said to him, "Lord, why can I not follow you now? I will lay down my life for you." ³⁸Jesus answered, "Will you lay down your life for me? Very truly, I tell you, before the cock crows, you will have denied me three times.

JESUS THE WAY TO THE FATHER

14 "Do not let your hearts be troubled. Believe*e* in God, believe also in me. ²In my Father's house there are many dwelling places. If it were not so,

---

a Gk *dipped it*   *b* Other ancient authorities read *Judas Iscariot son of Simon;* others, *Judas son of Simon from Karyot* (Kerioth)
c Gk *After the piece of bread*   *d* Other ancient authorities lack *If God has been glorified in him*   *e* Or *You believe*

would I have told you that I go to prepare a place for you?*a* *3*And if I go and prepare a place for you, I will come again and will take you to myself, so that where I am, there you may be also. *4*And you know the way to the place where I am going."*b* *5*Thomas said to him, "Lord, we do not know where you are going. How can we know the way?" *6*Jesus said to him, "I am the way, and the truth, and the life. No one comes to the Father except through me. *7*If you know me, you will know*c* my Father also. From now on you do know him and have seen him."

8 Philip said to him, "Lord, show us the Father, and we will be satisfied." *9*Jesus said to him, "Have I been with you all this time, Philip, and you still do not know me? Whoever has seen me has seen the Father. How can you say, 'Show us the Father'? *10*Do you not believe that I am in the Father and the Father is in me? The words that I say to you I do not speak on my own; but the Father who dwells in me does his works. *11*Believe me that I am in the Father and the Father is in me; but if you do not, then believe me because of the works themselves. *12*Very truly, I tell you, the one who believes in me will also do the works that I do and, in fact, will do greater works than these, because I am going to the Father. *13*I will do whatever you ask in my name, so that the Father may be glorified in the Son. *14*If in my name you ask me*d* for anything, I will do it.

THE PROMISE OF THE HOLY SPIRIT

15 "If you love me, you will keep*e* my commandments. *16*And I will ask the Father, and he will give you another Advocate,*f* to be with you forever. *17*This is the Spirit of truth, whom the world cannot receive, because it neither sees him nor knows him. You know him, because he abides with you, and he will be in*g* you.

18 "I will not leave you orphaned; I am coming to you. *19*In a little while the world will no longer see me, but you will see me; because I live, you also will live. *20*On that day you will know that I am in my Father, and you in me, and I in you. *21*They who have my commandments and keep them are those who love me; and those who love me will be loved by my Father, and I will love them and reveal myself to them." *22*Judas (not Iscariot) said to him, "Lord, how is it that you will reveal yourself to us, and not to the world?" *23*Jesus answered him, "Those who love me will keep my word, and my Father will love them, and we will come to them and make our home with them. *24*Whoever does not love me does not keep my words; and the word that you hear is not mine, but is from the Father who sent me.

---

a Or *If it were not so, I would have told you; for I go to prepare a place for you*   *b* Other ancient authorities read *Where I am going you know, and the way you know*   *c* Other ancient authorities read *If you had known me, you would have known*   *d* Other ancient authorities lack *me*   *e* Other ancient authorities read *me, keep*   *f* Or *Helper*   *g* Or *among*

25 "I have said these things to you while I am still with you. ²⁶But the Advocate,ᵃ the Holy Spirit, whom the Father will send in my name, will teach you everything, and remind you of all that I have said to you. ²⁷Peace I leave with you; my peace I give to you. I do not give to you as the world gives. Do not let your hearts be troubled, and do not let them be afraid. ²⁸You heard me say to you, 'I am going away, and I am coming to you.' If you loved me, you would rejoice that I am going to the Father, because the Father is greater than I. ²⁹And now I have told you this before it occurs, so that when it does occur, you may believe. ³⁰I will no longer talk much with you, for the ruler of this world is coming. He has no power over me; ³¹but I do as the Father has commanded me, so that the world may know that I love the Father. Rise, let us be on our way.

JESUS THE TRUE VINE

15 "I am the true vine, and my Father is the vinegrower. ²He removes every branch in me that bears no fruit. Every branch that bears fruit he prunesᵇ to make it bear more fruit. ³You have already been cleansedᵇ by the word that I have spoken to you. ⁴Abide in me as I abide in you. Just as the branch cannot bear fruit by itself unless it abides in the vine, neither can you unless you abide in me. ⁵I am the vine, you are the branches. Those who abide in me and I in them bear much fruit, because apart from me you can do nothing. ⁶Whoever does not abide in me is thrown away like a branch and withers; such branches are gathered, thrown into the fire, and burned. ⁷If you abide in me, and my words abide in you, ask for whatever you wish, and it will be done for you. ⁸My Father is glorified by this, that you bear much fruit and becomeᶜ my disciples. ⁹As the Father has loved me, so I have loved you; abide in my love. ¹⁰If you keep my commandments, you will abide in my love, just as I have kept my Father's commandments and abide in his love. ¹¹I have said these things to you so that my joy may be in you, and that your joy may be complete.

12 "This is my commandment, that you love one another as I have loved you. ¹³No one has greater love than this, to lay down one's life for one's friends. ¹⁴You are my friends if you do what I command you. ¹⁵I do not call you servants*ᵈ* any longer, because the servant*ᵉ* does not know what the master is doing; but I have called you friends, because I have made known to you everything that I have heard from my Father. ¹⁶You did not choose me but I chose you. And I appointed you to go and bear fruit, fruit that will last, so that the Father will give you whatever you ask him in my name. ¹⁷I am giving you these commands so that you may love one another.

ᵃ Or *Helper*   ᵇ The same Greek root refers to pruning and cleansing   ᶜ Or *be*   ᵈ Gk *slaves*   ᵉ Gk *slave*

THE WORLD'S HATRED

18 "If the world hates you, be aware that it hated me before it hated you. ¹⁹If you belonged to the world,ᵃ the world would love you as its own. Because you do not belong to the world, but I have chosen you out of the world—therefore the world hates you. ²⁰Remember the word that I said to you, 'Servantsᵇ are not greater than their master.' If they persecuted me, they will persecute you; if they kept my word, they will keep yours also. ²¹But they will do all these things to you on account of my name, because they do not know him who sent me. ²²If I had not come and spoken to them, they would not have sin; but now they have no excuse for their sin. ²³Whoever hates me hates my Father also. ²⁴If I had not done among them the works that no one else did, they would not have sin. But now they have seen and hated both me and my Father. ²⁵It was to fulfill the word that is written in their law, 'They hated me without a cause.'

26 "When the Advocateᶜ comes, whom I will send to you from the Father, the Spirit of truth who comes from the Father, he will testify on my behalf. ²⁷You also are to testify because you have been with me from the beginning.

16 "I have said these things to you to keep you from stumbling. ²They will put you out of the synagogues. Indeed, an hour is coming when those who kill you will think that by doing so they are offering worship to God. ³And they will do this because they have not known the Father or me. ⁴But I have said these things to you so that when their hour comes you may remember that I told you about them.

THE WORK OF THE SPIRIT

"I did not say these things to you from the beginning, because I was with you. ⁵But now I am going to him who sent me; yet none of you asks me, 'Where are you going?' ⁶But because I have said these things to you, sorrow has filled your hearts. ⁷Nevertheless I tell you the truth: it is to your advantage that I go away, for if I do not go away, the Advocateᶜ will not come to you; but if I go, I will send him to you. ⁸And when he comes, he will prove the world wrong aboutᵈ sin and righteousness and judgment: ⁹about sin, because they do not believe in me; ¹⁰about righteousness, because I am going to the Father and you will see me no longer; ¹¹about judgment, because the ruler of this world has been condemned.

12 "I still have many things to say to you, but you cannot bear them now. ¹³When the Spirit of truth comes, he will guide you into all the truth; for he will not speak on his own, but will speak whatever he hears, and he will declare to

---

a Gk were of the world   *b* Gk Slaves   *c* Or Helper   *d* Or convict the world of you the things that are to come. ¹⁴He will glorify me, because he will take what is mine and declare it to you. ¹⁵All that the Father has is mine. For this reason I said that he will take what is mine and declare it to you.

SORROW WILL TURN INTO JOY

16 "A little while, and you will no longer see me, and again a little while, and you will see me." ¹⁷Then some of his disciples said to one another, "What does he mean by saying to us, 'A little while, and you will no longer see me, and again a little while, and you will see me'; and 'Because I am going to the Father'?" ¹⁸They said, "What does he mean by this 'a little while'? We do not know what he is talking about." ¹⁹Jesus knew that they wanted to ask him, so he said to them, "Are you discussing among yourselves what I meant when I said, 'A little while, and you will no longer see me, and again a little while, and you will see me'? ²⁰Very truly, I tell you, you will weep and mourn, but the world will rejoice; you will have pain, but your pain will turn into joy. ²¹When a woman is in labor, she has pain, because her hour has come. But when her child is born, she no longer remembers the anguish because of the joy of having brought a human being into the world. ²²So you have pain now; but I will see you again, and your hearts will rejoice, and no one will take your joy from you. ²³On that day you will ask nothing of me.ᵃ Very truly, I tell you, if you ask anything of the Father in my name, he will give it to you.ᵇ ²⁴Until now you have not asked for anything in my name. Ask and you will receive, so that your joy may be complete.

PEACE FOR THE DISCIPLES

25 "I have said these things to you in figures of speech. The hour is coming when I will no longer speak to you in figures, but will tell you plainly of the Father. ²⁶On that day you will ask in my name. I do not say to you that I will ask the Father on your behalf; ²⁷for the Father himself loves you, because you have loved me and have believed that I came from God.ᶜ ²⁸I came from the Father and have come into the world; again, I am leaving the world and am going to the Father."

29 His disciples said, "Yes, now you are speaking plainly, not in any figure of speech! ³⁰Now we know that you know all things, and do not need to have anyone question you; by this we believe that you came from God." ³¹Jesus answered them, "Do you now believe? ³²The hour is coming, indeed it has come,

---

a Or *will ask me no question*   *b* Other ancient authorities read *Father, he will give it to you in my name*   *c* Other ancient authorities read *the Father* when you will be scattered, each one to his home, and you will leave me alone. Yet I am not alone because the Father is with me. [33]I have said this to you, so that in me you may have peace. In the world you face persecution. But take courage; I have conquered the world!"

JESUS PRAYS FOR HIS DISCIPLES

17 After Jesus had spoken these words, he looked up to heaven and said, "Father, the hour has come; glorify your Son so that the Son may glorify you, [2]since you have given him authority over all people,[a] to give eternal life to all whom you have given him. [3]And this is eternal life, that they may know you, the only true God, and Jesus Christ whom you have sent. [4]I glorified you on earth by finishing the work that you gave me to do. [5]So now, Father, glorify me in your own presence with the glory that I had in your presence before the world existed.

6 "I have made your name known to those whom you gave me from the world. They were yours, and you gave them to me, and they have kept your word. [7]Now they know that everything you have given me is from you; [8]for the words that you gave to me I have given to them, and they have received them and know in truth that I came from you; and they have believed that you sent me. [9]I am asking on their behalf; I am not asking on behalf of the world, but on behalf of those whom you gave me, because they are yours. [10]All mine are yours, and yours are mine; and I have been glorified in them. [11]And now I am no longer in the world, but they are in the world, and I am coming to you. Holy Father, protect them in your name that you have given me, so that they may be one, as we are one. [12]While I was with them, I protected them in your name that[b] you have given me. I guarded them, and not one of them was lost except the one destined to be lost,[c] so that the scripture might be fulfilled. [13]But now I am coming to you, and I speak these things in the world so that they may have my joy made complete in themselves.[d] [14]I have given them your word, and the world has hated them because they do not belong to the world, just as I do not belong to the world. [15]I am not asking you to take them out of the world, but I ask you to protect them from the evil one.[e] [16]They do not belong to the world, just as I do not belong to the world. [17]Sanctify them in the truth; your word is truth. [18]As you have sent me into the world, so I have sent them into the world. [19]And for their sakes I sanctify myself, so that they also may be sanctified in truth.

---

a Gk *flesh*   *b* Other ancient authorities read *protected in your name those whom*   *c* Gk *except the son of destruction*   *d* Or *among themselves*   *e* Or *from evil*

20 "I ask not only on behalf of these, but also on behalf of those who will believe in me through their word, ²¹that they may all be one. As you, Father, are in me and I am in you, may they also be in us,ª so that the world may believe that you have sent me. ²²The glory that you have given me I have given them, so that they may be one, as we are one, ²³I in them and you in me, that they may become completely one, so that the world may know that you have sent me and have loved them even as you have loved me. ²⁴Father, I desire that those also, whom you have given me, may be with me where I am, to see my glory, which you have given me because you loved me before the foundation of the world.

25 "Righteous Father, the world does not know you, but I know you; and these know that you have sent me. ²⁶I made your name known to them, and I will make it known, so that the love with which you have loved me may be in them, and I in them."

THE BETRAYAL AND ARREST OF JESUS

18 After Jesus had spoken these words, he went out with his disciples across the Kidron valley to a place where there was a garden, which he and his disciples entered. ²Now Judas, who betrayed him, also knew the place, because Jesus often met there with his disciples. ³So Judas brought a detachment of soldiers together with police from the chief priests and the Pharisees, and they came there with lanterns and torches and weapons. ⁴Then Jesus, knowing all that was to happen to him, came forward and asked them, "Whom are you looking for?" ⁵They answered, "Jesus of Nazareth."ᵇ Jesus replied, "I am he."ᶜ Judas, who betrayed him, was standing with them. ⁶When Jesusᵈ said to them, "I am he,"ᶜ they stepped back and fell to the ground. ⁷Again he asked them, "Whom are you looking for?" And they said, "Jesus of Nazareth."ᵇ ⁸Jesus answered, "I told you that I am he.ᶜ So if you are looking for me, let these men go." ⁹This was to fulfill the word that he had spoken, "I did not lose a single one of those whom you gave me." ¹⁰Then Simon Peter, who had a sword, drew it, struck the high priest's slave, and cut off his right ear. The slave's name was Malchus. ¹¹Jesus said to Peter, "Put your sword back into its sheath. Am I not to drink the cup that the Father has given me?"

JESUS BEFORE THE HIGH PRIEST

12 So the soldiers, their officer, and the Jewish police arrested Jesus and bound him. ¹³First they took him to Annas, who was the father-in-law of Caiaphas, the

---

a Other ancient authorities read *be one in us*   b Gk *the Nazorean*   c Gk *I am*   d Gk *he* high priest that year. [14]Caiaphas was the one who had advised the Jews that it was better to have one person die for the people.

PETER DENIES JESUS

15 Simon Peter and another disciple followed Jesus. Since that disciple was known to the high priest, he went with Jesus into the courtyard of the high priest, [16]but Peter was standing outside at the gate. So the other disciple, who was known to the high priest, went out, spoke to the woman who guarded the gate, and brought Peter in. [17]The woman said to Peter, "You are not also one of this man's disciples, are you?" He said, "I am not." [18]Now the slaves and the police had made a charcoal fire because it was cold, and they were standing around it and warming themselves. Peter also was standing with them and warming himself.

THE HIGH PRIEST QUESTIONS JESUS

19 Then the high priest questioned Jesus about his disciples and about his teaching. [20]Jesus answered, "I have spoken openly to the world; I have always taught in synagogues and in the temple, where all the Jews come together. I have said nothing in secret. [21]Why do you ask me? Ask those who heard what I said to them; they know what I said." [22]When he had said this, one of the police standing nearby struck Jesus on the face, saying, "Is that how you answer the high priest?" [23]Jesus answered, "If I have spoken wrongly, testify to the wrong. But if I have spoken rightly, why do you strike me?" [24]Then Annas sent him bound to Caiaphas the high priest.

PETER DENIES JESUS AGAIN

25 Now Simon Peter was standing and warming himself. They asked him, "You are not also one of his disciples, are you?" He denied it and said, "I am not." [26]One of the slaves of the high priest, a relative of the man whose ear Peter had cut off, asked, "Did I not see you in the garden with him?" [27]Again Peter denied it, and at that moment the cock crowed.

JESUS BEFORE PILATE

28 Then they took Jesus from Caiaphas to Pilate's headquarters.[a] It was early in the morning. They themselves did not enter the headquarters,[a] so as to avoid ritual defilement and to be able to eat the Passover. [29]So Pilate went out to them

---

a Gk *the praetorium*

and said, "What accusation do you bring against this man?" [30]They answered, "If this man were not a criminal, we would not have handed him over to you." [31]Pilate said to them, "Take him yourselves and judge him according to your law." The Jews replied, "We are not permitted to put anyone to death." [32](This was to fulfill what Jesus had said when he indicated the kind of death he was to die.)

33 Then Pilate entered the headquarters[a] again, summoned Jesus, and asked him, "Are you the King of the Jews?" [34]Jesus answered, "Do you ask this on your own, or did others tell you about me?" [35]Pilate replied, "I am not a Jew, am I? Your own nation and the chief priests have handed you over to me. What have you done?" [36]Jesus answered, "My kingdom is not from this world. If my kingdom were from this world, my followers would be fighting to keep me from being handed over to the Jews. But as it is, my kingdom is not from here." [37]Pilate asked him, "So you are a king?" Jesus answered, "You say that I am a king. For this I was born, and for this I came into the world, to testify to the truth. Everyone who belongs to the truth listens to my voice." [38]Pilate asked him, "What is truth?"

JESUS SENTENCED TO DEATH

After he had said this, he went out to the Jews again and told them, "I find no case against him. [39]But you have a custom that I release someone for you at the Passover. Do you want me to release for you the King of the Jews?" [40]They shouted in reply, "Not this man, but Barabbas!" Now Barabbas was a bandit.

19 Then Pilate took Jesus and had him flogged. [2]And the soldiers wove a crown of thorns and put it on his head, and they dressed him in a purple robe. [3]They kept coming up to him, saying, "Hail, King of the Jews!" and striking him on the face. [4]Pilate went out again and said to them, "Look, I am bringing him out to you to let you know that I find no case against him." [5]So Jesus came out, wearing the crown of thorns and the purple robe. Pilate said to them, "Here is the man!" [6]When the chief priests and the police saw him, they shouted, "Crucify him! Crucify him!" Pilate said to them, "Take him yourselves and crucify him; I find no case against him." [7]The Jews answered him, "We have a law, and according to that law he ought to die because he has claimed to be the Son of God."

8 Now when Pilate heard this, he was more afraid than ever. [9]He entered his headquarters[a] again and asked Jesus, "Where are you from?" But Jesus gave him no answer. [10]Pilate therefore said to him, "Do you refuse to speak to me?

a Gk the praetorium

Do you not know that I have power to release you, and power to crucify you?" [11]Jesus answered him, "You would have no power over me unless it had been given you from above; therefore the one who handed me over to you is guilty of a greater sin." [12]From then on Pilate tried to release him, but the Jews cried out, "If you release this man, you are no friend of the emperor. Everyone who claims to be a king sets himself against the emperor."

13 When Pilate heard these words, he brought Jesus outside and sat[a] on the judge's bench at a place called The Stone Pavement, or in Hebrew[b] Gabbatha. [14]Now it was the day of Preparation for the Passover; and it was about noon. He said to the Jews, "Here is your King!" [15]They cried out, "Away with him! Away with him! Crucify him!" Pilate asked them, "Shall I crucify your King?" The chief priests answered, "We have no king but the emperor." [16]Then he handed him over to them to be crucified.

THE CRUCIFIXION OF JESUS

So they took Jesus; [17]and carrying the cross by himself, he went out to what is called The Place of the Skull, which in Hebrew[b] is called Golgotha. [18]There they crucified him, and with him two others, one on either side, with Jesus between them. [19]Pilate also had an inscription written and put on the cross. It read, "Jesus of Nazareth,[c] the King of the Jews." [20]Many of the Jews read this inscription, because the place where Jesus was crucified was near the city; and it was written in Hebrew,[b] in Latin, and in Greek. [21]Then the chief priests of the Jews said to Pilate, "Do not write, 'The King of the Jews,' but, 'This man said, I am King of the Jews.'" [22]Pilate answered, "What I have written I have written." [23]When the soldiers had crucified Jesus, they took his clothes and divided them into four parts, one for each soldier. They also took his tunic; now the tunic was seamless, woven in one piece from the top. [24]So they said to one another, "Let us not tear it, but cast lots for it to see who will get it." This was to fulfill what the scripture says,

> "They divided my clothes among themselves,
> and for my clothing they cast lots."

25 And that is what the soldiers did.

Meanwhile, standing near the cross of Jesus were his mother, and his mother's sister, Mary the wife of Clopas, and Mary Magdalene. [26]When Jesus saw his mother and the disciple whom he loved standing beside her, he said to his mother, "Woman, here is your son." [27]Then he said to the disciple, "Here is your mother." And from that hour the disciple took her into his own home.

---

a Or *seated him* *b* That is, *Aramaic* *c* Gk *the Nazorean*

28 After this, when Jesus knew that all was now finished, he said (in order to fulfill the scripture), "I am thirsty." ²⁹A jar full of sour wine was standing there. So they put a sponge full of the wine on a branch of hyssop and held it to his mouth. ³⁰When Jesus had received the wine, he said, "It is finished." Then he bowed his head and gave up his spirit.

JESUS' SIDE IS PIERCED

31 Since it was the day of Preparation, the Jews did not want the bodies left on the cross during the sabbath, especially because that sabbath was a day of great solemnity. So they asked Pilate to have the legs of the crucified men broken and the bodies removed. ³²Then the soldiers came and broke the legs of the first and of the other who had been crucified with him. ³³But when they came to Jesus and saw that he was already dead, they did not break his legs. ³⁴Instead, one of the soldiers pierced his side with a spear, and at once blood and water came out. ³⁵(He who saw this has testified so that you also may believe. His testimony is true, and he knows*a* that he tells the truth.) ³⁶These things occurred so that the scripture might be fulfilled, "None of his bones shall be broken." ³⁷And again another passage of scripture says, "They will look on the one whom they have pierced."

THE BURIAL OF JESUS

38 After these things, Joseph of Arimathea, who was a disciple of Jesus, though a secret one because of his fear of the Jews, asked Pilate to let him take away the body of Jesus. Pilate gave him permission; so he came and removed his body. ³⁹Nicodemus, who had at first come to Jesus by night, also came, bringing a mixture of myrrh and aloes, weighing about a hundred pounds. ⁴⁰They took the body of Jesus and wrapped it with the spices in linen cloths, according to the burial custom of the Jews. ⁴¹Now there was a garden in the place where he was crucified, and in the garden there was a new tomb in which no one had ever been laid. ⁴²And so, because it was the Jewish day of Preparation, and the tomb was nearby, they laid Jesus there.

THE RESURRECTION OF JESUS

20 Early on the first day of the week, while it was still dark, Mary Magdalene came to the tomb and saw that the stone had been removed from the tomb. ²So she ran and went to Simon Peter and the other disciple, the one whom Jesus loved, and said to them, "They have taken the Lord out of the

---

a Or there is one who knows

tomb, and we do not know where they have laid him." ³Then Peter and the other disciple set out and went toward the tomb. ⁴The two were running together, but the other disciple outran Peter and reached the tomb first. ⁵He bent down to look in and saw the linen wrappings lying there, but he did not go in. ⁶Then Simon Peter came, following him, and went into the tomb. He saw the linen wrappings lying there, ⁷and the cloth that had been on Jesus' head, not lying with the linen wrappings but rolled up in a place by itself. ⁸Then the other disciple, who reached the tomb first, also went in, and he saw and believed; ⁹for as yet they did not understand the scripture, that he must rise from the dead. ¹⁰Then the disciples returned to their homes.

JESUS APPEARS TO MARY MAGDALENE

11 But Mary stood weeping outside the tomb. As she wept, she bent over to look*a* into the tomb; ¹²and she saw two angels in white, sitting where the body of Jesus had been lying, one at the head and the other at the feet. ¹³They said to her, "Woman, why are you weeping?" She said to them, "They have taken away my Lord, and I do not know where they have laid him." ¹⁴When she had said this, she turned around and saw Jesus standing there, but she did not know that it was Jesus. ¹⁵Jesus said to her, "Woman, why are you weeping? Whom are you looking for?" Supposing him to be the gardener, she said to him, "Sir, if you have carried him away, tell me where you have laid him, and I will take him away." ¹⁶Jesus said to her, "Mary!" She turned and said to him in Hebrew,*b* "Rabbouni!" (which means Teacher). ¹⁷Jesus said to her, "Do not hold on to me, because I have not yet ascended to the Father. But go to my brothers and say to them, 'I am ascending to my Father and your Father, to my God and your God.'" ¹⁸Mary Magdalene went and announced to the disciples, "I have seen the Lord"; and she told them that he had said these things to her.

JESUS APPEARS TO THE DISCIPLES

19 When it was evening on that day, the first day of the week, and the doors of the house where the disciples had met were locked for fear of the Jews, Jesus came and stood among them and said, "Peace be with you." ²⁰After he said this, he showed them his hands and his side. Then the disciples rejoiced when they saw the Lord. ²¹Jesus said to them again, "Peace be with you. As the Father has sent me, so I send you." ²²When he had said this, he breathed on them and said to them, "Receive the Holy Spirit. ²³If you forgive the sins of any, they are forgiven them; if you retain the sins of any, they are retained."

---

a Gk lacks *to look*   *b* That is, *Aramaic*

JESUS AND THOMAS

24 But Thomas (who was called the Twin*ᵃ*), one of the twelve, was not with them when Jesus came. ²⁵So the other disciples told him, "We have seen the Lord." But he said to them, "Unless I see the mark of the nails in his hands, and put my finger in the mark of the nails and my hand in his side, I will not believe."

26 A week later his disciples were again in the house, and Thomas was with them. Although the doors were shut, Jesus came and stood among them and said, "Peace be with you." ²⁷Then he said to Thomas, "Put your finger here and see my hands. Reach out your hand and put it in my side. Do not doubt but believe." ²⁸Thomas answered him, "My Lord and my God!" ²⁹Jesus said to him, "Have you believed because you have seen me? Blessed are those who have not seen and yet have come to believe."

THE PURPOSE OF THIS BOOK

30 Now Jesus did many other signs in the presence of his disciples, which are not written in this book. ³¹But these are written so that you may come to believe*ᵇ* that Jesus is the Messiah,*ᶜ* the Son of God, and that through believing you may have life in his name.

JESUS APPEARS TO SEVEN DISCIPLES

21 After these things Jesus showed himself again to the disciples by the Sea of Tiberias; and he showed himself in this way. ²Gathered there together were Simon Peter, Thomas called the Twin,*ᵃ* Nathanael of Cana in Galilee, the sons of Zebedee, and two others of his disciples. ³Simon Peter said to them, "I am going fishing." They said to him, "We will go with you." They went out and got into the boat, but that night they caught nothing.

4 Just after daybreak, Jesus stood on the beach; but the disciples did not know that it was Jesus. ⁵Jesus said to them, "Children, you have no fish, have you?" They answered him, "No." ⁶He said to them, "Cast the net to the right side of the boat, and you will find some." So they cast it, and now they were not able to haul it in because there were so many fish. ⁷That disciple whom Jesus loved said to Peter, "It is the Lord!" When Simon Peter heard that it was the Lord, he put on some clothes, for he was naked, and jumped into the sea. ⁸But the other disciples came in the boat, dragging the net full of fish, for they were not far from the land, only about a hundred yards*ᵈ* off.

---

a Gk *Didymus*   *b* Other ancient authorities read *may continue to believe*   *c* Or *the Christ*   *d* Gk *two hundred cubits*

9 When they had gone ashore, they saw a charcoal fire there, with fish on it, and bread. [10]Jesus said to them, "Bring some of the fish that you have just caught." [11]So Simon Peter went aboard and hauled the net ashore, full of large fish, a hundred fifty-three of them; and though there were so many, the net was not torn. [12]Jesus said to them, "Come and have breakfast." Now none of the disciples dared to ask him, "Who are you?" because they knew it was the Lord. [13]Jesus came and took the bread and gave it to them, and did the same with the fish. [14]This was now the third time that Jesus appeared to the disciples after he was raised from the dead.

JESUS AND PETER

15 When they had finished breakfast, Jesus said to Simon Peter, "Simon son of John, do you love me more than these?" He said to him, "Yes, Lord; you know that I love you." Jesus said to him, "Feed my lambs." [16]A second time he said to him, "Simon son of John, do you love me?" He said to him, "Yes, Lord; you know that I love you." Jesus said to him, "Tend my sheep." [17]He said to him the third time, "Simon son of John, do you love me?" Peter felt hurt because he said to him the third time, "Do you love me?" And he said to him, "Lord, you know everything; you know that I love you." Jesus said to him, "Feed my sheep. [18]Very truly, I tell you, when you were younger, you used to fasten your own belt and to go wherever you wished. But when you grow old, you will stretch out your hands, and someone else will fasten a belt around you and take you where you do not wish to go." [19](He said this to indicate the kind of death by which he would glorify God.) After this he said to him, "Follow me."

JESUS AND THE BELOVED DISCIPLE

20 Peter turned and saw the disciple whom Jesus loved following them; he was the one who had reclined next to Jesus at the supper and had said, "Lord, who is it that is going to betray you?" [21]When Peter saw him, he said to Jesus, "Lord, what about him?" [22]Jesus said to him, "If it is my will that he remain until I come, what is that to you? Follow me!" [23]So the rumor spread in the community[a] that this disciple would not die. Yet Jesus did not say to him that he would not die, but, "If it is my will that he remain until I come, what is that to you?"[b]

24 This is the disciple who is testifying to these things and has written them, and we know that his testimony is true. [25]But there are also many other things that Jesus did; if every one of them were written down, I suppose that the world itself could not contain the books that would be written.

---

a Gk *among the brothers*   *b* Other ancient authorities lack *what is that to you*

Ephesians

Like Colossians, Ephesians is one of the "disputed" letters of Paul. A minority of modern scholars argue that it was written by Paul, but a majority have concluded that it was written a generation or so after Paul's death. Though it has the typical form of a Pauline letter and echoes some important themes from the seven genuine letters of Paul, it also differs in a number of ways.

The differences include style and subject matter. In Ephesians, as in Colossians, many of the sentences are very long, unlike the commonly short and energized sentences of Paul's genuine letters. For example, 1.3–14 is one sentence in Greek, as is 1.15–23 (English translations commonly break these up into several sentences). Differences in subject matter include the emphasis of Ephesians on "the church" and its extended "household codes," about which more will be said later.

We are not even certain that it was written to Ephesus. The best ancient manuscripts lack the words "in Ephesus" in verse 1. In them, it reads simply: "Paul, an apostle of Christ Jesus by the will of God, to the saints who are faithful in Christ Jesus." "In Ephesus" was added later.

The rest of the letter contains features that suggest it was not addressed to a specific Christ-community. Unlike the seven genuine letters of Paul, there are no references to the circumstances of a particular community. Instead, it seems to be a "general" or "circular" letter meant to be read and heard within many Christian communities. The use of the Greek word translated into English as "church" also suggests this. In Paul's genuine letters, the word always refers to a specific local community. In Ephesians, it refers to "the church" in general, "the household of God," what is often called "the church universal." The framework for dating it is created by its close parallels to parts of Colossians that indicate that Colossians is earlier; and it seems to have been known by the Christian author Ignatius around the year 100. This suggests a date around 90.

The Unity of Jew and Gentile in Christ

A central theme of Ephesians is the unity of Christian Jews and Christian Gentiles that has happened in Christ. One of its best-known passages is 2.11–20:

> Remember that at one time you Gentiles by birth, called "the uncircumcision" by those who are called "the circumcision"—a physical circumcision made in the flesh by human hands—remember that you were at that time without Christ, being aliens from the commonwealth of Israel, and strangers to the covenants of promise. . . . But now in Christ Jesus you who once were far off have been brought near. . . . For he is our peace; in his flesh, he has made both groups into one and has broken down the dividing wall, that is, the hostility between us, . . . that he might create in himself one new humanity. . . . So then you are no longer strangers and aliens, but you are citizens with the saints and also members of the household of God, built upon the foundation of the apostles and prophets, with Christ Jesus himself as the cornerstone.

Note that the text treats the controversy about the full status of Gentile Christians as in the past, settled, and resolved. It does not argue for unity, but celebrates a unity achieved. Note also that it refers to "the apostles" as if they were figures of the past.

The theme of Christian unity sounds again with the repeated use of "one" in another passage well known to Christians:

> There is one body and one Spirit, just as you were called to the one hope of your calling, one Lord, one faith, one baptism, one God and Father of all, who is above all and through all and in all. (4.4–6)

"Ecclesiology"—a technical theological term for doctrine or teaching about "the church"—is central to Ephesians. Its ecclesiology is as splendid as anything in the New Testament.

The Armor of God

Another familiar passage in Ephesians uses the imagery of military conflict to describe the struggle "against the rulers, against the authorities, against the cosmic powers of this present darkness" (6.12), what Paul in his genuine letters calls "this world":

> Take up the whole armor of God, . . . the belt of truth around your waist, . . .
> the breastplate of righteousness, . . . the shield of faith, . . . the helmet of
> salvation, and the sword of the Spirit, which is the word of God. (6.13–17)

Though the imagery is drawn from warfare, it is clear that it is metaphorical: the
"armor of God" and Christians is truth, righteousness (justice), faith, salvation, the
Spirit, and the word of God.

The Christian Household

Ephesians also includes "rules," or directives, for the structuring of Christian life.
The "household code" for Christians that appears for the first time in nine verses in
Colossians (3.18–4.1) is expanded in Ephesians (5.21–6.9) to twenty-two verses.
Some of its language is familiar from its use in Christian marriage rituals:

> Wives, be subject to your husbands as you are to the Lord. For the husband
> is the head of the wife just as Christ is the head of the church, the body of
> which he is the Savior. Just as the church is subject to Christ, so also wives
> ought to be, in everything, to their husbands. Husbands, love your wives,
> just as Christ loved the church. (5.22–25)

Though these verses affirm that both wives and husbands have obligations to each
other, they are not equal: wives are to be subject. This is quite different from the
equality and mutuality recommended in Galatians 3.28 and 1 Corinthians 7.

The household code continues with an admonition to children to be obedient
to their parents. The Paul of the seven genuine letters would not have opposed
this—but he never mentioned it. His passion was not for reinforcing conventional
patterns of behavior, but proclaiming "Christ crucified," "Jesus is Lord," and "the
new creation."

The household code concludes with the relationship between slaves and masters:

> Slaves, obey your earthly masters with fear and trembling, in singleness
> of heart, as you obey Christ; not only while being watched, and in order to
> please them, but as slaves of Christ, doing the will of God from the heart.
> Render service with enthusiasm, as to the Lord and not to men and women,
> knowing that whatever good we do, we will receive the same again from the
> Lord, whether we are slaves or free. (6.5–8)

The author adds, "And, masters, do the same to them. Stop threatening them,
for you know that both of you have the same Master in heaven, and with him there
is no partiality" (6.9). The author is speaking to Christian "masters," Christian slave

owners; there is no reason to think he was addressing Christian slaves of non-Christian masters. The letter takes it for granted that Christians may have Christian slaves, and this text has often been used in the history of Christianity to legitimate slavery. But this position is very different from the one espoused by Paul in Galatians and Philemon. Ephesians, like Colossians and, as we will see, the pastoral letters to Timothy and Titus, is part of the process of late first-century Christian accommodation to the hierarchical values of the Roman world.

The Author as "Pauline"

Despite the fact that Ephesians not only goes beyond and sometimes compromises what Paul wrote in his seven genuine letters, the letter also echoes some of what was central to Paul's thought. For example, 2.7–10 concisely summarizes Paul's affirmation of justification by grace through faith, found in Galatians and Romans. The author proclaims

> . . . the immeasurable riches of [God's] grace in kindness toward us in Christ Jesus. For by grace you have been saved through faith, and this is not your own doing; it is the gift of God—not the result of works, so that no one may boast. For we are what [God] has made us, created in Christ Jesus for good works, which God prepared beforehand to be our way of life.

The point is not that the author knew Paul's letters to Rome and Galatia, but that he lived within a Pauline tradition and sought to be faithful to it. His vocation was to express what Paul meant to a later generation. He preserved even as he also accommodated.

THE LETTER OF PAUL TO THE

Ephesians

SALUTATION

1 Paul, an apostle of Christ Jesus by the will of God,
   To the saints who are in Ephesus and are faithful*a* in Christ Jesus:
2 Grace to you and peace from God our Father and the Lord Jesus Christ.

SPIRITUAL BLESSINGS IN CHRIST

3 Blessed be the God and Father of our Lord Jesus Christ, who has blessed us in Christ with every spiritual blessing in the heavenly places, ⁴just as he chose us in Christ*b* before the foundation of the world to be holy and blameless before him in love. ⁵He destined us for adoption as his children through Jesus Christ, according to the good pleasure of his will, ⁶to the praise of his glorious grace that he freely bestowed on us in the Beloved. ⁷In him we have redemption through his blood, the forgiveness of our trespasses, according to the riches of his grace ⁸that he lavished on us. With all wisdom and insight ⁹he has made known to us the mystery of his will, according to his good pleasure that he set forth in Christ, ¹⁰as a plan for the fullness of time, to gather up all things in him, things in heaven and things on earth. ¹¹In Christ we have also obtained an inheritance,*c* having been destined according to the purpose of him who accomplishes all things according to his counsel and will, ¹²so that we, who were the first to set our hope on Christ, might live for the praise of his glory. ¹³In him you also, when you had heard the word of truth, the gospel of your

---

a Other ancient authorities lack *in Ephesus*, reading *saints who are also faithful*   b Gk *in him*   c Or *been made a heritage* salvation, and had believed in him, were marked with the seal of the promised Holy Spirit; [14]this[a] is the pledge of our inheritance toward redemption as God's own people, to the praise of his glory.

PAUL'S PRAYER

15 I have heard of your faith in the Lord Jesus and your love[b] toward all the saints, and for this reason [16]I do not cease to give thanks for you as I remember you in my prayers. [17]I pray that the God of our Lord Jesus Christ, the Father of glory, may give you a spirit of wisdom and revelation as you come to know him, [18]so that, with the eyes of your heart enlightened, you may know what is the hope to which he has called you, what are the riches of his glorious inheritance among the saints, [19]and what is the immeasurable greatness of his power for us who believe, according to the working of his great power. [20]God[c] put this power to work in Christ when he raised him from the dead and seated him at his right hand in the heavenly places, [21]far above all rule and authority and power and dominion, and above every name that is named, not only in this age but also in the age to come. [22]And he has put all things under his feet and has made him the head over all things for the church, [23]which is his body, the fullness of him who fills all in all.

FROM DEATH TO LIFE

2 You were dead through the trespasses and sins [2]in which you once lived, following the course of this world, following the ruler of the power of the air, the spirit that is now at work among those who are disobedient. [3]All of us once lived among them in the passions of our flesh, following the desires of flesh and senses, and we were by nature children of wrath, like everyone else. [4]But God, who is rich in mercy, out of the great love with which he loved us [5]even when we were dead through our trespasses, made us alive together with Christ[d]—by grace you have been saved— [6]and raised us up with him and seated us with him in the heavenly places in Christ Jesus, [7]so that in the ages to come he might show the immeasurable riches of his grace in kindness toward us in Christ Jesus. [8]For by grace you have been saved through faith, and this is not your own doing; it is the gift of God— [9]not the result of works, so that no one may boast. [10]For we are what he has made us, created in Christ Jesus for good works, which God prepared beforehand to be our way of life.

---

a Other ancient authorities read *who*   b Other ancient authorities lack *and your love*   c Gk *He*   d Other ancient authorities read *in Christ*

ONE IN CHRIST

11 So then, remember that at one time you Gentiles by birth,[a] called "the uncircumcision" by those who are called "the circumcision"—a physical circumcision made in the flesh by human hands— [12]remember that you were at that time without Christ, being aliens from the commonwealth of Israel, and strangers to the covenants of promise, having no hope and without God in the world. [13]But now in Christ Jesus you who once were far off have been brought near by the blood of Christ. [14]For he is our peace; in his flesh he has made both groups into one and has broken down the dividing wall, that is, the hostility between us. [15]He has abolished the law with its commandments and ordinances, that he might create in himself one new humanity in place of the two, thus making peace, [16]and might reconcile both groups to God in one body[b] through the cross, thus putting to death that hostility through it.[c] [17]So he came and proclaimed peace to you who were far off and peace to those who were near; [18]for through him both of us have access in one Spirit to the Father. [19]So then you are no longer strangers and aliens, but you are citizens with the saints and also members of the household of God, [20]built upon the foundation of the apostles and prophets, with Christ Jesus himself as the cornerstone.[d] [21]In him the whole structure is joined together and grows into a holy temple in the Lord; [22]in whom you also are built together spiritually[e] into a dwelling place for God.

PAUL'S MINISTRY TO THE GENTILES

3 This is the reason that I Paul am a prisoner for[f] Christ Jesus for the sake of you Gentiles— [2]for surely you have already heard of the commission of God's grace that was given me for you, [3]and how the mystery was made known to me by revelation, as I wrote above in a few words, [4]a reading of which will enable you to perceive my understanding of the mystery of Christ. [5]In former generations this mystery[g] was not made known to humankind, as it has now been revealed to his holy apostles and prophets by the Spirit: [6]that is, the Gentiles have become fellow heirs, members of the same body, and sharers in the promise in Christ Jesus through the gospel.

7 Of this gospel I have become a servant according to the gift of God's grace that was given me by the working of his power. [8]Although I am the very least of all the saints, this grace was given to me to bring to the Gentiles the news of the boundless riches of Christ, [9]and to make everyone see[h] what is the plan of

---

a Gk *in the flesh*   b Or *reconcile both of us in one body for God*   c Or *in him*, or *in himself*   d Or *keystone*   e Gk *in the Spirit*
f Or *of*   g Gk *it*   h Other ancient authorities read *to bring to light*

the mystery hidden for ages in*a* God who created all things; [10]so that through the church the wisdom of God in its rich variety might now be made known to the rulers and authorities in the heavenly places. [11]This was in accordance with the eternal purpose that he has carried out in Christ Jesus our Lord, [12]in whom we have access to God in boldness and confidence through faith in him.*b* [13]I pray therefore that you*c* may not lose heart over my sufferings for you; they are your glory.

PRAYER FOR THE READERS

14 For this reason I bow my knees before the Father,*d* [15]from whom every family*e* in heaven and on earth takes its name. [16]I pray that, according to the riches of his glory, he may grant that you may be strengthened in your inner being with power through his Spirit, [17]and that Christ may dwell in your hearts through faith, as you are being rooted and grounded in love. [18]I pray that you may have the power to comprehend, with all the saints, what is the breadth and length and height and depth, [19]and to know the love of Christ that surpasses knowledge, so that you may be filled with all the fullness of God.

20 Now to him who by the power at work within us is able to accomplish abundantly far more than all we can ask or imagine, [21]to him be glory in the church and in Christ Jesus to all generations, forever and ever. Amen.

UNITY IN THE BODY OF CHRIST

4 I therefore, the prisoner in the Lord, beg you to lead a life worthy of the calling to which you have been called, [2]with all humility and gentleness, with patience, bearing with one another in love, [3]making every effort to maintain the unity of the Spirit in the bond of peace. [4]There is one body and one Spirit, just as you were called to the one hope of your calling, [5]one Lord, one faith, one baptism, [6]one God and Father of all, who is above all and through all and in all.

7 But each of us was given grace according to the measure of Christ's gift. [8]Therefore it is said,

"When he ascended on high he made captivity itself a captive;
　　he gave gifts to his people."

9 (When it says, "He ascended," what does it mean but that he had also descended*f* into the lower parts of the earth? [10]He who descended is the same one who ascended far above all the heavens, so that he might fill all things.) [11]The gifts he gave were that some would be apostles, some prophets, some evange-

---

a Or *by*　*b* Or *the faith of him*　*c* Or *I*　*d* Other ancient authorities add *of our Lord Jesus Christ*　*e* Gk *fatherhood*　*f* Other ancient authorities add *first* lists, some pastors and teachers, [12] to equip the saints for the work of ministry, for building up the body of Christ, [13] until all of us come to the unity of the faith and of the knowledge of the Son of God, to maturity, to the measure of the full stature of Christ. [14] We must no longer be children, tossed to and fro and blown about by every wind of doctrine, by people's trickery, by their craftiness in deceitful scheming. [15] But speaking the truth in love, we must grow up in every way into him who is the head, into Christ, [16] from whom the whole body, joined and knit together by every ligament with which it is equipped, as each part is working properly, promotes the body's growth in building itself up in love.

THE OLD LIFE AND THE NEW

17 Now this I affirm and insist on in the Lord: you must no longer live as the Gentiles live, in the futility of their minds. [18] They are darkened in their understanding, alienated from the life of God because of their ignorance and hardness of heart. [19] They have lost all sensitivity and have abandoned themselves to licentiousness, greedy to practice every kind of impurity. [20] That is not the way you learned Christ! [21] For surely you have heard about him and were taught in him, as truth is in Jesus. [22] You were taught to put away your former way of life, your old self, corrupt and deluded by its lusts, [23] and to be renewed in the spirit of your minds, [24] and to clothe yourselves with the new self, created according to the likeness of God in true righteousness and holiness.

RULES FOR THE NEW LIFE

25 So then, putting away falsehood, let all of us speak the truth to our neighbors, for we are members of one another. [26] Be angry but do not sin; do not let the sun go down on your anger, [27] and do not make room for the devil. [28] Thieves must give up stealing; rather let them labor and work honestly with their own hands, so as to have something to share with the needy. [29] Let no evil talk come out of your mouths, but only what is useful for building up,[a] as there is need, so that your words may give grace to those who hear. [30] And do not grieve the Holy Spirit of God, with which you were marked with a seal for the day of redemption. [31] Put away from you all bitterness and wrath and anger and wrangling and slander, together with all malice, [32] and be kind to one another, tenderhearted, forgiving one another, as God in Christ has forgiven you.[b]

5 Therefore be imitators of God, as beloved children, [2] and live in love, as Christ loved us[c] and gave himself up for us, a fragrant offering and sacrifice to God.

---

a Other ancient authorities read *building up faith*   b Other ancient authorities read *us*   c Other ancient authorities read *you*

RENOUNCE PAGAN WAYS

3 But fornication and impurity of any kind, or greed, must not even be mentioned among you, as is proper among saints. [4]Entirely out of place is obscene, silly, and vulgar talk; but instead, let there be thanksgiving. [5]Be sure of this, that no fornicator or impure person, or one who is greedy (that is, an idolater), has any inheritance in the kingdom of Christ and of God.

6 Let no one deceive you with empty words, for because of these things the wrath of God comes on those who are disobedient. [7]Therefore do not be associated with them. [8]For once you were darkness, but now in the Lord you are light. Live as children of light— [9]for the fruit of the light is found in all that is good and right and true. [10]Try to find out what is pleasing to the Lord. [11]Take no part in the unfruitful works of darkness, but instead expose them. [12]For it is shameful even to mention what such people do secretly; [13]but everything exposed by the light becomes visible, [14]for everything that becomes visible is light. Therefore it says,

> "Sleeper, awake!
> Rise from the dead,
> and Christ will shine on you."

15 Be careful then how you live, not as unwise people but as wise, [16]making the most of the time, because the days are evil. [17]So do not be foolish, but understand what the will of the Lord is. [18]Do not get drunk with wine, for that is debauchery; but be filled with the Spirit, [19]as you sing psalms and hymns and spiritual songs among yourselves, singing and making melody to the Lord in your hearts, [20]giving thanks to God the Father at all times and for everything in the name of our Lord Jesus Christ.

THE CHRISTIAN HOUSEHOLD

21 Be subject to one another out of reverence for Christ.

22 Wives, be subject to your husbands as you are to the Lord. [23]For the husband is the head of the wife just as Christ is the head of the church, the body of which he is the Savior. [24]Just as the church is subject to Christ, so also wives ought to be, in everything, to their husbands.

25 Husbands, love your wives, just as Christ loved the church and gave himself up for her, [26]in order to make her holy by cleansing her with the washing of water by the word, [27]so as to present the church to himself in splendor, without a spot or wrinkle or anything of the kind—yes, so that she may be holy and without blemish. [28]In the same way, husbands should love their wives as they do their own bodies. He who loves his wife loves himself. [29]For no one ever

hates his own body, but he nourishes and tenderly cares for it, just as Christ does for the church, [30]because we are members of his body.[a] [31]"For this reason a man will leave his father and mother and be joined to his wife, and the two will become one flesh." [32]This is a great mystery, and I am applying it to Christ and the church. [33]Each of you, however, should love his wife as himself, and a wife should respect her husband.

CHILDREN AND PARENTS

6 Children, obey your parents in the Lord,[b] for this is right. [2]"Honor your father and mother"—this is the first commandment with a promise: [3]"so that it may be well with you and you may live long on the earth."

4 And, fathers, do not provoke your children to anger, but bring them up in the discipline and instruction of the Lord.

SLAVES AND MASTERS

5 Slaves, obey your earthly masters with fear and trembling, in singleness of heart, as you obey Christ; [6]not only while being watched, and in order to please them, but as slaves of Christ, doing the will of God from the heart. [7]Render service with enthusiasm, as to the Lord and not to men and women, [8]knowing that whatever good we do, we will receive the same again from the Lord, whether we are slaves or free.

9 And, masters, do the same to them. Stop threatening them, for you know that both of you have the same Master in heaven, and with him there is no partiality.

THE WHOLE ARMOR OF GOD

10 Finally, be strong in the Lord and in the strength of his power. [11]Put on the whole armor of God, so that you may be able to stand against the wiles of the devil. [12]For our[c] struggle is not against enemies of blood and flesh, but against the rulers, against the authorities, against the cosmic powers of this present darkness, against the spiritual forces of evil in the heavenly places. [13]Therefore take up the whole armor of God, so that you may be able to withstand on that evil day, and having done everything, to stand firm. [14]Stand therefore, and fasten the belt of truth around your waist, and put on the breastplate of righteousness. [15]As shoes for your feet put on whatever will make you ready to proclaim the gospel of peace. [16]With all of these,[d] take the shield of faith, with

---

a Other ancient authorities add *of his flesh and of his bones*   b Other ancient authorities lack *in the Lord*   c Other ancient authorities read *your*   d Or *In all circumstances* which you will be able to quench all the flaming arrows of the evil one. [17]Take the helmet of salvation, and the sword of the Spirit, which is the word of God.

18 Pray in the Spirit at all times in every prayer and supplication. To that end keep alert and always persevere in supplication for all the saints. [19]Pray also for me, so that when I speak, a message may be given to me to make known with boldness the mystery of the gospel,[a] [20]for which I am an ambassador in chains. Pray that I may declare it boldly, as I must speak.

PERSONAL MATTERS AND BENEDICTION

21 So that you also may know how I am and what I am doing, Tychicus will tell you everything. He is a dear brother and a faithful minister in the Lord. [22]I am sending him to you for this very purpose, to let you know how we are, and to encourage your hearts.

23 Peace be to the whole community,[b] and love with faith, from God the Father and the Lord Jesus Christ. [24]Grace be with all who have an undying love for our Lord Jesus Christ.[c]

---

a Other ancient authorities lack *of the gospel*   b Gk *to the brothers*   c Other ancient authorities add *Amen*

Revelation

Revelation is the last document in the canonical New Testament, because it speaks of the second coming of Jesus, the ending of "this world," and its replacement by a new heaven and a new earth. Its final two chapters describe the "new Jerusalem" descending to earth, a glorious city in which mourning, crying, pain, and death are no more. In it is the throne of God and the Lamb. From it flows the river of life, on whose banks stands the tree of life, whose leaves are for the healing of the nations. It is a city of light. In the final verse of the vision: "There will be no more night; they need no light of lamp or sun, for the Lord God will be their light" (22.5). It is difficult to imagine a more powerful way to end the New Testament.

Because Revelation speaks about the second coming of Jesus and the events preceding it, it has often been understood by Christians to refer to events that are still in the future. To say the obvious, the second coming of Jesus hasn't happened. Therefore, what Revelation speaks about must still be in the future, and it could be soon.

This is the premise of Christian churches today that emphasize that the second coming may be near: what Revelation says will happen someday. It is also the premise of the recent series of Left Behind novels. All were bestsellers, totaling more than 70 million copies in the United States alone. They are about the final seven years of the world's history, based on Revelation as interpreted by their authors. What are commonly called "prophecy conferences" share the same premise, that Revelation reveals what will happen someday. It tells us about the signs of the end—and they may be happening now.

This chronological and contextual New Testament sees Revelation very differently. It locates Revelation in its time and place. What does it tell us about the author and his message to the early Christian communities to whom he wrote? What did he say and what did he expect? What it did it mean to those to whom it was written in their historical context?

Authorship

The author identifies himself as "John." For much of Christian history, it was taken for granted that he was the same John who wrote the gospel and letters of John and who was one of the twelve disciples of Jesus. Modern mainstream scholarship does not think so.

The author does not claim to be one of the twelve apostles. Indeed, he refers to them as revered figures of the past (21.14). Moreover, John was a common Jewish name, and there are several Johns in the New Testament: John the Baptizer; John, one of the twelve disciples; John, the name associated with the gospel; and John "the elder," who wrote one or more of the three letters of John.

The author names his location as the island of Patmos in the Aegean Sea, about fifty miles west of Asia Minor. Thus he is often called "John of Patmos" to distinguish him from the other Johns of the New Testament.

From Revelation itself, we learn a bit about him. Because it is addressed to Christian communities in seven cities of Asia Minor, scholars surmise that he was known to them, probably as an itinerant teacher and prophet. He was steeped in the Jewish Bible, the Old Testament; two-thirds of his 404 verses allude to it. His Greek suggests that his native language was Aramaic, which has led to speculation that he grew up in the Jewish homeland as a Palestinian Jew and then traveled to Asia Minor as a Christian missionary, perhaps after the destruction of Jerusalem and the temple in the year 70.

Finally, he was a religious ecstatic. He had visions. In 1.9–20, he describes a vision in which "one like the Son of Man" (the risen Christ) calls and commissions him: "Write what you have seen, what is, and what is to take place." Most of the rest of the document, chapters 4–22, is a series of visions. Whether they are "transcripts" of visions he actually had, literary creations, or a combination of the two is impossible to discern.

An Apocalypse

What John wrote is an apocalypse. Indeed, the document is commonly known among Catholics as "The Apocalypse." Originally a Greek word, it means an unveiling, disclosure, revelation. Apocalypses were relatively common in Judaism in the centuries before and after Jesus. They were sometimes revelations of the "other world," the heavenly world, sometimes revelations of the future of "this world," and sometimes both. Revelation combines both. Jewish apocalypses come out of a time of oppression and suffering inflicted by the powers that rule this world and contrast the present evil age with a future blessed age that will come soon through a dramatic intervention by God.

Like that of other apocalypses, the language of Revelation is highly symbolic. Some numbers are symbolic, especially "seven." It appears sixty times and also structures major portions of the document: seven letters, a scroll with seven seals, seven angels with seven trumpets, seven bowls of wrath. The number "twelve" appears twenty-two times. So also the number 144,000 is symbolic—twelve times twelve times one thousand.

There are symbolic animals: "the Lamb"; a pale green horse; locusts with crowns of gold, teeth like lions, and tails like scorpions; horses with lions' heads and tails like serpents; a red dragon with seven heads, ten horns, and seven crowns; a beast rising from the sea whose number is 666; another beast with two horns like a lamb who speaks like a dragon.

Among the symbolic women is one clothed with the sun; she has the moon under her feet and wears a crown with twelve stars. She is pregnant and about to give birth, and a dragon waits to devour her child. Another, the "great whore," is clothed in scarlet and purple and adorned with gold, jewels, and pearls. She rides on a red beast with seven heads and ten horns. Her name is "Babylon the Great," and she is the "great city" that rules the earth.

Dating

Because Revelation refers to persecution, it has been commonly dated either in the mid to late 60s, shortly after Nero's persecution, or in the mid–90s near the end of the reign of the emperor Domitian (d. 96 CE). But Nero's persecution of Christians was confined to the city of Rome and did not affect Asia Minor, and the historical evidence for official Roman persecution under Domitian is very weak.

Moreover, the document itself does not indicate that large-scale persecution was already under way. The letter to Smyrna warns that suffering is imminent, but has not yet begun: "Do not fear what you are about to suffer. Beware, the devil is about to throw some of you into prison so that you may be tested, and for ten days you will have affliction. Be faithful until death" (2.10). The letter to Pergamum names one Christian who has already been killed (2.13). One of the visions refers to "those who had been slaughtered for the word of God and for the testimony they had given" and to future persecution of "their brothers and sisters, who were soon to be killed" (6.9–11). But the massive persecution of which it warns is still future from its point in time.

Thus most contemporary scholars affirm that the persecutions in Revelation were unofficial, local, sporadic, and not official Roman persecution. With the link to Roman persecution severed, the primary reason for dating it in the 60s or the 90s is gone. Along with most scholars, I date it no earlier than the 90s, in part because its criticism of Christians in the seven communities sounds as though it is directed to second- or third-generation followers of Jesus who have begun to accommodate themselves to the norms and values of dominant culture. But it is also possible that it was written in the early decades of the second century.

Content

After the introduction and inaugural vision in chapter 1, chapters 2–3 are letters to Christian communities in seven cities in Asia Minor. Two—Ephesus and Laodicea—are referred to in letters attributed to Paul. Acts refers to Thyatira, but only in the context of identifying Lydia as a native of that city. The others, Smyrna (modern Izmir), Philadelphia, Pergamum, and Sardis, are not mentioned elsewhere in the New Testament. We do not know who founded the Christian communities there. Perhaps John of Patmos did.

The letters include an evaluation of each community, condemnation or commendation, and promise. Nothing bad is said about Smyrna and Philadelphia; nothing good is said about Sardis and Laodicea. Ephesus, Pergamum, and Thyatira receive mixed verdicts.

The rest of the document until its closing greetings is filled with visions:

> Worship in heaven and the Lamb with the scroll (4.1–5.14). Near the end are words familiar from Handel's *Messiah:* "Worthy is the Lamb that was slaughtered to receive power and wealth and wisdom and might and honor and glory and blessing . . . forever and ever."

> The Lamb opening the seven seals (6.1–8.5). War, famine, plague, death, and earthquake ensue; the sun becomes black, the moon blood red; stars fall from the sky; the rulers of this world call on the mountains to fall on them to protect them from the wrath of God and the Lamb.

> Seven angels blowing seven trumpets (8.6–11.19). A third of the earth burns up, a third of sea creatures and ships are destroyed, a third of earth's rivers become poisonous, a third of the sun, moon, and stars are darkened. Giant locusts ascend from the smoke-filled "bottomless pit," a great army of two hundred million cavalry invades, and a third of humankind is killed. This series ends with words that Handel also used: "The kingdom of the world

has become the kingdom of our Lord and of his Messiah, and he will reign forever and ever."

The cosmic woman and the dragon (12.1–13.18). As a woman clothed with the sun, with the moon under her feet, and wearing a crown with twelve stars gives birth to a male child who will rule the world, a dragon waits to devour him. She and the child are rescued. War breaks out in heaven between Michael and the dragon, the "ancient serpent," who is thrown down to earth. There he makes war on the woman's children. The dragon, the ancient serpent, now called "the beast," rises from the sea and rules the world. A second beast orders that all people worship the first beast, whose number is "666."

The final plagues and the seven bowls of God's wrath (14.1–16.21). Some of the language echoes the plagues that came upon Egypt in the story of the exodus: boils, seas and rivers turning to blood, and darkness. A great earthquake destroys the "great city," splitting it into three parts, and hailstones weighing a hundred pounds each fall upon people.

The destruction and fall of "Babylon the Great" (17.1–18.24). Personified as a royal, wealthy, and seductive woman, the "great whore" with whom the rulers of this world have committed fornication, she is identified as the city that rules the world, built on seven hills.

The defeat of the beast and his armies (19.1–21). The chapter includes the second coming of Jesus, riding a white horse and leading the armies of heaven in a final battle (at Armageddon, according to 16.16). The beast and his false prophet (the second beast of Revelation 13) are thrown alive into a lake of fire, and his armies are killed. The vision ends with a vivid image of carrion birds eating the corpses of kings and captains and soldiers: "All the birds were gorged with their flesh."

The thousand years (20.1–14). The dragon, the ancient serpent, "who is the Devil and Satan," is imprisoned in the "bottomless pit." After a thousand years, he escapes and once again attacks the "saints." Fire from heaven consumes his army, and he is thrown into a lake of fire and eternal torment.

The new Jerusalem (21.1–22.5). After the final destruction of Satan, the beast, a city descends from the sky like "a bride adorned for her husband." It is the "new Jerusalem," the place of God's presence, the dwelling place of God on earth. It is paradise restored—no tears, no death, no mourning, crying, or pain. From it flows the river of life and in it is the tree of life. There is no more darkness or night, for God is its light.

There the visions end. The rest of chapter 22 contains concluding affirmations, warnings, and promises. It ends: "The one who testifies to these things says, 'Surely I am coming soon.' Amen. Come, Lord Jesus! The grace of the Lord Jesus be with all the saints. Amen."

Interpreting Revelation

Recall that some Christians believe that the image-filled visions of Revelation are to be interpreted as referring to events that are still in the future—that it speaks in veiled but perhaps decipherable language about the signs of the end and the second coming of Jesus. Christians throughout the centuries have often interpreted it this way. There was a flurry of end-of-the-world expectation around the year 1000 as the first millennium ended. In the Reformation in the sixteenth century, Luther and others identified the "great whore," "Babylon the Great," "the beast," as Rome and the pope and thought the second coming might be near.

Closer to our own time, some Protestants from the nineteenth century on have proclaimed that the second coming is at hand. The expectation continues. One poll suggests that as many as 40 percent of American Protestants think it certainly or probably will happen in the next fifty years, a conviction based on the futurist interpretation of Revelation.

In contrast, this chronological New Testament sets Revelation in its late first-century context and asks what it meant (past tense) then. What did its language mean to its author and to the early Christian communities to which it was addressed? Within their shared field of meaning, what did he communicate to them?

To illustrate with a few illuminating and important examples:

> The author expected the events he describes to happen in his near future. Seven times (note the number seven again), he writes, "The time is near," "what must soon take place," "I am coming soon." "Soon" and "near" cannot plausibly be extended to two thousand years and counting. Like the authors of a number of New Testament documents, John of Patmos thought the second coming would happen soon.

> The author identified the dragon, the ancient serpent, Babylon the Great, the great whore, the beast whose number is 666. It was Rome—not just the city, but the Roman Empire. The identification is unmistakable in a late first-century context. Because of the Roman destruction of Jerusalem

in 70, Jews and Christians spoke of Rome as "Babylon"—because the Babylonian Empire was the previous destroyer of the holy city and its temple. The woman and the beast live in a city built on seven hills, a designation for Rome that goes back to antiquity. It is the city that rules the world; in a first-century context, that could only be Rome. The number 666 is a numerical code for Caesar Nero, the first Roman persecutor of Christians. The beast is the Roman Empire of the first century—not some future beast from our point in time.

The author chastised most of the communities to whom Revelation was addressed for their accommodation to the imperial way of life. They had abandoned their first love, forgotten what they received and heard, and become lukewarm.

The author's message of the imminent destruction of Rome and the second coming of Jesus encouraged his followers to hold fast. The powers who ruled and oppressed that world and rejected the vision of a new world, the kingdom of God proclaimed by Jesus and his followers, would soon be no more. "Be steady, take courage, do not be afraid," they were told.

John expected the destruction of Rome and the second coming of Jesus to occur soon. Obviously, he was wrong. They didn't happen.

This realization raises an interpretive question. What is a faithful interpretation of Revelation in our time? Is it one that affirms that what it says will still happen? That there will be a future beast who in a final battle at Armageddon will be vanquished by Jesus at the head of an army of heaven? That the plagues and wars and earthquakes and other signs of the end are still going to occur as signs of the second coming?

Or is it one that takes seriously what John was saying to Christians in his time? That accommodation to imperial ways is wrong. That the struggle between the lordship of Christ and the lordship of Caesar is the great conflict. That it is important to persevere even when it looks like the beast is winning. That, appearances to the contrary, the beast does not have the final word and is not the final Word. In its first-century context, Revelation is a pervasively anti-imperial document. What might this mean for Christians today, especially American Christians in a time of the American Empire? Was the problem with the Roman Empire that it was Roman? Or was the problem that it was an empire?

Note that a historical and contextual approach to Revelation does not restrict its meaning to the past. It begins with its past meaning, but is not confined to that. It asks: If this is what Revelation meant then, what might it mean now?

Revelation is full of contrasts. It uses the dualistic contrast between the forces of good and the forces of evil, an ancient archetypal image that continues to have power in the present. Think of the *Star Wars* movies with their battles between the evil empire of Darth Vader and the forces of light symbolized by Luke Skywalker and his light saber. Revelation particularizes the dualistic contrast into a conflict between the lordship of Christ and the lordship of Caesar.

It is full of contrasts in another sense as well. It is very violent, and much of the violence is done by God. God sends suffering, plagues, earthquakes, and death upon the world as the seals are opened, the trumpets blown, and the bowls of God's wrath are poured out. God destroys Babylon the Great and the armies of the beast. The victory song in chapter 18 is filled with gloating over divine violence. At the same time, Revelation includes some of the most magnificent language in the Bible, much of which has found its way into Christian worship and hymns.

It is thus an ambiguous document as regards its role in Christianity. On the one hand, it has been understood as a justification for vengeful and violent actions against "enemies." If God can be this violent, then so can we. Indeed, an increase in violence will be part of the end times leading up to the second coming of Jesus. Perhaps Christians will even be called to be part of what the Left Behind novels call the "tribulation force," an army of Christians using modern military weaponry to do battle with the forces of the "beast."

On the other hand, its language expresses the human yearning for a different kind of world, one lived in the presence of God, in which the sufferings of this world are no more. It has not only inspired Christian worship; its vision of the new Jerusalem in which every tear will be wiped away has comforted many in the face of suffering and death. And thus the final word about Revelation: handle with care.

THE
Revelation
TO JOHN

INTRODUCTION AND SALUTATION

1 The revelation of Jesus Christ, which God gave him to show his servants*
what must soon take place; he made* it known by sending his angel to his
servant* John, ²who testified to the word of God and to the testimony of Jesus
Christ, even to all that he saw.

3 Blessed is the one who reads aloud the words of the prophecy, and blessed
are those who hear and who keep what is written in it; for the time is near.

4 John to the seven churches that are in Asia:

Grace to you and peace from him who is and who was and who is to come,
and from the seven spirits who are before his throne, ⁵and from Jesus Christ,
the faithful witness, the firstborn of the dead, and the ruler of the kings of the
earth.

To him who loves us and freed* us from our sins by his blood, ⁶and made*
us to be a kingdom, priests serving* his God and Father, to him be glory and
dominion forever and ever. Amen.

> 7 Look! He is coming with the clouds;
>> every eye will see him,
>> even those who pierced him;
>>> and on his account all the tribes of the earth will wail.

So it is to be. Amen.

---

a Gk *slaves*   *b* Gk *and he made*   *c* Gk *slave*   *d* Other ancient authorities read *washed*   *e* Gk *priests to*

8 "I am the Alpha and the Omega," says the Lord God, who is and who was and who is to come, the Almighty.

A VISION OF CHRIST

9 I, John, your brother who share with you in Jesus the persecution and the kingdom and the patient endurance, was on the island called Patmos because of the word of God and the testimony of Jesus.*a* *10*I was in the spirit*b* on the Lord's day, and I heard behind me a loud voice like a trumpet *11*saying, "Write in a book what you see and send it to the seven churches, to Ephesus, to Smyrna, to Pergamum, to Thyatira, to Sardis, to Philadelphia, and to Laodicea."

12 Then I turned to see whose voice it was that spoke to me, and on turning I saw seven golden lampstands, *13*and in the midst of the lampstands I saw one like the Son of Man, clothed with a long robe and with a golden sash across his chest. *14*His head and his hair were white as white wool, white as snow; his eyes were like a flame of fire, *15*his feet were like burnished bronze, refined as in a furnace, and his voice was like the sound of many waters. *16*In his right hand he held seven stars, and from his mouth came a sharp, two-edged sword, and his face was like the sun shining with full force.

17 When I saw him, I fell at his feet as though dead. But he placed his right hand on me, saying, "Do not be afraid; I am the first and the last, *18*and the living one. I was dead, and see, I am alive forever and ever; and I have the keys of Death and of Hades. *19*Now write what you have seen, what is, and what is to take place after this. *20*As for the mystery of the seven stars that you saw in my right hand, and the seven golden lampstands: the seven stars are the angels of the seven churches, and the seven lampstands are the seven churches.

THE MESSAGE TO EPHESUS

2 "To the angel of the church in Ephesus write: These are the words of him who holds the seven stars in his right hand, who walks among the seven golden lampstands:

2 "I know your works, your toil and your patient endurance. I know that you cannot tolerate evildoers; you have tested those who claim to be apostles but are not, and have found them to be false. *3*I also know that you are enduring patiently and bearing up for the sake of my name, and that you have not grown weary. *4*But I have this against you, that you have abandoned the love you had at first. *5*Remember then from what you have fallen; repent, and do the works you did at first. If not, I will come to you and remove your lampstand from its

---

a Or *testimony to Jesus*　*b* Or *in the Spirit*

place, unless you repent. ⁶Yet this is to your credit: you hate the works of the Nicolaitans, which I also hate. ⁷Let anyone who has an ear listen to what the Spirit is saying to the churches. To everyone who conquers, I will give permission to eat from the tree of life that is in the paradise of God.

THE MESSAGE TO SMYRNA

8 "And to the angel of the church in Smyrna write: These are the words of the first and the last, who was dead and came to life:

9 "I know your affliction and your poverty, even though you are rich. I know the slander on the part of those who say that they are Jews and are not, but are a synagogue of Satan. ¹⁰Do not fear what you are about to suffer. Beware, the devil is about to throw some of you into prison so that you may be tested, and for ten days you will have affliction. Be faithful until death, and I will give you the crown of life. ¹¹Let anyone who has an ear listen to what the Spirit is saying to the churches. Whoever conquers will not be harmed by the second death.

THE MESSAGE TO PERGAMUM

12 "And to the angel of the church in Pergamum write: These are the words of him who has the sharp two-edged sword:

13 "I know where you are living, where Satan's throne is. Yet you are holding fast to my name, and you did not deny your faith in me*a* even in the days of Antipas my witness, my faithful one, who was killed among you, where Satan lives. ¹⁴But I have a few things against you: you have some there who hold to the teaching of Balaam, who taught Balak to put a stumbling block before the people of Israel, so that they would eat food sacrificed to idols and practice fornication. ¹⁵So you also have some who hold to the teaching of the Nicolaitans. ¹⁶Repent then. If not, I will come to you soon and make war against them with the sword of my mouth. ¹⁷Let anyone who has an ear listen to what the Spirit is saying to the churches. To everyone who conquers I will give some of the hidden manna, and I will give a white stone, and on the white stone is written a new name that no one knows except the one who receives it.

THE MESSAGE TO THYATIRA

18 "And to the angel of the church in Thyatira write: These are the words of the Son of God, who has eyes like a flame of fire, and whose feet are like burnished bronze:

---

a Or *deny my faith*

19 "I know your works—your love, faith, service, and patient endurance. I know that your last works are greater than the first. ²⁰But I have this against you: you tolerate that woman Jezebel, who calls herself a prophet and is teaching and beguiling my servants*a* to practice fornication and to eat food sacrificed to idols. ²¹I gave her time to repent, but she refuses to repent of her fornication. ²²Beware, I am throwing her on a bed, and those who commit adultery with her I am throwing into great distress, unless they repent of her doings; ²³and I will strike her children dead. And all the churches will know that I am the one who searches minds and hearts, and I will give to each of you as your works deserve. ²⁴But to the rest of you in Thyatira, who do not hold this teaching, who have not learned what some call 'the deep things of Satan,' to you I say, I do not lay on you any other burden; ²⁵only hold fast to what you have until I come. ²⁶To everyone who conquers and continues to do my works to the end,

> I will give authority over the nations;
> 27 to rule*b* them with an iron rod,
>> as when clay pots are shattered—

28 even as I also received authority from my Father. To the one who conquers I will also give the morning star. ²⁹Let anyone who has an ear listen to what the Spirit is saying to the churches.

THE MESSAGE TO SARDIS

3 "And to the angel of the church in Sardis write: These are the words of him who has the seven spirits of God and the seven stars:

"I know your works; you have a name of being alive, but you are dead. ²Wake up, and strengthen what remains and is on the point of death, for I have not found your works perfect in the sight of my God. ³Remember then what you received and heard; obey it, and repent. If you do not wake up, I will come like a thief, and you will not know at what hour I will come to you. ⁴Yet you have still a few persons in Sardis who have not soiled their clothes; they will walk with me, dressed in white, for they are worthy. ⁵If you conquer, you will be clothed like them in white robes, and I will not blot your name out of the book of life; I will confess your name before my Father and before his angels. ⁶Let anyone who has an ear listen to what the Spirit is saying to the churches.

THE MESSAGE TO PHILADELPHIA

7 "And to the angel of the church in Philadelphia write:

> These are the words of the holy one, the true one,
>> who has the key of David,

---

a Gk *slaves* *b* Or *to shepherd*

>who opens and no one will shut,
>
>who shuts and no one opens:

8 "I know your works. Look, I have set before you an open door, which no one is able to shut. I know that you have but little power, and yet you have kept my word and have not denied my name. [9]I will make those of the synagogue of Satan who say that they are Jews and are not, but are lying—I will make them come and bow down before your feet, and they will learn that I have loved you. [10]Because you have kept my word of patient endurance, I will keep you from the hour of trial that is coming on the whole world to test the inhabitants of the earth. [11]I am coming soon; hold fast to what you have, so that no one may seize your crown. [12]If you conquer, I will make you a pillar in the temple of my God; you will never go out of it. I will write on you the name of my God, and the name of the city of my God, the new Jerusalem that comes down from my God out of heaven, and my own new name. [13]Let anyone who has an ear listen to what the Spirit is saying to the churches.

THE MESSAGE TO LAODICEA

14 "And to the angel of the church in Laodicea write: The words of the Amen, the faithful and true witness, the origin[a] of God's creation:

15 "I know your works; you are neither cold nor hot. I wish that you were either cold or hot. [16]So, because you are lukewarm, and neither cold nor hot, I am about to spit you out of my mouth. [17]For you say, 'I am rich, I have prospered, and I need nothing.' You do not realize that you are wretched, pitiable, poor, blind, and naked. [18]Therefore I counsel you to buy from me gold refined by fire so that you may be rich; and white robes to clothe you and to keep the shame of your nakedness from being seen; and salve to anoint your eyes so that you may see. [19]I reprove and discipline those whom I love. Be earnest, therefore, and repent. [20]Listen! I am standing at the door, knocking; if you hear my voice and open the door, I will come in to you and eat with you, and you with me. [21]To the one who conquers I will give a place with me on my throne, just as I myself conquered and sat down with my Father on his throne. [22]Let anyone who has an ear listen to what the Spirit is saying to the churches."

THE HEAVENLY WORSHIP

4 After this I looked, and there in heaven a door stood open! And the first voice, which I had heard speaking to me like a trumpet, said, "Come up here, and I will show you what must take place after this." [2]At once I was in the

---

a Or beginning

spirit,*a* and there in heaven stood a throne, with one seated on the throne! ³And the one seated there looks like jasper and carnelian, and around the throne is a rainbow that looks like an emerald. ⁴Around the throne are twenty-four thrones, and seated on the thrones are twenty-four elders, dressed in white robes, with golden crowns on their heads. ⁵Coming from the throne are flashes of lightning, and rumblings and peals of thunder, and in front of the throne burn seven flaming torches, which are the seven spirits of God; ⁶and in front of the throne there is something like a sea of glass, like crystal.

Around the throne, and on each side of the throne, are four living creatures, full of eyes in front and behind: ⁷the first living creature like a lion, the second living creature like an ox, the third living creature with a face like a human face, and the fourth living creature like a flying eagle. ⁸And the four living creatures, each of them with six wings, are full of eyes all around and inside. Day and night without ceasing they sing,

> "Holy, holy, holy,
> the Lord God the Almighty,
> who was and is and is to come."

9 And whenever the living creatures give glory and honor and thanks to the one who is seated on the throne, who lives forever and ever, ¹⁰the twenty-four elders fall before the one who is seated on the throne and worship the one who lives forever and ever; they cast their crowns before the throne, singing,

> 11 "You are worthy, our Lord and God,
> to receive glory and honor and power,
> for you created all things,
> and by your will they existed and were created."

THE SCROLL AND THE LAMB

5 Then I saw in the right hand of the one seated on the throne a scroll written on the inside and on the back, sealed*b* with seven seals; ²and I saw a mighty angel proclaiming with a loud voice, "Who is worthy to open the scroll and break its seals?" ³And no one in heaven or on earth or under the earth was able to open the scroll or to look into it. ⁴And I began to weep bitterly because no one was found worthy to open the scroll or to look into it. ⁵Then one of the elders said to me, "Do not weep. See, the Lion of the tribe of Judah, the Root of David, has conquered, so that he can open the scroll and its seven seals."

6 Then I saw between the throne and the four living creatures and among the elders a Lamb standing as if it had been slaughtered, having seven horns

---

a Or *in the Spirit*   *b* Or *written on the inside, and sealed on the back* and seven eyes, which are the seven spirits of God sent out into all the earth. [7]He went and took the scroll from the right hand of the one who was seated on the throne. [8]When he had taken the scroll, the four living creatures and the twenty-four elders fell before the Lamb, each holding a harp and golden bowls full of incense, which are the prayers of the saints. [9]They sing a new song:

> "You are worthy to take the scroll
>   and to open its seals,
>   for you were slaughtered and by your blood you ransomed for God
>   saints from[a] every tribe and language and people and nation;
>   10 you have made them to be a kingdom and priests serving[b] our God,
>   and they will reign on earth."

11 Then I looked, and I heard the voice of many angels surrounding the throne and the living creatures and the elders; they numbered myriads of myriads and thousands of thousands, [12]singing with full voice,

> "Worthy is the Lamb that was slaughtered
> to receive power and wealth and wisdom and might
> and honor and glory and blessing!"

13 Then I heard every creature in heaven and on earth and under the earth and in the sea, and all that is in them, singing,

> "To the one seated on the throne and to the Lamb
> be blessing and honor and glory and might
> forever and ever!"

14 And the four living creatures said, "Amen!" And the elders fell down and worshiped.

THE SEVEN SEALS

6 Then I saw the Lamb open one of the seven seals, and I heard one of the four living creatures call out, as with a voice of thunder, "Come!"[c] [2]I looked, and there was a white horse! Its rider had a bow; a crown was given to him, and he came out conquering and to conquer.

3 When he opened the second seal, I heard the second living creature call out, "Come!"[c] [4]And out came[d] another horse, bright red; its rider was permitted to take peace from the earth, so that people would slaughter one another; and he was given a great sword.

5 When he opened the third seal, I heard the third living creature call out, "Come!"[c] I looked, and there was a black horse! Its rider held a pair of scales in his hand, [6]and I heard what seemed to be a voice in the midst of the four living

---

a Gk ransomed for God from   b Gk priests to   c Or "Go!"   d Or went creatures saying, "A quart of wheat for a day's pay,[a] and three quarts of barley for a day's pay,[a] but do not damage the olive oil and the wine!"

7 When he opened the fourth seal, I heard the voice of the fourth living creature call out, "Come!"[b] [8]I looked and there was a pale green horse! Its rider's name was Death, and Hades followed with him; they were given authority over a fourth of the earth, to kill with sword, famine, and pestilence, and by the wild animals of the earth.

9 When he opened the fifth seal, I saw under the altar the souls of those who had been slaughtered for the word of God and for the testimony they had given; [10]they cried out with a loud voice, "Sovereign Lord, holy and true, how long will it be before you judge and avenge our blood on the inhabitants of the earth?" [11]They were each given a white robe and told to rest a little longer, until the number would be complete both of their fellow servants[c] and of their brothers and sisters,[d] who were soon to be killed as they themselves had been killed.

12 When he opened the sixth seal, I looked, and there came a great earthquake; the sun became black as sackcloth, the full moon became like blood, [13]and the stars of the sky fell to the earth as the fig tree drops its winter fruit when shaken by a gale. [14]The sky vanished like a scroll rolling itself up, and every mountain and island was removed from its place. [15]Then the kings of the earth and the magnates and the generals and the rich and the powerful, and everyone, slave and free, hid in the caves and among the rocks of the mountains, [16]calling to the mountains and rocks, "Fall on us and hide us from the face of the one seated on the throne and from the wrath of the Lamb; [17]for the great day of their wrath has come, and who is able to stand?"

THE 144,000 OF ISRAEL SEALED

7 After this I saw four angels standing at the four corners of the earth, holding back the four winds of the earth so that no wind could blow on earth or sea or against any tree. [2]I saw another angel ascending from the rising of the sun, having the seal of the living God, and he called with a loud voice to the four angels who had been given power to damage earth and sea, [3]saying, "Do not damage the earth or the sea or the trees, until we have marked the servants[c] of our God with a seal on their foreheads."

4 And I heard the number of those who were sealed, one hundred forty-four thousand, sealed out of every tribe of the people of Israel:

---

a Gk a denarius   b Or "Go!"   c Gk slaves   d Gk brothers

5 From the tribe of Judah twelve thousand sealed,
   from the tribe of Reuben twelve thousand,
   from the tribe of Gad twelve thousand,
6 from the tribe of Asher twelve thousand,
   from the tribe of Naphtali twelve thousand,
   from the tribe of Manasseh twelve thousand,
7 from the tribe of Simeon twelve thousand,
   from the tribe of Levi twelve thousand,
   from the tribe of Issachar twelve thousand,
8 from the tribe of Zebulun twelve thousand,
   from the tribe of Joseph twelve thousand,
   from the tribe of Benjamin twelve thousand sealed.

THE MULTITUDE FROM EVERY NATION

9 After this I looked, and there was a great multitude that no one could count, from every nation, from all tribes and peoples and languages, standing before the throne and before the Lamb, robed in white, with palm branches in their hands. [10]They cried out in a loud voice, saying,

> "Salvation belongs to our God who is seated on the throne, and to the
>   Lamb!"

11 And all the angels stood around the throne and around the elders and the four living creatures, and they fell on their faces before the throne and worshiped God, [12]singing,

> "Amen! Blessing and glory and wisdom
> and thanksgiving and honor
> and power and might
> be to our God forever and ever! Amen."

13 Then one of the elders addressed me, saying, "Who are these, robed in white, and where have they come from?" [14]I said to him, "Sir, you are the one that knows." Then he said to me, "These are they who have come out of the great ordeal; they have washed their robes and made them white in the blood of the Lamb.

15 For this reason they are before the throne of God,
   and worship him day and night within his temple,
   and the one who is seated on the throne will shelter them.
16 They will hunger no more, and thirst no more;
   the sun will not strike them,
   nor any scorching heat;

17 for the Lamb at the center of the throne will be their shepherd,
     and he will guide them to springs of the water of life,
   and God will wipe away every tear from their eyes."

THE SEVENTH SEAL AND THE GOLDEN CENSER

8 When the Lamb opened the seventh seal, there was silence in heaven for
about half an hour. ²And I saw the seven angels who stand before God, and
seven trumpets were given to them.

3 Another angel with a golden censer came and stood at the altar; he was
given a great quantity of incense to offer with the prayers of all the saints on
the golden altar that is before the throne. ⁴And the smoke of the incense, with
the prayers of the saints, rose before God from the hand of the angel. ⁵Then the
angel took the censer and filled it with fire from the altar and threw it on the
earth; and there were peals of thunder, rumblings, flashes of lightning, and an
earthquake.

THE SEVEN TRUMPETS

6 Now the seven angels who had the seven trumpets made ready to blow them.

7 The first angel blew his trumpet, and there came hail and fire, mixed with
blood, and they were hurled to the earth; and a third of the earth was burned
up, and a third of the trees were burned up, and all green grass was burned up.

8 The second angel blew his trumpet, and something like a great mountain,
burning with fire, was thrown into the sea. ⁹A third of the sea became blood,
a third of the living creatures in the sea died, and a third of the ships were
destroyed.

10 The third angel blew his trumpet, and a great star fell from heaven, blazing like a torch, and it fell on a third of the rivers and on the springs of water.
¹¹The name of the star is Wormwood. A third of the waters became wormwood,
and many died from the water, because it was made bitter.

12 The fourth angel blew his trumpet, and a third of the sun was struck,
and a third of the moon, and a third of the stars, so that a third of their light
was darkened; a third of the day was kept from shining, and likewise the night.

13 Then I looked, and I heard an eagle crying with a loud voice as it flew in
midheaven, "Woe, woe, woe to the inhabitants of the earth, at the blasts of the
other trumpets that the three angels are about to blow!"

9 And the fifth angel blew his trumpet, and I saw a star that had fallen from
heaven to earth, and he was given the key to the shaft of the bottomless pit;
²he opened the shaft of the bottomless pit, and from the shaft rose smoke like

the smoke of a great furnace, and the sun and the air were darkened with the smoke from the shaft. ³Then from the smoke came locusts on the earth, and they were given authority like the authority of scorpions of the earth. ⁴They were told not to damage the grass of the earth or any green growth or any tree, but only those people who do not have the seal of God on their foreheads. ⁵They were allowed to torture them for five months, but not to kill them, and their torture was like the torture of a scorpion when it stings someone. ⁶And in those days people will seek death but will not find it; they will long to die, but death will flee from them.

7 In appearance the locusts were like horses equipped for battle. On their heads were what looked like crowns of gold; their faces were like human faces, ⁸their hair like women's hair, and their teeth like lions' teeth; ⁹they had scales like iron breastplates, and the noise of their wings was like the noise of many chariots with horses rushing into battle. ¹⁰They have tails like scorpions, with stingers, and in their tails is their power to harm people for five months. ¹¹They have as king over them the angel of the bottomless pit; his name in Hebrew is Abaddon,ᵃ and in Greek he is called Apollyon.ᵇ

12 The first woe has passed. There are still two woes to come.

13 Then the sixth angel blew his trumpet, and I heard a voice from the fourᶜ horns of the golden altar before God, ¹⁴saying to the sixth angel who had the trumpet, "Release the four angels who are bound at the great river Euphrates." ¹⁵So the four angels were released, who had been held ready for the hour, the day, the month, and the year, to kill a third of humankind. ¹⁶The number of the troops of cavalry was two hundred million; I heard their number. ¹⁷And this was how I saw the horses in my vision: the riders wore breastplates the color of fire and of sapphireᵈ and of sulfur; the heads of the horses were like lions' heads, and fire and smoke and sulfur came out of their mouths. ¹⁸By these three plagues a third of humankind was killed, by the fire and smoke and sulfur coming out of their mouths. ¹⁹For the power of the horses is in their mouths and in their tails; their tails are like serpents, having heads; and with them they inflict harm.

20 The rest of humankind, who were not killed by these plagues, did not repent of the works of their hands or give up worshiping demons and idols of gold and silver and bronze and stone and wood, which cannot see or hear or walk. ²¹And they did not repent of their murders or their sorceries or their fornication or their thefts.

---

a That is, *Destruction*   *b* That is, *Destroyer*   *c* Other ancient authorities lack *four*   *d* Gk *hyacinth*

THE ANGEL WITH THE LITTLE SCROLL

10 And I saw another mighty angel coming down from heaven, wrapped in a cloud, with a rainbow over his head; his face was like the sun, and his legs like pillars of fire. ²He held a little scroll open in his hand. Setting his right foot on the sea and his left foot on the land, ³he gave a great shout, like a lion roaring. And when he shouted, the seven thunders sounded. ⁴And when the seven thunders had sounded, I was about to write, but I heard a voice from heaven saying, "Seal up what the seven thunders have said, and do not write it down." ⁵Then the angel whom I saw standing on the sea and the land

raised his right hand to heaven

6 and swore by him who lives forever and ever,

who created heaven and what is in it, the earth and what is in it, and the sea and what is in it: "There will be no more delay, ⁷but in the days when the seventh angel is to blow his trumpet, the mystery of God will be fulfilled, as he announced to his servants*a* the prophets."

8 Then the voice that I had heard from heaven spoke to me again, saying, "Go, take the scroll that is open in the hand of the angel who is standing on the sea and on the land." ⁹So I went to the angel and told him to give me the little scroll; and he said to me, "Take it, and eat; it will be bitter to your stomach, but sweet as honey in your mouth." ¹⁰So I took the little scroll from the hand of the angel and ate it; it was sweet as honey in my mouth, but when I had eaten it, my stomach was made bitter.

11 Then they said to me, "You must prophesy again about many peoples and nations and languages and kings."

THE TWO WITNESSES

11 Then I was given a measuring rod like a staff, and I was told, "Come and measure the temple of God and the altar and those who worship there, ²but do not measure the court outside the temple; leave that out, for it is given over to the nations, and they will trample over the holy city for forty-two months. ³And I will grant my two witnesses authority to prophesy for one thousand two hundred sixty days, wearing sackcloth."

4 These are the two olive trees and the two lampstands that stand before the Lord of the earth. ⁵And if anyone wants to harm them, fire pours from their mouth and consumes their foes; anyone who wants to harm them must be killed in this manner. ⁶They have authority to shut the sky, so that no rain

---

a Gk *slaves*

may fall during the days of their prophesying, and they have authority over the waters to turn them into blood, and to strike the earth with every kind of plague, as often as they desire.

7 When they have finished their testimony, the beast that comes up from the bottomless pit will make war on them and conquer them and kill them, [8]and their dead bodies will lie in the street of the great city that is prophetically[a] called Sodom and Egypt, where also their Lord was crucified. [9]For three and a half days members of the peoples and tribes and languages and nations will gaze at their dead bodies and refuse to let them be placed in a tomb; [10]and the inhabitants of the earth will gloat over them and celebrate and exchange presents, because these two prophets had been a torment to the inhabitants of the earth.

11 But after the three and a half days, the breath[b] of life from God entered them, and they stood on their feet, and those who saw them were terrified. [12]Then they[c] heard a loud voice from heaven saying to them, "Come up here!" And they went up to heaven in a cloud while their enemies watched them. [13]At that moment there was a great earthquake, and a tenth of the city fell; seven thousand people were killed in the earthquake, and the rest were terrified and gave glory to the God of heaven.

14 The second woe has passed. The third woe is coming very soon.

THE SEVENTH TRUMPET

15 Then the seventh angel blew his trumpet, and there were loud voices in heaven, saying,

> "The kingdom of the world has become the kingdom of our Lord
>   and of his Messiah,[d]
> and he will reign forever and ever."

16 Then the twenty-four elders who sit on their thrones before God fell on their faces and worshiped God, [17]singing,

> "We give you thanks, Lord God Almighty,
>   who are and who were,
> for you have taken your great power
>   and begun to reign.

18 The nations raged,
>   but your wrath has come,
>   and the time for judging the dead,
> for rewarding your servants,[e] the prophets
>   and saints and all who fear your name,

---

a Or *allegorically;* Gk *spiritually*   b Or *the spirit*   c Other ancient authorities read *I*   d Gk *Christ*   e Gk *slaves*

both small and great,
and for destroying those who destroy the earth."

19 Then God's temple in heaven was opened, and the ark of his covenant was seen within his temple; and there were flashes of lightning, rumblings, peals of thunder, an earthquake, and heavy hail.

THE WOMAN AND THE DRAGON

12 A great portent appeared in heaven: a woman clothed with the sun, with the moon under her feet, and on her head a crown of twelve stars. ²She was pregnant and was crying out in birth pangs, in the agony of giving birth. ³Then another portent appeared in heaven: a great red dragon, with seven heads and ten horns, and seven diadems on his heads. ⁴His tail swept down a third of the stars of heaven and threw them to the earth. Then the dragon stood before the woman who was about to bear a child, so that he might devour her child as soon as it was born. ⁵And she gave birth to a son, a male child, who is to rule*ᵃ* all the nations with a rod of iron. But her child was snatched away and taken to God and to his throne; ⁶and the woman fled into the wilderness, where she has a place prepared by God, so that there she can be nourished for one thousand two hundred sixty days.

MICHAEL DEFEATS THE DRAGON

7 And war broke out in heaven; Michael and his angels fought against the dragon. The dragon and his angels fought back, ⁸but they were defeated, and there was no longer any place for them in heaven. ⁹The great dragon was thrown down, that ancient serpent, who is called the Devil and Satan, the deceiver of the whole world—he was thrown down to the earth, and his angels were thrown down with him.

10 Then I heard a loud voice in heaven, proclaiming,

"Now have come the salvation and the power
and the kingdom of our God
and the authority of his Messiah,*ᵇ*
for the accuser of our comrades*ᶜ* has been thrown down,
who accuses them day and night before our God.
11 But they have conquered him by the blood of the Lamb
and by the word of their testimony,
for they did not cling to life even in the face of death.

---

a Or *to shepherd*   *b* Gk *Christ*   *c* Gk *brothers*

12 Rejoice then, you heavens
    and those who dwell in them!
But woe to the earth and the sea,
    for the devil has come down to you
with great wrath,
    because he knows that his time is short!"

THE DRAGON FIGHTS AGAIN ON EARTH

13 So when the dragon saw that he had been thrown down to the earth, he pursued[a] the woman who had given birth to the male child. [14]But the woman was given the two wings of the great eagle, so that she could fly from the serpent into the wilderness, to her place where she is nourished for a time, and times, and half a time. [15]Then from his mouth the serpent poured water like a river after the woman, to sweep her away with the flood. [16]But the earth came to the help of the woman; it opened its mouth and swallowed the river that the dragon had poured from his mouth. [17]Then the dragon was angry with the woman, and went off to make war on the rest of her children, those who keep the commandments of God and hold the testimony of Jesus.

THE FIRST BEAST

18 Then the dragon[b] took his stand on the sand of the seashore.

13 And I saw a beast rising out of the sea, having ten horns and seven heads; and on its horns were ten diadems, and on its heads were blasphemous names. [2]And the beast that I saw was like a leopard, its feet were like a bear's, and its mouth was like a lion's mouth. And the dragon gave it his power and his throne and great authority. [3]One of its heads seemed to have received a death-blow, but its mortal wound[c] had been healed. In amazement the whole earth followed the beast. [4]They worshiped the dragon, for he had given his authority to the beast, and they worshiped the beast, saying, "Who is like the beast, and who can fight against it?"

5 The beast was given a mouth uttering haughty and blasphemous words, and it was allowed to exercise authority for forty-two months. [6]It opened its mouth to utter blasphemies against God, blaspheming his name and his dwelling, that is, those who dwell in heaven. [7]Also it was allowed to make war on the saints and to conquer them.[d] It was given authority over every tribe and people

---

a Or *persecuted*   *b* Gk *Then he;* other ancient authorities read *Then I stood*   *c* Gk *the plague of its death*   *d* Other ancient authorities lack this sentence and language and nation, [8]and all the inhabitants of the earth will worship it, everyone whose name has not been written from the foundation of the world in the book of life of the Lamb that was slaughtered.[a]

9 Let anyone who has an ear listen:

10 If you are to be taken captive,

    into captivity you go;

  if you kill with the sword,

    with the sword you must be killed.

Here is a call for the endurance and faith of the saints.

THE SECOND BEAST

11 Then I saw another beast that rose out of the earth; it had two horns like a lamb and it spoke like a dragon. [12]It exercises all the authority of the first beast on its behalf, and it makes the earth and its inhabitants worship the first beast, whose mortal wound[b] had been healed. [13]It performs great signs, even making fire come down from heaven to earth in the sight of all; [14]and by the signs that it is allowed to perform on behalf of the beast, it deceives the inhabitants of earth, telling them to make an image for the beast that had been wounded by the sword[c] and yet lived; [15]and it was allowed to give breath[d] to the image of the beast so that the image of the beast could even speak and cause those who would not worship the image of the beast to be killed. [16]Also it causes all, both small and great, both rich and poor, both free and slave, to be marked on the right hand or the forehead, [17]so that no one can buy or sell who does not have the mark, that is, the name of the beast or the number of its name. [18]This calls for wisdom: let anyone with understanding calculate the number of the beast, for it is the number of a person. Its number is six hundred sixty-six.[e]

THE LAMB AND THE 144,000

14 Then I looked, and there was the Lamb, standing on Mount Zion! And with him were one hundred forty-four thousand who had his name and his Father's name written on their foreheads. [2]And I heard a voice from heaven like the sound of many waters and like the sound of loud thunder; the voice I heard was like the sound of harpists playing on their harps, [3]and they sing a new song before the throne and before the four living creatures and before the elders. No one could learn that song except the one hundred forty-four thousand who have been redeemed from the earth. [4]It is these who have not

---

a Or written in the book of life of the Lamb that was slaughtered from the foundation of the world   b Gk whose plague of its death
c Or that had received the plague of the sword   d Or spirit   e Other ancient authorities read six hundred sixteen

defiled themselves with women, for they are virgins; these follow the Lamb wherever he goes. They have been redeemed from humankind as first fruits for God and the Lamb, [5]and in their mouth no lie was found; they are blameless.

THE MESSAGES OF THE THREE ANGELS

6 Then I saw another angel flying in midheaven, with an eternal gospel to proclaim to those who live[a] on the earth—to every nation and tribe and language and people. [7]He said in a loud voice, "Fear God and give him glory, for the hour of his judgment has come; and worship him who made heaven and earth, the sea and the springs of water."

8 Then another angel, a second, followed, saying, "Fallen, fallen is Babylon the great! She has made all nations drink of the wine of the wrath of her fornication."

9 Then another angel, a third, followed them, crying with a loud voice, "Those who worship the beast and its image, and receive a mark on their foreheads or on their hands, [10]they will also drink the wine of God's wrath, poured unmixed into the cup of his anger, and they will be tormented with fire and sulfur in the presence of the holy angels and in the presence of the Lamb. [11]And the smoke of their torment goes up forever and ever. There is no rest day or night for those who worship the beast and its image and for anyone who receives the mark of its name."

12 Here is a call for the endurance of the saints, those who keep the commandments of God and hold fast to the faith of[b] Jesus.

13 And I heard a voice from heaven saying, "Write this: Blessed are the dead who from now on die in the Lord." "Yes," says the Spirit, "they will rest from their labors, for their deeds follow them."

REAPING THE EARTH'S HARVEST

14 Then I looked, and there was a white cloud, and seated on the cloud was one like the Son of Man, with a golden crown on his head, and a sharp sickle in his hand! [15]Another angel came out of the temple, calling with a loud voice to the one who sat on the cloud, "Use your sickle and reap, for the hour to reap has come, because the harvest of the earth is fully ripe." [16]So the one who sat on the cloud swung his sickle over the earth, and the earth was reaped.

17 Then another angel came out of the temple in heaven, and he too had a sharp sickle. [18]Then another angel came out from the altar, the angel who has authority over fire, and he called with a loud voice to him who had the sharp

---

a Gk *sit*   b Or *to their faith in*

sickle, "Use your sharp sickle and gather the clusters of the vine of the earth, for its grapes are ripe." ¹⁹So the angel swung his sickle over the earth and gathered the vintage of the earth, and he threw it into the great wine press of the wrath of God. ²⁰And the wine press was trodden outside the city, and blood flowed from the wine press, as high as a horse's bridle, for a distance of about two hundred miles.ᵃ

THE ANGELS WITH THE SEVEN LAST PLAGUES

15 Then I saw another portent in heaven, great and amazing: seven angels with seven plagues, which are the last, for with them the wrath of God is ended.

2 And I saw what appeared to be a sea of glass mixed with fire, and those who had conquered the beast and its image and the number of its name, standing beside the sea of glass with harps of God in their hands. ³And they sing the song of Moses, the servantᵇ of God, and the song of the Lamb:

> "Great and amazing are your deeds,
>> Lord God the Almighty!
> Just and true are your ways,
>> King of the nations!ᶜ
> 4 Lord, who will not fear
>> and glorify your name?
> For you alone are holy.
>> All nations will come
>> and worship before you,
>> for your judgments have been revealed."

5 After this I looked, and the temple of the tentᵈ of witness in heaven was opened, ⁶and out of the temple came the seven angels with the seven plagues, robed in pure bright linen,ᵉ with golden sashes across their chests. ⁷Then one of the four living creatures gave the seven angels seven golden bowls full of the wrath of God, who lives forever and ever; ⁸and the temple was filled with smoke from the glory of God and from his power, and no one could enter the temple until the seven plagues of the seven angels were ended.

THE BOWLS OF GOD'S WRATH

16 Then I heard a loud voice from the temple telling the seven angels, "Go and pour out on the earth the seven bowls of the wrath of God."

---

a Gk *one thousand six hundred stadia* b Gk *slave* c Other ancient authorities read *the ages* d Or *tabernacle* e Other ancient authorities read *stone*

2 So the first angel went and poured his bowl on the earth, and a foul and painful sore came on those who had the mark of the beast and who worshiped its image.

3 The second angel poured his bowl into the sea, and it became like the blood of a corpse, and every living thing in the sea died.

4 The third angel poured his bowl into the rivers and the springs of water, and they became blood. ⁵And I heard the angel of the waters say,

> "You are just, O Holy One, who are and were,
>> for you have judged these things;
> 6 because they shed the blood of saints and prophets,
>> you have given them blood to drink.
> It is what they deserve!"

7 And I heard the altar respond,

> "Yes, O Lord God, the Almighty,
>> your judgments are true and just!"

8 The fourth angel poured his bowl on the sun, and it was allowed to scorch people with fire; ⁹they were scorched by the fierce heat, but they cursed the name of God, who had authority over these plagues, and they did not repent and give him glory.

10 The fifth angel poured his bowl on the throne of the beast, and its kingdom was plunged into darkness; people gnawed their tongues in agony, ¹¹and cursed the God of heaven because of their pains and sores, and they did not repent of their deeds.

12 The sixth angel poured his bowl on the great river Euphrates, and its water was dried up in order to prepare the way for the kings from the east. ¹³And I saw three foul spirits like frogs coming from the mouth of the dragon, from the mouth of the beast, and from the mouth of the false prophet. ¹⁴These are demonic spirits, performing signs, who go abroad to the kings of the whole world, to assemble them for battle on the great day of God the Almighty. ¹⁵("See, I am coming like a thief! Blessed is the one who stays awake and is clothed,ª not going about naked and exposed to shame.") ¹⁶And they assembled them at the place that in Hebrew is called Harmagedon.

17 The seventh angel poured his bowl into the air, and a loud voice came out of the temple, from the throne, saying, "It is done!" ¹⁸And there came flashes of lightning, rumblings, peals of thunder, and a violent earthquake, such as had not occurred since people were upon the earth, so violent was that earthquake. ¹⁹The great city was split into three parts, and the cities of the nations fell. God

---

a Gk *and keeps his robes*

remembered great Babylon and gave her the wine-cup of the fury of his wrath. [20]And every island fled away, and no mountains were to be found; [21]and huge hailstones, each weighing about a hundred pounds,[a] dropped from heaven on people, until they cursed God for the plague of the hail, so fearful was that plague.

THE GREAT WHORE AND THE BEAST

17 Then one of the seven angels who had the seven bowls came and said to me, "Come, I will show you the judgment of the great whore who is seated on many waters, [2]with whom the kings of the earth have committed fornication, and with the wine of whose fornication the inhabitants of the earth have become drunk." [3]So he carried me away in the spirit[b] into a wilderness, and I saw a woman sitting on a scarlet beast that was full of blasphemous names, and it had seven heads and ten horns. [4]The woman was clothed in purple and scarlet, and adorned with gold and jewels and pearls, holding in her hand a golden cup full of abominations and the impurities of her fornication; [5]and on her forehead was written a name, a mystery: "Babylon the great, mother of whores and of earth's abominations." [6]And I saw that the woman was drunk with the blood of the saints and the blood of the witnesses to Jesus.

When I saw her, I was greatly amazed. [7]But the angel said to me, "Why are you so amazed? I will tell you the mystery of the woman, and of the beast with seven heads and ten horns that carries her. [8]The beast that you saw was, and is not, and is about to ascend from the bottomless pit and go to destruction. And the inhabitants of the earth, whose names have not been written in the book of life from the foundation of the world, will be amazed when they see the beast, because it was and is not and is to come.

[9] "This calls for a mind that has wisdom: the seven heads are seven mountains on which the woman is seated; also, they are seven kings, [10]of whom five have fallen, one is living, and the other has not yet come; and when he comes, he must remain only a little while. [11]As for the beast that was and is not, it is an eighth but it belongs to the seven, and it goes to destruction. [12]And the ten horns that you saw are ten kings who have not yet received a kingdom, but they are to receive authority as kings for one hour, together with the beast. [13]These are united in yielding their power and authority to the beast; [14]they will make war on the Lamb, and the Lamb will conquer them, for he is Lord of lords and King of kings, and those with him are called and chosen and faithful."

---

a Gk weighing about a talent   b Or in the Spirit

15 And he said to me, "The waters that you saw, where the whore is seated, are peoples and multitudes and nations and languages. ¹⁶And the ten horns that you saw, they and the beast will hate the whore; they will make her desolate and naked; they will devour her flesh and burn her up with fire. ¹⁷For God has put it into their hearts to carry out his purpose by agreeing to give their kingdom to the beast, until the words of God will be fulfilled. ¹⁸The woman you saw is the great city that rules over the kings of the earth."

THE FALL OF BABYLON

18 After this I saw another angel coming down from heaven, having great authority; and the earth was made bright with his splendor. ²He called out with a mighty voice,

"Fallen, fallen is Babylon the great!
It has become a dwelling place of demons,
a haunt of every foul spirit,
a haunt of every foul bird,
a haunt of every foul and hateful beast.ᵃ
3 For all the nations have drunkᵇ
of the wine of the wrath of her fornication,
and the kings of the earth have committed fornication with her,
and the merchants of the earth have grown rich from the powerᶜ
of her luxury."
4 Then I heard another voice from heaven saying,
"Come out of her, my people,
so that you do not take part in her sins,
and so that you do not share in her plagues;
5 for her sins are heaped high as heaven,
and God has remembered her iniquities.
6 Render to her as she herself has rendered,
and repay her double for her deeds;
mix a double draught for her in the cup she mixed.
7 As she glorified herself and lived luxuriously,
so give her a like measure of torment and grief.
Since in her heart she says,
'I rule as a queen;
I am no widow,
and I will never see grief,'

---

a Other ancient authorities lack the words *a haunt of every foul beast* and attach the words *and hateful* to the previous line so as to read *a haunt of every foul and hateful bird*   b Other ancient authorities read *She has made all nations drink*   c Or *resources*

8 therefore her plagues will come in a single day—
>   pestilence and mourning and famine—
> and she will be burned with fire;
>   for mighty is the Lord God who judges her."

9 And the kings of the earth, who committed fornication and lived in luxury with her, will weep and wail over her when they see the smoke of her burning; [10]they will stand far off, in fear of her torment, and say,

>   "Alas, alas, the great city,
>   Babylon, the mighty city!
> For in one hour your judgment has come."

11 And the merchants of the earth weep and mourn for her, since no one buys their cargo anymore, [12]cargo of gold, silver, jewels and pearls, fine linen, purple, silk and scarlet, all kinds of scented wood, all articles of ivory, all articles of costly wood, bronze, iron, and marble, [13]cinnamon, spice, incense, myrrh, frankincense, wine, olive oil, choice flour and wheat, cattle and sheep, horses and chariots, slaves—and human lives.[a]

14 "The fruit for which your soul longed
>   has gone from you,
> and all your dainties and your splendor
>   are lost to you,
>   never to be found again!"

15 The merchants of these wares, who gained wealth from her, will stand far off, in fear of her torment, weeping and mourning aloud,

16 "Alas, alas, the great city,
>   clothed in fine linen,
>   in purple and scarlet,
>   adorned with gold,
>   with jewels, and with pearls!

17 For in one hour all this wealth has been laid waste!"

And all shipmasters and seafarers, sailors and all whose trade is on the sea, stood far off [18]and cried out as they saw the smoke of her burning,

>   "What city was like the great city?"

19 And they threw dust on their heads, as they wept and mourned, crying out,

>   "Alas, alas, the great city,
>   where all who had ships at sea
>   grew rich by her wealth!
> For in one hour she has been laid waste."

---

a Or chariots, and human bodies and souls

20 Rejoice over her, O heaven, you saints and apostles and prophets! For God has given judgment for you against her.

21 Then a mighty angel took up a stone like a great millstone and threw it into the sea, saying,

> "With such violence Babylon the great city
>> will be thrown down,
>> and will be found no more;
> 22 and the sound of harpists and minstrels and of flutists and
>> trumpeters
>> will be heard in you no more;
> and an artisan of any trade
>> will be found in you no more;
> and the sound of the millstone
>> will be heard in you no more;
> 23 and the light of a lamp
>> will shine in you no more;
> and the voice of bridegroom and bride
>> will be heard in you no more;
> for your merchants were the magnates of the earth,
>> and all nations were deceived by your sorcery.
> 24 And in you*a* was found the blood of prophets and of saints,
>> and of all who have been slaughtered on earth."

THE REJOICING IN HEAVEN

19 After this I heard what seemed to be the loud voice of a great multitude in heaven, saying,

> "Hallelujah!
> Salvation and glory and power to our God,
> 2 for his judgments are true and just;
> he has judged the great whore
>> who corrupted the earth with her fornication,
> and he has avenged on her the blood of his servants."*b*

3 Once more they said,

> "Hallelujah!
> The smoke goes up from her forever and ever."

4 And the twenty-four elders and the four living creatures fell down and worshiped God who is seated on the throne, saying,

---

a Gk *her*   *b* Gk *slaves*

"Amen. Hallelujah!"

5 And from the throne came a voice saying,

> "Praise our God,
>> all you his servants,[a]
> and all who fear him,
>> small and great."

6 Then I heard what seemed to be the voice of a great multitude, like the sound of many waters and like the sound of mighty thunderpeals, crying out,

> "Hallelujah!
> For the Lord our God
>> the Almighty reigns.

7 Let us rejoice and exult
>> and give him the glory,
> for the marriage of the Lamb has come,
>> and his bride has made herself ready;

8 to her it has been granted to be clothed
>> with fine linen, bright and pure"—

for the fine linen is the righteous deeds of the saints.

9 And the angel said[b] to me, "Write this: Blessed are those who are invited to the marriage supper of the Lamb." And he said to me, "These are true words of God." [10]Then I fell down at his feet to worship him, but he said to me, "You must not do that! I am a fellow servant[c] with you and your comrades[d] who hold the testimony of Jesus.[e] Worship God! For the testimony of Jesus[e] is the spirit of prophecy."

THE RIDER ON THE WHITE HORSE

11 Then I saw heaven opened, and there was a white horse! Its rider is called Faithful and True, and in righteousness he judges and makes war. [12]His eyes are like a flame of fire, and on his head are many diadems; and he has a name inscribed that no one knows but himself. [13]He is clothed in a robe dipped in[f] blood, and his name is called The Word of God. [14]And the armies of heaven, wearing fine linen, white and pure, were following him on white horses. [15]From his mouth comes a sharp sword with which to strike down the nations, and he will rule[g] them with a rod of iron; he will tread the wine press of the fury of the wrath of God the Almighty. [16]On his robe and on his thigh he has a name inscribed, "King of kings and Lord of lords."

---

a Gk slaves b Gk he said c Gk slave d Gk brothers e Or to Jesus f Other ancient authorities read sprinkled with g Or will shepherd

THE BEAST AND ITS ARMIES DEFEATED

17 Then I saw an angel standing in the sun, and with a loud voice he called to all the birds that fly in midheaven, "Come, gather for the great supper of God, [18]to eat the flesh of kings, the flesh of captains, the flesh of the mighty, the flesh of horses and their riders—flesh of all, both free and slave, both small and great." [19]Then I saw the beast and the kings of the earth with their armies gathered to make war against the rider on the horse and against his army. [20]And the beast was captured, and with it the false prophet who had performed in its presence the signs by which he deceived those who had received the mark of the beast and those who worshiped its image. These two were thrown alive into the lake of fire that burns with sulfur. [21]And the rest were killed by the sword of the rider on the horse, the sword that came from his mouth; and all the birds were gorged with their flesh.

THE THOUSAND YEARS

20 Then I saw an angel coming down from heaven, holding in his hand the key to the bottomless pit and a great chain. [2]He seized the dragon, that ancient serpent, who is the Devil and Satan, and bound him for a thousand years, [3]and threw him into the pit, and locked and sealed it over him, so that he would deceive the nations no more, until the thousand years were ended. After that he must be let out for a little while.

4 Then I saw thrones, and those seated on them were given authority to judge. I also saw the souls of those who had been beheaded for their testimony to Jesus[a] and for the word of God. They had not worshiped the beast or its image and had not received its mark on their foreheads or their hands. They came to life and reigned with Christ a thousand years. [5](The rest of the dead did not come to life until the thousand years were ended.) This is the first resurrection. [6]Blessed and holy are those who share in the first resurrection. Over these the second death has no power, but they will be priests of God and of Christ, and they will reign with him a thousand years.

SATAN'S DOOM

7 When the thousand years are ended, Satan will be released from his prison [8]and will come out to deceive the nations at the four corners of the earth, Gog and Magog, in order to gather them for battle; they are as numerous as the sands of the sea. [9]They marched up over the breadth of the earth and surrounded the

---

a Or for the testimony of Jesus

camp of the saints and the beloved city. And fire came down from heaven[a] and consumed them. [10]And the devil who had deceived them was thrown into the lake of fire and sulfur, where the beast and the false prophet were, and they will be tormented day and night forever and ever.

THE DEAD ARE JUDGED

11 Then I saw a great white throne and the one who sat on it; the earth and the heaven fled from his presence, and no place was found for them. [12]And I saw the dead, great and small, standing before the throne, and books were opened. Also another book was opened, the book of life. And the dead were judged according to their works, as recorded in the books. [13]And the sea gave up the dead that were in it, Death and Hades gave up the dead that were in them, and all were judged according to what they had done. [14]Then Death and Hades were thrown into the lake of fire. This is the second death, the lake of fire; [15]and anyone whose name was not found written in the book of life was thrown into the lake of fire.

THE NEW HEAVEN AND THE NEW EARTH

21 Then I saw a new heaven and a new earth; for the first heaven and the first earth had passed away, and the sea was no more. [2]And I saw the holy city, the new Jerusalem, coming down out of heaven from God, prepared as a bride adorned for her husband. [3]And I heard a loud voice from the throne saying,

>"See, the home[b] of God is among mortals.
>He will dwell[c] with them;
>they will be his peoples,[d]
>and God himself will be with them;[e]
>4 he will wipe every tear from their eyes.
>Death will be no more;
>mourning and crying and pain will be no more,
>for the first things have passed away."

5 And the one who was seated on the throne said, "See, I am making all things new." Also he said, "Write this, for these words are trustworthy and true." [6]Then he said to me, "It is done! I am the Alpha and the Omega, the beginning and the end. To the thirsty I will give water as a gift from the spring of the water of life. [7]Those who conquer will inherit these things, and I will be

---

a Other ancient authorities read *from God, out of heaven*, or *out of heaven from God* b Gk *the tabernacle* c Gk *will tabernacle*
d Other ancient authorities read *people* e Other ancient authorities add *and be their God*

their God and they will be my children. [8]But as for the cowardly, the faithless,[a] the polluted, the murderers, the fornicators, the sorcerers, the idolaters, and all liars, their place will be in the lake that burns with fire and sulfur, which is the second death."

VISION OF THE NEW JERUSALEM

9 Then one of the seven angels who had the seven bowls full of the seven last plagues came and said to me, "Come, I will show you the bride, the wife of the Lamb." [10]And in the spirit[b] he carried me away to a great, high mountain and showed me the holy city Jerusalem coming down out of heaven from God. [11]It has the glory of God and a radiance like a very rare jewel, like jasper, clear as crystal. [12]It has a great, high wall with twelve gates, and at the gates twelve angels, and on the gates are inscribed the names of the twelve tribes of the Israelites; [13]on the east three gates, on the north three gates, on the south three gates, and on the west three gates. [14]And the wall of the city has twelve foundations, and on them are the twelve names of the twelve apostles of the Lamb.

15 The angel[c] who talked to me had a measuring rod of gold to measure the city and its gates and walls. [16]The city lies foursquare, its length the same as its width; and he measured the city with his rod, fifteen hundred miles;[d] its length and width and height are equal. [17]He also measured its wall, one hundred forty-four cubits[e] by human measurement, which the angel was using. [18]The wall is built of jasper, while the city is pure gold, clear as glass. [19]The foundations of the wall of the city are adorned with every jewel; the first was jasper, the second sapphire, the third agate, the fourth emerald, [20]the fifth onyx, the sixth carnelian, the seventh chrysolite, the eighth beryl, the ninth topaz, the tenth chrysoprase, the eleventh jacinth, the twelfth amethyst. [21]And the twelve gates are twelve pearls, each of the gates is a single pearl, and the street of the city is pure gold, transparent as glass.

22 I saw no temple in the city, for its temple is the Lord God the Almighty and the Lamb. [23]And the city has no need of sun or moon to shine on it, for the glory of God is its light, and its lamp is the Lamb. [24]The nations will walk by its light, and the kings of the earth will bring their glory into it. [25]Its gates will never be shut by day—and there will be no night there. [26]People will bring into it the glory and the honor of the nations. [27]But nothing unclean will enter it, nor anyone who practices abomination or falsehood, but only those who are written in the Lamb's book of life.

---

a Or the unbelieving   b Or in the Spirit   c Gk He   d Gk twelve thousand stadia   e That is, almost seventy-five yards

THE RIVER OF LIFE

22 Then the angel[a] showed me the river of the water of life, bright as crystal, flowing from the throne of God and of the Lamb [2]through the middle of the street of the city. On either side of the river is the tree of life[b] with its twelve kinds of fruit, producing its fruit each month; and the leaves of the tree are for the healing of the nations. [3]Nothing accursed will be found there any more. But the throne of God and of the Lamb will be in it, and his servants[c] will worship him; [4]they will see his face, and his name will be on their foreheads. [5]And there will be no more night; they need no light of lamp or sun, for the Lord God will be their light, and they will reign forever and ever.

6 And he said to me, "These words are trustworthy and true, for the Lord, the God of the spirits of the prophets, has sent his angel to show his servants[c] what must soon take place."

7 "See, I am coming soon! Blessed is the one who keeps the words of the prophecy of this book."

EPILOGUE AND BENEDICTION

8 I, John, am the one who heard and saw these things. And when I heard and saw them, I fell down to worship at the feet of the angel who showed them to me; [9]but he said to me, "You must not do that! I am a fellow servant[d] with you and your comrades[e] the prophets, and with those who keep the words of this book. Worship God!"

10 And he said to me, "Do not seal up the words of the prophecy of this book, for the time is near. [11]Let the evildoer still do evil, and the filthy still be filthy, and the righteous still do right, and the holy still be holy."

12 "See, I am coming soon; my reward is with me, to repay according to everyone's work. [13]I am the Alpha and the Omega, the first and the last, the beginning and the end."

14 Blessed are those who wash their robes,[f] so that they will have the right to the tree of life and may enter the city by the gates. [15]Outside are the dogs and sorcerers and fornicators and murderers and idolaters, and everyone who loves and practices falsehood.

16 "It is I, Jesus, who sent my angel to you with this testimony for the churches. I am the root and the descendant of David, the bright morning star."

---

a Gk *he*   b Or *the Lamb.* [2]*In the middle of the street of the city, and on either side of the river, is the tree of life*   c Gk *slaves*
d Gk *slave*   e Gk *brothers*   f Other ancient authorities read *do his commandments*

17 The Spirit and the bride say, "Come."

And let everyone who hears say, "Come."

And let everyone who is thirsty come.

Let anyone who wishes take the water of life as a gift.

18 I warn everyone who hears the words of the prophecy of this book: if anyone adds to them, God will add to that person the plagues described in this book; [19]if anyone takes away from the words of the book of this prophecy, God will take away that person's share in the tree of life and in the holy city, which are described in this book.

20 The one who testifies to these things says, "Surely I am coming soon." Amen. Come, Lord Jesus!

21 The grace of the Lord Jesus be with all the saints. Amen.[a]

---

a Other ancient authorities lack *all;* others lack *the saints;* others lack *Amen*

Jude

Jude is perhaps the strangest document in the New Testament. It is one of the shortest, about a page long, and is the most enigmatic. Its authorship, the community to which it was addressed, and its date involve more "guesswork" than any other document.

The author identifies himself as "Jude, a servant of Jesus Christ and brother of James" (v. 1). Jude (Judas) was a common name in New Testament times. According to Mark 6.3, one of Jesus's brothers was named Jude. Because the author of this letter also identifies himself as "brother of James," another brother of Jesus and leader of the Christ-community in Jerusalem, it was taken for granted until recently that the author was also a brother of Jesus.

If so, that would make Jude one of the earliest documents in the New Testament. But modern mainline scholars have concluded that it was written much later. Though precision is impossible, most date it around 100. It contains nothing that suggests the location of either the author or its recipients, though it appears to have been written to a particular community in which "certain intruders have stolen in . . . who pervert the grace of our God into licentiousness and deny our only Master and Lord, Jesus Christ" (v. 4).

Much of the rest of the letter is a condemnation of these "intruders" as "dreamers," "scoffers," "worldly people," "waterless clouds," "wild waves of the sea," and "wandering stars"; they are accused of being "bombastic in speech" and "flattering people to their own advantage." But what the conflict was about is unclear. Most likely it was a form of antinomianism, that is, the conviction that God's grace means that behavior doesn't matter very much, if at all.

Jude and 2 Peter share so many distinctive phrases in common that it is clear that one author knew the letter of the other. The scholarly consensus is that 2 Peter used Jude rather than vice versa, and so Jude is earlier than 2 Peter.

Jude is distinctive in two other ways. It is the only New Testament document that clearly echoes nonbiblical Jewish sources. Verses 6, 14–15 refer to *1 Enoch,* a Jewish document not included in the Jewish Bible. Verse 9 refers to the archangel Michael and Satan disputing about the burial of Moses, which may come from another nonbiblical Jewish text.

Finally, it is the most judgmental and condemnatory of all the New Testament documents. Of course, these themes are found in other places in the New Testament, but even Revelation is not as consistently judgmental and condemnatory. Perhaps we should be grateful that it was not written by the brother of Jesus and James.

THE LETTER OF
Jude

SALUTATION

1 Jude,*a* a servant*b* of Jesus Christ and brother of James,

To those who are called, who are beloved*c* in*d* God the Father and kept safe for*d* Jesus Christ:

2 May mercy, peace, and love be yours in abundance.

OCCASION OF THE LETTER

3 Beloved, while eagerly preparing to write to you about the salvation we share, I find it necessary to write and appeal to you to contend for the faith that was once for all entrusted to the saints. ⁴For certain intruders have stolen in among you, people who long ago were designated for this condemnation as ungodly, who pervert the grace of our God into licentiousness and deny our only Master and Lord, Jesus Christ.*e*

JUDGMENT ON FALSE TEACHERS

5 Now I desire to remind you, though you are fully informed, that the Lord, who once for all saved*f* a people out of the land of Egypt, afterward destroyed those who did not believe. ⁶And the angels who did not keep their own position, but left their proper dwelling, he has kept in eternal chains in deepest darkness for the judgment of the great day. ⁷Likewise, Sodom and Gomorrah and the surrounding cities, which, in the same manner as they, indulged in sexual immorality and pursued unnatural lust,*g* serve as an example by undergoing a punishment of eternal fire.

---

a Gk *Judas*   *b* Gk *slave*   *c* Other ancient authorities read *sanctified*   *d* Or *by*   *e* Or *the only Master and our Lord Jesus Christ*
f Other ancient authorities read *though you were once for all fully informed, that Jesus* (or *Joshua*) *who saved*   *g* Gk *went after other flesh*

8 Yet in the same way these dreamers also defile the flesh, reject authority, and slander the glorious ones.*ᵃ* ⁹But when the archangel Michael contended with the devil and disputed about the body of Moses, he did not dare to bring a condemnation of slander*ᵇ* against him, but said, "The Lord rebuke you!" ¹⁰But these people slander whatever they do not understand, and they are destroyed by those things that, like irrational animals, they know by instinct. ¹¹Woe to them! For they go the way of Cain, and abandon themselves to Balaam's error for the sake of gain, and perish in Korah's rebellion. ¹²These are blemishes*ᶜ* on your love-feasts, while they feast with you without fear, feeding themselves.*ᵈ* They are waterless clouds carried along by the winds; autumn trees without fruit, twice dead, uprooted; ¹³wild waves of the sea, casting up the foam of their own shame; wandering stars, for whom the deepest darkness has been reserved forever.

14 It was also about these that Enoch, in the seventh generation from Adam, prophesied, saying, "See, the Lord is coming*ᵉ* with ten thousands of his holy ones, ¹⁵to execute judgment on all, and to convict everyone of all the deeds of ungodliness that they have committed in such an ungodly way, and of all the harsh things that ungodly sinners have spoken against him." ¹⁶These are grumblers and malcontents; they indulge their own lusts; they are bombastic in speech, flattering people to their own advantage.

WARNINGS AND EXHORTATIONS

17 But you, beloved, must remember the predictions of the apostles of our Lord Jesus Christ; ¹⁸for they said to you, "In the last time there will be scoffers, indulging their own ungodly lusts." ¹⁹It is these worldly people, devoid of the Spirit, who are causing divisions. ²⁰But you, beloved, build yourselves up on your most holy faith; pray in the Holy Spirit; ²¹keep yourselves in the love of God; look forward to the mercy of our Lord Jesus Christ that leads to*ᶠ* eternal life. ²²And have mercy on some who are wavering; ²³save others by snatching them out of the fire; and have mercy on still others with fear, hating even the tunic defiled by their bodies.*ᵍ*

BENEDICTION

24 Now to him who is able to keep you from falling, and to make you stand without blemish in the presence of his glory with rejoicing, ²⁵to the only God our Savior, through Jesus Christ our Lord, be glory, majesty, power, and authority, before all time and now and forever. Amen.

---

a Or *angels; Gk glories*   *b* Or *condemnation for blasphemy*   *c* Or *reefs*   *d* Or *without fear. They are shepherds who care only for themselves*   *e* Gk *came*   *f* Gk *Christ to*   *g* Gk *by the flesh.* The Greek text of verses 22–23 is uncertain at several points

1 John

Three letters are attributed to "John" in the New Testament. The first is the most substantial and important. Five chapters long, it emphasizes love as much as any document in the New Testament. The other two are less than a page long and are among the shortest documents in Christian scripture.

Authorship and Date

Who wrote these letters is unknown. A consensus of mainstream biblical scholarship agrees that the author was neither the John who was one of Jesus's twelve disciples nor the same person who wrote the gospel of John. The author's name could have been "John," even if not one of the above. Or it could have been someone writing in the name of "John."

There are strong similarities between 1 John and the gospel of John, as we will see, but also differences. The similarities are best explained not by common authorship, but by supposing a "Johannine community"—that is a community (and probably communities) out of which both the gospel and the letters of John came.

There is no consensus about whether the author of 1 John also wrote 2 and 3 John. Some scholars think so, some don't. But all agree that 2 and 3 John came out of the same early Christian milieu as the gospel and 1 John.

Dating these letters is difficult. There is a consensus that they are later than the gospel of John, most likely written around the year 100. But there is no way of knowing whether all were written at about the same time or whether they might be separated by a decade or more. I have decided to keep them together without any particularly good reason to do so, just as there is no particularly good reason to separate them chronologically.

Though called a letter, 1 John does not have the typical characteristics of a letter. Its introduction does not refer to the sender or the community to which it was written, and it does not end as a New Testament letter most often does. In contrast, 2 and 3 John clearly are letters to particular individuals and their communities.

Similarities to the Gospel of John

With good reason, 1 John has been associated with the gospel of John from the second century on. The two documents have many themes in common:

Light and darkness (1.5–7; 2.8–11)

Word and incarnation (1.1; 4.1–3; 5.6–8)

Abiding in Jesus, God, the Spirit (2.6, 14, 24; 3.23–24; 4.13–16)

Eternal life (1.2; 2.25; 3.15; 5.11–13, 20)

Those who are born of Jesus, God, the Spirit as children of God (2.29–3.2; 3.7–10; 5.4, 18)

"The world" as that which stands in opposition to God as known in Jesus (not the created world of nature, but "the world" as organized by humans; 2.15–16; 3.13; 4.4–5; 5.5)

"Love one another" and "God is love," the dominant theme of the letter (reaching its climax in 4.7–8, 16, 18–19)

Historical Context

From 1 John itself, we learn that the late first-century community to which it was written had recently experienced conflict and division. Some "went out from [them]" (2.19), and much of the letter treats the division.

Strikingly, those who left the community are called "antichrist," used in both singular and plural forms (2.18, 22; 4.3). Only in this letter is the term used; it does not appear in Revelation or any other New Testament document. Here it means denying that Jesus is the Messiah and denying "the Father and the Son" (2.22–23), denying that Jesus came "in the flesh" (4.1–3) and that he came "by water and blood" (5.6–8).

Most historical scholars think that the issue was an early form of "Docetism," a way of seeing Jesus that was later declared to be "unorthodox." "Docetism" comes from a Greek word that means "seems" or "appears." Applied to Jesus, it means that though he seemed and appeared to be human, he was divine and not really human. First John counters this by insisting that Jesus came "in the flesh" and "by water and blood"—not just by birth and baptism, but also by blood. He was mortal and suffered death. Of course, the author also believed that Jesus had been raised and vindicated by God. But he affirmed the full humanity of Jesus as the incarnation of God's love.

THE FIRST LETTER OF
John

THE WORD OF LIFE

1 We declare to you what was from the beginning, what we have heard, what we have seen with our eyes, what we have looked at and touched with our hands, concerning the word of life— ²this life was revealed, and we have seen it and testify to it, and declare to you the eternal life that was with the Father and was revealed to us— ³we declare to you what we have seen and heard so that you also may have fellowship with us; and truly our fellowship is with the Father and with his Son Jesus Christ. ⁴We are writing these things so that our*a* joy may be complete.

GOD IS LIGHT

5 This is the message we have heard from him and proclaim to you, that God is light and in him there is no darkness at all. ⁶If we say that we have fellowship with him while we are walking in darkness, we lie and do not do what is true; ⁷but if we walk in the light as he himself is in the light, we have fellowship with one another, and the blood of Jesus his Son cleanses us from all sin. ⁸If we say that we have no sin, we deceive ourselves, and the truth is not in us. ⁹If we confess our sins, he who is faithful and just will forgive us our sins and cleanse us from all unrighteousness. ¹⁰If we say that we have not sinned, we make him a liar, and his word is not in us.

---

a Other ancient authorities read *your*

CHRIST OUR ADVOCATE

2 My little children, I am writing these things to you so that you may not sin. But if anyone does sin, we have an advocate with the Father, Jesus Christ the righteous; [2]and he is the atoning sacrifice for our sins, and not for ours only but also for the sins of the whole world.

3 Now by this we may be sure that we know him, if we obey his commandments. [4]Whoever says, "I have come to know him," but does not obey his commandments, is a liar, and in such a person the truth does not exist; [5]but whoever obeys his word, truly in this person the love of God has reached perfection. By this we may be sure that we are in him: [6]whoever says, "I abide in him," ought to walk just as he walked.

A NEW COMMANDMENT

7 Beloved, I am writing you no new commandment, but an old commandment that you have had from the beginning; the old commandment is the word that you have heard. [8]Yet I am writing you a new commandment that is true in him and in you, because[a] the darkness is passing away and the true light is already shining. [9]Whoever says, "I am in the light," while hating a brother or sister,[b] is still in the darkness. [10]Whoever loves a brother or sister[c] lives in the light, and in such a person[d] there is no cause for stumbling. [11]But whoever hates another believer[e] is in the darkness, walks in the darkness, and does not know the way to go, because the darkness has brought on blindness.

12 I am writing to you, little children,
> because your sins are forgiven on account of his name.

13 I am writing to you, fathers,
> because you know him who is from the beginning.

I am writing to you, young people,
> because you have conquered the evil one.

14 I write to you, children,
> because you know the Father.

I write to you, fathers,
> because you know him who is from the beginning.

I write to you, young people,
> because you are strong
> and the word of God abides in you,
>> and you have overcome the evil one.

---

a Or that b Gk hating a brother c Gk loves a brother d Or in it e Gk hates a brother

15 Do not love the world or the things in the world. The love of the Father is not in those who love the world; ¹⁶for all that is in the world—the desire of the flesh, the desire of the eyes, the pride in riches—comes not from the Father but from the world. ¹⁷And the world and its desire*ᵃ* are passing away, but those who do the will of God live forever.

WARNING AGAINST ANTICHRISTS

18 Children, it is the last hour! As you have heard that antichrist is coming, so now many antichrists have come. From this we know that it is the last hour. ¹⁹They went out from us, but they did not belong to us; for if they had belonged to us, they would have remained with us. But by going out they made it plain that none of them belongs to us. ²⁰But you have been anointed by the Holy One, and all of you have knowledge.*ᵇ* ²¹I write to you, not because you do not know the truth, but because you know it, and you know that no lie comes from the truth. ²²Who is the liar but the one who denies that Jesus is the Christ?*ᶜ* This is the antichrist, the one who denies the Father and the Son. ²³No one who denies the Son has the Father; everyone who confesses the Son has the Father also. ²⁴Let what you heard from the beginning abide in you. If what you heard from the beginning abides in you, then you will abide in the Son and in the Father. ²⁵And this is what he has promised us,*ᵈ* eternal life.

26 I write these things to you concerning those who would deceive you. ²⁷As for you, the anointing that you received from him abides in you, and so you do not need anyone to teach you. But as his anointing teaches you about all things, and is true and is not a lie, and just as it has taught you, abide in him.*ᵉ*

28 And now, little children, abide in him, so that when he is revealed we may have confidence and not be put to shame before him at his coming.

CHILDREN OF GOD

29 If you know that he is righteous, you may be sure that everyone who does right has been born of him.

3 See what love the Father has given us, that we should be called children of God; and that is what we are. The reason the world does not know us is that it did not know him. ²Beloved, we are God's children now; what we will be has not yet been revealed. What we do know is this: when he*ᵉ* is revealed, we will be like him, for we will see him as he is. ³And all who have this hope in him purify themselves, just as he is pure.

---

a Or *the desire for it*   *b* Other ancient authorities read *you know all things*   *c* Or *the Messiah*   *d* Other ancient authorities read *you*   *e* Or *it*

4 Everyone who commits sin is guilty of lawlessness; sin is lawlessness. [5]You know that he was revealed to take away sins, and in him there is no sin. [6]No one who abides in him sins; no one who sins has either seen him or known him. [7]Little children, let no one deceive you. Everyone who does what is right is righteous, just as he is righteous. [8]Everyone who commits sin is a child of the devil; for the devil has been sinning from the beginning. The Son of God was revealed for this purpose, to destroy the works of the devil. [9]Those who have been born of God do not sin, because God's seed abides in them;[a] they cannot sin, because they have been born of God. [10]The children of God and the children of the devil are revealed in this way: all who do not do what is right are not from God, nor are those who do not love their brothers and sisters.[b]

LOVE ONE ANOTHER

11 For this is the message you have heard from the beginning, that we should love one another. [12]We must not be like Cain who was from the evil one and murdered his brother. And why did he murder him? Because his own deeds were evil and his brother's righteous. [13]Do not be astonished, brothers and sisters,[c] that the world hates you. [14]We know that we have passed from death to life because we love one another. Whoever does not love abides in death. [15]All who hate a brother or sister[b] are murderers, and you know that murderers do not have eternal life abiding in them. [16]We know love by this, that he laid down his life for us—and we ought to lay down our lives for one another. [17]How does God's love abide in anyone who has the world's goods and sees a brother or sister[d] in need and yet refuses help?

18 Little children, let us love, not in word or speech, but in truth and action. [19]And by this we will know that we are from the truth and will reassure our hearts before him [20]whenever our hearts condemn us; for God is greater than our hearts, and he knows everything. [21]Beloved, if our hearts do not condemn us, we have boldness before God; [22]and we receive from him whatever we ask, because we obey his commandments and do what pleases him.

23 And this is his commandment, that we should believe in the name of his Son Jesus Christ and love one another, just as he has commanded us. [24]All who obey his commandments abide in him, and he abides in them. And by this we know that he abides in us, by the Spirit that he has given us.

TESTING THE SPIRITS

4 Beloved, do not believe every spirit, but test the spirits to see whether they are from God; for many false prophets have gone out into the world. [2]By

---

a Or *because the children of God abide in him*   *b* Gk *his brother*   *c* Gk *brothers*   *d* Gk *brother* this you know the Spirit of God: every spirit that confesses that Jesus Christ has come in the flesh is from God, ³and every spirit that does not confess Jesus*a* is not from God. And this is the spirit of the antichrist, of which you have heard that it is coming; and now it is already in the world. ⁴Little children, you are from God, and have conquered them; for the one who is in you is greater than the one who is in the world. ⁵They are from the world; therefore what they say is from the world, and the world listens to them. ⁶We are from God. Whoever knows God listens to us, and whoever is not from God does not listen to us. From this we know the spirit of truth and the spirit of error.

GOD IS LOVE

7 Beloved, let us love one another, because love is from God; everyone who loves is born of God and knows God. ⁸Whoever does not love does not know God, for God is love. ⁹God's love was revealed among us in this way: God sent his only Son into the world so that we might live through him. ¹⁰In this is love, not that we loved God but that he loved us and sent his Son to be the atoning sacrifice for our sins. ¹¹Beloved, since God loved us so much, we also ought to love one another. ¹²No one has ever seen God; if we love one another, God lives in us, and his love is perfected in us.

13 By this we know that we abide in him and he in us, because he has given us of his Spirit. ¹⁴And we have seen and do testify that the Father has sent his Son as the Savior of the world. ¹⁵God abides in those who confess that Jesus is the Son of God, and they abide in God. ¹⁶So we have known and believe the love that God has for us.

God is love, and those who abide in love abide in God, and God abides in them. ¹⁷Love has been perfected among us in this: that we may have boldness on the day of judgment, because as he is, so are we in this world. ¹⁸There is no fear in love, but perfect love casts out fear; for fear has to do with punishment, and whoever fears has not reached perfection in love. ¹⁹We love*b* because he first loved us. ²⁰Those who say, "I love God," and hate their brothers or sisters,*c* are liars; for those who do not love a brother or sister*d* whom they have seen, cannot love God whom they have not seen. ²¹The commandment we have from him is this: those who love God must love their brothers and sisters*c* also.

FAITH CONQUERS THE WORLD

5 Everyone who believes that Jesus is the Christ*e* has been born of God, and everyone who loves the parent loves the child. ²By this we know that we

---

a Other ancient authorities read *does away with Jesus* (Gk *dissolves Jesus*)   *b* Other ancient authorities add *him;* others add *God*
c Gk *brothers*   *d* Gk *brother*   *e* Or *the Messiah*

love the children of God, when we love God and obey his commandments. ³For the love of God is this, that we obey his commandments. And his commandments are not burdensome, ⁴for whatever is born of God conquers the world. And this is the victory that conquers the world, our faith. ⁵Who is it that conquers the world but the one who believes that Jesus is the Son of God?

TESTIMONY CONCERNING THE SON OF GOD

6 This is the one who came by water and blood, Jesus Christ, not with the water only but with the water and the blood. And the Spirit is the one that testifies, for the Spirit is the truth. ⁷There are three that testify:ᵃ ⁸the Spirit and the water and the blood, and these three agree. ⁹If we receive human testimony, the testimony of God is greater; for this is the testimony of God that he has testified to his Son. ¹⁰Those who believe in the Son of God have the testimony in their hearts. Those who do not believe in Godᵇ have made him a liar by not believing in the testimony that God has given concerning his Son. ¹¹And this is the testimony: God gave us eternal life, and this life is in his Son. ¹²Whoever has the Son has life; whoever does not have the Son of God does not have life.

EPILOGUE

13 I write these things to you who believe in the name of the Son of God, so that you may know that you have eternal life.

14 And this is the boldness we have in him, that if we ask anything according to his will, he hears us. ¹⁵And if we know that he hears us in whatever we ask, we know that we have obtained the requests made of him. ¹⁶If you see your brother or sisterᶜ committing what is not a mortal sin, you will ask, and Godᵈ will give life to such a one—to those whose sin is not mortal. There is sin that is mortal; I do not say that you should pray about that. ¹⁷All wrongdoing is sin, but there is sin that is not mortal.

18 We know that those who are born of God do not sin, but the one who was born of God protects them, and the evil one does not touch them. ¹⁹We know that we are God's children, and that the whole world lies under the power of the evil one. ²⁰And we know that the Son of God has come and has given us understanding so that we may know him who is true;ᵉ and we are in him who is true, in his Son Jesus Christ. He is the true God and eternal life.

21 Little children, keep yourselves from idols.ᶠ

---

a A few other authorities read (with variations) ⁷*There are three that testify in heaven, the Father, the Word, and the Holy Spirit, and these three are one.* ⁸*And there are three that testify on earth:*　b Other ancient authorities read *in the Son*　c Gk *your brother*　d Gk *he*　e Other ancient authorities read *know the true God*　f Other ancient authorities add *Amen*

2 John

Unlike 1 John, 2 John has the typical characteristics of a letter. It begins by naming the sender ("the elder") and recipient ("the elect lady and her children"), continues with a greeting and thanksgiving followed by a brief body, and concludes with a closing. It is very short, only thirteen verses.

The body has two themes, both sounded in 1 John as well. The author reminds the recipients not of "a new commandment," but one they have known "from the beginning": "Let us love one another" (v. 5). Then the author refers to "deceivers" who "do not confess that Jesus Christ has come in the flesh" and then calls them "the antichrist" (v. 7). These similarities to 1 John are the reason that many scholars think 2 John was written by the same person. There are others who discern subtle differences and conclude that it was written by someone else. In either case, it comes from about the same time period—around 100 or slightly later.

Especially interesting is the address in verse 1: "to the elect lady and her children." In verse 5, the author calls the recipient "dear lady." At the end, the author sends greetings from "the children of your elect sister." For centuries, it has been taken for granted that "elect lady" and "elect sister" refer to Christian communities, just as "the church" in the New Testament is occasionally referred to as the bride of Christ.

But the natural meaning of this language in 2 John is that the author is writing to a woman who is the leader of an early Christian community. The closing greeting from the children of "your elect sister" suggests another Christian community headed by a woman. Thus the letter may provide evidence for women in leadership roles in Johannine communities, consistent with what we see in the genuine letters of Paul.

SALUTATION

1 The elder to the elect lady and her children, whom I love in the truth, and not only I but also all who know the truth, ²because of the truth that abides in us and will be with us forever:

3 Grace, mercy, and peace will be with us from God the Father and from*a* Jesus Christ, the Father's Son, in truth and love.

TRUTH AND LOVE

4 I was overjoyed to find some of your children walking in the truth, just as we have been commanded by the Father. ⁵But now, dear lady, I ask you, not as though I were writing you a new commandment, but one we have had from the beginning, let us love one another. ⁶And this is love, that we walk according to his commandments; this is the commandment just as you have heard it from the beginning—you must walk in it.

7 Many deceivers have gone out into the world, those who do not confess that Jesus Christ has come in the flesh; any such person is the deceiver and the antichrist! ⁸Be on your guard, so that you do not lose what we*b* have worked for, but may receive a full reward. ⁹Everyone who does not abide in the teaching of Christ, but goes beyond it, does not have God; whoever abides in the teaching has both the Father and the Son. ¹⁰Do not receive into the house or welcome anyone who comes to you and does not bring this teaching; ¹¹for to welcome is to participate in the evil deeds of such a person.

---

a Other ancient authorities add *the Lord* *b* Other ancient authorities read *you*

FINAL GREETINGS

12 Although I have much to write to you, I would rather not use paper and ink; instead I hope to come to you and talk with you face to face, so that our joy may be complete.

13 The children of your elect sister send you their greetings.^a

---

3 John

Like 2 John, 3 John is a letter and very brief, just fifteen verses. Also like 2 John, the sender is "the elder," but the recipient is specified as a man named "Gaius." Though the author is the same, there is no reason to think that this letter was sent to the same community as 2 John.

The letter commends Gaius and his community for showing hospitality to Christians: "the friends" (or "brothers and sisters"), even though they were strangers (vv. 3–8). Then it condemns an otherwise unknown Christian named "Diotrephes" for refusing the elder's authority, spreading false charges, and not providing hospitality to "the friends" (vv. 9–10).

It continues with a general exhortation: "Beloved, do not imitate what is evil but imitate what is good. Whoever does good is from God; whoever does evil has not seen God" (v. 11). It concludes with a commendation of another otherwise unknown early Christian named "Demetrius," presumably a teacher; they are to trust him (v. 12). Its closing echoes the end of 2 John. The elder declares, "I have much to write to you, but I would rather not write with pen and ink; instead I hope to see you soon, and we will talk together face to face" (vv. 13–14).

THE THIRD LETTER OF
John

SALUTATION

1 The elder to the beloved Gaius, whom I love in truth.

GAIUS COMMENDED FOR HIS HOSPITALITY

2 Beloved, I pray that all may go well with you and that you may be in good health, just as it is well with your soul. ³I was overjoyed when some of the friends*a* arrived and testified to your faithfulness to the truth, namely how you walk in the truth. ⁴I have no greater joy than this, to hear that my children are walking in the truth.

5 Beloved, you do faithfully whatever you do for the friends,*a* even though they are strangers to you; ⁶they have testified to your love before the church. You will do well to send them on in a manner worthy of God; ⁷for they began their journey for the sake of Christ,*b* accepting no support from non-believers.*c* ⁸Therefore we ought to support such people, so that we may become co-workers with the truth.

DIOTREPHES AND DEMETRIUS

9 I have written something to the church; but Diotrephes, who likes to put himself first, does not acknowledge our authority. ¹⁰So if I come, I will call attention to what he is doing in spreading false charges against us. And not content with those charges, he refuses to welcome the friends,*a* and even prevents those who want to do so and expels them from the church.

---

a Gk brothers   *b* Gk for the sake of the name   *c* Gk the Gentiles

11 Beloved, do not imitate what is evil but imitate what is good. Whoever does good is from God; whoever does evil has not seen God. [12]Everyone has testified favorably about Demetrius, and so has the truth itself. We also testify for him,[a] and you know that our testimony is true.

FINAL GREETINGS

13 I have much to write to you, but I would rather not write with pen and ink; [14]instead I hope to see you soon, and we will talk together face to face.

15 Peace to you. The friends send you their greetings. Greet the friends there, each by name.

---

a Gk lacks *for him*

Luke

The gospel of Luke and the Acts of the Apostles belong together. As we will see, they were written by the same person and share unifying themes, suggesting that the author conceived them as a single work in two volumes. But for about seventeen hundred years, they have been separated by the gospel of John. Because the canonical New Testament places all four gospels first, John follows the synoptic gospels of Matthew, Mark, and Luke.

That Luke and Acts were written by the same person is obvious from their introductions. Both are addressed to "Theophilus." Moreover, the first verse of Acts refers back to the gospel: "In the first book, Theophilus, I wrote about all that Jesus did and taught from the beginning." The name could refer to an individual—but it also means "lover of God," so it could be addressed to a group, namely, the "God-lovers."

Their thematic unity is also apparent. One major theme is the geographical progression of the Jesus movement from Galilee to Jerusalem, the center of Judaism (in the gospel), and then from Jerusalem to Rome, the center of the empire (in Acts).

A second major theme is their common emphasis on the "Spirit." In the gospel, Jesus is conceived by the Spirit; then the Spirit descends upon him at his baptism; and the first words of his public activity are, "The Spirit of the Lord is upon me" (4.18). His last words from the cross are, "Into your hands, I commend my spirit" (23.46). The Spirit of God that animated Jesus returns to God, and the gospel ends with the promise that the Spirit will descend upon his followers.

That promise is fulfilled in the opening chapters of Acts with the descent of the Spirit upon the community at Pentecost. Throughout the rest of Acts, the "Spirit" guides and leads the expansion of the Jesus movement from the homeland to the "ends of the earth" (1.8).

There was a practical reason that the author wrote this single work in two volumes. In the ancient world, the maximum length of a scroll was about 30 feet (interestingly, the word "volume" comes from the Latin word for "scroll"). Anything longer was heavy and awkward to use; finding a text meant unrolling the scroll to the appropriate place. And so the author wrote two volumes, each a scroll about 30 feet long. More of the New Testament was written by him than anybody else. Luke and Acts are about 30 percent of the New Testament—longer than the letters of Paul combined, and 80 percent as long as Matthew, Mark, and John combined.

We do not know who the author was. The documents do not name him. Second-century Christians assigned authorship to "Luke" and identified him with the "Luke" who was a companion of Paul in the 50s. This would make the author an eyewitness to some of what is narrated in Acts. It would also affect the dating of Luke-Acts. But the majority of modern scholars are skeptical or at least very uncertain that Luke-Acts was written by a companion of Paul. When I speak of the author as "Luke," I do so without supposing that he was a companion of Paul.

Dating

For about a century, the conventional wisdom of mainline scholarship has dated Luke and Acts to the late 80s or 90s. But in the last decade, a growing number of scholars have dated them significantly later, in the first decade or two of the second century.

Thus there is no consensus about their dating, though probably at least a slight majority still favor the 80s to early 90s. They see Luke, like Matthew, as written a decade or two after Mark and thus as a voice from a generation or so later. In this view, there is no compelling reason to date Matthew earlier than Luke or vice versa. Thus Luke and Acts would belong in the first half of the New Testament chronologically—not long after Mark, roughly contemporary with Matthew, and before John, Revelation, and several letters. Dating them later, as I do, is the exception to the rule that I have sought to follow, which is to reflect consensus conclusion when possible and, when there is no consensus, to follow majority opinion.

Some scholars, especially those in conservative Christian traditions, date Luke and Acts even earlier, to the early 60s rather than the 80s or 90s. They correctly note that Acts ends without mentioning the death of Paul, who was executed in Rome around the middle of the 60s. For them, this is evidence that Acts must have been written while Paul was still alive. And because Luke is the first volume, Luke must have been written at least a bit before Acts.

But mainstream scholars are not convinced by this argument for more than one reason. Even though Paul is the central character in Acts, the purpose of Acts was not to provide a biography of Paul, but to narrate the spread of early Christianity from Jerusalem to Rome. Thus its ending is perfect—Paul is teaching in Rome. For it to have ended with Paul's death—with words like, "And then they killed him"— would have been contrary to its purpose. Moreover, the author of Luke obviously used Mark. Given the consensus conclusion that Mark was written around 70, Luke-Acts must be later than 70.

The growing movement to date Luke and Acts in the early second century has more than one foundation. Some scholars argue that the author knew passages from the works of Josephus, a Jewish historian who wrote in the 90s, thus making Luke-Acts later than that. Though the evidence that the author did know the writings of Josephus is not completely persuasive, there is another reason for a date a decade or two later than Matthew, namely, both Luke and Acts emphasize the consistent rejection of Jesus by "the Jews."

In the gospel, the rejection theme is announced in the opening scene, the inaugural scene, of Jesus's public activity in his hometown of Nazareth (4.16–30). Jesus's fellow villagers react positively to his message until he refers to two Old Testament prophets whose activity extended to Gentiles—a widow and a leper. The scene anticipates the plan and theme of the two-volume work, which is the expansion of the Jesus movement from the Jewish homeland to the Gentile world.

What is striking is the reaction of Jesus's townsfolk. When he mentions Gentiles favorably, they reject him and try to kill him:

> All in the synagogue were filled with rage. They got up, drove him out of the town, and led him to the brow of the hill on which their town was built, so that they might hurl him off the cliff. (4.28–29)

Jesus, of course, escaped: "He passed through the midst of them and went on his way" (4.30). What is noteworthy is that Luke's story of Jesus begins with rejection by those "in the synagogue."

In Acts, the theme of rejection by the "synagogue" and "the Jews" begins to occur as Paul's mission to the Gentiles unfolds:

> "The Jews" incited devout women of high standing and leading men of the city, and stirred up persecution against Paul and Barnabas and drove them out of Antioch in Asia Minor (13.50).

> In Iconium, the next city in the itinerary of Paul in Acts, "The same thing occurred," and both Jews and Gentiles began to stone Paul and Barnabas (14.1–6).

In Lystra, the next city, "Jews" won over the crowd, "stoned Paul and dragged him out of the city, supposing that he was dead" (14.19).

In Thessalonica, "the Jews" formed a mob, set the city in an uproar, and searched for Paul (17.1–5). They followed Paul to Beroea, and there stirred up the crowds against him (17.13).

In Corinth, "the Jews" opposed and reviled Paul (18.5–6). They—"the Jews"—made "a united attack" against him and brought him before a Roman tribunal (18.12).

"The Jews" plotted against Paul in Greece, and so Paul left Greece (20.3).

"The Jews from Asia" tried to kill Paul in Jerusalem (21.27–36).

After Paul's speech in defense of himself, Jews cried out for Paul's condemnation and death (22.22).

The day after Paul appeared before the council, "the Jews" planned to ambush and kill him (23.12–24).

In Caesarea, a Jewish lawyer told the Roman governor that Paul was a "pestilent fellow, an agitator," and "the Jews" affirmed the accusation (24.5–9).

At a hearing before the Roman governor, "the Jews" from Jerusalem brought many serious charges against Paul (25.7).

"The whole Jewish community" petitioned the Roman governor to execute Paul (25.24).

That Acts reports that Paul experienced opposition from some Jews is not itself a reason for a late date. Historically, Paul did. Rather, it is the way Acts characterizes Paul's opposition as "the Jews" and the "synagogue." They are virtually generic terms in Acts.

This suggests that when Acts was written, "the parting of the ways" between Judaism and early Christianity was more than well under way—it had happened. Of course, many Christians during the time of Luke-Acts were Jewish in origin. But the emphasis upon the rejection of Paul and his mission by "the Jews" suggests that the division into two different religions was occurring. Hence the relatively late date for Acts and thus also for Luke. Most likely, they are from the first two decades of the second century.

Introduction to the Gospel

Luke used Mark as a major source, as did Matthew, but Luke used Mark differently. He included less of Mark—about 65 percent compared to Matthew's 90 percent. And, rather than taking over large blocks of material from Mark and editing them only lightly, as Matthew most often did, Luke wove material from Mark together with his other sources. But his basic story line follows Mark's threefold pattern of Galilee, journey to Jerusalem, and Jerusalem. Interestingly, he expands the journey section from roughly three chapters in Mark and Matthew to nine chapters.

Like Matthew, Luke combined Mark with Q, editing and shaping both as he did so. In addition, again like Matthew, Luke has several hundred verses that are only in his gospel. Sometimes called "special Luke" or simply "L," this material includes stories of Jesus's conception and birth and parables like the good Samaritan, the prodigal son, the woman and the lost coin, the Pharisee and the tax collector, the dishonest steward, and the widow and the unjust judge.

Luke shares the story of the empty tomb with Mark and Matthew. He also adds his own Easter stories, the most famous of which is Jesus appearing to two of his followers as an unrecognized stranger on the road to Emmaus. The gospel concludes with an ascension story, as does Matthew. But in Luke it happens just outside Jerusalem, whereas in Matthew it occurs on "the mountain" in Galilee. Thus, even as Luke and Matthew both proclaim that Jesus is risen, they narrate this shared affirmation in different ways and place it in different locations.

Luke's Story of Jesus's Birth

Luke begins with two chapters about the birth of Jesus, as does Matthew. But they tell the stories very differently. Recall that Matthew's is dominated by King Herod's plot to kill Jesus. It echoes the story of Pharaoh's attempt to kill Moses as an infant before the exodus from Egypt. It sets up Matthew's theme of Jesus as the new Moses, the gospel as a new Pentateuch, and what happened in Jesus as a new exodus. Matthew's birth story is an overture to his gospel.

So also Luke's birth story is an overture to his gospel, but it is very different from Matthew's. There is no mention of Herod's plot, no star of Bethlehem, no wise men, and no flight into Egypt. In Luke, Mary is the main character, not Joseph, as in Matthew. There are more differences. In Matthew, the holy family lives in Bethlehem, and Jesus is born at home. In Luke, they live in Nazareth, and Jesus is born in a stable in Bethlehem, because they had to travel there for a Roman census. Matthew's story is dark and full of foreboding, dominated by Herod's attempt to kill

Jesus. Luke's is full of joy. Three "hymns," known by Christians ever since as the Benedictus, the Magnificat, and the Nunc Dimittis, herald the coming of Jesus. Angels sing in the night sky to shepherds, "Glory to God in the highest."

Like Luke-Acts as a whole, Luke's first two chapters emphasize the "Spirit." They do so five times (1.15, 35, 41, 67; 2.25–27). Luke also emphasizes marginalized people more than any other gospel. Jesus is born among them in a stable, and angels appear to shepherds, who were among the outcast. Women—Elizabeth and Mary and Anna—are prominent in his story of Jesus's birth.

So also are Gentiles. The final hymn, the Nunc Dimittis, ends with an affirmation of the significance of Jesus not only for Jews, but also for Gentiles; he is the "salvation" that God has "prepared in the presence of *all peoples,* a light for revelation to *the Gentiles*" (2.30–32; italics added). Yet the very last line of the Nunc Dimittis reads: "and for glory to your people Israel." Luke does not overlook or negate Jews, but he does emphasize the expansion of early Christ-communities into the Gentile world and the full inclusion of Gentiles into what began as a Jewish movement.

Thus from the vantage point of the early second century, Luke and Acts look back on what had happened since the time of Jesus. The author proclaims in both volumes that the inclusion of Gentiles as well as Jews in the Jesus movement was divinely and providentially ordained from the beginning of Jesus's life. It was neither an accident nor a mistake.

THE GOSPEL ACCORDING TO
Luke

DEDICATION TO THEOPHILUS

1 Since many have undertaken to set down an orderly account of the events that have been fulfilled among us, ²just as they were handed on to us by those who from the beginning were eyewitnesses and servants of the word, ³I too decided, after investigating everything carefully from the very first,ᵃ to write an orderly account for you, most excellent Theophilus, ⁴so that you may know the truth concerning the things about which you have been instructed.

THE BIRTH OF JOHN THE BAPTIST FORETOLD

5 In the days of King Herod of Judea, there was a priest named Zechariah, who belonged to the priestly order of Abijah. His wife was a descendant of Aaron, and her name was Elizabeth. ⁶Both of them were righteous before God, living blamelessly according to all the commandments and regulations of the Lord. ⁷But they had no children, because Elizabeth was barren, and both were getting on in years.

8 Once when he was serving as priest before God and his section was on duty, ⁹he was chosen by lot, according to the custom of the priesthood, to enter the sanctuary of the Lord and offer incense. ¹⁰Now at the time of the incense offering, the whole assembly of the people was praying outside. ¹¹Then there appeared to him an angel of the Lord, standing at the right side of the altar of incense. ¹²When Zechariah saw him, he was terrified; and fear overwhelmed him. ¹³But the angel said to him, "Do not be afraid, Zechariah, for your prayer

---

a Or for a long time

has been heard. Your wife Elizabeth will bear you a son, and you will name him John. [14]You will have joy and gladness, and many will rejoice at his birth, [15]for he will be great in the sight of the Lord. He must never drink wine or strong drink; even before his birth he will be filled with the Holy Spirit. [16]He will turn many of the people of Israel to the Lord their God. [17]With the spirit and power of Elijah he will go before him, to turn the hearts of parents to their children, and the disobedient to the wisdom of the righteous, to make ready a people prepared for the Lord." [18]Zechariah said to the angel, "How will I know that this is so? For I am an old man, and my wife is getting on in years." [19]The angel replied, "I am Gabriel. I stand in the presence of God, and I have been sent to speak to you and to bring you this good news. [20]But now, because you did not believe my words, which will be fulfilled in their time, you will become mute, unable to speak, until the day these things occur."

21 Meanwhile the people were waiting for Zechariah, and wondered at his delay in the sanctuary. [22]When he did come out, he could not speak to them, and they realized that he had seen a vision in the sanctuary. He kept motioning to them and remained unable to speak. [23]When his time of service was ended, he went to his home.

24 After those days his wife Elizabeth conceived, and for five months she remained in seclusion. She said, [25]"This is what the Lord has done for me when he looked favorably on me and took away the disgrace I have endured among my people."

THE BIRTH OF JESUS FORETOLD

26 In the sixth month the angel Gabriel was sent by God to a town in Galilee called Nazareth, [27]to a virgin engaged to a man whose name was Joseph, of the house of David. The virgin's name was Mary. [28]And he came to her and said, "Greetings, favored one! The Lord is with you."[a] [29]But she was much perplexed by his words and pondered what sort of greeting this might be. [30]The angel said to her, "Do not be afraid, Mary, for you have found favor with God. [31]And now, you will conceive in your womb and bear a son, and you will name him Jesus. [32]He will be great, and will be called the Son of the Most High, and the Lord God will give to him the throne of his ancestor David. [33]He will reign over the house of Jacob forever, and of his kingdom there will be no end." [34]Mary said to the angel, "How can this be, since I am a virgin?"[b] [35]The angel said to her, "The Holy Spirit will come upon you, and the power of the Most High will overshadow you; therefore the child to be born[c] will be holy; he will be

---

a Other ancient authorities add *Blessed are you among women*   b Gk *I do not know a man*   e Other ancient authorities add *of you* called Son of God. [36]And now, your relative Elizabeth in her old age has also conceived a son; and this is the sixth month for her who was said to be barren. [37]For nothing will be impossible with God." [38]Then Mary said, "Here am I, the servant of the Lord; let it be with me according to your word." Then the angel departed from her.

MARY VISITS ELIZABETH

39 In those days Mary set out and went with haste to a Judean town in the hill country, [40]where she entered the house of Zechariah and greeted Elizabeth. [41]When Elizabeth heard Mary's greeting, the child leaped in her womb. And Elizabeth was filled with the Holy Spirit [42]and exclaimed with a loud cry, "Blessed are you among women, and blessed is the fruit of your womb. [43]And why has this happened to me, that the mother of my Lord comes to me? [44]For as soon as I heard the sound of your greeting, the child in my womb leaped for joy. [45]And blessed is she who believed that there would be[a] a fulfillment of what was spoken to her by the Lord."

MARY'S SONG OF PRAISE

46 And Mary[b] said,
> "My soul magnifies the Lord,
> 47 and my spirit rejoices in God my Savior,
> 48 for he has looked with favor on the lowliness of his servant.
>   Surely, from now on all generations will call me blessed;
> 49 for the Mighty One has done great things for me,
>   and holy is his name.
> 50 His mercy is for those who fear him
>   from generation to generation.
> 51 He has shown strength with his arm;
>   he has scattered the proud in the thoughts of their hearts.
> 52 He has brought down the powerful from their thrones,
>   and lifted up the lowly;
> 53 he has filled the hungry with good things,
>   and sent the rich away empty.
> 54 He has helped his servant Israel,
>   in remembrance of his mercy,
> 55 according to the promise he made to our ancestors,
>   to Abraham and to his descendants forever."

---

a Or believed, for there will be   b Other ancient authorities read Elizabeth

56 And Mary remained with her about three months and then returned to her home.

THE BIRTH OF JOHN THE BAPTIST

57 Now the time came for Elizabeth to give birth, and she bore a son. [58]Her neighbors and relatives heard that the Lord had shown his great mercy to her, and they rejoiced with her.

59 On the eighth day they came to circumcise the child, and they were going to name him Zechariah after his father. [60]But his mother said, "No; he is to be called John." [61]They said to her, "None of your relatives has this name." [62]Then they began motioning to his father to find out what name he wanted to give him. [63]He asked for a writing tablet and wrote, "His name is John." And all of them were amazed. [64]Immediately his mouth was opened and his tongue freed, and he began to speak, praising God. [65]Fear came over all their neighbors, and all these things were talked about throughout the entire hill country of Judea. [66]All who heard them pondered them and said, "What then will this child become?" For, indeed, the hand of the Lord was with him.

ZECHARIAH'S PROPHECY

67 Then his father Zechariah was filled with the Holy Spirit and spoke this prophecy:

68 "Blessed be the Lord God of Israel,
        for he has looked favorably on his people and redeemed them.
69 He has raised up a mighty savior[a] for us
        in the house of his servant David,
70 as he spoke through the mouth of his holy prophets from of old,
    71 that we would be saved from our enemies and from the hand of all
        who hate us.
72 Thus he has shown the mercy promised to our ancestors,
        and has remembered his holy covenant,
73 the oath that he swore to our ancestor Abraham,
        to grant us [74]that we, being rescued from the hands of our
        enemies,
    might serve him without fear, [75]in holiness and righteousness
        before him all our days.
76 And you, child, will be called the prophet of the Most High;
        for you will go before the Lord to prepare his ways,

---

a Gk a horn of salvation

77 to give knowledge of salvation to his people
>   by the forgiveness of their sins.
78 By the tender mercy of our God,
>   the dawn from on high will break upon*a* us,
79 to give light to those who sit in darkness and in the shadow of death,
>   to guide our feet into the way of peace."

80 The child grew and became strong in spirit, and he was in the wilderness until the day he appeared publicly to Israel.

THE BIRTH OF JESUS

2 In those days a decree went out from Emperor Augustus that all the world should be registered. ²This was the first registration and was taken while Quirinius was governor of Syria. ³All went to their own towns to be registered. ⁴Joseph also went from the town of Nazareth in Galilee to Judea, to the city of David called Bethlehem, because he was descended from the house and family of David. ⁵He went to be registered with Mary, to whom he was engaged and who was expecting a child. ⁶While they were there, the time came for her to deliver her child. ⁷And she gave birth to her firstborn son and wrapped him in bands of cloth, and laid him in a manger, because there was no place for them in the inn.

THE SHEPHERDS AND THE ANGELS

8 In that region there were shepherds living in the fields, keeping watch over their flock by night. ⁹Then an angel of the Lord stood before them, and the glory of the Lord shone around them, and they were terrified. ¹⁰But the angel said to them, "Do not be afraid; for see—I am bringing you good news of great joy for all the people: ¹¹to you is born this day in the city of David a Savior, who is the Messiah,*b* the Lord. ¹²This will be a sign for you: you will find a child wrapped in bands of cloth and lying in a manger." ¹³And suddenly there was with the angel a multitude of the heavenly host,*c* praising God and saying,

14 "Glory to God in the highest heaven,
>   and on earth peace among those whom he favors!"*d*

15 When the angels had left them and gone into heaven, the shepherds said to one another, "Let us go now to Bethlehem and see this thing that has taken place, which the Lord has made known to us." ¹⁶So they went with haste and found Mary and Joseph, and the child lying in the manger. ¹⁷When they saw this, they made known what had been told them about this child; ¹⁸and all who

---

a Other ancient authorities read *has broken upon* *b* Or *the Christ* *c* Gk *army* *d* Other ancient authorities read *peace, goodwill among people* heard it were amazed at what the shepherds told them. [19]But Mary treasured all these words and pondered them in her heart. [20]The shepherds returned, glorifying and praising God for all they had heard and seen, as it had been told them.

JESUS IS NAMED

21 After eight days had passed, it was time to circumcise the child; and he was called Jesus, the name given by the angel before he was conceived in the womb.

JESUS IS PRESENTED IN THE TEMPLE

22 When the time came for their purification according to the law of Moses, they brought him up to Jerusalem to present him to the Lord [23](as it is written in the law of the Lord, "Every firstborn male shall be designated as holy to the Lord"), [24]and they offered a sacrifice according to what is stated in the law of the Lord, "a pair of turtledoves or two young pigeons."

25 Now there was a man in Jerusalem whose name was Simeon;[a] this man was righteous and devout, looking forward to the consolation of Israel, and the Holy Spirit rested on him. [26]It had been revealed to him by the Holy Spirit that he would not see death before he had seen the Lord's Messiah.[b] [27]Guided by the Spirit, Simeon[c] came into the temple; and when the parents brought in the child Jesus, to do for him what was customary under the law, [28]Simeon[d] took him in his arms and praised God, saying,

29 "Master, now you are dismissing your servant[e] in peace,
         according to your word;
30 for my eyes have seen your salvation,
31   which you have prepared in the presence of all peoples,
32 a light for revelation to the Gentiles
         and for glory to your people Israel."

33 And the child's father and mother were amazed at what was being said about him. [34]Then Simeon[a] blessed them and said to his mother Mary, "This child is destined for the falling and the rising of many in Israel, and to be a sign that will be opposed [35]so that the inner thoughts of many will be revealed—and a sword will pierce your own soul too."

36 There was also a prophet, Anna[f] the daughter of Phanuel, of the tribe of Asher. She was of a great age, having lived with her husband seven years after her marriage, [37]then as a widow to the age of eighty-four. She never left the

---

a Gk *Symeon*   b Or *the Lord's Christ*   c Gk *In the Spirit, he*   d Gk *he*   e Gk *slave*   f Gk *Hanna* temple but worshiped there with fasting and prayer night and day. [38]At that moment she came, and began to praise God and to speak about the child[a] to all who were looking for the redemption of Jerusalem.

THE RETURN TO NAZARETH

39 When they had finished everything required by the law of the Lord, they returned to Galilee, to their own town of Nazareth. [40]The child grew and became strong, filled with wisdom; and the favor of God was upon him.

THE BOY JESUS IN THE TEMPLE

41 Now every year his parents went to Jerusalem for the festival of the Passover. [42]And when he was twelve years old, they went up as usual for the festival. [43]When the festival was ended and they started to return, the boy Jesus stayed behind in Jerusalem, but his parents did not know it. [44]Assuming that he was in the group of travelers, they went a day's journey. Then they started to look for him among their relatives and friends. [45]When they did not find him, they returned to Jerusalem to search for him. [46]After three days they found him in the temple, sitting among the teachers, listening to them and asking them questions. [47]And all who heard him were amazed at his understanding and his answers. [48]When his parents[b] saw him they were astonished; and his mother said to him, "Child, why have you treated us like this? Look, your father and I have been searching for you in great anxiety." [49]He said to them, "Why were you searching for me? Did you not know that I must be in my Father's house?"[c] [50]But they did not understand what he said to them. [51]Then he went down with them and came to Nazareth, and was obedient to them. His mother treasured all these things in her heart.

52 And Jesus increased in wisdom and in years,[d] and in divine and human favor.

THE PROCLAMATION OF JOHN THE BAPTIST

3 In the fifteenth year of the reign of Emperor Tiberius, when Pontius Pilate was governor of Judea, and Herod was ruler[e] of Galilee, and his brother Philip ruler[e] of the region of Ituraea and Trachonitis, and Lysanias ruler[e] of Abilene, [2]during the high priesthood of Annas and Caiaphas, the word of God came to John son of Zechariah in the wilderness. [3]He went into all the region around the Jordan, proclaiming a baptism of repentance for the forgiveness of sins, [4]as it is written in the book of the words of the prophet Isaiah,

---

a Gk him   b Gk they   c Or be about my Father's interests?   d Or in stature   e Gk tetrarch

"The voice of one crying out in the wilderness:
'Prepare the way of the Lord,
> make his paths straight.

5 Every valley shall be filled,
> and every mountain and hill shall be made low,

and the crooked shall be made straight,
> and the rough ways made smooth;

6 and all flesh shall see the salvation of God.'"

7 John said to the crowds that came out to be baptized by him, "You brood of vipers! Who warned you to flee from the wrath to come? ⁸Bear fruits worthy of repentance. Do not begin to say to yourselves, 'We have Abraham as our ancestor'; for I tell you, God is able from these stones to raise up children to Abraham. ⁹Even now the ax is lying at the root of the trees; every tree therefore that does not bear good fruit is cut down and thrown into the fire."

10 And the crowds asked him, "What then should we do?" ¹¹In reply he said to them, "Whoever has two coats must share with anyone who has none; and whoever has food must do likewise." ¹²Even tax collectors came to be baptized, and they asked him, "Teacher, what should we do?" ¹³He said to them, "Collect no more than the amount prescribed for you." ¹⁴Soldiers also asked him, "And we, what should we do?" He said to them, "Do not extort money from anyone by threats or false accusation, and be satisfied with your wages."

15 As the people were filled with expectation, and all were questioning in their hearts concerning John, whether he might be the Messiah,ᵃ ¹⁶John answered all of them by saying, "I baptize you with water; but one who is more powerful than I is coming; I am not worthy to untie the thong of his sandals. He will baptize you withᵇ the Holy Spirit and fire. ¹⁷His winnowing fork is in his hand, to clear his threshing floor and to gather the wheat into his granary; but the chaff he will burn with unquenchable fire."

18 So, with many other exhortations, he proclaimed the good news to the people. ¹⁹But Herod the ruler,ᶜ who had been rebuked by him because of Herodias, his brother's wife, and because of all the evil things that Herod had done, ²⁰added to them all by shutting up John in prison.

THE BAPTISM OF JESUS

21 Now when all the people were baptized, and when Jesus also had been baptized and was praying, the heaven was opened, ²²and the Holy Spirit descended

---

a Or *the Christ*   *b* Or *in*   *c* Gk *tetrarch*

upon him in bodily form like a dove. And a voice came from heaven, "You are my Son, the Beloved;[a] with you I am well pleased."[b]

THE ANCESTORS OF JESUS

23 Jesus was about thirty years old when he began his work. He was the son (as was thought) of Joseph son of Heli, [24]son of Matthat, son of Levi, son of Melchi, son of Jannai, son of Joseph, [25]son of Mattathias, son of Amos, son of Nahum, son of Esli, son of Naggai, [26]son of Maath, son of Mattathias, son of Semein, son of Josech, son of Joda, [27]son of Joanan, son of Rhesa, son of Zerubbabel, son of Shealtiel,[c] son of Neri, [28]son of Melchi, son of Addi, son of Cosam, son of Elmadam, son of Er, [29]son of Joshua, son of Eliezer, son of Jorim, son of Matthat, son of Levi, [30]son of Simeon, son of Judah, son of Joseph, son of Jonam, son of Eliakim, [31]son of Melea, son of Menna, son of Mattatha, son of Nathan, son of David, [32]son of Jesse, son of Obed, son of Boaz, son of Sala,[d] son of Nahshon, [33]son of Amminadab, son of Admin, son of Arni,[e] son of Hezron, son of Perez, son of Judah, [34]son of Jacob, son of Isaac, son of Abraham, son of Terah, son of Nahor, [35]son of Serug, son of Reu, son of Peleg, son of Eber, son of Shelah, [36]son of Cainan, son of Arphaxad, son of Shem, son of Noah, son of Lamech, [37]son of Methuselah, son of Enoch, son of Jared, son of Mahalaleel, son of Cainan, [38]son of Enos, son of Seth, son of Adam, son of God.

THE TEMPTATION OF JESUS

4 Jesus, full of the Holy Spirit, returned from the Jordan and was led by the Spirit in the wilderness, [2]where for forty days he was tempted by the devil. He ate nothing at all during those days, and when they were over, he was famished. [3]The devil said to him, "If you are the Son of God, command this stone to become a loaf of bread." [4]Jesus answered him, "It is written, 'One does not live by bread alone.'"

5 Then the devil[f] led him up and showed him in an instant all the kingdoms of the world. [6]And the devil[f] said to him, "To you I will give their glory and all this authority; for it has been given over to me, and I give it to anyone I please. [7]If you, then, will worship me, it will all be yours." [8]Jesus answered him, "It is written,

> 'Worship the Lord your God,
>   and serve only him.'"

---

a Or my beloved Son   b Other ancient authorities read You are my Son, today I have begotten you   c Gk Salathiel   d Other ancient authorities read Salmon   e Other ancient authorities read Amminadab, son of Aram; others vary widely   f Gk he

9 Then the devil[a] took him to Jerusalem, and placed him on the pinnacle of the temple, saying to him, "If you are the Son of God, throw yourself down from here, [10]for it is written,

> 'He will command his angels concerning you,
>> to protect you,'

11 and

> 'On their hands they will bear you up,
>> so that you will not dash your foot against a stone.'"

12 Jesus answered him, "It is said, 'Do not put the Lord your God to the test.'" [13]When the devil had finished every test, he departed from him until an opportune time.

THE BEGINNING OF THE GALILEAN MINISTRY

14 Then Jesus, filled with the power of the Spirit, returned to Galilee, and a report about him spread through all the surrounding country. [15]He began to teach in their synagogues and was praised by everyone.

THE REJECTION OF JESUS AT NAZARETH

16 When he came to Nazareth, where he had been brought up, he went to the synagogue on the sabbath day, as was his custom. He stood up to read, [17]and the scroll of the prophet Isaiah was given to him. He unrolled the scroll and found the place where it was written:

> 18 "The Spirit of the Lord is upon me,
>> because he has anointed me
>>> to bring good news to the poor.
> He has sent me to proclaim release to the captives
>> and recovery of sight to the blind,
>>> to let the oppressed go free,
>> 19 to proclaim the year of the Lord's favor."

20 And he rolled up the scroll, gave it back to the attendant, and sat down. The eyes of all in the synagogue were fixed on him. [21]Then he began to say to them, "Today this scripture has been fulfilled in your hearing." [22]All spoke well of him and were amazed at the gracious words that came from his mouth. They said, "Is not this Joseph's son?" [23]He said to them, "Doubtless you will quote to me this proverb, 'Doctor, cure yourself!' And you will say, 'Do here also in your hometown the things that we have heard you did at Capernaum.'" [24]And he said, "Truly I tell you, no prophet is accepted in the prophet's hometown. [25]But

---

a Gk he

the truth is, there were many widows in Israel in the time of Elijah, when the heaven was shut up three years and six months, and there was a severe famine over all the land; ²⁶yet Elijah was sent to none of them except to a widow at Zarephath in Sidon. ²⁷There were also many lepers*ᵃ* in Israel in the time of the prophet Elisha, and none of them was cleansed except Naaman the Syrian." ²⁸When they heard this, all in the synagogue were filled with rage. ²⁹They got up, drove him out of the town, and led him to the brow of the hill on which their town was built, so that they might hurl him off the cliff. ³⁰But he passed through the midst of them and went on his way.

THE MAN WITH AN UNCLEAN SPIRIT

31 He went down to Capernaum, a city in Galilee, and was teaching them on the sabbath. ³²They were astounded at his teaching, because he spoke with authority. ³³In the synagogue there was a man who had the spirit of an unclean demon, and he cried out with a loud voice, ³⁴"Let us alone! What have you to do with us, Jesus of Nazareth? Have you come to destroy us? I know who you are, the Holy One of God." ³⁵But Jesus rebuked him, saying, "Be silent, and come out of him!" When the demon had thrown him down before them, he came out of him without having done him any harm. ³⁶They were all amazed and kept saying to one another, "What kind of utterance is this? For with authority and power he commands the unclean spirits, and out they come!" ³⁷And a report about him began to reach every place in the region.

HEALINGS AT SIMON'S HOUSE

38 After leaving the synagogue he entered Simon's house. Now Simon's mother-in-law was suffering from a high fever, and they asked him about her. ³⁹Then he stood over her and rebuked the fever, and it left her. Immediately she got up and began to serve them.

40 As the sun was setting, all those who had any who were sick with various kinds of diseases brought them to him; and he laid his hands on each of them and cured them. ⁴¹Demons also came out of many, shouting, "You are the Son of God!" But he rebuked them and would not allow them to speak, because they knew that he was the Messiah.*ᵇ*

JESUS PREACHES IN THE SYNAGOGUES

42 At daybreak he departed and went into a deserted place. And the crowds were looking for him; and when they reached him, they wanted to prevent him

---

a The terms *leper* and *leprosy* can refer to several diseases   *b* Or *the Christ* from leaving them. ⁴³But he said to them, "I must proclaim the good news of the kingdom of God to the other cities also; for I was sent for this purpose." ⁴⁴So he continued proclaiming the message in the synagogues of Judea.ᵃ

JESUS CALLS THE FIRST DISCIPLES

5 Once while Jesusᵇ was standing beside the lake of Gennesaret, and the crowd was pressing in on him to hear the word of God, ²he saw two boats there at the shore of the lake; the fishermen had gone out of them and were washing their nets. ³He got into one of the boats, the one belonging to Simon, and asked him to put out a little way from the shore. Then he sat down and taught the crowds from the boat. ⁴When he had finished speaking, he said to Simon, "Put out into the deep water and let down your nets for a catch." ⁵Simon answered, "Master, we have worked all night long but have caught nothing. Yet if you say so, I will let down the nets." ⁶When they had done this, they caught so many fish that their nets were beginning to break. ⁷So they signaled their partners in the other boat to come and help them. And they came and filled both boats, so that they began to sink. ⁸But when Simon Peter saw it, he fell down at Jesus' knees, saying, "Go away from me, Lord, for I am a sinful man!" ⁹For he and all who were with him were amazed at the catch of fish that they had taken; ¹⁰and so also were James and John, sons of Zebedee, who were partners with Simon. Then Jesus said to Simon, "Do not be afraid; from now on you will be catching people." ¹¹When they had brought their boats to shore, they left everything and followed him.

JESUS CLEANSES A LEPER

12 Once, when he was in one of the cities, there was a man covered with leprosy.ᶜ When he saw Jesus, he bowed with his face to the ground and begged him, "Lord, if you choose, you can make me clean." ¹³Then Jesusᵇ stretched out his hand, touched him, and said, "I do choose. Be made clean." Immediately the leprosyᶜ left him. ¹⁴And he ordered him to tell no one. "Go," he said, "and show yourself to the priest, and, as Moses commanded, make an offering for your cleansing, for a testimony to them." ¹⁵But now more than ever the word about Jesusᵈ spread abroad; many crowds would gather to hear him and to be cured of their diseases. ¹⁶But he would withdraw to deserted places and pray.

JESUS HEALS A PARALYTIC

17 One day, while he was teaching, Pharisees and teachers of the law were sitting near by (they had come from every village of Galilee and Judea and from

---

a Other ancient authorities read *Galilee*   b Gk *he*   c The terms *leper* and *leprosy* can refer to several diseases   d Gk *him*

Jerusalem); and the power of the Lord was with him to heal.*ᵃ* ¹⁸Just then some men came, carrying a paralyzed man on a bed. They were trying to bring him in and lay him before Jesus;*ᵇ* ¹⁹but finding no way to bring him in because of the crowd, they went up on the roof and let him down with his bed through the tiles into the middle of the crowd*ᶜ* in front of Jesus. ²⁰When he saw their faith, he said, "Friend,*ᵈ* your sins are forgiven you." ²¹Then the scribes and the Pharisees began to question, "Who is this who is speaking blasphemies? Who can forgive sins but God alone?" ²²When Jesus perceived their questionings, he answered them, "Why do you raise such questions in your hearts? ²³Which is easier, to say, 'Your sins are forgiven you,' or to say, 'Stand up and walk'? ²⁴But so that you may know that the Son of Man has authority on earth to forgive sins"—he said to the one who was paralyzed—"I say to you, stand up and take your bed and go to your home." ²⁵Immediately he stood up before them, took what he had been lying on, and went to his home, glorifying God. ²⁶Amazement seized all of them, and they glorified God and were filled with awe, saying, "We have seen strange things today."

JESUS CALLS LEVI

27 After this he went out and saw a tax collector named Levi, sitting at the tax booth; and he said to him, "Follow me." ²⁸And he got up, left everything, and followed him.

29 Then Levi gave a great banquet for him in his house; and there was a large crowd of tax collectors and others sitting at the table*ᵉ* with them. ³⁰The Pharisees and their scribes were complaining to his disciples, saying, "Why do you eat and drink with tax collectors and sinners?" ³¹Jesus answered, "Those who are well have no need of a physician, but those who are sick; ³²I have come to call not the righteous but sinners to repentance."

THE QUESTION ABOUT FASTING

33 Then they said to him, "John's disciples, like the disciples of the Pharisees, frequently fast and pray, but your disciples eat and drink." ³⁴Jesus said to them, "You cannot make wedding guests fast while the bridegroom is with them, can you? ³⁵The days will come when the bridegroom will be taken away from them, and then they will fast in those days." ³⁶He also told them a parable: "No one tears a piece from a new garment and sews it on an old garment; otherwise the new will be torn, and the piece from the new will not match the old. ³⁷And no one puts new wine into old wineskins; otherwise the new wine will burst the

---

a Other ancient authorities read *was present to heal them*   *b* Gk *him*   *c* Gk *into the midst*   *d* Gk *Man*   *e* Gk *reclining* skins and will be spilled, and the skins will be destroyed. [38]But new wine must be put into fresh wineskins. [39]And no one after drinking old wine desires new wine, but says, 'The old is good.'"[a]

THE QUESTION ABOUT THE SABBATH

6 One sabbath[b] while Jesus[c] was going through the grainfields, his disciples plucked some heads of grain, rubbed them in their hands, and ate them. [2]But some of the Pharisees said, "Why are you doing what is not lawful[d] on the sabbath?" [3]Jesus answered, "Have you not read what David did when he and his companions were hungry? [4]He entered the house of God and took and ate the bread of the Presence, which it is not lawful for any but the priests to eat, and gave some to his companions?" [5]Then he said to them, "The Son of Man is lord of the sabbath."

THE MAN WITH A WITHERED HAND

6 On another sabbath he entered the synagogue and taught, and there was a man there whose right hand was withered. [7]The scribes and the Pharisees watched him to see whether he would cure on the sabbath, so that they might find an accusation against him. [8]Even though he knew what they were thinking, he said to the man who had the withered hand, "Come and stand here." He got up and stood there. [9]Then Jesus said to them, "I ask you, is it lawful to do good or to do harm on the sabbath, to save life or to destroy it?" [10]After looking around at all of them, he said to him, "Stretch out your hand." He did so, and his hand was restored. [11]But they were filled with fury and discussed with one another what they might do to Jesus.

JESUS CHOOSES THE TWELVE APOSTLES

12 Now during those days he went out to the mountain to pray; and he spent the night in prayer to God. [13]And when day came, he called his disciples and chose twelve of them, whom he also named apostles: [14]Simon, whom he named Peter, and his brother Andrew, and James, and John, and Philip, and Bartholomew, [15]and Matthew, and Thomas, and James son of Alphaeus, and Simon, who was called the Zealot, [16]and Judas son of James, and Judas Iscariot, who became a traitor.

---

a Other ancient authorities read *better;* others lack verse 39   b Other ancient authorities read *On the second first sabbath*
c Gk *he*   d Other ancient authorities add *to do*

JESUS TEACHES AND HEALS

17 He came down with them and stood on a level place, with a great crowd of his disciples and a great multitude of people from all Judea, Jerusalem, and the coast of Tyre and Sidon. ¹⁸They had come to hear him and to be healed of their diseases; and those who were troubled with unclean spirits were cured. ¹⁹And all in the crowd were trying to touch him, for power came out from him and healed all of them.

BLESSINGS AND WOES

20 Then he looked up at his disciples and said:
>"Blessed are you who are poor,
>>for yours is the kingdom of God.
>21 "Blessed are you who are hungry now,
>>for you will be filled.
>"Blessed are you who weep now,
>>for you will laugh.

22 "Blessed are you when people hate you, and when they exclude you, revile you, and defame you*a* on account of the Son of Man. ²³Rejoice in that day and leap for joy, for surely your reward is great in heaven; for that is what their ancestors did to the prophets.
>24 "But woe to you who are rich,
>>for you have received your consolation.
>25 "Woe to you who are full now,
>>for you will be hungry.
>"Woe to you who are laughing now,
>>for you will mourn and weep.

26 "Woe to you when all speak well of you, for that is what their ancestors did to the false prophets.

LOVE FOR ENEMIES

27 "But I say to you that listen, Love your enemies, do good to those who hate you, ²⁸bless those who curse you, pray for those who abuse you. ²⁹If anyone strikes you on the cheek, offer the other also; and from anyone who takes away your coat do not withhold even your shirt. ³⁰Give to everyone who begs from

---

a Gk *cast out your name as evil*

you; and if anyone takes away your goods, do not ask for them again. ³¹Do to others as you would have them do to you.

32 "If you love those who love you, what credit is that to you? For even sinners love those who love them. ³³If you do good to those who do good to you, what credit is that to you? For even sinners do the same. ³⁴If you lend to those from whom you hope to receive, what credit is that to you? Even sinners lend to sinners, to receive as much again. ³⁵But love your enemies, do good, and lend, expecting nothing in return.*^a Your reward will be great, and you will be children of the Most High; for he is kind to the ungrateful and the wicked. ³⁶Be merciful, just as your Father is merciful.

JUDGING OTHERS

37 "Do not judge, and you will not be judged; do not condemn, and you will not be condemned. Forgive, and you will be forgiven; ³⁸give, and it will be given to you. A good measure, pressed down, shaken together, running over, will be put into your lap; for the measure you give will be the measure you get back."

39 He also told them a parable: "Can a blind person guide a blind person? Will not both fall into a pit? ⁴⁰A disciple is not above the teacher, but everyone who is fully qualified will be like the teacher. ⁴¹Why do you see the speck in your neighbor's*^b eye, but do not notice the log in your own eye? ⁴²Or how can you say to your neighbor,*^c 'Friend,*^d let me take out the speck in your eye,' when you yourself do not see the log in your own eye? You hypocrite, first take the log out of your own eye, and then you will see clearly to take the speck out of your neighbor's*^b eye.

A TREE AND ITS FRUIT

43 "No good tree bears bad fruit, nor again does a bad tree bear good fruit; ⁴⁴for each tree is known by its own fruit. Figs are not gathered from thorns, nor are grapes picked from a bramble bush. ⁴⁵The good person out of the good treasure of the heart produces good, and the evil person out of evil treasure produces evil; for it is out of the abundance of the heart that the mouth speaks.

THE TWO FOUNDATIONS

46 "Why do you call me 'Lord, Lord,' and do not do what I tell you? ⁴⁷I will show you what someone is like who comes to me, hears my words, and acts on them. ⁴⁸That one is like a man building a house, who dug deeply and laid the

---

a Other ancient authorities read *despairing of no one*   *b* Gk *brother's*   *c* Gk *brother*   *d* Gk *Brother* foundation on rock; when a flood arose, the river burst against that house but could not shake it, because it had been well built.ᵃ ⁴⁹But the one who hears and does not act is like a man who built a house on the ground without a foundation. When the river burst against it, immediately it fell, and great was the ruin of that house."

JESUS HEALS A CENTURION'S SERVANT

7 After Jesusᵇ had finished all his sayings in the hearing of the people, he entered Capernaum. ²A centurion there had a slave whom he valued highly, and who was ill and close to death. ³When he heard about Jesus, he sent some Jewish elders to him, asking him to come and heal his slave. ⁴When they came to Jesus, they appealed to him earnestly, saying, "He is worthy of having you do this for him, ⁵for he loves our people, and it is he who built our synagogue for us." ⁶And Jesus went with them, but when he was not far from the house, the centurion sent friends to say to him, "Lord, do not trouble yourself, for I am not worthy to have you come under my roof; ⁷therefore I did not presume to come to you. But only speak the word, and let my servant be healed. ⁸For I also am a man set under authority, with soldiers under me; and I say to one, 'Go,' and he goes, and to another, 'Come,' and he comes, and to my slave, 'Do this,' and the slave does it." ⁹When Jesus heard this he was amazed at him, and turning to the crowd that followed him, he said, "I tell you, not even in Israel have I found such faith." ¹⁰When those who had been sent returned to the house, they found the slave in good health.

JESUS RAISES THE WIDOW'S SON AT NAIN

11 Soon afterwardsᶜ he went to a town called Nain, and his disciples and a large crowd went with him. ¹²As he approached the gate of the town, a man who had died was being carried out. He was his mother's only son, and she was a widow; and with her was a large crowd from the town. ¹³When the Lord saw her, he had compassion for her and said to her, "Do not weep." ¹⁴Then he came forward and touched the bier, and the bearers stood still. And he said, "Young man, I say to you, rise!" ¹⁵The dead man sat up and began to speak, and Jesusᵇ gave him to his mother. ¹⁶Fear seized all of them; and they glorified God, saying, "A great prophet has risen among us!" and "God has looked favorably on his people!" ¹⁷This word about him spread throughout Judea and all the surrounding country.

---

a Other ancient authorities read *founded upon the rock*   *b* Gk *he*   *c* Other ancient authorities read *Next day*

MESSENGERS FROM JOHN THE BAPTIST

18 The disciples of John reported all these things to him. So John summoned two of his disciples ¹⁹and sent them to the Lord to ask, "Are you the one who is to come, or are we to wait for another?" ²⁰When the men had come to him, they said, "John the Baptist has sent us to you to ask, 'Are you the one who is to come, or are we to wait for another?'" ²¹Jesus*a* had just then cured many people of diseases, plagues, and evil spirits, and had given sight to many who were blind. ²²And he answered them, "Go and tell John what you have seen and heard: the blind receive their sight, the lame walk, the lepers*b* are cleansed, the deaf hear, the dead are raised, the poor have good news brought to them. ²³And blessed is anyone who takes no offense at me."

24 When John's messengers had gone, Jesus*c* began to speak to the crowds about John:*d* "What did you go out into the wilderness to look at? A reed shaken by the wind? ²⁵What then did you go out to see? Someone*e* dressed in soft robes? Look, those who put on fine clothing and live in luxury are in royal palaces. ²⁶What then did you go out to see? A prophet? Yes, I tell you, and more than a prophet. ²⁷This is the one about whom it is written,

'See, I am sending my messenger ahead of you,
who will prepare your way before you.'

28 I tell you, among those born of women no one is greater than John; yet the least in the kingdom of God is greater than he." ²⁹(And all the people who heard this, including the tax collectors, acknowledged the justice of God,*f* because they had been baptized with John's baptism. ³⁰But by refusing to be baptized by him, the Pharisees and the lawyers rejected God's purpose for themselves.)

31 "To what then will I compare the people of this generation, and what are they like? ³²They are like children sitting in the marketplace and calling to one another,

'We played the flute for you, and you did not dance;
we wailed, and you did not weep.'

33 For John the Baptist has come eating no bread and drinking no wine, and you say, 'He has a demon'; ³⁴the Son of Man has come eating and drinking, and you say, 'Look, a glutton and a drunkard, a friend of tax collectors and sinners!' ³⁵Nevertheless, wisdom is vindicated by all her children."

---

a Gk He   *b* The terms *leper* and *leprosy* can refer to several diseases   *c* Gk *he*   *d* Gk *him*   *e* Or *Why then did you go out? To see someone*   *f* Or *praised God*

A SINFUL WOMAN FORGIVEN

36 One of the Pharisees asked Jesus*a* to eat with him, and he went into the Pharisee's house and took his place at the table. ³⁷And a woman in the city, who was a sinner, having learned that he was eating in the Pharisee's house, brought an alabaster jar of ointment. ³⁸She stood behind him at his feet, weeping, and began to bathe his feet with her tears and to dry them with her hair. Then she continued kissing his feet and anointing them with the ointment. ³⁹Now when the Pharisee who had invited him saw it, he said to himself, "If this man were a prophet, he would have known who and what kind of woman this is who is touching him—that she is a sinner." ⁴⁰Jesus spoke up and said to him, "Simon, I have something to say to you." "Teacher," he replied, "speak." ⁴¹"A certain creditor had two debtors; one owed five hundred denarii,*b* and the other fifty. ⁴²When they could not pay, he canceled the debts for both of them. Now which of them will love him more?" ⁴³Simon answered, "I suppose the one for whom he canceled the greater debt." And Jesus*c* said to him, "You have judged rightly." ⁴⁴Then turning toward the woman, he said to Simon, "Do you see this woman? I entered your house; you gave me no water for my feet, but she has bathed my feet with her tears and dried them with her hair. ⁴⁵You gave me no kiss, but from the time I came in she has not stopped kissing my feet. ⁴⁶You did not anoint my head with oil, but she has anointed my feet with ointment. ⁴⁷Therefore, I tell you, her sins, which were many, have been forgiven; hence she has shown great love. But the one to whom little is forgiven, loves little." ⁴⁸Then he said to her, "Your sins are forgiven." ⁴⁹But those who were at the table with him began to say among themselves, "Who is this who even forgives sins?" ⁵⁰And he said to the woman, "Your faith has saved you; go in peace."

SOME WOMEN ACCOMPANY JESUS

8 Soon afterwards he went on through cities and villages, proclaiming and bringing the good news of the kingdom of God. The twelve were with him, ²as well as some women who had been cured of evil spirits and infirmities: Mary, called Magdalene, from whom seven demons had gone out, ³and Joanna, the wife of Herod's steward Chuza, and Susanna, and many others, who provided for them*d* out of their resources.

---

a Gk *him*   *b* The denarius was the usual day's wage for a laborer   *c* Gk *he*   *d* Other ancient authorities read *him*

THE PARABLE OF THE SOWER

4 When a great crowd gathered and people from town after town came to him, he said in a parable: ⁵"A sower went out to sow his seed; and as he sowed, some fell on the path and was trampled on, and the birds of the air ate it up. ⁶Some fell on the rock; and as it grew up, it withered for lack of moisture. ⁷Some fell among thorns, and the thorns grew with it and choked it. ⁸Some fell into good soil, and when it grew, it produced a hundredfold." As he said this, he called out, "Let anyone with ears to hear listen!"

THE PURPOSE OF THE PARABLES

9 Then his disciples asked him what this parable meant. ¹⁰He said, "To you it has been given to know the secrets*a* of the kingdom of God; but to others I speak*b* in parables, so that

> 'looking they may not perceive,
>> and listening they may not understand.'

THE PARABLE OF THE SOWER EXPLAINED

11 "Now the parable is this: The seed is the word of God. ¹²The ones on the path are those who have heard; then the devil comes and takes away the word from their hearts, so that they may not believe and be saved. ¹³The ones on the rock are those who, when they hear the word, receive it with joy. But these have no root; they believe only for a while and in a time of testing fall away. ¹⁴As for what fell among the thorns, these are the ones who hear; but as they go on their way, they are choked by the cares and riches and pleasures of life, and their fruit does not mature. ¹⁵But as for that in the good soil, these are the ones who, when they hear the word, hold it fast in an honest and good heart, and bear fruit with patient endurance.

A LAMP UNDER A JAR

16 "No one after lighting a lamp hides it under a jar, or puts it under a bed, but puts it on a lampstand, so that those who enter may see the light. ¹⁷For nothing is hidden that will not be disclosed, nor is anything secret that will not become known and come to light. ¹⁸Then pay attention to how you listen; for to those who have, more will be given; and from those who do not have, even what they seem to have will be taken away."

---

a Or *mysteries*   *b* Gk lacks *I speak*

THE TRUE KINDRED OF JESUS

19 Then his mother and his brothers came to him, but they could not reach him because of the crowd. ²⁰And he was told, "Your mother and your brothers are standing outside, wanting to see you." ²¹But he said to them, "My mother and my brothers are those who hear the word of God and do it."

JESUS CALMS A STORM

22 One day he got into a boat with his disciples, and he said to them, "Let us go across to the other side of the lake." So they put out, ²³and while they were sailing he fell asleep. A windstorm swept down on the lake, and the boat was filling with water, and they were in danger. ²⁴They went to him and woke him up, shouting, "Master, Master, we are perishing!" And he woke up and rebuked the wind and the raging waves; they ceased, and there was a calm. ²⁵He said to them, "Where is your faith?" They were afraid and amazed, and said to one another, "Who then is this, that he commands even the winds and the water, and they obey him?"

JESUS HEALS THE GERASENE DEMONIAC

26 Then they arrived at the country of the Gerasenes,ᵃ which is opposite Galilee. ²⁷As he stepped out on land, a man of the city who had demons met him. For a long time he had wornᵇ no clothes, and he did not live in a house but in the tombs. ²⁸When he saw Jesus, he fell down before him and shouted at the top of his voice, "What have you to do with me, Jesus, Son of the Most High God? I beg you, do not torment me"— ²⁹for Jesusᶜ had commanded the unclean spirit to come out of the man. (For many times it had seized him; he was kept under guard and bound with chains and shackles, but he would break the bonds and be driven by the demon into the wilds.) ³⁰Jesus then asked him, "What is your name?" He said, "Legion"; for many demons had entered him. ³¹They begged him not to order them to go back into the abyss.

32 Now there on the hillside a large herd of swine was feeding; and the demonsᵈ begged Jesusᵉ to let them enter these. So he gave them permission. ³³Then the demons came out of the man and entered the swine, and the herd rushed down the steep bank into the lake and was drowned.

34 When the swineherds saw what had happened, they ran off and told it in the city and in the country. ³⁵Then people came out to see what had happened,

---

a Other ancient authorities read *Gadarenes*; others, *Gergesenes*   b Other ancient authorities read *a man of the city who had had demons for a long time met him. He wore*   c Gk *he*   d Gk *they*   e Gk *him* and when they came to Jesus, they found the man from whom the demons had gone sitting at the feet of Jesus, clothed and in his right mind. And they were afraid. [36]Those who had seen it told them how the one who had been possessed by demons had been healed. [37]Then all the people of the surrounding country of the Gerasenes[a] asked Jesus[b] to leave them; for they were seized with great fear. So he got into the boat and returned. [38]The man from whom the demons had gone begged that he might be with him; but Jesus[c] sent him away, saying, [39]"Return to your home, and declare how much God has done for you." So he went away, proclaiming throughout the city how much Jesus had done for him.

A GIRL RESTORED TO LIFE AND A WOMAN HEALED

40 Now when Jesus returned, the crowd welcomed him, for they were all waiting for him. [41]Just then there came a man named Jairus, a leader of the synagogue. He fell at Jesus' feet and begged him to come to his house, [42]for he had an only daughter, about twelve years old, who was dying.

As he went, the crowds pressed in on him. [43]Now there was a woman who had been suffering from hemorrhages for twelve years; and though she had spent all she had on physicians,[d] no one could cure her. [44]She came up behind him and touched the fringe of his clothes, and immediately her hemorrhage stopped. [45]Then Jesus asked, "Who touched me?" When all denied it, Peter[e] said, "Master, the crowds surround you and press in on you." [46]But Jesus said, "Someone touched me; for I noticed that power had gone out from me." [47]When the woman saw that she could not remain hidden, she came trembling; and falling down before him, she declared in the presence of all the people why she had touched him, and how she had been immediately healed. [48]He said to her, "Daughter, your faith has made you well; go in peace."

49 While he was still speaking, someone came from the leader's house to say, "Your daughter is dead; do not trouble the teacher any longer." [50]When Jesus heard this, he replied, "Do not fear. Only believe, and she will be saved." [51]When he came to the house, he did not allow anyone to enter with him, except Peter, John, and James, and the child's father and mother. [52]They were all weeping and wailing for her; but he said, "Do not weep; for she is not dead but sleeping." [53]And they laughed at him, knowing that she was dead. [54]But he took her by the hand and called out, "Child, get up!" [55]Her spirit returned, and she got up at once. Then he directed them to give her something to eat. [56]Her parents were astounded; but he ordered them to tell no one what had happened.

---

a Other ancient authorities read *Gadarenes;* others, *Gergesenes*   b Gk *him*   c Gk *he*   d Other ancient authorities lack *and though she had spent all she had on physicians*   e Other ancient authorities add *and those who were with him*

THE MISSION OF THE TWELVE

9 Then Jesus*a* called the twelve together and gave them power and authority over all demons and to cure diseases, ²and he sent them out to proclaim the kingdom of God and to heal. ³He said to them, "Take nothing for your journey, no staff, nor bag, nor bread, nor money—not even an extra tunic. ⁴Whatever house you enter, stay there, and leave from there. ⁵Wherever they do not welcome you, as you are leaving that town shake the dust off your feet as a testimony against them." ⁶They departed and went through the villages, bringing the good news and curing diseases everywhere.

HEROD'S PERPLEXITY

7 Now Herod the ruler*b* heard about all that had taken place, and he was perplexed, because it was said by some that John had been raised from the dead, ⁸by some that Elijah had appeared, and by others that one of the ancient prophets had arisen. ⁹Herod said, "John I beheaded; but who is this about whom I hear such things?" And he tried to see him.

FEEDING THE FIVE THOUSAND

10 On their return the apostles told Jesus*c* all they had done. He took them with him and withdrew privately to a city called Bethsaida. ¹¹When the crowds found out about it, they followed him; and he welcomed them, and spoke to them about the kingdom of God, and healed those who needed to be cured.

12 The day was drawing to a close, and the twelve came to him and said, "Send the crowd away, so that they may go into the surrounding villages and countryside, to lodge and get provisions; for we are here in a deserted place." ¹³But he said to them, "You give them something to eat." They said, "We have no more than five loaves and two fish—unless we are to go and buy food for all these people." ¹⁴For there were about five thousand men. And he said to his disciples, "Make them sit down in groups of about fifty each." ¹⁵They did so and made them all sit down. ¹⁶And taking the five loaves and the two fish, he looked up to heaven, and blessed and broke them, and gave them to the disciples to set before the crowd. ¹⁷And all ate and were filled. What was left over was gathered up, twelve baskets of broken pieces.

---

a Gk *he*   *b* Gk *tetrarch*   *c* Gk *him*

PETER'S DECLARATION ABOUT JESUS

18 Once when Jesus*a* was praying alone, with only the disciples near him, he asked them, "Who do the crowds say that I am?" [19]They answered, "John the Baptist; but others, Elijah; and still others, that one of the ancient prophets has arisen." [20]He said to them, "But who do you say that I am?" Peter answered, "The Messiah*b* of God."

JESUS FORETELLS HIS DEATH AND RESURRECTION

21 He sternly ordered and commanded them not to tell anyone, [22]saying, "The Son of Man must undergo great suffering, and be rejected by the elders, chief priests, and scribes, and be killed, and on the third day be raised."

23 Then he said to them all, "If any want to become my followers, let them deny themselves and take up their cross daily and follow me. [24]For those who want to save their life will lose it, and those who lose their life for my sake will save it. [25]What does it profit them if they gain the whole world, but lose or forfeit themselves? [26]Those who are ashamed of me and of my words, of them the Son of Man will be ashamed when he comes in his glory and the glory of the Father and of the holy angels. [27]But truly I tell you, there are some standing here who will not taste death before they see the kingdom of God."

THE TRANSFIGURATION

28 Now about eight days after these sayings Jesus*a* took with him Peter and John and James, and went up on the mountain to pray. [29]And while he was praying, the appearance of his face changed, and his clothes became dazzling white. [30]Suddenly they saw two men, Moses and Elijah, talking to him. [31]They appeared in glory and were speaking of his departure, which he was about to accomplish at Jerusalem. [32]Now Peter and his companions were weighed down with sleep; but since they had stayed awake,*c* they saw his glory and the two men who stood with him. [33]Just as they were leaving him, Peter said to Jesus, "Master, it is good for us to be here; let us make three dwellings,*d* one for you, one for Moses, and one for Elijah"—not knowing what he said. [34]While he was saying this, a cloud came and overshadowed them; and they were terrified as they entered the cloud. [35]Then from the cloud came a voice that said, "This is my Son, my Chosen;*e* listen to him!" [36]When the voice had spoken, Jesus was found alone. And they kept silent and in those days told no one any of the things they had seen.

---

a Gk *he*   *b* Or *The Christ*   *c* Or *but when they were fully awake*   *d* Or *tents*   *e* Other ancient authorities read *my Beloved*

JESUS HEALS A BOY WITH A DEMON

37 On the next day, when they had come down from the mountain, a great crowd met him. [38]Just then a man from the crowd shouted, "Teacher, I beg you to look at my son; he is my only child. [39]Suddenly a spirit seizes him, and all at once he*a* shrieks. It convulses him until he foams at the mouth; it mauls him and will scarcely leave him. [40]I begged your disciples to cast it out, but they could not." [41]Jesus answered, "You faithless and perverse generation, how much longer must I be with you and bear with you? Bring your son here." [42]While he was coming, the demon dashed him to the ground in convulsions. But Jesus rebuked the unclean spirit, healed the boy, and gave him back to his father. [43]And all were astounded at the greatness of God.

JESUS AGAIN FORETELLS HIS DEATH

While everyone was amazed at all that he was doing, he said to his disciples, [44]"Let these words sink into your ears: The Son of Man is going to be betrayed into human hands." [45]But they did not understand this saying; its meaning was concealed from them, so that they could not perceive it. And they were afraid to ask him about this saying.

TRUE GREATNESS

46 An argument arose among them as to which one of them was the greatest. [47]But Jesus, aware of their inner thoughts, took a little child and put it by his side, [48]and said to them, "Whoever welcomes this child in my name welcomes me, and whoever welcomes me welcomes the one who sent me; for the least among all of you is the greatest."

ANOTHER EXORCIST

49 John answered, "Master, we saw someone casting out demons in your name, and we tried to stop him, because he does not follow with us." [50]But Jesus said to him, "Do not stop him; for whoever is not against you is for you."

A SAMARITAN VILLAGE REFUSES TO RECEIVE JESUS

51 When the days drew near for him to be taken up, he set his face to go to Jerusalem. [52]And he sent messengers ahead of him. On their way they entered a village of the Samaritans to make ready for him; [53]but they did not receive him, because his face was set toward Jerusalem. [54]When his disciples James and John

---

a Or *it*

saw it, they said, "Lord, do you want us to command fire to come down from heaven and consume them?"*a* 55But he turned and rebuked them. 56Then*b* they went on to another village.

WOULD-BE FOLLOWERS OF JESUS

57 As they were going along the road, someone said to him, "I will follow you wherever you go." 58And Jesus said to him, "Foxes have holes, and birds of the air have nests; but the Son of Man has nowhere to lay his head." 59To another he said, "Follow me." But he said, "Lord, first let me go and bury my father." 60But Jesus*c* said to him, "Let the dead bury their own dead; but as for you, go and proclaim the kingdom of God." 61Another said, "I will follow you, Lord; but let me first say farewell to those at my home." 62Jesus said to him, "No one who puts a hand to the plow and looks back is fit for the kingdom of God."

THE MISSION OF THE SEVENTY

10 After this the Lord appointed seventy*d* others and sent them on ahead of him in pairs to every town and place where he himself intended to go. 2He said to them, "The harvest is plentiful, but the laborers are few; therefore ask the Lord of the harvest to send out laborers into his harvest. 3Go on your way. See, I am sending you out like lambs into the midst of wolves. 4Carry no purse, no bag, no sandals; and greet no one on the road. 5Whatever house you enter, first say, 'Peace to this house!' 6And if anyone is there who shares in peace, your peace will rest on that person; but if not, it will return to you. 7Remain in the same house, eating and drinking whatever they provide, for the laborer deserves to be paid. Do not move about from house to house. 8Whenever you enter a town and its people welcome you, eat what is set before you; 9cure the sick who are there, and say to them, 'The kingdom of God has come near to you.'*e* 10But whenever you enter a town and they do not welcome you, go out into its streets and say, 11'Even the dust of your town that clings to our feet, we wipe off in protest against you. Yet know this: the kingdom of God has come near.'*f* 12I tell you, on that day it will be more tolerable for Sodom than for that town.

WOES TO UNREPENTANT CITIES

13 "Woe to you, Chorazin! Woe to you, Bethsaida! For if the deeds of power done in you had been done in Tyre and Sidon, they would have repented long

---

a Other ancient authorities add *as Elijah did*   *b* Other ancient authorities read *rebuked them, and said, "You do not know what spirit you are of, 56for the Son of Man has not come to destroy the lives of human beings but to save them." Then*   *c* Gk *he*   *d* Other ancient authorities read *seventy-two*   *e* Or *is at hand for you*   *f* Or *is at hand* ago, sitting in sackcloth and ashes. [14]But at the judgment it will be more tolerable for Tyre and Sidon than for you. [15]And you, Capernaum,

> will you be exalted to heaven?
>
> No, you will be brought down to Hades.

16 "Whoever listens to you listens to me, and whoever rejects you rejects me, and whoever rejects me rejects the one who sent me."

THE RETURN OF THE SEVENTY

17 The seventy[a] returned with joy, saying, "Lord, in your name even the demons submit to us!" [18]He said to them, "I watched Satan fall from heaven like a flash of lightning. [19]See, I have given you authority to tread on snakes and scorpions, and over all the power of the enemy; and nothing will hurt you. [20]Nevertheless, do not rejoice at this, that the spirits submit to you, but rejoice that your names are written in heaven."

JESUS REJOICES

21 At that same hour Jesus[b] rejoiced in the Holy Spirit[c] and said, "I thank[d] you, Father, Lord of heaven and earth, because you have hidden these things from the wise and the intelligent and have revealed them to infants; yes, Father, for such was your gracious will.[e] [22]All things have been handed over to me by my Father; and no one knows who the Son is except the Father, or who the Father is except the Son and anyone to whom the Son chooses to reveal him."

23 Then turning to the disciples, Jesus[b] said to them privately, "Blessed are the eyes that see what you see! [24]For I tell you that many prophets and kings desired to see what you see, but did not see it, and to hear what you hear, but did not hear it."

THE PARABLE OF THE GOOD SAMARITAN

25 Just then a lawyer stood up to test Jesus.[f] "Teacher," he said, "what must I do to inherit eternal life?" [26]He said to him, "What is written in the law? What do you read there?" [27]He answered, "You shall love the Lord your God with all your heart, and with all your soul, and with all your strength, and with all your mind; and your neighbor as yourself." [28]And he said to him, "You have given the right answer; do this, and you will live."

29 But wanting to justify himself, he asked Jesus, "And who is my neighbor?" [30]Jesus replied, "A man was going down from Jerusalem to Jericho, and

---

a Other ancient authorities read *seventy-two* b Gk *he* c Other authorities read *in the spirit* d Or *praise* e Or *for so it was well-pleasing in your sight* f Gk *him* fell into the hands of robbers, who stripped him, beat him, and went away, leaving him half dead. ³¹Now by chance a priest was going down that road; and when he saw him, he passed by on the other side. ³²So likewise a Levite, when he came to the place and saw him, passed by on the other side. ³³But a Samaritan while traveling came near him; and when he saw him, he was moved with pity. ³⁴He went to him and bandaged his wounds, having poured oil and wine on them. Then he put him on his own animal, brought him to an inn, and took care of him. ³⁵The next day he took out two denarii,ᵃ gave them to the innkeeper, and said, 'Take care of him; and when I come back, I will repay you whatever more you spend.' ³⁶Which of these three, do you think, was a neighbor to the man who fell into the hands of the robbers?" ³⁷He said, "The one who showed him mercy." Jesus said to him, "Go and do likewise."

JESUS VISITS MARTHA AND MARY

38 Now as they went on their way, he entered a certain village, where a woman named Martha welcomed him into her home. ³⁹She had a sister named Mary, who sat at the Lord's feet and listened to what he was saying. ⁴⁰But Martha was distracted by her many tasks; so she came to him and asked, "Lord, do you not care that my sister has left me to do all the work by myself? Tell her then to help me." ⁴¹But the Lord answered her, "Martha, Martha, you are worried and distracted by many things; ⁴²there is need of only one thing.ᵇ Mary has chosen the better part, which will not be taken away from her."

THE LORD'S PRAYER

11 He was praying in a certain place, and after he had finished, one of his disciples said to him, "Lord, teach us to pray, as John taught his disciples." ²He said to them, "When you pray, say:
>   Father,ᶜ hallowed be your name.
>   Your kingdom come.ᵈ
>   3 Give us each day our daily bread.ᵉ
>   4 And forgive us our sins,
>   for we ourselves forgive everyone indebted to us.
>   And do not bring us to the time of trial."ᶠ

ᵃ The denarius was the usual day's wage for a laborer   ᵇ Other ancient authorities read *few things are necessary, or only one*
ᶜ Other ancient authorities read *Our Father in heaven*   ᵈ A few ancient authorities read *Your Holy Spirit come upon us and cleanse us.* Other ancient authorities add *Your will be done, on earth as in heaven*   ᵉ Or *our bread for tomorrow*   ᶠ Or *us into temptation.* Other ancient authorities add *but rescue us from the evil one* (or *from evil*)

PERSEVERANCE IN PRAYER

5 And he said to them, "Suppose one of you has a friend, and you go to him at midnight and say to him, 'Friend, lend me three loaves of bread; ⁶for a friend of mine has arrived, and I have nothing to set before him.' ⁷And he answers from within, 'Do not bother me; the door has already been locked, and my children are with me in bed; I cannot get up and give you anything.' ⁸I tell you, even though he will not get up and give him anything because he is his friend, at least because of his persistence he will get up and give him whatever he needs.

9 "So I say to you, Ask, and it will be given you; search, and you will find; knock, and the door will be opened for you. ¹⁰For everyone who asks receives, and everyone who searches finds, and for everyone who knocks, the door will be opened. ¹¹Is there anyone among you who, if your child asks for ª a fish, will give a snake instead of a fish? ¹²Or if the child asks for an egg, will give a scorpion? ¹³If you then, who are evil, know how to give good gifts to your children, how much more will the heavenly Father give the Holy Spirit ᵇ to those who ask him!"

JESUS AND BEELZEBUL

14 Now he was casting out a demon that was mute; when the demon had gone out, the one who had been mute spoke, and the crowds were amazed. ¹⁵But some of them said, "He casts out demons by Beelzebul, the ruler of the demons." ¹⁶Others, to test him, kept demanding from him a sign from heaven. ¹⁷But he knew what they were thinking and said to them, "Every kingdom divided against itself becomes a desert, and house falls on house. ¹⁸If Satan also is divided against himself, how will his kingdom stand? —for you say that I cast out the demons by Beelzebul. ¹⁹Now if I cast out the demons by Beelzebul, by whom do your exorcists ᶜ cast them out? Therefore they will be your judges. ²⁰But if it is by the finger of God that I cast out the demons, then the kingdom of God has come to you. ²¹When a strong man, fully armed, guards his castle, his property is safe. ²²But when one stronger than he attacks him and overpowers him, he takes away his armor in which he trusted and divides his plunder. ²³Whoever is not with me is against me, and whoever does not gather with me scatters.

THE RETURN OF THE UNCLEAN SPIRIT

24 "When the unclean spirit has gone out of a person, it wanders through waterless regions looking for a resting place, but not finding any, it says, 'I will

---

a Other ancient authorities add *bread, will give a stone; or if your child asks for*   b Other ancient authorities read *the Father give the Holy Spirit from heaven*   c Gk *sons* return to my house from which I came.' [25]When it comes, it finds it swept and put in order. [26]Then it goes and brings seven other spirits more evil than itself, and they enter and live there; and the last state of that person is worse than the first."

TRUE BLESSEDNESS

27 While he was saying this, a woman in the crowd raised her voice and said to him, "Blessed is the womb that bore you and the breasts that nursed you!" [28]But he said, "Blessed rather are those who hear the word of God and obey it!"

THE SIGN OF JONAH

29 When the crowds were increasing, he began to say, "This generation is an evil generation; it asks for a sign, but no sign will be given to it except the sign of Jonah. [30]For just as Jonah became a sign to the people of Nineveh, so the Son of Man will be to this generation. [31]The queen of the South will rise at the judgment with the people of this generation and condemn them, because she came from the ends of the earth to listen to the wisdom of Solomon, and see, something greater than Solomon is here! [32]The people of Nineveh will rise up at the judgment with this generation and condemn it, because they repented at the proclamation of Jonah, and see, something greater than Jonah is here!

THE LIGHT OF THE BODY

33 "No one after lighting a lamp puts it in a cellar,[a] but on the lampstand so that those who enter may see the light. [34]Your eye is the lamp of your body. If your eye is healthy, your whole body is full of light; but if it is not healthy, your body is full of darkness. [35]Therefore consider whether the light in you is not darkness. [36]If then your whole body is full of light, with no part of it in darkness, it will be as full of light as when a lamp gives you light with its rays."

JESUS DENOUNCES PHARISEES AND LAWYERS

37 While he was speaking, a Pharisee invited him to dine with him; so he went in and took his place at the table. [38]The Pharisee was amazed to see that he did not first wash before dinner. [39]Then the Lord said to him, "Now you Pharisees clean the outside of the cup and of the dish, but inside you are full of greed and wickedness. [40]You fools! Did not the one who made the outside make the inside also? [41]So give for alms those things that are within; and see, everything will be clean for you.

---

a Other ancient authorities add *or under the bushel basket*

42 "But woe to you Pharisees! For you tithe mint and rue and herbs of all kinds, and neglect justice and the love of God; it is these you ought to have practiced, without neglecting the others. [43]Woe to you Pharisees! For you love to have the seat of honor in the synagogues and to be greeted with respect in the marketplaces. [44]Woe to you! For you are like unmarked graves, and people walk over them without realizing it."

45 One of the lawyers answered him, "Teacher, when you say these things, you insult us too." [46]And he said, "Woe also to you lawyers! For you load people with burdens hard to bear, and you yourselves do not lift a finger to ease them. [47]Woe to you! For you build the tombs of the prophets whom your ancestors killed. [48]So you are witnesses and approve of the deeds of your ancestors; for they killed them, and you build their tombs. [49]Therefore also the Wisdom of God said, 'I will send them prophets and apostles, some of whom they will kill and persecute,' [50]so that this generation may be charged with the blood of all the prophets shed since the foundation of the world, [51]from the blood of Abel to the blood of Zechariah, who perished between the altar and the sanctuary. Yes, I tell you, it will be charged against this generation. [52]Woe to you lawyers! For you have taken away the key of knowledge; you did not enter yourselves, and you hindered those who were entering."

53 When he went outside, the scribes and the Pharisees began to be very hostile toward him and to cross-examine him about many things, [54]lying in wait for him, to catch him in something he might say.

A WARNING AGAINST HYPOCRISY

12 Meanwhile, when the crowd gathered by the thousands, so that they trampled on one another, he began to speak first to his disciples, "Beware of the yeast of the Pharisees, that is, their hypocrisy. [2]Nothing is covered up that will not be uncovered, and nothing secret that will not become known. [3]Therefore whatever you have said in the dark will be heard in the light, and what you have whispered behind closed doors will be proclaimed from the housetops.

EXHORTATION TO FEARLESS CONFESSION

4 "I tell you, my friends, do not fear those who kill the body, and after that can do nothing more. [5]But I will warn you whom to fear: fear him who, after he has killed, has authority[a] to cast into hell.[b] Yes, I tell you, fear him! [6]Are not five sparrows sold for two pennies? Yet not one of them is forgotten in God's sight.

---

a Or power   b Gk Gehenna

[7]But even the hairs of your head are all counted. Do not be afraid; you are of more value than many sparrows.

8 "And I tell you, everyone who acknowledges me before others, the Son of Man also will acknowledge before the angels of God; [9]but whoever denies me before others will be denied before the angels of God. [10]And everyone who speaks a word against the Son of Man will be forgiven; but whoever blasphemes against the Holy Spirit will not be forgiven. [11]When they bring you before the synagogues, the rulers, and the authorities, do not worry about how[a] you are to defend yourselves or what you are to say; [12]for the Holy Spirit will teach you at that very hour what you ought to say."

THE PARABLE OF THE RICH FOOL

13 Someone in the crowd said to him, "Teacher, tell my brother to divide the family inheritance with me." [14]But he said to him, "Friend, who set me to be a judge or arbitrator over you?" [15]And he said to them, "Take care! Be on your guard against all kinds of greed; for one's life does not consist in the abundance of possessions." [16]Then he told them a parable: "The land of a rich man produced abundantly. [17]And he thought to himself, 'What should I do, for I have no place to store my crops?' [18]Then he said, 'I will do this: I will pull down my barns and build larger ones, and there I will store all my grain and my goods. [19]And I will say to my soul, Soul, you have ample goods laid up for many years; relax, eat, drink, be merry.' [20]But God said to him, 'You fool! This very night your life is being demanded of you. And the things you have prepared, whose will they be?' [21]So it is with those who store up treasures for themselves but are not rich toward God."

DO NOT WORRY

22 He said to his disciples, "Therefore I tell you, do not worry about your life, what you will eat, or about your body, what you will wear. [23]For life is more than food, and the body more than clothing. [24]Consider the ravens: they neither sow nor reap, they have neither storehouse nor barn, and yet God feeds them. Of how much more value are you than the birds! [25]And can any of you by worrying add a single hour to your span of life?[b] [26]If then you are not able to do so small a thing as that, why do you worry about the rest? [27]Consider the lilies, how they grow: they neither toil nor spin;[c] yet I tell you, even Solomon in all his glory was not clothed like one of these. [28]But if God so clothes the grass of the field,

---

a Other ancient authorities add *or what* *b* Or *add a cubit to your stature* *c* Other ancient authorities read *Consider the lilies; they neither spin nor weave* which is alive today and tomorrow is thrown into the oven, how much more will he clothe you—you of little faith! ²⁹ And do not keep striving for what you are to eat and what you are to drink, and do not keep worrying. ³⁰For it is the nations of the world that strive after all these things, and your Father knows that you need them. ³¹Instead, strive for his^a kingdom, and these things will be given to you as well.

32 "Do not be afraid, little flock, for it is your Father's good pleasure to give you the kingdom. ³³Sell your possessions, and give alms. Make purses for yourselves that do not wear out, an unfailing treasure in heaven, where no thief comes near and no moth destroys. ³⁴For where your treasure is, there your heart will be also.

WATCHFUL SLAVES

35 "Be dressed for action and have your lamps lit; ³⁶be like those who are waiting for their master to return from the wedding banquet, so that they may open the door for him as soon as he comes and knocks. ³⁷Blessed are those slaves whom the master finds alert when he comes; truly I tell you, he will fasten his belt and have them sit down to eat, and he will come and serve them. ³⁸If he comes during the middle of the night, or near dawn, and finds them so, blessed are those slaves.

39 "But know this: if the owner of the house had known at what hour the thief was coming, he^b would not have let his house be broken into. ⁴⁰You also must be ready, for the Son of Man is coming at an unexpected hour."

THE FAITHFUL OR THE UNFAITHFUL SLAVE

41 Peter said, "Lord, are you telling this parable for us or for everyone?" ⁴²And the Lord said, "Who then is the faithful and prudent manager whom his master will put in charge of his slaves, to give them their allowance of food at the proper time? ⁴³Blessed is that slave whom his master will find at work when he arrives. ⁴⁴Truly I tell you, he will put that one in charge of all his possessions. ⁴⁵But if that slave says to himself, 'My master is delayed in coming,' and if he begins to beat the other slaves, men and women, and to eat and drink and get drunk, ⁴⁶the master of that slave will come on a day when he does not expect him and at an hour that he does not know, and will cut him in pieces,^c and put him with the unfaithful. ⁴⁷That slave who knew what his master wanted, but did not prepare himself or do what was wanted, will receive a severe beating. ⁴⁸But the one who did not know and did what deserved a beating will receive

---

_a Other ancient authorities read *God's*   b Other ancient authorities add *would have watched and*   c Or *cut him off*

a light beating. From everyone to whom much has been given, much will be required; and from the one to whom much has been entrusted, even more will be demanded.

JESUS THE CAUSE OF DIVISION

49 "I came to bring fire to the earth, and how I wish it were already kindled! [50]I have a baptism with which to be baptized, and what stress I am under until it is completed! [51]Do you think that I have come to bring peace to the earth? No, I tell you, but rather division! [52]From now on five in one household will be divided, three against two and two against three; [53]they will be divided:

> father against son
>   and son against father,
> mother against daughter
>   and daughter against mother,
> mother-in-law against her daughter-in-law
>   and daughter-in-law against mother-in-law."

INTERPRETING THE TIME

54 He also said to the crowds, "When you see a cloud rising in the west, you immediately say, 'It is going to rain'; and so it happens. [55]And when you see the south wind blowing, you say, 'There will be scorching heat'; and it happens. [56]You hypocrites! You know how to interpret the appearance of earth and sky, but why do you not know how to interpret the present time?

SETTLING WITH YOUR OPPONENT

57 "And why do you not judge for yourselves what is right? [58]Thus, when you go with your accuser before a magistrate, on the way make an effort to settle the case,[a] or you may be dragged before the judge, and the judge hand you over to the officer, and the officer throw you in prison. [59]I tell you, you will never get out until you have paid the very last penny."

REPENT OR PERISH

13 At that very time there were some present who told him about the Galileans whose blood Pilate had mingled with their sacrifices. [2]He asked

---

a Gk settle with him

them, "Do you think that because these Galileans suffered in this way they were worse sinners than all other Galileans? ³No, I tell you; but unless you repent, you will all perish as they did. ⁴Or those eighteen who were killed when the tower of Siloam fell on them—do you think that they were worse offenders than all the others living in Jerusalem? ⁵No, I tell you; but unless you repent, you will all perish just as they did."

THE PARABLE OF THE BARREN FIG TREE

6 Then he told this parable: "A man had a fig tree planted in his vineyard; and he came looking for fruit on it and found none. ⁷So he said to the gardener, 'See here! For three years I have come looking for fruit on this fig tree, and still I find none. Cut it down! Why should it be wasting the soil?' ⁸He replied, 'Sir, let it alone for one more year, until I dig around it and put manure on it. ⁹If it bears fruit next year, well and good; but if not, you can cut it down.'"

JESUS HEALS A CRIPPLED WOMAN

10 Now he was teaching in one of the synagogues on the sabbath. ¹¹And just then there appeared a woman with a spirit that had crippled her for eighteen years. She was bent over and was quite unable to stand up straight. ¹²When Jesus saw her, he called her over and said, "Woman, you are set free from your ailment." ¹³When he laid his hands on her, immediately she stood up straight and began praising God. ¹⁴But the leader of the synagogue, indignant because Jesus had cured on the sabbath, kept saying to the crowd, "There are six days on which work ought to be done; come on those days and be cured, and not on the sabbath day." ¹⁵But the Lord answered him and said, "You hypocrites! Does not each of you on the sabbath untie his ox or his donkey from the manger, and lead it away to give it water? ¹⁶And ought not this woman, a daughter of Abraham whom Satan bound for eighteen long years, be set free from this bondage on the sabbath day?" ¹⁷When he said this, all his opponents were put to shame; and the entire crowd was rejoicing at all the wonderful things that he was doing.

THE PARABLE OF THE MUSTARD SEED

18 He said therefore, "What is the kingdom of God like? And to what should I compare it? ¹⁹It is like a mustard seed that someone took and sowed in the garden; it grew and became a tree, and the birds of the air made nests in its branches."

THE PARABLE OF THE YEAST

20 And again he said, "To what should I compare the kingdom of God? ²¹It is like yeast that a woman took and mixed in with*ᵃ* three measures of flour until all of it was leavened."

THE NARROW DOOR

22 Jesus*ᵇ* went through one town and village after another, teaching as he made his way to Jerusalem. ²³Someone asked him, "Lord, will only a few be saved?" He said to them, ²⁴"Strive to enter through the narrow door; for many, I tell you, will try to enter and will not be able. ²⁵When once the owner of the house has got up and shut the door, and you begin to stand outside and to knock at the door, saying, 'Lord, open to us,' then in reply he will say to you, 'I do not know where you come from.' ²⁶Then you will begin to say, 'We ate and drank with you, and you taught in our streets.' ²⁷But he will say, 'I do not know where you come from; go away from me, all you evildoers!' ²⁸There will be weeping and gnashing of teeth when you see Abraham and Isaac and Jacob and all the prophets in the kingdom of God, and you yourselves thrown out. ²⁹Then people will come from east and west, from north and south, and will eat in the kingdom of God. ³⁰Indeed, some are last who will be first, and some are first who will be last."

THE LAMENT OVER JERUSALEM

31 At that very hour some Pharisees came and said to him, "Get away from here, for Herod wants to kill you." ³²He said to them, "Go and tell that fox for me,*ᶜ* 'Listen, I am casting out demons and performing cures today and tomorrow, and on the third day I finish my work. ³³Yet today, tomorrow, and the next day I must be on my way, because it is impossible for a prophet to be killed outside of Jerusalem.' ³⁴Jerusalem, Jerusalem, the city that kills the prophets and stones those who are sent to it! How often have I desired to gather your children together as a hen gathers her brood under her wings, and you were not willing! ³⁵See, your house is left to you. And I tell you, you will not see me until the time comes when*ᵈ* you say, 'Blessed is the one who comes in the name of the Lord.'"

JESUS HEALS THE MAN WITH DROPSY

14 On one occasion when Jesus*ᵉ* was going to the house of a leader of the Pharisees to eat a meal on the sabbath, they were watching him closely.

---

a Gk *hid in*   *b* Gk *He*   *c* Gk lacks *for me*   *d* Other ancient authorities lack *the time comes when*   *e* Gk *he*

²Just then, in front of him, there was a man who had dropsy. ³And Jesus asked the lawyers and Pharisees, "Is it lawful to cure people on the sabbath, or not?" ⁴But they were silent. So Jesus*a* took him and healed him, and sent him away. ⁵Then he said to them, "If one of you has a child*b* or an ox that has fallen into a well, will you not immediately pull it out on a sabbath day?" ⁶And they could not reply to this.

HUMILITY AND HOSPITALITY

7 When he noticed how the guests chose the places of honor, he told them a parable. ⁸"When you are invited by someone to a wedding banquet, do not sit down at the place of honor, in case someone more distinguished than you has been invited by your host; ⁹and the host who invited both of you may come and say to you, 'Give this person your place,' and then in disgrace you would start to take the lowest place. ¹⁰But when you are invited, go and sit down at the lowest place, so that when your host comes, he may say to you, 'Friend, move up higher'; then you will be honored in the presence of all who sit at the table with you. ¹¹For all who exalt themselves will be humbled, and those who humble themselves will be exalted."

12 He said also to the one who had invited him, "When you give a luncheon or a dinner, do not invite your friends or your brothers or your relatives or rich neighbors, in case they may invite you in return, and you would be repaid. ¹³But when you give a banquet, invite the poor, the crippled, the lame, and the blind. ¹⁴And you will be blessed, because they cannot repay you, for you will be repaid at the resurrection of the righteous."

THE PARABLE OF THE GREAT DINNER

15 One of the dinner guests, on hearing this, said to him, "Blessed is anyone who will eat bread in the kingdom of God!" ¹⁶Then Jesus*a* said to him, "Someone gave a great dinner and invited many. ¹⁷At the time for the dinner he sent his slave to say to those who had been invited, 'Come; for everything is ready now.' ¹⁸But they all alike began to make excuses. The first said to him, 'I have bought a piece of land, and I must go out and see it; please accept my regrets.' ¹⁹Another said, 'I have bought five yoke of oxen, and I am going to try them out; please accept my regrets.' ²⁰Another said, 'I have just been married, and therefore I cannot come.' ²¹So the slave returned and reported this to his master. Then the owner of the house became angry and said to his slave, 'Go out at once into the streets and lanes of the town and bring in the poor, the crippled,

---

a Gk *he* *b* Other ancient authorities read *a donkey*

the blind, and the lame.' ²²And the slave said, 'Sir, what you ordered has been done, and there is still room.' ²³Then the master said to the slave, 'Go out into the roads and lanes, and compel people to come in, so that my house may be filled. ²⁴For I tell you,ᵃ none of those who were invited will taste my dinner.'"

THE COST OF DISCIPLESHIP

25 Now large crowds were traveling with him; and he turned and said to them, ²⁶"Whoever comes to me and does not hate father and mother, wife and children, brothers and sisters, yes, and even life itself, cannot be my disciple. ²⁷Whoever does not carry the cross and follow me cannot be my disciple. ²⁸For which of you, intending to build a tower, does not first sit down and estimate the cost, to see whether he has enough to complete it? ²⁹Otherwise, when he has laid a foundation and is not able to finish, all who see it will begin to ridicule him, ³⁰saying, 'This fellow began to build and was not able to finish.' ³¹Or what king, going out to wage war against another king, will not sit down first and consider whether he is able with ten thousand to oppose the one who comes against him with twenty thousand? ³²If he cannot, then, while the other is still far away, he sends a delegation and asks for the terms of peace. ³³So therefore, none of you can become my disciple if you do not give up all your possessions.

ABOUT SALT

34 "Salt is good; but if salt has lost its taste, how can its saltiness be restored?ᵇ ³⁵It is fit neither for the soil nor for the manure pile; they throw it away. Let anyone with ears to hear listen!"

THE PARABLE OF THE LOST SHEEP

15 Now all the tax collectors and sinners were coming near to listen to him. ²And the Pharisees and the scribes were grumbling and saying, "This fellow welcomes sinners and eats with them."

3 So he told them this parable: ⁴"Which one of you, having a hundred sheep and losing one of them, does not leave the ninety-nine in the wilderness and go after the one that is lost until he finds it? ⁵When he has found it, he lays it on his shoulders and rejoices. ⁶And when he comes home, he calls together his friends and neighbors, saying to them, 'Rejoice with me, for I have found my sheep that was lost.' ⁷Just so, I tell you, there will be more joy in heaven over one sinner who repents than over ninety-nine righteous persons who need no repentance.

---

a The Greek word for *you* here is plural   *b* Or *how can it be used for seasoning?*

THE PARABLE OF THE LOST COIN

8 "Or what woman having ten silver coins,ᵃ if she loses one of them, does not light a lamp, sweep the house, and search carefully until she finds it? ⁹When she has found it, she calls together her friends and neighbors, saying, 'Rejoice with me, for I have found the coin that I had lost.' ¹⁰Just so, I tell you, there is joy in the presence of the angels of God over one sinner who repents."

THE PARABLE OF THE PRODIGAL AND HIS BROTHER

11 Then Jesusᵇ said, "There was a man who had two sons. ¹²The younger of them said to his father, 'Father, give me the share of the property that will belong to me.' So he divided his property between them. ¹³A few days later the younger son gathered all he had and traveled to a distant country, and there he squandered his property in dissolute living. ¹⁴When he had spent everything, a severe famine took place throughout that country, and he began to be in need. ¹⁵So he went and hired himself out to one of the citizens of that country, who sent him to his fields to feed the pigs. ¹⁶He would gladly have filled himself withᶜ the pods that the pigs were eating; and no one gave him anything. ¹⁷But when he came to himself he said, 'How many of my father's hired hands have bread enough and to spare, but here I am dying of hunger! ¹⁸I will get up and go to my father, and I will say to him, "Father, I have sinned against heaven and before you; ¹⁹I am no longer worthy to be called your son; treat me like one of your hired hands."' ²⁰So he set off and went to his father. But while he was still far off, his father saw him and was filled with compassion; he ran and put his arms around him and kissed him. ²¹Then the son said to him, 'Father, I have sinned against heaven and before you; I am no longer worthy to be called your son.'ᵈ ²²But the father said to his slaves, 'Quickly, bring out a robe—the best one—and put it on him; put a ring on his finger and sandals on his feet. ²³And get the fatted calf and kill it, and let us eat and celebrate; ²⁴for this son of mine was dead and is alive again; he was lost and is found!' And they began to celebrate.

25 "Now his elder son was in the field; and when he came and approached the house, he heard music and dancing. ²⁶He called one of the slaves and asked what was going on. ²⁷He replied, 'Your brother has come, and your father has killed the fatted calf, because he has got him back safe and sound.' ²⁸Then he became angry and refused to go in. His father came out and began to plead

---

a Gk *drachmas*, each worth about a day's wage for a laborer   b Gk *he*   c Other ancient authorities read *filled his stomach with*
d Other ancient authorities add *Treat me like one of your hired servants*

with him. ²⁹But he answered his father, 'Listen! For all these years I have been working like a slave for you, and I have never disobeyed your command; yet you have never given me even a young goat so that I might celebrate with my friends. ³⁰But when this son of yours came back, who has devoured your property with prostitutes, you killed the fatted calf for him!' ³¹Then the father*a* said to him, 'Son, you are always with me, and all that is mine is yours. ³²But we had to celebrate and rejoice, because this brother of yours was dead and has come to life; he was lost and has been found.'"

THE PARABLE OF THE DISHONEST MANAGER

16 Then Jesus*a* said to the disciples, "There was a rich man who had a manager, and charges were brought to him that this man was squandering his property. ²So he summoned him and said to him, 'What is this that I hear about you? Give me an accounting of your management, because you cannot be my manager any longer.' ³Then the manager said to himself, 'What will I do, now that my master is taking the position away from me? I am not strong enough to dig, and I am ashamed to beg. ⁴I have decided what to do so that, when I am dismissed as manager, people may welcome me into their homes.' ⁵So, summoning his master's debtors one by one, he asked the first, 'How much do you owe my master?' ⁶He answered, 'A hundred jugs of olive oil.' He said to him, 'Take your bill, sit down quickly, and make it fifty.' ⁷Then he asked another, 'And how much do you owe?' He replied, 'A hundred containers of wheat.' He said to him, 'Take your bill and make it eighty.' ⁸And his master commended the dishonest manager because he had acted shrewdly; for the children of this age are more shrewd in dealing with their own generation than are the children of light. ⁹And I tell you, make friends for yourselves by means of dishonest wealth*b* so that when it is gone, they may welcome you into the eternal homes.*c*

10 "Whoever is faithful in a very little is faithful also in much; and whoever is dishonest in a very little is dishonest also in much. ¹¹If then you have not been faithful with the dishonest wealth,*b* who will entrust to you the true riches? ¹²And if you have not been faithful with what belongs to another, who will give you what is your own? ¹³No slave can serve two masters; for a slave will either hate the one and love the other, or be devoted to the one and despise the other. You cannot serve God and wealth."*b*

---

a Gk *he*   *b* Gk *mammon*   *c* Gk *tents*

THE LAW AND THE KINGDOM OF GOD

14 The Pharisees, who were lovers of money, heard all this, and they ridiculed him. ¹⁵So he said to them, "You are those who justify yourselves in the sight of others; but God knows your hearts; for what is prized by human beings is an abomination in the sight of God.

16 "The law and the prophets were in effect until John came; since then the good news of the kingdom of God is proclaimed, and everyone tries to enter it by force.ᵃ ¹⁷But it is easier for heaven and earth to pass away, than for one stroke of a letter in the law to be dropped.

18 "Anyone who divorces his wife and marries another commits adultery, and whoever marries a woman divorced from her husband commits adultery.

THE RICH MAN AND LAZARUS

19 "There was a rich man who was dressed in purple and fine linen and who feasted sumptuously every day. ²⁰And at his gate lay a poor man named Lazarus, covered with sores, ²¹who longed to satisfy his hunger with what fell from the rich man's table; even the dogs would come and lick his sores. ²²The poor man died and was carried away by the angels to be with Abraham.ᵇ The rich man also died and was buried. ²³In Hades, where he was being tormented, he looked up and saw Abraham far away with Lazarus by his side.ᶜ ²⁴He called out, 'Father Abraham, have mercy on me, and send Lazarus to dip the tip of his finger in water and cool my tongue; for I am in agony in these flames.' ²⁵But Abraham said, 'Child, remember that during your lifetime you received your good things, and Lazarus in like manner evil things; but now he is comforted here, and you are in agony. ²⁶Besides all this, between you and us a great chasm has been fixed, so that those who might want to pass from here to you cannot do so, and no one can cross from there to us.' ²⁷He said, 'Then, father, I beg you to send him to my father's house— ²⁸for I have five brothers—that he may warn them, so that they will not also come into this place of torment.' ²⁹Abraham replied, 'They have Moses and the prophets; they should listen to them.' ³⁰He said, 'No, father Abraham; but if someone goes to them from the dead, they will repent.' ³¹He said to him, 'If they do not listen to Moses and the prophets, neither will they be convinced even if someone rises from the dead.'"

---

a Or *everyone is strongly urged to enter it*   *b* Gk *to Abraham's bosom*   *c* Gk *in his bosom*

SOME SAYINGS OF JESUS

17 Jesus[a] said to his disciples, "Occasions for stumbling are bound to come, but woe to anyone by whom they come! [2]It would be better for you if a millstone were hung around your neck and you were thrown into the sea than for you to cause one of these little ones to stumble. [3]Be on your guard! If another disciple[b] sins, you must rebuke the offender, and if there is repentance, you must forgive. [4]And if the same person sins against you seven times a day, and turns back to you seven times and says, 'I repent,' you must forgive."

5 The apostles said to the Lord, "Increase our faith!" [6]The Lord replied, "If you had faith the size of a[c] mustard seed, you could say to this mulberry tree, 'Be uprooted and planted in the sea,' and it would obey you.

7 "Who among you would say to your slave who has just come in from plowing or tending sheep in the field, 'Come here at once and take your place at the table'? [8]Would you not rather say to him, 'Prepare supper for me, put on your apron and serve me while I eat and drink; later you may eat and drink'? [9]Do you thank the slave for doing what was commanded? [10]So you also, when you have done all that you were ordered to do, say, 'We are worthless slaves; we have done only what we ought to have done!'"

JESUS CLEANSES TEN LEPERS

11 On the way to Jerusalem Jesus[d] was going through the region between Samaria and Galilee. [12]As he entered a village, ten lepers[e] approached him. Keeping their distance, [13]they called out, saying, "Jesus, Master, have mercy on us!" [14]When he saw them, he said to them, "Go and show yourselves to the priests." And as they went, they were made clean. [15]Then one of them, when he saw that he was healed, turned back, praising God with a loud voice. [16]He prostrated himself at Jesus'[f] feet and thanked him. And he was a Samaritan. [17]Then Jesus asked, "Were not ten made clean? But the other nine, where are they? [18]Was none of them found to return and give praise to God except this foreigner?" [19]Then he said to him, "Get up and go on your way; your faith has made you well."

THE COMING OF THE KINGDOM

20 Once Jesus[d] was asked by the Pharisees when the kingdom of God was coming, and he answered, "The kingdom of God is not coming with things that can

---

a Gk *He*   *b* Gk *your brother*   *c* Gk *faith as a grain of*   *d* Gk *he*   *e* The terms *leper* and *leprosy* can refer to several diseases
f Gk *his*

be observed; ²¹nor will they say, 'Look, here it is!' or 'There it is!' For, in fact, the kingdom of God is among[a] you."

22 Then he said to the disciples, "The days are coming when you will long to see one of the days of the Son of Man, and you will not see it. ²³They will say to you, 'Look there!' or 'Look here!' Do not go, do not set off in pursuit. ²⁴For as the lightning flashes and lights up the sky from one side to the other, so will the Son of Man be in his day.[b] ²⁵But first he must endure much suffering and be rejected by this generation. ²⁶Just as it was in the days of Noah, so too it will be in the days of the Son of Man. ²⁷They were eating and drinking, and marrying and being given in marriage, until the day Noah entered the ark, and the flood came and destroyed all of them. ²⁸Likewise, just as it was in the days of Lot: they were eating and drinking, buying and selling, planting and building, ²⁹but on the day that Lot left Sodom, it rained fire and sulfur from heaven and destroyed all of them ³⁰—it will be like that on the day that the Son of Man is revealed. ³¹On that day, anyone on the housetop who has belongings in the house must not come down to take them away; and likewise anyone in the field must not turn back. ³²Remember Lot's wife. ³³Those who try to make their life secure will lose it, but those who lose their life will keep it. ³⁴I tell you, on that night there will be two in one bed; one will be taken and the other left. ³⁵There will be two women grinding meal together; one will be taken and the other left."[c] ³⁷Then they asked him, "Where, Lord?" He said to them, "Where the corpse is, there the vultures will gather."

THE PARABLE OF THE WIDOW AND THE UNJUST JUDGE

18 Then Jesus[d] told them a parable about their need to pray always and not to lose heart. ²He said, "In a certain city there was a judge who neither feared God nor had respect for people. ³In that city there was a widow who kept coming to him and saying, 'Grant me justice against my opponent.' ⁴For a while he refused; but later he said to himself, 'Though I have no fear of God and no respect for anyone, ⁵yet because this widow keeps bothering me, I will grant her justice, so that she may not wear me out by continually coming.' "[e] ⁶And the Lord said, "Listen to what the unjust judge says. ⁷And will not God grant justice to his chosen ones who cry to him day and night? Will he delay long in helping them? ⁸I tell you, he will quickly grant justice to them. And yet, when the Son of Man comes, will he find faith on earth?"

a Or within   b Other ancient authorities lack in his day   c Other ancient authorities add verse 36, "Two will be in the field; one will be taken and the other left."   d Gk he   e Or so that she may not finally come and slap me in the face

THE PARABLE OF THE PHARISEE AND THE TAX COLLECTOR

9 He also told this parable to some who trusted in themselves that they were righteous and regarded others with contempt: [10]"Two men went up to the temple to pray, one a Pharisee and the other a tax collector. [11]The Pharisee, standing by himself, was praying thus, 'God, I thank you that I am not like other people: thieves, rogues, adulterers, or even like this tax collector. [12]I fast twice a week; I give a tenth of all my income.' [13]But the tax collector, standing far off, would not even look up to heaven, but was beating his breast and saying, 'God, be merciful to me, a sinner!' [14]I tell you, this man went down to his home justified rather than the other; for all who exalt themselves will be humbled, but all who humble themselves will be exalted."

JESUS BLESSES LITTLE CHILDREN

15 People were bringing even infants to him that he might touch them; and when the disciples saw it, they sternly ordered them not to do it. [16]But Jesus called for them and said, "Let the little children come to me, and do not stop them; for it is to such as these that the kingdom of God belongs. [17]Truly I tell you, whoever does not receive the kingdom of God as a little child will never enter it."

THE RICH RULER

18 A certain ruler asked him, "Good Teacher, what must I do to inherit eternal life?" [19]Jesus said to him, "Why do you call me good? No one is good but God alone. [20]You know the commandments: 'You shall not commit adultery; You shall not murder; You shall not steal; You shall not bear false witness; Honor your father and mother.'" [21]He replied, "I have kept all these since my youth." [22]When Jesus heard this, he said to him, "There is still one thing lacking. Sell all that you own and distribute the money[a] to the poor, and you will have treasure in heaven; then come, follow me." [23]But when he heard this, he became sad; for he was very rich. [24]Jesus looked at him and said, "How hard it is for those who have wealth to enter the kingdom of God! [25]Indeed, it is easier for a camel to go through the eye of a needle than for someone who is rich to enter the kingdom of God."

26 Those who heard it said, "Then who can be saved?" [27]He replied, "What is impossible for mortals is possible for God."

28 Then Peter said, "Look, we have left our homes and followed you." [29]And

---

a Gk lacks *the money*

he said to them, "Truly I tell you, there is no one who has left house or wife or brothers or parents or children, for the sake of the kingdom of God, [30]who will not get back very much more in this age, and in the age to come eternal life."

A THIRD TIME JESUS FORETELLS HIS DEATH AND RESURRECTION

31 Then he took the twelve aside and said to them, "See, we are going up to Jerusalem, and everything that is written about the Son of Man by the prophets will be accomplished. [32]For he will be handed over to the Gentiles; and he will be mocked and insulted and spat upon. [33]After they have flogged him, they will kill him, and on the third day he will rise again." [34]But they understood nothing about all these things; in fact, what he said was hidden from them, and they did not grasp what was said.

JESUS HEALS A BLIND BEGGAR NEAR JERICHO

35 As he approached Jericho, a blind man was sitting by the roadside begging. [36]When he heard a crowd going by, he asked what was happening. [37]They told him, "Jesus of Nazareth[a] is passing by." [38]Then he shouted, "Jesus, Son of David, have mercy on me!" [39]Those who were in front sternly ordered him to be quiet; but he shouted even more loudly, "Son of David, have mercy on me!" [40]Jesus stood still and ordered the man to be brought to him; and when he came near, he asked him, [41]"What do you want me to do for you?" He said, "Lord, let me see again." [42]Jesus said to him, "Receive your sight; your faith has saved you." [43]Immediately he regained his sight and followed him, glorifying God; and all the people, when they saw it, praised God.

JESUS AND ZACCHAEUS

19 He entered Jericho and was passing through it. [2]A man was there named Zacchaeus; he was a chief tax collector and was rich. [3]He was trying to see who Jesus was, but on account of the crowd he could not, because he was short in stature. [4]So he ran ahead and climbed a sycamore tree to see him, because he was going to pass that way. [5]When Jesus came to the place, he looked up and said to him, "Zacchaeus, hurry and come down; for I must stay at your house today." [6]So he hurried down and was happy to welcome him. [7]All who saw it began to grumble and said, "He has gone to be the guest of one who is a sinner." [8]Zacchaeus stood there and said to the Lord, "Look, half of my possessions, Lord, I will give to the poor; and if I have defrauded anyone of anything, I will pay back four times as much." [9]Then Jesus said to him, "Today salvation

---

a Gk the Nazorean

has come to this house, because he too is a son of Abraham. ¹⁰For the Son of Man came to seek out and to save the lost."

THE PARABLE OF THE TEN POUNDS

11 As they were listening to this, he went on to tell a parable, because he was near Jerusalem, and because they supposed that the kingdom of God was to appear immediately. ¹²So he said, "A nobleman went to a distant country to get royal power for himself and then return. ¹³He summoned ten of his slaves, and gave them ten pounds,ᵃ and said to them, 'Do business with these until I come back.' ¹⁴But the citizens of his country hated him and sent a delegation after him, saying, 'We do not want this man to rule over us.' ¹⁵When he returned, having received royal power, he ordered these slaves, to whom he had given the money, to be summoned so that he might find out what they had gained by trading. ¹⁶The first came forward and said, 'Lord, your pound has made ten more pounds.' ¹⁷He said to him, 'Well done, good slave! Because you have been trustworthy in a very small thing, take charge of ten cities.' ¹⁸Then the second came, saying, 'Lord, your pound has made five pounds.' ¹⁹He said to him, 'And you, rule over five cities.' ²⁰Then the other came, saying, 'Lord, here is your pound. I wrapped it up in a piece of cloth, ²¹for I was afraid of you, because you are a harsh man; you take what you did not deposit, and reap what you did not sow.' ²²He said to him, 'I will judge you by your own words, you wicked slave! You knew, did you, that I was a harsh man, taking what I did not deposit and reaping what I did not sow? ²³Why then did you not put my money into the bank? Then when I returned, I could have collected it with interest.' ²⁴He said to the bystanders, 'Take the pound from him and give it to the one who has ten pounds.' ²⁵(And they said to him, 'Lord, he has ten pounds!') ²⁶'I tell you, to all those who have, more will be given; but from those who have nothing, even what they have will be taken away. ²⁷But as for these enemies of mine who did not want me to be king over them—bring them here and slaughter them in my presence.'"

JESUS' TRIUMPHAL ENTRY INTO JERUSALEM

28 After he had said this, he went on ahead, going up to Jerusalem.

29 When he had come near Bethphage and Bethany, at the place called the Mount of Olives, he sent two of the disciples, ³⁰saying, "Go into the village ahead of you, and as you enter it you will find tied there a colt that has never

---

a The mina, rendered here by *pound*, was about three months' wages for a laborer been ridden. Untie it and bring it here. ³¹If anyone asks you, 'Why are you untying it?' just say this, 'The Lord needs it.'" ³²So those who were sent departed and found it as he had told them. ³³As they were untying the colt, its owners asked them, "Why are you untying the colt?" ³⁴They said, "The Lord needs it." ³⁵Then they brought it to Jesus; and after throwing their cloaks on the colt, they set Jesus on it. ³⁶As he rode along, people kept spreading their cloaks on the road. ³⁷As he was now approaching the path down from the Mount of Olives, the whole multitude of the disciples began to praise God joyfully with a loud voice for all the deeds of power that they had seen, ³⁸saying,

> "Blessed is the king
>> who comes in the name of the Lord!
> Peace in heaven,
>> and glory in the highest heaven!"

39 Some of the Pharisees in the crowd said to him, "Teacher, order your disciples to stop." ⁴⁰He answered, "I tell you, if these were silent, the stones would shout out."

JESUS WEEPS OVER JERUSALEM

41 As he came near and saw the city, he wept over it, ⁴²saying, "If you, even you, had only recognized on this day the things that make for peace! But now they are hidden from your eyes. ⁴³Indeed, the days will come upon you, when your enemies will set up ramparts around you and surround you, and hem you in on every side. ⁴⁴They will crush you to the ground, you and your children within you, and they will not leave within you one stone upon another; because you did not recognize the time of your visitation from God."[a]

JESUS CLEANSES THE TEMPLE

45 Then he entered the temple and began to drive out those who were selling things there; ⁴⁶and he said, "It is written,

> 'My house shall be a house of prayer';
>> but you have made it a den of robbers."

47 Every day he was teaching in the temple. The chief priests, the scribes, and the leaders of the people kept looking for a way to kill him; ⁴⁸but they did not find anything they could do, for all the people were spellbound by what they heard.

---

a Gk lacks *from God*

THE AUTHORITY OF JESUS QUESTIONED

20 One day, as he was teaching the people in the temple and telling the good news, the chief priests and the scribes came with the elders ²and said to him, "Tell us, by what authority are you doing these things? Who is it who gave you this authority?" ³He answered them, "I will also ask you a question, and you tell me: ⁴Did the baptism of John come from heaven, or was it of human origin?" ⁵They discussed it with one another, saying, "If we say, 'From heaven,' he will say, 'Why did you not believe him?' ⁶But if we say, 'Of human origin,' all the people will stone us; for they are convinced that John was a prophet." ⁷So they answered that they did not know where it came from. ⁸Then Jesus said to them, "Neither will I tell you by what authority I am doing these things."

THE PARABLE OF THE WICKED TENANTS

9 He began to tell the people this parable: "A man planted a vineyard, and leased it to tenants, and went to another country for a long time. ¹⁰When the season came, he sent a slave to the tenants in order that they might give him his share of the produce of the vineyard; but the tenants beat him and sent him away empty-handed. ¹¹Next he sent another slave; that one also they beat and insulted and sent away empty-handed. ¹²And he sent still a third; this one also they wounded and threw out. ¹³Then the owner of the vineyard said, 'What shall I do? I will send my beloved son; perhaps they will respect him.' ¹⁴But when the tenants saw him, they discussed it among themselves and said, 'This is the heir; let us kill him so that the inheritance may be ours.' ¹⁵So they threw him out of the vineyard and killed him. What then will the owner of the vineyard do to them? ¹⁶He will come and destroy those tenants and give the vineyard to others." When they heard this, they said, "Heaven forbid!" ¹⁷But he looked at them and said, "What then does this text mean:

'The stone that the builders rejected
    has become the cornerstone'?ᵃ

18 Everyone who falls on that stone will be broken to pieces; and it will crush anyone on whom it falls." ¹⁹When the scribes and chief priests realized that he had told this parable against them, they wanted to lay hands on him at that very hour, but they feared the people.

---

a Or keystone

THE QUESTION ABOUT PAYING TAXES

20 So they watched him and sent spies who pretended to be honest, in order to trap him by what he said, so as to hand him over to the jurisdiction and authority of the governor. ²¹So they asked him, "Teacher, we know that you are right in what you say and teach, and you show deference to no one, but teach the way of God in accordance with truth. ²²Is it lawful for us to pay taxes to the emperor, or not?" ²³But he perceived their craftiness and said to them, ²⁴"Show me a denarius. Whose head and whose title does it bear?" They said, "The emperor's." ²⁵He said to them, "Then give to the emperor the things that are the emperor's, and to God the things that are God's." ²⁶And they were not able in the presence of the people to trap him by what he said; and being amazed by his answer, they became silent.

THE QUESTION ABOUT THE RESURRECTION

27 Some Sadducees, those who say there is no resurrection, came to him ²⁸and asked him a question, "Teacher, Moses wrote for us that if a man's brother dies, leaving a wife but no children, the man*^a* shall marry the widow and raise up children for his brother. ²⁹Now there were seven brothers; the first married, and died childless; ³⁰then the second ³¹and the third married her, and so in the same way all seven died childless. ³²Finally the woman also died. ³³In the resurrection, therefore, whose wife will the woman be? For the seven had married her."

34 Jesus said to them, "Those who belong to this age marry and are given in marriage; ³⁵but those who are considered worthy of a place in that age and in the resurrection from the dead neither marry nor are given in marriage. ³⁶Indeed they cannot die anymore, because they are like angels and are children of God, being children of the resurrection. ³⁷And the fact that the dead are raised Moses himself showed, in the story about the bush, where he speaks of the Lord as the God of Abraham, the God of Isaac, and the God of Jacob. ³⁸Now he is God not of the dead, but of the living; for to him all of them are alive." ³⁹Then some of the scribes answered, "Teacher, you have spoken well." ⁴⁰For they no longer dared to ask him another question.

THE QUESTION ABOUT DAVID'S SON

41 Then he said to them, "How can they say that the Messiah*^b* is David's son? ⁴²For David himself says in the book of Psalms,

---

a Gk *his brother* *b* Or *the Christ*

'The Lord said to my Lord,
   "Sit at my right hand,
   43 until I make your enemies your footstool."'
44 David thus calls him Lord; so how can he be his son?"

JESUS DENOUNCES THE SCRIBES

45 In the hearing of all the people he said to the[a] disciples, [46]"Beware of the scribes, who like to walk around in long robes, and love to be greeted with respect in the marketplaces, and to have the best seats in the synagogues and places of honor at banquets. [47]They devour widows' houses and for the sake of appearance say long prayers. They will receive the greater condemnation."

THE WIDOW'S OFFERING

21 He looked up and saw rich people putting their gifts into the treasury; [2]he also saw a poor widow put in two small copper coins. [3]He said, "Truly I tell you, this poor widow has put in more than all of them; [4]for all of them have contributed out of their abundance, but she out of her poverty has put in all she had to live on."

THE DESTRUCTION OF THE TEMPLE FORETOLD

5 When some were speaking about the temple, how it was adorned with beautiful stones and gifts dedicated to God, he said, [6]"As for these things that you see, the days will come when not one stone will be left upon another; all will be thrown down."

SIGNS AND PERSECUTIONS

7 They asked him, "Teacher, when will this be, and what will be the sign that this is about to take place?" [8]And he said, "Beware that you are not led astray; for many will come in my name and say, 'I am he!'[b] and, 'The time is near!'[c] Do not go after them.

9 "When you hear of wars and insurrections, do not be terrified; for these things must take place first, but the end will not follow immediately." [10]Then he said to them, "Nation will rise against nation, and kingdom against kingdom; [11]there will be great earthquakes, and in various places famines and plagues; and there will be dreadful portents and great signs from heaven.

12 "But before all this occurs, they will arrest you and persecute you; they

---

a Other ancient authorities read *his* *b* Gk *I am* *c* Or *at hand* will hand you over to synagogues and prisons, and you will be brought before kings and governors because of my name. [13]This will give you an opportunity to testify. [14]So make up your minds not to prepare your defense in advance; [15]for I will give you words[a] and a wisdom that none of your opponents will be able to withstand or contradict. [16]You will be betrayed even by parents and brothers, by relatives and friends; and they will put some of you to death. [17]You will be hated by all because of my name. [18]But not a hair of your head will perish. [19]By your endurance you will gain your souls.

THE DESTRUCTION OF JERUSALEM FORETOLD

20 "When you see Jerusalem surrounded by armies, then know that its desolation has come near.[b] [21]Then those in Judea must flee to the mountains, and those inside the city must leave it, and those out in the country must not enter it; [22]for these are days of vengeance, as a fulfillment of all that is written. [23]Woe to those who are pregnant and to those who are nursing infants in those days! For there will be great distress on the earth and wrath against this people; [24]they will fall by the edge of the sword and be taken away as captives among all nations; and Jerusalem will be trampled on by the Gentiles, until the times of the Gentiles are fulfilled.

THE COMING OF THE SON OF MAN

25 "There will be signs in the sun, the moon, and the stars, and on the earth distress among nations confused by the roaring of the sea and the waves. [26]People will faint from fear and foreboding of what is coming upon the world, for the powers of the heavens will be shaken. [27]Then they will see 'the Son of Man coming in a cloud' with power and great glory. [28]Now when these things begin to take place, stand up and raise your heads, because your redemption is drawing near."

THE LESSON OF THE FIG TREE

29 Then he told them a parable: "Look at the fig tree and all the trees; [30]as soon as they sprout leaves you can see for yourselves and know that summer is already near. [31]So also, when you see these things taking place, you know that the kingdom of God is near. [32]Truly I tell you, this generation will not pass away until all things have taken place. [33]Heaven and earth will pass away, but my words will not pass away.

---

a Gk *a mouth* *b* Or *is at hand*

EXHORTATION TO WATCH

34 "Be on guard so that your hearts are not weighed down with dissipation and drunkenness and the worries of this life, and that day does not catch you unexpectedly, ³⁵like a trap. For it will come upon all who live on the face of the whole earth. ³⁶Be alert at all times, praying that you may have the strength to escape all these things that will take place, and to stand before the Son of Man."

37 Every day he was teaching in the temple, and at night he would go out and spend the night on the Mount of Olives, as it was called. ³⁸And all the people would get up early in the morning to listen to him in the temple.

THE PLOT TO KILL JESUS

22 Now the festival of Unleavened Bread, which is called the Passover, was near. ²The chief priests and the scribes were looking for a way to put Jesus*ᵃ* to death, for they were afraid of the people.

3 Then Satan entered into Judas called Iscariot, who was one of the twelve; ⁴he went away and conferred with the chief priests and officers of the temple police about how he might betray him to them. ⁵They were greatly pleased and agreed to give him money. ⁶So he consented and began to look for an opportunity to betray him to them when no crowd was present.

THE PREPARATION OF THE PASSOVER

7 Then came the day of Unleavened Bread, on which the Passover lamb had to be sacrificed. ⁸So Jesus*ᵇ* sent Peter and John, saying, "Go and prepare the Passover meal for us that we may eat it." ⁹They asked him, "Where do you want us to make preparations for it?" ¹⁰"Listen," he said to them, "when you have entered the city, a man carrying a jar of water will meet you; follow him into the house he enters ¹¹and say to the owner of the house, 'The teacher asks you, "Where is the guest room, where I may eat the Passover with my disciples?" ' ¹²He will show you a large room upstairs, already furnished. Make preparations for us there." ¹³So they went and found everything as he had told them; and they prepared the Passover meal.

THE INSTITUTION OF THE LORD'S SUPPER

14 When the hour came, he took his place at the table, and the apostles with him. ¹⁵He said to them, "I have eagerly desired to eat this Passover with you before I suffer; ¹⁶for I tell you, I will not eat it*ᶜ* until it is fulfilled in the kingdom

---

a Gk *him*   *b* Gk *he*   *c* Other ancient authorities read *never eat it again* of God." ¹⁷Then he took a cup, and after giving thanks he said, "Take this and divide it among yourselves; ¹⁸for I tell you that from now on I will not drink of the fruit of the vine until the kingdom of God comes." ¹⁹Then he took a loaf of bread, and when he had given thanks, he broke it and gave it to them, saying, "This is my body, which is given for you. Do this in remembrance of me." ²⁰And he did the same with the cup after supper, saying, "This cup that is poured out for you is the new covenant in my blood.ᵃ ²¹But see, the one who betrays me is with me, and his hand is on the table. ²²For the Son of Man is going as it has been determined, but woe to that one by whom he is betrayed!" ²³Then they began to ask one another which one of them it could be who would do this.

THE DISPUTE ABOUT GREATNESS

24 A dispute also arose among them as to which one of them was to be regarded as the greatest. ²⁵But he said to them, "The kings of the Gentiles lord it over them; and those in authority over them are called benefactors. ²⁶But not so with you; rather the greatest among you must become like the youngest, and the leader like one who serves. ²⁷For who is greater, the one who is at the table or the one who serves? Is it not the one at the table? But I am among you as one who serves.

28 "You are those who have stood by me in my trials; ²⁹and I confer on you, just as my Father has conferred on me, a kingdom, ³⁰so that you may eat and drink at my table in my kingdom, and you will sit on thrones judging the twelve tribes of Israel.

JESUS PREDICTS PETER'S DENIAL

31 "Simon, Simon, listen! Satan has demandedᵇ to sift all of you like wheat, ³²but I have prayed for you that your own faith may not fail; and you, when once you have turned back, strengthen your brothers." ³³And he said to him, "Lord, I am ready to go with you to prison and to death!" ³⁴Jesusᶜ said, "I tell you, Peter, the cock will not crow this day, until you have denied three times that you know me."

PURSE, BAG, AND SWORD

35 He said to them, "When I sent you out without a purse, bag, or sandals, did you lack anything?" They said, "No, not a thing." ³⁶He said to them, "But now, the one who has a purse must take it, and likewise a bag. And the one who has

---

a Other ancient authorities lack, in whole or in part, verses 19b–20 (which is given . . . in my blood)   b Or has obtained permission   c Gk He no sword must sell his cloak and buy one. ³⁷For I tell you, this scripture must be fulfilled in me, 'And he was counted among the lawless'; and indeed what is written about me is being fulfilled." ³⁸They said, "Lord, look, here are two swords." He replied, "It is enough."

JESUS PRAYS ON THE MOUNT OF OLIVES

39 He came out and went, as was his custom, to the Mount of Olives; and the disciples followed him. ⁴⁰When he reached the place, he said to them, "Pray that you may not come into the time of trial."ᵃ ⁴¹Then he withdrew from them about a stone's throw, knelt down, and prayed, ⁴²"Father, if you are willing, remove this cup from me; yet, not my will but yours be done." [[⁴³Then an angel from heaven appeared to him and gave him strength. ⁴⁴In his anguish he prayed more earnestly, and his sweat became like great drops of blood falling down on the ground.]]ᵇ ⁴⁵When he got up from prayer, he came to the disciples and found them sleeping because of grief, ⁴⁶and he said to them, "Why are you sleeping? Get up and pray that you may not come into the time of trial."ᵃ

THE BETRAYAL AND ARREST OF JESUS

47 While he was still speaking, suddenly a crowd came, and the one called Judas, one of the twelve, was leading them. He approached Jesus to kiss him; ⁴⁸but Jesus said to him, "Judas, is it with a kiss that you are betraying the Son of Man?" ⁴⁹When those who were around him saw what was coming, they asked, "Lord, should we strike with the sword?" ⁵⁰Then one of them struck the slave of the high priest and cut off his right ear. ⁵¹But Jesus said, "No more of this!" And he touched his ear and healed him. ⁵²Then Jesus said to the chief priests, the officers of the temple police, and the elders who had come for him, "Have you come out with swords and clubs as if I were a bandit? ⁵³When I was with you day after day in the temple, you did not lay hands on me. But this is your hour, and the power of darkness!"

PETER DENIES JESUS

54 Then they seized him and led him away, bringing him into the high priest's house. But Peter was following at a distance. ⁵⁵When they had kindled a fire in the middle of the courtyard and sat down together, Peter sat among them. ⁵⁶Then a servant-girl, seeing him in the firelight, stared at him and said, "This man also was with him." ⁵⁷But he denied it, saying, "Woman, I do not know him." ⁵⁸A little later someone else, on seeing him, said, "You also are one of

---

a Or *into temptation*　*b* Other ancient authorities lack verses 43 and 44 them." But Peter said, "Man, I am not!" [59]Then about an hour later still another kept insisting, "Surely this man also was with him; for he is a Galilean." [60]But Peter said, "Man, I do not know what you are talking about!" At that moment, while he was still speaking, the cock crowed. [61]The Lord turned and looked at Peter. Then Peter remembered the word of the Lord, how he had said to him, "Before the cock crows today, you will deny me three times." [62]And he went out and wept bitterly.

THE MOCKING AND BEATING OF JESUS

63 Now the men who were holding Jesus began to mock him and beat him; [64]they also blindfolded him and kept asking him, "Prophesy! Who is it that struck you?" [65]They kept heaping many other insults on him.

JESUS BEFORE THE COUNCIL

66 When day came, the assembly of the elders of the people, both chief priests and scribes, gathered together, and they brought him to their council. [67]They said, "If you are the Messiah,[a] tell us." He replied, "If I tell you, you will not believe; [68]and if I question you, you will not answer. [69]But from now on the Son of Man will be seated at the right hand of the power of God." [70]All of them asked, "Are you, then, the Son of God?" He said to them, "You say that I am." [71]Then they said, "What further testimony do we need? We have heard it ourselves from his own lips!"

JESUS BEFORE PILATE

23 Then the assembly rose as a body and brought Jesus[b] before Pilate. [2]They began to accuse him, saying, "We found this man perverting our nation, forbidding us to pay taxes to the emperor, and saying that he himself is the Messiah, a king."[c] [3]Then Pilate asked him, "Are you the king of the Jews?" He answered, "You say so." [4]Then Pilate said to the chief priests and the crowds, "I find no basis for an accusation against this man." [5]But they were insistent and said, "He stirs up the people by teaching throughout all Judea, from Galilee where he began even to this place."

JESUS BEFORE HEROD

6 When Pilate heard this, he asked whether the man was a Galilean. [7]And when he learned that he was under Herod's jurisdiction, he sent him off to Herod, who was himself in Jerusalem at that time. [8]When Herod saw Jesus, he was

---

a Or *the Christ*   *b* Gk *him*   *c* Or *is an anointed king* very glad, for he had been wanting to see him for a long time, because he had heard about him and was hoping to see him perform some sign. ⁹He questioned him at some length, but Jesus*ᵃ* gave him no answer. ¹⁰The chief priests and the scribes stood by, vehemently accusing him. ¹¹Even Herod with his soldiers treated him with contempt and mocked him; then he put an elegant robe on him, and sent him back to Pilate. ¹²That same day Herod and Pilate became friends with each other; before this they had been enemies.

JESUS SENTENCED TO DEATH

13 Pilate then called together the chief priests, the leaders, and the people, ¹⁴and said to them, "You brought me this man as one who was perverting the people; and here I have examined him in your presence and have not found this man guilty of any of your charges against him. ¹⁵Neither has Herod, for he sent him back to us. Indeed, he has done nothing to deserve death. ¹⁶I will therefore have him flogged and release him."*ᵇ*

18 Then they all shouted out together, "Away with this fellow! Release Barabbas for us!" ¹⁹(This was a man who had been put in prison for an insurrection that had taken place in the city, and for murder.) ²⁰Pilate, wanting to release Jesus, addressed them again; ²¹but they kept shouting, "Crucify, crucify him!" ²²A third time he said to them, "Why, what evil has he done? I have found in him no ground for the sentence of death; I will therefore have him flogged and then release him." ²³But they kept urgently demanding with loud shouts that he should be crucified; and their voices prevailed. ²⁴So Pilate gave his verdict that their demand should be granted. ²⁵He released the man they asked for, the one who had been put in prison for insurrection and murder, and he handed Jesus over as they wished.

THE CRUCIFIXION OF JESUS

26 As they led him away, they seized a man, Simon of Cyrene, who was coming from the country, and they laid the cross on him, and made him carry it behind Jesus. ²⁷A great number of the people followed him, and among them were women who were beating their breasts and wailing for him. ²⁸But Jesus turned to them and said, "Daughters of Jerusalem, do not weep for me, but weep for yourselves and for your children. ²⁹For the days are surely coming when they will say, 'Blessed are the barren, and the wombs that never bore, and the breasts that never nursed.' ³⁰Then they will begin to say to the mountains, 'Fall on us';

---

a Gk *he*   *b* Here, or after verse 19, other ancient authorities add verse 17, *Now he was obliged to release someone for them at the festival* and to the hills, 'Cover us.' ³¹For if they do this when the wood is green, what will happen when it is dry?"

32 Two others also, who were criminals, were led away to be put to death with him. ³³When they came to the place that is called The Skull, they crucified Jesus*a* there with the criminals, one on his right and one on his left. [[³⁴Then Jesus said, "Father, forgive them; for they do not know what they are doing."]]*b* And they cast lots to divide his clothing. ³⁵And the people stood by, watching; but the leaders scoffed at him, saying, "He saved others; let him save himself if he is the Messiah*c* of God, his chosen one!" ³⁶The soldiers also mocked him, coming up and offering him sour wine, ³⁷and saying, "If you are the King of the Jews, save yourself!" ³⁸There was also an inscription over him,*d* "This is the King of the Jews."

39 One of the criminals who were hanged there kept deriding*e* him and saying, "Are you not the Messiah?*c* Save yourself and us!" ⁴⁰But the other rebuked him, saying, "Do you not fear God, since you are under the same sentence of condemnation? ⁴¹And we indeed have been condemned justly, for we are getting what we deserve for our deeds, but this man has done nothing wrong." ⁴²Then he said, "Jesus, remember me when you come into*f* your kingdom." ⁴³He replied, "Truly I tell you, today you will be with me in Paradise."

THE DEATH OF JESUS

44 It was now about noon, and darkness came over the whole land*g* until three in the afternoon, ⁴⁵while the sun's light failed;*h* and the curtain of the temple was torn in two. ⁴⁶Then Jesus, crying with a loud voice, said, "Father, into your hands I commend my spirit." Having said this, he breathed his last. ⁴⁷When the centurion saw what had taken place, he praised God and said, "Certainly this man was innocent."*i* ⁴⁸And when all the crowds who had gathered there for this spectacle saw what had taken place, they returned home, beating their breasts. ⁴⁹But all his acquaintances, including the women who had followed him from Galilee, stood at a distance, watching these things.

THE BURIAL OF JESUS

50 Now there was a good and righteous man named Joseph, who, though a member of the council, ⁵¹had not agreed to their plan and action. He came from the Jewish town of Arimathea, and he was waiting expectantly for the kingdom of God. ⁵²This man went to Pilate and asked for the body of Jesus.

---

a Gk *him*   b Other ancient authorities lack the sentence *Then Jesus . . . what they are doing*   c Or *the Christ*   d Other ancient
authorities add *written in Greek and Latin and Hebrew* (that is, *Aramaic*)   e Or *blaspheming*   f Other ancient authorities read *in*
g Or *earth*   h Or *the sun was eclipsed*. Other ancient authorities read *the sun was darkened*   i Or *righteous*

⁵³Then he took it down, wrapped it in a linen cloth, and laid it in a rock-hewn tomb where no one had ever been laid. ⁵⁴It was the day of Preparation, and the sabbath was beginning.ᵃ ⁵⁵The women who had come with him from Galilee followed, and they saw the tomb and how his body was laid. ⁵⁶Then they returned, and prepared spices and ointments.

On the sabbath they rested according to the commandment.

THE RESURRECTION OF JESUS

24 But on the first day of the week, at early dawn, they came to the tomb, taking the spices that they had prepared. ²They found the stone rolled away from the tomb, ³but when they went in, they did not find the body.ᵇ ⁴While they were perplexed about this, suddenly two men in dazzling clothes stood beside them. ⁵The womenᶜ were terrified and bowed their faces to the ground, but the menᵈ said to them, "Why do you look for the living among the dead? He is not here, but has risen.ᵉ ⁶Remember how he told you, while he was still in Galilee, ⁷that the Son of Man must be handed over to sinners, and be crucified, and on the third day rise again." ⁸Then they remembered his words, ⁹and returning from the tomb, they told all this to the eleven and to all the rest. ¹⁰Now it was Mary Magdalene, Joanna, Mary the mother of James, and the other women with them who told this to the apostles. ¹¹But these words seemed to them an idle tale, and they did not believe them. ¹²But Peter got up and ran to the tomb; stooping and looking in, he saw the linen cloths by themselves; then he went home, amazed at what had happened.ᶠ

THE WALK TO EMMAUS

13 Now on that same day two of them were going to a village called Emmaus, about seven milesᵍ from Jerusalem, ¹⁴and talking with each other about all these things that had happened. ¹⁵While they were talking and discussing, Jesus himself came near and went with them, ¹⁶but their eyes were kept from recognizing him. ¹⁷And he said to them, "What are you discussing with each other while you walk along?" They stood still, looking sad.ʰ ¹⁸Then one of them, whose name was Cleopas, answered him, "Are you the only stranger in Jerusalem who does not know the things that have taken place there in these days?" ¹⁹He asked them, "What things?" They replied, "The things about Jesus of Nazareth,ⁱ who was a prophet mighty in deed and word before God and all

---

a Gk *was dawning* b Other ancient authorities add *of the Lord Jesus* c Gk *They* d Gk *but they* e Other ancient authorities lack *He is not here, but has risen* f Other ancient authorities lack verse 12 g Gk *sixty stadia;* other ancient authorities read *a hundred sixty stadia* h Other ancient authorities read *walk along, looking sad?"* i Other ancient authorities read *Jesus the Nazorean* the people, [20]and how our chief priests and leaders handed him over to be condemned to death and crucified him. [21]But we had hoped that he was the one to redeem Israel.[a] Yes, and besides all this, it is now the third day since these things took place. [22]Moreover, some women of our group astounded us. They were at the tomb early this morning, [23]and when they did not find his body there, they came back and told us that they had indeed seen a vision of angels who said that he was alive. [24]Some of those who were with us went to the tomb and found it just as the women had said; but they did not see him." [25]Then he said to them, "Oh, how foolish you are, and how slow of heart to believe all that the prophets have declared! [26]Was it not necessary that the Messiah[b] should suffer these things and then enter into his glory?" [27]Then beginning with Moses and all the prophets, he interpreted to them the things about himself in all the scriptures.

28 As they came near the village to which they were going, he walked ahead as if he were going on. [29]But they urged him strongly, saying, "Stay with us, because it is almost evening and the day is now nearly over." So he went in to stay with them. [30]When he was at the table with them, he took bread, blessed and broke it, and gave it to them. [31]Then their eyes were opened, and they recognized him; and he vanished from their sight. [32]They said to each other, "Were not our hearts burning within us[c] while he was talking to us on the road, while he was opening the scriptures to us?" [33]That same hour they got up and returned to Jerusalem; and they found the eleven and their companions gathered together. [34]They were saying, "The Lord has risen indeed, and he has appeared to Simon!" [35]Then they told what had happened on the road, and how he had been made known to them in the breaking of the bread.

JESUS APPEARS TO HIS DISCIPLES

36 While they were talking about this, Jesus himself stood among them and said to them, "Peace be with you."[d] [37]They were startled and terrified, and thought that they were seeing a ghost. [38]He said to them, "Why are you frightened, and why do doubts arise in your hearts? [39]Look at my hands and my feet; see that it is I myself. Touch me and see; for a ghost does not have flesh and bones as you see that I have." [40]And when he had said this, he showed them his hands and his feet.[e] [41]While in their joy they were disbelieving and still wondering, he said to them, "Have you anything here to eat?" [42]They gave him a piece of broiled fish, [43]and he took it and ate in their presence.

---

a Or *to set Israel free*   b Or *the Christ*   c Other ancient authorities lack *within us*   d Other ancient authorities lack *and said to them, "Peace be with you."*   e Other ancient authorities lack verse 40

44 Then he said to them, "These are my words that I spoke to you while I was still with you—that everything written about me in the law of Moses, the prophets, and the psalms must be fulfilled." ⁴⁵Then he opened their minds to understand the scriptures, ⁴⁶and he said to them, "Thus it is written, that the Messiah* is to suffer and to rise from the dead on the third day, ⁴⁷and that repentance and forgiveness of sins is to be proclaimed in his name to all nations, beginning from Jerusalem. ⁴⁸You are witnesses* of these things. ⁴⁹And see, I am sending upon you what my Father promised; so stay here in the city until you have been clothed with power from on high."

THE ASCENSION OF JESUS

50 Then he led them out as far as Bethany, and, lifting up his hands, he blessed them. ⁵¹While he was blessing them, he withdrew from them and was carried up into heaven.* ⁵²And they worshiped him, and* returned to Jerusalem with great joy; ⁵³and they were continually in the temple blessing God.*

---

a Or *the Christ*   b Or *nations. Beginning from Jerusalem* ⁴⁸*you are witnesses*   c Other ancient authorities lack *and was carried up into heaven*   d Other ancient authorities lack *worshiped him, and*   e Other ancient authorities add *Amen*

Acts

As mentioned in the introduction to Luke, both Luke and Acts were written by the same author, they share major themes in common, and there are reasons for dating them early in the second century.

A Story of Expansion

Acts is the story of the expansion of the Jesus movement from the Jewish homeland into the Gentile world and ultimately to Rome. The theme is announced in 1.8, the final words of Jesus to his followers just before his ascension into heaven: "You will be my witnesses in Jerusalem, in all Judea and Samaria, and to the ends of the earth."

This geographical expansion structures the book. Chapters 1–7 take place in Jerusalem. At the beginning of chapter 8, persecution scatters Jesus's followers into Judea and Samaria (8.1). By chapter 9, the movement has reached Damascus in Syria. Chapters 10–12 are transitional; though set in the Jewish homeland, they narrate Peter's conversion to accepting Gentiles, thus presaging the mission to the Gentile world that dominates the rest of Acts (chaps. 13–28). The general directional pattern is to the north and west, from Syria to Cyprus and central and western Asia Minor, then to Greece and Rome.

Expansion into the Gentile world raised a major issue in early Christianity that Paul also addressed, especially in Galatians; namely, under what conditions may Gentiles become part of Christ-communities? Do Gentile males need to be circumcised? Do Gentile converts, male and female, need to observe at least some of the Jewish law? Must they in effect become Jewish in order to be Christian?

According to Acts 15, this issue was resolved early on at a meeting of Jesus's followers in Jerusalem around the year 50. Often called the Jerusalem Council, it was convened especially to address the question of whether "it is necessary for them [Gentiles] to be circumcised and ordered to keep the law of Moses" (15.5). The verdict of "the apostles and the elders, with the consent of the whole" (15.22) invokes the guidance and blessing of the Holy Spirit: "It has seemed good to the Holy Spirit and to us to impose on you [Gentiles] no further burden" (15.28). Gentiles need not be circumcised and need not observe Jewish laws except for a few general essentials.

Thus, as Acts tells the story, the Gentile mission was approved by unanimous consent of Christian Jewish leaders in Jerusalem—and before most of Paul's activity among Gentiles. Thus what Paul did was in accord with the directions of the Jerusalem community. It is a story of early Christian unity. Indeed, according to the two volumes of Luke and Acts, the mission to the Gentiles was prefigured in the story of Jesus from its beginning—in his birth story and in the story of his "inaugural address." It was even anticipated in the Old Testament. It was "writ."

Scholars suspect that this portrayal of early Christian unity is an idealized picture projected backward from the time when Acts was written early in the second century. By then, Christ-communities containing many Gentiles (including "God-lovers") had become common in Gentile areas of the empire. Mixed communities of Christian Gentiles and Christian Jews were probably the norm, though some communities may have been primarily Gentile. From the author's place in time, what had happened was approved, even destined, from the beginning.

Acts and Paul

Paul is the central character in Acts. He first appears in chapter 7, consenting to the stoning of Stephen. Chapter 9 narrates his conversion experience and its immediate aftermath (repeated with somewhat different details in chapters 22 and 26). From chapter 13 on, every chapter is about Paul—well over half of Acts.

What are commonly called "Paul's three missionary journeys" dominate the middle of Acts (chaps. 13–20). All began in Antioch in Syria. On the first, he went from Antioch to cities in Cyprus and central Asia Minor and returned to Antioch. On the second, he went from Antioch to cities in central and western Asia Minor—and then to Europe, specifically Greece. On the third, he went from Antioch through Asia Minor to Ephesus and then north along its west coast and once again to cities in Greece. The return was mostly by sea, as he made his way to the journey's end in Jerusalem.

The rest of Acts—over a fourth—is the story of Paul's journey to Jerusalem, arrest, imprisonment, and arrival in Rome in chains (chaps. 21–28). Though Acts does not narrate the death of Paul, these chapters are Paul's passion story. Just as the story of Jesus's journey to Jerusalem and passion dominate the last part of the gospels, so the story of Paul's passion dominates the last part of Acts.

In Acts 20.17–38, Paul anticipates his death, just as Jesus does in Luke (and in all the gospels). On his sea trip to Jerusalem, Paul stops in Miletus, a city on the west coast of Asia Minor, in order to meet with elders of the Christ-community from nearby Ephesus. He tells them he is going to Jerusalem and that none of them "will ever see [his] face again" (20.25). At the end of the powerfully described scene, they are praying, weeping, embracing, and "grieving, especially because of what [Paul] had said, that they would not see him again" (20.37–38).

In Acts 21, Paul arrives in Jerusalem. By the end of the chapter, he has been attacked by a Jewish mob and arrested (and rescued by a Roman tribune, a military rank above centurion). For the rest of Acts, Paul is a prisoner. Though Roman officials again and again find no reason to confine him, "the Jews" and Jewish authorities insist that action be taken against him. According to Acts, Paul did not challenge Roman imperial authority. Rather, Jewish acrimony was responsible for the accusations made against him. Rome saw no problem with him. The Jews did.

Acts ends with Paul under house arrest in Rome. There he preached and taught (28.23–31). He "welcomed all who came to him, proclaiming the kingdom of God and teaching about the Lord Jesus Christ" (28.30–31). Some Jews responded, but others did not. Paul's final words affirm the mission to the Gentiles: the "salvation of God has been sent to the Gentiles; they will listen" (28.28).

Yet Paul was executed in Rome by Roman authority. As already mentioned, the author of Acts does not report this. It would have undermined his portrait of early Christianity as posing no challenge or threat to the imperial way of ordering the world. Acts, even though it contains the memory of Jesus's followers "turning the world upside down," is also an early second-century Christian accommodation to life within the empire. It belongs with other New Testament documents accommodating the early Christian movement to life in "this world."

THE

Acts

OF THE APOSTLES

THE PROMISE OF THE HOLY SPIRIT

1 In the first book, Theophilus, I wrote about all that Jesus did and taught from the beginning ²until the day when he was taken up to heaven, after giving instructions through the Holy Spirit to the apostles whom he had chosen. ³After his suffering he presented himself alive to them by many convincing proofs, appearing to them during forty days and speaking about the kingdom of God. ⁴While staying*ᵃ* with them, he ordered them not to leave Jerusalem, but to wait there for the promise of the Father. "This," he said, "is what you have heard from me; ⁵for John baptized with water, but you will be baptized with*ᵇ* the Holy Spirit not many days from now."

THE ASCENSION OF JESUS

6 So when they had come together, they asked him, "Lord, is this the time when you will restore the kingdom to Israel?" ⁷He replied, "It is not for you to know the times or periods that the Father has set by his own authority. ⁸But you will receive power when the Holy Spirit has come upon you; and you will be my witnesses in Jerusalem, in all Judea and Samaria, and to the ends of the earth." ⁹When he had said this, as they were watching, he was lifted up, and a cloud took him out of their sight. ¹⁰While he was going and they were gazing up toward heaven, suddenly two men in white robes stood by them. ¹¹They said, "Men of Galilee, why do you stand looking up toward heaven? This Jesus, who

---

a Or *eating* *b* Or *by*

has been taken up from you into heaven, will come in the same way as you saw him go into heaven."

MATTHIAS CHOSEN TO REPLACE JUDAS

12 Then they returned to Jerusalem from the mount called Olivet, which is near Jerusalem, a sabbath day's journey away. [13]When they had entered the city, they went to the room upstairs where they were staying, Peter, and John, and James, and Andrew, Philip and Thomas, Bartholomew and Matthew, James son of Alphaeus, and Simon the Zealot, and Judas son of[a] James. [14]All these were constantly devoting themselves to prayer, together with certain women, including Mary the mother of Jesus, as well as his brothers.

15 In those days Peter stood up among the believers[b] (together the crowd numbered about one hundred twenty persons) and said, [16]"Friends,[c] the scripture had to be fulfilled, which the Holy Spirit through David foretold concerning Judas, who became a guide for those who arrested Jesus— [17]for he was numbered among us and was allotted his share in this ministry." [18](Now this man acquired a field with the reward of his wickedness; and falling headlong,[d] he burst open in the middle and all his bowels gushed out. [19]This became known to all the residents of Jerusalem, so that the field was called in their language Hakeldama, that is, Field of Blood.) [20]"For it is written in the book of Psalms,

> 'Let his homestead become desolate,
>> and let there be no one to live in it';

and

>> 'Let another take his position of overseer.'

21 So one of the men who have accompanied us during all the time that the Lord Jesus went in and out among us, [22]beginning from the baptism of John until the day when he was taken up from us—one of these must become a witness with us to his resurrection." [23]So they proposed two, Joseph called Barsabbas, who was also known as Justus, and Matthias. [24]Then they prayed and said, "Lord, you know everyone's heart. Show us which one of these two you have chosen [25]to take the place[e] in this ministry and apostleship from which Judas turned aside to go to his own place." [26]And they cast lots for them, and the lot fell on Matthias; and he was added to the eleven apostles.

THE COMING OF THE HOLY SPIRIT

2 When the day of Pentecost had come, they were all together in one place. [2]And suddenly from heaven there came a sound like the rush of a violent

---

a Or the brother of   b Gk brothers   c Gk Men, brothers   d Or swelling up   e Other ancient authorities read the share wind, and it filled the entire house where they were sitting. ³Divided tongues, as of fire, appeared among them, and a tongue rested on each of them. ⁴All of them were filled with the Holy Spirit and began to speak in other languages, as the Spirit gave them ability.

5 Now there were devout Jews from every nation under heaven living in Jerusalem. ⁶And at this sound the crowd gathered and was bewildered, because each one heard them speaking in the native language of each. ⁷Amazed and astonished, they asked, "Are not all these who are speaking Galileans? ⁸And how is it that we hear, each of us, in our own native language? ⁹Parthians, Medes, Elamites, and residents of Mesopotamia, Judea and Cappadocia, Pontus and Asia, ¹⁰Phrygia and Pamphylia, Egypt and the parts of Libya belonging to Cyrene, and visitors from Rome, both Jews and proselytes, ¹¹Cretans and Arabs—in our own languages we hear them speaking about God's deeds of power." ¹²All were amazed and perplexed, saying to one another, "What does this mean?" ¹³But others sneered and said, "They are filled with new wine."

PETER ADDRESSES THE CROWD

14 But Peter, standing with the eleven, raised his voice and addressed them, "Men of Judea and all who live in Jerusalem, let this be known to you, and listen to what I say. ¹⁵Indeed, these are not drunk, as you suppose, for it is only nine o'clock in the morning. ¹⁶No, this is what was spoken through the prophet Joel:

17 'In the last days it will be, God declares,
    that I will pour out my Spirit upon all flesh,
        and your sons and your daughters shall prophesy,
    and your young men shall see visions,
        and your old men shall dream dreams.
18 Even upon my slaves, both men and women,
        in those days I will pour out my Spirit;
            and they shall prophesy.
19 And I will show portents in the heaven above
        and signs on the earth below,
            blood, and fire, and smoky mist.
20 The sun shall be turned to darkness
        and the moon to blood,
            before the coming of the Lord's great and glorious day.
21 Then everyone who calls on the name of the Lord shall be saved.'
22 "You that are Israelites,ᵃ listen to what I have to say: Jesus of Nazareth,ᵇ a

---

a Gk Men, Israelites   b Gk the Nazorean

man attested to you by God with deeds of power, wonders, and signs that God did through him among you, as you yourselves know— ²³this man, handed over to you according to the definite plan and foreknowledge of God, you crucified and killed by the hands of those outside the law. ²⁴But God raised him up, having freed him from death,ᵃ because it was impossible for him to be held in its power. ²⁵For David says concerning him,

'I saw the Lord always before me,
    for he is at my right hand so that I will not be shaken;
26 therefore my heart was glad, and my tongue rejoiced;
    moreover my flesh will live in hope.
27 For you will not abandon my soul to Hades,
    or let your Holy One experience corruption.
28 You have made known to me the ways of life;
    you will make me full of gladness with your presence.'

29 "Fellow Israelites,ᵇ I may say to you confidently of our ancestor David that he both died and was buried, and his tomb is with us to this day. ³⁰Since he was a prophet, he knew that God had sworn with an oath to him that he would put one of his descendants on his throne. ³¹Foreseeing this, Davidᶜ spoke of the resurrection of the Messiah,ᵈ saying,

'He was not abandoned to Hades,
    nor did his flesh experience corruption.'

32 This Jesus God raised up, and of that all of us are witnesses. ³³Being therefore exalted atᵉ the right hand of God, and having received from the Father the promise of the Holy Spirit, he has poured out this that you both see and hear. ³⁴For David did not ascend into the heavens, but he himself says,

'The Lord said to my Lord,
    "Sit at my right hand,
35 until I make your enemies your footstool."'

36 Therefore let the entire house of Israel know with certainty that God has made him both Lord and Messiah,ᶠ this Jesus whom you crucified."

THE FIRST CONVERTS

37 Now when they heard this, they were cut to the heart and said to Peter and to the other apostles, "Brothers,ᵇ what should we do?" ³⁸Peter said to them, "Repent, and be baptized every one of you in the name of Jesus Christ so that your sins may be forgiven; and you will receive the gift of the Holy Spirit. ³⁹For the promise is for you, for your children, and for all who are far away, everyone

---

ᵃ Gk the pains of death   ᵇ Gk Men, brothers   ᶜ Gk he   ᵈ Or the Christ   ᵉ Or by   ᶠ Or Christ whom the Lord our God calls to him." [40]And he testified with many other arguments and exhorted them, saying, "Save yourselves from this corrupt generation." [41]So those who welcomed his message were baptized, and that day about three thousand persons were added. [42]They devoted themselves to the apostles' teaching and fellowship, to the breaking of bread and the prayers.

LIFE AMONG THE BELIEVERS

43 Awe came upon everyone, because many wonders and signs were being done by the apostles. [44]All who believed were together and had all things in common; [45]they would sell their possessions and goods and distribute the proceeds[a] to all, as any had need. [46]Day by day, as they spent much time together in the temple, they broke bread at home[b] and ate their food with glad and generous[c] hearts, [47]praising God and having the goodwill of all the people. And day by day the Lord added to their number those who were being saved.

PETER HEALS A CRIPPLED BEGGAR

3 One day Peter and John were going up to the temple at the hour of prayer, at three o'clock in the afternoon. [2]And a man lame from birth was being carried in. People would lay him daily at the gate of the temple called the Beautiful Gate so that he could ask for alms from those entering the temple. [3]When he saw Peter and John about to go into the temple, he asked them for alms. [4]Peter looked intently at him, as did John, and said, "Look at us." [5]And he fixed his attention on them, expecting to receive something from them. [6]But Peter said, "I have no silver or gold, but what I have I give you; in the name of Jesus Christ of Nazareth,[d] stand up and walk." [7]And he took him by the right hand and raised him up; and immediately his feet and ankles were made strong. [8]Jumping up, he stood and began to walk, and he entered the temple with them, walking and leaping and praising God. [9]All the people saw him walking and praising God, [10]and they recognized him as the one who used to sit and ask for alms at the Beautiful Gate of the temple; and they were filled with wonder and amazement at what had happened to him.

PETER SPEAKS IN SOLOMON'S PORTICO

11 While he clung to Peter and John, all the people ran together to them in the portico called Solomon's Portico, utterly astonished. [12]When Peter saw it, he addressed the people, "You Israelites,[e] why do you wonder at this, or why do you stare at us, as though by our own power or piety we had made him walk?

---

a Gk *them*   *b* Or *from house to house*   *c* Or *sincere*   *d* Gk *the Nazorean*   *e* Gk *Men, Israelites*

¹³The God of Abraham, the God of Isaac, and the God of Jacob, the God of our ancestors has glorified his servant^a Jesus, whom you handed over and rejected in the presence of Pilate, though he had decided to release him. ¹⁴But you rejected the Holy and Righteous One and asked to have a murderer given to you, ¹⁵and you killed the Author of life, whom God raised from the dead. To this we are witnesses. ¹⁶And by faith in his name, his name itself has made this man strong, whom you see and know; and the faith that is through Jesus^b has given him this perfect health in the presence of all of you.

17 "And now, friends,^c I know that you acted in ignorance, as did also your rulers. ¹⁸In this way God fulfilled what he had foretold through all the prophets, that his Messiah^d would suffer. ¹⁹Repent therefore, and turn to God so that your sins may be wiped out, ²⁰so that times of refreshing may come from the presence of the Lord, and that he may send the Messiah^e appointed for you, that is, Jesus, ²¹who must remain in heaven until the time of universal restoration that God announced long ago through his holy prophets. ²²Moses said, 'The Lord your God will raise up for you from your own people^c a prophet like me. You must listen to whatever he tells you. ²³And it will be that everyone who does not listen to that prophet will be utterly rooted out of the people.' ²⁴And all the prophets, as many as have spoken, from Samuel and those after him, also predicted these days. ²⁵You are the descendants of the prophets and of the covenant that God gave to your ancestors, saying to Abraham, 'And in your descendants all the families of the earth shall be blessed.' ²⁶When God raised up his servant,^a he sent him first to you, to bless you by turning each of you from your wicked ways."

PETER AND JOHN BEFORE THE COUNCIL

4 While Peter and John^f were speaking to the people, the priests, the captain of the temple, and the Sadducees came to them, ²much annoyed because they were teaching the people and proclaiming that in Jesus there is the resurrection of the dead. ³So they arrested them and put them in custody until the next day, for it was already evening. ⁴But many of those who heard the word believed; and they numbered about five thousand.

5 The next day their rulers, elders, and scribes assembled in Jerusalem, ⁶with Annas the high priest, Caiaphas, John,^g and Alexander, and all who were of the high-priestly family. ⁷When they had made the prisoners^h stand in their midst, they inquired, "By what power or by what name did you do this?" ⁸Then Peter, filled with the Holy Spirit, said to them, "Rulers of the

---

a Or *child* *b* Gk *him* *c* Gk *brothers* *d* Or *his Christ* *e* Or *the Christ* *f* Gk *While they* *g* Other ancient authorities read *Jonathan* *h* Gk *them* people and elders, [9]if we are questioned today because of a good deed done to someone who was sick and are asked how this man has been healed, [10]let it be known to all of you, and to all the people of Israel, that this man is standing before you in good health by the name of Jesus Christ of Nazareth,[a] whom you crucified, whom God raised from the dead. [11]This Jesus[b] is

> 'the stone that was rejected by you, the builders;
> it has become the cornerstone.'[c]

12 There is salvation in no one else, for there is no other name under heaven given among mortals by which we must be saved."

13 Now when they saw the boldness of Peter and John and realized that they were uneducated and ordinary men, they were amazed and recognized them as companions of Jesus. [14]When they saw the man who had been cured standing beside them, they had nothing to say in opposition. [15]So they ordered them to leave the council while they discussed the matter with one another. [16]They said, "What will we do with them? For it is obvious to all who live in Jerusalem that a notable sign has been done through them; we cannot deny it. [17]But to keep it from spreading further among the people, let us warn them to speak no more to anyone in this name." [18]So they called them and ordered them not to speak or teach at all in the name of Jesus. [19]But Peter and John answered them, "Whether it is right in God's sight to listen to you rather than to God, you must judge; [20]for we cannot keep from speaking about what we have seen and heard." [21]After threatening them again, they let them go, finding no way to punish them because of the people, for all of them praised God for what had happened. [22]For the man on whom this sign of healing had been performed was more than forty years old.

THE BELIEVERS PRAY FOR BOLDNESS

23 After they were released, they went to their friends[d] and reported what the chief priests and the elders had said to them. [24]When they heard it, they raised their voices together to God and said, "Sovereign Lord, who made the heaven and the earth, the sea, and everything in them, [25]it is you who said by the Holy Spirit through our ancestor David, your servant:[e]

> 'Why did the Gentiles rage,
>   and the peoples imagine vain things?
> 26 The kings of the earth took their stand,
>   and the rulers have gathered together
>   against the Lord and against his Messiah.'[f]

---

a Gk the Nazorean   b Gk This   c Or keystone   d Gk their own   e Or child   f Or his Christ

27 For in this city, in fact, both Herod and Pontius Pilate, with the Gentiles and the peoples of Israel, gathered together against your holy servant*a* Jesus, whom you anointed, [28]to do whatever your hand and your plan had predestined to take place. [29]And now, Lord, look at their threats, and grant to your servants*b* to speak your word with all boldness, [30]while you stretch out your hand to heal, and signs and wonders are performed through the name of your holy servant*a* Jesus." [31]When they had prayed, the place in which they were gathered together was shaken; and they were all filled with the Holy Spirit and spoke the word of God with boldness.

THE BELIEVERS SHARE THEIR POSSESSIONS

32 Now the whole group of those who believed were of one heart and soul, and no one claimed private ownership of any possessions, but everything they owned was held in common. [33]With great power the apostles gave their testimony to the resurrection of the Lord Jesus, and great grace was upon them all. [34]There was not a needy person among them, for as many as owned lands or houses sold them and brought the proceeds of what was sold. [35]They laid it at the apostles' feet, and it was distributed to each as any had need. [36]There was a Levite, a native of Cyprus, Joseph, to whom the apostles gave the name Barnabas (which means "son of encouragement"). [37]He sold a field that belonged to him, then brought the money, and laid it at the apostles' feet.

ANANIAS AND SAPPHIRA

5 But a man named Ananias, with the consent of his wife Sapphira, sold a piece of property; [2]with his wife's knowledge, he kept back some of the proceeds, and brought only a part and laid it at the apostles' feet. [3]"Ananias," Peter asked, "why has Satan filled your heart to lie to the Holy Spirit and to keep back part of the proceeds of the land? [4]While it remained unsold, did it not remain your own? And after it was sold, were not the proceeds at your disposal? How is it that you have contrived this deed in your heart? You did not lie to us*c* but to God!" [5]Now when Ananias heard these words, he fell down and died. And great fear seized all who heard of it. [6]The young men came and wrapped up his body,*d* then carried him out and buried him.

7 After an interval of about three hours his wife came in, not knowing what had happened. [8]Peter said to her, "Tell me whether you and your husband sold the land for such and such a price." And she said, "Yes, that was the price." [9]Then Peter said to her, "How is it that you have agreed together to put the

---

a Or *child*   *b* Gk *slaves*   *c* Gk *to men*   *d* Meaning of Gk uncertain

Spirit of the Lord to the test? Look, the feet of those who have buried your husband are at the door, and they will carry you out." [10]Immediately she fell down at his feet and died. When the young men came in they found her dead, so they carried her out and buried her beside her husband. [11]And great fear seized the whole church and all who heard of these things.

THE APOSTLES HEAL MANY

12 Now many signs and wonders were done among the people through the apostles. And they were all together in Solomon's Portico. [13]None of the rest dared to join them, but the people held them in high esteem. [14]Yet more than ever believers were added to the Lord, great numbers of both men and women, [15]so that they even carried out the sick into the streets, and laid them on cots and mats, in order that Peter's shadow might fall on some of them as he came by. [16]A great number of people would also gather from the towns around Jerusalem, bringing the sick and those tormented by unclean spirits, and they were all cured.

THE APOSTLES ARE PERSECUTED

17 Then the high priest took action; he and all who were with him (that is, the sect of the Sadducees), being filled with jealousy, [18]arrested the apostles and put them in the public prison. [19]But during the night an angel of the Lord opened the prison doors, brought them out, and said, [20]"Go, stand in the temple and tell the people the whole message about this life." [21]When they heard this, they entered the temple at daybreak and went on with their teaching.

When the high priest and those with him arrived, they called together the council and the whole body of the elders of Israel, and sent to the prison to have them brought. [22]But when the temple police went there, they did not find them in the prison; so they returned and reported, [23]"We found the prison securely locked and the guards standing at the doors, but when we opened them, we found no one inside." [24]Now when the captain of the temple and the chief priests heard these words, they were perplexed about them, wondering what might be going on. [25]Then someone arrived and announced, "Look, the men whom you put in prison are standing in the temple and teaching the people!" [26]Then the captain went with the temple police and brought them, but without violence, for they were afraid of being stoned by the people.

27 When they had brought them, they had them stand before the council. The high priest questioned them, [28]saying, "We gave you strict orders not to teach in this name,[a] yet here you have filled Jerusalem with your teaching

---

a Other ancient authorities read *Did we not give you strict orders not to teach in this name?*

and you are determined to bring this man's blood on us." ²⁹But Peter and the apostles answered, "We must obey God rather than any human authority.*ᵃ* ³⁰The God of our ancestors raised up Jesus, whom you had killed by hanging him on a tree. ³¹God exalted him at his right hand as Leader and Savior that he might give repentance to Israel and forgiveness of sins. ³²And we are witnesses to these things, and so is the Holy Spirit whom God has given to those who obey him."

33 When they heard this, they were enraged and wanted to kill them. ³⁴But a Pharisee in the council named Gamaliel, a teacher of the law, respected by all the people, stood up and ordered the men to be put outside for a short time. ³⁵Then he said to them, "Fellow Israelites,*ᵇ* consider carefully what you propose to do to these men. ³⁶For some time ago Theudas rose up, claiming to be somebody, and a number of men, about four hundred, joined him; but he was killed, and all who followed him were dispersed and disappeared. ³⁷After him Judas the Galilean rose up at the time of the census and got people to follow him; he also perished, and all who followed him were scattered. ³⁸So in the present case, I tell you, keep away from these men and let them alone; because if this plan or this undertaking is of human origin, it will fail; ³⁹but if it is of God, you will not be able to overthrow them—in that case you may even be found fighting against God!"

They were convinced by him, ⁴⁰and when they had called in the apostles, they had them flogged. Then they ordered them not to speak in the name of Jesus, and let them go. ⁴¹As they left the council, they rejoiced that they were considered worthy to suffer dishonor for the sake of the name. ⁴²And every day in the temple and at home*ᶜ* they did not cease to teach and proclaim Jesus as the Messiah.*ᵈ*

SEVEN CHOSEN TO SERVE

6 Now during those days, when the disciples were increasing in number, the Hellenists complained against the Hebrews because their widows were being neglected in the daily distribution of food. ²And the twelve called together the whole community of the disciples and said, "It is not right that we should neglect the word of God in order to wait on tables.*ᵉ* ³Therefore, friends,*ᶠ* select from among yourselves seven men of good standing, full of the Spirit and of wisdom, whom we may appoint to this task, ⁴while we, for our part, will devote ourselves to prayer and to serving the word." ⁵What they said pleased the whole community, and they chose Stephen, a man full of faith and the Holy

---

a Gk *than men*   *b* Gk *Men, Israelites*   *c* Or *from house to house*   *d* Or *the Christ*   *e* Or *keep accounts*   *f* Gk *brothers*

Spirit, together with Philip, Prochorus, Nicanor, Timon, Parmenas, and Nico-
laus, a proselyte of Antioch. ⁶They had these men stand before the apostles,
who prayed and laid their hands on them.

7 The word of God continued to spread; the number of the disciples increased greatly in Jerusalem, and a great many of the priests became obedient
to the faith.

THE ARREST OF STEPHEN

8 Stephen, full of grace and power, did great wonders and signs among the
people. ⁹Then some of those who belonged to the synagogue of the Freedmen
(as it was called), Cyrenians, Alexandrians, and others of those from Cilicia
and Asia, stood up and argued with Stephen. ¹⁰But they could not withstand
the wisdom and the Spirit*ᵃ* with which he spoke. ¹¹Then they secretly instigated
some men to say, "We have heard him speak blasphemous words against Moses
and God." ¹²They stirred up the people as well as the elders and the scribes;
then they suddenly confronted him, seized him, and brought him before the
council. ¹³They set up false witnesses who said, "This man never stops saying
things against this holy place and the law; ¹⁴for we have heard him say that this
Jesus of Nazareth*ᵇ* will destroy this place and will change the customs that
Moses handed on to us." ¹⁵And all who sat in the council looked intently at
him, and they saw that his face was like the face of an angel.

STEPHEN'S SPEECH TO THE COUNCIL

7 Then the high priest asked him, "Are these things so?" ²And Stephen
replied:

"Brothers*ᶜ* and fathers, listen to me. The God of glory appeared to our ancestor Abraham when he was in Mesopotamia, before he lived in Haran, ³and
said to him, 'Leave your country and your relatives and go to the land that
I will show you.' ⁴Then he left the country of the Chaldeans and settled in
Haran. After his father died, God had him move from there to this country
in which you are now living. ⁵He did not give him any of it as a heritage, not
even a foot's length, but promised to give it to him as his possession and to his
descendants after him, even though he had no child. ⁶And God spoke in these
terms, that his descendants would be resident aliens in a country belonging to
others, who would enslave them and mistreat them during four hundred years.
⁷'But I will judge the nation that they serve,' said God, 'and after that they shall
come out and worship me in this place.' ⁸Then he gave him the covenant of

---

a Or *spirit*   *b* Gk *the Nazorean*   *c* Gk *Men, brothers* circumcision. And so Abraham*a* became the father of Isaac and circumcised him on the eighth day; and Isaac became the father of Jacob, and Jacob of the twelve patriarchs.

9 "The patriarchs, jealous of Joseph, sold him into Egypt; but God was with him, [10]and rescued him from all his afflictions, and enabled him to win favor and to show wisdom when he stood before Pharaoh, king of Egypt, who appointed him ruler over Egypt and over all his household. [11]Now there came a famine throughout Egypt and Canaan, and great suffering, and our ancestors could find no food. [12]But when Jacob heard that there was grain in Egypt, he sent our ancestors there on their first visit. [13]On the second visit Joseph made himself known to his brothers, and Joseph's family became known to Pharaoh. [14]Then Joseph sent and invited his father Jacob and all his relatives to come to him, seventy-five in all; [15]so Jacob went down to Egypt. He himself died there as well as our ancestors, [16]and their bodies*b* were brought back to Shechem and laid in the tomb that Abraham had bought for a sum of silver from the sons of Hamor in Shechem.

17 "But as the time drew near for the fulfillment of the promise that God had made to Abraham, our people in Egypt increased and multiplied [18]until another king who had not known Joseph ruled over Egypt. [19]He dealt craftily with our race and forced our ancestors to abandon their infants so that they would die. [20]At this time Moses was born, and he was beautiful before God. For three months he was brought up in his father's house; [21]and when he was abandoned, Pharaoh's daughter adopted him and brought him up as her own son. [22]So Moses was instructed in all the wisdom of the Egyptians and was powerful in his words and deeds.

23 "When he was forty years old, it came into his heart to visit his relatives, the Israelites.*c* [24]When he saw one of them being wronged, he defended the oppressed man and avenged him by striking down the Egyptian. [25]He supposed that his kinsfolk would understand that God through him was rescuing them, but they did not understand. [26]The next day he came to some of them as they were quarreling and tried to reconcile them, saying, 'Men, you are brothers; why do you wrong each other?' [27]But the man who was wronging his neighbor pushed Moses*d* aside, saying, 'Who made you a ruler and a judge over us? [28]Do you want to kill me as you killed the Egyptian yesterday?' [29]When he heard this, Moses fled and became a resident alien in the land of Midian. There he became the father of two sons.

30 "Now when forty years had passed, an angel appeared to him in the

---

a Gk *he* *b* Gk *they* *c* Gk *his brothers, the sons of Israel* *d* Gk *him* wilderness of Mount Sinai, in the flame of a burning bush. [31]When Moses saw it, he was amazed at the sight; and as he approached to look, there came the voice of the Lord: [32]'I am the God of your ancestors, the God of Abraham, Isaac, and Jacob.' Moses began to tremble and did not dare to look. [33]Then the Lord said to him, 'Take off the sandals from your feet, for the place where you are standing is holy ground. [34]I have surely seen the mistreatment of my people who are in Egypt and have heard their groaning, and I have come down to rescue them. Come now, I will send you to Egypt.'

35 "It was this Moses whom they rejected when they said, 'Who made you a ruler and a judge?' and whom God now sent as both ruler and liberator through the angel who appeared to him in the bush. [36]He led them out, having performed wonders and signs in Egypt, at the Red Sea, and in the wilderness for forty years. [37]This is the Moses who said to the Israelites, 'God will raise up a prophet for you from your own people[a] as he raised me up.' [38]He is the one who was in the congregation in the wilderness with the angel who spoke to him at Mount Sinai, and with our ancestors; and he received living oracles to give to us. [39]Our ancestors were unwilling to obey him; instead, they pushed him aside, and in their hearts they turned back to Egypt, [40]saying to Aaron, 'Make gods for us who will lead the way for us; as for this Moses who led us out from the land of Egypt, we do not know what has happened to him.' [41]At that time they made a calf, offered a sacrifice to the idol, and reveled in the works of their hands. [42]But God turned away from them and handed them over to worship the host of heaven, as it is written in the book of the prophets:

'Did you offer to me slain victims and sacrifices
forty years in the wilderness, O house of Israel?
43 No; you took along the tent of Moloch,
and the star of your god Rephan,
the images that you made to worship;
so I will remove you beyond Babylon.'

44 "Our ancestors had the tent of testimony in the wilderness, as God[b] directed when he spoke to Moses, ordering him to make it according to the pattern he had seen. [45]Our ancestors in turn brought it in with Joshua when they dispossessed the nations that God drove out before our ancestors. And it was there until the time of David, [46]who found favor with God and asked that he might find a dwelling place for the house of Jacob.[c] [47]But it was Solomon who built a house for him. [48]Yet the Most High does not dwell in houses made with human hands;[d] as the prophet says,

---

a Gk *your brothers*   *b* Gk *he*   *c* Other ancient authorities read *for the God of Jacob*   *d* Gk *with hands*

49 'Heaven is my throne,
>   and the earth is my footstool.
>   What kind of house will you build for me, says the Lord,
>   or what is the place of my rest?
50 Did not my hand make all these things?'

51 "You stiff-necked people, uncircumcised in heart and ears, you are forever opposing the Holy Spirit, just as your ancestors used to do. ⁵²Which of the prophets did your ancestors not persecute? They killed those who foretold the coming of the Righteous One, and now you have become his betrayers and murderers. ⁵³You are the ones that received the law as ordained by angels, and yet you have not kept it."

THE STONING OF STEPHEN

54 When they heard these things, they became enraged and ground their teeth at Stephen.ᵃ ⁵⁵But filled with the Holy Spirit, he gazed into heaven and saw the glory of God and Jesus standing at the right hand of God. ⁵⁶"Look," he said, "I see the heavens opened and the Son of Man standing at the right hand of God!" ⁵⁷But they covered their ears, and with a loud shout all rushed together against him. ⁵⁸Then they dragged him out of the city and began to stone him; and the witnesses laid their coats at the feet of a young man named Saul. ⁵⁹While they were stoning Stephen, he prayed, "Lord Jesus, receive my spirit." ⁶⁰Then he knelt down and cried out in a loud voice, "Lord, do not hold this sin against them." When he had said this, he died.ᵇ

8 And Saul approved of their killing him.

SAUL PERSECUTES THE CHURCH

That day a severe persecution began against the church in Jerusalem, and all except the apostles were scattered throughout the countryside of Judea and Samaria. ²Devout men buried Stephen and made loud lamentation over him. ³But Saul was ravaging the church by entering house after house; dragging off both men and women, he committed them to prison.

PHILIP PREACHES IN SAMARIA

4 Now those who were scattered went from place to place, proclaiming the word. ⁵Philip went down to the cityᶜ of Samaria and proclaimed the Messiahᵈ to them. ⁶The crowds with one accord listened eagerly to what was said by

---

a Gk *him*   *b* Gk *fell asleep*   *c* Other ancient authorities read *a city*   *d* Or *the Christ*

Philip, hearing and seeing the signs that he did, [7]for unclean spirits, crying with loud shrieks, came out of many who were possessed; and many others who were paralyzed or lame were cured. [8]So there was great joy in that city.

9 Now a certain man named Simon had previously practiced magic in the city and amazed the people of Samaria, saying that he was someone great. [10]All of them, from the least to the greatest, listened to him eagerly, saying, "This man is the power of God that is called Great." [11]And they listened eagerly to him because for a long time he had amazed them with his magic. [12]But when they believed Philip, who was proclaiming the good news about the kingdom of God and the name of Jesus Christ, they were baptized, both men and women. [13]Even Simon himself believed. After being baptized, he stayed constantly with Philip and was amazed when he saw the signs and great miracles that took place.

14 Now when the apostles at Jerusalem heard that Samaria had accepted the word of God, they sent Peter and John to them. [15]The two went down and prayed for them that they might receive the Holy Spirit [16](for as yet the Spirit had not come[a] upon any of them; they had only been baptized in the name of the Lord Jesus). [17]Then Peter and John[b] laid their hands on them, and they received the Holy Spirit. [18]Now when Simon saw that the Spirit was given through the laying on of the apostles' hands, he offered them money, [19]saying, "Give me also this power so that anyone on whom I lay my hands may receive the Holy Spirit." [20]But Peter said to him, "May your silver perish with you, because you thought you could obtain God's gift with money! [21]You have no part or share in this, for your heart is not right before God. [22]Repent therefore of this wickedness of yours, and pray to the Lord that, if possible, the intent of your heart may be forgiven you. [23]For I see that you are in the gall of bitterness and the chains of wickedness." [24]Simon answered, "Pray for me to the Lord, that nothing of what you[c] have said may happen to me."

25 Now after Peter and John[d] had testified and spoken the word of the Lord, they returned to Jerusalem, proclaiming the good news to many villages of the Samaritans.

PHILIP AND THE ETHIOPIAN EUNUCH

26 Then an angel of the Lord said to Philip, "Get up and go toward the south[e] to the road that goes down from Jerusalem to Gaza." (This is a wilderness road.) [27]So he got up and went. Now there was an Ethiopian eunuch, a court official of the Candace, queen of the Ethiopians, in charge of her entire treasury.

---

a Gk *fallen*   *b* Gk *they*   *c* The Greek word for *you* and the verb *pray* are plural   *d* Gk *after they*   *e* Or *go at noon*

He had come to Jerusalem to worship ²⁸and was returning home; seated in his chariot, he was reading the prophet Isaiah. ²⁹Then the Spirit said to Philip, "Go over to this chariot and join it." ³⁰So Philip ran up to it and heard him reading the prophet Isaiah. He asked, "Do you understand what you are reading?" ³¹He replied, "How can I, unless someone guides me?" And he invited Philip to get in and sit beside him. ³²Now the passage of the scripture that he was reading was this:

> "Like a sheep he was led to the slaughter,
>> and like a lamb silent before its shearer,
>>> so he does not open his mouth.
> 33 In his humiliation justice was denied him.
>> Who can describe his generation?
>> For his life is taken away from the earth."

34 The eunuch asked Philip, "About whom, may I ask you, does the prophet say this, about himself or about someone else?" ³⁵Then Philip began to speak, and starting with this scripture, he proclaimed to him the good news about Jesus. ³⁶As they were going along the road, they came to some water; and the eunuch said, "Look, here is water! What is to prevent me from being baptized?"^a ³⁸He commanded the chariot to stop, and both of them, Philip and the eunuch, went down into the water, and Philip^b baptized him. ³⁹When they came up out of the water, the Spirit of the Lord snatched Philip away; the eunuch saw him no more, and went on his way rejoicing. ⁴⁰But Philip found himself at Azotus, and as he was passing through the region, he proclaimed the good news to all the towns until he came to Caesarea.

THE CONVERSION OF SAUL

9 Meanwhile Saul, still breathing threats and murder against the disciples of the Lord, went to the high priest ²and asked him for letters to the synagogues at Damascus, so that if he found any who belonged to the Way, men or women, he might bring them bound to Jerusalem. ³Now as he was going along and approaching Damascus, suddenly a light from heaven flashed around him. ⁴He fell to the ground and heard a voice saying to him, "Saul, Saul, why do you persecute me?" ⁵He asked, "Who are you, Lord?" The reply came, "I am Jesus, whom you are persecuting. ⁶But get up and enter the city, and you will be told what you are to do." ⁷The men who were traveling with him stood speechless because they heard the voice but saw no one. ⁸Saul got up from the ground, and

---

a Other ancient authorities add all or most of verse 37, *And Philip said, "If you believe with all your heart, you may." And he replied, "I believe that Jesus Christ is the Son of God."* b Gk *he* though his eyes were open, he could see nothing; so they led him by the hand and brought him into Damascus. [9]For three days he was without sight, and neither ate nor drank.

10 Now there was a disciple in Damascus named Ananias. The Lord said to him in a vision, "Ananias." He answered, "Here I am, Lord." [11]The Lord said to him, "Get up and go to the street called Straight, and at the house of Judas look for a man of Tarsus named Saul. At this moment he is praying, [12]and he has seen in a vision[a] a man named Ananias come in and lay his hands on him so that he might regain his sight." [13]But Ananias answered, "Lord, I have heard from many about this man, how much evil he has done to your saints in Jerusalem; [14]and here he has authority from the chief priests to bind all who invoke your name." [15]But the Lord said to him, "Go, for he is an instrument whom I have chosen to bring my name before Gentiles and kings and before the people of Israel; [16]I myself will show him how much he must suffer for the sake of my name." [17]So Ananias went and entered the house. He laid his hands on Saul[b] and said, "Brother Saul, the Lord Jesus, who appeared to you on your way here, has sent me so that you may regain your sight and be filled with the Holy Spirit." [18]And immediately something like scales fell from his eyes, and his sight was restored. Then he got up and was baptized, [19]and after taking some food, he regained his strength.

SAUL PREACHES IN DAMASCUS

For several days he was with the disciples in Damascus, [20]and immediately he began to proclaim Jesus in the synagogues, saying, "He is the Son of God." [21]All who heard him were amazed and said, "Is not this the man who made havoc in Jerusalem among those who invoked this name? And has he not come here for the purpose of bringing them bound before the chief priests?" [22]Saul became increasingly more powerful and confounded the Jews who lived in Damascus by proving that Jesus[c] was the Messiah.[d]

SAUL ESCAPES FROM THE JEWS

23 After some time had passed, the Jews plotted to kill him, [24]but their plot became known to Saul. They were watching the gates day and night so that they might kill him; [25]but his disciples took him by night and let him down through an opening in the wall,[e] lowering him in a basket.

---

a Other ancient authorities lack *in a vision*   b Gk *him*   c Gk *that this*   d Or *the Christ*   e Gk *through the wall*

SAUL IN JERUSALEM

26 When he had come to Jerusalem, he attempted to join the disciples; and they were all afraid of him, for they did not believe that he was a disciple. [27]But Barnabas took him, brought him to the apostles, and described for them how on the road he had seen the Lord, who had spoken to him, and how in Damascus he had spoken boldly in the name of Jesus. [28]So he went in and out among them in Jerusalem, speaking boldly in the name of the Lord. [29]He spoke and argued with the Hellenists; but they were attempting to kill him. [30]When the believers[a] learned of it, they brought him down to Caesarea and sent him off to Tarsus.

31 Meanwhile the church throughout Judea, Galilee, and Samaria had peace and was built up. Living in the fear of the Lord and in the comfort of the Holy Spirit, it increased in numbers.

THE HEALING OF AENEAS

32 Now as Peter went here and there among all the believers,[b] he came down also to the saints living in Lydda. [33]There he found a man named Aeneas, who had been bedridden for eight years, for he was paralyzed. [34]Peter said to him, "Aeneas, Jesus Christ heals you; get up and make your bed!" And immediately he got up. [35]And all the residents of Lydda and Sharon saw him and turned to the Lord.

PETER IN LYDDA AND JOPPA

36 Now in Joppa there was a disciple whose name was Tabitha, which in Greek is Dorcas.[c] She was devoted to good works and acts of charity. [37]At that time she became ill and died. When they had washed her, they laid her in a room upstairs. [38]Since Lydda was near Joppa, the disciples, who heard that Peter was there, sent two men to him with the request, "Please come to us without delay." [39]So Peter got up and went with them; and when he arrived, they took him to the room upstairs. All the widows stood beside him, weeping and showing tunics and other clothing that Dorcas had made while she was with them. [40]Peter put all of them outside, and then he knelt down and prayed. He turned to the body and said, "Tabitha, get up." Then she opened her eyes, and seeing Peter, she sat up. [41]He gave her his hand and helped her up. Then calling the saints and widows, he showed her to be alive. [42]This became known throughout

---

a Gk *brothers* b Gk *all of them* c The name Tabitha in Aramaic and the name Dorcas in Greek mean *a gazelle*

Joppa, and many believed in the Lord. ⁴³Meanwhile he stayed in Joppa for some time with a certain Simon, a tanner.

PETER AND CORNELIUS

10 In Caesarea there was a man named Cornelius, a centurion of the Italian Cohort, as it was called. ²He was a devout man who feared God with all his household; he gave alms generously to the people and prayed constantly to God. ³One afternoon at about three o'clock he had a vision in which he clearly saw an angel of God coming in and saying to him, "Cornelius." ⁴He stared at him in terror and said, "What is it, Lord?" He answered, "Your prayers and your alms have ascended as a memorial before God. ⁵Now send men to Joppa for a certain Simon who is called Peter; ⁶he is lodging with Simon, a tanner, whose house is by the seaside." ⁷When the angel who spoke to him had left, he called two of his slaves and a devout soldier from the ranks of those who served him, ⁸and after telling them everything, he sent them to Joppa.

9 About noon the next day, as they were on their journey and approaching the city, Peter went up on the roof to pray. ¹⁰He became hungry and wanted something to eat; and while it was being prepared, he fell into a trance. ¹¹He saw the heaven opened and something like a large sheet coming down, being lowered to the ground by its four corners. ¹²In it were all kinds of four-footed creatures and reptiles and birds of the air. ¹³Then he heard a voice saying, "Get up, Peter; kill and eat." ¹⁴But Peter said, "By no means, Lord; for I have never eaten anything that is profane or unclean." ¹⁵The voice said to him again, a second time, "What God has made clean, you must not call profane." ¹⁶This happened three times, and the thing was suddenly taken up to heaven.

17 Now while Peter was greatly puzzled about what to make of the vision that he had seen, suddenly the men sent by Cornelius appeared. They were asking for Simon's house and were standing by the gate. ¹⁸They called out to ask whether Simon, who was called Peter, was staying there. ¹⁹While Peter was still thinking about the vision, the Spirit said to him, "Look, three*ᵃ* men are searching for you. ²⁰Now get up, go down, and go with them without hesitation; for I have sent them." ²¹So Peter went down to the men and said, "I am the one you are looking for; what is the reason for your coming?" ²²They answered, "Cornelius, a centurion, an upright and God-fearing man, who is well spoken of by the whole Jewish nation, was directed by a holy angel to send for you to come to his house and to hear what you have to say." ²³So Peter*ᵇ* invited them in and gave them lodging.

---

a One ancient authority reads *two;* others lack the word   *b* Gk *he*

The next day he got up and went with them, and some of the believers[a] from Joppa accompanied him. [24]The following day they came to Caesarea. Cornelius was expecting them and had called together his relatives and close friends. [25]On Peter's arrival Cornelius met him, and falling at his feet, worshiped him. [26]But Peter made him get up, saying, "Stand up; I am only a mortal." [27]And as he talked with him, he went in and found that many had assembled; [28]and he said to them, "You yourselves know that it is unlawful for a Jew to associate with or to visit a Gentile; but God has shown me that I should not call anyone profane or unclean. [29]So when I was sent for, I came without objection. Now may I ask why you sent for me?"

30 Cornelius replied, "Four days ago at this very hour, at three o'clock, I was praying in my house when suddenly a man in dazzling clothes stood before me. [31]He said, 'Cornelius, your prayer has been heard and your alms have been remembered before God. [32]Send therefore to Joppa and ask for Simon, who is called Peter; he is staying in the home of Simon, a tanner, by the sea.' [33]Therefore I sent for you immediately, and you have been kind enough to come. So now all of us are here in the presence of God to listen to all that the Lord has commanded you to say."

GENTILES HEAR THE GOOD NEWS

34 Then Peter began to speak to them: "I truly understand that God shows no partiality, [35]but in every nation anyone who fears him and does what is right is acceptable to him. [36]You know the message he sent to the people of Israel, preaching peace by Jesus Christ—he is Lord of all. [37]That message spread throughout Judea, beginning in Galilee after the baptism that John announced: [38]how God anointed Jesus of Nazareth with the Holy Spirit and with power; how he went about doing good and healing all who were oppressed by the devil, for God was with him. [39]We are witnesses to all that he did both in Judea and in Jerusalem. They put him to death by hanging him on a tree; [40]but God raised him on the third day and allowed him to appear, [41]not to all the people but to us who were chosen by God as witnesses, and who ate and drank with him after he rose from the dead. [42]He commanded us to preach to the people and to testify that he is the one ordained by God as judge of the living and the dead. [43]All the prophets testify about him that everyone who believes in him receives forgiveness of sins through his name."

---

a Gk brothers

GENTILES RECEIVE THE HOLY SPIRIT

44 While Peter was still speaking, the Holy Spirit fell upon all who heard the word. ⁴⁵The circumcised believers who had come with Peter were astounded that the gift of the Holy Spirit had been poured out even on the Gentiles, ⁴⁶for they heard them speaking in tongues and extolling God. Then Peter said, ⁴⁷"Can anyone withhold the water for baptizing these people who have received the Holy Spirit just as we have?" ⁴⁸So he ordered them to be baptized in the name of Jesus Christ. Then they invited him to stay for several days.

PETER'S REPORT TO THE CHURCH AT JERUSALEM

11 Now the apostles and the believers[a] who were in Judea heard that the Gentiles had also accepted the word of God. ²So when Peter went up to Jerusalem, the circumcised believers[b] criticized him, ³saying, "Why did you go to uncircumcised men and eat with them?" ⁴Then Peter began to explain it to them, step by step, saying, ⁵"I was in the city of Joppa praying, and in a trance I saw a vision. There was something like a large sheet coming down from heaven, being lowered by its four corners; and it came close to me. ⁶As I looked at it closely I saw four-footed animals, beasts of prey, reptiles, and birds of the air. ⁷I also heard a voice saying to me, 'Get up, Peter; kill and eat.' ⁸But I replied, 'By no means, Lord; for nothing profane or unclean has ever entered my mouth.' ⁹But a second time the voice answered from heaven, 'What God has made clean, you must not call profane.' ¹⁰This happened three times; then everything was pulled up again to heaven. ¹¹At that very moment three men, sent to me from Caesarea, arrived at the house where we were. ¹²The Spirit told me to go with them and not to make a distinction between them and us.[c] These six brothers also accompanied me, and we entered the man's house. ¹³He told us how he had seen the angel standing in his house and saying, 'Send to Joppa and bring Simon, who is called Peter; ¹⁴he will give you a message by which you and your entire household will be saved.' ¹⁵And as I began to speak, the Holy Spirit fell upon them just as it had upon us at the beginning. ¹⁶And I remembered the word of the Lord, how he had said, 'John baptized with water, but you will be baptized with the Holy Spirit.' ¹⁷If then God gave them the same gift that he gave us when we believed in the Lord Jesus Christ, who was I that I could hinder God?" ¹⁸When they heard this, they were silenced. And they praised God, saying, "Then God has given even to the Gentiles the repentance that leads to life."

---

a Gk *brothers*　*b* Gk lacks *believers*　*c* Or *not to hesitate*

THE CHURCH IN ANTIOCH

19 Now those who were scattered because of the persecution that took place over Stephen traveled as far as Phoenicia, Cyprus, and Antioch, and they spoke the word to no one except Jews. [20]But among them were some men of Cyprus and Cyrene who, on coming to Antioch, spoke to the Hellenists[a] also, proclaiming the Lord Jesus. [21]The hand of the Lord was with them, and a great number became believers and turned to the Lord. [22]News of this came to the ears of the church in Jerusalem, and they sent Barnabas to Antioch. [23]When he came and saw the grace of God, he rejoiced, and he exhorted them all to remain faithful to the Lord with steadfast devotion; [24]for he was a good man, full of the Holy Spirit and of faith. And a great many people were brought to the Lord. [25]Then Barnabas went to Tarsus to look for Saul, [26]and when he had found him, he brought him to Antioch. So it was that for an entire year they met with[b] the church and taught a great many people, and it was in Antioch that the disciples were first called "Christians."

27 At that time prophets came down from Jerusalem to Antioch. [28]One of them named Agabus stood up and predicted by the Spirit that there would be a severe famine over all the world; and this took place during the reign of Claudius. [29]The disciples determined that according to their ability, each would send relief to the believers[c] living in Judea; [30]this they did, sending it to the elders by Barnabas and Saul.

JAMES KILLED AND PETER IMPRISONED

12 About that time King Herod laid violent hands upon some who belonged to the church. [2]He had James, the brother of John, killed with the sword. [3]After he saw that it pleased the Jews, he proceeded to arrest Peter also. (This was during the festival of Unleavened Bread.) [4]When he had seized him, he put him in prison and handed him over to four squads of soldiers to guard him, intending to bring him out to the people after the Passover. [5]While Peter was kept in prison, the church prayed fervently to God for him.

PETER DELIVERED FROM PRISON

6 The very night before Herod was going to bring him out, Peter, bound with two chains, was sleeping between two soldiers, while guards in front of the door were keeping watch over the prison. [7]Suddenly an angel of the Lord appeared and a light shone in the cell. He tapped Peter on the side and woke him,

---

a Other ancient authorities read *Greeks*   *b* Or *were guests of*   *c* Gk *brothers* saying, "Get up quickly." And the chains fell off his wrists. [8]The angel said to him, "Fasten your belt and put on your sandals." He did so. Then he said to him, "Wrap your cloak around you and follow me." [9]Peter[a] went out and followed him; he did not realize that what was happening with the angel's help was real; he thought he was seeing a vision. [10]After they had passed the first and the second guard, they came before the iron gate leading into the city. It opened for them of its own accord, and they went outside and walked along a lane, when suddenly the angel left him. [11]Then Peter came to himself and said, "Now I am sure that the Lord has sent his angel and rescued me from the hands of Herod and from all that the Jewish people were expecting."

12 As soon as he realized this, he went to the house of Mary, the mother of John whose other name was Mark, where many had gathered and were praying. [13]When he knocked at the outer gate, a maid named Rhoda came to answer. [14]On recognizing Peter's voice, she was so overjoyed that, instead of opening the gate, she ran in and announced that Peter was standing at the gate. [15]They said to her, "You are out of your mind!" But she insisted that it was so. They said, "It is his angel." [16]Meanwhile Peter continued knocking; and when they opened the gate, they saw him and were amazed. [17]He motioned to them with his hand to be silent, and described for them how the Lord had brought him out of the prison. And he added, "Tell this to James and to the believers."[b] Then he left and went to another place.

18 When morning came, there was no small commotion among the soldiers over what had become of Peter. [19]When Herod had searched for him and could not find him, he examined the guards and ordered them to be put to death. Then he went down from Judea to Caesarea and stayed there.

THE DEATH OF HEROD

20 Now Herod[c] was angry with the people of Tyre and Sidon. So they came to him in a body; and after winning over Blastus, the king's chamberlain, they asked for a reconciliation, because their country depended on the king's country for food. [21]On an appointed day Herod put on his royal robes, took his seat on the platform, and delivered a public address to them. [22]The people kept shouting, "The voice of a god, and not of a mortal!" [23]And immediately, because he had not given the glory to God, an angel of the Lord struck him down, and he was eaten by worms and died.

---

a Gk He   b Gk brothers   c Gk he

24 But the word of God continued to advance and gain adherents. [25]Then after completing their mission Barnabas and Saul returned to[a] Jerusalem and brought with them John, whose other name was Mark.

BARNABAS AND SAUL COMMISSIONED

13 Now in the church at Antioch there were prophets and teachers: Barnabas, Simeon who was called Niger, Lucius of Cyrene, Manaen a member of the court of Herod the ruler,[b] and Saul. [2]While they were worshiping the Lord and fasting, the Holy Spirit said, "Set apart for me Barnabas and Saul for the work to which I have called them." [3]Then after fasting and praying they laid their hands on them and sent them off.

THE APOSTLES PREACH IN CYPRUS

4 So, being sent out by the Holy Spirit, they went down to Seleucia; and from there they sailed to Cyprus. [5]When they arrived at Salamis, they proclaimed the word of God in the synagogues of the Jews. And they had John also to assist them. [6]When they had gone through the whole island as far as Paphos, they met a certain magician, a Jewish false prophet, named Bar-Jesus. [7]He was with the proconsul, Sergius Paulus, an intelligent man, who summoned Barnabas and Saul and wanted to hear the word of God. [8]But the magician Elymas (for that is the translation of his name) opposed them and tried to turn the proconsul away from the faith. [9]But Saul, also known as Paul, filled with the Holy Spirit, looked intently at him [10]and said, "You son of the devil, you enemy of all righteousness, full of all deceit and villainy, will you not stop making crooked the straight paths of the Lord? [11]And now listen—the hand of the Lord is against you, and you will be blind for a while, unable to see the sun." Immediately mist and darkness came over him, and he went about groping for someone to lead him by the hand. [12]When the proconsul saw what had happened, he believed, for he was astonished at the teaching about the Lord.

PAUL AND BARNABAS IN ANTIOCH OF PISIDIA

13 Then Paul and his companions set sail from Paphos and came to Perga in Pamphylia. John, however, left them and returned to Jerusalem; [14]but they went on from Perga and came to Antioch in Pisidia. And on the sabbath day they went into the synagogue and sat down. [15]After the reading of the law and the

---

a Other ancient authorities read from   b Gk tetrarch

prophets, the officials of the synagogue sent them a message, saying, "Brothers, if you have any word of exhortation for the people, give it." [16]So Paul stood up and with a gesture began to speak:

"You Israelites,[a] and others who fear God, listen. [17]The God of this people Israel chose our ancestors and made the people great during their stay in the land of Egypt, and with uplifted arm he led them out of it. [18]For about forty years he put up with[b] them in the wilderness. [19]After he had destroyed seven nations in the land of Canaan, he gave them their land as an inheritance [20]for about four hundred fifty years. After that he gave them judges until the time of the prophet Samuel. [21]Then they asked for a king; and God gave them Saul son of Kish, a man of the tribe of Benjamin, who reigned for forty years. [22]When he had removed him, he made David their king. In his testimony about him he said, 'I have found David, son of Jesse, to be a man after my heart, who will carry out all my wishes.' [23]Of this man's posterity God has brought to Israel a Savior, Jesus, as he promised; [24]before his coming John had already proclaimed a baptism of repentance to all the people of Israel. [25]And as John was finishing his work, he said, 'What do you suppose that I am? I am not he. No, but one is coming after me; I am not worthy to untie the thong of the sandals[c] on his feet.'

26 "My brothers, you descendants of Abraham's family, and others who fear God, to us[d] the message of this salvation has been sent. [27]Because the residents of Jerusalem and their leaders did not recognize him or understand the words of the prophets that are read every sabbath, they fulfilled those words by condemning him. [28]Even though they found no cause for a sentence of death, they asked Pilate to have him killed. [29]When they had carried out everything that was written about him, they took him down from the tree and laid him in a tomb. [30]But God raised him from the dead; [31]and for many days he appeared to those who came up with him from Galilee to Jerusalem, and they are now his witnesses to the people. [32]And we bring you the good news that what God promised to our ancestors [33]he has fulfilled for us, their children, by raising Jesus; as also it is written in the second psalm,

'You are my Son;
    today I have begotten you.'

34 As to his raising him from the dead, no more to return to corruption, he has spoken in this way,

'I will give you the holy promises made to David.'

35 Therefore he has also said in another psalm,

'You will not let your Holy One experience corruption.'

---

a Gk Men, Israelites   b Other ancient authorities read cared for   c Gk untie the sandals   d Other ancient authorities read you

36 For David, after he had served the purpose of God in his own generation, died,^a was laid beside his ancestors, and experienced corruption; ³⁷but he whom God raised up experienced no corruption. ³⁸Let it be known to you therefore, my brothers, that through this man forgiveness of sins is proclaimed to you; ³⁹by this Jesus^b everyone who believes is set free from all those sins^c from which you could not be freed by the law of Moses. ⁴⁰Beware, therefore, that what the prophets said does not happen to you:

41 'Look, you scoffers!

Be amazed and perish,

for in your days I am doing a work,

a work that you will never believe, even if someone tells you.' "

42 As Paul and Barnabas^d were going out, the people urged them to speak about these things again the next sabbath. ⁴³When the meeting of the synagogue broke up, many Jews and devout converts to Judaism followed Paul and Barnabas, who spoke to them and urged them to continue in the grace of God.

44 The next sabbath almost the whole city gathered to hear the word of the Lord.^e ⁴⁵But when the Jews saw the crowds, they were filled with jealousy; and blaspheming, they contradicted what was spoken by Paul. ⁴⁶Then both Paul and Barnabas spoke out boldly, saying, "It was necessary that the word of God should be spoken first to you. Since you reject it and judge yourselves to be unworthy of eternal life, we are now turning to the Gentiles. ⁴⁷For so the Lord has commanded us, saying,

'I have set you to be a light for the Gentiles,

so that you may bring salvation to the ends of the earth.' "

48 When the Gentiles heard this, they were glad and praised the word of the Lord; and as many as had been destined for eternal life became believers. ⁴⁹Thus the word of the Lord spread throughout the region. ⁵⁰But the Jews incited the devout women of high standing and the leading men of the city, and stirred up persecution against Paul and Barnabas, and drove them out of their region. ⁵¹So they shook the dust off their feet in protest against them, and went to Iconium. ⁵²And the disciples were filled with joy and with the Holy Spirit.

PAUL AND BARNABAS IN ICONIUM

14 The same thing occurred in Iconium, where Paul and Barnabas^d went into the Jewish synagogue and spoke in such a way that a great number of both Jews and Greeks became believers. ²But the unbelieving Jews stirred up the Gentiles and poisoned their minds against the brothers. ³So they remained

---

a Gk *fell asleep*   *b* Gk *this*   *c* Gk *all*   *d* Gk *they*   *e* Other ancient authorities read *God* for a long time, speaking boldly for the Lord, who testified to the word of his grace by granting signs and wonders to be done through them. ⁴But the residents of the city were divided; some sided with the Jews, and some with the apostles. ⁵And when an attempt was made by both Gentiles and Jews, with their rulers, to mistreat them and to stone them, ⁶the apostles*a* learned of it and fled to Lystra and Derbe, cities of Lycaonia, and to the surrounding country; ⁷and there they continued proclaiming the good news.

PAUL AND BARNABAS IN LYSTRA AND DERBE

8 In Lystra there was a man sitting who could not use his feet and had never walked, for he had been crippled from birth. ⁹He listened to Paul as he was speaking. And Paul, looking at him intently and seeing that he had faith to be healed, ¹⁰said in a loud voice, "Stand upright on your feet." And the man*b* sprang up and began to walk. ¹¹When the crowds saw what Paul had done, they shouted in the Lycaonian language, "The gods have come down to us in human form!" ¹²Barnabas they called Zeus, and Paul they called Hermes, because he was the chief speaker. ¹³The priest of Zeus, whose temple was just outside the city,*c* brought oxen and garlands to the gates; he and the crowds wanted to offer sacrifice. ¹⁴When the apostles Barnabas and Paul heard of it, they tore their clothes and rushed out into the crowd, shouting, ¹⁵"Friends,*d* why are you doing this? We are mortals just like you, and we bring you good news, that you should turn from these worthless things to the living God, who made the heaven and the earth and the sea and all that is in them. ¹⁶In past generations he allowed all the nations to follow their own ways; ¹⁷yet he has not left himself without a witness in doing good—giving you rains from heaven and fruitful seasons, and filling you with food and your hearts with joy." ¹⁸Even with these words, they scarcely restrained the crowds from offering sacrifice to them.

19 But Jews came there from Antioch and Iconium and won over the crowds. Then they stoned Paul and dragged him out of the city, supposing that he was dead. ²⁰But when the disciples surrounded him, he got up and went into the city. The next day he went on with Barnabas to Derbe.

THE RETURN TO ANTIOCH IN SYRIA

21 After they had proclaimed the good news to that city and had made many disciples, they returned to Lystra, then on to Iconium and Antioch. ²²There they strengthened the souls of the disciples and encouraged them to continue in the faith, saying, "It is through many persecutions that we must enter the

---

a Gk *they*   *b* Gk *he*   *c* Or *The priest of Zeus-Outside-the-City*   *d* Gk *Men* kingdom of God." [23]And after they had appointed elders for them in each church, with prayer and fasting they entrusted them to the Lord in whom they had come to believe.

24 Then they passed through Pisidia and came to Pamphylia. [25]When they had spoken the word in Perga, they went down to Attalia. [26]From there they sailed back to Antioch, where they had been commended to the grace of God for the work[a] that they had completed. [27]When they arrived, they called the church together and related all that God had done with them, and how he had opened a door of faith for the Gentiles. [28]And they stayed there with the disciples for some time.

THE COUNCIL AT JERUSALEM

15 Then certain individuals came down from Judea and were teaching the brothers, "Unless you are circumcised according to the custom of Moses, you cannot be saved." [2]And after Paul and Barnabas had no small dissension and debate with them, Paul and Barnabas and some of the others were appointed to go up to Jerusalem to discuss this question with the apostles and the elders. [3]So they were sent on their way by the church, and as they passed through both Phoenicia and Samaria, they reported the conversion of the Gentiles, and brought great joy to all the believers.[b] [4]When they came to Jerusalem, they were welcomed by the church and the apostles and the elders, and they reported all that God had done with them. [5]But some believers who belonged to the sect of the Pharisees stood up and said, "It is necessary for them to be circumcised and ordered to keep the law of Moses."

6 The apostles and the elders met together to consider this matter. [7]After there had been much debate, Peter stood up and said to them, "My brothers,[c] you know that in the early days God made a choice among you, that I should be the one through whom the Gentiles would hear the message of the good news and become believers. [8]And God, who knows the human heart, testified to them by giving them the Holy Spirit, just as he did to us; [9]and in cleansing their hearts by faith he has made no distinction between them and us. [10]Now therefore why are you putting God to the test by placing on the neck of the disciples a yoke that neither our ancestors nor we have been able to bear? [11]On the contrary, we believe that we will be saved through the grace of the Lord Jesus, just as they will."

12 The whole assembly kept silence, and listened to Barnabas and Paul as they told of all the signs and wonders that God had done through them among

---

a Or *committed in the grace of God to the work*   *b* Gk *brothers*   *c* Gk *Men, brothers* the Gentiles. ¹³After they finished speaking, James replied, "My brothers,ᵃ listen to me. ¹⁴Simeon has related how God first looked favorably on the Gentiles, to take from among them a people for his name. ¹⁵This agrees with the words of the prophets, as it is written,

16 'After this I will return,
>   and I will rebuild the dwelling of David, which has fallen;
>>   from its ruins I will rebuild it,
>>   and I will set it up,
17 so that all other peoples may seek the Lord—
>   even all the Gentiles over whom my name has been called.
>>   Thus says the Lord, who has been making these things ¹⁸known
>>   from long ago.'ᵇ

19 Therefore I have reached the decision that we should not trouble those Gentiles who are turning to God, ²⁰but we should write to them to abstain only from things polluted by idols and from fornication and from whatever has been strangledᶜ and from blood. ²¹For in every city, for generations past, Moses has had those who proclaim him, for he has been read aloud every sabbath in the synagogues."

THE COUNCIL'S LETTER TO GENTILE BELIEVERS

22 Then the apostles and the elders, with the consent of the whole church, decided to choose men from among their membersᵈ and to send them to Antioch with Paul and Barnabas. They sent Judas called Barsabbas, and Silas, leaders among the brothers, ²³with the following letter: "The brothers, both the apostles and the elders, to the believersᵉ of Gentile origin in Antioch and Syria and Cilicia, greetings. ²⁴Since we have heard that certain persons who have gone out from us, though with no instructions from us, have said things to disturb you and have unsettled your minds,ᶠ ²⁵we have decided unanimously to choose representativesᵍ and send them to you, along with our beloved Barnabas and Paul, ²⁶who have risked their lives for the sake of our Lord Jesus Christ. ²⁷We have therefore sent Judas and Silas, who themselves will tell you the same things by word of mouth. ²⁸For it has seemed good to the Holy Spirit and to us to impose on you no further burden than these essentials: ²⁹that you abstain from what has been sacrificed to idols and from blood and from what is strangledʰ and from fornication. If you keep yourselves from these, you will do well. Farewell."

30 So they were sent off and went down to Antioch. When they gathered

---

a Gk Men, brothers   b Other ancient authorities read things. ¹⁸'Known to God from of old are all his works.'   c Other ancient authorities lack and from whatever has been strangled   d Gk from among them   e Gk brothers   f Other ancient authorities add saying, 'You must be circumcised and keep the law,'   g Gk men   h Other ancient authorities lack and from what is strangled the congregation together, they delivered the letter. [31]When its members[a] read it, they rejoiced at the exhortation. [32]Judas and Silas, who were themselves prophets, said much to encourage and strengthen the believers.[b] [33]After they had been there for some time, they were sent off in peace by the believers[b] to those who had sent them.[c] [35]But Paul and Barnabas remained in Antioch, and there, with many others, they taught and proclaimed the word of the Lord.

PAUL AND BARNABAS SEPARATE

36 After some days Paul said to Barnabas, "Come, let us return and visit the believers[b] in every city where we proclaimed the word of the Lord and see how they are doing." [37]Barnabas wanted to take with them John called Mark. [38]But Paul decided not to take with them one who had deserted them in Pamphylia and had not accompanied them in the work. [39]The disagreement became so sharp that they parted company; Barnabas took Mark with him and sailed away to Cyprus. [40]But Paul chose Silas and set out, the believers[b] commending him to the grace of the Lord. [41]He went through Syria and Cilicia, strengthening the churches.

TIMOTHY JOINS PAUL AND SILAS

16 Paul[d] went on also to Derbe and to Lystra, where there was a disciple named Timothy, the son of a Jewish woman who was a believer; but his father was a Greek. [2]He was well spoken of by the believers[b] in Lystra and Iconium. [3]Paul wanted Timothy to accompany him; and he took him and had him circumcised because of the Jews who were in those places, for they all knew that his father was a Greek. [4]As they went from town to town, they delivered to them for observance the decisions that had been reached by the apostles and elders who were in Jerusalem. [5]So the churches were strengthened in the faith and increased in numbers daily.

PAUL'S VISION OF THE MAN OF MACEDONIA

6 They went through the region of Phrygia and Galatia, having been forbidden by the Holy Spirit to speak the word in Asia. [7]When they had come opposite Mysia, they attempted to go into Bithynia, but the Spirit of Jesus did not allow them; [8]so, passing by Mysia, they went down to Troas. [9]During the night Paul had a vision: there stood a man of Macedonia pleading with him and saying, "Come over to Macedonia and help us." [10]When he had seen the vision, we

---

a Gk *When they*   *b* Gk *brothers*   *c* Other ancient authorities add verse 34, *But it seemed good to Silas to remain there*   *d* Gk *He* immediately tried to cross over to Macedonia, being convinced that God had called us to proclaim the good news to them.

THE CONVERSION OF LYDIA

11 We set sail from Troas and took a straight course to Samothrace, the following day to Neapolis, [12]and from there to Philippi, which is a leading city of the district[a] of Macedonia and a Roman colony. We remained in this city for some days. [13]On the sabbath day we went outside the gate by the river, where we supposed there was a place of prayer; and we sat down and spoke to the women who had gathered there. [14]A certain woman named Lydia, a worshiper of God, was listening to us; she was from the city of Thyatira and a dealer in purple cloth. The Lord opened her heart to listen eagerly to what was said by Paul. [15]When she and her household were baptized, she urged us, saying, "If you have judged me to be faithful to the Lord, come and stay at my home." And she prevailed upon us.

PAUL AND SILAS IN PRISON

16 One day, as we were going to the place of prayer, we met a slave-girl who had a spirit of divination and brought her owners a great deal of money by fortune-telling. [17]While she followed Paul and us, she would cry out, "These men are slaves of the Most High God, who proclaim to you[b] a way of salvation." [18]She kept doing this for many days. But Paul, very much annoyed, turned and said to the spirit, "I order you in the name of Jesus Christ to come out of her." And it came out that very hour.

19 But when her owners saw that their hope of making money was gone, they seized Paul and Silas and dragged them into the marketplace before the authorities. [20]When they had brought them before the magistrates, they said, "These men are disturbing our city; they are Jews [21]and are advocating customs that are not lawful for us as Romans to adopt or observe." [22]The crowd joined in attacking them, and the magistrates had them stripped of their clothing and ordered them to be beaten with rods. [23]After they had given them a severe flogging, they threw them into prison and ordered the jailer to keep them securely. [24]Following these instructions, he put them in the innermost cell and fastened their feet in the stocks.

25 About midnight Paul and Silas were praying and singing hymns to God, and the prisoners were listening to them. [26]Suddenly there was an earthquake, so violent that the foundations of the prison were shaken; and immediately

---

a Other authorities read *a city of the first district*   b Other ancient authorities read *to us* all the doors were opened and everyone's chains were unfastened. ²⁷When the jailer woke up and saw the prison doors wide open, he drew his sword and was about to kill himself, since he supposed that the prisoners had escaped. ²⁸But Paul shouted in a loud voice, "Do not harm yourself, for we are all here." ²⁹The jailer[a] called for lights, and rushing in, he fell down trembling before Paul and Silas. ³⁰Then he brought them outside and said, "Sirs, what must I do to be saved?" ³¹They answered, "Believe on the Lord Jesus, and you will be saved, you and your household." ³²They spoke the word of the Lord[b] to him and to all who were in his house. ³³At the same hour of the night he took them and washed their wounds; then he and his entire family were baptized without delay. ³⁴He brought them up into the house and set food before them; and he and his entire household rejoiced that he had become a believer in God.

35 When morning came, the magistrates sent the police, saying, "Let those men go." ³⁶And the jailer reported the message to Paul, saying, "The magistrates sent word to let you go; therefore come out now and go in peace." ³⁷But Paul replied, "They have beaten us in public, uncondemned, men who are Roman citizens, and have thrown us into prison; and now are they going to discharge us in secret? Certainly not! Let them come and take us out themselves." ³⁸The police reported these words to the magistrates, and they were afraid when they heard that they were Roman citizens; ³⁹so they came and apologized to them. And they took them out and asked them to leave the city. ⁴⁰After leaving the prison they went to Lydia's home; and when they had seen and encouraged the brothers and sisters[c] there, they departed.

THE UPROAR IN THESSALONICA

17 After Paul and Silas[d] had passed through Amphipolis and Apollonia, they came to Thessalonica, where there was a synagogue of the Jews. ²And Paul went in, as was his custom, and on three sabbath days argued with them from the scriptures, ³explaining and proving that it was necessary for the Messiah[e] to suffer and to rise from the dead, and saying, "This is the Messiah,[e] Jesus whom I am proclaiming to you." ⁴Some of them were persuaded and joined Paul and Silas, as did a great many of the devout Greeks and not a few of the leading women. ⁵But the Jews became jealous, and with the help of some ruffians in the marketplaces they formed a mob and set the city in an uproar. While they were searching for Paul and Silas to bring them out to the assembly, they attacked Jason's house. ⁶When they could not find them, they dragged Jason and some believers[c] before the city authorities,[f] shouting, "These people

---

a Gk He b Other ancient authorities read *word of God* c Gk *brothers* d Gk *they* e Or *the Christ* f Gk *politarchs* who have been turning the world upside down have come here also, [7]and Jason has entertained them as guests. They are all acting contrary to the decrees of the emperor, saying that there is another king named Jesus." [8]The people and the city officials were disturbed when they heard this, [9]and after they had taken bail from Jason and the others, they let them go.

PAUL AND SILAS IN BEROEA

10 That very night the believers[a] sent Paul and Silas off to Beroea; and when they arrived, they went to the Jewish synagogue. [11]These Jews were more receptive than those in Thessalonica, for they welcomed the message very eagerly and examined the scriptures every day to see whether these things were so. [12]Many of them therefore believed, including not a few Greek women and men of high standing. [13]But when the Jews of Thessalonica learned that the word of God had been proclaimed by Paul in Beroea as well, they came there too, to stir up and incite the crowds. [14]Then the believers[a] immediately sent Paul away to the coast, but Silas and Timothy remained behind. [15]Those who conducted Paul brought him as far as Athens; and after receiving instructions to have Silas and Timothy join him as soon as possible, they left him.

PAUL IN ATHENS

16 While Paul was waiting for them in Athens, he was deeply distressed to see that the city was full of idols. [17]So he argued in the synagogue with the Jews and the devout persons, and also in the marketplace[b] every day with those who happened to be there. [18]Also some Epicurean and Stoic philosophers debated with him. Some said, "What does this babbler want to say?" Others said, "He seems to be a proclaimer of foreign divinities." (This was because he was telling the good news about Jesus and the resurrection.) [19]So they took him and brought him to the Areopagus and asked him, "May we know what this new teaching is that you are presenting? [20]It sounds rather strange to us, so we would like to know what it means." [21]Now all the Athenians and the foreigners living there would spend their time in nothing but telling or hearing something new.

22 Then Paul stood in front of the Areopagus and said, "Athenians, I see how extremely religious you are in every way. [23]For as I went through the city and looked carefully at the objects of your worship, I found among them an altar with the inscription, 'To an unknown god.' What therefore you worship as unknown, this I proclaim to you. [24]The God who made the world and everything in it, he who is Lord of heaven and earth, does not live in shrines made

---

a Gk *brothers*   *b* Or *civic center;* Gk *agora*

by human hands, [25]nor is he served by human hands, as though he needed anything, since he himself gives to all mortals life and breath and all things. [26]From one ancestor[a] he made all nations to inhabit the whole earth, and he allotted the times of their existence and the boundaries of the places where they would live, [27]so that they would search for God[b] and perhaps grope for him and find him—though indeed he is not far from each one of us. [28]For 'In him we live and move and have our being'; as even some of your own poets have said,

'For we too are his offspring.'

[29]Since we are God's offspring, we ought not to think that the deity is like gold, or silver, or stone, an image formed by the art and imagination of mortals. [30]While God has overlooked the times of human ignorance, now he commands all people everywhere to repent, [31]because he has fixed a day on which he will have the world judged in righteousness by a man whom he has appointed, and of this he has given assurance to all by raising him from the dead."

32 When they heard of the resurrection of the dead, some scoffed; but others said, "We will hear you again about this." [33]At that point Paul left them. [34]But some of them joined him and became believers, including Dionysius the Areopagite and a woman named Damaris, and others with them.

PAUL IN CORINTH

18 After this Paul[c] left Athens and went to Corinth. [2]There he found a Jew named Aquila, a native of Pontus, who had recently come from Italy with his wife Priscilla, because Claudius had ordered all Jews to leave Rome. Paul[d] went to see them, [3]and, because he was of the same trade, he stayed with them, and they worked together—by trade they were tentmakers. [4]Every sabbath he would argue in the synagogue and would try to convince Jews and Greeks.

5 When Silas and Timothy arrived from Macedonia, Paul was occupied with proclaiming the word,[e] testifying to the Jews that the Messiah[f] was Jesus. [6]When they opposed and reviled him, in protest he shook the dust from his clothes[g] and said to them, "Your blood be on your own heads! I am innocent. From now on I will go to the Gentiles." [7]Then he left the synagogue[h] and went to the house of a man named Titius[i] Justus, a worshiper of God; his house was next door to the synagogue. [8]Crispus, the official of the synagogue, became a believer in the Lord, together with all his household; and many of the Corinthians who heard Paul became believers and were baptized. [9]One night the

---

a Gk *From one;* other ancient authorities read *From one blood*   b Other ancient authorities read *the Lord*   c Gk *he*   d Gk *He*
e Gk *with the word*   f Or *the Christ*   g Gk *reviled him, he shook out his clothes*   h Gk *left there*   i Other ancient authorities read
Titus

Lord said to Paul in a vision, "Do not be afraid, but speak and do not be silent; [10]for I am with you, and no one will lay a hand on you to harm you, for there are many in this city who are my people." [11]He stayed there a year and six months, teaching the word of God among them.

12 But when Gallio was proconsul of Achaia, the Jews made a united attack on Paul and brought him before the tribunal. [13]They said, "This man is persuading people to worship God in ways that are contrary to the law." [14]Just as Paul was about to speak, Gallio said to the Jews, "If it were a matter of crime or serious villainy, I would be justified in accepting the complaint of you Jews; [15]but since it is a matter of questions about words and names and your own law, see to it yourselves; I do not wish to be a judge of these matters." [16]And he dismissed them from the tribunal. [17]Then all of them[a] seized Sosthenes, the official of the synagogue, and beat him in front of the tribunal. But Gallio paid no attention to any of these things.

PAUL'S RETURN TO ANTIOCH

18 After staying there for a considerable time, Paul said farewell to the believers[b] and sailed for Syria, accompanied by Priscilla and Aquila. At Cenchreae he had his hair cut, for he was under a vow. [19]When they reached Ephesus, he left them there, but first he himself went into the synagogue and had a discussion with the Jews. [20]When they asked him to stay longer, he declined; [21]but on taking leave of them, he said, "I[c] will return to you, if God wills." Then he set sail from Ephesus.

22 When he had landed at Caesarea, he went up to Jerusalem[d] and greeted the church, and then went down to Antioch. [23]After spending some time there he departed and went from place to place through the region of Galatia[e] and Phrygia, strengthening all the disciples.

MINISTRY OF APOLLOS

24 Now there came to Ephesus a Jew named Apollos, a native of Alexandria. He was an eloquent man, well-versed in the scriptures. [25]He had been instructed in the Way of the Lord; and he spoke with burning enthusiasm and taught accurately the things concerning Jesus, though he knew only the baptism of John. [26]He began to speak boldly in the synagogue; but when Priscilla and Aquila heard him, they took him aside and explained the Way of God to him more accurately. [27]And when he wished to cross over to Achaia, the believers[b] encouraged him and wrote to the disciples to welcome him. On his arrival he greatly

---

a Other ancient authorities read *all the Greeks*   b Gk *brothers*   c Other ancient authorities read *I must at all costs keep the approaching festival in Jerusalem, but I*   d Gk *went up*   e Gk *the Galatian region* helped those who through grace had become believers, [28]for he powerfully refuted the Jews in public, showing by the scriptures that the Messiah[a] is Jesus.

PAUL IN EPHESUS

19 While Apollos was in Corinth, Paul passed through the interior regions and came to Ephesus, where he found some disciples. [2]He said to them, "Did you receive the Holy Spirit when you became believers?" They replied, "No, we have not even heard that there is a Holy Spirit." [3]Then he said, "Into what then were you baptized?" They answered, "Into John's baptism." [4]Paul said, "John baptized with the baptism of repentance, telling the people to believe in the one who was to come after him, that is, in Jesus." [5]On hearing this, they were baptized in the name of the Lord Jesus. [6]When Paul had laid his hands on them, the Holy Spirit came upon them, and they spoke in tongues and prophesied— [7]altogether there were about twelve of them.

8 He entered the synagogue and for three months spoke out boldly, and argued persuasively about the kingdom of God. [9]When some stubbornly refused to believe and spoke evil of the Way before the congregation, he left them, taking the disciples with him, and argued daily in the lecture hall of Tyrannus.[b] [10]This continued for two years, so that all the residents of Asia, both Jews and Greeks, heard the word of the Lord.

THE SONS OF SCEVA

11 God did extraordinary miracles through Paul, [12]so that when the handkerchiefs or aprons that had touched his skin were brought to the sick, their diseases left them, and the evil spirits came out of them. [13]Then some itinerant Jewish exorcists tried to use the name of the Lord Jesus over those who had evil spirits, saying, "I adjure you by the Jesus whom Paul proclaims." [14]Seven sons of a Jewish high priest named Sceva were doing this. [15]But the evil spirit said to them in reply, "Jesus I know, and Paul I know; but who are you?" [16]Then the man with the evil spirit leaped on them, mastered them all, and so overpowered them that they fled out of the house naked and wounded. [17]When this became known to all residents of Ephesus, both Jews and Greeks, everyone was awestruck; and the name of the Lord Jesus was praised. [18]Also many of those who became believers confessed and disclosed their practices. [19]A number of those who practiced magic collected their books and burned them publicly; when the value of these books[c] was calculated, it was found to come to fifty thousand silver coins. [20]So the word of the Lord grew mightily and prevailed.

---

a Or the Christ b Other ancient authorities read of a certain Tyrannus, from eleven o'clock in the morning to four in the afternoon
c Gk them

THE RIOT IN EPHESUS

21 Now after these things had been accomplished, Paul resolved in the Spirit to go through Macedonia and Achaia, and then to go on to Jerusalem. He said, "After I have gone there, I must also see Rome." 22So he sent two of his helpers, Timothy and Erastus, to Macedonia, while he himself stayed for some time longer in Asia.

23 About that time no little disturbance broke out concerning the Way. 24A man named Demetrius, a silversmith who made silver shrines of Artemis, brought no little business to the artisans. 25These he gathered together, with the workers of the same trade, and said, "Men, you know that we get our wealth from this business. 26You also see and hear that not only in Ephesus but in almost the whole of Asia this Paul has persuaded and drawn away a considerable number of people by saying that gods made with hands are not gods. 27And there is danger not only that this trade of ours may come into disrepute but also that the temple of the great goddess Artemis will be scorned, and she will be deprived of her majesty that brought all Asia and the world to worship her."

28 When they heard this, they were enraged and shouted, "Great is Artemis of the Ephesians!" 29The city was filled with the confusion; and people*a* rushed together to the theater, dragging with them Gaius and Aristarchus, Macedonians who were Paul's travel companions. 30Paul wished to go into the crowd, but the disciples would not let him; 31even some officials of the province of Asia,*b* who were friendly to him, sent him a message urging him not to venture into the theater. 32Meanwhile, some were shouting one thing, some another; for the assembly was in confusion, and most of them did not know why they had come together. 33Some of the crowd gave instructions to Alexander, whom the Jews had pushed forward. And Alexander motioned for silence and tried to make a defense before the people. 34But when they recognized that he was a Jew, for about two hours all of them shouted in unison, "Great is Artemis of the Ephesians!" 35But when the town clerk had quieted the crowd, he said, "Citizens of Ephesus, who is there that does not know that the city of the Ephesians is the temple keeper of the great Artemis and of the statue that fell from heaven?*c* 36Since these things cannot be denied, you ought to be quiet and do nothing rash. 37You have brought these men here who are neither temple robbers nor blasphemers of our*d* goddess. 38If therefore Demetrius and the artisans with him have a complaint against anyone, the courts are open, and there are proconsuls; let them bring charges there against one another. 39If there is anything

---

a Gk they   b Gk some of the Asiarchs   c Meaning of Gk uncertain   d Other ancient authorities read your further *a* you want to know, it must be settled in the regular assembly. [40]For we are in danger of being charged with rioting today, since there is no cause that we can give to justify this commotion." [41]When he had said this, he dismissed the assembly.

PAUL GOES TO MACEDONIA AND GREECE

20 After the uproar had ceased, Paul sent for the disciples; and after encouraging them and saying farewell, he left for Macedonia. [2]When he had gone through those regions and had given the believers*b* much encouragement, he came to Greece, [3]where he stayed for three months. He was about to set sail for Syria when a plot was made against him by the Jews, and so he decided to return through Macedonia. [4]He was accompanied by Sopater son of Pyrrhus from Beroea, by Aristarchus and Secundus from Thessalonica, by Gaius from Derbe, and by Timothy, as well as by Tychicus and Trophimus from Asia. [5]They went ahead and were waiting for us in Troas; [6]but we sailed from Philippi after the days of Unleavened Bread, and in five days we joined them in Troas, where we stayed for seven days.

PAUL'S FAREWELL VISIT TO TROAS

7 On the first day of the week, when we met to break bread, Paul was holding a discussion with them; since he intended to leave the next day, he continued speaking until midnight. [8]There were many lamps in the room upstairs where we were meeting. [9]A young man named Eutychus, who was sitting in the window, began to sink off into a deep sleep while Paul talked still longer. Overcome by sleep, he fell to the ground three floors below and was picked up dead. [10]But Paul went down, and bending over him took him in his arms, and said, "Do not be alarmed, for his life is in him." [11]Then Paul went upstairs, and after he had broken bread and eaten, he continued to converse with them until dawn; then he left. [12]Meanwhile they had taken the boy away alive and were not a little comforted.

THE VOYAGE FROM TROAS TO MILETUS

13 We went ahead to the ship and set sail for Assos, intending to take Paul on board there; for he had made this arrangement, intending to go by land himself. [14]When he met us in Assos, we took him on board and went to Mitylene. [15]We sailed from there, and on the following day we arrived opposite Chios. The

---

a Other ancient authorities read *about other matters* *b* Gk *given them* next day we touched at Samos, and*a* the day after that we came to Miletus. ¹⁶For Paul had decided to sail past Ephesus, so that he might not have to spend time in Asia; he was eager to be in Jerusalem, if possible, on the day of Pentecost.

PAUL SPEAKS TO THE EPHESIAN ELDERS

17 From Miletus he sent a message to Ephesus, asking the elders of the church to meet him. ¹⁸When they came to him, he said to them:

"You yourselves know how I lived among you the entire time from the first day that I set foot in Asia, ¹⁹serving the Lord with all humility and with tears, enduring the trials that came to me through the plots of the Jews. ²⁰I did not shrink from doing anything helpful, proclaiming the message to you and teaching you publicly and from house to house, ²¹as I testified to both Jews and Greeks about repentance toward God and faith toward our Lord Jesus. ²²And now, as a captive to the Spirit,*b* I am on my way to Jerusalem, not knowing what will happen to me there, ²³except that the Holy Spirit testifies to me in every city that imprisonment and persecutions are waiting for me. ²⁴But I do not count my life of any value to myself, if only I may finish my course and the ministry that I received from the Lord Jesus, to testify to the good news of God's grace.

25 "And now I know that none of you, among whom I have gone about proclaiming the kingdom, will ever see my face again. ²⁶Therefore I declare to you this day that I am not responsible for the blood of any of you, ²⁷for I did not shrink from declaring to you the whole purpose of God. ²⁸Keep watch over yourselves and over all the flock, of which the Holy Spirit has made you overseers, to shepherd the church of God*c* that he obtained with the blood of his own Son.*d* ²⁹I know that after I have gone, savage wolves will come in among you, not sparing the flock. ³⁰Some even from your own group will come distorting the truth in order to entice the disciples to follow them. ³¹Therefore be alert, remembering that for three years I did not cease night or day to warn everyone with tears. ³²And now I commend you to God and to the message of his grace, a message that is able to build you up and to give you the inheritance among all who are sanctified. ³³I coveted no one's silver or gold or clothing. ³⁴You know for yourselves that I worked with my own hands to support myself and my companions. ³⁵In all this I have given you an example that by such work we must support the weak, remembering the words of the Lord Jesus, for he himself said, 'It is more blessed to give than to receive.'"

---

a Other ancient authorities add *after remaining at Trogyllium*   *b* Or *And now, bound in the spirit*   *c* Other ancient authorities read *of the Lord*   *d* Or *with his own blood;* Gk *with the blood of his Own*

36 When he had finished speaking, he knelt down with them all and prayed. ³⁷There was much weeping among them all; they embraced Paul and kissed him, ³⁸grieving especially because of what he had said, that they would not see him again. Then they brought him to the ship.

PAUL'S JOURNEY TO JERUSALEM

21 When we had parted from them and set sail, we came by a straight course to Cos, and the next day to Rhodes, and from there to Patara.ᵃ ²When we found a ship bound for Phoenicia, we went on board and set sail. ³We came in sight of Cyprus; and leaving it on our left, we sailed to Syria and landed at Tyre, because the ship was to unload its cargo there. ⁴We looked up the disciples and stayed there for seven days. Through the Spirit they told Paul not to go on to Jerusalem. ⁵When our days there were ended, we left and proceeded on our journey; and all of them, with wives and children, escorted us outside the city. There we knelt down on the beach and prayed ⁶and said farewell to one another. Then we went on board the ship, and they returned home.

7 When we had finishedᵇ the voyage from Tyre, we arrived at Ptolemais; and we greeted the believersᶜ and stayed with them for one day. ⁸The next day we left and came to Caesarea; and we went into the house of Philip the evangelist, one of the seven, and stayed with him. ⁹He had four unmarried daughtersᵈ who had the gift of prophecy. ¹⁰While we were staying there for several days, a prophet named Agabus came down from Judea. ¹¹He came to us and took Paul's belt, bound his own feet and hands with it, and said, "Thus says the Holy Spirit, 'This is the way the Jews in Jerusalem will bind the man who owns this belt and will hand him over to the Gentiles.'" ¹²When we heard this, we and the people there urged him not to go up to Jerusalem. ¹³Then Paul answered, "What are you doing, weeping and breaking my heart? For I am ready not only to be bound but even to die in Jerusalem for the name of the Lord Jesus." ¹⁴Since he would not be persuaded, we remained silent except to say, "The Lord's will be done."

15 After these days we got ready and started to go up to Jerusalem. ¹⁶Some of the disciples from Caesarea also came along and brought us to the house of Mnason of Cyprus, an early disciple, with whom we were to stay.

PAUL VISITS JAMES AT JERUSALEM

17 When we arrived in Jerusalem, the brothers welcomed us warmly. ¹⁸The next day Paul went with us to visit James; and all the elders were present.

---

a Other ancient authorities add *and Myra*   *b* Or *continued*   *c* Gk *brothers*   *d* Gk *four daughters, virgins,*

¹⁹After greeting them, he related one by one the things that God had done among the Gentiles through his ministry. ²⁰When they heard it, they praised God. Then they said to him, "You see, brother, how many thousands of believers there are among the Jews, and they are all zealous for the law. ²¹They have been told about you that you teach all the Jews living among the Gentiles to forsake Moses, and that you tell them not to circumcise their children or observe the customs. ²²What then is to be done? They will certainly hear that you have come. ²³So do what we tell you. We have four men who are under a vow. ²⁴Join these men, go through the rite of purification with them, and pay for the shaving of their heads. Thus all will know that there is nothing in what they have been told about you, but that you yourself observe and guard the law. ²⁵But as for the Gentiles who have become believers, we have sent a letter with our judgment that they should abstain from what has been sacrificed to idols and from blood and from what is strangled^a and from fornication." ²⁶Then Paul took the men, and the next day, having purified himself, he entered the temple with them, making public the completion of the days of purification when the sacrifice would be made for each of them.

PAUL ARRESTED IN THE TEMPLE

27 When the seven days were almost completed, the Jews from Asia, who had seen him in the temple, stirred up the whole crowd. They seized him, ²⁸shouting, "Fellow Israelites, help! This is the man who is teaching everyone everywhere against our people, our law, and this place; more than that, he has actually brought Greeks into the temple and has defiled this holy place." ²⁹For they had previously seen Trophimus the Ephesian with him in the city, and they supposed that Paul had brought him into the temple. ³⁰Then all the city was aroused, and the people rushed together. They seized Paul and dragged him out of the temple, and immediately the doors were shut. ³¹While they were trying to kill him, word came to the tribune of the cohort that all Jerusalem was in an uproar. ³²Immediately he took soldiers and centurions and ran down to them. When they saw the tribune and the soldiers, they stopped beating Paul. ³³Then the tribune came, arrested him, and ordered him to be bound with two chains; he inquired who he was and what he had done. ³⁴Some in the crowd shouted one thing, some another; and as he could not learn the facts because of the uproar, he ordered him to be brought into the barracks. ³⁵When Paul^b came to the steps, the violence of the mob was so great that he had to be carried by the soldiers. ³⁶The crowd that followed kept shouting, "Away with him!"

---

a Other ancient authorities lack *and from what is strangled*   *b* Gk *he*

PAUL DEFENDS HIMSELF

37 Just as Paul was about to be brought into the barracks, he said to the tribune, "May I say something to you?" The tribune[a] replied, "Do you know Greek? [38]Then you are not the Egyptian who recently stirred up a revolt and led the four thousand assassins out into the wilderness?" [39]Paul replied, "I am a Jew, from Tarsus in Cilicia, a citizen of an important city; I beg you, let me speak to the people." [40]When he had given him permission, Paul stood on the steps and motioned to the people for silence; and when there was a great hush, he addressed them in the Hebrew[b] language, saying:

22 "Brothers and fathers, listen to the defense that I now make before you." 2 When they heard him addressing them in Hebrew,[b] they became even more quiet. Then he said:

3 "I am a Jew, born in Tarsus in Cilicia, but brought up in this city at the feet of Gamaliel, educated strictly according to our ancestral law, being zealous for God, just as all of you are today. [4]I persecuted this Way up to the point of death by binding both men and women and putting them in prison, [5]as the high priest and the whole council of elders can testify about me. From them I also received letters to the brothers in Damascus, and I went there in order to bind those who were there and to bring them back to Jerusalem for punishment.

PAUL TELLS OF HIS CONVERSION

6 "While I was on my way and approaching Damascus, about noon a great light from heaven suddenly shone about me. [7]I fell to the ground and heard a voice saying to me, 'Saul, Saul, why are you persecuting me?' [8]I answered, 'Who are you, Lord?' Then he said to me, 'I am Jesus of Nazareth[c] whom you are persecuting.' [9]Now those who were with me saw the light but did not hear the voice of the one who was speaking to me. [10]I asked, 'What am I to do, Lord?' The Lord said to me, 'Get up and go to Damascus; there you will be told everything that has been assigned to you to do.' [11]Since I could not see because of the brightness of that light, those who were with me took my hand and led me to Damascus.

12 "A certain Ananias, who was a devout man according to the law and well spoken of by all the Jews living there, [13]came to me; and standing beside me, he said, 'Brother Saul, regain your sight!' In that very hour I regained my sight and saw him. [14]Then he said, 'The God of our ancestors has chosen you to know his will, to see the Righteous One and to hear his own voice; [15]for you will be

---

a Gk He   b That is, *Aramaic*   c Gk *the Nazorean*

his witness to all the world of what you have seen and heard. ¹⁶And now why do you delay? Get up, be baptized, and have your sins washed away, calling on his name.'

PAUL SENT TO THE GENTILES

17 "After I had returned to Jerusalem and while I was praying in the temple, I fell into a trance ¹⁸and saw Jesus*ᵃ* saying to me, 'Hurry and get out of Jerusalem quickly, because they will not accept your testimony about me.' ¹⁹And I said, 'Lord, they themselves know that in every synagogue I imprisoned and beat those who believed in you. ²⁰And while the blood of your witness Stephen was shed, I myself was standing by, approving and keeping the coats of those who killed him.' ²¹Then he said to me, 'Go, for I will send you far away to the Gentiles.'"

PAUL AND THE ROMAN TRIBUNE

22 Up to this point they listened to him, but then they shouted, "Away with such a fellow from the earth! For he should not be allowed to live." ²³And while they were shouting, throwing off their cloaks, and tossing dust into the air, ²⁴the tribune directed that he was to be brought into the barracks, and ordered him to be examined by flogging, to find out the reason for this outcry against him. ²⁵But when they had tied him up with thongs,*ᵇ* Paul said to the centurion who was standing by, "Is it legal for you to flog a Roman citizen who is uncondemned?" ²⁶When the centurion heard that, he went to the tribune and said to him, "What are you about to do? This man is a Roman citizen." ²⁷The tribune came and asked Paul,*ᵃ* "Tell me, are you a Roman citizen?" And he said, "Yes." ²⁸The tribune answered, "It cost me a large sum of money to get my citizenship." Paul said, "But I was born a citizen." ²⁹Immediately those who were about to examine him drew back from him; and the tribune also was afraid, for he realized that Paul was a Roman citizen and that he had bound him.

PAUL BEFORE THE COUNCIL

30 Since he wanted to find out what Paul*ᶜ* was being accused of by the Jews, the next day he released him and ordered the chief priests and the entire council to meet. He brought Paul down and had him stand before them.

23 While Paul was looking intently at the council he said, "Brothers,*ᵈ* up to this day I have lived my life with a clear conscience before God." ²Then the high priest Ananias ordered those standing near him to strike him on the

---

a Gk *him*   *b* Or *up for the lashes*   *c* Gk *he*   *d* Gk *Men, brothers* mouth. [3]At this Paul said to him, "God will strike you, you whitewashed wall! Are you sitting there to judge me according to the law, and yet in violation of the law you order me to be struck?" [4]Those standing nearby said, "Do you dare to insult God's high priest?" [5]And Paul said, "I did not realize, brothers, that he was high priest; for it is written, 'You shall not speak evil of a leader of your people.'"

6 When Paul noticed that some were Sadducees and others were Pharisees, he called out in the council, "Brothers, I am a Pharisee, a son of Pharisees. I am on trial concerning the hope of the resurrection[a] of the dead." [7]When he said this, a dissension began between the Pharisees and the Sadducees, and the assembly was divided. [8](The Sadducees say that there is no resurrection, or angel, or spirit; but the Pharisees acknowledge all three.) [9]Then a great clamor arose, and certain scribes of the Pharisees' group stood up and contended, "We find nothing wrong with this man. What if a spirit or an angel has spoken to him?" [10]When the dissension became violent, the tribune, fearing that they would tear Paul to pieces, ordered the soldiers to go down, take him by force, and bring him into the barracks.

11 That night the Lord stood near him and said, "Keep up your courage! For just as you have testified for me in Jerusalem, so you must bear witness also in Rome."

THE PLOT TO KILL PAUL

12 In the morning the Jews joined in a conspiracy and bound themselves by an oath neither to eat nor drink until they had killed Paul. [13]There were more than forty who joined in this conspiracy. [14]They went to the chief priests and elders and said, "We have strictly bound ourselves by an oath to taste no food until we have killed Paul. [15]Now then, you and the council must notify the tribune to bring him down to you, on the pretext that you want to make a more thorough examination of his case. And we are ready to do away with him before he arrives."

16 Now the son of Paul's sister heard about the ambush; so he went and gained entrance to the barracks and told Paul. [17]Paul called one of the centurions and said, "Take this young man to the tribune, for he has something to report to him." [18]So he took him, brought him to the tribune, and said, "The prisoner Paul called me and asked me to bring this young man to you; he has something to tell you." [19]The tribune took him by the hand, drew him aside privately, and asked, "What is it that you have to report to me?" [20]He answered,

---

a Gk *concerning hope and resurrection*

"The Jews have agreed to ask you to bring Paul down to the council tomorrow, as though they were going to inquire more thoroughly into his case. ²¹But do not be persuaded by them, for more than forty of their men are lying in ambush for him. They have bound themselves by an oath neither to eat nor drink until they kill him. They are ready now and are waiting for your consent." ²²So the tribune dismissed the young man, ordering him, "Tell no one that you have informed me of this."

PAUL SENT TO FELIX THE GOVERNOR

23 Then he summoned two of the centurions and said, "Get ready to leave by nine o'clock tonight for Caesarea with two hundred soldiers, seventy horsemen, and two hundred spearmen. ²⁴Also provide mounts for Paul to ride, and take him safely to Felix the governor." ²⁵He wrote a letter to this effect:

26 "Claudius Lysias to his Excellency the governor Felix, greetings. ²⁷This man was seized by the Jews and was about to be killed by them, but when I had learned that he was a Roman citizen, I came with the guard and rescued him. ²⁸Since I wanted to know the charge for which they accused him, I had him brought to their council. ²⁹I found that he was accused concerning questions of their law, but was charged with nothing deserving death or imprisonment. ³⁰When I was informed that there would be a plot against the man, I sent him to you at once, ordering his accusers also to state before you what they have against him." ᵃ

31 So the soldiers, according to their instructions, took Paul and brought him during the night to Antipatris. ³²The next day they let the horsemen go on with him, while they returned to the barracks. ³³When they came to Caesarea and delivered the letter to the governor, they presented Paul also before him. ³⁴On reading the letter, he asked what province he belonged to, and when he learned that he was from Cilicia, ³⁵he said, "I will give you a hearing when your accusers arrive." Then he ordered that he be kept under guard in Herod's headquarters.ᵇ

PAUL BEFORE FELIX AT CAESAREA

24 Five days later the high priest Ananias came down with some elders and an attorney, a certain Tertullus, and they reported their case against Paul to the governor. ²When Paulᶜ had been summoned, Tertullus began to accuse him, saying:

---

a Other ancient authorities add *Farewell*   b Gk *praetorium*   c Gk *he*

"Your Excellency,[a] because of you we have long enjoyed peace, and reforms have been made for this people because of your foresight. [3]We welcome this in every way and everywhere with utmost gratitude. [4]But, to detain you no further, I beg you to hear us briefly with your customary graciousness. [5]We have, in fact, found this man a pestilent fellow, an agitator among all the Jews throughout the world, and a ringleader of the sect of the Nazarenes.[b] [6]He even tried to profane the temple, and so we seized him.[c] [8]By examining him yourself you will be able to learn from him concerning everything of which we accuse him."

9 The Jews also joined in the charge by asserting that all this was true.

PAUL'S DEFENSE BEFORE FELIX

10 When the governor motioned to him to speak, Paul replied:

"I cheerfully make my defense, knowing that for many years you have been a judge over this nation. [11]As you can find out, it is not more than twelve days since I went up to worship in Jerusalem. [12]They did not find me disputing with anyone in the temple or stirring up a crowd either in the synagogues or throughout the city. [13]Neither can they prove to you the charge that they now bring against me. [14]But this I admit to you, that according to the Way, which they call a sect, I worship the God of our ancestors, believing everything laid down according to the law or written in the prophets. [15]I have a hope in God—a hope that they themselves also accept—that there will be a resurrection of both[d] the righteous and the unrighteous. [16]Therefore I do my best always to have a clear conscience toward God and all people. [17]Now after some years I came to bring alms to my nation and to offer sacrifices. [18]While I was doing this, they found me in the temple, completing the rite of purification, without any crowd or disturbance. [19]But there were some Jews from Asia—they ought to be here before you to make an accusation, if they have anything against me. [20]Or let these men here tell what crime they had found when I stood before the council, [21]unless it was this one sentence that I called out while standing before them, 'It is about the resurrection of the dead that I am on trial before you today.'"

22 But Felix, who was rather well informed about the Way, adjourned the hearing with the comment, "When Lysias the tribune comes down, I will decide your case." [23]Then he ordered the centurion to keep him in custody, but to let him have some liberty and not to prevent any of his friends from taking care of his needs.

---

a Gk lacks *Your Excellency* b Gk *Nazoreans* c Other ancient authorities add *and we would have judged him according to our law.* [7]*But the chief captain Lysias came and with great violence took him out of our hands,* [8]*commanding his accusers to come before you.* d Other ancient authorities read *of the dead, both of*

PAUL HELD IN CUSTODY

24 Some days later when Felix came with his wife Drusilla, who was Jewish, he sent for Paul and heard him speak concerning faith in Christ Jesus. ²⁵And as he discussed justice, self-control, and the coming judgment, Felix became frightened and said, "Go away for the present; when I have an opportunity, I will send for you." ²⁶At the same time he hoped that money would be given him by Paul, and for that reason he used to send for him very often and converse with him.

27 After two years had passed, Felix was succeeded by Porcius Festus; and since he wanted to grant the Jews a favor, Felix left Paul in prison.

PAUL APPEALS TO THE EMPEROR

25 Three days after Festus had arrived in the province, he went up from Caesarea to Jerusalem ²where the chief priests and the leaders of the Jews gave him a report against Paul. They appealed to him ³and requested, as a favor to them against Paul,^a to have him transferred to Jerusalem. They were, in fact, planning an ambush to kill him along the way. ⁴Festus replied that Paul was being kept at Caesarea, and that he himself intended to go there shortly. ⁵"So," he said, "let those of you who have the authority come down with me, and if there is anything wrong about the man, let them accuse him."

6 After he had stayed among them not more than eight or ten days, he went down to Caesarea; the next day he took his seat on the tribunal and ordered Paul to be brought. ⁷When he arrived, the Jews who had gone down from Jerusalem surrounded him, bringing many serious charges against him, which they could not prove. ⁸Paul said in his defense, "I have in no way committed an offense against the law of the Jews, or against the temple, or against the emperor." ⁹But Festus, wishing to do the Jews a favor, asked Paul, "Do you wish to go up to Jerusalem and be tried there before me on these charges?" ¹⁰Paul said, "I am appealing to the emperor's tribunal; this is where I should be tried. I have done no wrong to the Jews, as you very well know. ¹¹Now if I am in the wrong and have committed something for which I deserve to die, I am not trying to escape death; but if there is nothing to their charges against me, no one can turn me over to them. I appeal to the emperor." ¹²Then Festus, after he had conferred with his council, replied, "You have appealed to the emperor; to the emperor you will go."

---

a Gk *him*

FESTUS CONSULTS KING AGRIPPA

13 After several days had passed, King Agrippa and Bernice arrived at Caesarea to welcome Festus. ¹⁴Since they were staying there several days, Festus laid Paul's case before the king, saying, "There is a man here who was left in prison by Felix. ¹⁵When I was in Jerusalem, the chief priests and the elders of the Jews informed me about him and asked for a sentence against him. ¹⁶I told them that it was not the custom of the Romans to hand over anyone before the accused had met the accusers face to face and had been given an opportunity to make a defense against the charge. ¹⁷So when they met here, I lost no time, but on the next day took my seat on the tribunal and ordered the man to be brought. ¹⁸When the accusers stood up, they did not charge him with any of the crimes*a* that I was expecting. ¹⁹Instead they had certain points of disagreement with him about their own religion and about a certain Jesus, who had died, but whom Paul asserted to be alive. ²⁰Since I was at a loss how to investigate these questions, I asked whether he wished to go to Jerusalem and be tried there on these charges.*b* ²¹But when Paul had appealed to be kept in custody for the decision of his Imperial Majesty, I ordered him to be held until I could send him to the emperor." ²²Agrippa said to Festus, "I would like to hear the man myself." "Tomorrow," he said, "you will hear him."

PAUL BROUGHT BEFORE AGRIPPA

23 So on the next day Agrippa and Bernice came with great pomp, and they entered the audience hall with the military tribunes and the prominent men of the city. Then Festus gave the order and Paul was brought in. ²⁴And Festus said, "King Agrippa and all here present with us, you see this man about whom the whole Jewish community petitioned me, both in Jerusalem and here, shouting that he ought not to live any longer. ²⁵But I found that he had done nothing deserving death; and when he appealed to his Imperial Majesty, I decided to send him. ²⁶But I have nothing definite to write to our sovereign about him. Therefore I have brought him before all of you, and especially before you, King Agrippa, so that, after we have examined him, I may have something to write— ²⁷for it seems to me unreasonable to send a prisoner without indicating the charges against him."

---

a Other ancient authorities read *with anything*   *b* Gk *on them*

PAUL DEFENDS HIMSELF BEFORE AGRIPPA

26 Agrippa said to Paul, "You have permission to speak for yourself." Then Paul stretched out his hand and began to defend himself:

2 "I consider myself fortunate that it is before you, King Agrippa, I am to make my defense today against all the accusations of the Jews, ³because you are especially familiar with all the customs and controversies of the Jews; therefore I beg of you to listen to me patiently.

4 "All the Jews know my way of life from my youth, a life spent from the beginning among my own people and in Jerusalem. ⁵They have known for a long time, if they are willing to testify, that I have belonged to the strictest sect of our religion and lived as a Pharisee. ⁶And now I stand here on trial on account of my hope in the promise made by God to our ancestors, ⁷a promise that our twelve tribes hope to attain, as they earnestly worship day and night. It is for this hope, your Excellency,ᵃ that I am accused by Jews! ⁸Why is it thought incredible by any of you that God raises the dead?

9 "Indeed, I myself was convinced that I ought to do many things against the name of Jesus of Nazareth.ᵇ ¹⁰And that is what I did in Jerusalem; with authority received from the chief priests, I not only locked up many of the saints in prison, but I also cast my vote against them when they were being condemned to death. ¹¹By punishing them often in all the synagogues I tried to force them to blaspheme; and since I was so furiously enraged at them, I pursued them even to foreign cities.

PAUL TELLS OF HIS CONVERSION

12 "With this in mind, I was traveling to Damascus with the authority and commission of the chief priests, ¹³when at midday along the road, your Excellency,ᵃ I saw a light from heaven, brighter than the sun, shining around me and my companions. ¹⁴When we had all fallen to the ground, I heard a voice saying to me in the Hebrewᶜ language, 'Saul, Saul, why are you persecuting me? It hurts you to kick against the goads.' ¹⁵I asked, 'Who are you, Lord?' The Lord answered, 'I am Jesus whom you are persecuting. ¹⁶But get up and stand on your feet; for I have appeared to you for this purpose, to appoint you to serve and testify to the things in which you have seen meᵈ and to those in which I will appear to you. ¹⁷I will rescue you from your people and from the Gentiles— to whom I am sending you ¹⁸to open their eyes so that they may turn from

---

a Gk O king   b Gk the Nazorean   c That is, Aramaic   d Other ancient authorities read the things that you have seen darkness to light and from the power of Satan to God, so that they may receive forgiveness of sins and a place among those who are sanctified by faith in me.'

PAUL TELLS OF HIS PREACHING

19 "After that, King Agrippa, I was not disobedient to the heavenly vision, [20]but declared first to those in Damascus, then in Jerusalem and throughout the countryside of Judea, and also to the Gentiles, that they should repent and turn to God and do deeds consistent with repentance. [21]For this reason the Jews seized me in the temple and tried to kill me. [22]To this day I have had help from God, and so I stand here, testifying to both small and great, saying nothing but what the prophets and Moses said would take place: [23]that the Messiah[a] must suffer, and that, by being the first to rise from the dead, he would proclaim light both to our people and to the Gentiles."

PAUL APPEALS TO AGRIPPA TO BELIEVE

24 While he was making this defense, Festus exclaimed, "You are out of your mind, Paul! Too much learning is driving you insane!" [25]But Paul said, "I am not out of my mind, most excellent Festus, but I am speaking the sober truth. [26]Indeed the king knows about these things, and to him I speak freely; for I am certain that none of these things has escaped his notice, for this was not done in a corner. [27]King Agrippa, do you believe the prophets? I know that you believe." [28]Agrippa said to Paul, "Are you so quickly persuading me to become a Christian?"[b] [29]Paul replied, "Whether quickly or not, I pray to God that not only you but also all who are listening to me today might become such as I am—except for these chains."

30 Then the king got up, and with him the governor and Bernice and those who had been seated with them; [31]and as they were leaving, they said to one another, "This man is doing nothing to deserve death or imprisonment." [32]Agrippa said to Festus, "This man could have been set free if he had not appealed to the emperor."

PAUL SAILS FOR ROME

27 When it was decided that we were to sail for Italy, they transferred Paul and some other prisoners to a centurion of the Augustan Cohort, named Julius. [2]Embarking on a ship of Adramyttium that was about to set sail to the ports along the coast of Asia, we put to sea, accompanied by Aristarchus,

---

a Or *the Christ*   *b* Or *Quickly you will persuade me to play the Christian* a Macedonian from Thessalonica. ³The next day we put in at Sidon; and Julius treated Paul kindly, and allowed him to go to his friends to be cared for. ⁴Putting out to sea from there, we sailed under the lee of Cyprus, because the winds were against us. ⁵After we had sailed across the sea that is off Cilicia and Pamphylia, we came to Myra in Lycia. ⁶There the centurion found an Alexandrian ship bound for Italy and put us on board. ⁷We sailed slowly for a number of days and arrived with difficulty off Cnidus, and as the wind was against us, we sailed under the lee of Crete off Salmone. ⁸Sailing past it with difficulty, we came to a place called Fair Havens, near the city of Lasea.

9 Since much time had been lost and sailing was now dangerous, because even the Fast had already gone by, Paul advised them, ¹⁰saying, "Sirs, I can see that the voyage will be with danger and much heavy loss, not only of the cargo and the ship, but also of our lives." ¹¹But the centurion paid more attention to the pilot and to the owner of the ship than to what Paul said. ¹²Since the harbor was not suitable for spending the winter, the majority was in favor of putting to sea from there, on the chance that somehow they could reach Phoenix, where they could spend the winter. It was a harbor of Crete, facing southwest and northwest.

THE STORM AT SEA

13 When a moderate south wind began to blow, they thought they could achieve their purpose; so they weighed anchor and began to sail past Crete, close to the shore. ¹⁴But soon a violent wind, called the northeaster, rushed down from Crete.ᵃ ¹⁵Since the ship was caught and could not be turned head-on into the wind, we gave way to it and were driven. ¹⁶By running under the lee of a small island called Caudaᵇ we were scarcely able to get the ship's boat under control. ¹⁷After hoisting it up they took measuresᶜ to undergird the ship; then, fearing that they would run on the Syrtis, they lowered the sea anchor and so were driven. ¹⁸We were being pounded by the storm so violently that on the next day they began to throw the cargo overboard, ¹⁹and on the third day with their own hands they threw the ship's tackle overboard. ²⁰When neither sun nor stars appeared for many days, and no small tempest raged, all hope of our being saved was at last abandoned.

21 Since they had been without food for a long time, Paul then stood up among them and said, "Men, you should have listened to me and not have set sail from Crete and thereby avoided this damage and loss. ²²I urge you now to keep up your courage, for there will be no loss of life among you, but only

---

a Gk *it*   *b* Other ancient authorities read *Clauda*   *c* Gk *helps* of the ship. [23]For last night there stood by me an angel of the God to whom I belong and whom I worship, [24]and he said, 'Do not be afraid, Paul; you must stand before the emperor; and indeed, God has granted safety to all those who are sailing with you.' [25]So keep up your courage, men, for I have faith in God that it will be exactly as I have been told. [26]But we will have to run aground on some island."

27 When the fourteenth night had come, as we were drifting across the sea of Adria, about midnight the sailors suspected that they were nearing land. [28]So they took soundings and found twenty fathoms; a little farther on they took soundings again and found fifteen fathoms. [29]Fearing that we might run on the rocks, they let down four anchors from the stern and prayed for day to come. [30]But when the sailors tried to escape from the ship and had lowered the boat into the sea, on the pretext of putting out anchors from the bow, [31]Paul said to the centurion and the soldiers, "Unless these men stay in the ship, you cannot be saved." [32]Then the soldiers cut away the ropes of the boat and set it adrift.

33 Just before daybreak, Paul urged all of them to take some food, saying, "Today is the fourteenth day that you have been in suspense and remaining without food, having eaten nothing. [34]Therefore I urge you to take some food, for it will help you survive; for none of you will lose a hair from your heads." [35]After he had said this, he took bread; and giving thanks to God in the presence of all, he broke it and began to eat. [36]Then all of them were encouraged and took food for themselves. [37](We were in all two hundred seventy-six[a] persons in the ship.) [38]After they had satisfied their hunger, they lightened the ship by throwing the wheat into the sea.

THE SHIPWRECK

39 In the morning they did not recognize the land, but they noticed a bay with a beach, on which they planned to run the ship ashore, if they could. [40]So they cast off the anchors and left them in the sea. At the same time they loosened the ropes that tied the steering-oars; then hoisting the foresail to the wind, they made for the beach. [41]But striking a reef,[b] they ran the ship aground; the bow stuck and remained immovable, but the stern was being broken up by the force of the waves. [42]The soldiers' plan was to kill the prisoners, so that none might swim away and escape; [43]but the centurion, wishing to save Paul, kept them from carrying out their plan. He ordered those who could swim to jump overboard first and make for the land, [44]and the rest to follow, some on planks and others on pieces of the ship. And so it was that all were brought safely to land.

---

a Other ancient authorities read *seventy-six*; others, *about seventy-six*   b Gk *place of two seas*

PAUL ON THE ISLAND OF MALTA

28 After we had reached safety, we then learned that the island was called Malta. [2]The natives showed us unusual kindness. Since it had begun to rain and was cold, they kindled a fire and welcomed all of us around it. [3]Paul had gathered a bundle of brushwood and was putting it on the fire, when a viper, driven out by the heat, fastened itself on his hand. [4]When the natives saw the creature hanging from his hand, they said to one another, "This man must be a murderer; though he has escaped from the sea, justice has not allowed him to live." [5]He, however, shook off the creature into the fire and suffered no harm. [6]They were expecting him to swell up or drop dead, but after they had waited a long time and saw that nothing unusual had happened to him, they changed their minds and began to say that he was a god.

7 Now in the neighborhood of that place were lands belonging to the leading man of the island, named Publius, who received us and entertained us hospitably for three days. [8]It so happened that the father of Publius lay sick in bed with fever and dysentery. Paul visited him and cured him by praying and putting his hands on him. [9]After this happened, the rest of the people on the island who had diseases also came and were cured. [10]They bestowed many honors on us, and when we were about to sail, they put on board all the provisions we needed.

PAUL ARRIVES AT ROME

11 Three months later we set sail on a ship that had wintered at the island, an Alexandrian ship with the Twin Brothers as its figurehead. [12]We put in at Syracuse and stayed there for three days; [13]then we weighed anchor and came to Rhegium. After one day there a south wind sprang up, and on the second day we came to Puteoli. [14]There we found believers[a] and were invited to stay with them for seven days. And so we came to Rome. [15]The believers[a] from there, when they heard of us, came as far as the Forum of Appius and Three Taverns to meet us. On seeing them, Paul thanked God and took courage.

16 When we came into Rome, Paul was allowed to live by himself, with the soldier who was guarding him.

---

a Gk brothers

PAUL AND JEWISH LEADERS IN ROME

17 Three days later he called together the local leaders of the Jews. When they had assembled, he said to them, "Brothers, though I had done nothing against our people or the customs of our ancestors, yet I was arrested in Jerusalem and handed over to the Romans. ¹⁸When they had examined me, the Romans*a* wanted to release me, because there was no reason for the death penalty in my case. ¹⁹But when the Jews objected, I was compelled to appeal to the emperor— even though I had no charge to bring against my nation. ²⁰For this reason therefore I have asked to see you and speak with you,*b* since it is for the sake of the hope of Israel that I am bound with this chain." ²¹They replied, "We have received no letters from Judea about you, and none of the brothers coming here has reported or spoken anything evil about you. ²²But we would like to hear from you what you think, for with regard to this sect we know that everywhere it is spoken against."

PAUL PREACHES IN ROME

23 After they had set a day to meet with him, they came to him at his lodgings in great numbers. From morning until evening he explained the matter to them, testifying to the kingdom of God and trying to convince them about Jesus both from the law of Moses and from the prophets. ²⁴Some were convinced by what he had said, while others refused to believe. ²⁵So they disagreed with each other; and as they were leaving, Paul made one further statement: "The Holy Spirit was right in saying to your ancestors through the prophet Isaiah,

26 'Go to this people and say,
You will indeed listen, but never understand,
and you will indeed look, but never perceive.
27 For this people's heart has grown
dull,
and their ears are hard of hearing,
and they have shut their eyes;
so that they might not look with their eyes,
and listen with their ears,
and understand with their heart and turn—
and I would heal them.'

---

a Gk *they*   *b* Or *I have asked you to see me and speak with me*

28 Let it be known to you then that this salvation of God has been sent to the Gentiles; they will listen."*

30 He lived there two whole years at his own expense*b* and welcomed all who came to him, ³¹proclaiming the kingdom of God and teaching about the Lord Jesus Christ with all boldness and without hindrance.

---

a Other ancient authorities add verse 29, *And when he had said these words, the Jews departed, arguing vigorously among themselves*
b Or *in his own hired dwelling*

2 Thessalonians

Paul's first letter to the Christ-community in Thessalonica in northern Greece is the earliest document in the New Testament, but 2 Thessalonians is one of the disputed letters of Paul. The majority of mainstream scholars do not think it was written by Paul, but by someone writing in his name some three to four decades after his martyrdom in the 60s.

Because 2 Thessalonians echoes the structure and language of 1 Thessalonians, a minority of scholars think this suggests that Paul wrote it soon after 1 Thessalonians. But a majority of scholars think the similarities are a conscious and deliberate imitation of 1 Thessalonians by an author writing in Paul's name around the year 100 or soon thereafter. The letter addresses two questions that belong to a time period later than Paul: the delay of the second coming of Jesus and the issue of "freeloaders"—people who became part of a Christ-community not because they were passionate about Jesus, but in order to receive free food.

After an opening greeting and thanksgiving similar to those in 1 Thessalonians, the letter continues with an explanation of why the second coming of Jesus has not yet happened (2.1–12). Recall that Paul in 1 Thessalonians expected it soon. But this letter affirms that there are events that must happen first: the "rebellion," and the revelation of the "lawless one" who "opposes and exalts himself above every so-called god" and "takes his seat in the temple of God, declaring himself to be God" (2.3–4). Though the recipients of the letter most likely understood what the author was writing about, we do not. Was he writing about Roman soldiers offering sacrifices to the emperor in the temple after they had conquered Jerusalem in the year 70? Or about an event that had not happened yet? In either case, the situation reflects a time after Paul's death. The broader point is that there are still things that must happen before the second coming.

The issue of freeloaders is addressed in the last chapter of this letter. The issue arises in any religious movement that is made up of "share communities," those that provide the material basis of existence for its members.

The author warns his recipients about "believers" who live in "idleness and not according to the tradition that they received." They are "mere busybodies, not doing any work" (3.6, 11). The passage commands: "Anyone unwilling to work should not eat" (3.10). Unless people are willing to work and seeking work, they do not deserve to be financially supported by those in the community who do work. The issue, as we will see, is also addressed in 1 Timothy, one of the letters attributed to Paul, but written around the same time as 2 Thessalonians, perhaps a decade or so later.

The letter concludes with the theme of peace: "Now may the Lord of peace himself give you peace at all times in all ways. The Lord be with all of you" (3.16). It, like a few other letters in the New Testament, is a "slight" letter—a minor one that would not be missed if it were not included. But it is a window into a Pauline community around the year 100.

THE SECOND LETTER OF PAUL TO THE
Thessalonians

SALUTATION

1 Paul, Silvanus, and Timothy,
To the church of the Thessalonians in God our Father and the Lord Jesus Christ:

2 Grace to you and peace from God our *a* Father and the Lord Jesus Christ.

THANKSGIVING

3 We must always give thanks to God for you, brothers and sisters,*b* as is right, because your faith is growing abundantly, and the love of every one of you for one another is increasing. ⁴Therefore we ourselves boast of you among the churches of God for your steadfastness and faith during all your persecutions and the afflictions that you are enduring.

THE JUDGMENT AT CHRIST'S COMING

5 This is evidence of the righteous judgment of God, and is intended to make you worthy of the kingdom of God, for which you are also suffering. ⁶For it is indeed just of God to repay with affliction those who afflict you, ⁷and to give relief to the afflicted as well as to us, when the Lord Jesus is revealed from heaven with his mighty angels ⁸in flaming fire, inflicting vengeance on those who do not know God and on those who do not obey the gospel of our Lord Jesus. ⁹These will suffer the punishment of eternal destruction, separated from the presence of the Lord and from the glory of his might, ¹⁰when he comes to

---

a Other ancient authorities read *the*   *b* Gk *brothers* be glorified by his saints and to be marveled at on that day among all who have believed, because our testimony to you was believed. [11]To this end we always pray for you, asking that our God will make you worthy of his call and will fulfill by his power every good resolve and work of faith, [12]so that the name of our Lord Jesus may be glorified in you, and you in him, according to the grace of our God and the Lord Jesus Christ.

THE MAN OF LAWLESSNESS

2 As to the coming of our Lord Jesus Christ and our being gathered together to him, we beg you, brothers and sisters,[a] [2]not to be quickly shaken in mind or alarmed, either by spirit or by word or by letter, as though from us, to the effect that the day of the Lord is already here. [3]Let no one deceive you in any way; for that day will not come unless the rebellion comes first and the lawless one[b] is revealed, the one destined for destruction.[c] [4]He opposes and exalts himself above every so-called god or object of worship, so that he takes his seat in the temple of God, declaring himself to be God. [5]Do you not remember that I told you these things when I was still with you? [6]And you know what is now restraining him, so that he may be revealed when his time comes. [7]For the mystery of lawlessness is already at work, but only until the one who now restrains it is removed. [8]And then the lawless one will be revealed, whom the Lord Jesus[d] will destroy[e] with the breath of his mouth, annihilating him by the manifestation of his coming. [9]The coming of the lawless one is apparent in the working of Satan, who uses all power, signs, lying wonders, [10]and every kind of wicked deception for those who are perishing, because they refused to love the truth and so be saved. [11]For this reason God sends them a powerful delusion, leading them to believe what is false, [12]so that all who have not believed the truth but took pleasure in unrighteousness will be condemned.

CHOSEN FOR SALVATION

13 But we must always give thanks to God for you, brothers and sisters[a] beloved by the Lord, because God chose you as the first fruits[f] for salvation through sanctification by the Spirit and through belief in the truth. [14]For this purpose he called you through our proclamation of the good news,[g] so that you may obtain the glory of our Lord Jesus Christ. [15]So then, brothers and sisters,[a] stand firm and hold fast to the traditions that you were taught by us, either by word of mouth or by our letter.

---

a Gk *brothers*   b Gk *the man of lawlessness;* other ancient authorities read *the man of sin*   c Gk *the son of destruction*   d Other ancient authorities lack *Jesus*   e Other ancient authorities read *consume*   f Other ancient authorities read *from the beginning*   g Or *through our gospel*

16 Now may our Lord Jesus Christ himself and God our Father, who loved us and through grace gave us eternal comfort and good hope, [17]comfort your hearts and strengthen them in every good work and word.

REQUEST FOR PRAYER

3 Finally, brothers and sisters,[a] pray for us, so that the word of the Lord may spread rapidly and be glorified everywhere, just as it is among you, [2]and that we may be rescued from wicked and evil people; for not all have faith. [3]But the Lord is faithful; he will strengthen you and guard you from the evil one.[b] [4]And we have confidence in the Lord concerning you, that you are doing and will go on doing the things that we command. [5]May the Lord direct your hearts to the love of God and to the steadfastness of Christ.

WARNING AGAINST IDLENESS

6 Now we command you, beloved,[a] in the name of our Lord Jesus Christ, to keep away from believers who are[c] living in idleness and not according to the tradition that they[d] received from us. [7]For you yourselves know how you ought to imitate us; we were not idle when we were with you, [8]and we did not eat anyone's bread without paying for it; but with toil and labor we worked night and day, so that we might not burden any of you. [9]This was not because we do not have that right, but in order to give you an example to imitate. [10]For even when we were with you, we gave you this command: Anyone unwilling to work should not eat. [11]For we hear that some of you are living in idleness, mere busybodies, not doing any work. [12]Now such persons we command and exhort in the Lord Jesus Christ to do their work quietly and to earn their own living. [13]Brothers and sisters,[e] do not be weary in doing what is right.

14 Take note of those who do not obey what we say in this letter; have nothing to do with them, so that they may be ashamed. [15]Do not regard them as enemies, but warn them as believers.[f]

FINAL GREETINGS AND BENEDICTION

16 Now may the Lord of peace himself give you peace at all times in all ways. The Lord be with all of you.

17 I, Paul, write this greeting with my own hand. This is the mark in every letter of mine; it is the way I write. [18]The grace of our Lord Jesus Christ be with all of you.[g]

---

a Gk *brothers*   b Or *from evil*   c Gk *from every brother who is*   d Other ancient authorities read *you*   e Gk *Brothers*   f Gk *a brother*   g Other ancient authorities add *Amen*

1 Peter

Two letters in the New Testament are attributed to Peter, the most important of Jesus's male disciples, who was executed in Rome around the year 64. But the majority of mainstream scholars do not think that either one was written by Peter. The letters reflect a later historical context. Moreover, they were not written by the same person. Second Peter is significantly later than 1 Peter.

Date, Author, and Historical Setting

First Peter was most likely written from Rome. Rome is suggested by its closing, which contains greetings from those "in Babylon" (5.13). As in Revelation, "Babylon" had become a name among both Jews and Christians for Rome after Rome destroyed Jerusalem and the temple in the year 70. Babylon was the previous destroyer of Jerusalem and the temple in 586 BCE. Rome was the new "Babylon."

But there is no unanimity about its date. Some mainline scholars date it to around 90 or as early as the 80s. The reason is that some think that the author of *1 Clement*, an early Christian letter not in the New Testament but dated by some to around the year 96, knew of 1 Peter. If so, 95 or so is the latest possible date for 1 Peter. But it is not clear that *1 Clement* was written that early. Moreover, because both *1 Clement* and 1 Peter were most likely written in Rome, their authors might well have known each other. Given that, similarity of language need not mean literary dependence. Some of its themes, especially its endorsement of Roman authority and imperial conventions about slavery, suggest a date early in the second century.

The author identifies himself as "Peter, an apostle of Jesus Christ" (1.1). Recall that most scholars do not think that Peter the disciple wrote the letter. Later, the author refers to himself as "an elder" among "elders" (5.1), which implies that he was a leader in a Christ-community in Rome.

The letter is addressed to Christ-communities in five regions of Asia Minor (Turkey). It was thus a "circular" letter, carried and read to a number of communities in different locations. The recipients had been experiencing suffering because they were followers of Jesus (1.6–7; 4.12–19; 5.8–10). The persecution seems not to have been lethal; no deaths are mentioned. It probably consisted of social ostracism, which could have been severe because it meant the severing of familial, friendship, and financial relationships and perhaps occasional acts of violence, even though they were not institutionally sponsored.

These communities were mostly made up of Gentile "God-lovers." That they were Christian Gentiles is indicated in the letter. "You have already spent enough time in doing what the Gentiles like to do" (4.3) is an unlikely sentence if the letter was addressed primarily to Jewish Christ-communities. Then the author lists a series of typically Gentile vices as seen from a Jewish point of view. The recipients were not Jews who had become Christian, but Gentile "God-lovers" who had become Christian.

Unlike many letters in the New Testament, this one does not refer to conflict within the Christ-communities. The conflict is with outsiders. There are no chastisements, though there are warnings and cautions about the situation of suffering being faced.

Main Themes

The letter combines affirmations about Jesus, God, and the new life with exhortations, moral teaching, and encouragement. The rhythm is repeated again and again: affirmation in 1.3–12, exhortation in 1.13–17; affirmation in 1.18–25, exhortation in 2.1–3; affirmation in 2.4–10, exhortation in 2.11–4.11 (the longest section of the letter).

Some of the exhortation is quite general:

> Prepare your minds for action; discipline yourselves; set all your hope on the grace that Jesus Christ will bring you when he is revealed. Like obedient children, do not be conformed to the desires that you formerly had in ignorance. (1.13–14)

> Rid yourselves, therefore, of all malice, and all guile, insincerity, envy, and all slander. (2.1)

> Have unity of spirit, sympathy, love for one another, a tender heart, and a humble mind. (3.8)

Some is very specific. For example, 2.13–3.7 is an extended passage about obeying authority. The recipients are to "accept the authority of every human institution," including the emperor and governors (2.13–14). Slaves are to accept the authority of their masters, and wives, the authority of their husbands. This teaching about slaves and wives is also found in Colossians, Ephesians, and 1 Timothy, documents from the later part of the first century and early second century. They reflect the growing accommodation of early Christianity to conventional cultural values, a movement away from the radicalism of Jesus and Paul.

The letter is distinctive for a number of reasons. It is one of only two documents in the New Testament that uses the word "Christian" (4.16; also in Acts 11.26; 26.28). It is the only document in addition to John that uses "born again" (or "born anew"; 1.23). This does not reduce the power or significance of the phrase. What it means is widespread in early Christianity; it has the same meaning as Paul's "dying and rising" with Christ—dying to an old way of life and being raised into a new way of life. But the specific phrase is found only in this letter and in John.

It also uses a distinctive metaphor for Jesus. He is "a living stone" (2.4). In John, Jesus is the "light of the world," the "bread of life," the "gate for the sheep," the "true vine," and so forth; in Hebrews, he is the "great high priest" and "sacrifice." Here he is a "living stone," indeed the "cornerstone" (2.6–7) of "a spiritual house" (2.5). This is temple imagery—Jesus is the living stone who is the cornerstone of a new temple, a new spiritual house. The author then calls the recipients to be "living stones" in "a spiritual house" and to be "a holy priesthood" offering "spiritual sacrifices" (2.5–7). The image of the community as priests leads to one of the best-known passages in 1 Peter:

> But you are a chosen race, a royal priesthood, a holy nation, God's own people, in order that you may proclaim the mighty acts of him who called you out of darkness into his marvelous light. (2.9)

Martin Luther is said to have loved this letter. It is easy to understand why. Like his contemporaries, he took it for granted that Peter wrote it. In this letter attributed to the first pope, Luther found a wonderfully egalitarian affirmation that all Christians are priests. The community is the royal priesthood, the living stones in a new spiritual house. The power and authority claimed by the Rome of his day were undermined by the first pope himself.

Finally, the letter's advice in a time of persecution is striking. The author instructs his readers how to respond to those who were persecuting them: "Do not fear what they fear, and do not be intimidated" (3.14). Their persecutors operated out of fear; they were not to be intimidated by them. Instead, they were to "cast all [their] anxiety" on God (5.7). "Fear not—do not be afraid" is the constant counsel of the Bible, Old and New Testament alike. Thus, though this letter is from the early second century, it preserves much that is authentically Jewish and Christian.

SALUTATION

1 Peter, an apostle of Jesus Christ,
To the exiles of the Dispersion in Pontus, Galatia, Cappadocia, Asia, and Bithynia, ²who have been chosen and destined by God the Father and sanctified by the Spirit to be obedient to Jesus Christ and to be sprinkled with his blood:

May grace and peace be yours in abundance.

A LIVING HOPE

3 Blessed be the God and Father of our Lord Jesus Christ! By his great mercy he has given us a new birth into a living hope through the resurrection of Jesus Christ from the dead, ⁴and into an inheritance that is imperishable, undefiled, and unfading, kept in heaven for you, ⁵who are being protected by the power of God through faith for a salvation ready to be revealed in the last time. ⁶In this you rejoice,ᵃ even if now for a little while you have had to suffer various trials, ⁷so that the genuineness of your faith—being more precious than gold that, though perishable, is tested by fire—may be found to result in praise and glory and honor when Jesus Christ is revealed. ⁸Although you have not seenᵇ him, you love him; and even though you do not see him now, you believe in him and rejoice with an indescribable and glorious joy, ⁹for you are receiving the outcome of your faith, the salvation of your souls.

---

a Or *Rejoice in this* b Other ancient authorities read *known*

10 Concerning this salvation, the prophets who prophesied of the grace that was to be yours made careful search and inquiry, [11]inquiring about the person or time that the Spirit of Christ within them indicated when it testified in advance to the sufferings destined for Christ and the subsequent glory. [12]It was revealed to them that they were serving not themselves but you, in regard to the things that have now been announced to you through those who brought you good news by the Holy Spirit sent from heaven—things into which angels long to look!

A CALL TO HOLY LIVING

13 Therefore prepare your minds for action;[a] discipline yourselves; set all your hope on the grace that Jesus Christ will bring you when he is revealed. [14]Like obedient children, do not be conformed to the desires that you formerly had in ignorance. [15]Instead, as he who called you is holy, be holy yourselves in all your conduct; [16]for it is written, "You shall be holy, for I am holy."

17 If you invoke as Father the one who judges all people impartially according to their deeds, live in reverent fear during the time of your exile. [18]You know that you were ransomed from the futile ways inherited from your ancestors, not with perishable things like silver or gold, [19]but with the precious blood of Christ, like that of a lamb without defect or blemish. [20]He was destined before the foundation of the world, but was revealed at the end of the ages for your sake. [21]Through him you have come to trust in God, who raised him from the dead and gave him glory, so that your faith and hope are set on God.

22 Now that you have purified your souls by your obedience to the truth[b] so that you have genuine mutual love, love one another deeply[c] from the heart.[d] [23]You have been born anew, not of perishable but of imperishable seed, through the living and enduring word of God.[e] [24]For

> "All flesh is like grass
> and all its glory like the flower of grass.
> The grass withers,
> and the flower falls,
> 25 but the word of the Lord endures forever."

That word is the good news that was announced to you.

THE LIVING STONE AND A CHOSEN PEOPLE

2 Rid yourselves, therefore, of all malice, and all guile, insincerity, envy, and all slander. [2]Like newborn infants, long for the pure, spiritual milk, so that

---

a Gk *gird up the loins of your mind* b Other ancient authorities add *through the Spirit* c Or *constantly* d Other ancient authorities read *a pure heart* e Or *through the word of the living and enduring God* by it you may grow into salvation— ³if indeed you have tasted that the Lord is good.

4 Come to him, a living stone, though rejected by mortals yet chosen and precious in God's sight, and ⁵like living stones, let yourselves be built*a* into a spiritual house, to be a holy priesthood, to offer spiritual sacrifices acceptable to God through Jesus Christ. ⁶For it stands in scripture:

> "See, I am laying in Zion a stone,
>> a cornerstone chosen and precious;
> and whoever believes in him*b* will not be put to shame."

7 To you then who believe, he is precious; but for those who do not believe,

> "The stone that the builders rejected
>> has become the very head of the corner,"

8 and

> "A stone that makes them stumble,
>> and a rock that makes them fall."

They stumble because they disobey the word, as they were destined to do.

9 But you are a chosen race, a royal priesthood, a holy nation, God's own people,*c* in order that you may proclaim the mighty acts of him who called you out of darkness into his marvelous light.

> 10 Once you were not a people,
>> but now you are God's people;
> once you had not received mercy,
>> but now you have received mercy.

LIVE AS SERVANTS OF GOD

11 Beloved, I urge you as aliens and exiles to abstain from the desires of the flesh that wage war against the soul. ¹²Conduct yourselves honorably among the Gentiles, so that, though they malign you as evildoers, they may see your honorable deeds and glorify God when he comes to judge.*d*

13 For the Lord's sake accept the authority of every human institution,*e* whether of the emperor as supreme, ¹⁴or of governors, as sent by him to punish those who do wrong and to praise those who do right. ¹⁵For it is God's will that by doing right you should silence the ignorance of the foolish. ¹⁶As servants*f* of God, live as free people, yet do not use your freedom as a pretext for evil. ¹⁷Honor everyone. Love the family of believers.*g* Fear God. Honor the emperor.

---

a Or *you yourselves are being built*   *b* Or *it*   *c* Gk *a people for his possession*   *d* Gk *God on the day of visitation*   *e* Or *every institution ordained for human beings*   *f* Gk *slaves*   *g* Gk *Love the brotherhood*

THE EXAMPLE OF CHRIST'S SUFFERING

18 Slaves, accept the authority of your masters with all deference, not only those who are kind and gentle but also those who are harsh. [19]For it is a credit to you if, being aware of God, you endure pain while suffering unjustly. [20]If you endure when you are beaten for doing wrong, what credit is that? But if you endure when you do right and suffer for it, you have God's approval. [21]For to this you have been called, because Christ also suffered for you, leaving you an example, so that you should follow in his steps.

22 "He committed no sin,
and no deceit was found in his mouth."

23 When he was abused, he did not return abuse; when he suffered, he did not threaten; but he entrusted himself to the one who judges justly. [24]He himself bore our sins in his body on the cross,[a] so that, free from sins, we might live for righteousness; by his wounds[b] you have been healed. [25]For you were going astray like sheep, but now you have returned to the shepherd and guardian of your souls.

WIVES AND HUSBANDS

3 Wives, in the same way, accept the authority of your husbands, so that, even if some of them do not obey the word, they may be won over without a word by their wives' conduct, [2]when they see the purity and reverence of your lives. [3]Do not adorn yourselves outwardly by braiding your hair, and by wearing gold ornaments or fine clothing; [4]rather, let your adornment be the inner self with the lasting beauty of a gentle and quiet spirit, which is very precious in God's sight. [5]It was in this way long ago that the holy women who hoped in God used to adorn themselves by accepting the authority of their husbands. [6]Thus Sarah obeyed Abraham and called him lord. You have become her daughters as long as you do what is good and never let fears alarm you.

7 Husbands, in the same way, show consideration for your wives in your life together, paying honor to the woman as the weaker sex,[c] since they too are also heirs of the gracious gift of life—so that nothing may hinder your prayers.

SUFFERING FOR DOING RIGHT

8 Finally, all of you, have unity of spirit, sympathy, love for one another, a tender heart, and a humble mind. [9]Do not repay evil for evil or abuse for abuse;

---

a Or carried up our sins in his body to the tree   b Gk bruise   c Gk vessel

but, on the contrary, repay with a blessing. It is for this that you were called—
that you might inherit a blessing. [10]For

> "Those who desire life
>   and desire to see good days,
>   let them keep their tongues from evil
>   and their lips from speaking deceit;
> 11 let them turn away from evil and do good;
>   let them seek peace and pursue it.
> 12 For the eyes of the Lord are on the righteous,
>   and his ears are open to their prayer.
>   But the face of the Lord is against those who do evil."

13 Now who will harm you if you are eager to do what is good? [14]But even if you do suffer for doing what is right, you are blessed. Do not fear what they fear,[a] and do not be intimidated, [15]but in your hearts sanctify Christ as Lord. Always be ready to make your defense to anyone who demands from you an accounting for the hope that is in you; [16]yet do it with gentleness and reverence.[b] Keep your conscience clear, so that, when you are maligned, those who abuse you for your good conduct in Christ may be put to shame. [17]For it is better to suffer for doing good, if suffering should be God's will, than to suffer for doing evil. [18]For Christ also suffered[c] for sins once for all, the righteous for the unrighteous, in order to bring you[d] to God. He was put to death in the flesh, but made alive in the spirit, [19]in which also he went and made a proclamation to the spirits in prison, [20]who in former times did not obey, when God waited patiently in the days of Noah, during the building of the ark, in which a few, that is, eight persons, were saved through water. [21]And baptism, which this prefigured, now saves you—not as a removal of dirt from the body, but as an appeal to God for[e] a good conscience, through the resurrection of Jesus Christ, [22]who has gone into heaven and is at the right hand of God, with angels, authorities, and powers made subject to him.

GOOD STEWARDS OF GOD'S GRACE

4 Since therefore Christ suffered in the flesh,[f] arm yourselves also with the same intention (for whoever has suffered in the flesh has finished with sin), [2]so as to live for the rest of your earthly life[g] no longer by human desires but by the will of God. [3]You have already spent enough time in doing what the Gentiles like to do, living in licentiousness, passions, drunkenness, revels, carousing, and lawless idolatry. [4]They are surprised that you no longer join

---

a Gk *their fear*   b Or *respect*   c Other ancient authorities read *died*   d Other ancient authorities read *us*   e Or *a pledge to God from*   f Other ancient authorities add *for us*; others, *for you*   g Gk *rest of the time in the flesh* them in the same excesses of dissipation, and so they blaspheme.*a 5But they will have to give an accounting to him who stands ready to judge the living and the dead. 6For this is the reason the gospel was proclaimed even to the dead, so that, though they had been judged in the flesh as everyone is judged, they might live in the spirit as God does.

7 The end of all things is near;*b therefore be serious and discipline yourselves for the sake of your prayers. 8Above all, maintain constant love for one another, for love covers a multitude of sins. 9Be hospitable to one another without complaining. 10Like good stewards of the manifold grace of God, serve one another with whatever gift each of you has received. 11Whoever speaks must do so as one speaking the very words of God; whoever serves must do so with the strength that God supplies, so that God may be glorified in all things through Jesus Christ. To him belong the glory and the power forever and ever. Amen.

SUFFERING AS A CHRISTIAN

12 Beloved, do not be surprised at the fiery ordeal that is taking place among you to test you, as though something strange were happening to you. 13But rejoice insofar as you are sharing Christ's sufferings, so that you may also be glad and shout for joy when his glory is revealed. 14If you are reviled for the name of Christ, you are blessed, because the spirit of glory,*c which is the Spirit of God, is resting on you.*d 15But let none of you suffer as a murderer, a thief, a criminal, or even as a mischief maker. 16Yet if any of you suffers as a Christian, do not consider it a disgrace, but glorify God because you bear this name. 17For the time has come for judgment to begin with the household of God; if it begins with us, what will be the end for those who do not obey the gospel of God? 18And

> "If it is hard for the righteous to be saved,
>
>   what will become of the ungodly and the sinners?"

19 Therefore, let those suffering in accordance with God's will entrust themselves to a faithful Creator, while continuing to do good.

TENDING THE FLOCK OF GOD

5 Now as an elder myself and a witness of the sufferings of Christ, as well as one who shares in the glory to be revealed, I exhort the elders among you 2to tend the flock of God that is in your charge, exercising the oversight,*e not under compulsion but willingly, as God would have you do it*f—not for sordid gain but eagerly. 3Do not lord it over those in your charge, but be

---

a Or they malign you b Or is at hand c Other ancient authorities add and of power d Other ancient authorities add On their part he is blasphemed, but on your part he is glorified e Other ancient authorities lack exercising the oversight f Other ancient authorities lack as God would have you do it examples to the flock. [4]And when the chief shepherd appears, you will win the crown of glory that never fades away. [5]In the same way, you who are younger must accept the authority of the elders.[a] And all of you must clothe yourselves with humility in your dealings with one another, for

> "God opposes the proud,
>> but gives grace to the humble."

6 Humble yourselves therefore under the mighty hand of God, so that he may exalt you in due time. [7]Cast all your anxiety on him, because he cares for you. [8]Discipline yourselves, keep alert.[b] Like a roaring lion your adversary the devil prowls around, looking for someone to devour. [9]Resist him, steadfast in your faith, for you know that your brothers and sisters[c] in all the world are undergoing the same kinds of suffering. [10]And after you have suffered for a little while, the God of all grace, who has called you to his eternal glory in Christ, will himself restore, support, strengthen, and establish you. [11]To him be the power forever and ever. Amen.

FINAL GREETINGS AND BENEDICTION

12 Through Silvanus, whom I consider a faithful brother, I have written this short letter to encourage you and to testify that this is the true grace of God. Stand fast in it. [13]Your sister church[d] in Babylon, chosen together with you, sends you greetings; and so does my son Mark. [14]Greet one another with a kiss of love.

Peace to all of you who are in Christ.[e]

---

a Or of those who are older   b Or be vigilant   c Gk your brotherhood   d Gk She who is   e Other ancient authorities add Amen

1 Timothy

In the canonical New Testament, 1 Timothy is the first of three letters known as the "pastoral letters" or "pastoral epistles." The other two are 2 Timothy and Titus. They are called "pastoral" in part because they are addressed to two early Christian "pastors," Timothy and Titus. "Pastor" did not yet refer to an official institutional role, but had its ancient meaning of shepherd, leader of the flock. Their themes are also pastoral, providing practical advice for ordering the community's life.

According to the seven genuine letters of Paul, Timothy and Titus were his associates, perhaps his most important ones. Timothy is mentioned in five of the letters (1 and 2 Corinthians, Philippians, Philemon, and 1 Thessalonians; and also in the later letters of Colossians, and 2 Thessalonians), and Titus, in two (Galatians and 2 Corinthians).

Though all three letters claim to be written by Paul, most modern scholars see them as written long after his death in the first decades of the second century. There is a consensus that they were all written by the same person. But was that person Paul? For more than one reason, authorship by Paul has been rejected:

- The vocabulary and style are very different from those in the seven letters we are sure that Paul wrote.

- The "tone" is very different. The passion that marks Paul's genuine letters is absent. Not just the passion of conflict, but the passion of insight, brilliance, and radiance. There are echoes of Paul's language in the pastorals, but they are just echoes.

- The issues addressed in the pastorals seem to belong to a later generation of early Christianity, the beginning of the process of "institutionalization."

Institutionalization was greatly to increase over the centuries, so we see
it here in nascent form. This includes the delineation of leadership roles
(qualifications for "bishops" and "deacons"), an emphasis on "official"
teaching (what 2 Tim. 4.3 calls "sound doctrine"), and even directives for
discerning which widows deserved the financial support of the community.
All of this suggests a later period of time.

There is yet another reason for thinking the pastorals are later than Paul—the
role of women is very different from that in the genuine letters of Paul. There Paul
pronounces the equality of male and female "in Christ Jesus" (Gal. 3.28), refers to
Junia as a prominent "apostle" (Rom. 16.7), and speaks of other women as early
Christian leaders (Rom. 16.1–16). He does not object to women prophesying in
the community in Corinth; his issue is whether they should do so with covered or
uncovered heads (1 Cor. 11.5).

The contrast to a particular passage in 1 Timothy is stark. Because of its importance in Christian history, the whole passage is quoted (2.8–15). It begins with roles
for men and women. Men should pray and women should dress modestly:

> I desire, then, that in every place the men should pray, lifting up holy hands
> without anger or argument; also that the women should dress themselves
> modestly and decently in suitable clothing, not with their hair braided, or
> with gold, pearls, or expensive clothes, but with good works, as is proper for
> women who profess reverence for God.

The issue is not whether men should pray and women dress modestly (and note
that "modestly" here means "inexpensively"); both might be good counsel. The
issue is the different hierarchical roles assigned to men and women.

That this is the case is apparent from the next two verses. They narrowly restrict
the role of women and disqualify them from leadership in the community:

> Let a woman learn in silence with full submission. I permit no woman to
> teach or to have authority over a man; she is to keep silent.

It is difficult to reconcile this with the Paul of the seven genuine letters.

Then the author provides the theological justification for this constriction of
women's role:

> For Adam was formed first, then Eve; and Adam was not deceived, but the
> woman was deceived and became a transgressor.

Women were responsible for bringing sin into the world. In the seven genuine letters,
Paul never blames Eve; for him, the image of life apart from Christ is life in Adam
(1 Cor. 15.21–22; Rom. 5.12–14).

As this text ends, it does affirm that women, despite being responsible for sin, can "be saved." How? Note the means: "Through childbearing, provided they continue in faith and love and holiness, with modesty." This does not sound like the Paul of the seven genuine letters.

Institutionalization

The letter includes lists of qualifications for "bishops" and "deacons." "Elders" are also mentioned, though nothing is said about their qualifications. To begin with "bishops," back then the word meant something quite different from what it does now. The Greek word *episkopos* meant "overseer," and in a late first- and early second-century Christian context could have referred to the "overseer" of a particular Christ-community or perhaps of a number of Christ-communities in a specific city. Only later did it refer to the chief ecclesiastical official of a larger geographical area. But clearly "bishops" were leaders when this letter was written.

Bishops' qualifications are interesting (3.1–7). They begin with positives: "A bishop must be above reproach, married only once, temperate, sensible, respectable, hospitable, an apt teacher." They continue with negatives: "not a drunkard, not violent but gentle, not quarrelsome, and not a lover of money. . . . He must not be a recent convert, or he may be puffed up with conceit and fall into the condemnation of the devil."

These are excellent qualifications. Who could disagree with temperate, sensible, respectable, hospitable, and a good teacher; neither a drunkard, violent, quarrelsome, greedy for money, nor puffed up with conceit?

But note also that he is to be "married only once." We do not know if this was a prohibition of polygamy or of divorce and remarriage. The point is that a bishop, an overseer, was supposed to be married. As the qualifications continue, it is taken for granted that he is the head of a family, a household: "He must manage his own household well, keeping his children submissive and respectful in every way—for if someone does not know how to manage his own household, how can he take care of God's church?"

Finally, "He must be well thought of by outsiders, so that he may not fall into disgrace and the snare of the devil." To be well thought of by outsiders may in some circumstances be a virtue, but this sounds like accommodation to the dominant culture. The qualifications for "deacons," though somewhat different, are consistent with the above. What we see in 1 Timothy is the process not only of institutionalization, but also of accommodation.

So also this letter accommodates the institution of slavery.

> Let all who are under the yoke of slavery regard their masters as worthy of all honor, so that the name of God and the teaching may not be blasphemed. Those who have believing masters must not be disrespectful to them on the ground that they are members of the church; rather they must serve them all the more, since those who benefit by their service are believers and beloved. (6.1–2)

This sounds very different from the Paul of the seven letters, especially Galatians and Philemon. The radicalism of the early Paul is toned down, indeed eliminated.

Institutionalization is also reflected in the letter's directives for deciding which widows qualify for financial support (5.3–16). From this section, we learn the following:

> The community was financially supporting widows. In that world, women were generally financially dependent on a man—a father, a husband, a son. Thus "widows" were often without financial support. The support of widows is consistent with the "share" practice of Paul's early communities; to be part of a Christ-community meant that you would not go without food, the material basis of existence.

> The support of widows had become a financial burden for the community, and so there was a need to define who the *real* widows are.

> The criteria include: (1) if a widow has children or grandchildren, they should support her, if possible; (2) a widow should "be put on the list" only if she is over sixty; younger widows should try to remarry (the text includes some negative remarks about young widows); (3) if a widow has a woman relative in the community who has any wealth to share, that woman should support her.

The text is interesting for more than one reason. It illustrates not only the development of practical regulations that are part of the process of institutionalization, but also a problem facing any movement that emphasizes the sharing of the material basis of existence. The problem is generated by limits on the community's resources and the issue of "freeloaders"—people who like the sharing aspect and take advantage of it. Hence the need to develop directives, rules, for allocating the community's resources.

In its final chapter, this letter deals with the question of wealth. This indicates that in at least some Christian communities by the time it was written, there were some who were "rich"—perhaps not superrich, but rich by the standards of the time. The author cautions against wanting to be rich:

We brought nothing into the world, so that we can take nothing out of it, but if we have food and clothing, we will be content with these. But those who want to be rich fall into temptation and are trapped by many senseless and harmful desires that plunge people into ruin and destruction. For the love of money is a root of all kinds of evil, and in their eagerness to be rich some have wandered away from the faith and pierced themselves with many pains. (6.7–10)

Having food and clothing—having what we need—is the basis for contentment. It is enough. Though wealth itself is not condemned, the desire for it is: "The love of money is a root of all kinds of evil." That is very strong language and it invites the question: Is that true?

In almost the last verses of the letter, the author suggests what to say to those who are already rich and yet Christian:

As for those who in the present age are rich, command them not to be haughty, or to set their hopes on the uncertainty of riches, but rather on God who richly provides us with everything for our enjoyment. They are to do good, to be rich in good works, generous, and ready to share. (6.17–18)

The list includes both negatives and positives: the rich are not to be haughty or to trust in riches; they are to trust in God, do good, and be rich in good works, generous, and sharing.

Thus, even as 1 Timothy reflects the settling down of Christianity and early stages of accommodation to the dominant culture, it also in its cautions about wealth preserves some of the radical impulse of Jesus and Paul and earliest Christianity. It is an accommodationist document, but that doesn't mean it is without value.

THE FIRST LETTER OF PAUL TO
Timothy

1 Paul, an apostle of Christ Jesus by the command of God our Savior and of Christ Jesus our hope,

2 To Timothy, my loyal child in the faith:

Grace, mercy, and peace from God the Father and Christ Jesus our Lord.

WARNING AGAINST FALSE TEACHERS

3 I urge you, as I did when I was on my way to Macedonia, to remain in Ephesus so that you may instruct certain people not to teach any different doctrine, [4]and not to occupy themselves with myths and endless genealogies that promote speculations rather than the divine training*a* that is known by faith. [5]But the aim of such instruction is love that comes from a pure heart, a good conscience, and sincere faith. [6]Some people have deviated from these and turned to meaningless talk, [7]desiring to be teachers of the law, without understanding either what they are saying or the things about which they make assertions.

8 Now we know that the law is good, if one uses it legitimately. [9]This means understanding that the law is laid down not for the innocent but for the lawless and disobedient, for the godless and sinful, for the unholy and profane, for those who kill their father or mother, for murderers, [10]fornicators, sodomites, slave traders, liars, perjurers, and whatever else is contrary to the sound teaching [11]that conforms to the glorious gospel of the blessed God, which he entrusted to me.

---

a Or *plan*

GRATITUDE FOR MERCY

12 I am grateful to Christ Jesus our Lord, who has strengthened me, because he judged me faithful and appointed me to his service, [13]even though I was formerly a blasphemer, a persecutor, and a man of violence. But I received mercy because I had acted ignorantly in unbelief, [14]and the grace of our Lord overflowed for me with the faith and love that are in Christ Jesus. [15]The saying is sure and worthy of full acceptance, that Christ Jesus came into the world to save sinners—of whom I am the foremost. [16]But for that very reason I received mercy, so that in me, as the foremost, Jesus Christ might display the utmost patience, making me an example to those who would come to believe in him for eternal life. [17]To the King of the ages, immortal, invisible, the only God, be honor and glory forever and ever.[a] Amen.

18 I am giving you these instructions, Timothy, my child, in accordance with the prophecies made earlier about you, so that by following them you may fight the good fight, [19]having faith and a good conscience. By rejecting conscience, certain persons have suffered shipwreck in the faith; [20]among them are Hymenaeus and Alexander, whom I have turned over to Satan, so that they may learn not to blaspheme.

INSTRUCTIONS CONCERNING PRAYER

2 First of all, then, I urge that supplications, prayers, intercessions, and thanksgivings be made for everyone, [2]for kings and all who are in high positions, so that we may lead a quiet and peaceable life in all godliness and dignity. [3]This is right and is acceptable in the sight of God our Savior, [4]who desires everyone to be saved and to come to the knowledge of the truth. [5]For

>   there is one God;
>   there is also one mediator between God and humankind,
>   Christ Jesus, himself human,
>   6 who gave himself a ransom for all

—this was attested at the right time. [7]For this I was appointed a herald and an apostle (I am telling the truth,[b] I am not lying), a teacher of the Gentiles in faith and truth.

8 I desire, then, that in every place the men should pray, lifting up holy hands without anger or argument; [9]also that the women should dress themselves modestly and decently in suitable clothing, not with their hair braided, or with gold, pearls, or expensive clothes, [10]but with good works, as is proper

---

a Gk to the ages of the ages   b Other ancient authorities add in Christ for women who profess reverence for God. [11]Let a woman[a] learn in silence with full submission. [12]I permit no woman[a] to teach or to have authority over a man;[b] she is to keep silent. [13]For Adam was formed first, then Eve; [14]and Adam was not deceived, but the woman was deceived and became a transgressor. [15]Yet she will be saved through childbearing, provided they continue in faith and love and holiness, with modesty.

QUALIFICATIONS OF BISHOPS

3 The saying is sure:[c] whoever aspires to the office of bishop[d] desires a noble task. [2]Now a bishop[e] must be above reproach, married only once,[f] temperate, sensible, respectable, hospitable, an apt teacher, [3]not a drunkard, not violent but gentle, not quarrelsome, and not a lover of money. [4]He must manage his own household well, keeping his children submissive and respectful in every way— [5]for if someone does not know how to manage his own household, how can he take care of God's church? [6]He must not be a recent convert, or he may be puffed up with conceit and fall into the condemnation of the devil. [7]Moreover, he must be well thought of by outsiders, so that he may not fall into disgrace and the snare of the devil.

QUALIFICATIONS OF DEACONS

8 Deacons likewise must be serious, not double-tongued, not indulging in much wine, not greedy for money; [9]they must hold fast to the mystery of the faith with a clear conscience. [10]And let them first be tested; then, if they prove themselves blameless, let them serve as deacons. [11]Women[g] likewise must be serious, not slanderers, but temperate, faithful in all things. [12]Let deacons be married only once,[h] and let them manage their children and their households well; [13]for those who serve well as deacons gain a good standing for themselves and great boldness in the faith that is in Christ Jesus.

THE MYSTERY OF OUR RELIGION

14 I hope to come to you soon, but I am writing these instructions to you so that, [15]if I am delayed, you may know how one ought to behave in the household of God, which is the church of the living God, the pillar and bulwark of the truth. [16]Without any doubt, the mystery of our religion is great:

> He[i] was revealed in flesh,
>   vindicated[j] in spirit,[k]

---

a Or *wife*   b Or *her husband*   c Some interpreters place these words at the end of the previous paragraph. Other ancient authorities read *The saying is commonly accepted*   d Or *overseer*   e Or *an overseer*   f Gk *the husband of one wife*   g Or *Their wives,* or *Women deacons*   h Gk *be husbands of one wife*   i Gk *Who;* other ancient authorities read *God;* others, *Which*   j Or *justified*   k Or *by the Spirit*

> seen by angels,
>> proclaimed among Gentiles,
>>> believed in throughout the world,
>>>> taken up in glory.

FALSE ASCETICISM

4 Now the Spirit expressly says that in later[a] times some will renounce the faith by paying attention to deceitful spirits and teachings of demons, [2] through the hypocrisy of liars whose consciences are seared with a hot iron. [3] They forbid marriage and demand abstinence from foods, which God created to be received with thanksgiving by those who believe and know the truth. [4] For everything created by God is good, and nothing is to be rejected, provided it is received with thanksgiving; [5] for it is sanctified by God's word and by prayer.

A GOOD MINISTER OF JESUS CHRIST

6 If you put these instructions before the brothers and sisters,[b] you will be a good servant[c] of Christ Jesus, nourished on the words of the faith and of the sound teaching that you have followed. [7] Have nothing to do with profane myths and old wives' tales. Train yourself in godliness, [8] for, while physical training is of some value, godliness is valuable in every way, holding promise for both the present life and the life to come. [9] The saying is sure and worthy of full acceptance. [10] For to this end we toil and struggle,[d] because we have our hope set on the living God, who is the Savior of all people, especially of those who believe.

11 These are the things you must insist on and teach. [12] Let no one despise your youth, but set the believers an example in speech and conduct, in love, in faith, in purity. [13] Until I arrive, give attention to the public reading of scripture,[e] to exhorting, to teaching. [14] Do not neglect the gift that is in you, which was given to you through prophecy with the laying on of hands by the council of elders.[f] [15] Put these things into practice, devote yourself to them, so that all may see your progress. [16] Pay close attention to yourself and to your teaching; continue in these things, for in doing this you will save both yourself and your hearers.

DUTIES TOWARD BELIEVERS

5 Do not speak harshly to an older man,[g] but speak to him as to a father, to younger men as brothers, [2] to older women as mothers, to younger women as sisters—with absolute purity.

---

a Or *the last* b Gk *brothers* c Or *deacon* d Other ancient authorities read *suffer reproach* e Gk *to the reading* f Gk *by the presbytery* g Or *an elder*, or *a presbyter*

3 Honor widows who are really widows. [4]If a widow has children or grand-children, they should first learn their religious duty to their own family and make some repayment to their parents; for this is pleasing in God's sight. [5]The real widow, left alone, has set her hope on God and continues in supplications and prayers night and day; [6]but the widow[a] who lives for pleasure is dead even while she lives. [7]Give these commands as well, so that they may be above reproach. [8]And whoever does not provide for relatives, and especially for family members, has denied the faith and is worse than an unbeliever.

9 Let a widow be put on the list if she is not less than sixty years old and has been married only once;[b] [10]she must be well attested for her good works, as one who has brought up children, shown hospitality, washed the saints' feet, helped the afflicted, and devoted herself to doing good in every way. [11]But refuse to put younger widows on the list; for when their sensual desires alienate them from Christ, they want to marry, [12]and so they incur condemnation for having violated their first pledge. [13]Besides that, they learn to be idle, gadding about from house to house; and they are not merely idle, but also gossips and busybodies, saying what they should not say. [14]So I would have younger widows marry, bear children, and manage their households, so as to give the adversary no occasion to revile us. [15]For some have already turned away to follow Satan. [16]If any believing woman[c] has relatives who are really widows, let her assist them; let the church not be burdened, so that it can assist those who are real widows.

17 Let the elders who rule well be considered worthy of double honor,[d] especially those who labor in preaching and teaching; [18]for the scripture says, "You shall not muzzle an ox while it is treading out the grain," and, "The laborer deserves to be paid." [19]Never accept any accusation against an elder except on the evidence of two or three witnesses. [20]As for those who persist in sin, rebuke them in the presence of all, so that the rest also may stand in fear. [21]In the presence of God and of Christ Jesus and of the elect angels, I warn you to keep these instructions without prejudice, doing nothing on the basis of partiality. [22]Do not ordain[e] anyone hastily, and do not participate in the sins of others; keep yourself pure.

23 No longer drink only water, but take a little wine for the sake of your stomach and your frequent ailments.

24 The sins of some people are conspicuous and precede them to judgment, while the sins of others follow them there. [25]So also good works are conspicuous; and even when they are not, they cannot remain hidden.

---

a Gk *she*   b Gk *the wife of one husband*   c Other ancient authorities read *believing man or woman;* others, *believing man*
d Or *compensation*   e Gk *Do not lay hands on*

6 Let all who are under the yoke of slavery regard their masters as worthy of all honor, so that the name of God and the teaching may not be blasphemed. [2]Those who have believing masters must not be disrespectful to them on the ground that they are members of the church;[a] rather they must serve them all the more, since those who benefit by their service are believers and beloved.[b]

FALSE TEACHING AND TRUE RICHES

Teach and urge these duties. [3]Whoever teaches otherwise and does not agree with the sound words of our Lord Jesus Christ and the teaching that is in accordance with godliness, [4]is conceited, understanding nothing, and has a morbid craving for controversy and for disputes about words. From these come envy, dissension, slander, base suspicions, [5]and wrangling among those who are depraved in mind and bereft of the truth, imagining that godliness is a means of gain.[c] [6]Of course, there is great gain in godliness combined with contentment; [7]for we brought nothing into the world, so that[d] we can take nothing out of it; [8]but if we have food and clothing, we will be content with these. [9]But those who want to be rich fall into temptation and are trapped by many senseless and harmful desires that plunge people into ruin and destruction. [10]For the love of money is a root of all kinds of evil, and in their eagerness to be rich some have wandered away from the faith and pierced themselves with many pains.

THE GOOD FIGHT OF FAITH

11 But as for you, man of God, shun all this; pursue righteousness, godliness, faith, love, endurance, gentleness. [12]Fight the good fight of the faith; take hold of the eternal life, to which you were called and for which you made[e] the good confession in the presence of many witnesses. [13]In the presence of God, who gives life to all things, and of Christ Jesus, who in his testimony before Pontius Pilate made the good confession, I charge you [14]to keep the commandment without spot or blame until the manifestation of our Lord Jesus Christ, [15]which he will bring about at the right time—he who is the blessed and only Sovereign, the King of kings and Lord of lords. [16]It is he alone who has immortality and dwells in unapproachable light, whom no one has ever seen or can see; to him be honor and eternal dominion. Amen.

17 As for those who in the present age are rich, command them not to be haughty, or to set their hopes on the uncertainty of riches, but rather on God who richly provides us with everything for our enjoyment. [18]They are to do

---

a Gk are brothers   b Or since they are believers and beloved, who devote themselves to good deeds   c Other ancient authorities add Withdraw yourself from such people   d Other ancient authorities read world—it is certain that   e Gk confessed good, to be rich in good works, generous, and ready to share, [19]thus storing up for themselves the treasure of a good foundation for the future, so that they may take hold of the life that really is life.

PERSONAL INSTRUCTIONS AND BENEDICTION

20 Timothy, guard what has been entrusted to you. Avoid the profane chatter and contradictions of what is falsely called knowledge; [21]by professing it some have missed the mark as regards the faith.

Grace be with you.[a]

---

a The Greek word for *you* here is plural; in other ancient authorities it is singular. Other ancient authorities add *Amen*

2 Timothy

Second Timothy is like and unlike 1 Timothy. Both begin as letters from Paul to Timothy. Both emphasize "sound teaching," guarding "the good treasure entrusted to you" (1.13–14) and "sound doctrine" (4.3). Both are almost certainly by the same author.

But 2 Timothy is much more personal. Paul is in prison (1.8, 16–17), expecting to die soon (4.6). The letter reads like a "farewell letter" that also commissions Timothy to continue what Paul has begun. There is nothing about qualifications for leadership or directives about who is a real widow. Rather, it is like a last testament from Paul to Timothy.

It begins with memories, naming Timothy's mother and grandmother, Eunice and Lois. Then the author refers to Paul's imprisonment and sense of abandonment (1.15; 4.9–16). It continues with a commendation to Timothy to be "a good soldier of Christ Jesus" and a worker approved by God (2.1–16). It warns of what will happen "in the last days":

> People will be lovers of themselves, lovers of money, boasters, arrogant, abusive, disobedient to their parents, ungrateful, unholy, inhuman, implacable, slanderers, profligates, brutes, haters of good, treacherous, reckless, swollen with conceit, lovers of pleasure rather than lovers of God, holding to the outward form of godliness but denying its power. (3.2–5)

This is not Paul. But it is not far from Paul.

Most of the rest of the letter, beginning with 3.10, is a "charge" to Timothy commissioning him to be Paul's successor and legatee:

Now you have observed my teaching, my conduct, my aim in life, my faith,
my patience, my love, my steadfastness, my persecutions, and my suffering
the things that happened to me. (3.10–11)

I solemnly urge you: proclaim the message; be persistent whether the time
is favorable or unfavorable; convince, rebuke, and encourage, with the
utmost patience in teaching. For the time is coming when people will not
put up with sound doctrine, but having itching ears, they will accumulate
for themselves teachers to suit their own desires. . . . As for you, always be
sober, endure suffering, do the work of an evangelist, carry out your ministry
fully. (4.1–5)

This section of the letter contains what is probably its best-known verse. It affirms that "all scripture is inspired by God" (3.16). It is one of the foundations of
Christian controversy about the authority of the Bible. Especially in the last hundred
years, many Protestants have thought, been taught, or have taken for granted that
"inspired by God" means that the Bible has a divine guarantee to be true. It commonly leads to the claim that the Bible is "inerrant" and "infallible." Some would
make a subtle distinction between those two terms, but in ordinary usage today
they are synonyms. This understanding of this verse and thus of the Bible as the
inerrant Word of God is the foundation of fundamentalist and most of conservative-
evangelical Protestantism. For these Protestants, the Bible as the inspired and
therefore inerrant and infallible Word of God defines who they are.

The verse is in the middle of a passage urging Timothy to maintain sound
doctrine:

As for you, continue in what you have learned and firmly believed, knowing from whom you learned it, and how from childhood you have known
the sacred writings that are able to instruct you for salvation through faith
in Christ Jesus. *All scripture is inspired by God and is useful for teaching,
for reproof, for correction, and for training in righteousness,* so that everyone who belongs to God may be proficient, equipped for every good work.
(3.14–17; v. 16 in italics)

Although the verse does say "all scripture is inspired by God," it does not say
that "inspired" means "inerrant and infallible." Rather, because it is inspired, it is
useful for teaching, reproof, correction, and training in righteousness (the last word
would be better translated "justice"). There is nothing controversial in that claim. Is
scripture useful for teaching and so forth? Of course.

Moreover, it is worth reflecting about what the word "inspired" means. The Greek word literally means "God-breathed," a manifest metaphor with an imprecise meaning. What does "inspired" as "breathed by God" suggest?

We might imagine what it means when we think of a person as "inspired." Sometimes we use the word very broadly to include rather everyday behaviors that seem to reflect exceptional wisdom. Somewhat more narrowly, we speak of great artists as "inspired": Michelangelo, Shakespeare, Bach, Mozart, Beethoven. Their quality and power transcend their time and place and seem to come from somewhere else. Even more narrowly, Christians think of the prophets of the Old Testament as "inspired." What do we imagine when we picture that? That they were deeply moved by the Spirit of God and spoke their words as passionately and powerfully as they could? Or do we imagine that they became "inerrant" and "infallible"? Inspiration—being moved by the Spirit of God, God-breathed—does not mean becoming "infallible."

Finally, note that within the historical context of this verse, "scripture" referred only to the Old Testament, the Jewish Bible. There was no New Testament yet. The verse does not refer to the Christian Bible as a whole, but to what was "scripture" for Christians around the year 100—the Jewish Bible.

Thus the author had a much more limited meaning in mind than the structure of biblical authority as inerrancy and infallibility that has been built on 3.16. In the context of the letter, he urges Timothy to take scripture seriously as foundational to his vocation of defending sound teaching and proclaiming the "message." Is the Bible inspired, important, and useful? The author's answer is, "Of course." But to think that the author meant inerrancy and infallibility goes beyond what he wrote.

Timothy

SALUTATION

1 Paul, an apostle of Christ Jesus by the will of God, for the sake of the promise of life that is in Christ Jesus,

2 To Timothy, my beloved child:

Grace, mercy, and peace from God the Father and Christ Jesus our Lord.

THANKSGIVING AND ENCOURAGEMENT

3 I am grateful to God—whom I worship with a clear conscience, as my ancestors did—when I remember you constantly in my prayers night and day. [4]Recalling your tears, I long to see you so that I may be filled with joy. [5]I am reminded of your sincere faith, a faith that lived first in your grandmother Lois and your mother Eunice and now, I am sure, lives in you. [6]For this reason I remind you to rekindle the gift of God that is within you through the laying on of my hands; [7]for God did not give us a spirit of cowardice, but rather a spirit of power and of love and of self-discipline.

8 Do not be ashamed, then, of the testimony about our Lord or of me his prisoner, but join with me in suffering for the gospel, relying on the power of God, [9]who saved us and called us with a holy calling, not according to our works but according to his own purpose and grace. This grace was given to us in Christ Jesus before the ages began, [10]but it has now been revealed through

the appearing of our Savior Christ Jesus, who abolished death and brought life and immortality to light through the gospel. [11]For this gospel I was appointed a herald and an apostle and a teacher,[a] [12]and for this reason I suffer as I do. But I am not ashamed, for I know the one in whom I have put my trust, and I am sure that he is able to guard until that day what I have entrusted to him.[b] [13]Hold to the standard of sound teaching that you have heard from me, in the faith and love that are in Christ Jesus. [14]Guard the good treasure entrusted to you, with the help of the Holy Spirit living in us.

15 You are aware that all who are in Asia have turned away from me, including Phygelus and Hermogenes. [16]May the Lord grant mercy to the household of Onesiphorus, because he often refreshed me and was not ashamed of my chain; [17]when he arrived in Rome, he eagerly[c] searched for me and found me [18]—may the Lord grant that he will find mercy from the Lord on that day! And you know very well how much service he rendered in Ephesus.

A GOOD SOLDIER OF CHRIST JESUS

2 You then, my child, be strong in the grace that is in Christ Jesus; [2]and what you have heard from me through many witnesses entrust to faithful people who will be able to teach others as well. [3]Share in suffering like a good soldier of Christ Jesus. [4]No one serving in the army gets entangled in everyday affairs; the soldier's aim is to please the enlisting officer. [5]And in the case of an athlete, no one is crowned without competing according to the rules. [6]It is the farmer who does the work who ought to have the first share of the crops. [7]Think over what I say, for the Lord will give you understanding in all things.

8 Remember Jesus Christ, raised from the dead, a descendant of David— that is my gospel, [9]for which I suffer hardship, even to the point of being chained like a criminal. But the word of God is not chained. [10]Therefore I endure everything for the sake of the elect, so that they may also obtain the salvation that is in Christ Jesus, with eternal glory. [11]The saying is sure:

> If we have died with him, we will also live with him;

12 if we endure, we will also reign with him;

> if we deny him, he will also deny us;

13 if we are faithless, he remains faithful—

> for he cannot deny himself.

---

a Other ancient authorities add *of the Gentiles* *b* Or *what has been entrusted to me* *c* Or *promptly*

A WORKER APPROVED BY GOD

14 Remind them of this, and warn them before God*a* that they are to avoid wrangling over words, which does no good but only ruins those who are listening. ¹⁵Do your best to present yourself to God as one approved by him, a worker who has no need to be ashamed, rightly explaining the word of truth. ¹⁶Avoid profane chatter, for it will lead people into more and more impiety, ¹⁷and their talk will spread like gangrene. Among them are Hymenaeus and Philetus, ¹⁸who have swerved from the truth by claiming that the resurrection has already taken place. They are upsetting the faith of some. ¹⁹But God's firm foundation stands, bearing this inscription: "The Lord knows those who are his," and, "Let everyone who calls on the name of the Lord turn away from wickedness."

20 In a large house there are utensils not only of gold and silver but also of wood and clay, some for special use, some for ordinary. ²¹All who cleanse themselves of the things I have mentioned*b* will become special utensils, dedicated and useful to the owner of the house, ready for every good work. ²²Shun youthful passions and pursue righteousness, faith, love, and peace, along with those who call on the Lord from a pure heart. ²³Have nothing to do with stupid and senseless controversies; you know that they breed quarrels. ²⁴And the Lord's servant*c* must not be quarrelsome but kindly to everyone, an apt teacher, patient, ²⁵correcting opponents with gentleness. God may perhaps grant that they will repent and come to know the truth, ²⁶and that they may escape from the snare of the devil, having been held captive by him to do his will.*d*

GODLESSNESS IN THE LAST DAYS

3 You must understand this, that in the last days distressing times will come. ²For people will be lovers of themselves, lovers of money, boasters, arrogant, abusive, disobedient to their parents, ungrateful, unholy, ³inhuman, implacable, slanderers, profligates, brutes, haters of good, ⁴treacherous, reckless, swollen with conceit, lovers of pleasure rather than lovers of God, ⁵holding to the outward form of godliness but denying its power. Avoid them! ⁶For among them are those who make their way into households and captivate silly women, overwhelmed by their sins and swayed by all kinds of desires, ⁷who are always being instructed and can never arrive at a knowledge of the truth. ⁸As Jannes and Jambres opposed Moses, so these people, of cor-

---

a Other ancient authorities read *the Lord*   *b* Gk *of these things*   *c* Gk *slave*   *d* Or *by him, to do his* (that is, God's) *will* rupt mind and counterfeit faith, also oppose the truth. [9]But they will not make much progress, because, as in the case of those two men,[a] their folly will become plain to everyone.

PAUL'S CHARGE TO TIMOTHY

10 Now you have observed my teaching, my conduct, my aim in life, my faith, my patience, my love, my steadfastness, [11]my persecutions, and my suffering the things that happened to me in Antioch, Iconium, and Lystra. What persecutions I endured! Yet the Lord rescued me from all of them. [12]Indeed, all who want to live a godly life in Christ Jesus will be persecuted. [13]But wicked people and impostors will go from bad to worse, deceiving others and being deceived. [14]But as for you, continue in what you have learned and firmly believed, knowing from whom you learned it, [15]and how from childhood you have known the sacred writings that are able to instruct you for salvation through faith in Christ Jesus. [16]All scripture is inspired by God and is[b] useful for teaching, for reproof, for correction, and for training in righteousness, [17]so that everyone who belongs to God may be proficient, equipped for every good work.

4 In the presence of God and of Christ Jesus, who is to judge the living and the dead, and in view of his appearing and his kingdom, I solemnly urge you: [2]proclaim the message; be persistent whether the time is favorable or unfavorable; convince, rebuke, and encourage, with the utmost patience in teaching. [3]For the time is coming when people will not put up with sound doctrine, but having itching ears, they will accumulate for themselves teachers to suit their own desires, [4]and will turn away from listening to the truth and wander away to myths. [5]As for you, always be sober, endure suffering, do the work of an evangelist, carry out your ministry fully.

6 As for me, I am already being poured out as a libation, and the time of my departure has come. [7]I have fought the good fight, I have finished the race, I have kept the faith. [8]From now on there is reserved for me the crown of righteousness, which the Lord, the righteous judge, will give me on that day, and not only to me but also to all who have longed for his appearing.

PERSONAL INSTRUCTIONS

9 Do your best to come to me soon, [10]for Demas, in love with this present world, has deserted me and gone to Thessalonica; Crescens has gone to

---

a Gk lacks two men b Or Every scripture inspired by God is also

Galatia,*a* Titus to Dalmatia. [11]Only Luke is with me. Get Mark and bring him with you, for he is useful in my ministry. [12]I have sent Tychicus to Ephesus. [13]When you come, bring the cloak that I left with Carpus at Troas, also the books, and above all the parchments. [14]Alexander the coppersmith did me great harm; the Lord will pay him back for his deeds. [15]You also must beware of him, for he strongly opposed our message.

16 At my first defense no one came to my support, but all deserted me. May it not be counted against them! [17]But the Lord stood by me and gave me strength, so that through me the message might be fully proclaimed and all the Gentiles might hear it. So I was rescued from the lion's mouth. [18]The Lord will rescue me from every evil attack and save me for his heavenly kingdom. To him be the glory forever and ever. Amen.

FINAL GREETINGS AND BENEDICTION

19 Greet Prisca and Aquila, and the household of Onesiphorus. [20]Erastus remained in Corinth; Trophimus I left ill in Miletus. [21]Do your best to come before winter. Eubulus sends greetings to you, as do Pudens and Linus and Claudia and all the brothers and sisters.*b*

22 The Lord be with your spirit. Grace be with you.*c*

---

a Other ancient authorities read *Gaul*   *b* Gk *all the brothers*   *c* The Greek word for *you* here is plural. Other ancient authorities add *Amen*

Titus

The third of the pastoral letters is addressed to Titus. Like Timothy, he was an important associate of Paul. According to Galatians 2.3, he was a Gentile convert, probably a "God-lover" who was with Paul in Jerusalem in the late 40s or 50s. In 2 Corinthians, he was an important mediator in Paul's conflicted relationship with the Christ-community in Corinth in the mid-50s.

In the letter, Titus is on Crete (1.5), the largest of the Greek islands. The reason is that the putative author Paul had left Titus there so that he "should put in order what remained to be done, and should appoint elders in every town" (1.5). The letter is about the need for order and the appointment of authorized leaders—in short, it is about institutionalization.

The author negatively stereotypes the inhabitants of Crete: "'Cretans are always liars, vicious brutes, lazy gluttons.' That testimony is true" (1.12–13). So, Titus is told, "Teach what is consistent with sound doctrine" (2.1).

The letter combines characteristics of 1 and 2 Timothy. The author calls Titus "my child," just as he did Timothy, and thus passes Paul's mantle to a later generation. It is concerned with "sound doctrine" (2.1). Like 1 Timothy, it is practical and pastoral. It includes a list of qualifications for bishops (1.5–9) and directions for what to teach older men and older women, younger women and younger men, and slaves (2.1–10).

Slaves are "to be submissive to their masters and to give satisfaction in every respect; they are not to talk back, not to pilfer, but to show complete and perfect fidelity, so that in everything they may be an ornament to the doctrine of God our Savior." If the counsel is directed to Christian slaves of non-Christian masters, it makes sense. But if the text presupposes that there are Christian masters of Christian slaves, it is very different from the radical Paul of the seven genuine letters.

Finally, like 2 Timothy, the letter commissions Titus to continue what Paul has been doing. It is about Paul's legacy perhaps a half century after his death.

Titus

SALUTATION

1 Paul, a servant*a* of God and an apostle of Jesus Christ, for the sake of the faith of God's elect and the knowledge of the truth that is in accordance with godliness, ²in the hope of eternal life that God, who never lies, promised before the ages began— ³in due time he revealed his word through the proclamation with which I have been entrusted by the command of God our Savior,

4 To Titus, my loyal child in the faith we share:

Grace*b* and peace from God the Father and Christ Jesus our Savior.

TITUS IN CRETE

5 I left you behind in Crete for this reason, so that you should put in order what remained to be done, and should appoint elders in every town, as I directed you: ⁶someone who is blameless, married only once,*c* whose children are believers, not accused of debauchery and not rebellious. ⁷For a bishop,*d* as God's steward, must be blameless; he must not be arrogant or quick-tempered or addicted to wine or violent or greedy for gain; ⁸but he must be hospitable, a lover of goodness, prudent, upright, devout, and self-controlled. ⁹He must have a firm grasp of the word that is trustworthy in accordance with the teaching, so that he may be able both to preach with sound doctrine and to refute those who contradict it.

10 There are also many rebellious people, idle talkers and deceivers, especially those of the circumcision; ¹¹they must be silenced, since they are upsetting

---

a Gk *slave*   *b* Other ancient authorities read *Grace, mercy,*   *c* Gk *husband of one wife*   *d* Or *an overseer* whole families by teaching for sordid gain what it is not right to teach. [12]It was one of them, their very own prophet, who said,

"Cretans are always liars, vicious brutes, lazy gluttons."

13 That testimony is true. For this reason rebuke them sharply, so that they may become sound in the faith, [14]not paying attention to Jewish myths or to commandments of those who reject the truth. [15]To the pure all things are pure, but to the corrupt and unbelieving nothing is pure. Their very minds and consciences are corrupted. [16]They profess to know God, but they deny him by their actions. They are detestable, disobedient, unfit for any good work.

TEACH SOUND DOCTRINE

2 But as for you, teach what is consistent with sound doctrine. [2]Tell the older men to be temperate, serious, prudent, and sound in faith, in love, and in endurance.

3 Likewise, tell the older women to be reverent in behavior, not to be slanderers or slaves to drink; they are to teach what is good, [4]so that they may encourage the young women to love their husbands, to love their children, [5]to be self-controlled, chaste, good managers of the household, kind, being submissive to their husbands, so that the word of God may not be discredited.

6 Likewise, urge the younger men to be self-controlled. [7]Show yourself in all respects a model of good works, and in your teaching show integrity, gravity, [8]and sound speech that cannot be censured; then any opponent will be put to shame, having nothing evil to say of us.

9 Tell slaves to be submissive to their masters and to give satisfaction in every respect; they are not to talk back, [10]not to pilfer, but to show complete and perfect fidelity, so that in everything they may be an ornament to the doctrine of God our Savior.

11 For the grace of God has appeared, bringing salvation to all,[a] [12]training us to renounce impiety and worldly passions, and in the present age to live lives that are self-controlled, upright, and godly, [13]while we wait for the blessed hope and the manifestation of the glory of our great God and Savior,[b] Jesus Christ. [14]He it is who gave himself for us that he might redeem us from all iniquity and purify for himself a people of his own who are zealous for good deeds.

15 Declare these things; exhort and reprove with all authority.[c] Let no one look down on you.

---

a Or has appeared to all, bringing salvation b Or of the great God and our Savior c Gk commandment

MAINTAIN GOOD DEEDS

3 Remind them to be subject to rulers and authorities, to be obedient, to be ready for every good work, ²to speak evil of no one, to avoid quarreling, to be gentle, and to show every courtesy to everyone. ³For we ourselves were once foolish, disobedient, led astray, slaves to various passions and pleasures, passing our days in malice and envy, despicable, hating one another. ⁴But when the goodness and loving kindness of God our Savior appeared, ⁵he saved us, not because of any works of righteousness that we had done, but according to his mercy, through the water *a* of rebirth and renewal by the Holy Spirit. ⁶This Spirit he poured out on us richly through Jesus Christ our Savior, ⁷so that, having been justified by his grace, we might become heirs according to the hope of eternal life. ⁸The saying is sure.

I desire that you insist on these things, so that those who have come to believe in God may be careful to devote themselves to good works; these things are excellent and profitable to everyone. ⁹But avoid stupid controversies, genealogies, dissensions, and quarrels about the law, for they are unprofitable and worthless. ¹⁰After a first and second admonition, have nothing more to do with anyone who causes divisions, ¹¹since you know that such a person is perverted and sinful, being self-condemned.

FINAL MESSAGES AND BENEDICTION

12 When I send Artemas to you, or Tychicus, do your best to come to me at Nicopolis, for I have decided to spend the winter there. ¹³Make every effort to send Zenas the lawyer and Apollos on their way, and see that they lack nothing. ¹⁴And let people learn to devote themselves to good works in order to meet urgent needs, so that they may not be unproductive.

15 All who are with me send greetings to you. Greet those who love us in the faith.

Grace be with all of you. *b*

---

a Gk *washing*   *b* Other ancient authorities add *Amen*

2 Peter

There is a strong scholarly consensus that 2 Peter is the last New Testament document to be written. Some date it as late as 150, and most date it between 120
and 150. Among the reasons for its late dating are its reference to 1 Peter (3.1),
its mention of the letters of Paul (3.15–16), and its use of phrases from the letter
of Jude. In addition, it offers an explanation for the delay of the second coming of
Jesus (3.3–10).

As in 1 Peter, the author identifies himself as "Peter, a servant and apostle of
Jesus Christ" (1.1). He refers to Peter's impending death (1.3–15). He refers to
himself as an eyewitness to the transfiguration of Jesus (1.17–18). As narrated in
Mark 9.2–8 (and in Matthew and Luke), only Peter, James, and John were with
Jesus on that occasion. But the letter is much too late to have been written by Peter
or the author of 1 Peter.

We know nothing about the location of the author or the letter's recipients. There
are no geographical clues at all. The letter is not addressed to a specific Christ-
community or region of communities. Thus it is classified as one of the "general" or
"catholic" (meaning universal) letters.

Content

The final chapter of the letter explains why the second coming of Jesus had not yet
happened. Recall that many early Christians shared the conviction that it was imminent, close at hand. The author refers to "scoffers" who will ask, "Where is the
promise of his coming?" Already their ancestors had died (once again suggesting a
late date for the letter), but still the world continued as it was (3.4).

The author offers a twofold explanation for the delay. First, God's time is not like our sense of time: "With the Lord one day is like a thousand years, and a thousand years are like one day" (3.8). Second, because of God's patience, God is providing more time for "all to come to repentance" (3.9).

The more general theme of the letter is separation from the ways of the world (1.3–11) and warnings about false prophets who seek to lure the recipients back into the ways of the world (2.1–22). The corruption of the world includes lust (1.4), deception, injustice (unrighteousness), slander, adultery, and greed (2.3–14). The words "lust" and "adultery" may refer to sexual desire and behavior, but often in the Bible they are metaphors for greed and idolatry. Those who entice them into the ways of the world are described as "bold and willful" (2.10), "irrational animals" who are "creatures of instinct" (2.12), "waterless springs and mists" (2.17) who speak "bombastic nonsense" and promise "freedom" even as they "are slaves of corruption" (2.18–19).

The antidote—the way of escaping the "corruption that is in the world"—is the power and promises of God, who has given them "everything needed for life and godliness" through Jesus. (1.3–4). On this foundation, the author writes:

> You must make every effort to support your faith with goodness, and good-ness with knowledge, and knowledge with self-control, and self-control with endurance, and endurance with godliness, and godliness with mutual affec-tion, and mutual affection with love. (1.5–7)

Thus, like the New Testament as a whole, its last letter emphasizes love as the climactic Christian virtue.

THE SECOND LETTER OF
Peter

SALUTATION

1 Simeon*a* Peter, a servant*b* and apostle of Jesus Christ,

To those who have received a faith as precious as ours through the righteousness of our God and Savior Jesus Christ:*c*

2 May grace and peace be yours in abundance in the knowledge of God and of Jesus our Lord.

THE CHRISTIAN'S CALL AND ELECTION

3 His divine power has given us everything needed for life and godliness, through the knowledge of him who called us by*d* his own glory and goodness. 4Thus he has given us, through these things, his precious and very great promises, so that through them you may escape from the corruption that is in the world because of lust, and may become participants of the divine nature. 5For this very reason, you must make every effort to support your faith with goodness, and goodness with knowledge, 6and knowledge with self-control, and self-control with endurance, and endurance with godliness, 7and godliness with mutual*e* affection, and mutual*e* affection with love. 8For if these things are yours and are increasing among you, they keep you from being ineffective and unfruitful in the knowledge of our Lord Jesus Christ. 9For anyone who lacks these things is short-sighted and blind, and is forgetful of the cleansing of past sins. 10Therefore, brothers and sisters,*f* be all the more eager to confirm

---

a Other ancient authorities read *Simon*   *b* Gk *slave*   *c* Or *of our God and the Savior Jesus Christ*   *d* Other ancient authorities read *through*   *e* Gk *brotherly*   *f* Gk *brothers* your call and election, for if you do this, you will never stumble. [11]For in this way, entry into the eternal kingdom of our Lord and Savior Jesus Christ will be richly provided for you.

12 Therefore I intend to keep on reminding you of these things, though you know them already and are established in the truth that has come to you. [13]I think it right, as long as I am in this body,[a] to refresh your memory, [14]since I know that my death[b] will come soon, as indeed our Lord Jesus Christ has made clear to me. [15]And I will make every effort so that after my departure you may be able at any time to recall these things.

EYEWITNESSES OF CHRIST'S GLORY

16 For we did not follow cleverly devised myths when we made known to you the power and coming of our Lord Jesus Christ, but we had been eyewitnesses of his majesty. [17]For he received honor and glory from God the Father when that voice was conveyed to him by the Majestic Glory, saying, "This is my Son, my Beloved,[c] with whom I am well pleased." [18]We ourselves heard this voice come from heaven, while we were with him on the holy mountain.

19 So we have the prophetic message more fully confirmed. You will do well to be attentive to this as to a lamp shining in a dark place, until the day dawns and the morning star rises in your hearts. [20]First of all you must understand this, that no prophecy of scripture is a matter of one's own interpretation, [21]because no prophecy ever came by human will, but men and women moved by the Holy Spirit spoke from God.[d]

FALSE PROPHETS AND THEIR PUNISHMENT

2 But false prophets also arose among the people, just as there will be false teachers among you, who will secretly bring in destructive opinions. They will even deny the Master who bought them—bringing swift destruction on themselves. [2]Even so, many will follow their licentious ways, and because of these teachers[e] the way of truth will be maligned. [3]And in their greed they will exploit you with deceptive words. Their condemnation, pronounced against them long ago, has not been idle, and their destruction is not asleep.

4 For if God did not spare the angels when they sinned, but cast them into hell[f] and committed them to chains[g] of deepest darkness to be kept until the judgment; [5]and if he did not spare the ancient world, even though he saved Noah, a herald of righteousness, with seven others, when he brought a flood on a world of the ungodly; [6]and if by turning the cities of Sodom and Gomorrah

---

a Gk *tent*   b Gk *the putting off of my tent*   c Other ancient authorities read *my beloved Son*   d Other ancient authorities read *but moved by the Holy Spirit saints of God spoke*   e Gk *because of them*   f Gk *Tartaros*   g Other ancient authorities read *pits* to ashes he condemned them to extinction[a] and made them an example of what is coming to the ungodly;[b] [7]and if he rescued Lot, a righteous man greatly distressed by the licentiousness of the lawless [8](for that righteous man, living among them day after day, was tormented in his righteous soul by their lawless deeds that he saw and heard), [9]then the Lord knows how to rescue the godly from trial, and to keep the unrighteous under punishment until the day of judgment [10]—especially those who indulge their flesh in depraved lust, and who despise authority.

Bold and willful, they are not afraid to slander the glorious ones,[c] [11]whereas angels, though greater in might and power, do not bring against them a slanderous judgment from the Lord.[d] [12]These people, however, are like irrational animals, mere creatures of instinct, born to be caught and killed. They slander what they do not understand, and when those creatures are destroyed,[e] they also will be destroyed, [13]suffering[f] the penalty for doing wrong. They count it a pleasure to revel in the daytime. They are blots and blemishes, reveling in their dissipation[g] while they feast with you. [14]They have eyes full of adultery, insatiable for sin. They entice unsteady souls. They have hearts trained in greed. Accursed children! [15]They have left the straight road and have gone astray, following the road of Balaam son of Bosor,[h] who loved the wages of doing wrong, [16]but was rebuked for his own transgression; a speechless donkey spoke with a human voice and restrained the prophet's madness.

17 These are waterless springs and mists driven by a storm; for them the deepest darkness has been reserved. [18]For they speak bombastic nonsense, and with licentious desires of the flesh they entice people who have just[i] escaped from those who live in error. [19]They promise them freedom, but they themselves are slaves of corruption; for people are slaves to whatever masters them. [20]For if, after they have escaped the defilements of the world through the knowledge of our Lord and Savior Jesus Christ, they are again entangled in them and overpowered, the last state has become worse for them than the first. [21]For it would have been better for them never to have known the way of righteousness than, after knowing it, to turn back from the holy commandment that was passed on to them. [22]It has happened to them according to the true proverb,

"The dog turns back to its own vomit,"

and,

"The sow is washed only to wallow in the mud."

---

a Other ancient authorities lack *to extinction*   b Other ancient authorities read *an example to those who were to be ungodly*
c Or *angels;* Gk *glories*   d Other ancient authorities read *before the Lord;* others lack the phrase   e Gk *in their destruction*
f Other ancient authorities read *receiving*   g Other ancient authorities read *love-feasts*   h Other ancient authorities read *Beor*
i Other ancient authorities read *actually*

THE PROMISE OF THE LORD'S COMING

3 This is now, beloved, the second letter I am writing to you; in them I am trying to arouse your sincere intention by reminding you [2] that you should remember the words spoken in the past by the holy prophets, and the commandment of the Lord and Savior spoken through your apostles. [3]First of all you must understand this, that in the last days scoffers will come, scoffing and indulging their own lusts [4]and saying, "Where is the promise of his coming? For ever since our ancestors died,[a] all things continue as they were from the beginning of creation!" [5]They deliberately ignore this fact, that by the word of God heavens existed long ago and an earth was formed out of water and by means of water, [6]through which the world of that time was deluged with water and perished. [7]But by the same word the present heavens and earth have been reserved for fire, being kept until the day of judgment and destruction of the godless.

8 But do not ignore this one fact, beloved, that with the Lord one day is like a thousand years, and a thousand years are like one day. [9]The Lord is not slow about his promise, as some think of slowness, but is patient with you,[b] not wanting any to perish, but all to come to repentance. [10]But the day of the Lord will come like a thief, and then the heavens will pass away with a loud noise, and the elements will be dissolved with fire, and the earth and everything that is done on it will be disclosed.[c]

11 Since all these things are to be dissolved in this way, what sort of persons ought you to be in leading lives of holiness and godliness, [12]waiting for and hastening[d] the coming of the day of God, because of which the heavens will be set ablaze and dissolved, and the elements will melt with fire? [13]But, in accordance with his promise, we wait for new heavens and a new earth, where righteousness is at home.

FINAL EXHORTATION AND DOXOLOGY

14 Therefore, beloved, while you are waiting for these things, strive to be found by him at peace, without spot or blemish; [15]and regard the patience of our Lord as salvation. So also our beloved brother Paul wrote to you according to the wisdom given him, [16]speaking of this as he does in all his letters. There are some things in them hard to understand, which the ignorant and unstable

---

a Gk our fathers fell asleep   b Other ancient authorities read on your account   c Other ancient authorities read will be burned up
d Or earnestly desiring

twist to their own destruction, as they do the other scriptures. [17]You therefore, beloved, since you are forewarned, beware that you are not carried away with the error of the lawless and lose your own stability. [18]But grow in the grace and knowledge of our Lord and Savior Jesus Christ. To him be the glory both now and to the day of eternity. Amen.[a]

---

[a] Other ancient authorities lack *Amen*